Privacy Defended

Protecting Yourself Online

Gary Bahadur
William Chan
Chris Weber

® 201 West 103rd Street
Indianapolis, Indiana 46290

Privacy Defended:
Protecting Yourself Online

International Standard Book Number: 0-7897-2605-X

Library of Congress Catalog Card Number: 2001098173

Printed in the United States of America

First Printing: *February 2002*

05   04   03   02   4   3   2   1

Trademarks

Warning and Disclaimer

Associate Publisher
Dean Miller

Acquisitions Editor
Lloyd Black

Development Editor
Gayle Johnson

Managing Editor
Thomas F. Hayes

Project Editor
Tonya Simpson

Production Editor
Megan Wade

Indexer
Ken Johnson

Proofreader
Suzanne Thomas

Technical Editor
Preethi Menon

Team Coordinator
Cindy Teeters

Interior Designer
Gary Adair

Cover Designer
Bill Thomas

Page Layout
Mark Walchle

Contents at a Glance

Contents

About the Authors

Gary Bahadur, cofounder and Chief Information Officer of Foundstone, Inc. (`http://www.foundstone.com`), has been providing security consulting and training services to Foundstone's clients for the past two years. He implements the technical infrastructure necessary to provide services to Foundstone's clients. Prior to starting Foundstone with his partners, he performed security consulting and training services for Fortune 500 companies as a consultant and manager for Price Waterhouse and Ernst & Young.

Bahadur has been involved with numerous ethical hacking tests and network reviews covering various firewalls, Unix, Windows NT, Novell networks, Web servers, Internet connectivity, and SAP security during the past seven years. He has helped develop methodologies for network security reviews and security classes. He is a frequent speaker at security conferences and writes for a number of security-related publications. Bahadur holds a Bachelor of Science degree in information systems/finance from New York University and is a Certified Information Systems Security Professional (CISSP). He can be reached at `gary@privacydefended.com` or `gary@foundstone.com`.

William Chan is a cofounder and the Vice President for Educational Services at Foundstone, Inc. He is responsible for managing and delivering Foundstone's "Ultimate Hacking" series of classes. These classes have been well-received by several hundred security professionals from the private sector as well as from security practitioners in the government and the military. Chan has been involved with information security and privacy for the past 10 years. He has performed numerous security consulting engagements, advising clients on security and privacy-related issues. He has worked primarily in the financial services industry and has spent several years providing consulting services to a wide variety of organizations. Chan holds a Bachelor of Science degree in computer science from Rensselaer Polytechnic Institute and a Master of Science in information systems from Pace University. He is also a Certified Information Systems Security Professional. He can be reached at `william@privacydefended.com` or `william@foundstone.com`.

Chris Weber is a security consultant for Foundstone, Inc. He is adept in many facets of information technology and secure network computing. He has performed numerous ethical hacking tests, security architecture reviews, and secure application analyses. Prior to working at Foundstone, he worked for VisionAir, performing enterprise network assessments and mission-critical system implementations for some of the largest police departments in the U.S. Weber's public work includes course development and advisory board membership at the SANS Institute. He has also been a security tutorial honoraria speaker at the USENIX 10th Annual Security Symposium in 2001 and a co-instructor at the Computer Security Institute's 2001 Network Security conference in New Orleans. Weber holds a Bachelor of Science in information systems and marketing from the University of North Carolina at Wilmington. He can be reached at chris@privacydefended.com or chris.weber@foundstone.com.

> "And progress is not intelligently planned,
> It's the facade of our heritage, the odor of our land…"

Greg Graffin, 1989

Dedications

For the years of sacrifice and patience with me, nothing I have ever done would be possible without the support of my mother. For my niece Alexa: May she grow up in a world that continues to cherish privacy.

Gary Bahadur

To my mother and sister, for all their love and support, and in memory of my father, for all his love and sacrifices.

William Chan

To my mom, dad, and relatives for believing in me. To Anne and our friends for understanding my passion for computer technology and for sharing years of good surfing.

Chris Weber

Acknowledgments

We would first like to thank Preethi Menon for all her hard work in technical editing of this book. We tend to write to very technical audiences in bits and bytes, and she kept the book on track. The late-night e-mails asking for a quick review of a new chapter and a sanity check of what we wrote made this book possible and readable.

Second, we would like to thank a strong supporting cast that is the Foundstone team. We work with some absolutely astounding people who have provided insight and motivation to write this book. Being surrounded by so many driven people, several of whom have been through the writing process, made it possible to give up the nights and weekends it took to complete this book.

Finally, we want to acknowledge the monumental efforts, self sacrifice, and dedication of privacy activists such as Phil Zimmerman and organizations such as the Electronic Privacy Information Center, the Electronic Frontier Foundation, and the hundreds of others who work tirelessly on a daily basis to keep us all informed about threats to our personal lives and who fight for our right to privacy.

All this technology means nothing if we can't live together in peace!

Tell Us What You Think!

As the reader of this book, *you* are our most important critic and commentator. We value your opinion and want to know what we're doing right, what we could do better, what areas you'd like to see us publish in, and any other words of wisdom you're willing to pass our way.

As an associate publisher for Que, I welcome your comments. You can fax, e-mail, or write me directly to let me know what you did or didn't like about this book—as well as what we can do to make our books stronger.

Please note that I cannot help you with technical problems related to the topic of this book, and that due to the high volume of mail I receive, I might not be able to reply to every message.

When you write, please be sure to include this book's title and authors as well as your name and phone or fax number. I will carefully review your comments and share them with the authors and editors who worked on the book.

Fax: 317-581-4666

E-mail: feedback@quepublishing.com

Mail: Dean Miller
Que
201 West 103rd Street
Indianapolis, IN 46290 USA

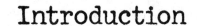

Introduction

Why write a book on privacy? Aren't there several technical books that deal with security? Even though many books cover computer security, there are no great resources on personal privacy.

Privacy used to mean making sure no one found your credit card sales receipt or got a copy of your e-mail. Within the past few years, the average person's personal information has become capable of being made available from dozens of sources. The worst part of the problem is that we freely give away our rights to privacy through all types of services, such as the Internet, e-mail, and surveys. We don't think about how little pieces of information about us can be pulled from many sources to create a full profile of what we buy, what we eat, where we live, and how may hours we spend on the Internet.

The recognition of data privacy issues has increased in the past few years because of high-profile security break-ins. It seems as if some company is always getting hacked and credit card or personal information is being stolen. The one benefit of these break-ins is that the level of awareness about information security and privacy issues has come to the forefront of public news sources.

The questions facing most non-technical users are, "How does all this security activity in the corporate world affect me? And how can I benefit from the expensive tools being used to protect the privacy and data of corporations?" As consultants to large corporations, we have seen the vast amounts of time and money that are dedicated to security and privacy issues. The problem is that the average user cannot afford to spend the time to learn all the various options to secure themselves, nor can he spend the money necessary to buy and then learn all these sophisticated tools. The market has not adequately addressed the needs of individuals when it comes to data privacy and security. Although many methods exist for distributing your personal information and being attacked by hostile users in the online world, few safeguards are available to the average user. Pockets of security resources do exist that apply to an individual, such as banking applications and credit card transaction processing. However, these functions all relate to monetary transactions. But as we have seen, these are not perfect. The major shortfall in the market relates to small, cost-effective tools that are easy to use by individuals to protect themselves in the savage online world. The consumer market has not been addressed when it comes to disseminating security information. Corporate administrators have all the technical information at their fingertips, but the everyday consumer has not been given practical advice on what steps to take and what tools to use to keep his information and home systems secure. We hope to address this lack in the security market that has forgotten the consumer.

With the advent of such technologies as cable modems and Digital Subscriber Line (DSL), the individual user has opened himself to attack from direct Internet connections. Sending data to companies for free e-mail accounts, buying merchandise online, and signing up for services over the Internet has opened a black hole for data collection. Every piece of information you send is being stored in a database somewhere that can and will be sold to agencies all over the world. Such information doesn't even need to be stolen anymore; companies can just buy everything there is to know about you.

Understanding the potential problems you face by using new technologies has not been communicated to the public. Such technologies as purchasing online, using cable modems, and using mobile phones to browse the Internet never advertise the potential privacy concerns and security risks. Such marketing material never quite makes it into a public forum until someone has been hacked and the news headlines broadcast the gory details.

One primary goal of this book is give the everyday user the practical knowledge to understand the sophisticated battle for data privacy and security. The technical jargon has been left to the reference manuals used in corporate information technology (IT) environments. Usability is our number one priority in presenting this material. You don't have to work in IT to understand how to keep your data private. A secondary goal is to balance your knowledge with practical tools and techniques to use today's technologies in a secure fashion.

You will need practical, cost-effective methods of keeping yourself secure once you understand the pitfalls that lie in your path on the road to newer and better technologies. Examples are given of how to use the tools we describe, as well as best practice cases and references to additional material that can increase your knowledge of the risks you face in keeping your data private.

What's So Special About This Book?

We wrote this book to educate you about your right to privacy. Technical folks have hundreds of books that are somewhat incomprehensible to people who are not in the IT industry. IT can appear to be black magic with all its acronyms; it's like casting a spell—ICMP TCP, IP, UDP, WEP, IEEE, IPSEC, poof! You just baked a network. This book should be your bridge between all the technical jargon and the practical advice you need to operate securely in an Internet environment. Consumers are faced with new technologies that no one has told them how to secure, and now their information is being attacked.

The Problem

You have just gotten your cable modem installed. After 2–3 weeks of fighting with the cable company and 4–6 hours of tech support, you are finally blazing away on the Internet, surfing your favorite Web pages and downloading some music from Napster. You then check your e-mail, and you see a joke from a friend sent as an attachment. You execute the attachment, and it has a dancing baby.

Your 733MHz Pentium III Windows 98 home system is pretty fast, you have a fast cable modem connection, you aren't doing anything too intensive, and yet your computer begins slowing down. You stop that file you were downloading, but you can barely surf a Web page. Nothing seems to be wrong with your computer, but the problem persists.

The Cause

Several things might be happening. First, cable modems give you an IP address that is reachable from the Internet. You now have a direct connection, so anyone on the Internet can see you. This leaves you open to a denial-of-service attack, in which the attacker attempts to disable your connection or computer through various means of attack. Another possibility is that the Web site you were surfing that asked you to download something or click some function could have performed hostile activity on your computer. Or, that e-mail attachment with the dancing baby could have installed a Trojan horse program (a program that is supposed to perform a task but also performs some other task, usually hostile, in the background) that is using up your system resources.

The Solution

Leaving your computer wide open to anyone on the Internet is the first problem that must be solved. Several good, inexpensive software products can be used to protect and hide your computer from attackers. The potential problems involved with surfing a site that you might not know is hostile can be solved through learning how to download programs securely and how to know when a program is trying to attack your computer. E-mail attachments can be checked with virus scanners that have to be kept up-to-date constantly.

Consumers often rely on third parties to keep them secure. For example, you assume that your bank is keeping your data secure when you pay bills online, that the Web site where you just bought a Palm Pilot has securely accepted your credit card information, and that your Internet service provider is doing something to protect your home computer. This is not enough in today's environment. Often, the large third-party corporation can't keep itself secure, so how will it keep its users secure? Security and privacy go hand in hand; you can't keep you data private if you're using an insecure technology.

For every potential weakness in the technologies we discuss, we will have a solution and countermeasure available for you to use. Privacy and security can be achieved with the right tools, techniques, and the knowledge of how to use them. You will not be able to secure an IT environment with this knowledge, but you will know how to securely use the technologies that apply to you on a daily basis.

Legislation has been severely lacking to accommodate the new needs of consumers. How our privacy is affected by new technologies is not yet understood by lawyers or courts, much less the consumer. We will strive to make some sense of the current legal environment and attempt to demystify the future of privacy when it comes to new laws.

Here to Help

This book explains why you are a target of attack, how the government is intricately involved with your privacy, and how you can take control of the mechanisms necessary in today's sophisticated environment to protect yourself. Through a combination of practical steps and forward-looking analysis of security measures you need to implement, we hope that you can secure your home and family with the information we provide.

We, the authors, come from a background of computer security consulting and training. For years we have been performing network penetration testing and computer security assessments for corporations around the world and in virtually every industry sector. Companies have taken a proactive stance regarding security and as a result, privacy of consumer information has benefited. We have seen all sorts of security breaches and have done testing to prove these breaches can and do occur. That experience is what we bring to this book.

We have tested and secured various technologies, and we now present that knowledge to the consumer market. We have seen how a hacker or disgruntled system administrator can invade your privacy by stealing your personal information from a company. The gap between corporate IT and the consumer's knowledge about security and privacy is vast; hopefully, we can help close that gap by giving you some practical advice to keep yourself and your systems private and secure.

Feel free to contact any of us—we are here to help:

```
gary@foundstone.com
william@foundstone.com
chris.weber@foundstone.com
```

I

Life in the Digital Age: Why We Want and Need Privacy

1

The Quest for Privacy in the Information Age

Anyone with an inkling of the world probably thinks that there is no such thing as privacy anymore. The growth of the Information Age and Internet has brought increased attention to privacy issues. On any given day, you will see at least one news story about privacy, or lack thereof. "You have zero privacy anyway." The CEO of Sun Microsystems, Scott McNealy, said this. It just about sums up the way the world is heading when it comes to privacy. Are we doomed to be open books for those wishing to know about our lives? There must be some reason that every futuristic movie shows individual privacy as an antiquated concept. Every person's life is encoded in a chip, a card, or a thumbprint that gives a semi-sentient machine complete access to his life and background. Is this where we are headed as a culture? Is there anything we can do about it? Perhaps. Perhaps not.

The steady progression of technology has had mostly beneficial results on our daily lives. Can you imagine not being able to look up information on the Internet about any subject with a couple clicks of the mouse? Instant access to information and communications is probably one of the greatest benefits of the Internet and all the peripheral technologies it has spawned. Having to perform research using the local library card catalogs and encyclopedias is almost a thing of the past. If you need to find out about a new product or that company you want to invest in, it's a matter of spending a few minutes to find what you need online. (You probably have to wade through some useless items first, but nothing is perfect!) Communication from companies to consumers and consumers to consumers has never been greater. To contact someone, you probably have several ways to track him down if he is wired. First, you try the cell phone, then maybe the pager, and after that, maybe a wireless device such as a Palm or RIM Blackberry device. And let's not forget about the online, instant gratification communication methods: Instant Messenger, ICQ, and so on. Communicating has never been easier. You can track people down with a number of ways that have almost become a virtual leash around our necks. (Sometimes you just don't want to be found!)

The most popular achievement of technology is probably online shopping. It seems trivial, but money makes the world go round—shopping online is just making it go round faster. As demonstrated by the Christmas sales reports each year, there is a steady progression in the number of people making purchases online. Who wants to hassle with crowds and parking when you can stay at home and finish your shopping in a fraction of the time? Internet shopping has made instant gratification an addiction when it comes to shopping. There is no need to visit five stores to find what you need when you can buy it on the Internet and have it delivered the next day to your doorstep. Comparison-shopping can be done for you with such sites as Pricewatch, CNET, and Pricegrabber, to name a few. They do all the work for you, and you pick what best suits your needs. Of course, you are submitting your personal preferences to them when shopping.

Wireless technology is probably the other achievement that will revolutionize how we conduct business and access information. For cell phone users, being without it is tantamount to losing a limb. Wireless shopping will push the adoption of this technology to the consumer market at a faster pace. Wireless will provide easier access to information and communications that will possibly supplant the way we access information today. Usage will increase at an exponential rate over the next several years. Soon you will be able to locate people via their cell phones; there will be no way of hiding from people or missing someone just around the corner.

Table 1.1 lists wireless subscriber (consumer) statistics from International Data Corp.

Table 1.1   **Wireless Subscriber Statistics**

	1999	**2003**
U.S.	560,000	73,100,000
Western Europe	91,000	72,000,000
Asia Pacific	460,000	143,400,000
Japan	3,800,000	40,900,000

Internet technology, which is more than just use of the Internet over a computer, has invaded our lives and become a necessity. As new products and services become available, consumers have shown that the adoption rate is becoming shorter as consumers become educated and sophisticated in technology usage. Features such as online shopping and wireless access to everything have spurred usage across every segment of society.

Growth Factors

As the telephone revolutionized how we communicate, so does the Internet and other modes of communications such as wireless technology. Within the last ten years, we have seen a fast and steady progression in communications between corporations and between individuals. The first stages were businesses interacting increasingly with the consumer. It became easy for companies to provide information and interaction with users through their Internet presence. At first, it was just displaying information on a static Web site—it was basically putting all their hardcopy marketing material on a Web site for the consumer to read through. As each company registered its domain name and linked it to a Web site, it became easier for the consumer to find the information she needed. This was not true "e-commerce." It was more like "e-information." Disseminating information to consumers over the Internet became easier. Companies have taken the information dissemination to the next stage, which is personal customizations of products and services a company can provide to the consumer. These customized products and services are based on data collected from hundreds of sources. True e-commerce developed between the company and the consumer and between companies. Companies could automate processes and transactions between each other, share information, and better serve the consumer. The consumer has the new, vast capabilities of giving direct feedback and providing information for customized services from the corporation.

When you buy a product on the Internet, say a digital camera, you get complete information about it, research it beforehand, and find every possible comparison that can help you make a decision. CNET information on digital cameras was found in less than 1 minute (see Figure 1.1). After you make a decision and a purchase, your confirmation via e-mail informs you that everything went well with the transaction. You can have your purchase shipped the next day to your home or office, and you can go to the shipping company's Web site and track the product's progress to your doorstep. If you have complaints about it when it arrives, you can e-mail all sorts of people, from within the company to the Better Business Bureau. If you need to return the product, you can ship it back the next day and have your credit card automatically credited. Of course, the company can now send you e-mail blasts about products you might like based on your shopping preferences. Isn't that nice of them? Every step of the process is filled with information and communications made possible by the widespread use by both the consumer and corporation of Internet technologies. e-Commerce has been driven by the ability to make money while new technologies are expanding the methods of making money.

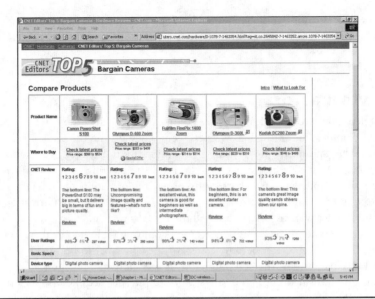

Figure 1.1   CNET digital camera search results.

The sophistication of the consumer has also impacted how much effort a company will put forth in developing technology and providing more products and services. As consumers use new technologies, they become more comfortable and make it a requirement in their lives. By catering to the needs of the consumer, which have become easier to gauge, a company can provide targeted products and marketing materials. After you make it onto an e-mail list, you have basically given a company free reign to send you product information and pass your name along to other companies that have services and products that might be of interest to you (unless the privacy policy says differently).

Costs have been greatly reduced because of new technologies. Companies can reach a wider audience with fewer costs and less resources. The Internet has created the "666" rule for marketing to consumers, as defined by Stephan Barnes. A small company can appear to have 600 people working for it by using Internet marketing tools when they are only 60 people. Those 60 people can work so hard because of all the business being generated through widespread contact with consumers that it feels like there are only 6 people in the company being overworked. (If you have ever worked for a small company, you probably know what it is like to do the work of 10 people.) Companies have been impacted with less time to market and better feedback from consumers on what they do and don't like. The adoption rate of technology by both consumers and corporations has been greatly affected in part by the decreasing costs of buying and selling. In addition, information dissemination and availability of services (resources) over the Internet has spurred growth in all areas regarding technology.

Technology has had the effect of leveling the playing field somewhat among large and small companies. Before these leaps were seen in technology, a small mom-and-pop store could not hope to achieve the marketing and recognition of large companies. With a good Web page and spam e-mail lists, a small company can generate the appearance of a vast presence on the Internet. Immediate feedback can be compiled regarding online purchases when a new marketing campaign is started. Small companies can appear huge through a Web site that makes a cool news story or gets voted number one for some reason. This, of course, gives consumers more choices and more places to make purchases and give up their personal information.

Some companies have almost intimate relationships with consumers because of the Internet and its related technologies. Data on what the consumers like, from underwear to favorite Web sites, is compiled somewhere on some company's server. A complete profile can be developed of the consumer's needs. This, of course, is good for providing targeted products and services to the consumer, but this also means the consumer can be overwhelmed with data and advertisements and be completely known to some unknown entity on the Internet. Is the trade-off worth it?

As technology advances, we see communications between individuals become widespread in a fashion never before seen. Becoming friends with people halfway across the globe whom you have never met is commonplace, and selling your products and services directly to consumers through online auctions and classified ads is easy. Consumer-to-consumer interaction will become more so commonplace as users become more sophisticated and technology caters to these desires. eBay (www.ebay.com) functionality has increased to match the desires of consumers to communicate and sell to each other. Napster, with all its legal problems, has been one vast network of consumers catering to the needs of each other, pushing the envelope of the laws, and pioneering new laws regarding e-commerce. Gnutella (http://gnutella.wego.com/) is another Napster-like technology. This enables consumers to communicate with each other and develop consumer-to-consumer markets. Traditional e-commerce between the consumer and corporation is changing based on these technologies. Consumers can share their information with each other, further disseminating their personal privacy. In scenarios such as these, we are giving our information to each other for the benefit of reaching a larger audience and reaching markets we could not in the past.

The Cost of Privacy

But as with any advancement, some sacrifices must be made. One sacrifice we seem to be making for an Internet-ready lifestyle is our privacy. With each new piece of technology we use—whether it's online banking or wireless Web surfing via cell phones—some bit about ourselves is given to the corporations and mass marketers. For each access point in technology, such as cell phone usage, online grocery shopping, stock trading, reading online newspapers, information about you is being compiled. Your credit card information is stored among numerous companies if you are at all into online shopping or even bill payments. Trading information about consumers has spawned a new field of businesses. Companies are dedicated to just compiling consumer information and reselling it to the next bidder. And this type of business is not illegal. Consumers are making both a conscious and an unconscious decision to trade their private information for the convenience that comes with new technology.

The question of how private we really are can be broken down into two areas of weakness: server side and client side (see Figure 1.2). *Server-side* privacy refers to the storage of consumer information on corporate servers or the vastness of cyberspace. This encompasses the data gathering done by companies you voluntarily give your information to, such as when you buy a product. When you buy a product, a company has information about where you live, your credit information, and what your product preferences are and can start building your profile. When you complete a purchase, you usually have an option to be added to the company's e-mail list. Whether you opt into the e-mail list or not, they can still target you for future marketing and sell your information to others. One such example is the TiVo recorder, a sophisticated VCR-type device used to record television shows. It can be accessed remotely. Information collected about consumer preferences was going to be resold to advertisers, although the company said individual user preferences would not be divulged. TiVo defended its practices by saying names of subscribers were stripped from the data. TiVo-collected data has not yet been resold. Simple technologies such as TiVo are capturing your information and compiling statistics on you.

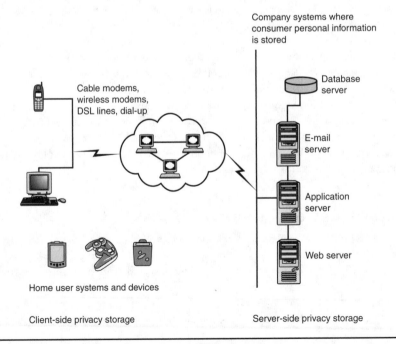

Figure 1.2   Client-side versus server-side privacy.

Collecting information for resale is the sole purpose of some companies. Figure 1.3 shows one example of how these companies make a living. Entire databases of consumer information are compiled, analyzed, and resold, and anyone can buy this information. The last part of server-side privacy is more malicious. It is those individuals, and perhaps companies, who are dedicated to gathering consumer information for nefarious purposes, such as using your credit card information to make purchases or take control of your home computer to launch attacks against someone else. Cyber terrorism activities have become better known and better publicized. In April 2001, news stories about Russian hackers were very publicized because they were targeting specific companies to gather financial information and make a profit through computer hacking.

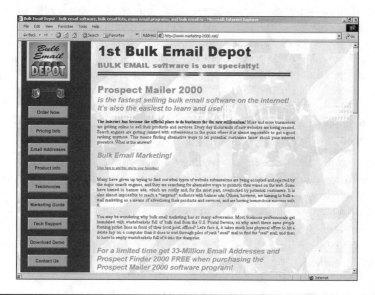

Figure 1.3   Consumer information database for sale.

Client-side privacy is dependent on the consumer. Technology has given us almost instant access to the rest of the world through our cable modems, digital subscriber line (DSL), e-mail, and cell phones. Each wired person has become a player on the world stage with the use of technology. Now, it's not just a company Web site that is a target for attacks and exploitation; consumers have connections to the Internet and have become the new target. The benefits of using the Internet are vast, but as we shall see, they are not without inherent costs. The consumer has been given technological tools but has not been told how to use them correctly or even given a manual on operating them. (But, then again, who reads the manual?) The consumer needs to learn how to secure his information on the Internet and in the coming wireless world that is being spawned with ever-growing technology.

The combination of server-side and client-side technology opens a new world of exploitation to the consumer. That is not to say this is uncontrollable. The consumer has resources and knowledge available that can be used to protect himself and his privacy. Learning the possibilities of the technologies we are using is the first step in securing our Internet connections and information. This book endeavors to bring that knowledge to the consumer.

Case Study: Online Identity Search

Debit and credit cards are currently the most convenient forms of purchase. Cybercash-type technologies have not yet made it into the mainstream of Internet technologies, although they eventually will. If all your bank account information is tied to a debit card, how easily can some malicious person gain that information? Let's break down what type of information the malicious attacker (for the rest of this book we will call him/her HackerX) needs to re-create your debit card information or gather every piece of information about you. The first piece of information used to track you down is your name. You might think this is the most important piece of information, but as we will see throughout the book, other information about you is even more important, and your name doesn't even factor into some methods of compromising your privacy.

So, HackerX uses your name to start finding out everything there is to know about you. Literally hundreds of online methods are available to find information about someone using her name. HackerX can be anyone trying to do this, from a credit card company checking your credit history to the system administrator who runs the computer network of your favorite online shopping site. It's pretty simple to gain all your pertinent information the old-fashioned way, by copying your credit card receipt at the checkout stand. However, the online world poses new forms of privacy risks that are far greater than a clerk simply copying your receipt.

To find out more by using your name online, HackerX can use several person-oriented search engines as a start. These search engines are dedicated to finding all references about you in the online world. A quick search of www.whowhere.lycos.com for "Gary Bahadur" produces the results shown in Figure 1.4. It found 913 references, and the first 2 are a resume and a speaking engagement at a trade show. So, within a few seconds of starting a search, a short biography of Gary has been found, as well as information about where he will be at a certain date. The next piece of information that would be useful for HackerX to know is a phone number. Using the same Web site, HackerX can use the person's name to look up any phone numbers associated with him. HackerX has easily gotten a brief background and phone number of his victim. Using other sites such as Whitepages (http://www.whitepages.com) or US Search (http://www.ussearch.com), you can use a person's name or phone number to find out more information about him, such as his address.

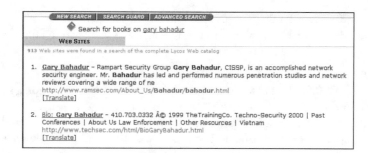

Figure 1.4   Lycos result from searching for Gary Bahadur.

To make a purchase on the Internet using that person's identity, HackerX must have all relevant address and phone number information. Next, he must get the actual credit card information. If HackerX is a good hacker, he can easily break into the online shopping site where his victim is known to make purchases and steal that information from the online merchant's computer systems. As we have seen in repeated news stories, this is becoming a frequent occurrence. A perfect example of this type of hacking was done to CD Universe in January 2001. A hacker compromised credit card information and even posted that information on a Web site. A malicious hacker tried to extort money out of the company and captured thousands of credit card numbers. Using a combination of methods, a good hacker, or even just someone looking to garner information about you, can easily create a detailed profile of his intended victim.

The short case study is meant to underline the brief process of gathering your personal information. The rest of this book goes into detail of how this is actually done and what the consumer can do to prevent such information disclosure. Our everyday life in the online world submits personal data to various entities in numerous ways. Information such as where you are logging in from, phone calls made from your wireless phone, who you are sending e-mail to, what you are buying, and what your online habits are gets stored in databases throughout the Internet. Information does not go away in the online world; it just gets stored somewhere and waits to be found by the wrong person. *Data mining*, which is the search for information using different resources, uses numerous techniques to find all possible information about you that is floating around the online world.

Points of Disclosure

The points of privacy compromised increase as technology moves ahead. Traditionally, you gave your personal information only to sources such as banks, stores where you made credit card purchases, car dealers where you needed financing, and other such hardcopy/brick-and-mortar sources. Controlling and tracking how you gave away your information was easier because the backend technologies were not in place to share your information with the rest of the world. However, the advent of the

Internet—and, more recently, personal technologies available to consumers—has greatly increased the potential point of information disclosure. These points of information access are discussed throughout the book.

Figure 1.5 is a basic outline of a simple Web shopping transaction, in which you make personal information available to the world at several points. If you are going to buy that digital camera you found on CNET, you would have to go through this basic process. Along the way are several points where your personal information can be subverted and captured for evil purposes. These are discussed in the following sections.

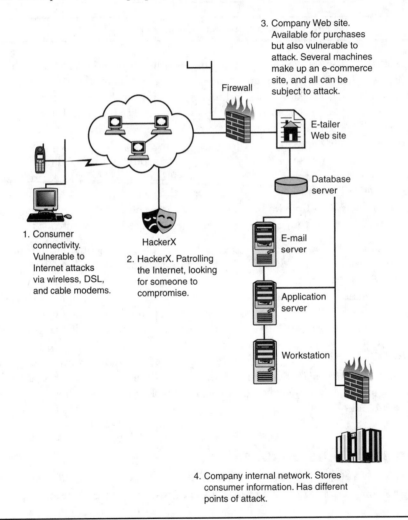

Figure 1.5   Potential points of information disclosure.

Potential Threat 1: Consumer Connectivity to the Internet

The consumer (you) is now present on the Internet through a variety of means, such as cable modems, dial-up connections, DSL, and wireless devices. You are now a node on the Internet and subject to attack, just as are large corporations. The goal of attackers, whether they are hackers or companies after your marketing information, are the same: find out as much about you as possible. How they use your information differs. In this step, you make a purchase from your favorite Web site. To do this, you connect to the Internet, browse through the Web site, make a purchase using your credit card, get an e-mail confirmation, and have the product sent to you. This basic transaction has many points of information dissemination.

With your computer always connected, using Windows 9.x, Windows Me, Windows NT, Windows 2000, Windows XP, Mac OS, or Linux variants, you leave yourself open to attack. If HackerX is after you, the first goal could possibly be hacking your computer and taking control of it. If you are not protected by security software, gaining control of your system is probably a simple five-minute exercise. This extreme example probably seems like it is prorogating fear, uncertainty, and doubt (the FUD factor), but we will strive to clarify all these steps throughout the book to give you a clear understanding of what is possible. On your computer are sensitive files, e-mail, and cookies (more to come on this later)—to name a few sources of information. HackerX now has a lot of information about you by taking advantage of you through client-side technologies, namely your own computer. If you are using wireless technologies to make a purchase, HackerX has a more difficult job of gaining your information and will probably target the server-side processes to invade your privacy.

If the attacker is a company looking for marketing material, it's a simple matter of buying your information from the product company. Each time you make a purchase, you have that option of subjecting yourself to mass marketing, in most cases. Of course, not all companies sell information. (We will discuss the merits of privacy polices to address this issue later.) There are ways of tracking your preferences other than purchasing your information from a product company. If you've used a search engine, the logs of what keywords you used and where you were surfing from can be compiled and sifted for relevant information, and geographic target segments of the population can be compiled based on such information.

Potential Threat 2: Hackers Searching the Internet

Hackers are patrolling the Internet looking for any opportunity to compromise a network or an individual user system. The reasons can vary from fun and profit to cyber terrorism. Hacker skills range from the "script kiddies" who just download and use tools in the hopes of compromising a computer to really knowledgeable hackers who write exploits, actually understand the underlying technologies, and know how to take advantage of weaknesses. HackerX can launch attacks at both the server-side information stores and client-side technologies. Both avenues of attack look for any weaknesses that can be exploited to gain access to your personal information. Hackers targeting individual user systems are mostly looking for resources to control, whereas individual information on the client side is usually secondary when attacking consumer systems. The reasons for attacking consumer systems can be

- To use the client-side launching points for further attacks
- To trade illegal software
- Excitement in testing skills
- To be used for distributed denial-of-service attacks
- To gather personal user information
- To destroy a user's systems
- Revenge

HackerX targets corporate networks for somewhat different reasons. Financial gain and cyber terrorism are becoming increasingly more prevalent in hacker attacks. In the past, it was usually to show off their skills, have bragging rights in the underground community, trade illegal software, and make a statement. Now attackers have more specific goals in mind. The end result of HackerX targeting server-side resources is your private information being compromised. It is easier to hack a corporate e-commerce site and retrieve a whole database of customer credit card information than it is to hack individual user systems and hope credit card information is stored there.

In the case of the consumer using a wireless device to make a purchase, HackerX must compromise a system on the corporate network to gain the consumer's private information. One other possibility is to be in range of the cell phone with a scanner and eavesdrop on conversations, and perhaps "sniff" wireless traffic. Wireless hacking can be very difficult, and the technology is generally more secure that older wire-based technologies. But exploitable weaknesses do exist in wireless technology that HackerX can take advantage of to gain information. For example, the Wireless Equivalent Privacy (WEP) algorithm, which is designed to protect wireless networks from eavesdropping has emerged with flaws. The weakness stems from the ability of an attacker to decrypt traffic based on statistical analysis, inject new traffic from unauthorized mobile stations, decrypt traffic, and launch dictionary attacks. As the technology becomes more complex, exploitation of the technology will move forward at a matching pace.

Potential Threat 3: Vendor Sites Are Vulnerable to Attack

The company's e-commerce site has multiple points of attack as well as multiple ways of disseminating consumer information. All the information it collects about the consumer is stored in databases that are easily mined, with information sold to the highest bidder. Server-side security of your personal information is wholly dependent on the security measures put in place by the company. The user has no rights or influence on how the company protects her information, but public image and revenue loss are usually the driving factors behind the security measures put in place by the company. If news of a compromise of user information were made public, the company would lose the trust of the public, and that translates directly into revenue dollars. There are numerous steps companies take in securing data, from in-house internal audit departments to outsourced third-party security companies that look for weaknesses in the security measures that are in place.

In our example, the consumer enters data through the Web interface, the purchase is made, the credit card information is accepted, and the credit card processing is handled by banks and processing companies. The result is a charge to your credit card and revenues posted to the company's bank account. In many cases, the credit card number might not even be stored on the company's servers, which just means that another company has your financial information and might be the target of a hacker. Several servers on the company's network have to be secured from unauthorized access. This increases the risk of exposure of your data. If HackerX were to compromise one system on the corporate network, he could launch further attacks or just watch the traffic on the network and capture the sensitive information. The attacker can install a *backdoor* that will allow him access at a later time or Trojan programs that can perform malicious activity after some trigger has been activated by hiding what he actually is from the consumer.

Potential Threat 4: Credit Card Companies Are Also Subject to Attack

Credit card processing done by third-party companies has the same risk exposure to your personal data as does the company from which you are buying the product. The credit card processor has its own networks that are at risk from attackers. There might be secure connections between the company and the credit card processor, but after the transaction is complete and your financial information is stored on the credit card processor's server, the connections need to be secured. If the network is compromised, the hacker can install a backdoor and Trojans again and capture all further incoming credit card information.

If HackerX is looking for financial reward, he can blackmail the company into paying some money to not be made a public spectacle. This was done in the CD Universe hacking incident. In this case, an attacker hacked into the company, stole credit card information, and tried to extort money from CD Universe; however, the company did not pay the attacker any money. An attacker can cause destruction of the Web site or to the backend processing servers to cause financial ruin to the company. Code can also be modified to allow the attacker to reroute financial transactions or even change prices on the Web site to buy products cheaply. This type of attack can affect public companies, which can lead to stock price manipulation for profit by the attacker. The attacker can be very stealthy, steal information over a period of months, and use credit card information without the company even knowing it has been breached. There are numerous methods of gaining your personal information from server-side risks.

Potential Threat 5: Internal Networks Are Vulnerable to Hackers and Disgruntled Employees

Assuming that the corporate internal network is secure and data stored on internal servers cannot be obtained from the Internet is a big mistake. Any company that has an Internet connection usually has some connection from its internal network to that Internet site; this is a necessity for easy administration. Protective measures such as firewalls usually are in place to control access, but attackers can still challenge that security to get to the internal environment. The internal network is usually less secure than Internet reachable networks. Stealing your personal information from the internal corporate database servers has the same effect as stealing it from the e-commerce database server.

Internal attacks from disgruntled employees or ex-employees make up the vast majority of internal hacking incidents. Employees can steal your information the same way a clerk in a store can copy your credit card information after you have made a purchase—only they can steal thousands of numbers by copying a whole database instead of just one or two handwritten copies a clerk can make.

These five potential threats to your privacy illustrate some of the points of access to your personal information that we will discuss in the rest of the book. Proactive techniques are needed to achieve personal privacy. In the preceding sections, we have identified points of weakness that we will illustrate in greater detail in coming chapters. Users and companies can manage the risk to consumer information by taking the necessary proactive steps. Server-side risks have been prevalent in the past, but with the advent of new technologies, the onus will be on the consumer to protect his privacy. The tools and procedures are available to fight the war on information dissemination; you just have to learn what they are and how to use them effectively.

Privacy Roadmap

After reading about all the risks to your privacy, you might be wondering how to combat all these attacks on your personal information. As technology advances, it's just a matter of time before someone comes up with an automated method of searching the Internet and compiling every bit of relevant piece of information about you. Privacy advocates such as the Electronic Frontier Foundation (EFF) (http://www.eff.org/) are leading the charge to keep us secure. But that is not enough. Consumers must take matters into their own hands about what type information is given out and how to protect themselves on the Internet and in the coming wireless environment. Data mining is becoming a science, and you do not want your information to be one of the nuggets mined from cyberspace.

Security measures need to be taken by the user to keep information private. Installing security systems on your computer is not synonymous with being private. *Privacy* refers to information about you, and it also includes your behavior and habits in using the online world, which can easily divulge information about you. *Security* is a process of keeping that information out of the hands of the wrong people, and security measures are tactical steps you can take to secure your data. Tangible assets and pieces of information can be made secure. On the client side of the privacy issue, the individual must implement measures such as personal firewalls and encryption to keep her data secure. On the server side, the corporation must take the same measures to secure information, only on a much larger scale. Consumer pressures and laws will have to be put forth to keep our information private on the server side. Companies understand such pressures and will do what is necessary to keep the revenues coming in and keep the customers happy.

Good security does not necessarily equal good privacy. As you will see through examples later in the book, a computer system can be made secure from hackers, but the user can still divulge information through several channels. All the information can be made secure on your home system, but after you send it to a company, you have no control of how it uses your data or who has access to that data. If you implement strong security measures to stop a hacker from breaking into your computer but download a file with a virus that wipes out your hard drive, you have still been compromised and your private information destroyed. Security can be compromised in a number of ways that we will cover later in detail. As an educated consumer, you will understand that you must play a large role in keeping your information from falling into the wrong hands.

The following chapters define steps that can be taken to secure yourself and your PC. The progression of the book lays out practical and legal aspects of privacy first. Next, the problems associated with information dissemination in the online environment are discussed in detail. Then, threats posed by other devices (such as game stations, Palm Pilots, and cell phones) that can share your personal information are discussed, as well as what threats they pose in the near future. Finally, security measures are explained that will show you how to secure your environments and be secure in the future.

The practical steps that can be taken by the consumer to secure their information include the following.

Understanding the Legal Environment

The laws are changing to address the issues of personal privacy, but they aren't changing fast enough to keep up with technology. You need to understand what these changes are and how they affect your daily life. Cybercrime prosecution has taken great leaps forward in recent years. More hackers are being prosecuted, and tangible measures for loss are being developed to help in prosecution. Cybercrime is a global problem that cannot be addressed by one country's laws alone. However, laws are also being passed that can be a liability to the consumer. Industries are lobbying for minimum controls in some areas to enable them to operate more freely and make large profits. For every new privacy law, there will be opponents that see a loss of revenue and therefore seek to bar such laws from being passed. The various privacy laws between countries are covered in Chapter 2, "Defining Privacy: Social and Legal Aspects."

Understanding the Corporate Environment

Companies generally tend to address consumer needs, so you will find a Privacy Statement on just about every company's Web site. If you actually read these, you can better understand what the company's stance is regarding your private information. Half of the time it is very vague, but you can tell somewhat about how they regard your data. If you are using some piece of software, such as RealPlayer, that is connected to the Internet and the company's corporate networks, you should understand what these programs are actually doing. Are they sending information back to the company about you and your system? To understand the companies you are dealing with, it is important to know the following:

- Do they resell information?
- Have they had any prior incidents regarding privacy issues or hacker attacks?
- Have they taken proactive steps to secure their own sites, such as with security testing or audits?
- Do they support privacy initiatives such as those of the EFF?
- What information are they capturing about you, and is it necessary?
- Do they use third-party agents who will also have access to your information?
- What security measures have been built into the software you have installed from a company?
- Does the software you installed perform unknown functions?
- How do they profile your preferences to see trends in your activities?
- If a company goes out of business (such as the dot-gones), what happens to your information?

Knowing Your System

Your personal computers and home networks have become a focal point of attacks and compromise. Cable modem and DSL providers tout the always-on access to the Internet but don't mention the "always-vulnerable" aspect of being on the Internet. You have become another node that can be attacked. Without software to protect your system, you are basically an easy target for any hacker. When your system starts to perform outside the norm, you need to know why. When using browser technology, information is being stored on your hard drive for later retrieval. If you use free e-mail such as with Yahoo!, you have the option to have the site remember who you are. That involves using stored information on your computer to remember you. You must understand how these services and technologies affect you computer. In addition, if you have a home network or your own personal Web site, the potential risks just increase with the additional technology you are using. To know your systems you must

- Understand the weaknesses in your computer systems.
- Understand some of the tools that typically are used against your home systems.
- Understand how to log and monitor your system.
- Know what legal actions you can take and what actions would be deemed illegal if you were to start executing attacks against your attackers.
- Know how to respond to a hacker compromise of your system.
- Learn how to implement secure environments as you use the Internet.

The home user must become a system administrator. This does not mean you must go out and learn all about technology and programming languages. What it means is that you must take some time and effort in becoming knowledgeable about the devices in your home and the software needed to protect yourself. Accepting the default settings and configurations from your DSL and cable modem provider will only lead to attacks by malicious folks on the Internet. Assuming that the Web site you browse and the online shopping carts you use are secure, using proper encryption on your credit card information will lead to someone "sniffing" and pilfering your personal information. Assuming you can browse the Web from your cell phone and use your wireless network card on your laptop securely will only lead to dispensing your information to anyone within close range of you. The end user has more responsibility for his own security and privacy and cannot wholly depend on third parties.

Understanding the Threats You Face

Primary threats against you will be directly related to hacker activity. In knowing the technologies you are using, you will better understand what is possible when it comes to exploiting your privacy. Hacker threats are becoming more mainstream and prevalent, and chances are you will be touched by some hacker activity in the near future. To understand hacker threats, you need to know what technologies you are using and how they might be vulnerable. To do this, you must

- Implement security features built into the technologies you are using.
- Keep current with vulnerabilities associated with technologies you are using.
- Know what information about you is available on your computer and what information is being sent out to companies and Internet service providers (ISPs) about your systems.
- Monitor your environment for attacks.
- Be aware that the threats facing the companies you do business with, are the same that you face on your home networks.
- Know who your enemies are—there are more out there than you think.

The secondary threats you face are from corporate entities that seek to use your information in any way possible to make a profit. Companies attack you from an information gathering standpoint rather than a security standpoint. Your profile translates into dollars to the right marketing company.

Using Proactive Measures

Being secure today does not equal being secure tomorrow. The same goes for keeping your information private. Although security and privacy are not the same thing, they are inseparable. To keep data private on a system, you need good practical security measures in place. Each day poses a new threat to whatever measure you have taken, so proactive steps must be in place to keep up with technology changes. Numerous sources of information about system security are available. These need to be sifted through for the information pertinent to your privacy. As you install new technology or use a new product, investigate the potential weaknesses it has that could affect you personally. New technologies bring new weaknesses on a daily basis. By continuously updating and upgrading your security measures, you can keep current with the latest threats you will be facing in the wired world.

Chapter Descriptions

The following sections describe the chapters in this book. Each chapter builds on the previous chapters to tie together the threats you face and show you how you can respond to threats to your personal information, systems, and devices.

Chapter 2, "Defining Privacy: Social and Legal Aspects"

To understand where privacy is headed, you need to understand the laws and societal pressures that affect your privacy. Do we as consumers have a right to keep our data private? We have voluntarily given out this information to companies and Web portals in return for free services and prizes. Should we expect the people we have given this data to will keep it secure? These issues are being debated in both the legal realm and the corporate realm. Privacy advocates are pushing legal standards, while corporations are pushing for standards of their own to voluntarily secure data. This stems from generating revenue by making the customer happy. But some companies make money by disseminating your personal information, so they are pushing for openness of data and loose privacy controls.

You need to understand the laws that are currently in place as well as the laws that are *not* yet in place. Each day brings a new challenge to current laws that were not written to address the Internet revolution. Copyright laws have been making the headlines based on the Napster case. Personal privacy has been prevalent in the resale of customer information, yet legal cases have not made the front pages as yet regarding this issue. Prosecution of cybercrime is being better understood, and the laws are being defined to address the new technologies involved in cybercrime.

Companies want to prosecute when they become the victim of a cybercrime, yet they have a very difficult time doing so because of the lack of clear-cut laws and precedents. For the consumer, it's almost impossible to do anything about being hacked. If your information is stolen from your systems, you will not be able to track the attacker. On the other hand, if your information is stolen from a company, you probably won't know unless a news story makes the theft public. The consumer must depend on the security of the company to keep her data from attackers. The root of the privacy measures begins with the company's privacy policy. For a company to have a good policy it must do the following:

- Take into account the needs of its target market; some customers might be more resistant to having their information captured.
- Capture only necessary data from the consumers. Using surveys and requiring consumers to fill out questionnaires can capture a lot of unnecessary information.
- Clearly identify what is done with the data after it is collected, how it is stored, and who has access to it.
- Give the user the choice of opting-out of any marketing based on the information she has submitted and of keeping her information from being sent to others.
- Comply with any laws regarding privacy and be familiar with pending legislation that might affect the business and consumer information.
- Define the security measures in place to secure the customer information and define what steps are in place to keep it secure on an ongoing basis.
- Define how third parties will use the consumer information if they provide a business function with the company.
- Provide for the enforcement of the policy through internal control structures.
- Give the customer a choice in not revealing her information and the ability to see what data has been collected about her.
- Keep the policy easy to read and understand. A policy that needs translation by a lawyer will not help consumers feel secure.

The problem faced by both companies and individuals is that there are no standards set for securing personal information. It's the Wild West of the electronic frontier, and so far consumers have been losing the battle. Corporate America has not come up with a standard set of guidelines, and neither has the government. For other countries, the same problems apply. Privacy rights are violated on a daily basis both knowingly and unknowingly. If one company has the best privacy practices and then gets bought out by another company, all the consumer data now falls under the control of another company who might not have such stringent privacy policies. When laws have not even been written to address privacy, there is not much the consumer can do for legal recourse.

Chapter 2 strives to highlight the current landscape of legal and societal issues regarding privacy. A number of initiatives are underway to better protect your privacy, and you need to know about them. By understanding both the problems you face and the proposed solutions, you can better secure your own information.

Chapter 3, "Privacy Organizations and Initiatives"

Several organizations have made it their goal to fight for the rights of the consumer. Much like *Consumer Reports*, which keeps tabs on companies and products, organizations are keeping tabs on the government and corporations who would seek to have the bare minimum of requirements and laws to protect your privacy. A grassroots effort has grown up around privacy, with the EFF leading the way. These organizations are pushing the legal community through lawsuits and lobbying to get new laws passed to help the consumer.

A significant trend among large corporations has been the adoption of a chief privacy officer (CPO). This position has been used to highlight the serious focus that some large companies have placed on consumer information. In financial institutions, this is a very key role because of the practical nature of having consumer information stolen and disseminated. Money has been the driving force behind many technologies and initiatives, and privacy is no different. When a company's bottom line is affected because of a loss of consumer confidence over privacy issues, corporations will respond to fill the hole. The CPO is a response to the growing need of consumers to feel secure about how their information is being stored and used.

For any large organization, documents such as a Privacy Policy and a Security Policy are standard initiatives. The quality of these documents, however, is a different matter. From experiences in the consulting arena, we have seen the trend toward having these documents reviewed and tested for validity. Companies are becoming more cognizant of how adversely they can be affected by negative consumer confidence if they are hacked and consumer information stolen. Testing these polices and determining how effective they are has been helpful for organizations to prove to the consumer that they are making every effort to secure customer data and keep the customer information private. Compliance with these types of documents and procedures in the past has not been a great issue. But with the media coverage of the exploitation of customer/consumer information, strict adherence to the actual policies is becoming the trend. Companies use their strict security procedures as a marketing tool to show how concerned they are about their customers.

Chapter 3 discusses the initiatives that affect how your information is collected, stored, and used. Several large companies, such as Microsoft, have taken proactive steps to try to set standards and meet the needs of consumers. Initiatives involving the Internet as well as mobile devices and wireless devices are underway, and you need to be aware of how they will interact with the technologies you use and will be using.

Chapter 4, "Legal Threats to Individual Privacy"

Because the laws are not clearly defined about what the line is when it comes to privacy, the consumer can easily be taken advantage of by companies that have no legal restrictions to curb their activities. Three entities pose legal threats to your privacy: individuals, businesses, and governments.

The low cost of technology has enabled individuals to become their own mini companies. Where once it took vast resources to set up a network, develop a Web site, sell a product on the Internet, process credit card information, and disseminate information, now Joe User can do all this for $39.95 a month. Where you could once expect some sort of controls and security measures from a company, you have no idea what individuals are doing on their sites. No laws exist that prevent a consumer from putting anything she wants on a Web site. The information collected through registrations, survey information, and information gathered from technology weaknesses (such as where you are coming from and the type of hardware and software you are using) is regulated, and individuals can do what ever they want with the information.

The second entity that poses a legal threat is the corporation. Possibly the largest threat, corporations help define the legal environment through lobbying and influencing politicians to pass favorable laws. Besides affecting which laws are passed regarding securing your information, corporations have almost no requirements in how they protect your information after they have collected it. As mentioned earlier, security has the role of keeping your data out of the wrong hands, but there are almost no regulations—from either government or regulatory bodies—as to how a company should secure consumer information. The beginnings of such regulations are now being developed. One government regulation that has already passed is the Health Insurance Portability and Accountability Act (HIPAA). This law is intended to ensure patient privacy and protect the interests of health-care consumers from large insurance companies. This is a case of some segment of the corporate world (namely the insurance companies), who desire to divulge consumer information, and the government stepping in to secure our privacy.

With the accessibility of hacker tools and such things as e-mail viruses and Trojan horses, companies are facing more attacks on a daily basis. This was never that important to the consumer before the advent of widespread usage of the Internet. Now, both you and the company face the same security threats. With all your private information being stored on the server side, you face an inadvertent threat from attackers targeting companies. If the corporate Web site is compromised and an attacker makes it into the internal network, he can find the server that has all your personal credit card information. The consumer has to rely on the internal polices and procedures developed by the company to secure her data.

Industry regulatory bodies have difficulty passing regulations that are detailed enough for good security. Unless a hacking incident makes the news, most consumers are unaware of the hacking activity going on every day. The Computer Security Institute's

(CSI) sixth annual survey, "Computer Crime and Security Survey," announced that based on responses from 538 computer security practitioners in U.S. corporations, government agencies, financial institutions, medical institutions, and universities, 85% of respondents detected computer security breaches within the last 12 months, and 64% acknowledged financial losses due to computer breaches. Yet how many of these were made public? The consumer must rely on corporate goodwill and consumer pressures to implement good security.

Companies can also be a threat to each other and therefore a threat to the consumer. If one company takes over another company, the consumer is at the mercy of the new company's policies regarding privacy and security. What if the company you have been doing business with is acquired and sold off in pieces? Its collections of data are just another asset to be sold. Again, there are no legal restrictions governing such situations, so the consumer has no recourse when such situations happen and cannot do anything to stop her information from being disseminated.

The third legal threat to consumer privacy is the government itself. The U.S. government has been hands-off for the most part in passing regulations to ensure user privacy and even corporate security. This stance has been difficult to change. For the most part, companies and most individuals would rather see self-regulation by industries rather than having numerous laws to keep information private. The sad state of computer security in general has forced more government involvement, and not always for the better. One side of the privacy issue regarding government regulations is that the government can pass laws to make accessing consumer information difficult. The other side of the privacy issue is that government can use its powers to invade the consumer's privacy.

One such example is the software DCS1000 (originally called Carnivore) developed by the FBI. DCS1000 was designed by the FBI to monitor e-mail communications of suspected criminals, but it can intercept and scrutinize e-mail transmissions by individuals who might have no connection to criminal activities. This Orwellian technology has privacy organizations fighting against it. The government has proposed this as a method of helping the public and keeping data secure, but others say it does just the opposite. Privacy advocates are using the Freedom of Information Act to get detailed information on this technology.

The Electronic Privacy Information Center (EPIC) has already filed a federal lawsuit. The same types of laws are also being enacted and challenged in other countries, such as the United Kingdom. The U.K. passed the Regulation of Investigatory Powers Act that allows the British government to access e-mail and other encrypted Internet communications for surveillance purposes. Privacy advocates have raised concerns that this law conflicts with the Human Rights Act of the European Union, which is meant to protect consumer privacy. As you can see, government can be helpful as well as a hindrance to consumer privacy concerns.

After the tragic terrorist events of September 11, 2001, in the U.S., the U.S. and several other countries quickly passed new laws strengthening the government's ability to monitor electronic traffic. Agencies such as the FBI and their equivalents around the world now have more capabilities and leeway in tracking and monitoring suspicious activity. DCS1000 has been implemented in some Internet service providers, and laws such as the Anti-Terrorism Act in the U.S. have been passed to expand the powers of wiretapping and electronic surveillance.

Chapter 4 goes into detail about pending laws and regulations that affect the consumer. Threats come from individuals, companies, and the government, and each entity has its own special set of circumstances that can lead to a compromise of your information.

Chapter 5, "Illegal Threats to Individual Privacy"

The distinction between legal threats and illegal threats is not always clear-cut when we discuss technology. Laws to protect your privacy are not in place yet. In addition, some laws might even compromise your privacy. Over the next several years, we will see legal regulations become more readily defined, which can be good or bad—new laws can be a detriment to your privacy. For now, we do have the ability to determine clear violations of some privacy issues based on current laws. Attacks against you and your data residing on the client side as well as the server side can be measured and tracked in numerous ways.

Illegal threats to privacy and therefore security have usually come from individuals. But, as we have discussed with legal threats, illegal threats can also come from corporations and even governments. The individual attackers are, for the most part, hackers, extortionists, and now *cyberterrorists*. Business threats can come in the form of companies disregarding laws and performing illegal activities that can place consumer information in jeopardy. Governments, on the other hand, can tacitly sponsor illegal activities against other governments and corporations of other governments by not prosecuting such activities or by turning a blind eye to its occurrence.

Illegal attacks can come in two forms against user information. The first is usually launched against the security of the system. This means targeting your computer network at home and at the office. Attackers can compromise your home systems to get your data or use your computer as a launching point for further attacks. The second form of attack is aimed at stealing information, not just systems and data. Information combines different bits of data to make up who you are in the online world. Information can be all the data needed to make purchases with your credit card, such as the card number itself, your billing address, and your phone numbers. This takes more effort and resources than just attacks against computer resources.

Identity theft is one complex form of information theft. This can be done in numerous ways. Identity theft began with physical theft of things, such as passports and driver licenses. One extreme example of this is having a house mover steal all your things. How do you prove that it was theft if the mover says he was robbed on the way to your new home? He now has all your personal belongs and every bit of information about you and can now become you and use your credit cards, and even open new cards. Physical theft is hard enough to defend against, but identity theft is even more complex because you have information in disparate locations and information that requires others to keep it secure.

The individual illegal attacks against your personal information include the following:

- **Hackers**—Hacking was originally used to describe a practical joke or modification of technology and software to solve a problem. But as technology and the Internet developed, it got the connotation of illegal activity.

- **Cyberterrorists**—A new breed of criminal has developed because of the global use of technology and connectivity of just about every country to the rest of the world through the Internet and communications lines. Cyberterrorists target governments or organizations for attack but rarely target individuals.

- **Businesses**—With access to a wealth of consumer information, it was inevitable that some businesses would take advantage of consumers through disguised business practices.

- **Credit card theft**—This activity most directly affects the consumer. Having your credit card information stolen from a site where you make a purchase can be readily understood by the consumer when she sees a charge on her credit card bill for a purchase she did not make.

- **Spyware**—These insidious products stealthily install themselves on your computer and can send out information about your system and your activities.

- **Governments**—Governments around the world have always covertly been involved in illegal activities. With access to the Internet, a government can easily sanction such tactics as cyberterrorism without being blamed.

- **Identity theft**—This is probably one of the most damaging forms of illegal attacks on the individual consumer. Identity theft can destroy your financial reputation and bilk you out of money, as well as make recovery a living nightmare.

- **Fraud**—Scams are prevalent on the Internet. Setting up fake companies and convincing people to spend money for products or services they will never get is easy. In the past, fraud happened only on an individual basis, but with Internet usage, whole groups of people can be deceived by a technologically savvy criminal.

Chapter 5 defines the threats you face. In later chapters, details of how these threats are actually launched in a practical manner are discussed.

Chapter 6, "Understanding the Online Environment: Addresses, Domains, and Anonymity"

The home user has vast capabilities in setting up a presence in the online world. You probably already have your own domain name (www.*yournameregistered*.com) and maybe even a Web site showing family pictures or talking about your pet. If you don't already have a domain name, you can register one for $20–$30 a year, set up a basic Web site, and talk about your love of knitting all in one day. You can make it very easy for someone to find you online by putting all this great or not so great information out there, but that only leads to giving up private information about yourself. This includes detailing your interests, how to reach you, what technologies you are using— all things that lead to a detailed profile. Any registered Web site can be tracked through WHOIS (whois.arin.net); this information shows the person registering a site and his contact and billing information (see Figure 1.6).

Figure 1.6   WHOIS results of a search on PrivacyDefended.com.

To get online, you obviously must have a connection through some service provider. America Online is one of the more popular Internet service providers. An ISP can be considered the same as any other company where you buy a product and give up your personal information, such as a credit card number. You must rely on the ISP to keep that data secure. Of course, one target of hackers is the ISP. Because the ISP has all your information—and in the case of a company using an ISP, access to the company information—compromising an ISP and installing a backdoor on the network can be easy. A backdoor can do several things, including leaving an open connection for later connectivity and capturing information such as your login ID and password as it is sent along the wire. You are now reliant on the ISP's security measures to keep your data secure. But ISPs have many connections to companies and users, leaving multiple points of attack open for the wily hacker. With all the traffic flowing through the ISP—possibly millions of user logins—tracking down one specific attacker and seeing what data he has accessed can be hard.

Being online, you almost have to resign yourself to potentially giving away all your information. Of course, there are many steps that you can take to keep this to a minimum. Using anonymous Internet portals and software can help hide who you are from prying eyes. Anonymous Web surfing allows you to visit a Web site without the site being able to track where you are coming from or track what you are browsing and what your preferences are. Free Internet service providers can also be a way of becoming anonymous, but they bring a whole other host of potential problems with using the Internet. Using a cyber café or public library for surfing can be another path to Internet anonymity.

Chapter 6 shows several means by which a user can be tracked down on the Internet, as well as how you can hide your access and surf anonymously. Being anonymous becomes harder each day with all the login requirements and methods of tracking how you use the Internet.

Chapter 7, "Understanding the Online Environment: Web Surfing and Online Payment Systems"

The Internet has become widespread because of Web surfing. To make money, companies started out with typical sales models, but trading goods and services for money just didn't seem to be enough for the Web. Freebies became a standard part of the Internet culture. Just about anything you want can be found on the Web somewhere. Many sites are just informational, using registration processes to allow entry but also to track users and what they are actually surfing.

Various technologies are involved with Web surfing, from encryption to cookies to information storage. All along the process are multiple points where your personal information can be captured. Having to register on vendor sites, free contest sites, and portal information sites allows the sites to build a profile on you. Many of these sites then resell that information or use it themselves for mass marketing.

The dangers of Web surfing come from two major angles. On the one hand is the personal information you know you are giving out through site registrations and such.

On the other hand is the information you unknowingly give out. The nature of computing in today's world basically comes down to this: You do not really own your computer. Even though you might own the hardware, such as hard drives and modems, software is licensed, and you do not have ownership rights to it; rather, you have a license to use it. The increasingly distributed environment of the Internet is leading many large companies to seek more control over your personal computer. Things such as active content enable centralized sites to exercise control of your PC by installing software of their choice on it. You might or might not be made aware of this.

Internet elements such as cookies are fed to your Web browser when you surf. They collect personal information about you and send that information back to either the originating Web site or a third-party Web site of which you are unaware. Cookies serve both good and bad purposes, and it is important to understand their nature and how you can control them.

Web bugs can be used similar to cookies. They might be designed to track your mouse clicks, or *clickstream*, across the Internet. Sometimes Web bugs are used in conjunction with cookies or spyware and might be designed to make your Web browser fetch software and install it on your computer. However, programs such as Bugnosis from `www.bugnosis.org` can be used to identify Web bugs on Web pages.

Spyware can come in many forms, including software you purposely download or install. Any legitimate software can be considered spyware if it collects and sends information about you back out to the Internet or to a specific organization. If you are unaware of or if you accept a program doing this, it is invading your privacy.

Throughout this first chapter, we have been using credit card theft as a good example of how your personal information can be stolen and used maliciously. Payment systems on the Internet go beyond simple credit cards. New forms of online payments systems are being developed, such as Cybercash, Checkfree, and Digicash. These are, of course, tied to your personal information as credit cards are but should be more difficult for the hacker to compromise and use against you. Theoretically. Technology such as that used by Microsoft's Passport.com enables the consumer to sign on once and then shop multiple sites without having to reenter credit card information each time. All charges come from one account from many sites that have become partners/users of Passport.com. Visa has a similar program using online wallets through several vendors. Your information is stored once through Visa and the vendor and then is used to pay for your transactions at sites you shop.

With all the various methods of surfing the Internet and making payments online, a number of weaknesses exist that can lead to a compromise of your privacy. Chapter 7 discusses how these technologies work and what the potential threats are to the consumer. As with every technology you use, there are correct and incorrect ways of using it.

Chapter 8, "E-mail Security"

E-mail is the basic current communications method on the Internet. Many wired folks have 2–3 e-mail accounts. They are provided free by many Web sites, and your ISP will of course provide an e-mail address. When you register a domain name, the domain registrant typically also provides free e-mail. E-mail is free everywhere because it keeps people coming back to the site and requires information about the user to be given up.

Most e-mail is sent in clear text. *Clear text* means that anyone on your network, whether it's your work network or your home network, can see traffic flowing on the network. This means they can "sniff" the traffic and read your e-mail. Because e-mail can carry some extremely private information, you are making that information available to anyone on your local network where you send and receive e-mail as well as on the network where you are sending the e-mail. In the case of cable modems, your local network can include all your neighbors using your cable company. They can be sniffing your e-mail ID and password and reading your e-mail. However, there are measures you can take to secure your e-mail through encryption that we will discuss.

As we have seen with all the major news stories about the "I Love You" virus, e-mail can be deadly to your computer. A virus attached to an e-mail can easily wipe out your hard drive or look for files on your system and send them to a malicious hacker. Targeting specific information on your computer through viruses will be the next wave of virus development.

Pretty Good Privacy (PGP) was primarily developed for keeping e-mail private. It uses a public key exchange mechanism. Each person has two keys: one public and the other private. These keys encrypt and decrypt the e-mail. If you are not the intended recipient of the e-mail, you will not be able to read it. Normal e-mail traffic is clear text as we have mentioned, but PGP e-mail is encrypted and can't be read by an attacker. There are ways around PGP, such as if you have decrypted the e-mail and keep an unencrypted copy of the message on your machine. If your security is then compromised, the intruder will have access to your text. PGP can also be used as a digital signature to ensure the authenticity of the message.

Chapter 8 demonstrates some of the vulnerabilities associated with using e-mail and gives you several alternatives for using e-mail securely. Encryption is your friend when it comes to e-mail, and you should understand how to use it correctly and safely.

Chapter 9, "Securing Your Internet Transactions with SSL and Digital Certificates"

Although this book is not focused in-depth on technical aspects of using technologies such as the Internet and wireless technology, it is important for the consumer who is heavily into these technologies and who will be using them more as new features get developed to understand the underlying technology and security of devices used on a daily basis. One key technology that makes security possible is Secure Sockets Layer (SSL). SSL works by encrypting data that is transferred over the SSL connection. All Web sites that process transactions or need to use encryption technology use SSL or some other form of secure transmission. Another protocol for transmitting data securely is Secure HTTP (S-HTTP). SSL creates a secure connection between a client and a server, whereas S-HTTP is designed to transmit individual messages securely. Information-only sites that require ID and password authentication usually use SSL if they do not want a hacker to sniff information and passwords. Of course, there are ways around the security mechanisms of SSL and S-HTTP. One of the major concerns with these security measures is implementation and configuration. Problems can occur both on the server side and client side. Therefore, the user must be aware of how these technologies are used to secure her private information.

On your home systems, if you set up a Web site or are running a business out of your home DSL or cable modem, you need to understand these technologies. You do not want your neighbor, who might happen to have hacker tendencies, to take over your Web site and make modifications or destroy your system. Say you were running a home business that sells clay pots. You might think you are not a target of an attacker, but as we have mentioned already, you can be used as a launching point for further attacks.

Another method of securing transactions and performing authorizations is by using *digital certificates*. Digital certificates are a verification of who you are and the integrity of your data. Certificates let consumers know that the company is legitimate and provides for authenticity and verification. Of course, as with all the technologies we have discussed, digital certificates are not perfect and are subject to attack. As recent as March 2001, Verisign was tricked into issuing a fake Microsoft digital certificate. The hacker could potentially use the certificate to pretend that his software product is a Microsoft product and thus is secure and trustworthy. If someone downloaded a software product with this certificate, she would think it was from Microsoft and not a hacker tool. As with any technology, the consumer must know the strengths and weaknesses that apply to their privacy.

Chapter 9 also discusses how to secure your transactions. Transactions can be anything from browsing Web pages to making a purchase. Securing the communications we use on the Internet and eventually through wireless technologies is necessary to keep our information secure.

Chapter 10, "Understanding Your PC Operating System and Its Security Features"

The first step in securing your data is implementing operating system security. Good security starts at home. Home systems have become very complex in the past 2–3 years with the advent of always-on technologies such as ISDN, DSL, cable modems, and sophisticated operating system software. Your computer is subject to attack

24/7/365. To understand how to secure your system, you must first understand how a hacker can find out information about your computer. A good hacker methodically discovers every piece of information about your network/PC and then starts hacking your system with known and sometimes unknown vulnerabilities.

Your home operating system can be a Microsoft Windows-based operating system such as Windows 98, Windows 2000, or Windows Me. Or it might be Mac OS or a Unix variant such as RedHat Linux. No matter what it is, there are ways it can be hacked. Hackers can try to compromise either the operating system or application you are running, such as a Web server, and they can launch denial-of-service attacks against your machine to take it off the network or destroy it. Application attacks are more common against companies that have to perform some type of business processing on their Web sites, such as online brokers. Most attackers try to take advantage of the home user through operating system attacks.

A number of Web sites are dedicated to hacking and teaching hacking skills that can be of benefit to the average user. If you understand the techniques being used in the real world, you will have a better understanding of how you are really vulnerable to a hacker compromise. Newsgroups and discussion forums are available to any user on the Internet for posting and reading about computer security. Good security practices require ongoing attention. In addition to these information sources, several free and for sale products are available that can help you in the quest for privacy and security.

The goal of Chapter 10 is to identify the method attackers use to gain access to your computer. The intent of the attacker can be to take over your system, destroy your system, or hide and use it as a launching point for further attacks. There are inherent weaknesses resident on operating systems and applications that need to be addressed before you should even get on the Internet. Chapter 10 details practical steps to understanding how your operating system can be taken advantage of and help develop the best practices for securing your operating system. We mainly focus on Windows variants and Unix variants of operating systems (sorry, Mac users; we will cover the Mac OS in the next edition).

Chapter 11, "Securing Your Standalone PC: Broadband Connections"

Operating system security is just the first step in your home security. Just as you have more than one lock on your front door, perhaps also using a security service such as ADT, your home network needs more than one layer of security. Just as all the windows and doors are entry points to your home, your computer has multiple entry points, too. Every application and service you are running on your computer can be a threat if it provides Internet access capability. If you run your own Web server, you have a port open on the computer that an attacker can use to reach your system. Open ports are what allow connectivity between systems. If you run Napster, a port is open on your system to allow Napster traffic.

To determine which ports are open and how the applications affect your system security, you use a number of tools. The home user must be a mini-system administrator and security officer to protect his computer. The tools you use to do this are compatible with whatever technology you are using to connect to the Internet, whether it's cable, DSL, dial-up, or some other form of connectivity. (Sorry, ESP is not covered.) We discuss various tools that can help you find weaknesses in your computer and network.

The major market share on online connectivity belongs to regular phone dial-up connections, DSL, and cable modems. Each of these technologies poses different threats to your home environment. These technologies are also frequently used by businesses, which face the same risks as home users. We discuss the relative capabilities of each technology and how to secure each.

Operating system security helps secure your files and the data on your computer. To secure the applications and other computers on your home network, you will probably want a *firewall*. A firewall is usually a software-based application used to allow you to protect your computer as well as a whole network of computers. Home firewalls are now inexpensive and relatively simple to install. The problem most home users face is that they do not understand the firewall settings and rules that allow traffic in and out. We discuss in detail several popular firewall options and show how you can easily configure them to secure your home network.

Home use of networking technology is also on the rise. Cost has been a large factor involved in allowing consumers to buy multiple computers, network them together, and have continuous access to the Internet. But more connectivity just means more areas of attacks from evildoers. Chapter 11 discusses detailed mechanisms to protect your home network.

Chapter 12, "Securing Your Standalone PC: Viruses, Chat, and Encryption"

The operating system is probably the key lynchpin to good security. After we discuss how to secure the operating system, we can move onto application security. Application attacks are prevalent against large corporations, but the home user faces the same challenges on a smaller scale. Internet applications such as Instant Messenger, ICQ, chat rooms, and e-mail are already subject to specific attacks. Everything from viruses to denial-of-service attacks can be launched over these types of Internet applications. However, these technologies all have some type of countermeasures. Security is a moving target that changes on a daily basis, but security software for these technologies is always just a half-step behind the hackers. The consumer must be vigilant to ensure that the gap in security is not wide and deep, causing compromises of her system from different sources.

Technologies such as ICQ and chat programs inadvertently give away system information to anyone on the connecting end or even anyone searching the Internet looking for these running programs. After an attacker knows you exist and can contact your machine, he can launch attacks, as described in Chapter 11. These programs have security options in some instances, but the user must be aware of their existence before they can be used. Combining these programs with technology such as encryption is an option most users are not aware of.

Encryption technology can be a mystical art if you do not know the basics behind how it works. It does not belong strictly to academic or corporate heavy weights. The home user has many options regarding how she encrypts data and communications to keep her information safe from eavesdroppers. If encryption is used correctly, an attacker could compromise the home network, but with disclosure kept to a minimum. Several freeware and for sale products are available; we discuss them and the benefits of each for different scenarios.

To use available Internet applications and yet be secure, you must understand how those applications can be attacked and compromised in the same vein as the operating system. Chapter 12 focuses on how to protect communications between your PC and the rest of the world and how to have a secure mini-domain, which is your PC.

Chapter 13, "Securing Your Home Network"

The connectivity provided by broadband connections has given the home user the ability to run his own networks. Personal firewalls provide functionality that allows you to network all the computers in your home.

But with more connectivity and more systems on the Internet, the risk of being attacked is increased beyond just being vulnerable on one machine on a dial-up connection—your network can be attacked. You therefore need to know how a real hacker goes about attacking your systems, where you have potential vulnerabilities, and how to fix them.

Chapter 13 outlines how attacks are performed. You will understand how you can test your own network's security before the bad guys do. After you find out where you might have a hole in your network, you can go about fixing it so a real attacker will not be able to gain access to your network.

Chapter 14, "Securing Your Privacy Using Other Digital Devices"

The realm of privacy concerns goes far beyond the Internet and your PC. PCs are no longer the sole technology for communications, shopping, and information dissemination. New functionality is being developed to use the Internet for everything from online gaming to watching movies to paying bills. Even as vast as the Internet is and with all the technologies it employs, new technology is creating new paths for Internet-like services in other mediums. The force driving this development of alternative technologies to replace what has been working on the Internet is the consumer's need for convenience. It's becoming easier to shop and talk to people everywhere in the world, and consumers want more and more.

Ease of communications is probably one of the greatest characteristics that has been ported to other mediums. Devices from personal digital assistants (PDAs) to cell phones have developed capabilities far beyond that of their original designs. They are allowing consumers to communicate anywhere at anytime, and this capability can become addictive. Many cell phones now have instant messaging—one of the key features of AOL. We have become addicted to instant messaging on the computer over the past several years, and now it's even easier to do with your cell phone. Cell phones are also capable of wireless Web access. You can shop and browse the Internet from tiny cell phone screens (although, if you have tried this, you know the technology is not quiet ready for prime time). What hasn't been discussed with these advancements is how your personal information is being transmitted and who is seeing it on the other end. If you make purchases on your cell phone, does your personal data get encrypted just as it would be if you were using your desktop?

Wireless technology is the latest frontier to be conquered. As cell phones and PDAs use wireless technology to bring shopping and Web browsing to handheld devices, consumers will have a greater range of possible avenues to spend their money and share their information with the rest of the world. Wireless technology has taken greater care with regard to security, such as encryption and authorization, but as we have mentioned, privacy is not the same as security. Is your data being kept private when it is transmitted via wireless protocols?

The manner in which your information is transmitted and stored is very vague, and consumers have very little knowledge about how these new devices and functionality will affect their privacy. We cover a number of devices and technologies in Chapter 14 and detail the threats they pose to your security and privacy of information. The industry trend is to move beyond the PC to perform different functions; however, advancements in technology are not without cost.

Chapter 15, "Parental Controls"

Using the Internet securely can be taught by reading books or practical experience. But how do you manage to impress the need for security of personal information on your kids? Many kids are even more knowledgeable about using the Internet than their parents, but that doesn't mean they know or even care whether they are giving away personal information to anyone in a chat room or by filling out a survey by using a service such as Napster or Morpheus.

As the parent and system administrator of your home, you need to understand how your family members are using computers in your home and how you can help them use technology securely. This can come close to invading your children's privacy, so it is a fine line that must be walked in securing your family in your home.

We cover several technologies in Chapter 15 that can help you protect your kids and allow you to monitor what they are doing. Much like you would not want children watching an R-rated movie, you will want to protect them from R-rated and X-rated material on the Internet.

Chapter 16, "Guarding Your System Against Hacking"

After we have discussed all the methods of securing your systems and devices and restricting access to your personal information, we discuss on-going security measures you must take to maintain your privacy. There will be continuous threats to your privacy, so you need constant vigilance to keep your information secure.

One key factor in maintaining good security is understanding how to detect a system compromise or detect someone making unauthorized access requests for your information. You will need to know how to respond to an attack and what steps are necessary to close the holes in your systems and maintain a good security posture.

Aside from technology monitoring of your systems and information, you do have legal rights in prosecuting attacks. Legal action is not as effective for home users as it is for corporations, but that will change over time. You must also know what the line is between securing your systems from a hacker and becoming a hacker yourself when you try to retaliate against someone. It's an easy step from victim to attacker, and you must know how to avoid stepping over the line. Chapter 16 is dedicated to understanding how to respond to attacks and maintain security over your information and systems on an ongoing basis.

Future Trends

The future is unknown. Well almost. For the next couple years, we can map the basic trends for technology growth. The current technology we have today will only get better and more sophisticated to meet the demands of the consumer. Ease of use has been driving technology, one great example of which is wireless technology. It has made information access and usability of computers and mobile devices so easy that consumers cannot get enough. This also applies to just about every device and technology we discuss in this book.

Mobile Devices

New devices and high-speed access technologies will allow more people to go online for less than it has cost in the past. Technology will invade every segment of society, and for those who cannot afford it, free portals will be available—such as libraries and schools—to meet the demand. The ways people use these devices will change how PCs are used. Mobility and ease of use will be the key factors in adoption by a larger portion of the population. Things once done on a PC and Web browser, such as stock quotes, auction bids, instant messaging, shopping, and information lookup, will be ported to other devices.

Communications

Consumer-to-consumer communications will become more prevalent. We have seen the beginnings in services such as eBay and Napster, in which consumers interact directly with each other. In addition, programs like Instant Messenger and ICQ have brought users together directly—they can share information and files and chat on a real-time basis without boundaries or borders. Cell phones are already widespread; as their functionality increases, so too will usage. Pagers have evolved into a whole new species of device, such as the Blackberry, which replicates many functions of Microsoft Outlook in a pager format. Global communications will be made easier through technology, and instant gratification by using a variety of devices to communicate will drive the marketplace.

Costs

Technology costs have been steadily dropping. The miniaturization of every device we use from laptops to cell phones has also seen a decrease in costs. Services we pay for are also becoming more inexpensive. Individuals can use their access and low costs to become players on the Internet, but the end result is that anyone who wants to do business, not matter how cheap the costs of entry, will have to make money. The days of free online access and giving away freebies, contests, prizes, and information are numbered. The dot.com crash has shown that free really isn't a way to make money (duh!).

Privacy

With the U.S. government using technology such as DCS1000 (snapping up your e-mail and watching what you say), it doesn't seem like we are heading in the right direction for keeping our lives and information private. Technology is making snooping on each other and stalking people in cyberspace easier. The government can be the best friend or worst enemy of privacy advocates, depending on how laws are created and interpreted. Legal reaction to changing technology has been getting better as government officials and lawyers begin to understand technology and anticipate advances in technology. In addition, users are becoming more educated about their rights and how people, corporations, and governments are encroaching upon them. Technology is keeping pace with consumer needs for privacy, and privacy protections will be more widespread and user-friendly through the use of technology. Consumers will be able to maintain some level of privacy, which is good because we really don't want to end up in Orwell's *1984*.

Summary

The control and security of our privacy is being spread over many new technologies. As we become more connected and part of the global economy, we will be faced with more threats. To combat these threats, consumers must understand the tools and techniques available to them. It is no longer enough to simply depend on companies and governments to protect us. In many cases, these entities will be the downfall of personal security. The everyday user must learn how he will be attacked and how to defend his information if he hopes to have any privacy in the coming wired environment.

The one thing that will doom all privacy rights is consumer acceptance. If the public accepts the government's and corporations' slow destruction of our rights to privacy, it will be we who are to blame. Organizations such as the EFF are out there fighting the battle for the rest of us, and we need to become active participants in our own fate. We as a community have the ability to rise up and say we need to be individuals and not databases of profiles and marketing fodder. Privacy will live or die by our hands.

2

Defining Privacy: Social and Legal Aspects

In the 1890s, U.S. Supreme Court Justice Louis Brandeis defined the concept of privacy as an individual's "right to be left alone." Brandeis said that privacy was the most cherished of freedoms of a democracy. If Justice Brandeis could see the state of our personal privacy today, he would have a heart attack.

The two forms of privacy we are concerned with in this book are

- **Information privacy**—Rules governing the collection and handling of personal data, such as credit information, personal preferences, home address information, and medical records. Closely tied to this concept is security of private data and privacy of communications.

- **Privacy of communications**—The security and privacy of mail, wireless telephones, e-mail, wireless devices, and other forms of communication.

Privacy is a value that is protected by the right to control one's personal information. The use of various forms of communications, with the Internet being the major channel, has raised legal and social aspects about the expectation of privacy. Prior to the communications revolution that we are facing today, securing your personal information was much simpler. Theft or compromise of your privacy required hardcopy materials and much effort. The ease with which this can now be done is frightening. The question we are faced with is this: Is privacy a right? If so, how do we go about achieving this right? Some might argue that we have voluntarily given up our right to privacy because of the use of technology and communications, and it will just be harder to keep our information secure in the coming technology environment.

The legal rights to privacy have taken several paths. In some countries, comprehensive laws have been defined to govern the collection, use, and dissemination of personal information in both the public and private sectors. Governing bodies then enforce compliance with these laws. Other countries have defined specific laws to address segments of privacy issues, such as child pornography. The U.S. government has taken a hands-off approach to regulations and relies on industry to come up with its own set of regulations. Laws that address privacy issues and self-regulation have been very disappointing. Those laws have not been very specific and therefore leave a lot of room for interpretation. Self-regulation is always in favor of the industry rather than the individual. Enforcement of laws and regulations is one of the major problems with privacy initiatives, so the individual must take control of her information and become knowledgeable in the art of privacy.

The Historical Right to Privacy

History has shown us that we care very much about our privacy. In 1361, the Justices of the Peace Act in England provided for the arrest of peeping toms and eavesdroppers. In 1776, the Swedish Parliament enacted the Access to Public Records Act that required that all government-held information be used for legitimate purposes. The 1948 Universal Declaration of Human Rights specifically protects territorial and communications privacy. Article 12 states, "No one should be subjected to arbitrary interference with his privacy, family, home or correspondence, nor to attacks on his honour or reputation. Everyone has the right to the protection of the law against such interferences or attacks." In 1995 and 1997, the European Union enacted two directives to ensure consistent levels of protection for its citizens. The directives set a common baseline level of privacy. The 1995 Data Protection Directive set a benchmark for national laws for processing personal information in electronic and manual files, and the 1997 Telecommunications Directive established specific protections covering telephone, digital television, mobile networks, and other telecommunications. In addition, the U.S. Constitution and subsequent laws have given us a right to be left alone.

If we assume that we have a right to privacy, we then have to figure out where the line is between our right to privacy and the rights of society in regard to having access to our information that would benefit society. Do criminals have a right to absolute privacy, as would a law-abiding citizen? To find that line, we have to look at how society defines privacy issues and how the law defines privacy. Advocacy groups such as the Electronic Frontier Foundation (EFF) drive privacy laws such as the Electronic Communications Privacy Act. This act attempts to determine privacy rights, but it also provides for dissemination of your information. Within the act, it is not illegal for anyone to view or disclose an electronic communication if the communication is "readily accessible" to the public. If you were to post a message to a bulletin board, with your name and e-mail address, this could be considered public access and anyone can use your information from this board. This information will be stored on multiple servers, and people can search these databases of information. Your information can never be retrieved and withheld from the public after you have put it out there for retrieval. Privacy laws have left a lot of room for interpretation, and a great deal of money has been spent on lawyers to argue both sides of the interpretation.

The Path to Privacy

The path your information follows as you use various technologies leaves many points of access open to information compromise. On the Internet, submitting your information to a Web site, such as when applying for a brokerage account, sends your information through a variety of public channels. All along the way, system administrators or hackers can track down and even watch your information. When you use your wireless laptop to connect to your office, anyone in your vicinity can attempt to capture your wireless traffic and hack into your wireless network with your information. All your data being stored along these access paths will linger for years and be accessible by many people. Different companies have different strategies as to how your data is stored, secured, and used.

If we examine the brokerage account sign-up process, we can see several points of information compromise:

- **Web browser**—When you open your Web browser, whether it is Netscape, Internet Explorer, Opera, or any other browser, you are surfing the Web with unencrypted traffic. As we will discuss in detail later, unencrypted traffic can be viewed by anyone who can capture your traffic along the path to its final destination. If the Web site you are browsing is not encrypting traffic, a hacker on the local segment from which you are surfing, such as your neighbor using the same cable company to connect, can see your traffic and all the information you type in a browser window, such as your name, phone number, and Social Security number.

- **Web administrator**—On the other side of the transaction are administrators who have complete access to all your information. Companies have to place trust in these people because without them, nothing would function. You have to assume that the company has hired ethical administrators and monitors actions so no rogue administrator can steal information and use it for evil purposes.

- **Site security**—The technological aspects of your information security are the most frequent points of attack. If the brokerage site does not implement strong security measures, an attacker can remotely gain access to databases that store your information.

- **Your home security**—As many brokerage companies are moving to completely electronic trading procedures, from making a trade on the Web site to receiving an e-mail confirmation rather than a hardcopy letter, you will store more personal and sensitive information on your system. If your home computer gets hacked, and the attacker has access to your e-mail, he can find very valuable information about you and access your brokerage account.

- **Your ISP**—Your Internet service provider (ISP) can be hacked and compromised just like any other company. If a hacker has a foothold on the ISP systems, he can install packet capture software that retrieves user information and login IDs and passwords.

The multitude of places where your information is stored and who can have access to it means that even if one entity has defined your privacy right with a privacy policy, all the other entities in any transaction you make have not agreed to keep your data secure. If you send your information to a brokerage site that has a good privacy policy, there is no guarantee that the ISP you are using is not watching your traffic or that the system administrator won't quit and steal all the user information. Your expectations of privacy must be tempered with the knowledge that there is no real guarantee that all these various points of access to your data will be secure and adhere to laws and privacy statements.

A false sense of security is probably worse than having no security at all. If a site says it requires a login and password from members, it might be somewhat secure. A user will feel that not everyone on the Internet will have access to her information. But that is wrong. What is to prevent a valid user on the system from taking your information and spreading it through other completely public forums?

One example of having a false sense of security is the compromise of the ICQ logs of the CEO of eFront. Private messages over ICQ were made public by a hacker. There were several things wrong with the use of ICQ in this case. First, ICQ is by default insecure. The messages are not encrypted, and data can be captured on the wire. Second, the log files are stored on the computer running ICQ and can be retrieved by someone with malicious intents. Lastly, there is no guarantee that the other party will not disclose your personal information and communications. Personal communications can be made public, such as in this book (see Figure 2.1), because there is no law or guarantee saying that the other party will not disseminate your information. It was easy for us to post a private ICQ message session.

Cases such as the ICQ log fiasco should not be a surprise to anyone because there was no expectation of privacy. It's true that a hacker made the logs available, but it could just have easily been one of the users of ICQ making the logs available. (Are you scrambling to erase your ICQ logs now?) Of course, for every problem there is a solution. eFront could have used secure messaging solutions; many are available, such as from Mercury Prime (http://www.mercuryprime.com). If the management team at eFront had better understood the security issues involving the programs they were using, they would have probably used a secure technology. Expectations of privacy were not in line with the actual use of the technology.

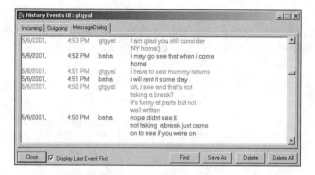

Figure 2.1　ICQ log message.

The flip side of this expectation of privacy is actual laws or policies that tell the user she can expect her information to be secure. The Federal Electronic Communications Privacy Act (ECPA) makes it unlawful for anyone to read or disclose the contents of an electronic communication (18 USC § 2511). E-mail service provided by online services is covered by this act. As mentioned earlier, this same act also provides for loopholes around the privacy safeguards. Three exceptions to the security of your e-mail messages are

- The provider can view private e-mail if it suspects damage or harm by the sender.

- The provider can legally view and disclose private e-mail if either the sender or the recipient of the message consents to disclosure.

- If an employer owns the e-mail system, the employer can inspect e-mail on the system.

Interpretations of these exceptions can just as easily disclose your personal e-mail messages as any hacker would. This is just a legal means of reading your personal e-mail. ECPA also provides for law enforcement to access e-mails with a court order. The points of access where your information is stored are all subject to these types of exceptions.

Your right to privacy is more like a right to *some* privacy, until you get hacked, the government decides it's necessary to view your personal information, or you unknowingly give it away. Everything you do online can be tracked or stored on some server somewhere in the vastness of cyberspace. There are no limitations on the amount of data that can be stored or how long it will exist. Even casual browsing of Web sites can capture information about your interests, where you are surfing from, and the type of software you are using. Web sites can use *cookies* to track your activity on their sites and remember you from the last time you visited them. Cookies are small text files containing user information collected by a Web site and sent by the user's browser to the site's server, and vice versa. The Netscape `cookie.txt` file saves information about your access to the site. We will discuss in detail what this file is actually doing in Chapter 7, "Understanding the Online Environment: Web Surfing and Online Payment Systems," and Chapter 8, "E-mail Security." The following example is a shortened cookies file:

```
# Netscape HTTP Cookie File
# http://www.netscape.com/newsref/std/cookie_spec.html
# This is a generated file!  Do not edit.

.euniverseads.com   TRUE  /  FALSE  1293839999  RMID  ce8739a23a097b70
ww2.weatherbug.com  FALSE /  FALSE  2114399909  WeatherBugAff
➥Value=1345100&Check=CHECK
216.60.197.200  FALSE  /  FALSE  2137622455  CFID  57776
216.60.197.200  FALSE  /  FALSE  2137622455  CFTOKEN  85398937
www.webfn.com   FALSE  /  FALSE  1262304053  UUID
➥77964445-b5c2-11d4-80f2-00508b72c54e
.msnbc.com  TRUE  /  FALSE  1893456052  MC1
➥GUID=517C7F0920764BB08CC39E24E442CEA0
.msn.com    TRUE  /  FALSE  1065294053  MC1
➥V=2&GUID=517C7F0920764BB08CC39E24E442CEA0
.msnbc.com  TRUE  /  FALSE  1893456052  P1  0
.avis.com   TRUE  /  FALSE  1293840056  RMID  ce8739a23a0ae410
www.avis.com  FALSE  /  FALSE  1293840056  AnalysisUserId  247973792274
.focalink.com  TRUE  /  FALSE  1293796800  SB_ID
➥09737922760000495248166096606
ads.link4ads.com TRUE  /  FALSE  1893456066  uid  0xd3cb1fad3.0xce8739a2
.dell.com   TRUE  /  FALSE  1293789606  Profile
➥%7B042D91E4%2D852E%2D11D4%2DA7CD%2D00D0B746BE7A%7D
.dell.com   TRUE  /  FALSE  1132094802  MenuState  6
hc2.humanclick.com  FALSE  /  FALSE  1005844596  HumanClickID
➥206.135.57.162-89709977
.mediaplex.com   TRUE  /  FALSE  1245629120  svid
➥97432691504076313734464968610
.highschoolalumni.com  TRUE  /  FALSE  1074326979  ATA
➥highschoolalumni.974327316640.206.135.57.162
.mediaplex.com   TRUE  /  FALSE  1245628772  mojo1  11f3988/1sb194358
.ac.com     TRUE  /  FALSE  1920408339  MKT_AC  5814277352806457
www.vmware.com  FALSE  /  FALSE  2137621928  CFTOKEN  6987391
www.vmware.com  FALSE  /  FALSE  2137621928  CFID  1084551
.dell.com   TRUE  /  FALSE  1009792806  rpoprodcode
➥dhs%5Fnotebooks%5Finspn
www.processor.com  FALSE  /  FALSE  1293775268  USERID  203646
stats.klsoft.com   FALSE  /  FALSE  1009581230  SYSTEM_USER_ID
➥{25B952BE-99BA-42d6-924A-C472CDFCA0B8}
ads.iboost.com:8080  FALSE  /  FALSE  1078099169  GUID
➥000093939AD80B0D46C2DBA72690574D
.valueclick.com  TRUE  /  FALSE  1762810659  ksa  0OhRTX9FVA7IAAUPjbfc3556f0ae
.linkexchange.com  TRUE  /  FALSE  1005946660  LE_COOKIE
```

Using the information about what you are looking at and keywords you are searching for, sites can develop patterns of usage and tailor ads and marketing material to these patterns. Do you expect this type of information to be kept private? Just from browsing Web sites, companies can track what items are being searched for, where people are coming from, and how they are using the Web. Figure 2.2 shows a sample of the information that can be collected from browsing a company Web site and tracking what users are doing. Using Web log analysis software, such as Webalizer, we can see the ISPs surfers are using.

	Top 30 of 54298 Total Sites								
#	Hits		Files		KBytes		Visits		Hostname
1	93076	4.39%	57610	4.26%	728397	4.13%	314	0.51%	home.com
2	52784	2.48%	30561	2.26%	387943	2.20%	358	0.59%	rr.com
3	50992	2.40%	34578	2.56%	394001	2.23%	310	0.51%	t-dialin.net
4	24139	1.13%	14703	1.09%	179099	1.02%	311	0.51%	uu.net
5	22657	1.07%	14532	1.07%	224983	1.28%	390	0.64%	aol.com
6	21884	1.03%	13440	0.99%	166936	0.95%	274	0.45%	pacbell.net
7	18800	0.88%	13718	1.01%	195905	1.11%	243	0.40%	co.uk
8	16803	0.79%	7365	0.54%	124845	0.71%	138	0.23%	workstation
9	16803	0.79%	7365	0.54%	124845	0.71%	138	0.23%	workstation
10	16115	0.76%	10091	0.75%	139060	0.79%	245	0.40%	mediaone.net
11	16033	0.75%	9944	0.74%	175335	0.99%	245	0.40%	wanadoo.fr
12	14457	0.68%	8677	0.64%	107563	0.61%	232	0.38%	bellsouth.net
13	13230	0.62%	8382	0.62%	96278	0.55%	191	0.31%	mindspring.com
14	12520	0.59%	6149	0.45%	79243	0.43%	190	0.31%	gtei.net
15	11975	0.56%	8274	0.61%	115423	0.65%	251	0.41%	net.au
16	11863	0.56%	7611	0.56%	79511	0.45%	300	0.49%	ne.jp
17	9669	0.45%	6473	0.48%	80896	0.46%	193	0.31%	bellatlantic.net
18	8689	0.41%	5817	0.43%	68313	0.39%	168	0.27%	btinternet.com
19	7963	0.37%	5392	0.40%	81208	0.46%	173	0.28%	com.au
20	7893	0.37%	5237	0.39%	67514	0.38%	150	0.24%	swbell.net
21	7766	0.37%	4702	0.35%	59376	0.34%	138	0.23%	att.net
22	7614	0.36%	4736	0.35%	63193	0.36%	150	0.24%	shawcable.net
23	7205	0.34%	4364	0.32%	57100	0.32%	112	0.18%	optonline.net
24	7182	0.34%	4600	0.34%	49267	0.28%	142	0.23%	uswest.net
25	7074	0.33%	4119	0.30%	64880	0.37%	217	0.35%	in-addr.arpa

Figure 2.2 Webalizer view of users' ISPs.

There are no guarantees or laws to provide anonymity through browsing or a host of other features you use on the Internet, such as chat rooms, message forums, and FTP (File Transfer Protocol). Companies can track how you use the features they provide to you and build profiles of your activities.

Privacy Policy Usage

Companies are defining your rights for you in their privacy policies. Because the laws are still very vague, the Internet industry is performing self-regulation. This does not mean users will receive the best care when it comes to their personal information. Advocacy groups and several laws are paving the way for the industry to develop privacy policies and secure your data, but the implementation and interpretation is still up to each company. The Federal Trade Commission is encouraging sites to post privacy policies, but it does not have the power to enforce privacy polices based on any current laws. Several organizations that are actively encouraging privacy polices are TRUSTe (www.truste.org), the Council of Better Business Bureaus (BBB, at www.bbbonline.org), the American Institute of Certified Public Accountants WebTrust program (www.aicpa.org/webtrust/index.htm), and a coalition of companies called the Online Privacy Alliance (www.privacyalliance.com). These organizations and others feel we have a right to privacy and are trying to develop standards for those rights.

Privacy polices define what rights you have on each site you visit. They can range from absolute security and privacy of your data to giving away all rights to your data to the company, who can then do whatever they want with it. One example of a privacy policy that both keeps your personal information private yet gives the company the right to resell it is from iWon (www.iwon.com). Among its many features, this Internet portal gives away prizes. When you sign up for iWon, your preferences and personal information are stored. Part of the privacy policy says the following:

> "We disclose our privacy policies and procedures in this document. We do not sell or rent your personally identifiable information to third parties for marketing purposes without providing you with a choice to opt out from such disclosure, which you can exercise at the "My profile" page. We allow all users to opt out at any time from receiving e-mail messages from iWon and third parties including selected iWon partners or from having information shared for marketing purposes with third parties including selected iWon sponsors or business partners. We allow users to access their user profiles and change information as they deem necessary."

This policy is securing your information, but by default you have opted to let iWon give your personal information and preferences to business partners for targeted advertisements. To change this, you have to modify your profile and *opt-out* of the marketing blitz. This type of opt-out strategy is popular with many product companies that generate revenue from sales or advertisements. They are saying you have a right to privacy, but only if you figure out that you can keep your information private. They are not making great efforts to keep your data out of the hands of the mass marketers. In many cases, they are going to make money if they are able to gather more information about you.

You might have a right to privacy, but that doesn't mean it will actually happen. Laws have been enacted and proposed that both restrict our privacy rights and secure them. Our right to privacy is an on-going battle that we as consumers must take part in if we want to keep our information from prying eyes.

Security Versus Privacy

Laws have not been capable of determining how privacy will be achieved in any practical sense. The ECPA is one step in privacy rights. But as we have mentioned, it can do harm as well as do good when it comes to your personal information. You can't have privacy of data without security, but you can have security with no privacy. *Privacy* refers to data, consumer characteristics, preferences, and any information that needs to be kept private and confidential. *Security*, on the other hand, refers to access mechanisms and control of data and devices. Security applies to both client-side and server-side aspects of user information. To attain privacy, security measures must be taken by both the corporation and the user.

To keep your information out of the hands of malicious hackers and very determined marketers, a company can install very good security measures over data transactions. Such an example is when you are buying a product with your credit card; a company typically encrypts all the information and stores it on a secure server in its organization. The whole transaction process has good security; SSL connectivity on the Web site and data encryption on the server end is performed. Your credit card information is verified, and no one can capture your traffic en route to the company. This secure transaction means nothing to you if all your information is then sold to a marketing company. Recently, one company, eTour, which stated in its privacy policy that it "will not give out your name, residence address, or e-mail address to any third parties without your permission, for any reason, at any time, ever," sold part of its customer database to Ask Jeeves. Even though the site had good security measures over consumer data, personal information still made its way to a marketing company. Your personal privacy has just been compromised even though great security features were used during the transaction.

Security begins with the privacy policy of any site you are using. These policies don't go into detail about what security measures the site is taking, but they can give you some comfort that the site takes security of data and transactions seriously and has dedicated resources to this end. Not many companies have put security clauses in their privacy policies, but hopefully that trend will change. Taking the Dell privacy policy as an example, it mentions Dell's commitment to security in one segment:

> "Internet Commerce: The online store at dell.com is designed to give you options concerning the privacy of your credit card information, name, address, e-mail and any other information you provide us. Dell is committed to data security with respect to information collected on our site. We offer the industry standard security measures available through your browser called SSL encryption, (please see Dell's Store Security page for details on these security measures). If at any time you would like to make a purchase, but do not want to provide your credit card information online, you can place an order without credit card information and a representative will contact you. Alternatively, you can always contact a sales representative over the telephone. Simply call 1-800-WWW-DELL. It has always been a Dell practice to contact customers in the event of a potential problem with your purchase or any normal business communication regarding your purchase."

This type of proactive measure regarding the security of your information gives the user some idea of the steps that might be taken by the site. But even if this type of information is included in a privacy policy on the site, how does the user know that security measures are actually in place to meet the privacy statements? The answer is that there is almost no way of knowing. Some organizations have come up with a certification process a site can go through to check security measures. After the site meets the requirements, it receives a seal of approval. Two such companies that provide this certification are Verisign (http://www.verisign.com/) and TruSecure (http://www.trusecure.com/). The problem with these certifications is that there is no standard set of checks and government regulations that can give the general public a baseline to understand what the certifications actually mean. Another problem with certifications is that it is merely a point-in-time process. The minute the certifying company has placed its seal on the site and finished testing the security measures, the actual security posture of the site might have already changed. Everyday, a new hacker exploit becomes known and can invalidate all the testing and certification of the site. Certifications do give the user some idea of the security over his data, and that is better than not having any idea of what steps a site takes to keep your data secure.

Online services can be particularly invasive when it comes to your personal information and your need to understand how they implement security over your data. One of the key aspects of securing your communications and transactions online is the use of *encryption*. Encryption is the technique of scrambling a message or transaction such that anyone who does not possess the right key does not have the ability to unscramble it. If you are chatting with someone using an encrypted connection, no one else can capture your information as it travels along the wire. Unintended recipients can't scrutinize your information. ICQ messaging is an example of *unencrypted* messages. Other people on the wire can intercept your messages and read them. Another benefit of encrypted messages and transactions is that the system administrators of the site you are using can't read your information.

You will notice a lock icon in the lower-left corner of the Netscape browser (see Figure 2.3) and a lock icon on the right side of Internet Explorer (see Figure 2.4). These indicate when encryption is being used. The lock is closed for Netscape and appears as yellow and closed in Internet Explorer when encryption is being used. This is just one example of the various security features that can be used by a site to ensure security of your data. Secure Sockets Layer (SSL) encryption is used in many Web applications to secure the transmission of data.

Figure 2.3   Netscape encryption indication.

Figure 2.4   Internet Explorer encryption indication.

Any message containing private or sensitive information that is encrypted is secure until it reaches its destination and is then unencrypted. Various strong encryption programs, such as Pretty Good Privacy (PGP), are available. PGP is used to encrypt your content, such as an e-mail message. If someone does not have the right key to unlock an encrypted message, all he will see is gibberish. Another form of encryption is the use of the data as it travels along the wire or whatever medium is being used. The data is encrypted as it travels along the transport mechanism rather than being encrypted and then transmitted. SSL, which is used by many secure Web applications, uses this form of encryption. But there are also weak forms of encryption that can give the user a false sense of security. If the encryption scheme is weak and can be cracked, your information will be exposed without you knowing it.

Anonymity is becoming harder to achieve with the technology we want to use. However, some methods of using the Internet anonymously are still available if you feel the security of your personal information through the services you use is not good enough. Anonymous re-mailers and Web browsing are available to you. Determining the name and e-mail address of anyone who posts messages or sends e-mail is easy, so programs that anonymously mail and enable you to surf the Internet have been developed. Hushmail (`http://www.hushmail.com`) is one example of secure e-mailing that provides anonymity and security over your messages. One popular anonymous browser site is Anonymizer (`http://www.anonymizer.com`). A Web surfer can use Anonymizer to browse sites, and no information about him will be captured unless the surfer specifically submits information, such as in a sign-up form. We will spend more time on these topics in Chapter 6, "Understanding the Online Environment: Addresses, Domains, and Anonymity," and Chapter 7.

If a site is using security in all your purchase transactions or in messaging on its site with functions like a forum board, what is the guarantee that after it has securely collected your information it will keep it secure in the future? Do you know whether it has good internal security measures? You have no real guarantees. You have no idea what it does in its network operation centers to secure your data after it has stored it. One example of good encryption and transaction security but bad backend processing security is the hack of A&B Sound's (`http://www.absound.ca/`) online store. This site took orders securely but was successfully hacked, and some online consumer credit card information was stolen and posted to the A&B Sound Web site. The backend systems were insecure even though the transaction process was encrypted and secure.

There is a trade-off between security and privacy from a law enforcement perspective. The more secure a system is and the more messages are kept private using such technologies as 128-bit encryption, the harder it is for law enforcement agencies to monitor criminal activities. If a hacker encrypts all messages with a very strong encryption scheme that law enforcement can't crack, they will not be able to prosecute the hacker with incriminating e-mail messages. If child pornographers have total anonymity on the Internet, they can post material and break laws with the possibility of capture being extremely low. If you have ever posted a message to a newsgroup, you will find that you can post anything, from pirated software to pornography without identifying yourself. Attorney General John Ashcroft, speaking at the Computer Privacy, Policy, and Security Institute, said, "On the Internet, it is easy for a criminal to create a fictitious identity to perpetrate frauds, extortions, and other crimes. Because many computer crimes—such as trading pirated software or child pornography—can be committed entirely online, this anonymity can significantly complicate an investigation." The Justice Department's Computer Crime and Intellectual Property Section, the FBI's Computer Crime Squads, and the National Infrastructure Protection Center (among other agencies) are faced with the problem of anonymous crimes online. For law enforcement officials to gain access to subscriber transactional records, they must obtain a court order demonstrating that the records are relevant to an ongoing criminal investigation (Communications Assistance for Law Enforcement Act, 18 USC § 2703(d)). Laws are both a help and hindrance to our security, which is different from our privacy.

Corporate security measures, as they pertain to the security of your personal information, are beyond your control. Security over your personal information on your own system is a totally different matter, though. Technologies such as personal firewalls, wireless devices, and encryption have enabled the consumer to more easily take security into her own hands. We have mentioned cookies as a method of tracking your use of some Web site and notifying the site when you return and what you have used on the site. To counter this invasion of your privacy, programs such as CookiePal have been developed (see Figure 2.5).

Figure 2.5   CookiePal cookie identification.

This program notifies you when a site is trying to store and use cookies to track your activity. (These technologies are covered in greater detail in Chapter 7.) You can implement your own security procedures to care for your personal information on your own system. After you understand how to implement security at home, you will have a better understanding of how companies implement security and keep your information private.

The cost of security measures necessary to ensure good consumer privacy is also a major roadblock that companies face when considering how much security should be in place. The bottom line usually drives most business decisions, and your privacy can be a casualty of that bottom-line dollar amount. A home user can implement a personal firewall, install a program such as CookiePal, encrypt e-mail, and have secure

Web browsing for a minimal amount of dollars. For a large corporation with thousands of users, however, the cost of security can be astronomical. For Web portal sites, security is usually not the highest priority. Making money is, and anything that impedes this goal will be removed. Security can be a roadblock to fast implementation of a new service or product.

Home user security has taken on new meaning with all the access we now have. Personal firewalls and personal intrusion detection systems are enabling the home user to implement strong security measures to keep his information and systems secure from the client side of connectivity. In the past, the consumer didn't have as much to worry about—companies were mostly the target of attackers. With consumers who have their own mini-networks and at-home businesses with Web sites, security over those connections has come to the forefront of technology. Numerous applications and devices exist to enable home security; we will discuss these in Chapter 10, "Understanding Your PC Operating System and Its Security Features." The consumer is not totally reliant on companies to keep his data secure; he's responsible for client security, and the company he submits his information to is responsible for server-side security.

On your home PC, security measures need to be put in place to cover the operating system, communication channels, and applications you use. The data you store on your computer is at risk from both attackers and legitimate companies. A company can easily store cookies and applications on your system if you are not careful. You have to understand what you are agreeing to do when using some Web sites. One such legal means being developed to trade consumer information is the Information Content and Exchange protocol (ICE). This protocol will be used to exchange consumer information more easily between businesses and will use the eXtensible Markup Language (XML) to provide businesses with a standardized method for exchanging users' personal information, preferences, and other types of data related to online business. The protocol is also designed to automate the process of negotiating the terms and conditions of syndication for this information. Consumers must be aware of the security issues with such technologies if they hope to keep their own information private and secure.

If you have ever downloaded freeware or shareware programs, you are taking a big risk that the maker hasn't installed some sort of backdoor or is retrieving more information than is necessary from your system. Freeware is great because it is free, but as we said, nothing is really free. Many hackers encode backdoors into free programs that can do anything from copy your data to destroy your computer.

One category of software that has developed recently is *spyware*. These are programs that perform hidden functions using the consumer's Internet connection, which the consumer has no knowledge about. One typical function is to send information to the producer of the software. A list of known spyware programs can be found at `http://www.infoforce.qc.ca/spyware/enknownlistfrm.html`. One example of spyware is

TSADBOT, which is installed as a Windows Service with AdGateway by TimeSink/Conducent Technologies. It is loaded onto your system and makes network connections even when behind a firewall and persists even after the software it came with has been uninstalled. It connects to the Internet, downloading ads—whether the advertising-supported application is running or not—and implements an unauthorized proxy server on the user's system. Then, *profiles* are stored in encrypted files on the user's system and can be transmitted to Conducent by the TSADBOT software. With programs such as these running on your system, your data can be used and abused without your knowledge. Security becomes paramount on the client side in situations such as these. You need to know whether unauthorized activity is taking place on your own desktop before you start worrying about what corporations are doing with your information.

When using services provided by companies, such as free Internet access, the consumer must be aware of what the security risks are and what information he is giving away. One example of losing control of your data and computer system is the case in which Juno (http://www.juno.com), a service that provides free online access, changed the terms of its agreement with customers in early 2001. The new agreement said that customers must allow the downloading of software that would perform computational tasks on the home user's computer. The consumer must also leave his computer on, and Juno would have the right to "initiate a telephone connection from your computer to Juno's central computers." So, the consumer loses control of his own computer, the service install software that the user has no idea about, and Juno can make phone calls from the user's computer. Your personal data would be at risk from the company itself. To get something for free, you would have to give away a lot of your rights to your own computer. There really isn't anything free anymore. You have no idea about what security breaches might be installed on your computer, with all your personal files at risk.

An industry-funded study by Robert W. Hahn, a Resident Scholar of the American Enterprise Institute, titled "An Assessment of the Costs of Proposed Online Privacy Legislation," estimates costs of $30 billion or more to comply with possible Internet privacy legislation. This study was sponsored by the Association for Competitive Technology, and the results of the study have been attacked by various privacy organizations. The independence of the study can be questioned, but it does highlight the fact that security of private information is not a trivial matter when it comes to dollar amounts. As laws are still being defined in the U.S. to address security and privacy, the costs can't be readily estimated to any degree of certainty, other than to say that it will not be inexpensive for companies to implement security. As mentioned earlier, the U.S. privacy initiatives are largely self-enforced with little guidance from the government as yet on how to implement security procedures to protect our privacy.

Can you have privacy without good security? No. As we discuss security risks in detail in the following chapters, you will see that any lack of security can lead to a compromise of your personal information, both from home user systems and corporate systems. But does this mean that companies can install vast security measures, such as e-mail monitoring and data capture technologies (sniffing), on their networks and Web sites to look for hacker activity? This would be a good security feature but could also lead to the invasion of our privacy.

The FBI has developed a sniffing technology called DCS1000 (originally called Carnivore), a controversial e-mail monitoring program. DCS1000 was designed by the FBI to monitor e-mail communications of suspected criminals by seeking out packets of data in e-mail messages, using keywords or just capturing all e-mail from or to a specific e-mail address. DCS1000 is implemented at the ISP (assuming that the ISP cooperates with the FBI). A terminal box loaded with the software is installed with the ISP's equipment and is then attached to the network. With the terrorist attacks on the U.S. on September 11, 2001, more ISPs are cooperating with the FBI in implementing DCS1000. It has not yet been implemented in many ISPs, though.

Do the security features touted in the FBI's DCS1000 project outweigh the possible loss of privacy we will face with its technology monitoring all our e-mail messages at the ISP level? In 2000, the U.K. passed the Regulation of Investigatory Powers Act that allows the British government to access e-mail and other encrypted Internet communications for surveillance purposes.

These programs and laws lead to better security through criminal investigation, but consumer privacy is being compromised because of these security steps. There are no clear-cut lines between the need for security versus the need for privacy. But they do go hand in hand. The terms *security* and *privacy* can't be used interchangeably, but they are codependent.

Privacy Laws

Several laws have been passed or are in various stages of development in the U.S. that affect consumer privacy. Two of the earliest privacy laws are the Freedom of Information Act (FOIA) and the Privacy Act of 1974. These acts allow consumers to make requests for information from government agencies, such as the FBI and the Department of Justice. The Privacy Act allows you to obtain your own records and amend or delete information about you that is inaccurate, irrelevant, outdated, or incomplete. You have the right to sue the agency if it refuses to correct or amend your record, or if it refuses to give you access to it. The FOIA applies only to federal agencies and does not create a right of access to records held by Congress, the courts, or state or local government agencies. Each state has its own public access laws. The FOIA requires an agency to decide within ten working days whether to comply with an FOIA request and to inform the person making the request.

Several differences exist between the two acts:

- Only U.S. citizens or permanent resident aliens can obtain access to records that can be retrieved from a system of records by your name, a number, a symbol, or some other identifying particular that is assigned to you, according to the Privacy Act. The FOIA allows any person to obtain access to any records, as stated previously.
- The Privacy Act carries broader exemptions than the FOIA does. Some law enforcement agencies can refuse your FOIA requests.
- The Privacy Act permits an agency to charge requesters for copying, but not for search costs.
- The statute of limitations for filing a lawsuit is only two years under the Privacy Act, but is six years under the FOIA.

Privacy advocates have made wide use of these acts in the past several years to promote individual privacy and learn how the government tracks consumer information.

One law that got passed but was determined to be unconstitutional in the U.S. is the Communications Decency Act (CDA), which was passed as part of the Telecommunications Act of 1996. The CDA prohibited Internet users from using the Internet to communicate material that, under contemporary community standards, would be deemed patently offensive to minors under the age of 18. The Supreme Court struck down this act on First Amendment grounds. The CDA provided two affirmative defenses to prosecution: (1) the use of a credit card or other age verification system, and (2) any good faith effort to restrict access by minors. Key terms were not defined in this act and were deemed unconstitutionally vague. The court found that this act was "wholly unprecedented" in that, for example, it was "not limited to commercial speech or commercial entities...[but rather] its open-ended prohibitions embrace all nonprofit entities and individuals posting indecent messages or displaying them on their own computers." The actions required on the part of Internet users and companies would be cost-prohibitive to doing business and technology was not yet developed to enable the restrictions designed by the act.

In response to the Supreme Court's decision on the CDA, the Children's Online Privacy Protection Act (COPPA) was enacted into law on October 21, 1998. This act subjected commercial Web publishers to the restrictions of ensuring that minors could not access harmful material on the Web. This act uses defined terms and is much smaller in scope than the CDA. However, the Third Circuit Court of Appeals found the COPPA to be unconstitutional. The Department of Justice has filed a petition for certiorari asking the U.S. Supreme Court to reverse the decision of the Third Circuit Court of Appeals. This appeal "presents a conflict between one of society's most cherished rights—freedom of expression—and one of the government's most profound obligations—the protection of minors." The COPPA is supposed to protect minors by using "contemporary community standards" to keep minors from viewing material knowingly posted on the World Wide Web for commercial purposes. The court found that because the Web is accessible by all Internet users worldwide, and because current technology does not permit a Web publisher to restrict access to its site based on the geographic locale, it is not possible for the Web publisher to conform to the act for each community where access to the Internet is available. The court also found that the act imposes an impermissible burden on constitutionally protected First Amendment speech. Current technology is not available to enact the law.

A similar law tries to protect the public use of the Internet in schools and libraries from questionable material. The Children's Internet Protection Act (CHIPA), which is supposed to block access to material from both adults and minors in schools and libraries, is being contested as being unconstitutional. Beyond the constitutional question is the question of how the technology is used. Blocking technology is not anywhere near perfect, and users will be blocked from resources they should have legitimate access to under the law. The EFF, along with the Online Policy Group (`http://www.onlinepolicy.org`) and the American Civil Liberties Union (`http://www.aclu.org`), have been leading the protests against the law.

A new attack on your privacy that has the force of law behind it is the Financial Services Modernization Act (also known as the Gramm-Leach-Bliley Act, or GLB). This act allows banks, insurance companies, and brokerage firms to operate as one. Companies now have the ability to merge customer data from several sources and sell it to third parties. Think about all the personal information collected through your bank, brokerage house, and insurance company. All your financial information, the companies you invest in, and your medical history can be aggregated into one large profile about you. Even before this act was passed in 2000, there were few restrictions on a financial institution's ability to share or sell your personal information.

Three key notices are required by GLB for financial institutions for consumers:

- **Privacy policy**—The types of information collected about you and how it uses that information must be disclosed.
- **Right to opt-out**—Institutions must explain your ability to prevent the sale of your customer data to third parties.
- **Safeguards**—Institutions are required to develop policies to prevent fraudulent access to confidential financial information.

Privacy notices will be sent from your institution to you from each company you belong to. Notices should arrive by July 1, 2001. Consumers are entitled to a "reasonable" time to respond before personal data can be disclosed. You must return the notice so that it reaches the company within 30 days after it was sent to you to opt out of the dissemination of information. You then have to follow precise instructions on how to inform the company that you don't want it to sell your information. You might receive more than 10 notices that you must read through and opt out of to keep your data secure. The law and regulations require only that you get a notice of the categories of information the financial institution collects and the categories of information that might be sold or shared with a third party; the details are not required by law to be sent to you. GLB and federal regulations only keep financial institutions from disclosing your account number or access code to a nonaffiliated third party.

Unless you opt out, sensitive information such as details about your health and treatments can be disclosed to a nonaffiliated third party or even sold to outside marketing companies. The status of these medical privacy rules is ever changing. The Bush administration is waiting on a study to determine what action to take. Individual states have passed their own laws, such as the one passed by California that makes it a crime for an insurance company to sell information to a financial institution for the purpose of granting credit (AB 2797 in the 2000 legislative session, California Civil Code 56.26). But the law does not cover information that flows from a financial institution to an insurance company. Aggregation of information can still occur from nonaffiliated third parties, consumer reporting agencies, or public records, all of which are not covered by the law.

Under GLB, a company can share your personal information with its affiliates, but you can opt out under the Fair Credit Reporting Act (FCRA). This law gives you the right to prevent a company from sharing information about your credit worthiness and information from your applications with an affiliate. Under federal rules, a credit reporting agency (CRA, such as Equifax, Experian, and Trans Union) can't sell so-called "credit header" information to third parties (your name, address, phone number, age, and Social Security number) unless your bank has given you the right to opt out. But, if you do not know you have the right to opt out of such activities, institutions will have free reign to do as they please with your information. GLB does not contain what is called a private right of action, so you have no recourse to take an agency to court under federal law; however, state laws might differ. Trying to opt out of the dissemination under GLB is almost a lost cause. A number of loopholes are in the act that allow your information to be traded like baseball cards. This does not paint a rosy picture for the future of our privacy.

One standard that is in the fledgling stages of acceptance for privacy is Safe Harbor, an international privacy agreement that took effect in 2000. It marks the line between acceptable privacy practices in Europe and the United States and is the result of an agreement between the U.S. Department of Commerce and the European Commission. The European Union is more concerned with privacy than the U.S. and has passed more stringent laws than the U.S. Safe Harbor governs the transatlantic flow of data. The agreement sets up a framework for certifying companies collecting data under privacy protection standards and is visible in the form of a new privacy-seal program. TRUSTe launched the new program to stamp a seal of approval for a company that complies with the EU Safe Harbor certification. The Safe Harbor is a compromise over problems for Web companies that started with the European Commission's Directive on Data Privacy. The directive went into effect in

October 1998 and blocks transfer of personal data to non–European Union nations that do not meet the European laws on privacy protection.

U.S. companies who voluntarily enter Safe Harbor will be deemed as having "adequate" privacy protection, and data transfers to those firms can continue. The problem as with all other self-regulation in the U.S. is that no law exists to force companies to comply with Safe Harbor. It does benefit them from a business perspective, which would get many companies to join. After a company gets Safe Harbor status, monitoring the company is left to private-sector groups, such as the Better Business Bureau or the American Arbitration Association.

The Council of the European Union (the 15 EU governments) will be supporting the EU "law enforcement agencies'" request for full access to all telecommunications data to be written into all community legislation in the future. Existing European Union laws will be reexamined with the goal of analyzing data retention (the archiving of all telecommunications for at least seven years). EU member states have been amending national laws on interception and storage of data to combat computer crime. This has the effect of opening up and storing personal data that the law enforcement agencies can have access to. Future laws, including the proposals currently being discussed on the protection of privacy and computer-aided crime should ensure the retention of data, which will greatly affect privacy of personal data. This case of strict EU controls has the same effect as some proposed and already passed U.S. laws in that it leaves personal information open to the government's perusal.

In Australia, the Privacy Amendment (Private Sector) Act 2000 establishes a national scheme for the handling of personal information by private sector organizations. This act is similar to the directives passed by the EU. This act was developed to provide Australian businesses with a framework that will help them in the global information economy to be compatible with the European Union directive on privacy issues. The legislation establishes the National Privacy Principles (NPP), which are a minimum set of privacy standards to regulate the collection, use, disclosure, and transfer of personal information. Organizations are required to keep accurate, up-to-date information and keep the data secure. Companies must also be open about how they manage personal information, provide access and correction rights to individuals, and allow people to deal with them anonymously. As more countries define privacy laws, we will see either more security and control of our data or loss of privacy to government and corporations, depending on which segment does the better lobbying—privacy advocate groups or corporations.

Privacy Cases

News stories abound with cases of privacy litigation and compromises. The laws are still being defined, and it's the Wild West when it comes to prosecution. One major topic being debated by courts throughout the U.S. is whether public court records detailing child abuse, financial records, or medical information should be posted on the Internet. Rules governing electronic publication of documents in civil and criminal cases are being defined and debated. A panel of state court administrators will propose national guidelines that try to balance the public's right to know against an individual's right to privacy. Each state currently decides whether to post court documents online and whether to withhold some information that is otherwise available to the public at courthouses. Los Angeles Superior Court Judge Kathleen Kennedy-Powell said online posting of information as seemingly non-controversial as traffic citations could enable the spouse of a domestic violence victim to discover the person's new address.

The government is also finding it difficult to define the line of where they have power to enforce laws and self-regulation. In one case, the FTC found it "likely" that Amazon and its subsidiary, Alexa, illegally deceived customers about their data collection practices. However, the FTC did not take any punitive action. Alexa produces a Web browser plug-in that helps users find Web sites that match their interests. The FTC started investigating the company in response to complaints that Alexa sometimes captured personal information such as street and e-mail addresses. Its privacy policy said all data collected "remains anonymous," but Alexa had changed its privacy policy to describe in more detail what types of data it collects. The FTC cited a number of reasons for not going after Amazon. Because the case was brought forth, Alexa has changed its practice and modified the policy.

Few laws address what a company can and can't do with information collected online. The FTC has taken on the burden of protecting online privacy. The problem is the FTC doesn't have the power to enforce self-regulation or even some laws that are passed. "The agency's jurisdiction is (over) deception," stated Lee Peeler, the FTC's associate director for advertising practices. "If a practice isn't deceptive, we can't prohibit them from collecting information. The agency doesn't have the jurisdiction to enforce privacy. It has the authority to challenge deceptive practices." The lack of government enforcement will continue until laws have clearly defined what is legal versus illegal.

In another case of invasion of privacy, the Supreme Court said a radio host can't be sued for airing an illegally taped telephone conversation. The cases are Bartnicki vs. Vopper, 99-1687, and U.S. vs. Vopper, 99-1728. In a 6–3 vote, the court said the First Amendment supercedes wiretap laws in the case of the host who played a recording made by someone else. "A stranger's illegal conduct does not suffice to remove the First Amendment shield from speech about a matter of public concern," said Justice John Paul Stevens. A lower court ruled in favor of a Pennsylvania radio host and others who aired a tape of an intercepted cellular phone call, saying the airing of a public concern was legal in the manner in which the radio host made the information public. In this case, someone's personal cell phone conversation was recorded and aired. Even though the conversation was about illegal matters, the question we face is can any phone conversation be made public? It could set a precedent for further invasion of our privacy. Cell phone conversations can be taped easily, and this case gives some legal precedent for not prosecuting the person eavesdropping on the calls.

The U.S. laws, and U.S. vs. Vopper, 99-1728. seem contradictory on the issue of right to privacy. As companies are facing the issue of how much legal leeway they have in using and abusing your personal information, the laws haven't even begun to come close to defining responsibility for transmission of information. The case of Napster being sued and losing the battle to share copyrighted information is one step toward defining responsibility. (People used Napster to download and share music files.) Even though Napster did not make copies of information itself, it hosted the servers that stored the files, which caused it to lose the case.

The next entity that could possibly face prosecution is the ISP. In the past, ISPs have argued that they are not responsible for data flowing through their systems. So, if a hacker attacks someone from an AOL account, AOL would not be held responsible. ISPs do not cut off people from their service even if they are performing illegal activities. If they were to do that, the ISPs would become the cybercops of the Internet. If the responsibility were placed on the ISPs, they would have to start monitoring your traffic and watching what you do to ensure you are not performing any illegal activities. The Digital Millennium Copyright Act (DMCA) already exempts ISPs from any obligation to monitor their networks for copyright violations and absolves them of liability for transient files. But ISPs are receiving more subpoenas for disclosure of information as more cases are brought to court. AOL processed more than 400 requests last year. Sharing of data in Napster-like fashion will probably develop into peer-to-peer networking, in which consumers can directly trade files between their computers. Peer-to-peer has the advantage of keeping identity information secure. Countries that have more relaxed laws than the U.S. will see an influx of Internet hubs and connectivity to avoid restrictions in countries such as the U.S. and EU.

The "Sex Spam" bill, called the Unsolicited Commercial Electronic Mail Act of 2001, was recently passed by the House Judiciary Committee and seemed like the government was helping us get rid of all *spam* (junk e-mail) related to sex. What some legitimate businesses that deal in sex-related issues are finding is that it can be illegal for them to operate also. One amendment that was adopted makes the bill apply to all e-mail advertisements related to sex—not just unsolicited ones. Instead of banning sex notes outright, the bill fines companies and doles out a one-year prison term to anyone who e-mails an advertisement relating to sex without including a special advisory to be drafted by the attorney general. This label can enable spammers to get around the intention of the bill, which in effect still subjects consumers to junk e-mails. The inability of consumers to sue breakers of the law further weakens the act. The government is still struggling to understand technology and implement laws that actually safeguard our privacy. Each law that is passed has loopholes to either let our personal information out the door or just outright weakens our rights.

Note

The next step in spam is cell phone spamming. Several companies are already sending out spam text messages to cell phones, which is much more intrusive than spam e-mail. AT&T's text messaging is pretty easy. Customers automatically get an e-mail address consisting of their phone numbers followed by @mobile.att.net, and this information is easy to get through all the mass-marketing lists available for sale. Marketing companies just have to buy cell phone lists and can then send out text advertisements.

The FOIA has helped advocacy groups gain information about the government invasions of our privacy in the U.S. One newsworthy attack on personal privacy is the DCS1000 program mentioned earlier. The FBI states that DCS1000, which is installed at the facilities of an ISP and can monitor all traffic moving through that ISP, filters data traffic and delivers to investigators only those packets that the FBI is lawfully authorized to obtain. The FBI's compliance with legal requirements is questionable because it has refused to submit some information that was in Electronic Privacy Information Center's (EPIC) FOIA request. The FBI is supposed to detail why it has refused to comply with the request. Monitoring of communications is becoming more pertinent in law enforcement because of the rise in technology crimes, but this places consumer privacy at risk. The Administrative Office of the U.S. Courts released its 2000 Wiretap Report that indicated 60% of wiretaps authorized in 2000 were for wireless devices such as cellular phones and pagers. The report also indicates that 22 investigations encountered encrypted communications, but it did not prevent access to plain text. Wireless devices will be subject to the intense scrutiny the Internet is facing by law enforcement.

Several laws that affect consumer privacy and personal information are as follows:

- **Electronic Communications Privacy Act of 1986**—The ECPA prohibits the unauthorized interception of cellular telephone calls and computer-to-computer transmissions. Violations can result in civil liability of not less than $100 for each day of violation. The protection of the ECPA also extends to unauthorized access or disclosure of stored electronic communications, and violators are liable for damages suffered or forfeiture of profits.

- **Telecommunications Act of 1996**—Under section 702, customer proprietary network information (CPNI) can't be used for any purpose other than to provide telecommunications services. Suits can be filed to recover damages. Carriers can use customer information to provide telecommunications service, including the publication of subscriber directories; provide customer information to others at the written request of the customer; and provide customer information in aggregate form. The act also allows telecommunications carriers an exception to use customer information: to initiate, render, bill, and collect for their services; to protect against fraudulent, abusive, or illegal conduct; and to provide telemarketing, referral, or administrative services during a call initiated by the customer.

- **Consumer Credit Reporting Reform Act of 1996**—The 1996 Act amends the Fair Credit Reporting Act of 1970 (FCRA) to require improved notice and right of access for credit reporting subjects. The Reform Act imposes new restrictions on resellers of consumer credit reports. Suits can be filed to recover damages and attorneys' fees. States have taken action to include bank records, cable television subscriptions, credit reports, employment records, government records, genetic information and medical records, insurance records, school records, electronic communications, and video rentals.

Privacy Compromise

The hacker community is extremely large and robust. With the ease of availability of hacking information and teaching manuals, it's obvious why we have seen many more news stories involving hacker activity. It does not take a genius anymore to compromise a Web site and gain consumer credit card information. Several sites dedicated to information about security breaches and teaching hacker techniques include the following:

Security Focus	`http://www.securityfocus.com`
PacketStorm	`http://packetstorm.securify.com`
Windows IT Security	`http://www.ntsecurity.net`
Security Bugware	`http://oliver.efri.hr/~crv/security/security.html`
Foundstone	`http://www.foundstone.com/advisories`

Attrition.org (`http://www.attrition.org/`) used to mirror hacked Web pages but has recently stopped because keeping track of all the hacked sites was becoming too much work. Some have said the popularity of being on Attrition.org encouraged hackers to deface Web sites. Through the increase in hacker skills and availability of automated tools to compromise Internet-connected companies, accessing private consumer information is easier than ever.

Tracking user information legally (it's pretty hard to track user information illegally with the weak laws that are in place) is a form of privacy compromise. A hacker doesn't have to break into your home system or some company site for your information to be abused. The Network Advertising Initiative (NAI) Principle, which is a response to advocacy groups trying to limit online *profiling* (the collection of information about Internet surfing behavior within an advertising network for the purpose of formulating a *profile* or representation of users' habits and interests), has been severely criticized for not actually being capable of curbing online profiling. Cookies have been the main culprits of capturing user information for profiles and linking data. The cookies allow information about user behavior to be collected, analyzed, and stored. The problem of online profiling was first presented to Congress in testimony before the Senate Commerce Committee in July 1999. The principles place the burden of privacy protection on the consumer, with opt-out strategies being the main force behind them. The consumer must be cognizant of her rights and abilities to opt out, which is generally very difficult for the consumer.

Selecting to opt-out of one company's database doesn't seem to make a dent in the data capture capabilities of the company after your personal information. A more intrusive manner of tracking Internet users takes place through the use of Web *bugs*, invisible images that also place cookies on users' computers. One newsworthy item was the use of bugs by DoubleClick. DoubleClick, the largest network advertiser, placed Web bugs on more than 60,000 Web pages. It presented advertisements for thousands of clients and placed billions of advertisements in one month. DoubleClick then wanted to link consumer names to information collected through cookies; however, it was severely attacked by privacy groups. The company dropped its plans because of the uproar, but it is estimated that DoubleClick has profiled millions of Internet users. DoubleClick is just one of many such advertisers collecting consumer information. It seems that companies do not change their policies and practices unless they are caught in the act and privacy groups become a nuisance to them.

We have all heard about viruses and worms that damage your system. Worms replicate themselves and send themselves to other computers. A new breed of worm is being used to either try to fix a problem or ferret out the bad guys. One such worm that was recently discovered (in June 2001) infects computers using Microsoft Outlook. It searches the infected computer for image files containing child pornography and alerts government agencies if any suspicious files are discovered. The alert e-mail contains an attached copy of one of the files that allegedly contains child pornography discovered during the worm's search of infected hard drives and also identifies the porn possessor's e-mail address. This is a serious invasion of privacy, even if the worm attempts to perform a public service. What if you had a file with a name the worm thinks is child pornography? It would send an e-mail to government agencies, and you could have someone knocking on your door. If the author took it another step further and just deleted all your files in retribution for assuming you had child pornography, you would lose all your personal data.

Compromise of information not only affects corporations and consumers. The government is at risk just as much as the rest of us. The National Infrastructure Protection Center was created in February 1998 to thwart cybercriminals. The new agency pursues criminals who attack or employ global networks and attempts to better secure the nation. After three years, the NIPC was found to be poorly organized and an ill-conceived agency that is ignored by other agencies. The General Accounting Office analyzed the NIPC and found that

- It's not clear where the agency belongs.
- Nobody seems to listen to the NIPC.
- Information is not shared with them.

- They can't define threats to national security.
- They are not reacting quickly enough to the needs of the government.

Privacy Violation Consequences

The consequences for violating privacy policies are minimal. As mentioned in the Amazon case, no punishment was levied against Amazon. In most cases, self-regulation by the industry is the only thing that even makes companies use a privacy policy. So breaking it carries no retribution other than public outcry. Although, public advocates have forced companies and the government to take privacy policies seriously and will continue to do so in the future. Laws such as COPPA will carry penalties for non-compliance, but these laws do not strictly enforce an actual privacy policy.

The U.S. has a history of punishing companies for blatant violations of privacy rights. In the case of Boling vs. Tennessee State Bank (1994), a bank was liable to borrowers for $14,825 in compensatory damages for disclosing borrowers' personal information and business plans to a bank president who had a conflicting interest. Fraudulent misrepresentation requires either actual knowledge or at least the belief that the representation is false. Liability can also be attached to the case for negligent misrepresentation of services or intent. Whoever makes a false statement in the course of his business, profession, employment, or any transaction can be held liable "if he fails to exercise reasonable care or competence in obtaining or communicating the information." This case was a use of information, not a collection of information judgment.

In another recent case, the Superior Court of Connecticut held that a failure by an electric utility to disclose its reporting of customer payment information to national credit agencies sustained a cause of action for misrepresentation, Brouillard vs. United Illuminating Co. The plaintiff was denied credit because the defendant reported payments not received within 30 days of the billing date as "late," and the plaintiff was not informed of the policy. The court specifically held that "a claim for negligent misrepresentation can be based on the defendant's failure to speak when he has a duty to do so." Fraudulent intent is not a necessary element in a cause of action for negligent misrepresentation. This type of case effects how information on what is collected and reported affects consumer personal information and privacy. Disclosing information without consent can be punished, and recent laws are making punishing such violations easier.

In the case of AmSouth Bancorporation, a class action lawsuit alleged the defendant "exploited the trust depositors placed in the Bank, by sharing confidential information regarding Bank depositors and their [consumers'] accounts" to enable a bank affiliate to sell mutual funds and other investments. This is, of course, prior to GLB. The legality of what companies have done that can compromise the privacy of consumers is not clearly defined by laws. Court cases will eventually determine what is lawful and what is not. Damages are often awarded in such cases when it is made clear that the consumer has been taken advantage of.

The litigation against Amazon and Alexa was of a similar type of action, but that was not prosecuted because Amazon and Alexa corrected the issues that brought the lawsuit. The Computer Fraud and Abuse Act was cited as using unlawful access to stored communications, and the Electronic Communications Privacy Act was cited for unlawful interception of electronic and wire communications. The unknowing collection of personal information was debated in the Amazon case. In cases such as AmSouth Bancorporation, laws could be cited that were broken. When it comes to companies collecting and sharing your information through legal means such as cookies and buying e-mail lists, as was the case with Amazon and Alexa, your legal rights are not being broken and you have no recourse to stop it until new laws are passed.

New laws and proposed laws are providing for more direct consequences to privacy violations against specific laws. The pending Online Privacy Protection Act of 2001 makes it unlawful for an operator of a Web site or online service to collect, use, or disclose personal information concerning an individual (age 13 and above) in a manner that violates regulations to be prescribed by the FTC. The operator must protect the confidentiality, security, and integrity of the personal information it collects. The FTC will be directed to provide incentives for self-regulation, and the government can bring action against a site on behalf of the public. It provides for enforcement of this act through the Federal Trade Commission Act. This is a step in enforcing protection of user information in a tangible manner because these punishments are specific to laws and not site privacy policies.

Privacy Policy Best Practices

What makes a good privacy policy? The reasons for a policy are varied and have been changing since the inception of such policies. The rights of the consumer are the number one reason to have a policy. Policies were first developed from market pressures, but as laws change we will see a requirement for policies based on legislation. The consumer's first step in learning how his personal information will be used and stored is the public availability of the company's policy. The policy's first goal is to define what data is collected on the user. The second goal is to identify how that data will be used, and the third goal is to give the user the option of reviewing his data and to provide some compliance measures to ensure that the policy is adhered to. The user might not be told all the security features of the system that protects his data, but the policy should give some comfort to the consumer that privacy is a concern.

The rights of the user are determined by the policy. Questions a user should consider when reviewing a company's privacy policy include the following:

- What types of information will be collected automatically from me (systems information, behavioral patterns, key word searches, and so on)?
- What information will be stored on my computer (such as cookies or downloaded applet programs)?

- What will registering with a site, whether for product use or using information on the site, track about me?
- What will be done with my data after it is collected?
- What information about my computer is collected?
- How will my information be protected?
- Can the company resell my information at a later time?
- Can I unregister or opt out of marketing campaigns and e-mail lists?
- Can I review the information collected about me?
- Can I change or delete the information collected about me?

Compliance to a privacy policy is probably one of the most difficult tasks for a company. The original goal of privacy policies was to placate consumers and give them some comfort about their rights and the security of their data. Now, though, polices have taken on real meaning and in some cases, have the force of law behind them. If the policy defines how the company will treat your information, but the practical steps are not taken to ensure compliance with the policy, the company can face repercussions both legally and through consumer actions.

The two main methods of breaking policy rules are market pressures forcing a company to sell off assets or conduct business in a different manner that would affect user information and third-party forces that cause inadvertent disclosure and breaking of the policy rules. The case of eTour selling its customer information to Ask Jeeves is an example of the first scenario. Other companies that have tried to sell their customer databases because they have failed include Boo.com, Toysmart, and CraftShop.com. The legality of this is still being debated.

The way market pressures can force disclosure of information also means that consumers can force more privacy protections on the industry. The Network Advertising Initiative (NAI, http://www.networkadvertising.org/) was created by ad networks to oppose legislation in Congress aimed at making opt out automatic. But, NAI does provide consumers a function of opting out of advertisements based on browsing preferences. This is a self-regulatory measure, however. Opting out is usually a hidden or hard-to-find feature on the Web site because companies do not want the consumer to opt out. Collecting customer data is a default action of many sites, and in some cases, customers are not even given an option to opt out. If you do not understand how data is captured and used about you, you can't decide to opt out.

An example of the second method of breaking the rules of the privacy policy is being hacked by a malicious attacker. Bibliofind.com was recently hacked, and approximately 98,000 credit cards were compromised. The hack was several months old before it was discovered. After the hack was discovered, the site shut down and took its customer information off its servers. But it can only be assumed that the information was already copied by the attackers and stored on some server somewhere on the Internet.

In cases such as this, the consumer will never know whether his information was compromised because of weak security at the site or because an attacker was extremely intelligent and came up with a never-before-seen attack or even if an internal employee or ex-employee gave access to some hacker. The following excerpt from the Privacy Policy of Bibliofind.com (now incorporated into Amazon.com) states the following:

"How Secure Is Information About Me?

"We work to protect the security of your information during transmission by using Secure Sockets Layer (SSL) software, which encrypts information you input.

"We reveal only the last five digits of your credit card numbers when confirming an order. Of course, we transmit the entire credit card number to the appropriate credit card company during order processing.

"It is important for you to protect against unauthorized access to your password and to your computer. Be sure to sign off when finished using a shared computer."

Because this chapter was written after the Biblio.com hack, we do not know whether this was part of the original privacy policy. Amazon is providing a statement about the security of user information, but this is no guarantee that your personal information will stay secure after it makes it way onto a company's servers. Privacy policies are a guideline to what *should* happen rather than what actually happens. A company that is very strict about its policy will have the practical steps in place to ensure compliance to that policy.

All information about the user collected through use of a company's systems should be readily identified and understood by the user. A functional and usable privacy policy for any company wishing to ensure the privacy of its customers will

- Take into account the needs of its target market; some customers might be more resistant to having their information captured.
- Capture only necessary data from the consumers. Using surveys and requiring consumers to fill out questionnaires can capture a lot of unnecessary information.
- Define why information is being collected.
- Clearly identify what is done with the data after it is collected, how it is stored, and who has access to it.
- Give the user a choice of opting out of any marketing based on the information he has submitted and keeping his information from being sent to others.
- Comply with any laws regarding privacy and be familiar with pending legislation that can affect the business and consumer information.
- Write a statement of the organization's commitment to data security.

- Define the security measures in place to secure the customer information and what steps are in place to keep it secure on an ongoing basis.

- Define how third parties will use the consumer information if they provide a business function to the company.

- Provide for enforcement of the policy through internal control structures.

- Explain how and whom to contact within the organization with privacy-related questions or concerns.

- Make reference to the use of technologies such as cookies and log files.

- Give the customer a choice in not revealing his information and the ability to see what data has been collected about him.

- Keep the policy easy to read and understand.

- Notify users that the site complies with all privacy laws.

- Explain the consequences of an individual's refusal to provide information.

One statement that is found in many policy documents is the right of the site to change its policy at any time without giving notice to the consumers. If it changes the policy, how are consumers to know unless they read the policy constantly or the company sends out an e-mail to all its customers? If you submitted your information based on one policy and then that is changed, is there still an expectation of privacy? These types of issues have not yet been determined in the courts. This type of modification and divergence in company policy will affect consumer confidence in the company to keep its data secure and not sell it to the highest bidder. As it is, consumers have little assurance about the security of their data.

The problem faced by both companies and individuals is that there is no standard set of procedures for securing personal information. It's the Wild West of the electronic frontier and so far consumers have been losing the battle. Corporate America has not come up with a standard set of guidelines, and neither has the government. For other countries, the same problems apply. Privacy rights are violated on a daily basis both knowingly and unknowingly. If one company has the best privacy practices and then gets acquired by another company, all the consumer data now falls under the control of the acquirer, and the parent entity might not have such stringent privacy policies. When laws have not been written to address privacy, there is not much the consumer can do for legal recourse.

Large organizations can afford to have outside third-party organizations perform auditing of both their computer systems for security weaknesses and their policies for completeness. Smaller organizations can't typically afford these services, and the consumer has no knowledge of the security stance of the company. If companies have third parties advertising on their sites and collecting consumer information, does the site have any responsibility for what is done with that information? Are the security measures of these third parties audited, and are their privacy polices actually being followed? For the corporation to gain the trust of the consumer, the consumer must understand how his data is being handled. For sites that have been subjected to an audit of their privacy policies, the consumer can have some confidence that his data is taken seriously and that the site will try to adhere to what the policy states. The policies on audited sites are probably more defined and sensitive to the consumers' right to privacy, but this is usually a self-administered audit. The problem with this type of auditing is when companies are compromised or knowingly break their privacy policies even though they have the seal of approval from some auditing company. Consumers will put less faith in these seals because they can't force a company to adhere to them after the audit. In addition, if the company has weak security mechanisms and a hacker steals consumer information, the seal will be meaningless.

eBay uses TRUSTe as its auditors of its privacy policy. Part of the eBay privacy policy states the following:

> "eBay Inc. is a licensee of the TRUSTe Privacy Program. What is TRUSTe? It is a non-profit organization dedicated to building trust in the Internet by having member organizations such as eBay disclose information practices. TRUSTe operates as a third-party "watch dog" by auditing our privacy practices to make sure that we are in compliance with TRUSTe's privacy standards."

In 1999, eBay was hacked. Whether the TRUSTe seal of approval was on the site before or after the hack does not matter. What consumers will remember is that eBay was hacked and their personal information potentially compromised. Even though the seal of approval from any company does not cover all aspects of security and privacy, consumers will not know that and assume any seal that is on a site guarantees that all aspects of that site are secure and that their data is secure.

The government has not forced the issue of auditing of privacy polices as it has in auditing financial statements. Without government intervention, consumers must rely on the self-regulation and standards developed by the industry. A company can either rely on a third party to audit its policy and hope that third party does a good job to secure consumer information or audit the policy themselves, meaning there is no objective analysis of the privacy policy. Auditing the policy means more than just reading it and adding the appropriate statements to make it comprehensive. The practical aspects of actually complying with the policy—measures such as security controls, encryption techniques, and testing of site security—must be done to gauge compliance. Different industry segments will go about compliance with policies in various ways. Because no baseline standards exist for developing and testing for compliance in policy initiatives, each will differ and consumers will not have an understanding of what actually works and which polices they can rely on.

One step in the right direction for one industry segment is the Health Insurance Portability and Accountability Act (HIPAA) of 1996. It sets standards for patient information handling and dissemination. Organizations in the healthcare industry are being held accountable for how they mange consumer information and will be punished for breaking the laws set fourth in HIPAA. But the problem companies are facing with

HIPAA is that the guidelines for how to actually comply with the act from a technology standpoint are not clear-cut. The American Hospital Association (AHA) has stressed an urgent need to suspend the rules governing "standards for privacy of individually identifiable health information" because it feels compliance is unfair. The AHA submits that the medical privacy rule needs to be fixed. As currently drafted, the rule frustrates patient care; complicates essential hospitals operations; threatens the financial viability of many of America's hospitals; and is needlessly complex, intrusive, and costly. The First Consulting Group (FCG) released a study in December 2000 that found that compliance could be as high as $22.5 billion over five years for hospitals to meet the requirements. Compliance can be approached from various points of view and cost different amounts of money because no standards have been set to implement practical compliance steps. We are still a long way from valid privacy polices that can be enforced.

Organizations creating, maintaining, using, or disseminating individually identifiable information should take steps to ensure that the data is accurate, complete, relevant, and timely. Data should not be collected that does not serve a specific purpose in the organization; plus, the information collected should be accessible by the user to ensure correctness of data and fix any problems found. Organizations should take other reasonable steps to ensure the quality of the data collected, including obtaining it from reliable and reputable sources. Full disclosure of what is done to the data collected as well as how long the data will be stored and used will provide consumers with a better understanding of how their personal information is being manipulated. Organizations need to dispel the fear, uncertainty, and doubt (FUD) factor about consumer's privacy issues. By allowing the consumer full access to the information collected about him, the organization can maintain an accurate database of information as well as gain the user's trust to keep that data secure and maintain a level of quality control over his personal information.

Summary

Privacy policies have been used to drive industry self-regulation and government laws. Self-regulation in the U.S. has been the dominant form of privacy protection. However, it is slowly giving way to government intervention. Companies that suffer no consequences when changing their privacy policies or outright ignoring them have constantly abused consumers. Even having a privacy policy is not always a given for many Web sites. Even though public outcry has caused privacy laws to be passed, tangible punishments for companies that violate these laws are not prevalent. With laws such as HIPAA and COPPA, among others, being passed and adhered to, consumer information can either be kept secure or be legally traded like baseball players in the off-season.

The global economy is taking consumer privacy more seriously, but that doesn't stop companies from using personal information to bombard you with junk e-mail and advertisements and using your surfing habits for targeted harassment. The EU has taken very aggressive steps toward keeping personal information secure. Other countries are moving toward more security and privacy laws because the global economy and consumers are pushing for change. No matter what laws are passed, the consumer still has to bear the weight of implementing steps to keep his home systems and personal information secure from the information brokers of the world.

3
Privacy Organizations and Initiatives

The consumer on his own stands no chance of defending his own privacy needs. The lack of power by the individual consumer has given rise to a number of organizations that should lessen the burden of fighting the "forces of evil" that would take away all our privacy rights. "Forces of evil" might be a strong term, but how else to describe companies and governments that would strip others of an inherent right to be left alone and to keep our personal information confidential?

The U.S. government has failed to set the standards and controls necessary to ensure our privacy. It has been the task of the privacy industry, organizations, and individuals to create these standards. The government has even failed to meet its responsibilities on the standards of privacy. In 2000, the government banned cookies from most government sites, yet reports of 51 inspectors general found 300 cookies on the Web sites of 23 agencies that should not have been there. *Cookies*, as we mentioned in earlier chapters, track user information and browsing preferences. "These reports document a real problem—the violation of Americans' privacy by their own government on the Internet," said Sen. Jay Inslee, (D-Wash). Auditors from that agency learned three contractors who maintained Web sites for government departments were collecting personal information, such as Social Security numbers, without disclosing how they used that information.

The findings also showed that Web *bugs* were found on 23 Commerce Department pages (these bugs collect information), and nearly 75% of State Department sites were not in compliance with government rules requiring agencies to post their privacy policies. Several contractors who maintain government sites were collecting personal information such as Social Security numbers without notifying users how this information would be used. Other government agencies, such as the Federal Trade Commission, are also not becoming involved in privacy issues. FTC Commissioner Thomas Leary said, "We're a lot more relaxed than we were before." It's hard to imagine the government being any more relaxed about our privacy rights. Leary also said, "This hysteria [over privacy] is misplaced." If the government can't even comply with it own privacy standards and has such little regard for our privacy, how will the consumer achieve any level of personal information security?

Although many think government involvement in privacy issues is desirable, some feel less government involvement and more private industry controls are the right way to achieve consumer privacy needs. According to a report released in May 2001 by Citizens Against Government Waste (CAGW), it would be cheaper on Americans for private industry to regulate itself rather than having Congress pass laws and trying to enforce those laws. CAGW's new study, "Keeping Big Brother From Watching You," concluded that "federal privacy regulations or legislation are unnecessary and that the private sector is more effective than government in this increasingly important area." The 107th session of Congress has put forth more than 40 bills aimed at privacy; whether all these pass or actually benefit the consumer has been highly debated. If the government can't handle the laws that have already been passed, how will new laws be enforced to protect the consumer? Organizations such as CAGW promote private sector policies to help consumers and want the government to continue with its hands-off approach to privacy.

Another study released in May 2001, underwritten by the Association for Competitive Technology (ACT), a Microsoft-backed lobbying organization, found that privacy laws could cost businesses between $9 billion and $36 billion. Firms were asked to estimate their charges to make the changes required under several pending bills to determine what the potential costs to the industry would be. The costs range anywhere from $100,000 on up to the millions. Fourteen of the 17 companies questioned are affiliated with ACT. This is not an impartial study, but it does shed some light on potential costs of privacy laws. Groups such as ACT also want a government hands-off approach but for different reasons from organization such as CAGW. With less government involvement, private industry can more easily turn a profit in just about anything it does.

Privacy Organizations

A lack of government intervention in protecting consumer privacy rights has caused grassroots efforts to spring up to address the void in privacy organizations. Publicly funded nonprofit organizations have taken on the challenge of fighting for consumer privacy rights. The following sections discuss several of the key players when it comes to organizations taking on the battle against business and government threats to your privacy.

Online Privacy Alliance

http://www.privacyalliance.org

The Online Privacy Alliance (OPA) is a group of corporations and associations that attempts to promote online privacy initiatives. The OPA is in favor of self-regulation of privacy concerns and less government involvement. The mission of the alliance is stated as follows:

"The Alliance will:

- identify and advance effective online privacy policies across the private sector
- support and foster the development and use of self-regulatory enforcement mechanisms and activities, as well as user empowerment technology tools, designed to protect individuals' privacy
- support compliance with and strong enforcement of applicable laws and regulations
- support and foster the development and use of practices and policies that protect the privacy of children
- promote broad awareness of and participation in Alliance initiatives by businesses, non-profits, policy makers, and consumers
- seek input and support for Alliance initiatives from consumer, business, academic, advocacy and other organizations that share its commitment to privacy protection."

Several of its larger members include IBM, Microsoft, Verizon, The American Institute of Certified Public Accounts, and Sun Microsystems. The OPA reports on privacy news and provides resources for companies and consumers to learn more about privacy issues. The OPA has set up guidelines for defining a privacy policy that companies can use and a framework for enforcing self-regulation. The guidelines have become an industry framework for the creation of a privacy policy.

OPA has been active in lobbying government officials to promote self-regulation. One such action was focused on the Congressional Privacy Caucus. The Privacy Caucus includes more than 30 members of Congress from the House and Senate. It is co-chaired by Sens. Richard Shelby (R–AL) and Chris Dodd (D-CT) and Reps. Joe Barton (R-TX) and Edward Markey (D-MA). The OPA wants laws to focus on privacy issues and not the technologies being used. "It's the behavior of businesses and not the technologies they use that determine whether consumer privacy is respected," said Christine Varney, an advisor to the OPA. Another initiative by the OPA was the submission of comments to the Department of Health and Human Services (HHS) regarding their proposed implementation of the provisions of the Health Insurance Portability and Accountability Act of 1996. The regulations are unclear, and the implementation of controls to comply with the regulations is not defined. The OPA attempts to empower and educate consumers on how to protect their privacy online.

BBBOnline

http://www.bbbonline.org

BBBOnline is a subsidiary of the Council of Better Business Bureaus. Its mission is to "promote trust and confidence on the Internet through the BBBOnline Reliability and BBBOnline Privacy programs." BBBOnline has three certification programs called the Reliability Seal Program, Kids Privacy Seal Program, and Privacy Seal Program. A Web site can get these seals to show that they promote privacy initiatives and give consumers some form of confidence that the site is trustworthy. This is a self-regulatory program for Web sites. Several of the criteria for a Web site getting the Seal include

- Being members of their local Better Business Bureaus
- Having been in business for at least one year
- Having agreed to abide by BBB standards of truth in advertising
- Having committed to work with the BBB to resolve consumer disputes that arise over goods or services promoted or advertised on their site
- Providing the BBB with information regarding company ownership and management and the street address and telephone number at which they do business
- Agreeing to participate in the BBB's advertising self-regulation program
- Responding promptly to all consumer complaints

After it's approved, a company is allowed to put on its Web site the seals shown in Figures 3.1, 3.2, and 3.3.

Figure 3.1   BBBOnline Reliability seal.

Figure 3.2   BBBOnline Kids Privacy seal.

Figure 3.3   BBBOnline Privacy seal.

The Kids Privacy Seal Program is used by a Web site to show that it is in compliance with the Children's Online Privacy Protection Act (COPPA). This law requires all businesses with any part of their Web sites (or online services) directed at children under the age of 13 or Web sites (or online services) that collect personally identifiable information from visitors actually known to be under the age of 13 to follow specific guidelines. These requirements to get this seal are based on the guidelines of the Council of Better Business Bureaus' Children's Advertising Review Unit (CARU), the industry standards suggested by the Online Privacy Alliance, and the Children's Online Privacy Protection Act.

Several of the criteria required to get this seal include

- The Web site must obtain parental consent before any personally identifiable information can be collected, used, or disclosed.
- The Web site must obtain parental consent before children are allowed to post or communicate directly with others.
- The Web site must provide warnings and explanations in easy-to-understand language.
- The Web site must avoid collecting more information than necessary when offering children's games and activities.
- The Web site must be careful in the way it provides hyperlinks.
- The Web site must follow strict rules when sending e-mail.
- The Web site must provide reasonable access to collected information.

BBBOnline is more of a resource for information than an enforcer of privacy initiatives. A company can tout that it has the seal, but no concrete measures or procedures define how a consumer's informationis handled. The seals do not say that the company will not resell your information or use cookies on its site to track your information. BBBOnline has little authority to do anything about a compromise of your information after a company has the seal. As we captured the image of the seal for this book, what is to stop a Web site from copying the image and putting it on it sites even if it is not a BBBOnline member?

It might even be said that these seals are counterproductive. If a consumer goes to a site with this seal, she might have a false sense of security, which is worse than knowing your data is insecure. If you think this seal will protect your private information and then submit personal data to a site, you do not really know how the company will treat your information if you did not read its privacy policy. If, at the time the company got the seal, it had great privacy measures in place, there is no guarantee that a week later its policies did not change. If it changed its policies after getting the seal, what is the follow-up mechanism for notifying consumers and notifying BBBOnline of the changes? The lack of defined procedures for ensuring the seal actually provides some value to the consumer makes these type of programs of limited value to the consumer. Several other such programs can also be misleading to the consumer, as we will discuss later.

TRUSTe

http://www.truste.org

TRUSTe is an endeavor similar to BBBOnline. Its goal is to promote Internet privacy and provide a seal of approval to sites that meet its requirements. It has a number of sponsors and contributor companies that help promote the seals. Like BBBOnline, it is also an information repository for privacy initiatives. To be approved for the Privacy Seal (see Figure 3.4), the Web site seeking approval must meet the following criteria:

- Adoption and implementation of a privacy policy that takes into account consumer anxiety over sharing personal information online
- Notice and disclosure of information collection and use practices
- Choice and consent, giving users the opportunity to exercise control over their information
- Data security and quality and access measures to help protect the security and accuracy of personally identifiable information

Figure 3.4   The TRUSTe Privacy seal.

The TRUSTe seal informs the consumer that the site will disclose the following:

- What personal information is being gathered about you
- How the information will be used
- Who the information will be shared with, if anyone
- Choices available to you regarding how collected information is used

- Safeguards in place to protect your information from loss, misuse, or alteration
- How you can update or correct inaccuracies in your information

Similar to BBBOnline, TRUSTe also has a Children's Privacy Seal, as shown in Figure 3.5. This applies to children under the age of 13. TRUSTe has also recently been approved as a "safe harbor" program under the terms of the Children's Online Privacy Protection Act. Safe harbor programs are industry self-regulatory guidelines that are deemed to implement the act. The Children's Privacy Seal notifies the consumer that the site will not

- Collect online contact information from a child under 13 without prior verifiable parental consent or direct parental notification of the nature and intended use of this information, which shall include an opportunity for the parent to prevent use of the information and participation in the activity. Where prior parental consent is not obtained, online contact information shall only be used to directly respond to the child's request and shall not be used to recontact the child for other purposes.
- Collect personally identifiable offline contact information from children under 13 without prior verifiable parental consent.
- Distribute to third parties any personally identifiable information collected from a child under 13 without prior verifiable parental consent.
- Give the ability to children under 13 to publicly post or otherwise distribute personally identifiable contact information without prior verifiable parental consent, and will make best efforts to prohibit a child from posting any contact information.
- Entice a child under 13 by the prospect of a special game, prize, or other activity to divulge more information than is needed to participate in such activity.

Figure 3.5   TRUSTe Kids Privacy seal.

Several differences exist between TRUSTe and BBBOnline. Although they both have a dispute resolution service for when a member carrying the seal does not comply with the requirements, the seal by TRUSTe has more details and a check mechanism to ensure that the site displaying a seal is actually a member of the program (see Figure 3.6). The mechanism to check whether a site is actually part of the TRUSTe program is very proactive and takes a step in the right direction. The only problem with this is that a consumer must click the icon to check the site. Most consumers do not check each site they visit to determine whether the site is actually a member of the TRUSTe Program.

Figure 3.6   TRUSTe Click-to-Verify seal.

As with the BBBOnline seal, after a company is approved for this seal, it's hard to continue to verify that its polices and practices haven't changed and therefore break the requirements of the seal. TRUSTe does make the attempt to keep sites in compliance, but there will be a window between the change and checkup by TRUSTe when a site could be compromising consumer privacy. TRUSTe's policy on checkup on compliance with its criteria is as follows:

- Initial and periodic reviews of the site by TRUSTe
- "Seeding," whereby the company submits personal user information online to verify that a site is following its stated privacy policies
- Compliance reviews by a CPA firm
- Feedback and complaints from the online community

Electronic Information Privacy Organization

http://www.epic.org

The Electronic Information Privacy Organization (EPIC) is a nonprofit organization dedicated to serving the public's civil liberties and privacy. EPIC is involved with other privacy organizations such as Privacy International (http://www.privacyinternational.org), the Global Internet Liberty Campaign (http://www.gilc.org), the Internet Free Expression Alliance (http://www.ifea.net), the Internet Privacy Coalition (http://www.crypto.org), the Internet Democracy Project (http://www.internetdemocracyproject.org), and the Trans Atlantic Consumer Dialogue (http://www.tacd.org). EPIC is actively pursuing government legislation and fighting laws that would compromise consumer privacy. The Web site provides a wealth of privacy information and keeps up-to-date with the latest laws being passed and that are being proposed. EPIC is funded by consumer and corporations who want to promote the fight for privacy.

Recently, EPIC's executive director, Marc Rotenberg, testified before the House Commerce Committee on Information Privacy urging Congress to pass privacy legislation and promote technology that would better secure consumer information. EPIC often brings privacy matters to the forefront of congressional business to protect consumers. One such matter brought to Congress's attention was the proposed sale of consumer domain name registration information by Network Solutions to direct marketing companies. The following is an excerpt from the letter sent to Congress by EPIC:

Electronic Privacy Information Center

February 16, 2001

Representative Fred Upton
2333 Rayburn House Office Building
Washington, DC 20515

Representative Edward J. Markey
2108 Rayburn House Office Building
Washington, DC 20515

Senator Conrad Burns
187 Dirksen Senate Office Building
Washington, DC 20510

Senator Fritz Hollings
125 Russell Senate Office Building
Washington, DC 20510

Dear Congressmen,

We are writing to you on behalf of the Electronic Privacy Information Center (EPIC) to bring your attention to a privacy issue of importance to Internet users around the world, and of particular concern to users in the United States who register domain names. According to a report in *The Wall Street Journal* today, Network Solutions, Inc., the largest domain registration company in the country, is now selling information on 6 million Internet customers to direct marketers. The information was obtained by Network Solutions, Inc. for the purpose of registration and is not unlike motor vehicle information for which Congress has passed important privacy legislation, The Drivers Privacy Protection Act of 1994, that was recently upheld by the United States Supreme Court in Reno v. Condon, 528 U.S. 141.

We are writing to you to urge you to examine whether this sale is currently permissible and if so, whether it is therefore necessary to adopt new legislation to safeguard the information that is provided by Internet users and companies as a condition of registering a domain name. We believe that the sale violates well established principles of U.S. law as well as international privacy standards, including privacy rules specifically developed to address concerns related to privacy in the context of domain name registration.

Thus far privacy has received only passing attention during the discussion of ICANN's authority. The Subcommittee on Communications recently held hearings on the Internet Corporation for Assigned Names and Numbers, otherwise known as ICANN. ICANN is the central authority for all Internet users worldwide that wish to register a domain name. As mentioned during the recent hearings held by your Subcommittee, part of ICANN's responsibility is to protect the privacy of its domain name registrants. Also mentioned during the hearings was the low level of privacy protection offered for this personal information. As you pursue further work on ICANN, we urge you to focus on the much-needed privacy protections for this personal information.

Another case of EPIC's fight for consumer privacy was when it filed a letter of complaint against the company eTour. The letter sent to the Federal Trade Commission (FTC) and the National Association of Attorneys General (NAAG) alleged that direct-marketing company eTour, Inc., violated consumer protection law by selling personal information about its 4.5 million customers to Ask Jeeves in early 2001, despite clear statements that it would never do so. eTour's privacy policy was vague on what constitutes a breach of its privacy policy.

EPIC also testified on Social Security number privacy in May of 2001 before the U.S. House of Representatives Subcommittee on Social Security. A hearing was held on "Protecting Privacy and Preventing Misuse of Social Security Numbers." EPIC argued the point that "legislation to limit the collection and use of the SSN is appropriate, necessary, and fully consistent with U.S. law."

Unlike ACT, EPIC seeks to have more government intervention, or at a minimum, the government intervention that actually promotes consumer privacy. EPIC launched an Internet Public Interest Opportunities Program (IPIOP) that will serve law students who have an interest in public interest law and the Internet. EPIC uses the Freedom of Information Act (FOIA) to obtain information from the government about cryptography and privacy policy. Several cases that EPIC has been involved with include the following:

- **Electronic Privacy Information Center v. Department of Justice & Federal Bureau of Investigation (C.A. No. 00-1849)**—EPIC wanted to make details of DCS1000 public.

- **Electronic Privacy Information Center v. National Security Agency (C.A. No. 99-3197)**—EPIC asked a federal court to order the release of controversial documents concerning government surveillance of American citizens and sought public disclosure of internal National Security Agency (NSA) documents.

- **Electronic Privacy Information Center v. Federal Trade Commission (C.A. No. 99-2689)**—Sought the disclosure of records about privacy complaints received by the Federal Trade Commission.

- **Electronic Privacy Information Center v. U.S. Department of State (C.A. No. 97-1401)**—Sought public disclosure of the travel records of Ambassador David Aaron, who has been promoting the Administration's controversial encryption policies in foreign countries. EPIC is seeking to open U.S. encryption policy to public scrutiny.

- **Electronic Privacy Information Center v. U.S. Department of State (C.A. No. 95-2228)**—Sought the release of a survey conducted by the Department of Commerce (DOC) on the foreign availability of encryption software.

- **Electronic Privacy Information Center v. National Security Council (C.A. No. 95-0461)**—Sought disclosure of information concerning the Security Policy Board.

Several of the laws discussed in Chapter 2, "Defining Privacy: Social and Legal Aspects," can either help or hurt consumer privacy rights. EPIC advocates laws that enforce privacy initiatives and protect the consumer. Fighting companies that take advantage of users is also one of EPIC main concerns as demonstrated by the fight against eTour and Network Solutions.

Federal Trade Commission

http://www.ftc.gov

The Federal Trade Commission (FTC) is one of the few government organizations that has been actively involved with privacy concerns of consumers. The Internet has led to an enlargement of the scope of the FTC's activities. No longer are they just concerned with communications mediums such as telephone, radio, and TV. The Internet has posed new challenges for the power and enforcement capabilities of the FTC. One of the main functions of the FTC Web site is to educate consumers about laws and privacy initiatives.

The FTC has launched various initiatives to safeguard consumer privacy. Some of the focus revolves around credit bureaus, the Department of Motor Vehicles (DMV), and Direct Marketers.

The three major credit bureaus the FTC has focused on helping consumers protect that privacy include

- Equifax, Inc., P.O. Box 740123, Atlanta, GA 30374-0123
- Experian, 701 Experian Parkway, Allen, TX 75013
- Trans Union, P.O. Box 97328, Jackson, MS 39288-7328

Each of these agencies has opt-out options the FTC wants consumers to know about.

Similar to credit bureaus, the DMV has a lot of personal information about you. Even though the Drivers Protection Act has some safeguards against distributing your personal information, the DMV still has a lot of leeway in disseminating information. Information can be given to law enforcement, driver safety agencies, background checking agencies, insurance brokers, and a host of other agencies. However, few people can get your DMV information. The FTC does make an effort to educate consumers of the possibilities of how your information can be used through DMV.

As we have plainly seen, direct marketing can be very intrusive, and direct marketers can easily find out a lot of information about your preferences. The Direct Marketing Association (http://www.the-dma.org) offers the Mail, Telephone, and E-mail Preference Services, which allow you to opt out of some marketing databases. The FTC publishes a free brochure on "Shopping by Phone or Mail" to assist consumers is taking some steps to protect themselves.

The FTC is also involved in policing efforts for numerous laws. One that concerns consumer privacy is the Gramm-Leach-Bliley Act. As mentioned in Chapter 2, the act removes certain restrictions on mergers, affiliations, and other business activities of banks that date to the Depression era. The concerns about privacy cause amendments to the act that try to protect consumer privacy and sharing of information between entities. The FTC is one of the agencies responsible for ensuring compliance with the act. Another major act the FTC has responsibility in policing is the HIPAA Act. HIPAA and Gramm-Leach-Bliley address similar regulatory concerns and contain several common compliance elements the FTC must address and ensure that companies are in compliance with. As with most government agencies' involvement with private industry, there is much confusion and no clear decision on compliance and how the FTC will address the necessary steps to ensure compliance.

The FTC has also been aggressively pursuing privacy violations. In one recent case, the FTC successfully prosecuted three Web sites that were in violation of the Children's Online Privacy Protection Rule (COPPA Rule). The FTC charged Monarch Services, Inc., and Girls Life, Inc., operators of www.girlslife.com; Bigmailbox.com, Inc., and Nolan Quan, operators of www.bigmailbox.com; and Looksmart Ltd., operator of www.insidetheweb.com, with illegally collecting personally identifying information from children under 13; these companies settled with the FTC on these charges. The FTC has also settled a case with Toysmate.com, which violated its privacy policy that stated it would never sell consumer information. The FTC also settled a case against several online pharmacies, including Worldwidemedicine.com and Focusmedical.com, which misrepresented information to consumers and did not handle consumer information securely. COPPA has helped increase the number of sites posting a privacy policy from 24% in 1998 to 91% today. The FTC also grants "safe harbor" status to companies and associations that prove they are in compliance with COPPA. The Children's Advertising Review Unit (CARU) of the Council of Better Business Bureaus—an arm of the advertising industry's self-regulatory program—won the first COPPA safe harbor approval, which the FTC is striving for many companies to achieve.

Government agencies such as the FTC that strive to assist companies with securing consumer privacy rights are themselves subject to privacy violations. In July 2001, the U.S. Department of Commerce's safe harbor Web site was hacked by attackers. Safe harbor participants were contacted about the attack. The lack of security on government sites can greatly discourage companies that are seeking guidance from government agencies regarding the steps they must take to protect their consumers.

Privacy International

`http://www.privacyinternational.org`

Privacy International (PI) is a human rights group formed in 1990 as a watchdog on surveillance by governments and corporations. It is based in London, England, and has an office in Washington, D.C. PI has conducted campaigns throughout the world on issues ranging from wiretapping and national security activities, to ID cards, video surveillance, data matching, police information systems, and medical privacy. This information portal does not have any authority or government powers and serves only as a consumer education site.

Several initiatives that PI has recently conducted include the following:

- **International Privacy Survey**—Reviews the state of privacy in more than 50 countries of privacy issues including, data protection, telephone tapping, genetic databases, ID systems, and freedom of information laws.
- **Project Compliance**—Monitors companies' compliance with the EU Data Protection and the U.S./EU negotiations on Safe Harbor.
- **Big Brother Awards**—"Awards" are given to the companies, government agencies, and individuals that have most directly undercut privacy.

Privacy.org

`http://www.privacy.org/`

Privacy.org is the site for daily news, information, and initiatives on privacy, striving to educate consumers about the actions of companies and governments to compromise their privacy. The Web site is a joint project of EPIC and Privacy International. On this site are a number of links and resources to further information to protect consumer privacy.

Internet Free Expression Alliance

`http://www.ifea.net`

The Internet Free Expression Alliance (IFEA) is another informational site that seeks to educate consumers on privacy issues with an emphasis on freedom of expression. The IFEA seeks to protect the privacy of such entities as Internet users, online publishers, libraries, and academic groups. A number of organizations belong to the IFEA to promote free speech issues.

From the IFEA Web site, the goals of the Internet Free Expression Alliance include

- Ensure the continuation of the Internet as a forum for open, diverse, and unimpeded expression and to maintain the vital role the Internet plays in providing an efficient and democratic means of distributing information around the world

- Promote openness and encourage informed public debate and discussion of proposals to rate and/or filter online content

- Identify new threats to free expression and First Amendment values on the Internet, whether legal or technological

- Oppose any governmental effort to promote, coerce, or mandate the rating or filtering of online content

- Protect the free speech and expression rights of both the speaker and the audience in the interactive online environment

- Ensure that Internet speakers are able to reach the broadest possible interested audience and that Internet listeners are able to access all material of interest to them

- Closely examine technical proposals to create filtering architectures and oppose approaches that conceal the filtering criteria employed, or irreparably damage the unique character of the Internet

- Encourage approaches that highlight "recommended" Internet content, rather than those that restrict access to materials labeled as "harmful" or otherwise objectionable, and emphasize that any rating that exists solely to enable specific content to be blocked from view can inhibit the flow of free expression

Electronic Frontier Foundation

http://www.eff.org

The Electronic Frontier Foundation (EFF) is a nonprofit, nonpartisan organization that is member supported. The organization seeks to protect civil liberties, including privacy and freedom of expression on the Internet. EFF was founded in 1990 and is based in San Francisco, California. Like other sites such as PI and IFEA, the EFF is a strong advocate for consumer freedom. The EFF speaks to law enforcement organizations, state attorney bar associations, conferences and summits, and university classes and takes an active role in pursuing legal action and helping victims of privacy invasion and freedom of speech restrictions. The EFF has taken active roles in many cases, including the following:

- **Felten v. RIAA**—EFF asked a federal court to rule that Princeton University professor Edward Felten and his research team have a First Amendment right to present their research on digital music access-control technologies at the USENIX Security Conference this August in Washington, D.C.

- **DVD-CCA v. Bunner**—The DVD Copy Control Association (DVD-CCA) is suing dozens of individuals who put DeCSS (a program to decrypt the protections placed on DVDs) on their Web sites. The EFF is paying for and coordinating the case.

- **Medinex_v._Awe2bad4mdnx**—The EFF is defending critics of a failing dot.com company to defend the right of anonymous critics to express their views online without fear of arbitrary disclosure of their identities. The company called Medinex Systems, Inc., seeks to learn the identities of 14 John Does who participated in a Yahoo! message board. On May 21, 2001, Medinex dismissed the suit before a hearing could be held. EFF provided pro bono defense for the anonymous posters.

EFF submits amicus briefs and finds pro bono counsel when possible for other free-speech cases. EFF has been very active in protecting the Children's Internet Protection Act. The EFF is also against implementation of Congressionally mandated Internet blocking in schools and libraries as outlined in this act and works with other privacy groups to protect such laws. Lisa Maldonado, field director for the American Civil Liberties Union of Northern California commented, "The government is trying to strangle the free flow of information on the Internet to those library patrons who need it the most. CHIPA would widen the 'digital divide' that already exists between those who can afford Internet access at home and those who rely on their public library for Internet access." "The government-mandated requirement for Internet blocking in schools and libraries violates the free expression rights of Americans, adults and minors alike," said Will Doherty, EFF online activist.

Global Internet Liberty Campaign

http://www.gilc.org

Another education and information dissemination organization, the Global Internet Liberty Campaign (GILC), was formed by members of the American Civil Liberties Union, the Electronic Privacy Information Center, Human Rights Watch, the Internet Society, Privacy International, the Association des Utilisateurs d'Internet, and other civil liberties and human rights organizations. GILC members speak out against laws and initiatives that can infringe on consumer privacy. Several statements released by the GILC include opposition to stealth blocking, which is the practice of some Internet service providers (ISPs) to block Internet access to particular hosts without the knowledge of end users and opposing the DVD Copy Control Association's (CCA) suit against people who have posted information about the DVD Content Scrambling System (CSS).

From the Organization's Web site, the GILC advocates the following:

- Prohibiting prior censorship of online communication
- Requiring that laws restricting the content of online speech distinguish between the liability of content providers and the liability of data carriers
- Insisting that online free expression not be restricted by indirect means such as excessively restrictive governmental or private controls over computer hardware or software, telecommunications infrastructure, or other essential components of the Internet

- Including citizens in the Global Information Infrastructure (GII) development process from countries that are currently unstable economically, have insufficient infrastructure, or lack sophisticated technology

- Prohibiting discrimination on the basis of race, color, sex, language, religion, political or other opinion, national or social origin, property, birth, or other status

- Ensuring that personal information generated on the GII for one purpose is not used for an unrelated purpose or disclosed without the person's informed consent and enabling individuals to review personal information on the Internet and to correct inaccurate information

- Enabling online users to encrypt their communications and information without restriction

Junkbusters

http://www.junkbusters.com

This site provides a great deal of information about removing yourself from mass mailing and e-mailing lists. The site mission is "to get rid of any junk mail, telemarketing calls, junk faxes, junk pages, junk e-mail, unwanted banner ads, and any other solicitations" you do not want. As we have seen so far, this is a major undertaking. The site provides educational information on such things as cookies, Web bugs, and how to reply to marketers to get your name off mailing lists.

New Initiatives

Privacy organizations are at the forefront of the fight against companies and governments to protect consumer privacy. As we have seen with just a sampling of the cases and initiatives that are underway, many fronts exist that require defending by privacy organizations. There are a number of new concerns, as well as positive defenses revolving consumer information that go beyond simple things such as spam e-mail and purchased information for direct mailings.

Chief Privacy Officer

One of the most positive changes in consumer privacy has been the emergency of the chief privacy officer (CPO) position in many large corporations. The goal of the CPO is to guide a company's privacy policies and practices. The need for a privacy officer has grown rapidly over the past couple years and is the focus of attention because of the new laws that affect a company's policies regarding consumer information. Legal requirements are forcing many companies to comply or face penalties. We have discussed laws such as HIPPA and Gramm-Leach-Bliley that have definite requirements and penalties for non-compliance of protecting consumer information. Fear is also a driving factor behind the ascension of the CPO. Companies are afraid of lawsuits and laws that could affect their reputations and business practices. The CPO role is more of a policy role than an implementation of technology.

Standards for the CPO role are still being developed, as are the requirements of the role. Some CPOs report to a director of compliance, whereas others report to the chief executive officer (CEO) or chief operations officer (COO). CPOs are former lawyers, marketing people, and compliance officers as well as people who have no experience in technology. Technology skills are not high on the list of requirements for the position; however, some of the requirements of the position include

- Developing privacy taskforces from cross-functional groups
- Making, coordinating, and implementing policy and activities
- Monitoring company products and services for compliance with policies
- Coordinating IT, management, and marketing departments
- Conducting privacy audits
- Training employees
- Dealing with the media
- Communicating legislation to management
- Recommending privacy strategies and policies
- Comparing the company's privacy policies with potential risks
- Keeping up-to-date with technology issues
- Managing a customer-privacy dispute and verification process

The role has spawned the Association of Chief Privacy Officers (www.pandab.org), a professional group for CPOs. Privacy issues have also spawned the Privacy Leadership Initiative, an alliance to study consumer privacy issues and lay out voluntary guidelines. The group will work with the New York-based Direct Marketing Association on a three-year, multimillion-dollar publicity blitz to convince consumers that their data is safe. CPOs are playing a prominent role is such initiatives. Doubleclick, one of the companies that has been in the news and in the courts over privacy issues, has filled their CPO role after the FTC and several states started to investigate it. AT&T's CPO has a hand in denying a deal that would compromise consumer data through a retail company partnership.

There are many potential and real problems with the CPO role, however. The main problem is that of actual authority to accomplish the privacy needs of a company. If the role is not invested with the proper authority, the company will not be capable of complying with laws and consumer pressures. The technological challenges are another obstacle the CPO must face. Even if the policies are in place, the implementers of the technology can make mistakes or even not comply with the company's policies without the CPO knowing or understanding how technology is compromising consumer information.

The CPO has no baseline from the government to follow to achieve consumer privacy. But the few laws passed on privacy issues do not address the guidelines necessary for the CPO to be successful. U.S. senators on the Commerce, Science, and Transportation Committee have been debating how to best implement privacy safeguards but can't come to a consensus on whether businesses should be required to seek consent, or "opt in," from users before collecting and sharing personal information.

Key areas of contention that must be addressed before online privacy legislation is adopted include the following:

- **The ability to sue, or "private right of action"**—Consumers need the ability to sue businesses that violate privacy rules as a means of ensuring that businesses comply with the law.
- **Online versus offline rules**—Offline merchants that do not require opt-in or opt-out choices should face the same rules as online merchants that need opt-in or opt-out choices from users.
- **Federal preemption of state laws**—States are free to adopt tougher privacy rules unless Congress says otherwise.

Other government agencies are facing the same dilemma, which is determining what the best method is of protecting consumer privacy. If corporate self-regulation doesn't work with the help of the CPO roles in many leading organizations, the government will be forced to come to some compromise that might not be in the best interests of consumers or corporations, as is typically the case with government intervention.

Privacy is stated as one of the roadblocks to successful e-commerce, yet consumers sometimes seem to not care at all about their privacy and assume it is a lost cause. The CPO role is evolving into a police role as well as a strategic role. When consumers do not understand how their privacy can be compromised and when it is inappropriate for a company to require information, the CPO has to step in and defend the consumers' rights. The need for a CPO might not be necessary in all organization; those companies that already have a CPO tend to be organizations that collect a lot of information about the consumer, including such things as credit card information and shopping preferences. In addition, diverse businesses, such as financial institutions and insurance companies, are finding the need for a CPO role. The public only seems to hear the stories about the small companies, such as dot.coms, that have privacy compromises or sell consumer data to get cash for the failing business. Government actions have not been targeted at the smaller players; recent regulations have affected the financial, insurance, and medical industries, where most of the CPO roles have been filled.

Some other notable companies that have installed a CPO role include IBM, Zero Knowledge Systems, Earthlink, and American Express. With such companies leading the way, the CPO role is becoming a reality in more and more companies, even down to small shops that are very concerned about consumer privacy. For companies that rely heavily on consumer personal information, the CPO can be a roadblock to doing business. If the company wants to sell consumer information or do mass marketing with information that goes against its policies, the CPO must step in and uphold the company's policies. The result of installing CPOs has not yet been fully realized. As more companies fill the role, we will see if it affects consumer privacy and helps companies comply with the laws being passed.

Internet Blocking

Internet blocking refers to software that has been designed to sort and filter content on the Internet. Its main focus has been the capability to block pornography. It's also called *filtering software* or *censorware*. Because each state or country has its own set of laws, such software has to work within the guidelines set up by the local authorities—whether it is governmental or societal. Several laws are in progress that would require censorship software in schools and libraries; if libraries and schools are not in compliance, they would lose funding from the government. The Children's Online Protection Act & Neighborhood Children's Online Protection Act make such software a requirement. Organizations such as the EFF are vigorously protesting these acts and calling for public support. Even SurfControl, maker of the Cyber Patrol blocking software, issued a statement against Massachusetts's attempt to make such software mandatory in public libraries. In the case of Multnomah Public Library v. U.S., the plaintiff, a diverse group of public libraries, library associations, library patrons, and Internet authors and publishers seek injunctive and declaratory relief against provisions of the Children's Internet Protection Act, as it relates to blocking software. CHIPA requires all public libraries that participate in certain federal programs to install and enforce blocking software. The software is supposed to filter obscene, child pornographic, or harmful materials a minor can access.

Rather than affecting consumer privacy directly, blocking software restricts the consumer's right to choose. This type of software faces right to free speech arguments from opponents. In public facilities, laws are being designed to tell consumer what they can and can't see. Many of the organizations mentioned previously have come out with strong statements and protests against the use of blocking software in public places.

Laws passed requiring blocking technology face many problems. Congress requires such technologies in schools and libraries, but those against such use of technology say that the technology is just not ready or capable of performing the necessary blocking. Several reason given include the following:

- **Underblocking**—No blocking technology is sophisticated enough to block even half of the pornography and explicit sites.
- **Overblocking**—Blocking technology can't filter correctly to just restrict pornography. Legitimate sites also get blocked, which can infringe on free

speech rights and civil liberties. Informative and useful sites can get blocked because of the inadequacies of such technology.

- **"Expert" control**—Average consumers will require expert help to use the software. Companies will decide what the consumer can and can't see.
- **Subjective**—No specific guidelines exist for what should be blocked. Blocked sites are purely subjective. It is hard to customize the software to meet the specific needs of different groups of people.
- **Error-Prone**—Frequent errors occur in the software and in the sites being blocked. Blocking sites is more art than science.
- **Censorship**—Government-mandated censorship is in direct conflict with the U.S. Constitutional guarantees to free expression and freedom of association and can be challenged by any of the advocate groups.
- **Discrimination**—Blocking can unfairly discriminate against whole communities of people accessing, publishing, or broadcasting on the Internet; there is no customization of who can see what material, or even by geographic location.
- **Vulnerable**—The technology can easily be bypassed.
- **Problematic**—Technical problems can occur with this type of software during installation, maintenance, upgrades, and removal. This would negatively affect the use of the Internet in public places.
- **Focus**—Having software attempt to monitor children's activities is probably not the best way to educate children about what is right and wrong.

The following paragraphs describe some blocking software.

X-Stop (http://www.xstop.com), shown in Figure 3.7, has both client and server software and charges a year fee for the product.

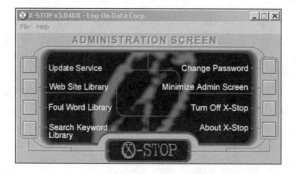

Figure 3.7   Xstop administration screen.

Cyber Patrol (http://www.surfcontrol.com), shown in Figure 3.8, is one of the more popular filter programs. Each year of service has some cost associated with it. Surf Control also has a version for education sites.

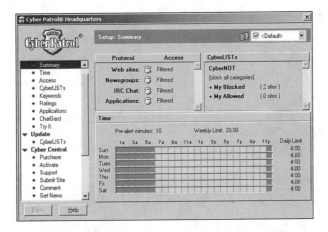

Figure 3.8   Cyber Patrol administration screen.

Bair (http://www.thebair.com), shown in Figure 3.9, is another filter program.

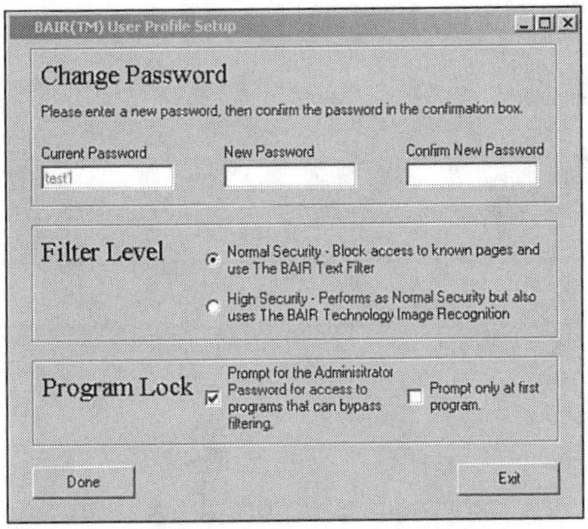

Figure 3.9   Bair administration screen.

We-Blocker (http://www.we-blocker.com), shown in Figure 3.10, is yet another filtering program.

The Censorware Project (http://censorware.net/), formed by a group of writers and activists in late 1997, is an anti-filtering advocacy group. This advocacy group analyzes Internet blocking software and decrypting and lists the sites blocked by these programs. These products block Internet users from receiving information, but the lists of sites blocked by each product are closely guarded secrets of the companies. Censorware programs take this blocking technology to the next level by censoring what information is sent *out* from your computer through mediums such as e-mail.

Censorware programs rely on automated aids such as spiders to review the Web for controversial material, but they do need human intervention because many such programs inadvertently block valid sites. Sites blocked by censorware have no idea that they are blocked, so legitimate sites would never know they were blocked unless they researched what the products block or people tell them they can't reach their sites. The Censorware Project found that the Utah Education Network's Internet "filtering" software blocked various sites offering information on safe-sex practices, legal issues concerning homosexuality, and the U.S. Constitution. As with other blocking programs, censorware faces court battles over freedom of speech.

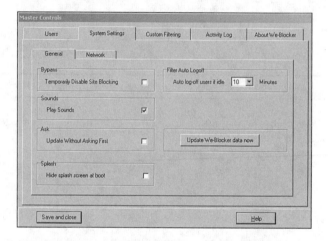

Figure 3.10   We-Blocker administration screen.

Privacy Pledge

The Privacy Coalition—a nonpartisan coalition of consumer, civil liberties, educational, library, labor, and family-based groups—launched a government-targeted initiative in February 2001 that is aimed at setting standards for privacy laws in the future. "The Privacy Pledge" is a document that the coalition urges federal and state government legislatures to sign to show their support for consumer privacy friendly laws. Members of the coalition include the American Association of Law Libraries, American Library Association, American Civil Liberties Union (ACLU), Center for Media Education, Consumer Federation of America, and Consumers Union.

The pledge that the coalition developed is in the following sidebar.

The Privacy Pledge

Privacy is one of America's most fundamental values.

The Fourth Amendment states that "The right of the people to be secure in their persons, houses, papers, and effects, against unreasonable searches and seizures, shall not be violated." In addition, the U.S. has adopted many laws protecting Americans from privacy invasive practices by both the public and private sectors.

Recognizing the need to protect this essential freedom, I, (insert Member's name), pledge to my constituents in (State and District) and to the American people that I will support a privacy framework to safeguard the rights of Americans in this information age.

This framework includes:

1. the Fair Information Practices: the right to notice, consent, security, access, correction, use limitations, and redress when information is improperly used,

2. independent enforcement and oversight,

3. promotion of genuine Privacy Enhancing Technologies that limit the collection of personal information and legal restrictions on surveillance technologies such as those used for locational tracking, video surveillance, electronic profiling, and workplace monitoring, and

4. a solid foundation of federal privacy safeguards that permit the private sector and states to implement supplementary protections as needed.

Platform for Privacy Preferences Project

The Platform for Privacy Preferences Project (P3P) is a new industry standard providing a simple, automated way for users to control information that is given to Web sites they visit. P3P covers a Web site's privacy policy with a number of multiple-choice questions. The answers give users of the site an understanding of how the Web site handles user information. P3P enables an automated process that can be used by applications to determine the privacy policy of a site. P3P-enabled browsers can "read" the answers about the privacy policy and compare the policy to user preferences. One of the problems consumers face is the inability to understand the legal language many privacy policies have or even understand what simple language polices actually mean. P3P might be the solution to giving users an understanding of what actually happens to their information. The machine-readable syntax of P3P automates and provides a guideline for future policy statements and promotes a standard for policy creation.

P3P is an industry self-regulation that has not gotten much support from federal legislatures. Government lawmakers remain unconvinced that P3P will be enough to regulate privacy policies and secure consumer information. One major contributor to the P3P push is Microsoft. In Internet Explorer 6, support for P3P will be built in. With P3P, users can configure their browsers to automatically determine whether a Web site collects personally identifiable information and creates profiles. Users can use the browser to opt in or opt out of information collection. P3P will be used to check advertisements' network privacy policies. If the policies are not in compliance with user preferences, the ads will not be capable of placing cookies on the user's system. Because ads require cookies, most leading ad networks will comply with P3P and IE standards. As P3P takes off, many companies will be out of compliance and will not be capable of using cookies and gathering consumer information. Netscape will also support P3P in its browser.

Microsoft and Netscape will face a number of challenges with promoting P3P in their browsers. The capability to manage cookies will be the first. Cookies enable a lot of Web site function as a well as store information for ad networks. If users can't understand how to manage cookies with the new capabilities provided by their browsers, they could lose functionality on a number of Web sites. The browser will automatically be capable of reading the privacy policies associated with cookies. The browser can then block or allow cookies, much the same as programs such as CookiePal can do, but extra software will not need to be installed. The new browser will enable users to use a lever to set their browsers to one of five settings, ranging from a low to high level of privacy protection. Ease of use is always a major stumbling block for any new technology. Another problem all industries face is the fact that governments will still become involved in privacy issues and pass laws that could adversely affect companies and how they handle consumer information. P3P has not proven that it can be the end-all solution to privacy policies and ensure information collected from consumers is justified and secured. A future obstacle for P3P might be the capability of new technology to get around the controls installed with P3P. This is almost a certainty given how quickly technology progresses. EPIC has come out with criticisms of P3P and the way Microsoft is using it, specifically that not enough has been done to protect consumer information.

European Union Privacy Laws

The EU has come out with very strong privacy standards regarding consumer information. The European Union's comprehensive privacy legislation, the Directive on Data Protection (the Directive), became effective on October 25, 1998. Only recently have the laws of the EU begun to impact other countries, namely the United States. The strict laws of the Directive require that transfers of personal data take place only to non-EU countries that provide an "adequate" level of privacy protection. The problem U.S. companies are facing with the stringent mandates of the Directive is that the United States uses a sectorial approach that relies on a mix of legislation, regulation, and self regulation, which do not meet all the requirements of the EU.

One of the points of the Directive states that consumers must have access to data collected about them and have the opportunity to destroy or change such data. U.S. companies can't as yet fulfill this requirement on a wide scale basis, and the exchange of such data across international borders will become a problem. The most effected of the industries is the financial sector. The U.S. Gramm–Leach–Bliley Act requires financial institutions, including insurance companies, brokerages, and banks, to let customers opt out of potential data-sharing practices among those three parties but is not as strict as the EU laws.

Along with the Directive, the EU and the U.S. have developed Safe Harbor. Safe Harbor is an arrangement negotiated by the Department of Commerce and the EU in which companies agree to abide by a set of guidelines dealing with the transfer of data. No legal requirements exist; this is a self-regulatory mechanism supported by both governments and a number of large, influential corporations. Microsoft, Intel, Hewlett-Packard, and Procter and Gamble have recently pledged to provide European-grade privacy protection to their customers in the United States and around the world along with 69 other companies. Safe Harbor will help U.S. companies comply with EU privacy laws and give them the right to transfer EU citizen information to the U.S.

The Safe Harbor principles are outlined in the following sidebar.

Safe Harbor Privacy Principles
Issued by the U.S. Department of Commerce on July 21, 2000

NOTICE: An organization must inform individuals about the purposes for which it collects and uses information about them, how to contact the organization with any inquiries or complaints, the types of third parties to which it discloses the information, and the choices and means the organization offers individuals for limiting its use and disclosure. This notice must be provided in clear and conspicuous language when individuals are first asked to provide personal information to the organization or as soon thereafter as is practicable, but in any event before the organization uses such information for a purpose other than that for which it was originally collected or processed by the transferring organization or discloses it for the first time to a third party[1].

CHOICE: An organization must offer individuals the opportunity to choose (opt out) whether their personal information is (a) to be disclosed to a third party or (b) to be used for a purpose that is incompatible with the purpose(s) for which it was originally collected or subsequently authorized by the individual. Individuals must be provided with clear and conspicuous, readily available, and affordable mechanisms to exercise choice.

For sensitive information (i.e. personal information specifying medical or health conditions, racial or ethnic origin, political opinions, religious or philosophical beliefs, trade union membership or information specifying the sex life of the individual), they must be given affirmative or explicit (opt in) choice if the information is to be disclosed to a third party or used for a purpose other than those for which it was originally collected or subsequently authorized by the individual through the exercise of opt in choice. In any case, an organization should treat as sensitive any information received from a third party where the third party treats and identifies it as sensitive.

ONWARD TRANSFER: To disclose information to a third party, organizations must apply the Notice and Choice Principles. Where an organization wishes to transfer information to a third party that is acting as an agent, as described in the endnote, it might do so if it first either ascertains that the third party subscribes to the Principles or is subject to the Directive or another adequacy finding or enters into a written agreement with such third party requiring that the third party provide at least the same level of privacy protection as is required by the relevant Principles. If the organization complies with these requirements, it shall not be held responsible (unless the organization agrees otherwise) when a third party to which it transfers such information processes it in a way contrary to any restrictions or representations, unless the organization knew or should have known the third party would process it in such a contrary way and the organization has not taken reasonable steps to prevent or stop such processing.

SECURITY: Organizations creating, maintaining, using or disseminating personal information must take reasonable precautions to protect it from loss, misuse and unauthorized access, disclosure, alteration and destruction.

DATA INTEGRITY: Consistent with the Principles, personal information must be relevant for the purposes for which it is to be used. An organization might not process personal information in a way that is incompatible with the purposes for which it has been collected or subsequently authorized by the individual. To the extent necessary for those purposes, an organization should take reasonable steps to ensure that data is reliable for its intended use, accurate, complete, and current.

ACCESS: Individuals must have access to personal information about them that an organization holds and be able to correct, amend, or delete that information where it is inaccurate, except where the burden or expense of providing access would be disproportionate to the risks to the individual's privacy in the case in question, or where the rights of persons other than the individual would be violated.

ENFORCEMENT: Effective privacy protection must include mechanisms for assuring compliance with the Principles, recourse for individuals to whom the data relate affected by non-compliance with the Principles, and consequences for the organization when the Principles are not followed. At a minimum, such mechanisms must include (a) readily available and affordable independent recourse mechanisms by which each individual's complaints and disputes are investigated and resolved by reference to the Principles and damages awarded where the applicable law or private sector initiatives so provide; (b) follow up procedures for verifying that the attestations and assertions businesses make about their privacy practices are true and that privacy practices have been implemented as presented; and (c) obligations to remedy problems arising out of failure to comply with the Principles by organizations announcing their adherence to them and consequences for such organizations. Sanctions must be sufficiently rigorous to ensure compliance by organizations.

U.S. Laws

In addition to the laws we have already mentioned, such as COPA, Gramm-Leach-Bliley, and HIPPA, a number of proposals for new laws regarding consumer information and privacy are before the various state and federal legislatures. The following list describes some of the numerous proposals for laws and regulations that are pending:

- **H.R.89 Online Privacy Protection Act of 2001**—Requires the Federal Trade Commission to prescribe regulations to protect the privacy of personal information collected from and about individuals who are not covered by the

Children's Online Privacy Protection Act of 1998 on the Internet, to provide greater individual control over the collection and use of that information, and for other purposes. Sponsor: Rep. Rodney P. Frelinghuysen, R-NJ. Latest major action: 1/3/2001 referred to House Energy and Commerce Committee.

- **H.R.90 Know Your Caller Act**—A bill to amend the Communications Act of 1934 to prohibit telemarketers from interfering with the caller identification service of any person to whom a telephone solicitation is made and for other purposes. Sponsor: Rep. Rodney P. Frelinghuysen, R-NJ. Latest major action: 3/12/2001 House preparation for floor.

- **H.R.91 Social Security On-line Privacy Protection Act**—Regulates the use by interactive computer services of Social Security account numbers and related personally identifiable information. Sponsor: Rep Rodney P. Frelinghuysen, R-NJ. Latest major action: 1/3/2001 referred to House Energy and Commerce Committee.

- **H.R.95 Unsolicited Commercial Electronic Mail Act of 2001**—Protects individuals, families, and Internet service providers from unsolicited and unwanted electronic mail. Sponsor: Rep. Gene Green, D-TX (introduced 1/3/2001). Latest major action: Referred to House Committees on Energy and Commerce and House Judiciary.

- **H.R.199 Law Enforcement Officers Privacy Protection Act**—Amends rule 26 of the Federal Rules of Civil Procedure to provide for the confidentiality of a personnel record or personal information of a law enforcement officer. Sponsor: Rep. John E. Sweeney, R-NY (introduced 1/3/2001). Latest major action: Referred to House Judiciary Committee.

- **H.R.220 Identity Theft Protection Act of 2001**—Amends title II of the Social Security Act and the Internal Revenue Code of 1986 to protect the integrity and confidentiality of Social Security account numbers issued under such title to prohibit the establishment in the federal government of any uniform national identifying number and to prohibit federal agencies from imposing standards for identification of individuals on other agencies or persons. Sponsor: Rep. Ron Paul, R-TX. Latest major action: 1/3/2001 referred to House Ways and Means and House Government Reform Committees.

- **H.R.232 Telemarketing Victims Protection Act**—Amends the Telemarketing and Consumer Fraud and Abuse Prevention Act to authorize the Federal Trade Commission to issue new rules regulating telemarketing firms, and for other purposes. Sponsor: Rep. Peter T. King, R-NY (introduced 1/6/2001). Latest major action: Referred to House Committee on Energy and Commerce.

- **H.R.237 Consumer Internet Privacy Enhancement Act**—Protects the privacy of consumers who use the Internet. Sponsor: Rep. Anna G. Eshoo, D-CA (introduced 1/20/2001). Latest major action: 1/20/2001 referred to House Committee on Energy and Commerce.

- **H.R.260 Wireless Privacy Protection Act of 2001**—Requires customer consent to the provision of wireless call location information. Sponsor: Rep. Rodney P. Frelinghuysen, R-NJ. Latest major action: 1/30/2001 referred to House Committee on Energy and Commerce.

- **H.R.333 Bankruptcy Abuse Prevention and Consumer Protection Act of 2001**—Amends title 11, United States Code, and for other purposes. Sponsor: Rep. George W. Gekas, R-IA. Latest major action: 3/5/2001 received in the Senate. Read twice. Placed on Senate Legislative Calendar under General Orders. Calendar No. 17.

- **H.R.347 Consumer Online Privacy and Disclosure Act**—Requires the Federal Trade Commission to prescribe regulations to protect the privacy of personal information collected from and about individuals on the Internet, to provide greater individual control over the collection and use of that information, and for other purposes. Sponsor: Rep. Gene Green, D-TX. Latest major action: 1/31/2001 referred to House Committee on Energy and Commerce.

- **H.R.583 Privacy Commission Act**—Establishes the Commission for the Comprehensive Study of Privacy Protection. Sponsor: Rep. Asa Hutchinson, R-AR. Latest major action: 2/13/2001 referred to House Committee on Government Reform.

- **H.R.733 Parent-Child Privilege Act of 2001**—Amends the Federal Rules of Evidence to establish a parent child privilege. Sponsor: Rep. Robert E. Andrews, D-NJ. Latest major action: 2/27/2001 referred to House Judiciary Committee.

- **H.R.1017 Anti-Spamming Act of 2001**—Prohibits the unsolicited e-mail known as *spam*. Sponsor: Rep. Bob Goodlatte, R-VA. Latest major action: 3/14/2001 referred to House Judiciary Committee.

- **H.R.1158 National Homeland Security Agency Act**—Establishes the National Homeland Security Agency. Sponsor: Rep. William (Mac) Thornberry, R-TX. Latest major action: 3/21/2001 referred to House Committee on Government Reform.

- **H.R.1176 Fair Credit Reporting Act Amendments of 2001**—Amends the Fair Credit Reporting Act to protect consumers from the adverse consequences of incomplete and inaccurate consumer credit reports, and for other purposes. Sponsor: Rep. Harold Ford, Jr., D-TN. Latest major action: 3/22/2001 referred to House Committee on Financial Services.

- **H.R.1215 Medical Information Protection and Research Enhancement Act of 2001**—Ensures confidentiality with respect to medical records and health care–related information, and for other purposes. Sponsor: Rep. James C. Greenwood, R-PA. Latest major action: 3/27/2001 referred to House Committee on Energy and Commerce and House Judiciary Committee.

- **H.R.1259 Computer Security Enhancement Act of 2001**—Amends the National Institute of Standards and Technology Act to enhance the ability of the National Institute of Standards and Technology to improve computer security, and for other purposes. Sponsor: Rep. Constance A. Morella, R–MD. Latest major action: 3/28/2001 referred to House Committee on Science.

- **H.R.1292 Homeland Security Strategy Act of 2001**—Requires the president to develop and implement a strategy for homeland security. Sponsor: Rep. Ike Skelton, D–MO. Latest major action: 3/29/2001 referred to House Committees on Armed Services, Judiciary, Transportation and Infrastructure, and the Select Committee on Intelligence.

- **H.R.1408 Financial Services Antifraud Network Act of 2001**—Safeguards the public from fraud in the financial services industry, streamlines and facilitates the antifraud information sharing efforts of federal and state regulators, and other purposes. Sponsor: Rep. Mike Rogers, R–MI. Latest major action: 4/4/2001 referred to House Committees on Agriculture, Financial Services, and Judiciary.

- **H.R.1478 Personal Information Privacy Act of 2001**—Protects the privacy of the individual with respect to the Social Security number and other personal information, and for other purposes. Sponsor: Rep. Gerald D. Kleczka, D–WI. Latest major action: 4/4/2001 referred to House Committees on Financial Services and Ways and Means.

- **H.R.1543 Civil Rights and Employee Investigation Clarification Act**—Amends the Fair Credit Reporting Act to exempt certain communications from the definition of consumer report, and for other purposes. Sponsor: Rep. Pete Sessions, R–TX. Latest major action: 4/24/2001 referred to House Committee on Financial Services.

- **H.R.1655 Personal Pictures Protection Act of 2001**—Amends title 18, United States Code, to punish the placing of sexually explicit photographs on the Internet without the permission of the persons photographed. Sponsor: Rep. Mark Green, R–WI. Latest major action: 5/1/2001 referred to House Judiciary Committee.

- **H.R.1846 Who Is E-Mailing Our Kids Act**—Amends section 254 of the Communications Act of 1934 to require schools and libraries receiving universal service assistance to block access to Internet services that enable users to access the World Wide Web and transfer electronic mail in an anonymous manner. Sponsor: Rep. Felix J. Grucci, Jr., R–NY. Latest major action: 5/22/2001 referred to House Subcommittee on Energy and Commerce.

- **H.R.1847 Hands Off Our Kids Act of 2001**—Requires the attorney general to identify organizations that recruit juveniles to participate in violent and illegal activities related to the environment or to animal rights, and to amend the Juvenile Justice and Delinquency Prevention Act of 1974 to provide assistance to states to carry out activities to prevent the participation of juveniles in such activities. Sponsor: Rep. Felix J. Grucci, Jr., R-NY. Latest major action: 5/15/2001 referred to House Committee on Education and the Workforce and the House Judiciary Committee.

- **H.R.1854 Parental Freedom of Information Act**—Amends the General Education Act to allow parents access to certain information about their children. Sponsor: Rep. Todd Tiahrt, R-KS. Latest major action: 5/15/2001 referred to House Committee on Education and the Workforce.

- **H.R.1877 Child Sex Crimes Wiretapping Act of 2001**—Amends title 18, United States Code, to provide that certain sexual crimes against children are predicate crimes for the interception of communications, and for other purposes. Sponsor: Rep. Nancy L. Johnson, R-CT. Latest major action: 5/16/2001 referred to House Judiciary Committee.

- **H.R.2031 Consumer Credit Report Accuracy and Privacy Act of 2001**—Amends the Fair Credit Reporting Act to enable any consumer to receive a free credit report annually from any consumer reporting agency. Sponsor: Rep. Lucille Roybal Allard, D-CA. Latest major action: 5/25/2001 referred to House Committee on Financial Services.

- **H.R.2036 Social Security Number Privacy and Identity Theft Prevention Act of 2001**—Amends the Social Security Act to enhance privacy protections for individuals, to prevent fraudulent misuse of the Social Security account number, and for other purposes. Sponsor: Rep. E. Clay Shaw, Jr., R-FA. Latest major action: 5/25/2001 referred to House Committees on Financial Services, Energy and Commerce, and Ways and Means.

- **H.R.2135 Consumer Privacy Protection Act**—Protects consumer privacy. Sponsor: Rep. Tom Sawyer, D-OH. Latest major action: 6/18/2001 referred to House Subcommittee on Energy and Commerce.

- **H.R.2136 Confidential Information Protection Act**—Protects the confidentiality of information acquired from the public for statistical purposes. Sponsor: Rep. Tom Sawyer, D-OH. Latest major action: 6/12/2001 referred to House Committee on Government Reform.

Federal Bureau of Investigation

Although the FBI certainly can't be called a new initiative, it has taken on a modified or even "new" role in computer security and privacy. The role of the FBI has traditionally been criminal investigations, but the rise of Internet hacking has spawned new skills and responsibilities for the agency. Within government enforcement agencies, there is a conflict between a centralizing tendency that would set uniform standards and link "intrusion detection" monitoring for all government and private systems and protect consumer information from unwanted dissemination using the current decentralized self-regulation of the industry. Security requirements between government systems, business systems, and consumer systems vary greatly, and government agencies have not come up with reliable or acceptable standards that address this issue.

Government agencies such as the FBI have increased spending on research and manpower to combat threats to privacy and security. They have also helped fund the education of new information security professionals, assisted in the development of best security testing procedures, and encouraged systems security improvements. Yet we see a rise in Internet hacking and information theft. The lack of standards and quantifiable metrics as far as what types of compromises and invasions have taken place all contribute to the trend toward more government intervention in security matters and law enforcement.

In association with the FBI, agencies such as the National Institute for Standards and Technology (NIST) and the National Security Agency (NSA) are attempting to define processes and standards for information protection and system protection to help both private industry and government sectors. The changing role of the FBI might cause long-term conflicts that have not been discussed to date, but for now, the FBI has taken the spotlight in many hacking cases and has become more publicly involved in computer security.

The FBI has been seen in many news stories for its prosecution of well-known hacker cases. The latest is the arrest of the Russian programmer Dmitry Skylarov at the DefCon convention in Las Vegas in July 2001. He was arrested on charges of criminal copyright violations, which sparked protests from privacy advocacy groups and the security/hacker community. Skylarov developed a crack for Adobe's Ebook and was charged under the Digital Millennium Copyright Act. "The U.S. government for the first time is prosecuting a programmer for building a tool that may be used for many purposes, including those that legitimate purchasers need in order to exercise their fair-use rights," said Robin Gross, an attorney with the EFF.

The FBI has also made prominent headlines with its DCS1000 tool (originally called Carnivore), which can capture a lot of user data and information that travels over the Internet from the ISP location. Not only does the program capture data for the suspect under investigation, but other user information is also captured. This is taking the "monitoring" role of the FBI to a new level in Internet security. Advocacy groups and public officials are questioning the FBI's extended capabilities. House Majority Leader Dick Armey said in a letter to Attorney General John Ashcroft, "I respectfully ask that you consider the serious constitutional questions Carnivore has raised and respond with how you intend to address them. This is an issue of great importance to the online public."

After the terrorist attacks in the U.S. on September 11, 2001, the FBI was granted more leeway in its use of DCS1000 and has gotten more cooperation from ISPs in capturing and turning user information over to the government. Both AOL and Earthlink have cooperated to track terrorist activities using their systems.

The USA Patriot Act makes it even easier to use DCS1000. This act gives federal authorities much wider capabilities in monitoring Internet use and expands the way such data is shared among government agencies. Even though this bill was passed to track down terrorists, it by no means restricts investigations to terrorists. It can easily be applied to anyone or any organization.

The FBI's more active role in prosecuting criminal hacking has led to it working with more corporations to track and prosecute hackers. However, most corporations still don't want to admit that they have been hacked and need help from the FBI. Corporations have always been very sensitive about letting the public know that they suffered a break-in and that consumer information such as credit card numbers or Social Security numbers could have been stolen. One of the reasons companies give for not notifying the FBI of a break-in is that the FBI can't guarantee that the information collected is limited to what is absolutely necessary for prosecution and that information will not be shared without proper consent of the corporation. The government tends to make mandatory requirements without much notice and forces private industry to comply without warning. The FBI can provide many services regarding information protection, but the history of government involvement and specifically FBI involvement has caused private industry to be very leery of any help. The DCS1000 case illustrates that capability of the FBI to garner consumer information even when there is no ongoing investigation. To alleviate the fears of private industry, the government must justify both the purpose and the use of information-gathering tools and clearly define how it will protect consumer information.

Summary

The United States has been conducting business in regard to consumer privacy on a self-regulatory basis until now. As we are seeing with the pending legislation, the time for self-regulation might be over. The laws that have already been passed are forcing companies into federal compliance based on consumer and advocate group pressure. The EU has already made the push to strong government-enforced privacy standards. To do business in the EU, U.S. companies are being forced to modify their privacy tactics.

Even as technology becomes more invasive, we see responses led by certain groups, such as the EFF and EPIC, that are still willing to protect consumer rights. Large companies such as Microsoft and IBM, which have a lot to gain from gathering consumer information, are also attempting to protect users with initiatives such as P3P. Perhaps they see that if the government steps in completely and regulates all industries as the EU has done, they will be adversely affected. Finding the right mixture of self-regulation and government regulation is probably something that we will never achieve. One of the fears of government intervention is the inflexibility and slow movement of laws. Self-regulation can be modified quickly or ignored when a company needs to make a profit. Legislation also carries a monetary cost that self-regulation could never come close to matching. As we know from experience, whenever the government becomes involved, someone will be paying a great deal of money, and any costs the corporation incurs will eventually be passed onto the consumer.

We have seen that the sectorial self-regulation approach does not provide a standard baseline and measurement system for compliance. Each industry has its own guidelines or no guidelines at all for consumer privacy. The answer has not been found to consumer privacy through the self-regulation method. Consumers are being pulled in many directions, and the guidelines for privacy are still not defined or protected. For consumers to feel secure in using the Internet and other technologies while protecting who they are from prying eyes, corporations and governments must find a mixture of government and corporate compromise that will ensure we remain anonymous in an ever more connected world.

II

The Enemy Is Out There: Threats to Individual Privacy

4

Legal Threats to Individual Privacy

Privacy is a fundamental human right recognized in the UN Declaration of Human Rights and the International Covenant on Civil and Political Rights. Many constitutions around the globe recognize privacy as a right. Privacy can be achieved, but there are many roadblocks in keeping data private and secure in our connected world. Threats to your privacy can come from many sources, some of which are legal according to the letter of the law. Different countries approach the privacy rights issue via various means; threats to individual privacy are addressed in laws and constitutions. But as any good lawyer will tell you, there are ways around the law to get what you desire. In countries such as the United States, privacy is not explicitly in the constitution, but laws that have been passed give some assurance of the right to privacy. International agreements, such as the International Covenant on Civil and Political Rights or the European Convention on Human Rights, recognize privacy rights. These international agreements provide some acknowledgement of the privacy issue between countries.

Legal threats to privacy come from different sectors. An organization that holds personal data does so usually for some valid purpose. The caretakers of personal information and the consumer each have an interest in the proper use of such information; it is mutually beneficial to share information. When a business invades or abuses the consumer's privacy, the consumer has been exploited for some reason other than was intended when the information was turned over to the business. The advancement of technology is the driving factor behind privacy violations. The ability to collect, analyze, and disseminate information on individuals has bypassed all previous laws dealing with consumer information. The use of technology is also a driving factor behind changes in legislation to address new threats to the consumer. New developments in medical research and care, telecommunications, and financial industries (to name a few) have increased the level of information generated by each individual and the need for laws to protect the consumer now and in the future. The ties between industries such as medical and insurance have increased the breadth of information disseminated. Laws such as the Health Insurance Portability and Accountability Act (HIPAA) that should protect consumers can also be used to share personal medical information with insurance companies. Comprehensive profiles on any person can be developed with information such as medical history, insurance claims, and financial history.

Technology has given these entities legal means of compromising consumer privacy. If your insurance company can determine how much money you make or know everything about your financial and medical history, it can use this information to market services to you or restrict access to insurance. For example, if it knows you have a bad heart condition, it won't sell you life insurance, or if it knows you make a million dollars a year, it can raise your premiums or spam you with marketing e-mails.

Reasons for Privacy Laws

There are several reasons that laws are being passed on a global basis to protect individual privacy. Countries pass laws for one or more of the following reasons:

- **Electronic commerce advancement**—As technology is being used to launch smaller countries into the world arena, laws protecting consumers have the added benefit of promoting commerce and driving business. Setting up rules and regulations for secure business transactions help develop economies. Larger countries such as those in the European Union (EU) use privacy regulations as a method of assuring consumers of the security of their data. To compete on a global scale, companies must take into account the restrictions between countries regarding privacy, or lack thereof.

- **Consistent application with Pan-European laws**—Countries in Central and Eastern Europe are adopting new laws based on the Council of Europe Convention and the European Union Data Protection Directive. The directive on the "Protection of Individuals with regard to the processing of personal data and on the free movement of such data" sets a benchmark for national law. Joining the EU in the near future is the goal of many countries. In addition, countries such as the U.S. and Canada must adapt to the EU laws to do business. More than 40 countries now have data protection or information privacy laws.

- **Consumer pressure**—Advocacy groups such as the Electronic Frontier Foundation (EFF) have brought consumer pressure to bear on laws that affect consumer privacy, and they campaign for laws to better protect consumers.

- **Technological advancement**—Technology development has exposed consumer information to just about anyone who has any technical savvy. Gaining information about someone is very easy, so laws are necessary to protect consumers. Technological tools that have been developed provide some consumer security, but laws are needed to provide the rest of our security needs.

Forms of privacy can be attacked through various means. The categories of privacy that can be taken advantage of by individuals, businesses, and governments are as follows:

- **Information privacy**—The laws, rules, and guidelines that govern the collection, analysis, usage, and dissemination of personal data. Where and how data that relates to you is stored are affected by technology and legal requirements.

- **Personal privacy**—Your physical attributes, such as fingerprints or retina scans. Your body can be invaded through such things as drug testing and cavity searches. Your personal space, whether it's at home, in the office, or walking down the street, can be invaded with monitoring devices; your actions also can be tracked.

- **Communications privacy**—Technologies such as e-mail, cell phones, faxes, and other forms of communication can be intercepted and monitored, or even changed to compromise your interaction with others. Your right to communicate freely without interruption or being monitored is under constant attack, mostly through the workplace and by law enforcement.

- **Legal privacy**—Your basic right to privacy can be attacked in the courts and in the laws that are passed. Although laws that allow technologies to be used to invade your privacy are already a reality, new laws can be passed that restrict your ability to have any privacy at all, regardless of technology.

Threats to Privacy

Even with the adoption of legal and other protections, individuals, businesses, and governments continue to invade consumer privacy, through both legal and illegal means. The illegal aspect of privacy invasion is easy to understand. A hacker who breaks into a company and steals credit card information has blatantly stolen personal information. But the scenario in which a marketing company sells all your personal information to anyone with money breaks no laws, but the result is the same—your personal data is compromised. In many countries, laws have not kept up with the technology, so technology has created significant gaps in protection for consumers. More functionality with the use of technology such as e-mail, Web surfing, and cell phones has not spawned equally aggressive technologies to keep personal data secure.

Without laws to support the enforcement of security of new technologies, the consumer will be easy prey for any individual or business who has access to information-gathering tools. The U.S. State Department's annual review of human rights violations finds that more than 90 countries engage in illegal monitoring of the communications of political opponents, human rights workers, journalists, and labor organizers. Even though we have laws in the U.S. against such illegal activities, they still occur. Legal violations of your rights are even easier for governments to commit. As with any law, interpretation is key in the implementation of the law. Significant breaches of personal privacy can be buried in bills before the House and Senate that get passed because lawmakers are always compromising to achieve a middle ground. Laws such as HIPAA, which is a set of federal regulations intended to protect and simplify the exchange of health care data, and Gramm-Leach-Bliley, which requires financial institutions to establish an effective security program, seem to help consumers, but as we have been discussing and will see later in this chapter, there are many instances in which these laws have actually compromised consumer privacy.

Individual Threats to Privacy

Over the past decade or more, computer security has taken on a public face with the general public being made aware of what security means. The Internet has rapidly expanded the availability of knowledge and tools to assist system administrators and users in securing their systems and networks. The consumer can take privacy protection into her own hands. The widespread use of the Internet enables anyone to easily find a security tool and implement it on her on computer. Where laws have not been fully developed to protect the user—such as protecting the consumer from cookies that capture and retain information—tools such as CookiePal have been developed to help the consumer fight back against that dreaded technology. The consumer has an abundance of tools and knowledge available, but she might not fully understand the implications of the tools she uses.

Internet users are a major legal threat to your privacy. Whether someone is a friend or an enemy, he can be a threat to you either maliciously or inadvertently. As already seen with some of the Web sites available to businesses, such as `www.discreetresearch.com`, the average Internet user can take advantage of these same sites to perform his own searches on you. The proliferation of Web site and software tools available for investigating someone enables even the most technically challenged person to easily gain information. With the aggregation of information through Web sites and government mandates, finding a central repository of information is easier to do; information is not as dispersed as it was in the past. Plus, the cost of information retrieval is negligible compared to what it was before the widespread use of the Internet.

Individuals have access to numerous technologies and new functionality through the Internet. Ease of use has been one of the key aspects that has caused the growth of the Internet. Some of the functions that let anyone easily and legally retrieve personal information about you include

- **Usenet messages**—Usenet is a worldwide distributed discussion system that consists of a set of newsgroups. One popular site for reading newsgroups is Google (`http://groups.google.com`). A *newsgroup* is a topic for discussion—for example, `alt.cars.bmw` would be focused on discussing BMW cars. Each message posted to a newsgroup is called an *article* or *message* and can be submitted by anyone. Software lets you connect to a newsgroup system, and the articles are then broadcast to other interconnected computer systems via a wide variety of networks. Much information can be posted in a Usenet message, such as your name, the type of software you are using, your IP address, what your interests are, and your e-mail address. These messages can provide valuable information for someone building a profile on you. Newsgroups can be searched for keywords or even names. So, for example, if someone posts a message about BMWs, you can search on her name and find out that she owns a BMW.

- **People finders**—These sites list addresses and similar information about people from public information sources. If you have ever signed up on your old high school's alumni page, the chances are that information will make it into one of the people finder search engines. Some of the more popular people finders are Switchboard (`http://switchboard.com`), Yahoo People Finder (`http://www.yahoo.com/search/people`), Big Book (`http://www.bigbook.com`), Bigfoot (`www.bigfoot.com`), and Lycos's WhoWhere? (`http://www.whowhere.com`). One site called Classmates (`http://www.classmates.com`) claims to have information from 30,000 high schools in the U.S. and Canada. Many of these sites require you to set up a login profile, further extracting information from you and adding it to their databases. With some of these sites, you can spend some money and get access to even more information.

- **Reverse directories**—A number of sites enable you to enter a telephone number or e-mail address and get the corresponding name and address. Several such sites include Connectpeople.com (`http://www.connectpeople.com/telephone.html`) and Anywho.com (`http://www.anywho.com`).

- **Online public records**—There are more sites than can be counted that display personal information on the Web. Although these are legal activities, personal information is exposed for anyone in the world to see. One example is the San Diego Sheriff's department Web site, which makes available inmate booking logs (`http://www.co.san-diego.ca.us/cnty/cntydepts/safety/sheriff/bookings.html`). You can enter a last name, such as `Smith`, and see all the Smiths booked and their dates of birth. One aggregate site of search tools is Know X (`http://www.knowx.com`). It requires registration and a fee, but anyone can have access to its research tools and track information about anyone they know. Many legal records are accessible, including home buyer and seller records, bankruptcies, judgments, lawsuits, and liens. As mentioned with the threats posed by businesses, users can also pay and perform credit checks on anyone with the credit checking Web sites that are available, including Experian (`www.experian.com`), Equifax (`www.equifax.com`), and Trans Union (`www.transunion.com`).

- **Hacker sites**—Even though hacking is against the law and a threat to your personal information, discussions, knowledge sharing, and software tools that can be used for hacking purposes are not against the law. Numerous Web sites and Usenet groups are dedicated to hacking everything from operating systems to telephone systems to software applications. Security knowledge used to be shared among a small community of technical people, but with the Internet, disseminating information and tools is easy. Several popular security/hacker Web sites include Security Focus (`www.securityfocus.com`), Packetstorm (`http://packetstormsecurity.org`), Technotronic (`http://www.technotronic.com/`), and Security Bugware (`http://oliver.efri.hr/~crv/security/security.html`).

With always-on online connectivity with such technologies as cable modems and DSL, individuals can have their own Web sites and run their own e-commerce applications and businesses that can fall outside the realm of privacy protections. If you use a chat room, or use ICQ to share messages and chat, or use a message board on a personal Web site that discusses cars or whatever happens to be your interest, the information you submit is in no way protected from dissemination. As discussed in Chapter 12, "Securing Your Standalone PC: Viruses, Chat, and Encryption," technologies such as ICQ can be used to share your personal information. There is no legal reason someone can't post your entire ICQ log history for your conversations on a Web site somewhere for all to see.

Another favorite technology that is used by individuals, as well as business, to share information is listserver technology. A mailing list is set up that anyone can join and post and receive information—much like a message board, only it's over e-mail. The generic term for the software that runs e-lists is *listserver software* or *mailing list management (MLM) software*. Two commonly used software products are listproc (`ftp://cs-ftp.bu.edu/pub/listserv`) and majordomo (`http://www.math.psu.edu/barr/majordomo-faq.html`). An individual can create a list and a consumer can sign up for the list on the Web site. Any data you send to the list goes to users, including possibly your name and e-mail address. Functionality such as listservers and Web site surveys gather and disseminate your information, and that data can be stored and sold by the individual running the Web site without your permission or even knowledge. As you can see, individuals can be inadvertent threats to your privacy.

Government Threats to Privacy

Government threats to individuals can be rather obscure. Approaches to privacy vary from country to country, but two basic models are followed. The first is a regulatory model adopted by the government to provide guidance, laws, and enforcement for privacy and security. The second model is one of self-regulation and sectoral laws. Sectoral laws are specific to certain industries, technologies, and states. Laws get developed as a last resort and follow technology development. In countries such as Hong Kong, Canada, Australia, and New Zealand and in Central and Eastern Europe, governments have taken a very active role in privacy rights. A public position also has been developed in several of these countries to enforce a comprehensive data protection law. This position monitors compliance with the law and conducts investigations.

Other countries, such as the United States, have avoided general nationwide laws until very recently in favor of specific sectoral laws and have relied on industry self-regulation. Enforcement is much more difficult in countries following this type of regulation. More mechanisms are needed to enforce privacy rights because taking advantage of the consumer is easier. The U.S. Privacy Act of 1974 regulates federal government agency record keeping and disclosure practices and gives individuals access to public records. It also requires that personal information in agency files be accurate, complete, relevant, and timely. Since 1974, the act has been amended several times, and new laws have been passed involving privacy. New legislation will be continuously needed with each new technology, so protections frequently lag behind, exposing the consumer to privacy invasion.

A major shift in the EU has forced other countries to upgrade their privacy policies. The 1995 Data Protection Directive is a benchmark for national laws for processing personal information in electronic and manual files. The 1997 Telecommunications Directive includes specific protections covering telephone, digital television, mobile networks, and other telecommunications systems. These Directives detail the rights of the consumer, such as the right to know where the data originated, the right to have inaccurate data rectified, the right of recourse in the event of unlawful processing, and the right to withhold permission to use data in some circumstances. The Data Protection Directive contains strengthened protections over the use of sensitive personal data. In the cases of industries, such as the finance and insurance industries, security of personal data is paramount and the laws generally require "explicit and unambiguous" consent of use of the data.

One of the major differences in the European model is the enforcement capability of the laws. The EU stance is that the consumer should have the ability to go to a person or an authority who can act on her behalf and advocate her rights. Every EU country has a privacy commissioner or agency that enforces the rules, which is far ahead of steps the U.S. has taken to enforce the rights of consumers. Countries with which Europe does business must have a similar level of oversight in the future, and as mentioned in Chapter 3, "Privacy Organizations and Initiatives," the Safe Harbor program is a step in this direction.

Even though this does sound great and we say that the EU has better enforcement procedures in place, practical implementation is still not ideal. EU businesses currently can do business with U.S. businesses that are not part of the Safe Harbor program. How these rules get enforced, by both EU and U.S. businesses and governments, is not well-defined. The rules on the books for the EU are stronger than U.S. rules and punishments, but all countries currently lack practical capabilities for enforcement.

Gramm–Leach–Bliley

Although the EU has taken steps to provide more security of data to the consumer, other countries such the U.S. have not been as progressive. The U.S. has been passing more laws recently, but a number of the laws have actually decreased the security of data and protection. One of the most far-reaching laws that has been passed is the Gramm-Leach-Bliley Act (GLB). Even though this law provides for more security of consumer data in the financial industry, it also opens up new paths to the dissemination of consumer data. GLB enables financial institutions to share information with "affiliated" companies, and they can share information with "nonaffiliated" companies following notice of a company's information sharing practices to the affected customers. However, consumers must be given an opt-out opportunity before the information can be shared with a nonaffiliated company.

Six key areas of security exist that GLB addresses that can also compromise consumer data protection mechanism. These areas are discussed in the following sections.

Assessing IT Environments and Understanding Security Risks

Of the industry sectors, the financial industry has generally been the most secure. When it comes to access to money, companies take very active measures regarding security. GLB mandates a higher level of security awareness and understanding. Organizations have to define both internal and Even though this law provides for more security of consumer external threats to security. Although the law recognizes the threats from both an internal and external perspective, the government is relying on industry self-regulation and sectoral laws to provide actual guidance and detailed steps to enforce the law. Organizations have general guidelines, but the interpretation of those guidelines has varied and can be misinterpreted. For the consumer, this means that while the government says that financial institutions must protect consumer data, the actual steps are left open. In the case of hackers gaining access to personal data such as credit card or bank account information, the devil is in the details.

Establishing Information Security Policies

GLB requires financial institutions to install risk controls for "foreseeable internal and external threats that could result in unauthorized disclosure, misuse, alteration or destruction of customer information or customer information systems." From an auditing perspective, such controls include authentication, access control, and encryption systems. The law doesn't specify what protections should be employed, leaving it up to individual organizations to Even though this law provides for more security of consumer determine how to best mitigate their risks, hire outside companies to perform audits, and implement the security fixes necessary to protect data. Intrusion-detection systems are encouraged, but no specific details are given on how these systems should operate or how they should be implemented. Even though it is not the function of laws to provide technical details, it is the function of the law to provide enforcement and guidelines one how these requirements should be met.

Regular Independent Assessments

The ever-changing IT environment requires constant updates for security weaknesses and updates of the knowledgebase of the individuals doing the actual testing of security and privacy weaknesses. For this reason, GLB requires regular independent third-party assessment testing of financial institutions' IT environments for security weaknesses that can allow an intruder to gain access to consumer information. The frequency of assessment testing, the credentials of the organization doing the testing, and the skill set required are all left to the discretion of the individual company. Regulation boards provide some insight into the assurance and sufficient analysis provided by third parties, but the law does not provide any real guidance on this issue. The consumer can't gain any comfort that the third party doing the testing actually conducts a thorough analysis of the environment and finds all potential Even though this law provides for more security of consumer avenues of information compromise. Again, the consumer must rely on industry self-regulation and sectoral laws for the enforcement and competence of the testing measures. A whitepaper published by Datamonitor in November 2000, titled "eSecurity—removing the roadblock to eBusiness," showed that more than 50% of businesses worldwide spend just 5% or less of their IT budgets on securing their networks.

As an example of where the IT budgets are being spent, we can look at the virus prevention industry. All the laws being passed focus mainly on hacker attacks and laws regarding computer use, but virus prevention is a good place to see where laws are lacking in the protection of computer systems. Laws such as GLB and HIPAA and the EU regulations for Safe Harbor status provide a lot of direction, but practical steps such as virus prevention are not built in to laws or can't be built in to laws because that would be too specific.

ICSA.Net released the "2000 Computer Virus Prevalence Survey" on virus attacks, which details the following statistics:

- The number of corporations infected by viruses has risen by 20% this year alone.
- 99.67% of companies surveyed experienced at least one virus encounter during the survey period.
- 51% claimed they had at least one "virus disaster" during the 12-month period before they were surveyed.
- The monthly rate of infection per 1,000 PCs has nearly doubled every year since 1996.
- 80% said the "LoveLetter" virus was their most recent virus disaster.
- The reported damage estimate from the "LoveLetter" virus is as much as $10 billion.
- The reported damage estimate from the "Melissa" virus was $385 million.
- Including hard and soft dollar figures, the true cost of virus disasters is between $100,000 and $1 million per company.

GLB does not specify the percentage of the IT budget or security budget required to secure environments or where money should be allocated, such as for virus protection. Hard numbers are difficult to apply to the need for security and the actual dollars spent on security. While the government would find determining and enforcing dollar figures for security very difficult, not providing any guidance on what statistics companies should strive to meet for security needs can be just as detrimental to the consumer.

User Training and Security Awareness Programs

For any company to keep up with the day-to-day changes in security of technology, constant knowledge transfer is required. IT employees must be made aware almost on a daily basis of advancements in technology as well as hacking techniques to provide a strong defense. GLB recognizes the need for training and security awareness and requires Even though this law provides for more security of consumer financial institutions to develop security awareness and education programs that ensure their employees are properly trained in security procedures and policies, but the extent of how detailed the programs must be or whether certification is required for employees is not covered. Each organization can define its own programs and determine how in-depth the knowledge of security issues needs to be. Enforcement of this part of GLB will be difficult because training can be a very subjective issue that can be addressed through various mechanisms, all of which have the potential of not helping one iota in securing consumer information.

If GLB specified some certification process that training would accomplish, business would have a benchmark to reach to be in compliance with this part of GLB. Leaving it up to each individual company to set its own training requirements is a sure way for poor training in security to be conducted—to the detriment of the consumer. Training costs money, and cutting the training budget is guaranteed to happen.

Scrutinizing Business Relationships

The financial sector, companies that handle money and securities, are the only ones covered by GLB. Although other laws are being passed, such as HIPAA, that address other sectors, the key strengths of GLB will not be applied to them. Within the scope of GLB are many partner companies that work with financial institutions that are not Even though this law provides for more security of consumer covered by GLB but still have full access to consumer financial information. Using the same self-regulation that is central to other U.S. privacy laws, GLB puts the onus on the financial institutions to scrutinize their business partners to ensure they have adequate security and implementations of security measures. Each company must inspect its partners' security programs and determine the credibility and accuracy of their security measures and whether it should do business with them. The consumer has to have faith in his financial institution to say no to a business partner who does not have very strict security polices. How often do we think this will happen?

An example is your credit card company teaming up with a telephone provider. The bank will tell you that if you sign up with its partner telephone company, it will give you reward points, free long-distance minutes, or some bonus for signing up. For the bank to send you this information, it might have already shared your information with its partner, and your information has been spread beyond the bank's control.

The restriction of GLB would apply only to the bank in this example. After your information is shared with its partner telephone company, it is not secured by GLB. The bank is responsible for determining whether its partner has adequate security in place. Many businesses don't have enough security to begin with. How will they determine if others are secure?

As with the benchmarks for training, the same problem exists with partners. No benchmarks, certifications, or criteria exist for business partners to meet security requirements. Each company can apply strong or weak security measures to its partners as it sees fit.

Reviewing and Updating Procedures

As mentioned already, security is a daily practice. A company is secure only at any given instance. New attacks are developed each day that can compromise consumer data, whether it's stored on a company's servers or on the home user's desktop. In the case in which financial institutions hold your information, GLB requires companies to have a program for reviewing, amending, and upgrading their security programs. How companies Even though this law provides for more security of consumer do this— whether on a daily, weekly, monthly, or quarterly basis—is not fully defined. Policies do not have to be updated daily, but practices and steps to keep the technology secure is a daily effort. In the example of viruses floating around on the Internet, a daily practice is required to ensure that a company's servers and data are not attacked and infected. As we saw in August 2001, the Code Red Worm infected thousands of servers and had the capability of modifying systems and destroying data if a server was vulnerable. Instead of just modifying Web pages and infecting systems, the Code Red virus could just have easily copied data or destroyed data, affecting the average consumer who has information on the infected system. According to Internet Security Systems, 71,402 virus attacks were reported in the fourth quarter of 2000 alone. IDC Asia/Pacific reported an estimated 25% of major companies in the Pacific Rim do not employ the use of virus protection on their systems. Without specific guidelines and enforcement provided by some governmental body, companies will be lax in their update procedures and always be behind the latest security breach, exposing consumer data to attack.

Most U.S. laws passed recently have been left intentionally ambiguous in how financial institutions, as well as other industry sectors, should protect consumer information. Although this does provide flexibility in how the law is interpreted, the flexibility can mean loss of security for consumers if companies feel that too much money must be spent on security issues. Without oversight bodies to enforce the ambiguous laws, consumer information will always be last on the priority list companies have for making money and staying in business. The compliance date has already passed for GLB to be enacted by companies, yet many are still not in compliance.

Enforcing compliance over the hundred or thousands of U.S. companies affected by GLB is next to impossible for the government. Penalties for noncompliance with GLB by insurers and health plans will be established under the state implementing laws and regulations, thus dispersing the responsibility and weakening the security model of the law. The government has yet to prosecute a company for violation of GLB. This results in differing punishments between states. Noncompliance so far doesn't really mean much, because prosecution or punishments have not yet been enforced.

Several government agencies are responsible for monitoring GLB, including the Federal Deposit Insurance Corporation (FDIC), the Federal Reserve System (FRS), the Federal Trade Commission (FTC), the Securities and Exchange Commission (SEC), the National Credit Union Administration (NCUA), the Office of the Comptroller of the Currency, and the Office of Thrift Supervision.

Health Insurance Portability and Accountability Act of 1996

The U.S. Department of Health and Human Services (HHS) published regulations establishing privacy standards that must be met to be in compliance with the Health Insurance Portability and Accountability Act of 1996 (HIPAA). Part of the challenge is the use of electronic communication of patient information (individually identifiable information transmitted or stored in any form, such as paper, oral, or electronic that concerns the individual's past, present, or future physical or mental health). Because all electronic communications are subject to attack, the HHS developed standards to protect patients' personal information. Several of the requirements of the law include

- Insurers and hospitals must obtain written consent to use or disclose information for treatment, payment, or health care operations.
- The use and disclosure of protected health information is permitted by any organization restricted by HIPAA *without* the individual's consent, authorization, or agreement for specified public policy purposes (for example, public health activities, law enforcement purposes, research, and serious threats to health or safety).
- Organizations restricted by HIPAA must "reasonably ensure" that all uses and disclosures of information are limited to the minimum amount of information required.
- Organizations restricted by HIPAA can disclose protected health information to "business associates," if the associate has security measures in place.
- Patients must have adequate notice of privacy practices by organizations restricted by HIPAA.
- Patients have the right to access protected health information stored by organizations restricted by HIPAA.
- Organizations restricted by HIPAA must implement administrative requirements (including designating a privacy official; training workforce members; and establishing administrative, technical, and physical safeguards for information).

Compliance with the privacy standards set forth in HIPAA is the responsibility of the HHS's Office of Civil Rights. It relies on a voluntary basis first, and then if that fails, it establishes civil and criminal penalties. As we see from just a brief look at the HIPAA implementation, it looks somewhat similar to the GLB rules on consumer information. Plenty of sharing of patient information occurs; the use of new technologies opens a vast area of attack simply because security has not been a mainstay of the health care environment in the past; patients do not have the right to restrict their information in certain scenarios; and specific guidelines have not been defined for terms such as "reasonably ensure." HIPAA is more strict in detailing requirements for administrative requirements and requiring security technologies be used to secure data.

For health plans and insurers, HIPAA and GLB address similar regulatory issues and can affect companies in the same way with regard to updating systems, implementing security, and sharing consumer data across companies and affiliates. HIPAA is not as weak and easy to abuse as GLB is. Because some companies will fall under both statues, regulations must be coordinated so that there are not dual hurdles that a company must go through. In the FTC's final rule on GLB, it is noted that "it appears likely there will be overlap between HIPAA and the financial privacy rules." The Department of Health and Human Services will be consulted by regulatory agencies to ensure no duplication of effort exists. HHS noted that "GLB has caused concern and confusion among health plans that are subject to our privacy regulation." Federal HIPAA regulations preempt all "contrary" state laws unless a state law is more stringent; this is one of the main problems faced by consumers in countries such as the U.S. The varying laws across states can cause confusion and allow the opportunity for government to take advantage of consumer privacy. Having multiple government agencies involved in anything is a sure way to cause confusion.

The Patriot Act of 2001

In the wake of the terrorist attacks in the U.S. on September 11, 2001, several U.S. laws have been considered to provide more power to law enforcement to track terrorists and other types of criminals. One law that was signed was the Provide Appropriate Tools Required to Intercept and Obstruct Terrorism (PATRIOT) Act of 2001. This law gives federal investigators broader authority to track phone and Internet activities. While aimed at terrorist activities, the language covers other types of activity as well.

Civil liberties activists protested the law, which would allow wiretap orders under foreign intelligence rules. The law also allows law enforcers to obtain Internet records under so-called "trap-and-trace" orders. The attacks on the U.S. helped push this law past the privacy concerns of many groups, but a provision in the law states that Congress will review it in two years. Part of the law expands the capabilities of the FBI's DCS1000 program. ISPs must make their systems more available to the DCS1000 program, although the law does provide for a judge to review the FBI's Internet wiretaps.

The Tax Man Giveth Away

When consumers fill out tax returns, very personal data is submitted to the government; in exchange for giving up this personal information, consumers usually have some right to the protection of their information. They expect that this information will be used for the purpose for which it was given and do not expect to be annoyed, pressured, harassed, or harmed by its use.

A benefit (or detriment) of technology advancement is the easy methods now available for paying taxes and checking tax information. Many consumers now pay taxes online, exposing themselves to entirely new hacking techniques. From the client side of the tax transaction, a hacker can gain access to your home computer and pull up your Quicken information and capture your data. From the server side of the tax transaction, government servers can be hacked, and information can be stolen directly from the server. You have the ability to secure your own information on your home computer, but you have no ability to affect the government server's security. Unlike the weak guidelines provided by GLB for companies, strict guidelines for government resources are followed for security. However, this doesn't mean they can't be hacked; it's just harder for an attacker to gain information. Although securing technology is defined by government standards, access through legal means to tax information without the consent of the consumer is a very real possibility.

One such example of legal information dissemination was featured in an MSNBC news story. Via a Web site, as shown in Figure 4.1, anyone can enter a name and state where the person filed taxes and see whether the IRS owes that person money. Do you really want the general public knowing you are owed money?

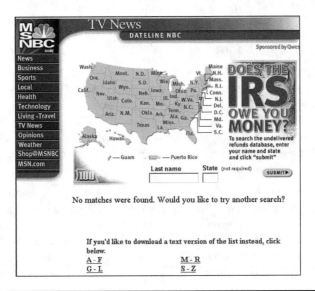

Figure 4.1   The IRS owes you money.

The FBI and You

The FBI, one of the U.S.'s protective agencies, has gotten into the privacy game. The government's evolving infrastructure protection program has placed the National Infrastructure Protection Center (NIPC) at the FBI. The FBI's new developing role of protection might conflict with the traditional criminal investigative and foreign counter-intelligence responsibilities. When hackers attack and compromise a company, rarely was the FBI notified. But more recently publicized cases have made it more acceptable and even necessary for a large company to call on the help of the FBI. With many attacks coming from abroad, companies have no other legal recourse but to notify the FBI. In the case where two Russian hackers broke into U.S. banks, the FBI was needed to lure the hackers to the U.S. and arrest them. The companies were unable to do anything without assistance from the FBI. But the FBI must still rely on voluntary cooperation from business to become involved in an attack.

But as with any government action or organization, the potential for it to overstep its boundaries is very real. In the case of the use of the FBI's information gathering tool, DCS1000 (Carnivore), consumer information can be easily captured by the FBI even if the consumer is not under surveillance. What happens to this information after it is captured is anybody's guess at this point in time. A bill has recently passed the House of Representatives in the U.S. to require the FBI and the attorney general to provide detailed reports on the use of DCS1000. Among requirements of the bill are how many times DCS1000 has been used, how the approval process to use it works, and any unauthorized information that has been gathered by the system. Justice Department officials have avoided complete details of the use of DCS1000, but what is known is that consumer e-mails and other information can be easily captured at the ISP level of communications on the Internet, subjecting thousands of consumers to privacy invasion during usage. This bill has not yet passed through the Senate, and consumers may be out of luck if it fails to pass into law.

When individuals and businesses ask for help from the FBI, there is no guarantee of how in-depth the FBI will take an investigation and what data will be captured and stored by the FBI. The data collected in cases is not guaranteed in any manner to be private and secure after it is obtained. How invasive the FBI will become when investigating a case might not be warranted or agreed on by the company needing help, but after the FBI is involved, control of the case usually falls to them and no recourse is available to the company or individual as to how their data is treated. There are no clear guidelines in the new role the FBI has taken on with regard to investigating a privacy compromise. Vague descriptions and assertions about technologies such as DCS1000 do not provide any assurance to consumers or businesses about how information will be collected, used, and stored.

Loss of Anonymity

Governments have been more assertive in cracking down on the right to anonymity in regard to distributing illegal pornographic materials, issuing libelous statements, and using technology in criminal activities. Courts in the U.S. have issued rulings requiring chat rooms or e-mail forums to reveal the names of people who post anonymous messages to support lawsuits. Making false claims on the Internet has resulted in prosecution. In one recent case, Mark S. Jakob, 23, accepted responsibility for one count of wire fraud and two counts of securities fraud for sending out a fake press release that affected the shares of Emulex. Shares of the Costa Mesa, California-based company fell by as much as 62% on August 25, the day Bloomberg News and other news organizations distributed the inaccurate information. Jakob was sentenced to jail time in August 2001. In early September 2000, a Canadian judge required an Internet service provider (ISP) to reveal a subscriber's identity after claims of defamation were made; the ISP complied. One anonymous remailer, `anon.penet.fi`, closed down after a Church of Scientology claimed copyright violations.

Chat rooms, which have always been a bastion of anonymity, have been forced to reveal users' personal information. In cases involving Yahoo! and AOL Time Warner, user information about people criticizing companies or revealing internal secrets has been revealed for lawsuits. AnswerThink took legal actions against 12 John Does in February 2000 for their negative comments posted in a Yahoo! chat room. The complaint claims defamation and breach of contract, and the user information was revealed. As you can see from these examples, anonymity on the Internet is no longer guaranteed.

Government Monitoring

Government monitoring of individuals and businesses has always been a mainstay of criminal investigations and prosecution. The changes we have seen in technology in the past several years and the laws that have been passed to increase the government's capability to monitor communications and activity of individuals have become more invasive. In addition to technologies such as DCS1000, the government is pressuring technology companies and ISPs to install monitoring devices. Laws being passed will force ISPs to reveal user information and show traffic generated by consumers under investigation.

The Federal Intrusion Detection Network (FIDNet), part of the National Security Plan, is another monitoring technology available to the government. The FIDNet described in the National Plan would be a government-wide system using artificial intelligence "intrusion detection" software to monitor contacts with sensitive government computers. Intrusion detection system would be connected, and data generated could be collated and analyzed. Plus, patterns and intruders could be identified across systems. FIDNet is available for civilian government computers, but it does not define which systems will be covered. Designated systems have been defined as the departments of Health and Human Services, Commerce, Transportation, and Treasury and the EPA. Although privacy groups have raised opposition to FIDNet, the government has said, "A preliminary legal review by the Justice Department has concluded that, subject to certain limitations, the FIDNet concept complies with the Electronic Communications Privacy Act (ECPA)." The owner of a system, including the government, is allowed to monitor use of its own system to protect itself, and FIDNet would not be breaking any laws against monitoring its own systems.

Updated Laws

A recent study by McConnell International (`http://www.mcconnellinternational.com`) titled "Cyber Crime and Punishment? ArchaicLaws Threaten Global Information," published in December 2000, shows the updates to the security and privacy laws for a number of countries (see Table 4.1).

From this study the following points can be made:

- No standard exists for laws on privacy and security between countries. Each country is approaching this issue in its own manner. Even different states in the U.S. have many different laws applying to privacy.

- No standard guidelines are developed that all countries can follow for a uniform code on security and privacy. The EU comes closest to codifying privacy laws across countries.

- Most laws have not advanced enough to prosecute cybercrimes. Countries still rely on antiquated laws that cannot apply to the technology being used. Cybercrime prosecution does not work in most cases because standards have not been developed on how to prosecute a cybercrime and what evidence is necessary.

- The punishment does not fit the crime in most privacy cases. It is hard to quantify data and personal information because it is not easily measurable.

- Protection is being kept in the hands of private industry. Governments are not taking enough action to protect individuals and corporations. This is slowly changing, with several recent laws and bills before many government legislatures.

- It is nearly impossible to prosecute across borders. The Council of Europe has come close to drafting standards for illegal access, illegal interception, data interference, system interference, computer-related forgery, computer-related fraud, and the aiding and abetting of these crimes.

Table 4.1   Countries with Updated Privacy

Country	DATA CRIMES			NETWORK CRIMES		ACCESS CRIMES		RELATED CRIMES		
	Data Interception	Data Modification	Data Theft	Network Interference	Network Sabotage	Unauthorized Access	Virus Dissemination	Aiding and Abetting Cyber Crimes	Computer-Related Forgery	Computer-Related Fraud
Australia	X	X	X	X		X			X	X
Brazil		X			X	X		X		
Canada	X	X	X	X	X	X	X			X
Chile	X	X	X	X	X		X			
China		X	X	X		X				
Czech Republic		X	X		X	X	X	X		X
Denmark		X	X	X	X	X	X	X		X
Estonia		X	X	X	X	X		X		X
India	X	X	X	X	X	X		X		X
Japan		X					X		X	
Malaysia	X	X	X	X	X	X		X		X
Mauritius	X	X	X	X	X	X		X	X	X
Peru	X	X	X	X			X	X	X	
Philippines		X	X					X		
Poland		X								
Spain	X	X	X	X				X	X	X
Turkey		X			X		X			X
United Kingdom		X		X	X	X		X		
United States	X	X	X	X	X	X	X	X		X

The following list describes several countries' monitoring agencies:

- **Russia**—The Federal Security Service (FSB) possesses investigatory powers. It conducts intelligence operations inside and outside Russia to enhance "the economic, scientific-technical and defense potential" of Russia. It can monitor Internet transmissions coming into and out of Russia. The Federal Agency for Government Communications and Information (FAPSI) has technical capabilities for monitoring communications and gathering intelligence.

- **People's Republic of China**—The People's Republic of China (PRC) created a Ministry of State Security to stop "enemy agents, spies, and counterrevolutionary activities designed to…overthrow China's socialist system." The Internet police agency was started in 1998.

- **Germany**—Germany's Bundesnachrichtendienst (BND) has been engaged in intelligence gathering for nearly 50 years.

- **Israel**—Israel has at least three official intelligence-gathering organizations: Mossad, Shin Bet, and Aman. Mossad handles surveillance outside of Israel, whereas Shin Bet conducts surveillance inside the country. Aman handles military intelligence.

- **France**—The Secretariat General de la Defense Nationale (SGDN), the Direction du Renseignement Militaire (DRM), and the Direction Generale de la Securite Exterieure (DGSE) conduct surveillance and information gathering.

- **India**—India's Central Bureau of Investigation (CBI) is tasked with the "preservation of values in public life" as well as "ensuring the health of the national economy."

One of the main problems faced by consumers in most countries is the patchwork system of laws that apply to privacy. The EU Directives are one of the few sets of statutes that provide a somewhat comprehensive approach to privacy. Rather than having many different laws applying to different aspects of the privacy issue, consumers would be better served with a uniform set of laws that are national in focus and can be applied to all sectors of business. In the U.S., the House Subcommittee on Commerce, Trade, and Consumer Protection has been examining the coverage of privacy laws in the U.S. and looking at the 30 federal statutes and numerous state laws that address privacy. "I will be one of the first to admit that the U.S. approach toward privacy has been piecemeal," said Commerce Committee Chairman Billy Tauzin (R-LA) in a statement. To meet the regulations that can often differ between states, companies that operate in the U.S. can incur large costs to abide by the laws. Often the costs are passed on to the consumer, or companies don't adhere to the laws correctly, so consumer privacy is compromised.

Council of Europe

One global initiative for protection against cybercrime is the treaty being developed by more than 40 countries, including the U.S., the EU, and Russia. The treaty will cover such aspects of computer crime as data crimes, network crimes, access crimes, computer forgery, and computer-related fraud. The cybercrime treaty is designed to aid police investigations by requiring Web sites and ISPs to collect and record information about their users. This has brought privacy groups to arms. The personal information that can be collected by ISPs and Web sites can be very damaging to consumers if it is disseminated. If a user is being investigated, he can be required to hand over "measures applied to protect the computer data," or in other words, his cryptographic keys he uses to secure personal data.

Another key aspect of the treaty is the move to make it illegal to distribute some security software that can assist system administrators in protecting their own networks. Only users such as law enforcement agencies that the Council of Europe chooses would be allowed to have such tools. By making it illegal for administrators to own such security testing tools, the treaty will basically ensure that only the hackers will have access to security testing tools.

Even though this treaty is aimed at defining standards and uniformity of cybercrimes, the onus of enforcing the treaty will be on each individual country. One key requirement not in the treaty is that of privacy. The council has found dealing with the diverse privacy laws from different countries too difficult and has left out privacy regulations. "We cannot find an acceptable international standard in terms of privacy as it applies to this treaty," said Henrik Kaspersen of the Council of Europe. The Global Internet Liberty Campaign says it believes "the draft treaty is contrary to well-established norms for the protection of the individual, that it improperly extends the police authority of national governments, that it will undermine the development of network security techniques, and that it will reduce government accountability in future law enforcement conduct." The U.S. Justice Department has been involved in the drafting process, and when the treaty is complete, Congress will have to review it and decide whether it should be passed in the U.S.

Lack of Enforcement

Government descriptions of privacy and security continue to emphasize indirect, market-based incentives, self-regulation, and sectoral laws rather than nationwide legislative mandates to keep data secure. These mechanisms include the measurement of industry adherence to new information security standards by insurers when writing liability coverage, incorporation of such standards in accounting evaluations, and the influence such standards will exert on the business relations with customers. Many privacy groups find this tactic beneficial to consumer rights, but it has led to weak overall privacy measurements. The key element in all such schemes is information security standards and enforcement of such standards—an area where the private sector might well be ahead of most government agencies and regulations. However, the difference between industry sectors and even companies is vast and leaves many holes for consumer privacy compromise.

A clear example of the lack of enforcement capability in government legislations is the Spam Bill that is before Congress. Legislation introduced in February 2001 would prevent or greatly reduce unsolicited commercial e-mail (*spam*). But when lobbying began by associations that promote spam and such marketing schemes, the bill was amended in a congressional committee and stripped of some of its enforcement provisions. The government continues to let the industry regulate itself and seems to step in only when a crisis point arises, and then with halfway measures. Privacy advocates have blasted the new bill, which is before the House Judiciary Committee. "This bill is far too weak," said Jason Catlett, president of Junkbusters Corp., a privacy advocacy organization in Green Brook, New Jersey. Junkbusters and the Coalition Against Unsolicited Commercial Email (CAUCE) are two of the privacy advocates that have vowed to fight the amended version of the bill, known as House Resolution 718. Insurers, accountants, lenders, and investors already understand the importance of information security and enforcement of security measures. However, without punishments that can affect a company if these measures are not met, consumers will continue to bear the brunt of attacks and loss of data and peace of mind.

Business Threats to Privacy

Which is more of a threat to your privacy, the government or the business community? Business has never been about doing what is best for the consumer. Business is concerned with making money, and a good way to make money is to keep the consumer happy and paying for more services and products. If consumer privacy happens to be one of the casualties of doing business, so be it. Only recently have we seen a real regard for consumer privacy by business entities and government agencies. The U.S. attitude toward the privacy issue has been that of an observer rather than of an active participant up until the last few years. As new laws are being passed that try to protect consumers, business entities have become more active in lobbying against such laws. The business community would rather use technology and industry pressure to keep consumer data secure than have government regulations in place to restrict and often cost them money in the implementation of the requirements of the laws.

Businesses operate on incentives. If consumers retaliate and advocacy groups provide a strong enough outcry, a business will change tactics and policies if its monetary rewards are affected. In the past, this has been enough to protect consumers in some fashion. But with the development of technology that has made violating a consumer's right to privacy very easy, the government has needed to step in and pass laws that adversely affect the business community.

Online Privacy Alliance

With the advent of legal action being a new threat to the business model when it concerns consumer privacy, businesses are finding they need to fight back and attempt to stem the tide of new privacy laws. One such initiative is the Online Privacy Alliance (OPA). This group of companies is organized to lobby against legislative proposals that infringe on privacy in three main aspects: identifying costs that regulations would impose on business and consumers, questioning how U.S. Internet laws would apply to non-Internet industries, and identifying the use of technology to secure privacy rather than the use of laws.

Members of the Online Privacy Alliance include Microsoft, AOL Time Warner, IBM, AT&T, BellSouth, and Sun Microsystems. In association with the Direct Marketing Association (DMA), they have been lobbying against privacy laws, as has the DMA been doing against laws that affect the advertising industry. These groups are concerned with the various laws of different states and pending legislation that makes doing business nationally difficult because of new costs that will be incurred to implement new privacy rules and build technology to address consumer privacy needs. The driving factor is cost to the industry. One set of numbers thrown around about costs conclude that proposals to limit companies from sharing or selling customer information could cost 90 of the largest financial institutions $17 billion a year of added expense. Of course, a large part of this cost will be passed on to the consumer. Although these numbers are not verifiable, all industry studies have found a large cost of following the proposed privacy laws, and businesses will do whatever they can to avoid those costs.

In much the same way that tobacco lobbyists persuade legislatures to limit tobacco laws, organizations such as the OPA seek to limit government control of their ability to limit consumer privacy rights. Many companies now have privacy policies because of market pressures, but they will do what they can to limit further restrictions on their ability to make a profit using consumer data.

Data Mining

One of the most invasive and damaging of business practices is *data mining*, which basically is the act of compiling databases of consumer information; aggregating it; and extracting useful information, such as geographic buy trends, personal preferences, financial information, and so on. With a large database, a company can perform specific target marketing or even sell pieces of that database for a profit. Database extraction techniques have become continuously more sophisticated, and marketing companies have developed a whole new service based on selling such information. Data miners espouse the benefits of their business; there is improved customer service by insurance firms, banks, and department stores. Everything is known about a customer when he calls in so the company can provide personalized service.

Data mining understandably worries privacy advocates. With laws such as HIPAA and GLB allowing the sharing of consumer information, aggregating personal medical, insurance, and financial information can lead to the development of large databases ripe for the plundering. With data being at the fingertips of businesses, they can control how much information and what type of data/advertising they send to consumers. Consumers now have no control over receiving spam mail. This is not illegal, but it does violate consumer privacy. Consumers now have no control over how a company can gain access to their information. When they submit pieces of information through Web site registrations or by browsing sites that retain data about them, the aggregation of all this data can profile the consumer without their explicit knowledge. Legislation is supposed to protect consumers from having their data shared and keep it secure through use of technology, but as we have discussed, companies just have to go through a few hurdles before they share consumer information.

Data mining is not a centralized activity. There is no one place you can restrict data to prevent data mining. Companies that want your information will go through numerous methods, from buying e-mail lists to purchasing lists of customers' buying habits from a merchant. The rest of this book covers steps and procedures you can follow to limit the information you make available to the world to limit the information gold that companies seek when it comes to your personal data.

Credit Bureaus and Information Brokers

If you have applied for a job recently, you know that many companies now check your credit history as part of their background checking processes. The U.S.'s big three credit bureaus—Experian Inc., Equifax Inc., and Trans Union Corp.—sell credit information to organizations doing background checks. Associated Credit Bureaus Inc., a Washington-based trade group, estimates that 600 million reports were sold in 2000, including such data as a person's name, age, Social Security number, and past and current addresses.

Several laws have been passed that attempt to protect consumer credit information, including the following:

- **Truth in Lending Act**—Credit grantors must provide you with the annual percentage rate (APR) of any loan prior to signing. This tells consumers what they will actually be paying for a loan.

- **Equal Credit Opportunity Act**—Prohibits discrimination against you because of age, sex, marital status, race, color, religion, national origin, or receipt of public assistance.

- **Fair Credit Billing Act**—Allows for the prompt correction of errors on a credit account and prevents damage to your credit record while disputing an item. This can often happen during an identity theft compromise.

- **Fair Credit Reporting Act**—Protects consumers from incorrect credit reporting to credit bureaus that can ruin their credit and hurt them in the future.

- **Fair Debt Collection Practices Act**—Prohibits debt collection agencies from abusive collection practices that could be a hassle to consumers.

With the advent of the Web, a number of companies sell reports with personal data online for such things as locating people and performing job background checks. Much of this data comes from credit reports. An example of a typical Web site that performs this function is Discreet Research (`http://www.discreetresearch.com/`), shown in Figure 4.2. By signing up using a credit card online, you can begin researching anyone and finding public information. Such information is purchased from other information brokers for a fee. Another popular search Web site is Whowhere.com (`http://www.whowhere.com`), which enables users to order a background check on any individual in the database. This public record report includes property ownership, civil judgments, driver's license physical description, and summary of assets. A vast amount of information is available out there that is public and that many people would really not want known by just anyone.

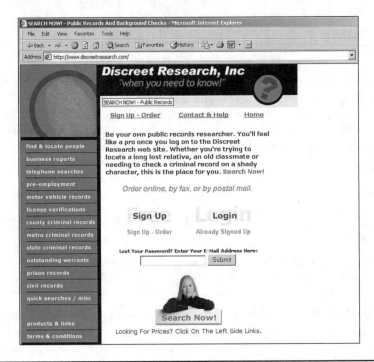

Figure 4.2   Discreet Research credit check.

If you want to obtain your own credit report, you can contact any of the major credit bureaus and provide the following information to receive a report:

- Full name, including any maiden name
- Current address
- Previous address (if needed for five-year credit history)
- Daytime telephone number
- Social Security number
- Date of birth
- Copy of driver's license (or utility bill to prove address)
- Signature
- Fee

Closely tied to the retrieval of credit history is the ability to find people more easily with the Internet. There has been a great reduction in costs of finding someone and delving into the details of his life. In the past, investigators were required to do this, but now it can be done for free or a small fee. The capability to link data from different sources to track someone has been a fundamental shift in finding and detailing a person's life. And it's all legal.

Companies that perform these searches get data from a variety of sources, such as paid subscriptions to credit bureaus, buying lists of information from marketers, capturing information through survey process, and so on. There are numerous ways to do this with the development of technology, and it will only become more invasive. One disturbing case of using data collected on the Internet was Aware Woman Center For Choice, Inc. v. Raney, No. 6:99cv00005 (M.D. Fla., filed January 21, 1999). An abortion clinic sued a number of ISPs, alleging that anti-abortionists had used Internet services accessible via the ISPs to trace names and addresses of visitors to the clinic, who they then sent harassing letters to in protest of abortion. Information can even be captured through mistakes made by companies. On January 20, 1999, a Fox News Web site displayed street and e-mail addresses of Ohio residents. On another occasion, Yahoo! admitted that it had revealed customer addresses, partial credit card numbers, products ordered, and amounts spent on nutritional products on a Yahoo! store demo site, and Nissan sent a listing of 24,000 addresses to everyone in its mailing list. All these sources of data lead to specific personal profiles that compromise every aspect of consumer information.

Mobile Phone Invasion

The proliferation of the cell phone as it relates to invasion of privacy is just beginning to be understood. Cell phone technology has already moved beyond just making a phone call. With cell phones you can wirelessly browse the Web, make purchases online, check your stock, and send e-mail. This technology will rapidly expand over the next several years, but we are already seeing abuses of individual privacy. The laws regarding mobile phone use are much weaker than those that apply to Internet use.

Cell phones can already be used to locate people within a certain distance. The U.S. Federal Communications Commission issued a mandate stating that by October 2001, all wireless 911 calls must be pinpointed within 410 feet. This technology could conceivably be turned over to business functions, such as rental car agencies, that can track a consumer in distress and be used to get traffic updates when you are driving. The applications are numerous, but so is the potential for abuse. The Big Brother metaphor will arise when law enforcement can track you down whenever you make a phone call. This geolocation technology will rapidly expand as the technology becomes more inexpensive and standardization occurs by companies on the technology.

We have already seen abuses of cell phone messaging technology with spam messages already arriving on consumers' phones. Unlike with e-mail spam, the customer must pay for incoming as well as outgoing calls and messages. Think about combining spam with location technology, and you can see that at some point, when you walk down the street and pass a store, the store will receive your cell phone location and send you an advertisement because you are nearby. That is a scary thought—personalization of advertisements based on where you are at any given time with your cell phone. The idea of a wireless spam bill has been discussed in the U.S. but has not made much progress. The Wireless Ad Association released a list of industry guidelines that says, "The WAA does not condone wireless targeted advertising or content (push messaging) intentionally or negligently sent to any subscriber's wireless mobile device without explicit subscriber permission and clear identification of the sender." This is one of the few positive steps in cell phone privacy concerns.

Another potential legal invasion of your privacy is Web-based caller ID. When you surf the Web with your cell phone, your cell phone number is broadcast to the Web site. You number can be logged and associated with the Web site you visit and purchases you make. It's easy to see how your cell number and shopping preferences can then be sold to a marketing company and mass mailings sent to you based on your cell phone browsing habits.

Today there are still few wireless Net subscribers in the United States, but the Asian and European markets are expanding rapidly. A Banc of America report said about 6.6 million people around the world subscribed to wireless phone data service at the end of 1999, but this number will increase to nearly 400 million by 2003. It is predicted companies will spend about $700 million on wireless advertising by 2005.

The use of wireless advertising and spamming is too far ahead of the current laws and even proposed laws for wireless security. It took years for laws to be passed on spamming, and it will probably take several years before sufficient laws are passed to protect wireless devices.

Forces Driving Legal Business Threats to Privacy

Business functions because of one reason—money. The growth of the Internet can be attributed to the need for businesses to expand and conquer new markets. There are a number of reasons that drive businesses to utilize personal information in the ways they do.

Globalization

The Internet and new technologies have made the global marketplace a reality. In the past, sharing information was not an easy process. With the advent of large multi-national networks and use of the Internet, transferring data, buying and selling data, and accessing data are easy. With all this access, more people and businesses have access to your information and can exploit your personal information. It is estimated that these connections are increasing by 10% every month, which means the threat to your privacy is increasing by 10% a month.

To compete on a global basis, companies must get customers from all over the world. Laws in different countries may be more or less restrictive when it comes to protecting consumers, but there are always ways around laws—especially the vague ones that currently exist regarding privacy.

Complexity

New technologies bring complexity to any network or organization, but implementations and usage can be flawed. Consumers have to rely on companies to protect their information, but the connectivity and technology has become so sophisticated, large corporations are having a difficult time keeping up with threats to new technologies. Detecting problems in a complex network can take weeks or months, and during this time consumer data can be subject to attack. The number of users, applications, and hardware is no longer static and usually not centrally controlled, providing many access points to data.

Training system administrators in just the use of the technology is time-consuming and fraught with problems. Now these same administrators must be concerned with security measures and protection of data. They also must understand how to respond to an attack, track down a break-in to their complex systems, and determine the damage, which can cross subdivisions of a company or different countries in which the company operates. With new functionality being brought to the organization because of technology, companies are forced to decrease their time to market with products and services. This fast-paced deployment of technology is usually one of the major reasons hackers can compromise a system and gain access to consumer information: A system weakness hasn't been patched because of the haste of implementation, and a backdoor is left open in to the environment. Security becomes an afterthought in implementing new technology.

Most legal and regulatory requirements do not state, in any depth or detail, what the security requirements are for consumer data and the controls surrounding access and implementation of the technology. Across countries, this becomes even more difficult when it comes to designing compatible computer systems and technologies while still keeping good security measures in place. The technology has become the access point to compromising consumer information. Because so many functions are provided by business applications and sharing among companies has become so widespread, it's next to impossible to understand how your information is being used and where it is going.

Legal Requirements

As stated earlier, in the section "Government Threats to Privacy," the legal environment directly affects the consumer. The same threats to the consumer posed by government agencies and laws can also be a threat to businesses. Business entities are usually the implementers of government laws involving consumer personal information. State and national boundaries have made coming up with standards on privacy issues that all businesses can follow difficult. What might be legal in one country might not be in another. The strict requirements of the EU Directives might protect consumer data in the EU, but after it gets transferred outside the EU, that data can be subject to lax laws in other countries and the consumer information could get compromised anyway.

Functioning on a global scale does not mean that your information will have the same security measures applied to it across countries. The lack of details in laws makes it easy for a business to interpret the law in such a fashion that enables it to do business easily and conveniently. This can mean that the intent of the law to protect your information does not materialize in practical applications of the law.

The legal controls over consumer data carry very weak or no punishments for lack of compliance in most cases. Only recently have hackers been prosecuted and sentenced to jail time. For businesses, such threats of punishment are almost nonexistent. Breaking the privacy laws currently in place, because of little consumer pressure or advocate group pressures, results in very little monetary or criminal punishments. If businesses face no real punishments in bending and even breaking legal restrictions on the privacy of your data, there is not much to stop them from making money off your information wherever possible.

Criminal Threat

Criminal hacker activity against businesses ends up being attacks against you as an individual. The data and credit card information do not belong to the business, but to the consumer. When a hacker breaks into a company and posts its customers' credit card information on the Web, it hurts the business, but the individuals are the ones ultimately being attacked. The perpetrator of criminal threats might be an insider or external to the organization. The activity might be from an individual, a loosely knit group, organized criminal elements, corporations, or governments. If the business does not take these threats seriously, it can have weaknesses in its environments. A compromise of its systems might not cause financial loss, but it can seriously affect the personal information of consumers.

It is not illegal to have weaknesses in a business network, and it is not illegal to now have standards and built-in security for the company's site. A consumer has no say in whether the business is actively trying to protect her information and no recourse should the business be hacked and data stolen.

A business that has weak security controls faces no real legal problems unless it does not adhere to very specific requirements in the laws covering computer security. If a hacker breaks into a company and steals all your data, there is no legal threat to the company. This weak stand on computer security by many companies can directly affect you, but it is perfectly valid for a business to have weak security standards without regard for your information.

Technologies for Legal Privacy Invasion

Individuals, businesses, and governments are the main culprits when it comes to legal threats to privacy. But the technology advancements we have seen over the past five years have led us to this current state of affairs. Many things are out of our control, such as direct access to passing laws and developing our own technology, but we can control how we use the technology and reduce some of the risk we face through legal means.

File Sharing

Anyone who has used the Internet is familiar with the concept of file sharing. Application technologies such as Napster have made the concept of file sharing commonplace. Although this technology is perfectly legal, it exposes your computer to other people on the Internet and possible attack. At a more sophisticated level, personal computers give you the ability to share files and printers over a network even without the use of Napster-like technologies. With the advent of technologies such as DSL and cable modems, incorrect configurations can allow your whole hard drive to be shared and captured by anyone on the Internet. The IPSs are not in the business of protecting their customers; they only provide access and leave security and privacy up to the consumer.

Legitimate companies search the Internet for computers that are sharing files. If files are shared, they can be copied and further disseminated. Sharing of a hard drive can also expose a lot of data about a person's preferences that can be used to build a profile about him. Computer worms and viruses can also be spread by shared hard drives and files. When ISPs do try to assist in providing security for computers, customers complain and the ISP is forced to revert to just providing access. Consumers must seek out technology to protect themselves and rely on their own skills in implementing security, which is usually a problem for the non-IT user.

Public Access

If you have stayed at a major hotel chain lately, you've seen that Internet access is now provided through dedicated connections as well as through phone lines. In addition, libraries and universities have high-speed access anyone can use. Cyber cafes, airport Internet kiosks, and conferences—to name a few venues—provide Internet access to the person on the go. Access is becoming very convenient, but does this mean a trade-off in privacy and security? In many cases, the answer is yes.

As mentioned earlier, cookies are a method of storing personal preferences that can track your bank account login information as well as what type of Web sites you like to browse. When using public access methods to connect, you are leaving data about yourself in public places. Web browsers cache Web pages, and the last Web page you viewed could be pulled up by the next user. (Think about the sites you really don't want other people knowing you visit.) You do not know who last used public access computers, so anyone could have put a keystroke capture program on the computer to capture your password. Programs such as Back Orifice could be used to capture your data and watch what you are doing on the computer. In places such as cyber cafes and schools, you do not know what the policies are on how these providers monitor the systems for "illegal" activities. In efforts to monitor activity, they could be capturing your personal data by accident. You can find out more about how you can keep your data secure in such instances in Chapter 7, "Understanding the Online Environment: Web Surfing and Online Payment Systems," and Chapter 11, "Securing Your Standalone PC: Broadband Connections."

E-mail Monitoring

If you are reading this book, there is a 99.99% chance that you have e-mail. It has become a de facto form of communication because of its ease of use, speed, and reliability. Yet even with its widespread use, most people do not understand the potential dangers in sending e-mail. Very personal information is being sent by millions of people each day without thought as to who can retrieve this e-mail. If you use public access places to check e-mail, a real possibility exists that anyone on that local area network can capture your e-mail as it is going across the wire and read it. The ISP who provides access to e-mail can capture your e-mails and read them. Also, the people reading your e-mail can find out what IP address you are coming from (IP addresses are discussed in Chapter 6, "Understanding the Online Environment: Addresses, Domains, and Anonymity") and details about the computer application and operating system you are using to send e-mail. The government can even access your e-mail in a criminal investigation.

Employers can easily monitor all e-mail into and out of a company. Searching e-mails for keywords or for specific employees is easy, and the laws do not restrict this type of access to employee e-mail by employers. Automated software can be used to search e-mails for damaging keywords or phrases that are not allowed by the company, and the employer can determine whether they are "legitimate" messages. Justification by employers for e-mail monitoring is simple: protecting intellectual property from being sent out, checking for sexually harassing e-mails, or just monitoring useless traffic being generated by employees. A Society for Human Resource Management survey found that roughly 20% of employers have gotten complaints about inappropriate e-mail. Salomon Smith Barney in 1998 fired two executives for electronically transmitting pornography. Officials said the material was discovered during routine e-mail monitoring. These types of actions have made it publicly acceptable to monitor e-mail.

Knowledge about the problems associated with e-mail and laws to help secure this technology are sadly lacking. Agencies around the world are developing programs for e-mail interception and analysis because of its popularity and means of communicating. We saw this type of development in government agencies to monitor telephone conversations, and we are seeing the same process develop for Internet communications. With all this monitoring of e-mail and information being transmitted, there is the very real possibility that data about you will be stored somewhere and kept for years. A very personal profile of you can be developed by anyone with access to this data. Even though this is legal on the surface, it is one of the major threats to personal privacy and communications.

Video Surveillance

Have you noticed that many traffic lights now have cameras that take a picture of your license plate if you run a red light? Video surveillance is becoming so widespread that we don't even think about it half the time. If you walk down any of the major streets around Wall Street, cameras could be watching your every move, especially around the major banks. In the U.K., between 150 and 300 million pounds per year are now spent on a surveillance industry involving an estimated 200,000 cameras monitoring public spaces, including cameras that watch for speeding traffic. Many public facilities have video surveillance, which most would argue is a good thing because they can watch for crime and record an incident. The growth rate of video surveillance is estimated at 15%–20% annually.

Private property surveillance is also increasing. Many families use technology such as the Nanny Cam (http://www.alerthome.com) to monitor their homes while they are away. The ability to watch your children and your house from work using a Web browser is very convenient. If you are on the receiving end of this surveillance, you can say you don't like all this monitoring, but there aren't any specific laws to stop such surveillance. So, watch what you do, whether you are in public or in private.

Communication Surveillance

It's very obvious that governments have surveillance over communication devices such as faxes, telephones, and Internet communications. Within one's own country, the average citizen need not fear direct interception of communications by government authorities. Legal surveillance does have to follow a process where most people who have nothing to fear will not be watched. Government agencies can push the envelope of when it is actually necessary for invasive surveillance. The chances of inadvertent monitoring are on the rise. The best example of this is when a law enforcement agency needs to review an ISP's log files for activity by someone under surveillance. The agency will have access to thousands of users and all their communications. The FBI's DCS1000 program can capture a lot of data not specific to one person. What happens to this data after it is collected is not detailed in the FBI's descriptions and documentation on DCS1000. Therefore, abuse of the new technologies by law enforcement agencies is very possible and easy to do.

Some law enforcement agencies are forcing ISPs to install surveillance systems that are secret to the general public. These systems monitor the traffic of their users and capture data for storage and analysis. Access to this data is restricted to law enforcement and the ISP staff. This data can be searched by keywords and phrases. One of the many problems is that the user has no knowledge of what is done to his data and how secure his information is after it is captured by these monitoring devices. In 1998, the Russian Federal Security Service (FSB) issued a decree on the System for Operational Research Actions on the Documentary Telecommunication Networks (SORM-2) that would require ISPs to install surveillance devices and high-speed links to the FSB. This access without a warrant was challenged successfully in court by the ISPs. In the Netherlands, the Telecommunications Act of 1998 requires that ISPs have the capability to intercept all traffic with a court order. The U.K. Parliament approved the Regulation of Investigatory Powers Act in July 2000. It requires that ISPs provide a "reasonable interception capability" in their networks. This trend of government requirements for ISP monitoring and data capture is on the rise.

Some countries, such as those in the EU, have been strong proponents of restricted access by law enforcement agencies to personal data and to perform such tactics as wiretaps. On the other hand, other countries, such as the U.S., have led the way in enhancing law enforcement powers to monitor personal communications to prosecute suspects.

Identity Systems

Trying to hide your identity on the Internet is one thing, but some situations require you to identify yourself, and you have no control over that information. The main place where you are forced to identify yourself is through your job. Many companies have ID card systems and biometric systems to track employee access. You really have no control over how your information is stored or used once you are required to identify yourself.

Identity Cards

If you work for a large company, the odds are you have some form of picture ID. This card lets you enter secured doors and gain access to restricted environments. If you carry a major credit card, your picture is on it in many cases. Plus, new debit cards link to your bank account. Why carry so many cards when technology can enable you to carry one national card with all your information on it that lets you access bank accounts, have credit-type functionality, access your building, and serve as identification instead of a driver's license? The countries that already have this type of card include Germany, France, Belgium, Greece, Luxembourg, Portugal, and Spain. Other countries have fought this type of functionality in a national card because it could be a great invasion of privacy. With this type of card, one central agency can know exactly where you are (they can see where you last made a purchase), what your preferences are for shopping (making it much easier for the marketers to sell to you), how much money you have in all your bank accounts, and what your credit history is like. A hundred other pieces of information about you would also be available on such a card. This is why many advocate groups are fighting against such a card.

Government agencies could easily track people and monitor where they are and what they are doing. Corrupt governments could use these cards for religious and political identification. There are many possible negative aspects of national cards that are still being debated in many countries. Even though the cards can provide services, they can also be a weapon in the hands of law enforcement that can be abused. How many futuristic movies have we seen in which a police officer just walks up to someone and demands to see her registration card? This type of card has been challenged on a constitutional basis in the Philippine Supreme Court and the Hungarian Constitutional Court for violating privacy rights. In the U.S., the Bush Administration has come out against a national ID card system, which has pleased privacy advocates.

There is not much support from individuals for this type of national ID card in the U.S. or in many other countries around the world. The convenience of such a system does not outweigh the potential loss of privacy that most people think will occur. Businesses are not fully behind such a card, and they drive many of the laws that get passed.

Several problems are readily apparent with a national ID card. The first is that the data entered can be forged before it even makes it into the system or can be entered incorrectly. The second is that implementations of such a widespread technology are guaranteed to have numerous technological problems. And third, having all that personal data in one place enables someone to easily take over your identity should it be compromised. Millions of people's information could be stolen during one hacker compromise.

Biometrics

Biometric technology collects, processes, and stores details about physical characteristics, such as fingerprints, retina information, hand geometry, voice recognition, and facial appearance for identification and authentication. It has seen widespread use in corporations and governments where ID cards are not enough security. Biometrics is harder to fake and provides increased security. National plans are being implemented using biometric data. In the 2001 Super Bowl, law enforcement officials used biometric technology that captured the images of people entering the stadium and compared them with a database of criminals' faces. In Spain, a national fingerprint system for unemployment benefits and healthcare entitlement is being developed. In Russia, plans were announced for a national electronic fingerprint system for banks. Jamaicans use thumb prints to qualify to vote. In the U.S., the Immigration and Naturalization Service (INS) uses hand geometry in its immigration system. This type of system can be used on a worldwide basis by travelers to streamline the transportation process. One company, EyeTicket, is using retinal pictures of travelers in conjunction with the International Air Transport Association as an identification method for travelers. The technology identifies people by the pattern of their irises—the colored ring around the pupil of the eye.

DNA identification has been used in criminal investigations but has not been used widely for identification purposes outside of the law. Creating national databases for DNA matches by law enforcement has been facing an uphill battle by privacy rights groups. One such group is Fight The Fingerprint (`http://www.networkusa.org/fingerprint.shtml`), which is dedicated to fighting biometric and Social Security identification schemes. The United States, Germany, and Canada are creating such databases. The Supreme Court has given its okay to centralized databases by reversing three lower court decisions which said that the Driver's Privacy Protection Act of 1994 was unconstitutional. This act allows national databases of driver information to be collected and used across states and allows access to this information by private investigators. This collects personal information that can be accessed by any state about any driver.

Restricting biometric collection of data is a losing battle. Technology is making biometrics great for authentication, and it will become cheaper and easier as the technology matures.

Workplace Surveillance

In many industry sectors, surveillance of the workplace has become common practice. Lawsuits against companies have helped drive the need for surveillance as has the threat of some crime happening. There are not too many laws against workplace surveillance, and many employees are forced to agree to being monitored as a requirement for employment. Surveillance can take many forms, including phone conversation recording, reading e-mail, watching computer screens, monitoring chat room conversations, video camera monitoring, drug testing, and tracking movements with ID card systems. Technologies to monitor activity can assist employers in determining whether employees are being productive, using the phone to make personal calls, or taking long coffee breaks. Technology has made it very simple for employers to watch everything an employee does. Software can track what has been done on a computer that can later be used as an audit trail if evidence is needed to prosecute some crime.

It is hard to say what types of monitoring are not legal. Even if it is all legal, your privacy can be easily compromised with no recourse because it is legal and laws have not been developed to address exactly where the line is in workplace monitoring. In workplaces, some technologies, such as anonymous remailers and anonymous Web browsers, are blocked because they avoid monitoring by employers.

Satellite Surveillance

Although not yet very popular, the use of satellites will become more widespread as costs and the technology advance to make it practical. Several companies provide satellite Internet access service, such as Starband and Optistreams. Satellite technology is becoming available to the consumer because of lower costs and increased competition.

Satellites can already see images as small as 1 meter in diameter. Spy technology that has been used by governments will become commercial and can be used to invade the privacy of individuals. Satellite monitoring can be used for such things as tracking forest fires, reporting on wars and natural disasters, detecting unlicensed building work, or looking for nuclear testing sites; the possibilities are expanding as the technology advances and the costs decrease.

Privacy groups have voiced concerns that satellites can watch anyone anywhere on earth and track activities, but the average consumer has little to fear just yet from satellite surveillance.

Telephone Monitoring

The monitoring of phone conversations is nothing new. Anytime you call a credit card company, you hear that they "may record this conversation for customer service." Every corporate call center that provides customer support records conversations, and they always say it's for your benefit. What these types of monitoring technologies also do is monitor how much work is being conducted by employees, how long they spend on each call, whether they are making personal calls, as well as how long they are not talking on the phone. Law enforcement and telephone monitoring go hand in hand. The capability to perform wiretaps without being detected has increased at a rapid pace. Technology allows the recording of all transactions and phone numbers, and voice identification can even be used with the monitoring technology.

Summary

The need for protection from legal attacks has never been greater than it is today. Providing privacy safeguards conflicts in many cases with individual, business, and government needs. The legitimate need governments and business have to use consumer information and the need of consumers to protect their privacy and confidentiality require legal and technological protections. Consumers are threatened by privacy invasion because they are not the "data owner" after they have submitted information to the black void that is business, government, and the Internet. Consumers have nothing to say about the use of information they have given about themselves or that has been collected about them and can never take that information out of circulation. Consumers also have no control over the data sources; the categories of data maintained; or the organizational policies and practices regarding data storage and protection by individuals, businesses, and governments. These three threats to your information have not identified a focal point to which complaints should be issued, have not taken positive steps to address violations of privacy, and have not been proactive in confirming the security and controls of partners or affiliates who receive your information and maintained detailed records of what happens to your information.

To better protect consumers from legal threats to their personal information, the right of refusal should be given to the consumer if possible. You do not have to hand over all your personal information every time you buy something or use a service. Consumers also should be informed about how their information will be used. The policies and procedures that govern how data is managed should be clearly stated before consumers are made to submit information. After data is collected, consumers should have the opportunity to inspect the record, challenge it, and make corrections. If the information is used for reasons other than the stated purpose, some practical punishments should be enforced. Tied closely to enforcement is the capability to monitor how consumer information is used and to detect violations of policies and procedures.

Despite the fact that the governments of the world are moving toward more legislation concerning threats to privacy, most categories of personal information are still wide open to legal and illegal attacks. Disclosure of information can be compelled by legal process, such as a subpoena issued by a court; gathered through online shopping sites, surveys, and cookies; and collected through marketing efforts and data mining technologies.

To provide protection against the multiple sources of data compromise, individuals, businesses, and governments can all agree that there will be a high cost associated with the protections that are necessary. From the inception of the U.S. Privacy Act of 1974 to the latest laws being passed by countries around the world, no practical costs have been developed. Even though real estimates of the costs have been made, the necessity exists because consumers are continuously being exploited. Such costs include research into necessary laws and technologies; analysis, design, and implementation of the protection requirements; improvement of current practices and upgrades to systems; management of the new privacy practices; and salaries of employees and the administrative cost of privacy inclusion in all systems and functionalities regarding consumer information.

5

Illegal Threats to Individual Privacy

In Chapter 4, "Legal Threats to Individual Privacy," you gained an understanding of how you can be attacked by individuals, businesses, and governments who want to use laws or the lack of laws to legally invade your privacy. Through legislation and industry self-regulation, consumer information is almost up for grabs by anyone who is willing to devote a bit of time to searching for personal information. Individuals have become empowered through the use of technology to perform their own data mining for personal gain using other people's information. As if the few legal activities were not enough of a threat against our privacy, we are faced with illegal activities that can be even more damaging.

With any change in society, there always seems to be an element that takes advantage of that change for personal benefit, and by illegal means. Technology has opened up a host of possibilities that a criminal can use to take advantage of the consumer. Cybercrime is one of the fastest-growing criminal activities because of the widespread use of technology and easy access of technology. It is becoming easier on a daily basis around the world for anyone to have access to technology, specifically the Internet. With the wealth of information available through technology, we are faced with illegal uses of that information. Illegal activities ranging from financial scams, computer hacking, pornography, virus attacks, and cyberstalking are easily conducted because of the Internet. This obviously does not mean we will shut down the Internet because of illegal activity, but we should know what threats we face from the new technological criminal.

Cybercrime compromises a vast range of illegal activity. The ease of using the Internet and new technologies has just made it easier for criminals to take advantage of the consumer. The cost of cybercrime is escalating every year, with one estimate of cybercrime at $40 billion a year. Although actually determining the amount is impossible, we can see from security spending by corporation that each year sees an increase in cybercrime.

The main threats to individuals through illegal activities that we will cover include

- **Hackers**—The term *hacking* was originally used to describe a practical joke or a modification of technology and software to solve a problem. But as technology and the Internet developed, it came to mean illegal activity.

- **Cyberterrorists**—This new breed of criminal has developed because of the global use of technology and connectivity of just about every country to the rest of the world through the Internet and communications lines. Cyberterrorists target governments or organizations for attack, but rarely individuals.

- **Businesses**—With access to a wealth of consumer information, it was inevitable that some businesses would take advantage of consumers through disguised business practices.

- **Credit card theft**—This activity most directly affects the consumer. Having your credit card information stolen from a site where you make a purchase can be readily understood by the consumer when he sees a purchase on his credit card bill he did not make.

- **Spyware**—These are insidious products that stealthily install themselves on your computer and can send out information about your system and your activities.

- **Governments**—Governments around the world have always been covertly involved with illegal activities. With access to the Internet, a government easily can sanction such tactics as cyberterrorism without being blamed.

- **Identify theft**—Probably one of the most damaging forms of illegal attacks on the individual consumer. Identity theft can destroy your financial reputation and bilk you out of money, as well as make recovery a living nightmare.

- **Fraud**—Scams are prevalent on the Internet. Setting up fake companies and convincing people to spend money for products or services they will never get is easy. Once fraud happened only on an individual basis, but with Internet usage, whole groups of people can be deceived by a technologically savvy criminal.

The escalation of computer crime is a global event. Ninety percent of U.S. companies that responded to a Computer Security Institute survey in 2000 detected computer security intrusions last year, and 74% acknowledged financial losses as a result of breaches of security. Of the 273 organizations that quantified their financial losses, the number was a staggering $265 million. Fraud has been much easier to achieve with the ability to set up fake companies on the Internet; after they capture enough credit cards or personal information, the company can then disappear. Identity theft used to be a paper exercise, but with the availability of consumer information on the Internet, cybercriminals can steal your identify in a virtual world without ever making contact with you or your paper-based information. It is one of the fastest growing crimes in the U.S. Tables 5.1 and 5.2 show the kinds of attacks businesses face as reported by the 2000 Information Security Industry Survey.

Table 5.1 **Reported Security Breaches**

Breach	Percentage of Respondents Who Experienced It
Viruses, Trojan horses, worms	80%
Denial-of-service attacks	37%
Scripting/mobile code attacks	37%
Protocol weakness attacks	26%
Insecure password attacks	25%
Buffer overflows	24%
Attacks on bugs in Web servers	24%

Table 5.2 **Breaches Experienced in the Past 12 Months**

Breach	Percentage of Respondents Who Experienced It
Installation of unauthorized software	76%
Infection of equipment via viruses/malicious code	70%
Illicit or illegal use of systems	63%
Abuse of computer access controls	58%
Unauthorized hardware installation	54%
Personal profit use (gambling and so on)	50%
Physical theft	42%
Electronic theft	24%
Fraud	13%

One *EWeek* Survey, shown in Table 5.3, found that virus attacks and hacker attacks were the most common breaches found in organizations.

Table 5.3 **Security Breaches**

Breach	Percentage of Respondents Who Experienced It
Virus attack	82%
Attack from hackers	50%
Breach of firewall policy	32%
Denial-of-service attack	31%
Authentication (identity fraud)	19%
e-Commerce fraud	7%
Other	4%

Lack of international laws has enabled criminals to easily avoid being caught and extradited if they're caught performing cybercrimes. Law enforcement must cross national boundaries to catch criminals, which currently poses many challenges for enforcement agencies around the world. National cyber boundaries pose the same threat as physical boundaries. Without the cooperation of other nations, prosecution of international criminals is next to impossible across national lines. Countries are very wary of cooperating even when it comes to hacking activities that affect more than one country and more than one group of people.

All is not lost to the cybercriminals, though. Many nations are making initiatives that can lead to the tracking and capturing of criminals. In the U.K., the National Hi-Tech Crime Unit is being set up with the intention of making the U.K. a safe place for consumers on the Internet. The U.S. FBI has a Computer Crime Squad with more than 200 agents across the United States that have become more tech savvy; they are now better at handling illegal attacks using technology. Recent virus epidemics around the world have made the lack of security on the Internet mainstream knowledge. With knowledge comes power—both for law enforcement agencies and consumers who can be cognizant of the dangers they now face. The Council of Europe produced a draft treaty on cybercrime that was instantly bombarded by privacy advocates. Laws that attempt to protect the consumer can end up doing as much harm as any criminal in some cases.

Consumers need to understand the changes in technology that have brought new threats to their security and personal information. These threats will only escalate in the future as technology expands and we are further tied together on a global basis. Criminal activity has been increasing because businesses are more connected and available to attack, a wider audience has access to knowledge and technology that can be used to an illegal end, and anonymity in committing crimes is easy using technology. Criminal activity in the real world will be completely duplicated eventually in the online world.

Hackers

The term *hacker* has evolved from its original meaning of someone who applied knowledge to fix some technological problem to someone who uses technology, frequently the Internet, to perform some illegal activity. The terms *hacker* and *cracker* have been used interchangeably, and there is strong opinion among techies on what each actually means. This book considers a hacker someone who attempts to gain or does gain unauthorized access to a computer system or network. (Crackers are discussed later.) Access can be through different means, such as phone lines, the Internet, or wireless networks. Telephone hackers are normally referred to as *phreakers* that break into phone companies and get free telephone calls. Good hackers often know several programming languages and understand why technology works and what is lacking in technology when it comes to security features. Hackers explore the systems searching for misconfigurations, bugs, and holes in the operating systems that would allow them access.

The original hackers were intelligent programmers who could manipulate software to get the results they desired. Today's hackers use software to get what they want, but mostly for illegal purposes. *Script kiddies* is a term used for unskilled people who use software tools and instructions created by skilled programmers/hackers to take advantage of a system.

The accessibility of hacking tools means a technically obtuse person can easily attack systems using tools to crack passwords, steal files, cause denial-of-service attacks, and install backdoors into computer networks. As we have seen in some of the denial-of-service attacks that have made the news, public tools created for this specific purpose can automate large-scale attacks and cause endless problems for individuals, businesses, and governments. Out of the hacker community was born the *cyber terrorist*, who uses hacker tools for destruction (this topic is also discussed later).

Motivation of the Hacker

The motivation of hackers in the past has been the challenge of figuring out something new, for coming up with a new method of doing something or developing a new technology or piece of software. Hacking is fun and exciting for many people; the challenge of breaking into a systems has developed in the hacker community over the years. It used to be a game with no detrimental consequences for both the system being hacked and the hacker. As pagers, handheld computers, personal digital assistants, and other wireless devices have grown in popularity; hackers have new areas on which to focus their attention. Knowledge is power, and hacking is a way of exerting power and showing others your skills as a hacker. The reasons for hacking are as varied as the hackers themselves.

Way of Life

Hacking, once started, becomes a life-long involvement for many people. Whether it is legal hacking, illegal hacking for a specific gain such as money or revenge, or just for the fun of doing it, those who get into hacking and computer security most likely stay with it for most of their lives. It can even be a form of addiction. Also, a virtual lifestyle in which you are connected to numerous smart and creative people around the world can satisfy a need for relationships that many techies might not have in their normal lives. Sustaining interpersonal relationships can be difficult for many people in the hacking community, so hacking becomes a lifestyle for them.

Thrill of the Kill

Hacking as a strictly illegal act with goals in mind other than increasing knowledge and creating something new has over the past decade become the predominant view of hackers. Performing an illegal act can be thrilling in and of itself to a hacker. Causing harm can be a thrill to some people, and this attitude has developed in the hacker community. Dominating the illegal underground based on their ability to hack, steal information, or cause destruction is a way of gaining recognition from the hacker community. Making a name for oneself in the hacker community has increasingly been based on illegal activities, whereas in the past it was the ability to do something that wasn't necessarily illegal and damage-causing. One popular method of making a name for oneself is by defacing Web sites. Several sites carry archives of hacked Web sites, but this seems to just encourage people to hack more Web sites. With all the weaknesses in Web software, that can be easy, and for hackers who are unknown, it's a quick way to gain notoriety. The hacker culture is ever evolving and publicly acknowledged illegal activities are in season at the moment.

Vigilantism

The opposite of the hacker who needs to make a name for himself by causing harm or stealing information are *hacktivists*—the vigilantes of computer security. Hacking Web sites that promote ideas (or even governments) that the hacker finds objectionable, such as Neo-Nazi sites or pornography sites, is seen as a worthy use of hacking skills. By defacing or destroying the Web site they find objectionable, the hacktivists feel they are doing some good. Much like the animal rights groups who commit minor crimes, such as illegal protests or attacking people wearing fur, these hactivists see their attacks on Web sites as spreading the message about problems with such sites as neo-nazi sites. This is all subjective opinion, of course. And it is illegal.

Other types of hacktivists use their skills to find and make known a security flaw in a program, an operating system, or a technology. This could be as simple as a Web site security vulnerability or as complex as breaking the encryption codes used for DVDs. They think they are actually doing good for the world by helping companies fix the problem, even if it means breaking the law. Hacktivists hack for some social concern. Even though this is useful to companies and consumers who could otherwise lose money or data to hackers bent on theft or destruction, it is still an illegal action, no matter the good intentions of the attacker.

Information Must Be Free

"Information should be free" is a mantra of the hacking community. They believe that software, source code, and information should be available to everyone. Some hackers are on a quest to make information free, no matter how much individuals, businesses, or governments might want to keep that information secure. Fighting "the Man" was not just a hippie movement. Hackers cross all races, religions, and national boundaries, and they believe the world should be open to everyone. Hacking as a means of increasing knowledge and causing damage to a system is not part of this type of hacker ethic. Script kiddies who do not understand the tools they are using or cause damage are viewed unfavorably by hackers who seek to learn and make information available to everyone. Although these types of hackers mostly stress not harming systems or people and do not seek financial gain from their activities, their hacking activities are still illegal.

Crossing the Line

Some hackers cross the line between legal and illegal hacking. Security consultants perform hacking functions, but if they are hired by a company to test its security measures, then it's legal. The problem occurs when the consultants hacks outside of a legal contract or when the government hires the hacker to perform some function, but which might still be illegal. The FBI has a reputation of using hackers who either cross the line themselves or are asked to cross the line between legal and illegal hacking. When hackers mature, they tend to take stable jobs, but the tendency to hack can still be there, and they can still perform illegal activities.

Anonymity

One reason the hacker community is referred to as being underground is its tendency toward secrecy. In the hacker community, many people use a *handle*, or hacker name, rather than using their own names. Hackers can hide behind that name and create a persona for themselves without people ever meeting them. Anonymity helps in performing crimes and makes it that much harder to track the real criminal. When sharing knowledge and information, it benefits the hacker to remain anonymous if that information is proprietary to some business that might have been hacked to steal the information. A hacker can gain notoriety based on his hacker name and be proud of the persona he has built. Eventually, the real name becomes associated with the handle. Fame is a strong allure for hacking, even if it is just within the small hacking community. Hiding their names as well as how they attack a system, such as using multiple hacked connections to reach their end targets, is built into the hacker community.

Power and Wealth

Power and wealth are becoming dominant reasons for hacking. The ability to steal information about consumers or companies that can lead to direct financial gain or increase in power can make hacking a very attractive option as a career. Plus, corporate espionage can be very lucrative indeed. Easy access to companies and individuals because of the growth of technology can make gaining information such as credit card numbers simple, which can lead to direct financial gain. One recently reported case involved a man in Mission Viejo, California, who plead guilty to hacking into computers at Oregon State University and using stolen credit card numbers in an attempt to wire transfer money using Western Union. He plead guilty to one count of obtaining information from a protected computer and one count of wire fraud. The hacker was also charged with hacking into NASA computers. FBI involvement in computer hacking cases has increased over the past several years because of financial losses that can be traced to hacking.

Revenge

Hacking has been on the rise from insiders because of revenge. In many cases, ex-employees are the attackers because they want revenge on the company that fired them. In one case, Patrick McKenna of Hampton, New Hampshire, was convicted and sentenced for "unauthorized computer intrusion" into the computer database of his former Portsmouth, New Hampshire, employer, Bricsnet U.S. This is another case that was tracked by the FBI. He hacked into his ex-employer's network, caused damage to computer files, modified systems, altered records, and sent fraudulent e-mails to clients to damage the reputation of the company.

Crackers

Crackers used to be what a hacker is now. The definition of a cracker has changed somewhat from someone who breaks into systems to someone who breaks software codes. Crackers have always had a very negative reputation, from being malicious to outright destructive. In the underground community, it is argued that hackers seek knowledge, while crackers are the ones who break into computer systems illegally. Public perception of hackers and crackers doesn't really take into account what the underground thinks of these terms. Today's hacker who causes harm is usually called a cracker in addition to those who break software codes. Crackers, in general, like to leave a calling card to show who they are by their handles. Just about all cracker activity, which is focused around breaking copyrights and software piracy, is illegal. Software piracy was estimated to have cost software companies $11 billion in lost revenue in 2000.

A key new U.S. law directed at crackers of software licenses and software piracy is the Digital Millennium Copyright Act of 1998 (DMCA). The DMCA prohibits the circumvention of copy protection and the distribution of devices that can be used to circumvent copyrights. Researchers who write programs to test copyright protection or encryption are faced with prosecution under this law. In mid-2001, a Russian encryption expert named Dmitry Sklyarov was arrested in the U.S. for writing a program that broke the copyright protection on Adobe software. Although this law is valuable in prosecuting crackers who perform illegal activities, such as cracking software and then selling the software or the cracking program, legitimate security specialists can face prosecution under the law, too. This has the potential to weaken research into security weaknesses in software and encryption technologies. A Web site dedicated to fighting the DCMA has been set up at Anti-DMCA.Org (`www.Anti-DMCA.org`).

Extortion

Online extortion is a natural extension of hackers. Whereas in the past, hackers sought fun and games, a challenge, and name recognition, increasing incidents are centered around monetary gain through extortion. In the U.S., the FBI found that more than one million credit cards were stolen by a Russian and Ukrainian extortion scheme in 2001. As we mentioned, it is easy for many hackers to break into a poorly secured small e-commerce site and steal the credit card database and then either extort money from the company to keep it quiet or use the cards to make purchases. In the extortion case of CDUniverse in 1999, more than 300,000 card numbers were stolen, and the hacker tried to extort money from CDUniverse. The same thing happened to Western Union and Creditcards.com. In all these cases, the extortion failed, but there could be cases in which the hackers successfully extort money that never make the evening news.

Many companies have turned to insurance against extortion and loss of business due to hacking. For many companies that can't protect themselves, insurance is a way to mitigate the risk. Insurance payouts have not made the news yet, and legal precedents for insurance claims and even insurance fraud have yet to be made, but eventually they will be.

To combat extortion, countries around the world are passing stiffer hacking laws. Europe is probably the most advanced in passing stiff antihacking laws to help combat extortion.

Cyberterrorists

Cyberterrorism is an offshoot of hacking. A cyberterrorist uses sophisticated programming skills and knowledge of operating systems, networking, and computer architectures to cause significant damage. His aim is to cause more than just denial of service. The same tools that are available to a hacker are available to a terrorist on the Internet. Tools that exploit security weaknesses in popular operating systems and common network protocols are commonly used to take advantage of a company or government Internet connection. A key fear of terrorism is assaults that could crash power grids, financial networks, transportation systems, and telecommunications. National security agencies around the world trace the threat to hostile governments, cartels, guerrilla groups, and individual terrorists. Cyberattacks such as those that damaged Web sites in February 2000, including Yahoo! Inc.'s Internet gateway, eBay Inc.'s auction service, and Amazon.com Inc.'s retail site, can be a precursor to major attacks. The infrastructure of the Internet is also subject to attack. The connections through phone companies that provide service to millions of people and route traffic around the world can be targets (although destroying such connections can be detrimental to the terrorists as well as everyone else). Hackers and programmers have made software available to everyone. The use of the software is up to the individual. When the hacker is a script kiddie with little knowledge of what he is actually doing with other people's software, he can cause great harm. The ease of use can create instant terrorists. Launching denial-of-service attacks is very easy with automated tools, but sophisticated attacks require a great deal of knowledge on the part of the attacker.

The software and hardware industries are more aware of attacks and work quickly to release patches as soon as a new security vulnerability is made known. Sophisticated attackers can create or modify tools to take advantage of publicly unknown holes before the vendor is aware of a problem. The infrastructure of the Internet is easier to attack through a denial of service rather than by exploiting security weaknesses that can lead to access to computer systems.

The U.S. is becoming a frequent target of cyberterrorists. The motives of cyberterrorists are usually the same as for normal terrorists, including political, financial, revenge, and just plain nasty attitudes. Malicious hackers can target the U.S. for terrorism for the prestige that comes from attacking U.S. properties. Destruction of systems brings down the wrath of law enforcement much more quickly that hacking for fun or exploration, though, so cyberterrorists face faster criminal investigations from law enforcement agencies around the world.

Large-scale acts by foreign terrorist groups are likely to increase in the future because of the small timeframe it takes to acquire basic computer skills to perform attacks. The script kiddies' ability of hacking is available to terrorists at very low costs. Terrorists can also hire outside expertise to perform more sophisticated attacks. The typical targets of terrorists are typically more protected than that of typical hackers. Although the average hacker targets companies for Web site defacement or stealing credit cards, terrorists target government agencies, banks, and critical infrastructure companies. These are, in general, well guarded and not easy targets for either denial-of-service attacks or in-depth exploitation. Elaborate security measures that are in place might not be completely secure, but putting up many roadblocks to attack give administrators time to respond to an attack.

Differing opinions exist on how easily terrorists can attack critical companies and governments on the Internet. Some believe that, because of the availability of tools and past experience with hackers, terrorists can do so easily and everyone should be very worried. Others, however, think that as attacks become more sophisticated, so will the countermeasures to attacks. Viruses, such as ILOVEYOU, Code Red, and Melissa, have caused millions of dollars in damage. Instead of just causing damage to systems, these viruses could have easily stolen information or tried to perform any number of other functions, such as stealing money to fund the terrorist attacks. But as soon as these viruses appeared, patches were released to fix the problems. Damage was caused only because many administrators did not implement the patches in time to save their systems, but this does illustrate the point that a countermeasure is always made available. When cyberterrorists combine technological attacks with physical attacks, the damage can be quite extensive. For example, if a terrorist damaged a hospital's computer systems and then set off a bomb in the vicinity, patient care would be greatly impacted. In August 2001 in Yugoslavia, attackers hacked into Telekom Serbia and threatened to disrupt Internet and phone service because the company had a monopoly on the telephone service and had increased prices. Service was disrupted for several hours, which could have caused widespread damage.

Hacktivism

Hacktivism is a term recently coined that refers to politically motivated hacking. Car bombs against the ruling government are one form of terrorism, and defacing the Web site of the party in power that the terrorist is trying to overthrow is another form. The impact of hacking a Web site is not the same as that of a car bomb, for now. But it is easy to see how simple Web defacement can expand into shutting down critical computer systems, such as 911 lines or power grids, all in the name of politics. The Internet as a means to counter social injustice is a motivator for the hacktivist.

Some hacktivists deface Web sites of organizations that have little or no control over the social injustice that is perceived by the terrorist. A group calling itself "Gforce Pakistan" defaced 11 pages belonging to the National Oceanic Atmospheric Administration with pleas for Kashmiri independence. In Malaysia, hackers have broken into numerous political Web sites protesting their own government and demanding greater press freedom and an end to corruption. Within all countries, hacktivism is a way of speaking out against the current government, like cyber graffiti that the whole world can see.

A case of group hacking occurred in November 2000. Arab computer hackers attacked Jewish Web sites in Israel and the U.S., marking the beginning of the cyberspace war between Israel and Palestine. Hacktivism efforts that marry political resistance with cybercrimes are becoming a favorite tool for guerrilla warfare in cyberspace. Pakistani groups have been attacking Indian sites and expounding on the political situation between the countries. Hacktivism affects governments, businesses, and individuals. If this trend continues, hacking for political purposes could easily target transportation systems or medical systems to make a major impact, as do car bombs and embassy bombings. Stealing credit cards from another country's people could easily lead to shutting down critical systems in another country. No cyberattacks have yet resulted in fatalities because the attackers are mostly interested in defacing Web sites and making a name for themselves or their country in the world of hacking.

Hacktivism and terrorism are usually difficult for most people to understand. As a motivator, cyberterrorism can be downright obscure. The message of cyberterrorists is hard to discern in many cases, and it's even easier for various groups to claim credit for some attack because of the anonymity of cyberattacks. Many such attacks are just a showcase for groups of hackers who have little regard for the actual message behind the attack. But the threat is real in cyberattacks; escalation of the destruction of such attacks will only get worse unless governments and companies take the initiative to see the global picture of these attacks. Minor cyberattacks are a testing ground for eventual large-scale attacks. The minimal damage so far should not cause a lack of concern but should identify the very real threat in the near future of these attacks. Even though it's currently disorganized, it's simple to extrapolate the evolution of focused attacks that can cause real damage on a national or even global basis.

Government Reaction

Fighting cyberterrorism is becoming a new challenge of world governments. The U.S. government, specifically the FBI, has made headway into making it publicly acceptable for a company to call for help when attacked and to admit to being compromised. Government agencies are being assigned the task of tracking and stopping cyberterrorism and cyberattacks proactively rather than reactively. Additionally, the U.S. National Security Council is developing the nation's strategy against cyberterrorists, hackers, electronic spies, and other threats to its information infrastructure. The National Security Council has formed the Cyberincident Steering Group, aimed at fostering cooperation between the private sector and government to secure systems from cyber-attacks. As we have mentioned in earlier chapters, the government's hands-off approach and it letting the private sector perform self-regulation has not worked very well. In the case of global attacks, governments have to take a proactive role in defending their countries' assets and work with other countries to stop global attacks. In the case of the National Security Council, the U.S. government has increased its budget to $1.5 billion. Future projects will include technical research and development to stop cyber-attacks.

On the other hand, governments can also use cyberterrorism as a hidden means of attacking their rivals. Whether it's turning the other cheek when criminals launch attacks against a foreign country or slyly funding cyberterrorism, governments can play an active role in attacks. The U.S. is frequently attacked from other countries. The FBI-led National Infrastructure Protection Center (NIPC) is on the forefront of protecting the U.S. from cyberattacks. Recent attacks against the U.S. have been linked to China. A virus that defaced the White House's home page in 2001 left behind a message linking the attack to the University of Foshan in China, although Beijing officials denied any connection to the virus or Chinese involvement. The infamous Code Red worm, which damaged many systems and caused millions in damages, has also been linked to China. Chinese Internet chat rooms have been fueled by anti-western sentiments recently, and hackers have been fanning the flames.

Business Threats

The illegal threats posed by businesses to the consumers are not as clear cut as those of hackers or cyberterrorists. The "New Economy" that has been built around the Internet is most subtle. Information is a form of currency on the Internet that can be stolen and traded. New technologies and concepts, such as profiling and targeting, are not strictly illegal. With these borderline functions on the rise, the Internet has quickly motivated privacy groups to take action against legal threats to consumer information.

Businesses have few legal restrictions as yet in compromising consumer personal information. Chapter 4 discusses various laws in place to either help or hinder businesses with regard to using personal information. With the lack of controls and laws, businesses can easily take advantage of the consumer without breaking any laws.

Companies can easily cross the few lines that have been drawn to secure personal information. Corporate espionage has always been a factor in doing business, but with the advent of the Internet and the connectivity of businesses, it's easier for one company to break into a rival and steal information, which can be anything from product specifications to customer lists. Customer information is increasingly more valuable with all the data mining techniques now available. The Computer Security Institute in conjunction with the FBI produces the "Computer Crime and Security Survey," which states that more than 50% of respondents said that the information sought in probes would be of use to U.S.-owned corporate competitors and U.S.-owned corporate competitors are likely sources of industrial espionage. Also in the survey, 26% cited foreign competitors as a likely source of attack. The prize in many cases can be customer and client information.

If you have ever filled out a survey on a company Web site when making a purchase, you might wonder why you must do that. How will that information be used? With recent acts being passed in the U.S. against how information is collected and used, the consumer might think he is protected. But it's very difficult to nearly impossible for any agency to monitor the millions of Web sites that can collect information and ensure they are in compliance with the changing privacy laws. How is the consumer to know which laws affect information collection and use when companies do not even know in many cases that they are breaking the law? Businesses today have an opportunity to use information technologies to their competitive advantage, and that enticement can cause them to go one step beyond what is strictly legal. The deadline for compliance with the Gramm-Leach-Bliley Act (GLB) has passed and left many companies out of compliance. A recent survey of banks, mortgage brokers, and insurance companies showed a failure to fully inform online customers of their privacy rights according to the requirements of the act. The Center for Democracy and Technology (CDT) examined 100 Web sites and privacy practices by organizations affected by GLB and found that 80 did not provide advice on how to restrict access to their information and 34 shared customer information outside the guidelines set by GLB. Of the 100 sites, only 22 offered customers clear and simple opt-out mechanisms.

Any large company or global company has connections to partners, vendors, and even customers. By letting other organizations and people connect to their systems, companies are opening up potential holes in their systems that can allow an attacker a chance to get to your information. If a company sets up a connection incorrectly with a partner that allows unrestricted access to corporate assets, what is to stop that partner from pilfering information? If a company sells products over its Web site and customers can log in and check their orders, an inadvertent misconfiguration or not applying a patch to the system can give someone access to customer information that can be stolen. The very fact that a large company can offer a diverse range of services and form partnerships and alliances with other companies can put your personal information in jeopardy from an attack.

As you will see in later chapters, security is not that easy to implement. Any company that has your information and is connected in some form to the outside world can be subject to attack. As we have discussed, security spending is on the rise because hacker attacks are on the rise. A company can be an unknown ally to the attacker if it implements weak security measures to protect your information. Secure information and communication systems enables e-commerce, but being complacent about such security can be the death of e-commerce. There is no way to guarantee a risk-free environment in which a business can operate and protect your personal information. Businesses can be your worst enemy by enabling malicious attackers to easily access their systems and your data by lack of security measures. Proper controls require planning and careful implementation, which is not really prevalent yet when it comes to security-related issues. Security has always been an afterthought in doing business until recently. Companies that are not proactive in monitoring and managing the risk to your information will enable illegal access to your data and invasion of your privacy. There are always new types of attacks, services, and vulnerabilities that must be addressed on a daily basis to do business in this new economy.

Employer Spying

Most companies have the capability to legally monitor the e-mail, phone conversations, and any other forms of communications by employees using company resources. Employers are concerned with raising worker productivity; preventing theft; avoiding legal liability, corporate espionage, and harassment; and preventing lawsuits through inappropriate use of company resources. Where that line is between what is legal monitoring of company resources and spying or breaking of eavesdropping laws is very vague. In one recent case, the U.S. federal court system's chief administrator dropped requirements on monitoring the Internet communications of the judicial branch because of the backlash from judges on invasion of privacy issues and laws that could potentially be broken. The monitoring policy would have asked all employees to waive their privacy rights while using the resources of the office. But what happens in companies in which the employee has no say?

Federal law, which regulates phone calls with persons outside the state, does enable unannounced monitoring for business-related calls. (See Electronic Communications Privacy Act, 18 U.S.C 2510.) Personal calls cannot be monitored, though, only business calls. Using cell phones or pay phones can help you keep conversations private, but you can inadvertently be monitored when making personal calls.

Numerous monitoring software programs are available that can let employers watch a computer screen and read all the e-mail messages of an employee. Such software can do everything from recording all applications being used to capturing every keystroke made and taking screen shots of the monitor every few seconds. A remote monitoring station can watch exactly what is being done on your computer and record all the actions you take. Several of the software packages that enable employers to monitor your actions include

- **Little Brother (www.littlebrother.com)**—This software, for $295, can be used to track up to 10 systems for Internet use and bandwidth consumption, can block sites, and can provide very detailed reports on employee surfing.

- **Cyber Snoop (www.pearlsw.com)**—This Internet monitoring and filtering package costs $49. Cyber Snoop gives the system administrator control over the Web, IRC chat, FTP, e-mail, and newsgroups and can report on employees' work activities on their computers.

- **Stealth Keylogger Interceptor Pro (www.keyloggers.com)**—For $69, this program covertly monitors keystrokes and saves them to a text-based `.log` file. The log is complete, retrieving times and dates, application and dialog names, filenames, pasted text, and keystroke actions. There is no evidence that the program is running on the target machine.

Even if you delete your e-mail, backup copies are always available, and even deleted e-mail can be recovered. Recovering deleted e-mail is actually quite simple. One of the many popular e-mail packages used by businesses is Microsoft Outlook, in which retrieving a deleted e-mail message is easy. In Outlook 2002, you can simply select Tools, Recover Deleted Items to undelete e-mail messages, as shown in Figure 5.1.

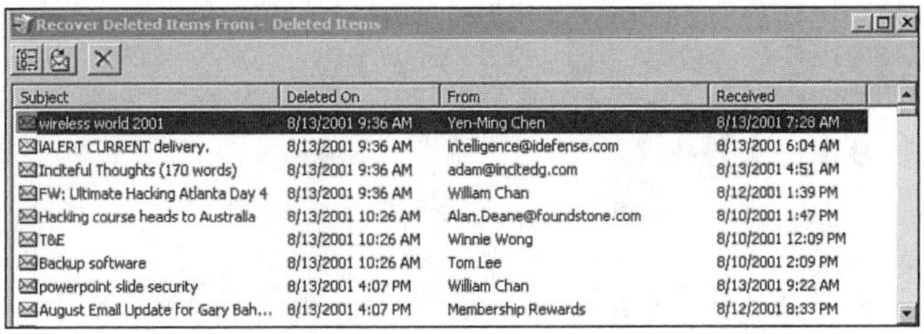

Figure 5.1   Recovering deleted e-mails.

Monitoring software can get around encryption of data on your machine if the employer can monitor what is on your screen. If data is transmitted in an encrypted form, no one can read it unless he can decrypt it. However, after you've decrypted your e-mail, your employer can easily have a screen-monitoring program running that can view the unencrypted data on your monitor. In some cases, even if the employer states that it has the right to monitor all e-mails, it can be breaking a local or federal law by doing so.

Even though monitoring employees seems like a way to better secure the environment, it can be a breach of moral and legal boundaries when it comes to privacy. Fostering such an environment can actually lead to employee dissatisfaction with the workplace and decreased productivity. If such actions are left to only extreme cases, perhaps when an employee is caught hacking, then a company should use such tools. On a daily basis, though, these tools will only cause problems in the workplace and weaken the already limited privacy rights of everyone.

Insider Threats

The insider threat is very real when it comes to system compromises. Employees are a serious and large threat to companies and individuals. The 1999 Computer Security Institute/FBI report notes that 55% of respondents reported malicious activity by insiders. In one case reported by the FBI before the Senate Committee on Appropriations, an FBI employee, Shakuntla Devi Singla, used her access to use another employee's ID and password to delete data from a U.S. Coast Guard personnel database system. The costs to recover included 115 agency employees and 1,800 hours. In another case reported by the FBI, in January and February 1999 the National Library of Medicine (NLM) computer system was hacked. Montgomery Johns Gray III, a former computer programmer for NLM, had left a backdoor into the system, stole patient information, and posed a public health threat by stealing such personal medical information.

Employees have access to systems without having to hack their way in. By stealing a customer list and selling it to a rival, an employee can easily make money. Ex-employees also are a threat because they know so much about the systems, and frequently all their access to the company is not terminated when they leave. This easy access can enable them to go back into the system as legitimate users and steal information.

Credit Card Theft

Credit card theft is experienced by many businesses and individuals. As a consumer, you are not usually held responsible for charges to a credit card that has been stolen. In some cases, however, you might have to pay $50 or whatever amount was charged, but other than that and the headache of having to get a new credit card, the cost is minimal. For businesses, though, the cost of credit card theft is astronomical. For everyone from the merchant who will not get paid because the credit card company can back out of the charge to the insurance company that has to pay out money each year for stolen merchandise to the credit card company that has to incur the cost of reissuing the card, the costs mount up along the way. When Egghead.com was hacked in late 2000, it spent numerous man hours tracking the attack; in addition, banks and credit unions paid millions of dollars to reissue credit cards (it costs a credit card issuer $2–$5 to cancel and reissue a card) and compensate workers for hours worked. Also, consumers had to check their bills to see whether their cards were stolen. In another case, an online credit card scam cost Visa USA at least $48 million last year. From this one hacker attack, millions of dollars were potentially spent and huge amounts of time were wasted. When one hacker failed to extort money from Creditcards.com, he posted about 55,000 credit card numbers on the Internet. The costs in contacting customers and replacing those cards, loss of revenue through use of those card numbers by other people, and time wasted were very high for all parties involved.

Who is to blame for credit card theft via the Internet or use of technology? Is it the consumer, who should be responsible for how he uses his cards, or is it companies for not using the correct technology to secure data, or maybe society for not putting a stop to hacker activity? This is a rhetorical question because we can't blame anyone—we can only attempt to make it difficult in the future to have credit card information stolen, especially with technology. It can be argued that a company with good security should be able to stop an attack. But security is just a point-in-time event. If you think your systems are secure today, tomorrow a brand new exploit can become known that will find a new hole in your security defenses. After an attacker does breach security defenses, it takes a lot of time and effort to track what was done to the systems and ensure that no other weaknesses were introduced to the environment by the attack, further escalating the costs of an attack.

The reason many attackers go after credit cards is because they're easy to use. On the Internet, no picture ID is required, and performing any kind of verification of who is making the purchase is difficult. In most cases, verification is not performed thoroughly because of the costs associated in doing so.

Older methods of stealing credit card information, such as shoulder surfing (peeking over your shoulder to get credit card, phone card, and personal identification numbers, as well as other private information) and searching the trash for credit card receipts, are no longer necessary for hi-tech crooks. Devices such as credit card skimmers are used in restaurants and stores to capture all the information on a card for later use. Programs that can generate legitimate credit card numbers are available to those in the know about such technology. It's not even illegal to write credit card number generators. A credit card number can be easily generated using a known algorithm. Many programs are available that can generate a seemingly valid credit card number. If the number is not checked at the time of purchase by the vendor for valid name, address, and number with the credit card company, the hacker can make purchases with a false yet seemingly valid credit card number.

For a small merchant who accepts credit cards, the sophisticated software security tools might not be cost effective to implement, enabling a hacker to more easily break into a small, poorly secured site and steal information. After he breaks into a site with your credit card information, the odds are very high that he can get more personal information, such as home address and telephone number, from the same database. Stolen credit card information is an easy path to stealing someone's identity.

The most recent event of credit card theft is that of a Russian hacker who stole thousands of credit card numbers. He even put a Web site up on the Internet to show the information. The site showed more than 25,000 numbers with cardholder names, addresses, and expiration dates. The hacker—known as Maxus—broke into CDUniverse to get this information. The database stolen had more than 300,000 customers in it. The site was put up by the hacker after a failed attempt at extorting money from CDUniverse. The ease of how this was done suggests that future attacks will follow along the same path, and some companies will end up paying the extortion bill to keep their names out of the press.

Measuring the result of credit card theft is extremely difficult. Merchants lose customers' trust, which can't be measured; fixing problems involves time and effort, which can be hard to measure; and the consumer might make fewer purchases because of fear, uncertainty, and doubt about using new technologies. The barriers to becoming knowledgeable about credit card theft are very low. With some time and effort, anyone can find information on how to hack, learn how to use credit card generators, or even find guides to stealing information on the Internet. The ability to be anonymous through this whole process makes it even harder for companies and law enforcement to track credit card theft. Even with the limited liability that consumers have because of theft, it still affects their use of the Internet and credit cards in immeasurable ways.

U.S. federal law protects credit card users against fraud online with the Fair Credit Billing Act. Liability is capped at $50 of unauthorized charges. For ATM cards, a cardholder's liability is $50 if the card is reported lost within 48 hours and up to $500 if reported stolen after a charge is made. The major issuers, such as Visa USA, MasterCard International, and American Express, do not make the consumer pay anything for unauthorized purchases. Even with these financial guarantees to the customer, having your information stolen can be a very personal and shocking event that causes you to distrust the Internet and shy away from its use, which is of no benefit to anyone.

Although we are not proponents of people stealing credit cards, it important for consumers to know several of the methods of how this could possibly be done. Some basic types of steps that cybercriminals can take to purchase in your name include the following:

- **Compromising a site**—A hacker simply breaks into a company and steals its database of credit card information.

- **Creating a card**—A hacker downloads a credit card account generator and makes a card based on the Luhn formula, which card companies use to make cards with 13–16 digits.

- **Skimming**—Retail and restaurant employees use skimmers to steal information. These devices read information from the magnetic strip and cost several hundred dollars.

- **Cloning a site**—On the Internet, a hacker can copy a site and redirect traffic to his site. He then captures the information and passes on the valid order to the real site. The consumer would not know the difference.

- **Creating false sites**—Fictional sites are created that purport to sell a service or product but just are set up temporarily to capture credit card information and then shut down.

From the consumer's point of view, a limited number of options is available for protecting credit card and other personal information stored in some company's database. After you have submitted that information, it's pretty much out of your control. What you can do to help protect yourself is know where you are submitting your information and what possible controls that company might have in place. Several steps you can take to better protect your information include

- **Check the site's security**—That little lock icon in your browser lets you know whether the site is using security and encryption. Each browser can bring up a site's security certificates, which you can check to see whether you are actually using the real site of the company you are buying from. The lock also lets you know your information is being encrypted as it is sent so you do not have to worry about someone stealing your traffic as it makes its way to the company.

- **Use specific credit cards**—Set aside a credit card that you use only for Internet shopping that you can always check and know it's only for Internet purchases. This card should have a low limit for spending, and you should have information readily on hand to cancel it if necessary.

- **Destroy receipts carefully**—If you throw out whole receipts in the trash, the possibility exists that someone can go through your trash and find that receipt, and then use it to make purchases.

- **Check your credit report**—You should periodically check your credit report to see whether activity is occurring that you do not know about or whether your credit history is being abused. The three main credit reporting agencies are Equifax (800-685-1111), Experian (800-311-4769), and Trans Union (800-888-4213).

- **Check the site's policies**—Each site you visit will have some form of a privacy policy or a statement regarding its stance on privacy and security. At a minimum, if it does not, you should probably not use that site.

Merchants have to take more responsibility to ensure that the consumer's credit card is not stolen. Simple things like securing the e-commerce site with necessary defense measures, such as with firewalls, routers, digital certificates, intrusion detection systems, antivirus software, and other forms of access controls, can greatly cut down on hacker attacks and compromises of smaller merchants. After the technology is in place, the processes need to be followed that provide additional security, such as verifying addresses with what the bank has on file for the credit card. If the criminal can't change the shipping address, the card can't be used to buy material goods. Credit cards also have a card verification value, (CVV and CVV2), which is a 3-digit to 4-digit value on the card that does not get imprinted. The purchaser must have the actual number for the order to be processed; a stolen database of card numbers would not have this number. If merchants would limit the amount of information they capture, stolen information would have less of an impact on the consumer. It's not always necessary to have every bit of information about the consumer in a database somewhere. And finally, insider threats are just as dangerous as outside hacker threats. Employees have much greater access to sensitive information, so limiting their access is a good idea.

A Gartner Group survey of 166 retailers—half of whom sell on the Internet—found that online credit card fraud equaled 1.13% of transactions. Online credit card fraud for Visa was approximately 0.15%, or $48 million. The Secret Service takes an active role in investigating credit card crimes, but little or nothing is actually ever done with minor cases or cases that involve only a few individuals. Because people sometimes do not report online fraud and companies especially want to avoid becoming known for being taken advantage of by fraud and cyberthefts, the exact numbers are difficult to calculate.

Spyware

Spyware crosses the line between legal and illegal acts. This type of software is very intrusive and stealthy. A variety of software products are building in functionality that installs unwanted and unknown software on your system, piggybacking on other software installations and sending out information to the company about you and your system that you might not want divulged. These products also are often used to download advertisements to your computer. The only way to find out that the software's there is when it starts making changes to your system settings, sending out traffic from your system that you can notice, or opening an Internet connection for its own purposes.

Spyware is an offshoot of adware, which is freeware that embeds ads into free programs, thereby generating revenue through advertisements and links to the company placing the ad. Adware programs usually have a free version with ads and a paid version without ads. Spyware is synonymous with its name: It masks itself as freeware or adware but has an alternative purpose, which is usually to track users' activities and monitor their actions. This type of activity is unwanted by just about all consumers, but no laws strictly prohibit this type of activity. Several lawsuits have been brought against spyware companies; one such case was a lawsuit against Radiate, which made spyware. The company settled a case in February 2001 that said it was using its software to collect demographic data and monitor viewing preferences without consumer knowledge. One bill in front of Congress addresses spyware—the Spyware Control and Privacy Protection Act, which would provide for the disclosure of the collection of information through computer software. This act would essentially make spyware illegal, but it has not been passed yet.

One other major problem with spyware is the removal process. Spyware does not enable the user to easily remove it. Just detecting it can be a problem is if it masks itself with the running of another program. Several products on the market, such as adware, can detect some spyware products and help in their removal. Two other products that can help clean up spyware are the following:

- **XCleaner**—A simple-to-use anti-spyware and privacy enhancement tool. No installation is required; you simply click and it starts. Users can check boxes to allow control of cleaning functions and spy software detection services. XCleaner clears temporary files, caches, cookies, and many other user artifacts.

- **Spyblocker**—Many Web sites have ads that are distracting and a drain on bandwidth. Some sites send cookies and other files to your computer. Still others acquire information about you, your machine, and your browsing habits by using single-pixel Web bugs and other methods. Spyblocker is one of the many programs that can block such activity from occurring. It can stop pop-up ads and cookie activity and keep some of your browsing habits from being sent out from your machine.

Another method of checking for spyware is by using Windows Task Manager to see which processes are running. In Windows 9x and Me, this can be done by pressing Ctrl+Alt+Tab. In Windows 2000 or NT, pressing these keys and then selecting Task Manager shows which applications and processes are running (see Figure 5.2). The problem you face is knowing which of these programs is valid and which is invalid. The blocking software can stop some hidden programs from running, but you must get to know your computer to understand what should and should not be running, which is a difficult process.

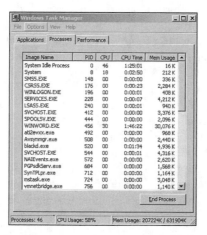

Figure 5.2   Windows 2000 Task Manager.

Spyware could potentially violate the Federal Trade Commission Act because it collects personal information and misrepresents its practices to the public. This applies to companies that collect information online or offline. The government has already taken steps to limit how companies can collect information without consumer knowledge with laws such as the Children' Online Privacy Protection Act (COPPA) and the Gramm-Leach-Bliley (GLB) Act. The problem, as we mentioned in earlier chapters, is enforcement of these laws. With millions of site available in the U.S. and around the world, it will be a great challenge to track use and enforce the laws. Part of the responsibilities of the FTC in the U.S. is to prohibit unfair and deceptive acts and practices in all industries, and Internet use falls under this jurisdiction.

Government Threats

The most significant threat the government poses in the realm of illegal activity is the lack of intervention that governments around the world have made in cybercrime. Even though several laws that have passed in some countries, such as the U.S. and Australia, and in Europe have made progress, the average consumer is still faced with threats to her privacy and security on many fronts with little or no help from law enforcement agencies. The right to anonymity in the online world is, of course, desired by everyone, but this anonymity does help criminals hide their activities from the average consumer. Government intervention is slowly making its way into cybercrime cases, such as when U.S. courts have issued rulings requiring chat rooms or e-mail forums to reveal the names of people who have posted anonymous messages. However, some of these cases have been overturned, and the government must find its way through new precedents every time a cybercrime case is brought into court.

As we have seen in recent international cases, such as with the Russian hackers in 2001 who stole bank information, extraditing criminals for cybercrimes is next to impossible. The FBI estimates that more than one million credit card numbers have been stolen from e-commerce Web sites in 2000 and 2001 from hacker groups in Russia and the Ukraine. The FBI's National Infrastructure Protection Center (NIPC) was the main task force in tracking these thefts. The two alleged network intruders, identified as 20-year-old Alexey Ivanov and 25-year-old Vasiliy Gorshkov, were recently indicted on counts of conspiracy, wire fraud, and violations of the Computer Crime and Abuse Act. The FBI and Department of Justice got a lot of information about the Russian and Ukrainian hacking of U.S. sites during this investigation. The FBI could not extradite the hackers, so it had to lure them to the U.S. with job offers and then arrest them. The great lengths the FBI had to go to to arrest these hackers is evidence of the weak cooperation between countries in tracking down hacking incidents.

Government-Sanctioned Hacking

A new threat facing consumers in an indirect way is hacking between governments. This type of illegal activity has become widely known within the past year based on a number of viruses, worms, and hacking groups that can be traced back to specific countries. The incident of the Russian hackers was not tied to the government, but it does display a lack of action on the part of many governments around the world to suppress illegal cybercrime activity. Some of the most dangerous worms and viruses have been linked to China in recent cases. The Code Red worm in July and August 2001 is estimated to have caused about $2.6 billion of damage and is linked to Chinese hackers. In other recent cases, Chinese hackers have attacked U.S. government information systems, including the White House and U.S. embassies around the world, in the new war in cyberspace. Chinese military writings have announced that the People's Liberation Army is developing information warfare capabilities designed to attack and destroy technology and communications systems. The FBI's NPIC has sent out alerts based on the monitoring of Chinese Web sites and chat rooms that are proponents of denial-of-service and e-mail attacks and disruptions of service against what they perceive as anti-Chinese governments and Web sites.

In most cases, a government does not take responsibility for such hacker attacks. Also, many governments do not attempt to stop such hackers, and some even covertly fund or assist in such attacks. The problem with tracking such connections between governments and hacker groups is the anonymity that we cherish with Internet use. In one case, Web sites for the U.S. Department of Health and Human Services, the Department of Labor, and the White House Historical Society were defaced with images of the Chinese flag and Weng Wei, the Chinese pilot who died in a crash between an American plane and a Chinese plane. A survey by the Web site China.com that found 85% of respondents were in favor of organized attacks against the United States.

By no means is it just China that has hackers targeting other countries. Numerous Chinese Web sites have been vandalized by American hackers in retaliation of Chinese hacking, and the U.S. has made no concerted effort to track these attackers.

Hacker Prosecution

As hacker attacks increase, the U.S. government is slowly making progress in prosecuting hackers who steal personal information. Table 5.4 shows a number of cases that are in the process of being tried.

Table 5.4 U.S. Cases for Prosecution

Computer Crimes Case Chart[1]	Interest Harmed[2]	Estimated Dollar Loss	Target[3]	Perpetrator Charged?[4]	Geography	Punishment[5]
U.S. v. Osowski (N.D. CA) August 20, 2001	C	6.3M	Private	No	TBD	TBD
U.S. v. Ivanov III (E.D. CA) August 16, 2001	C, I, A	Unknown	Private	Yes	TBD	TBD
U.S. v. Turner (N.D. OH) August 7, 2001	C, I, A	Unknown	Public	No	TBD	TBD
U.S. v. Diekman II (C.D. CA) August 1, 2001	—	Unknown	Private	No	TBD	TBD
U.S. v. Carpenter (D. MD) July 24, 2001	C, I, A	Unknown	Private	No	TBD	TBD
U.S. v. Brown (N.D. OH) July 6, 2001	C, I, A	Unknown	Private	No	TBD	TBD
U.S. v. Ivanov II (C.D. CA) June 20, 2001	C, I, A	Unknown	Private	Yes	TBD	TBD
U.S. v. McKenna (D. NH) June 18, 2001	C, I, A	13K	Private	No		6-month sentence; pay $13,000
U.S. v. Oquendo (S.D. NY) June 13, 2001	C, I, A	60K	Private	No		27-month sentence; pay $96,000

Table 5.4   Continued

Computer Crimes Case Chart[1]	Interest Harmed[2]	Estimated Dollar Loss	Target[3]	Perpetrator Charged?[4]	Geography	Punishment[5]
U.S. v. Ivanov (D. CT) May 7, 2001	C, I, A	Unknown	Private	Yes	TBD	TBD
U.S. v. Sullivan (W.D. NC) April 13, 2001	I, A	100K	Private	No		24-month sentence; pay $194,000
U.S. v. Morch (N.D. CA) March 21, 2001	C	5K	Private	No		36 months probation
U.S. v. Ventimiglia (M.D. FL) March 20, 2001	I, A	209K	Private	No		60 months probation; pay $233,000
U.S. v. Dennis (D. Alaska) January 22, 2001	A	Unknown	Public	No		6-month sentence; pay $5,000
U.S. v. Sanford (N.D. TX) December 6, 2000	C, I, A	45K	Private	Yes	Yes	60 months probation; pay $45,000
U.S. v. Torricelli (S.D. NY) December 1, 2000	C, I	Unknown	Private, public	Yes	TBD	TBD
U.S. v. Diekman I (C.D. CA) November 7, 2000	C, I	23K	Public	No	TBD	TBD

Table 5.4   **Continued**

Computer Crimes Case Chart[1]	Interest Harmed[2]	Estimated Dollar Loss	Target[3]	Perpetrator Charged?[4]	Geography	Punishment[5]
U.S. v. "cOmrade" (S.D. FL) September 21, 2000	C, A	41K	Public	Yes		6-month sentence
U.S. v. Gregory (N.D. TX) September 6, 2000	C	1.5M	Private	Yes		26-month sentence; pay $154,000
U.S. v. Zezov et al. (S.D. NY) August 14, 2000	C	Unknown	Private	Yes	TBD	TBD
U.S. v. Lloyd (D. NJ) May 9, 2000	I, A	10M	Private	No	TBD	TBD
U.S. v. Davis (E.D. WI) March 1, 2000	C, A	Unknown	Public	Yes		6-month sentence; pay $8,000
U.S. v. Iffih (D. Mass.) February 23, 2000	C, A	Unknown	Public	No	TBD	TBD

1. Colloquial case name (district), press release date
2. Confidentiality = C; Integrity = I; Availability = A
3. Private, public, or threat to public health or safety
4. Juvenile, group, or international
5. Sentence; fine, forfeiture, or restitution

The appropriate legislation is not in place to address all these cases. Legislators have been notorious for falling behind in addressing the way technology has affected criminal activity; they hope to apply the same old laws to attacks from cybercriminals. Urging companies to be more vigilant and implement security measures has failed in addressing new attacks against consumers and businesses as is proven by the numerous cases that go to trial and never send anyone to jail, or the numerous cases that can't even make it to court because the laws being broken are too vague or do not exist.

The U.K. is one of the few countries that has passed reasonable laws against hackers. In 2000, the U.K. passed the Terrorism Act of 2000; if a hacker endangers the life of the public through breaking into a computer system, he will be deemed a cyberterrorist and punished under the anti-terrorism law as a normal terrorist would be. The police can interpret how violent the break-ins are and whether they are terrorist acts. The U.S.-based Center for Strategic and International Studies (CSIS) warns that there could be a future cyberarms race, and the rise of terrorist groups will be Internet criminals. As we saw recently in the attacks on the World Trade Center, terrorists are using Internet message boards, Web sites, and encrypted data and images to transmit information to their people all over the world. The ease of use and availability of Internet communications helps businesses as well as terrorists. It would be easy for terrorists to learn hacking skills and then attack power utilities or other Internet-capable businesses that can have a dramatic impact on public safety.

Most countries make it illegal to hack through one law or another, but the lack of cooperation between countries enables political hacking to grow and become more detrimental. Subtle encouragement by some countries will definitely promote hacktivism in the future. It's easy to see how a company, becoming tired of being attacked by another country's hackers would launch an attack because it can't get any help from foreign governments. One company that did just that was the California ISP Conxion. It launched its own denial-of-service attack against hackers in mid-2001. Just detecting and securing your own sites might no longer be enough when governments and politically motivated groups become involved in hacking. Because laws do not currently provide the relief many people and businesses need, counter-hacking, which is as illegal as hacking, will be turned to as an alternative to getting attacked on a daily basis.

Identity Theft

Identify theft is the most damaging and personally invasive of new illegal cyberactivities. It is a crime in just about any country to steal someone's identify. The use of technology and the Internet has made it very simple to become someone else. When someone wrongfully obtains and uses another person's personal data that is *identity theft*. *Fraud* is very closely linked to identity theft in many cases. In the U.S., online databases carrying everything from your Social Security number to your driver license information, which can be hacked and stolen. When criminals try to become you, they steal as much information about you as they can, such as bank account or credit card numbers, telephone calling card numbers, your home address, your cell phone number, and your Social Security card number. All these bits of information can be used to re-create you for their own purposes, which in many cases is for financial gain. With access to all this information, someone can open a bank account, write bad checks, take money from your existing bank accounts, open credit cards, and ruin your financial standing. Running up huge debts and using your identify to commit a crime can even get you thrown in prison.

Even before the advent of sophisticated Internet technologies, identity theft was a problem. The easy ways to find information and cause identify theft have grown with Internet use. In the U.S., one of the most important pieces of information about you is your Social Security number, and probably next in line are your birthday and home address. With such information, a criminal can open credit card accounts, take out loans, and even get a driver's license. Crimes can be committed in your name after a criminal has this information.

Proving who you are and that you did not commit those crimes can be a problem. With credit card theft and usage, U.S. customers are responsible for only $50 of fraud because of the Truth in Lending Act. The problem with financial theft, though, is that your credit history is ruined and you will have a difficult time doing things such as getting a home loan or car loan. Cleaning up your credit report will be a nightmare and a time-consuming process.

Information is the key in doing battle against identity theft. For you to avoid being a victim, you should know how this can be done. Some of the things that can be done with your identity include

- Opening a credit card in your name with your Social Security number, home address, and phone number. Home address and phone number are easily found through public sources such as the phone company.
- Writing bad checks in your name.
- Opening bank accounts in your name.
- Getting a driver's license in your name with all the information the criminal now has.
- Getting a telephone or cell phone account that can be turned on.
- Filing bankruptcy in your name.
- Obtaining car and home loans in your name.

Here are the various ways identity thieves get your personal information:

- Finding your Social Security number in some fashion, whether by stealing your mail; going through your trash; or hacking into a database that has it, such as DMV records, a credit card company, or an employer database
- Stealing your wallet or purse, which invariably has a wealth of information about you

- Responding to a preapproved credit card application
- Changing your mailing address with the post office to forward your mail
- Obtaining a credit report on you and using that information for illegal purposes
- Obtaining information about you from your employer's human resources department
- Searching the Internet for any information about you, such as e-mail or news-group messages you have sent; hacking into companies that have information about you; and stealing such information
- Gaining information about you by having someone who works at your bank gather that information

Risk Reduction

After you understand the dangers posed by identity theft, your next step is to reduce your risk to such activity. As with any criminal activity involving personal information, keeping track of how you use information and how others use your information is the most important factor in keeping your data safe. But as we have mentioned already, after you let that information out, there isn't much you can do to protect it after it is entered into some company's database. As a consumer, you have no control over the security measures in place at your credit card company or at the Department of Motor Vehicles.

Some things you can control, however, include the following:

- Check your credit card statements every month and ensure that you receive one each month. Missing statements can mean that someone stole it or redirected your mail. Unknown charges on your card should obviously be investigated.
- Check with the post office if you stop receiving mail suddenly. Your mail should be delivered in a box that only you and the postal worker can access. Mail can be put on hold while you're on vacation by calling 800-275-8777.
- Password-protect your credit card accounts, bank accounts, and phone account using today's technology and services provided by these organizations. Changes can't be made unless you supply that password.
- In your wallet or purse, reduce the amount of cards you carry.
- Never give out personal information over the phone or to anyone who can't justify where they are from and what need they have for that information.
- Do not fill out Internet surveys or mailing surveys with personal information.
- Destroy any credit card receipts, bank account statements, credit card statements, brokerage statements, or other hardcopy material that is personally identifiable with a shredder before throwing it away.

- When signing up with new companies, such as when buying a product or getting a credit card, make sure the company is legitimate and has been in business a while. An easy way is to check with the Better Business Bureau (BBB).

- Check the privacy policy for any Internet site to which you submit personal information. It should have statements regarding sharing and security of your information. If there is no privacy policy, stay away!

- Check your credit report periodically to see what activity is happening and who is checking up on your credit status. If you are getting numerous credit card checks, perhaps someone is opening credit cards in your name. You can be charged up to $8.50 for a copy of your credit report. Any mistakes you see about yourself in your credit report should be followed up on immediately.

- When purchasing from a Web site, check the security measures as well as ensure that encryption is turned on (that little lock icon in the browser should be closed). Many sites use certificates, so check whether these certificates are for the legitimate company and not someone trying to impersonate that company. (We discuss certificates in detail in Chapter 8, "E-mail Security," and Chapter 9, "Securing Your Internet Transactions with SSL or Digital Certificates.") Many sites use certifications to prove their legitimacy, such as from BBB (www.bbbonline.org), the American Institute of Certified Public Accountants (www.cpawebtrust.org), and TRUSTe (www.truste.org). Never give out Social Security information online, and use only one credit card for all Internet purchases.

- Do not respond to a request for information through e-mail or Internet sites unless you know it is legitimate and how the information will be used and secured.

Recovering from a Theft

Even if you are vigilante about how you use your personal information and think you have been careful, you can fall victim to an identity theft. It's like a lightening strike—you never know when it might happen and sometimes there is just nothing you can do about it. If you become a victim, there are certain steps you can take to attempt to recover your life from the criminals. Several actions you can take include

- **Request that a fraud alert be placed on your account from the three major credit bureaus: Experian, Equifax, and Trans Union**—Making a statement to them that you have become a victim of identity theft lets them know that creditors should contact you about accounts and about making changes and canceling accounts. The credit bureau must give you the written results and a free copy of your report when disputes result in a change to your credit history.

- **Check the credit history from the time the activity started**—You can check for changes and inaccuracies in your credit report. Inquires on your account can be attempts to open accounts in your name. The Fair Credit Reporting Act (FCRA) establishes procedures for correcting mistakes on your credit record, and credit bureaus and organization that provided the information to the credit bureaus have to allow you to correct your information.

- **Contact all your creditors and notify them of what has happened**—These include credit card companies, phone companies and other utilities, banks, lenders, product companies where purchases have been made, and any other agencies where you do business or you see activity happening on your credit report. Provide your complete name and address and clearly identify each item in your report that you dispute. Also, be sure to give the facts and explain why you're disputing the information. You should also request the deletion or correction of the information.

- **File a report with the police in your community**—This will help you if crimes have been committed in your name and help you show proof of the theft to companies.

- **Write a letter to the collection agency telling them to stop contacting you and that you have no outstanding debt**—The Fair Debt Collection Practices Act prohibits debt collectors from using unfair or deceptive practices. You might still owe money, which will show up on your credit report, but you have some ability to stop debt collectors from harassing you when your identity has been stolen and give yourself time to resolve the problem before your credit is damaged further.

- **Add passwords to all your accounts**—This ensures that no further activity can occur on your accounts.

- **Check your bank statements and stop all check activity on your account.**

- **Cancel all credit and debit cards if they have been stolen**—Send letters to credit card companies via certified mail disputing charges.

- **Report your ATM card stolen within two business days**—You will be liable for only $50 loss. The Electronic Fund Transfer Act provides consumer protections for transactions involving an ATM or a debit card and limits liability. After two business days, but within 60 days, you can be responsible for up to $500 of withdrawals.

- **Check all brokerage accounts and ensure nothing has been changed in your accounts.**

- **If your Social Security number has been used, you can contact the Social Security Administration's Fraud Hotline**—Call 800-269-0271 and notify them of the incident. Check with the Department of Motor Vehicles to see whether any changes have been made to your diver's license or whether a new one has been issued.

- **Check whether a bankruptcy has been filed in your name with the U.S. Trustee Program in your region**—Information can be found at www.usdoj.gov/ust. You can provide information on the identity theft and file a complaint.

- **Contact the Internet Fraud Complaint Center**—Go to www.ifccfbi.gov/Default.asp to report online identity theft. A lot of information is available through this site.

- **Request a new Social Security number as a last resort**—Do this only as a last resort because it can cause a number of problems. A new SSN will not clear up your credit history and can cause problems in getting credit in the future. This can have very far-reaching effects, so try everything else first.

When you have determined that you are a victim, the previously mentioned actions should be taken immediately. In the U.S., the Federal Trade Commission is responsible for following up with identify theft. They can walk you through the process of recovering from a theft and put you in contact with the other necessary agencies. They can be reached at 877-IDTHEFT (438-4338). Next in line to contact are the three credit bureaus: Equifax at 800-525-6285, Experian at 888-397-3742, and Trans Union at 800-680-7289. These agencies are powerful and can help you track activity of using your name. This invasion of your privacy can have long-lasting effects on our credit history and reputation and should be resolved as soon as possible if you become a victim. You will have to work with government agencies and businesses over a period of time to clear up your name.

Legal Recourse

The Identity Theft and Assumption Deterrence Act of 1998 makes it a federal crime for someone to knowingly transfer or use the identification of another person with the intent to commit, or to aid or abet, any unlawful activity that constitutes a violation of federal law, or that constitutes a felony under any applicable state or local law. This law is used to prosecute identity thieves. Forms of identification include credit card number, cellular telephone number, name, Social Security number, and a host of other means. In the U.S., agencies that investigate identity theft include the Federal Trade Commission, U.S. Secret Service, Federal Bureau of Investigations, U.S. Postal Inspection Service, and Social Security Administration's Office of the Inspector General; federal cases are prosecuted by the U.S. Department of Justice. In addition to federal laws, each U.S. state has its own set of laws that address identity theft. Most state laws are listed in Table 5.5.

Table 5.5   State Identity Theft Laws

State	Law
Alabama	2001 Al. Pub. Act 312; 2001 Al. SB 144
Alaska	2000 Alaska Sess. Laws 65
Arizona	Ariz. Rev. Stat. § 13-2008

Table 5.5 **Continued**

State	Law
Arkansas	Ark. Code Ann. § 5-37-227
California	Cal. Penal Code § 530.5-530.7
Colorado	Colo. Rev. Stat. § 18-5-102
Connecticut	1999 Gen. Stat. § 53(a)-120(a)
Delaware	Del. Code Ann. tit. II, § 854
Florida	Fla. Stat. Ann. § 817.568
Georgia	Ga. Code Ann. § 16-9-121
Idaho	Idaho Code § 18-3126
Illinois	720 Ill. Comp. Stat. 5/16G
Indiana	Ind. Code Ann. § 35-43-5-4 (2000)
Iowa	Iowa Code § 715A.8
Kansas	Kan. Stat. Ann. § 21-4018
Kentucky	Ky. Rev. Stat. Ann. § 514.160
Louisiana	La. Rev. Stat. Ann. § 14:67.16
Maine	Me. Rev. Stat. Ann. § tit. 17-A, § 354-2A
Maryland	Md. Ann. Code art. 27, § 231
Massachusetts	Mass. Gen. Laws ch. 266, § 37E
Michigan	Mich. Comp. Laws § 750.285
Minnesota	Minn. Stat. Ann. § 609.527
Mississippi	Miss. Code Ann. § 97-19-85
Missouri	Mo. Rev. Stat. § 570.223
Montana	H.B. 331, 2001 Leg. (not yet codified)
Nevada	Nev. Rev. Stat. § 205.463-465
New Hampshire	N.H. Rev. Stat. Ann. § 638:26
New Jersey	N.J. Stat. Ann. § 2C:21-17
North Carolina	N.C. Gen. Stat. § 14-113.20
North Dakota	N.D.C.C. § 12.1-23
Ohio	Ohio Rev. Code Ann. 2913.49
Oklahoma	Okla. Stat. tit. 21, § 1533.1
Oregon	Or. Rev. Stat. § 165.800
Pennsylvania	18 Pa. Cons. State § 4120
Rhode Island	R.I. Gen. Laws § 11-49.1-1
South Carolina	S.C. Code Ann. § 16-13-500, 501
South Dakota	S.D. Codified Laws § 22-30A-3.1.
Tennessee	Tenn. Code Ann. § 39-14-150
Texas	Tex. Penal Code § 32.51
Utah	Utah Code Ann. § 76-6-1101-1104
Virginia	VA. Code Ann. § 18.2-186.3
Washington	Wash. Rev. Code § 9.35.020
West Virginia	W.Va. Code § 61-3-54
Wisconsin	Wis. Stat. § 943.201
Wyoming	Wyo. Stat. Ann. § 6-3-901
Guam	9 Guam Code Ann. § 46.80
U.S. Virgin Islands	14 VI Code Ann. § 3003

Resources

A number of governmental resources are available when you become a victim of an identity theft. Several of these resources include

- **Federal Trade Commission**—Its Web site is at www.ftc.gov or www.consumer.gov/idtheft. The FTC is the federal clearinghouse for identity theft complaints. It provides victims with information to help resolve the problems associated with identify theft. It also refers complaints to other agencies and can be reached at 877-IDTHEFT (438-4338) or Identity Theft Clearinghouse, Federal Trade Commission, 600 Pennsylvania Avenue, NW, Washington, D.C. 20580.

- **Office of Thrift Supervision (OTS)**—Its Web site is at www.ots.treas.gov. The OTS is the primary regulator of all federal and many state-chartered thrift institutions, including savings banks and savings and loan institutions. It can be reached at 202-906-6000 or at Office of Thrift Supervision, 1700 G Street, NW, Washington, D.C. 20552.

- **Department of Justice (DOJ)**—Its Web site is at www.usdoj.gov. The DOJ and its U.S. attorneys prosecute federal identity theft cases.

- **Federal Bureau of Investigation**—Its Web site is at www.fbi.gov, and it investigates cases of identity theft and assists in building cases for prosecution.

- **Internal Revenue Service**—Its Web site is at www.treas.gov/irs/ci. The IRS is responsible for administering and enforcing the internal revenue laws; if you have a problem with federal income tax returns, you can call 800-829-0433 or 877-777-4778.

- **U.S. Secret Service (USSS)**—Its Web site is at www.treas.gov/usss. The U.S. Secret Service investigates financial crimes, which can include identity theft.

- **Social Security Administration (SSA)**—Its Web site is at www.ssa.gov. The SSA can assign you a new SSN and handles problems with theft of your Social Security number. It can be contacted through the SSA Fraud Hotline at 800-269-0271 or by writing to SSA Fraud Hotline, P.O. Box 17768, Baltimore, MD 21235.

- **U.S. Postal Inspection Service (USPIS)**—Its Web site is at www.usps.gov/websites/depart/inspect. The USPIS is one of the federal law enforcement agencies that investigates cases of identity theft and is the law enforcement arm of the U.S. Postal Service.

- **U.S. Securities and Exchange Commission (SEC)**—Its Web site is at www.sec.gov. The SEC's Office of Investor Education and Assistance serves investor complaints of fraud or investment mishandling. Identity theft in connection with a securities transaction can be notified by writing SEC, 450 Fifth Street, NW, Washington, D.C. 20549-0213. You also can call 202-942-7040 or send an e-mail to help@sec.gov.

- **U.S. Trustee (UST)**—Its Web site is at www.usdoj.gov/ust. Someone filing a bankruptcy in your name would have to go through the UST. You can write to them to substantiate who you are and that your identity has been illegally used.

- **State and local governments**—Many state and local governments that have their own laws about identity theft can be reached through the state attorney general's office. A list can be found at www.naag.org, or the local consumer protection agency can be found at www.consumer.gov/idtheft/.

- **Credit bureaus**—The following are the three main bureaus:

    - **Equifax**—Its Web site is at www.equifax.com. To order your report, call 800-685-1111 or write P.O. Box 740241, Atlanta, GA 30374-0241. To report fraud, call 800-525-6285 and write P.O. Box 740241, Atlanta, GA 30374-0241.

    - **Experian**—Its Web site is at www.experian.com. To order your report, call 888-EXPERIAN (397-3742) or write P.O. Box 2104, Allen, TX 75013. To report fraud, call 888-EXPERIAN (397-3742) or write P.O. Box 9532, Allen, TX 75013.

    - **Trans Union**—Its Web site is at www.tuc.com. To order your report, call 800-916-8800 or write P.O. Box 1000, Chester, PA 19022. To report fraud, call 800-680-7289 or write Fraud Victim Assistance Division, P.O. Box 6790, Fullerton, CA 92634.

Fraud

Whereas identity theft can include fraud, fraud crimes can occur without someone becoming you by stealing all your personal information. Many fraud cases involve business crimes such as financial institution fraud, Internet fraud, fraud in the insurance industry, and international criminal activities, but fraud can just as easily happen to the average consumer. The anonymity of the Internet lets cybercriminals create any persona and even a fictitious company to fool people into thinking the fraud scheme is legitimate. Internet fraud has developed over the past several years as cybercriminals have gotten more access to people and information and become more sophisticated in their use of technology. Access to people makes fraud possible, and with the multiple ways of reaching people through the Internet, such as with chat rooms, e-mail, message boards, and Web sites, implementing fraud schemes to bilk consumers out of money and information is easy.

Fraud has been around longer than the Internet has existed, but with the advent of online communications, thousands of people can be duped at one time with the click of a mouse. The ease of use of technology makes it possible to set up a fake online e-commerce site and take advantage of people. In the U.K., a survey on cybercrime, called "Cybercrime Survey 2001," stated that two-thirds of U.K. firms suffered a form of cybercrime in 2000. The Confederation of British Industry (CBI) led this survey and is calling on the British government to centralize efforts to combat fraud on the Internet. The British Computer Misuse Act of 1990 does not include specific language to address failure of technology due to cybercrime. In all countries, online fraud results in loss of money by consumers but also affects the online industry as a whole by sowing mistrust in online applications and merchants.

Internet fraud cases can generally be categorized in several groups:

- **Auction and retail schemes**—Cybercriminals set up online auctions and online retail goods sites. After consumers makes purchases via credit cards, debit cards, or check, the site is shut down or counterfeit goods are sent out.

- **Business opportunity/"work-at-home" schemes**—Business opportunities have moved to the Internet, and consumers are guaranteed to make thousands of dollars very quickly. Consumers pay an upfront fee for some materials or registration, but nothing is ever delivered or the material is worthless.

- **Identity theft**—Using the online world to collect information about someone is easy and can be used to steal someone's identity, as discussed in the previous section.

- **Investment schemes**—Cybercriminals try to manipulate the market by falsifying a company's information to increase the stock price and then sell the stock. The opposite tactic can be used in short selling; the criminal disseminates information that negatively impacts a company's stock price.

The Internet Fraud Watch reported the following as the top 10 categories of Internet-related fraud complaints:

- Internet and online services that were misrepresented or never delivered

- General merchandise that was never delivered or not as advertised

- Auctions of items that were never delivered or whose value was inflated

- Pyramid and multilevel marketing schemes in which profits are made from fees to join the scheme rather than sales of actual items

- Business opportunities that were substantially less profitable than advertised

- Work-at-home schemes that sold materials to consumers with false promises to pay for the work performed

- Prizes and sweepstakes schemes in which prizes were never awarded

- Credit card offers in which consumers never received the promised cards

- Sales of self-help manuals that were misrepresented or never delivered

- Magazine subscriptions that were never delivered or for which the scheme's affiliation with legitimate publishers was misrepresented

Many fraud schemes are now feasible with the use of the Internet. The same theme runs through all fraud schemes: A promise of some service or goods is made in order for the consumer to pay out some money. The goods or services are never delivered, and the anonymity of the online world enables the cybercriminal to easily get away unscathed.

The Department of Justice established the Internet Fraud Initiative in 1999 to address online fraud. Criminal prosecutions of online fraud have been ongoing for several years. One such example is the prosecution of three men in Philadelphia on March 2, 2000 for their alleged roles in falsely offering the sale of Beanie Babies on the Internet. The products were never delivered, or incorrect products were sent. Another online fraud case charged four people in California in 1999 for sending out approximately 50 million e-mails that falsely advertised work-at-home opportunities for people. People paid a $35 fee but never received anything in return.

As with hacker activity, the lack of global cooperation just increases the risk consumers face. Defrauding consumers in other countries is easy because they have almost no legal recourse to track and prosecute the criminal due to the lack of international laws and online fraud cooperation. In the U.S., at least a national effort is being made to track and prosecute fraud with the Internet Fraud Initiative (IFI; at `http://www.usdoj.gov/criminal/fraud/Internet.htm`) and Internet Fraud Complaint Center (IFCC; at `http://www.ifccfbi.gov/`).

The IFI was approved in early 1999 and was started by the Department of Justice. The IFI is responsible for several initiatives:

- Researching Internet fraud and developing estimates
- Training prosecutors and agents on Internet fraud through the National Advocacy Center (NAC)
- Developing investigative and analytical resources to identify and investigate Internet-related fraud schemes along with the FBI/National White Collar Crime Center
- Providing and facilitating coordination among federal prosecutors and law enforcement agencies
- Advising prosecutors around the country and establishing a program of public education and prevention

The IFCC is a joint project of the FBI and the National White Collar Crime Center. The IFCC is responsible for federal, state, and local law enforcement agencies that receive online complaints, analysis of online schemes and crime trends, and compiling and notifying law enforcement of such schemes. Agents and analysts from the IRS and Postal Inspection Service are included in the group.

Telemarketing Fraud

Telemarketing fraud has been around for a very long time. It mainly deals with fraud over the phone. A fraudster calls you and tries to convince you to buy some goods or services that you will never receive, as with online fraud. Trying to get you to provide money to some charity is a favorite tactic of these criminals. They make money by either never delivering the promised goods or services or delivering inferior goods and services and pocketing the difference. Getting people to pay upfront for whatever the fraudster is selling is the simplest way for them to make money. They can then disappear with your money. By making the scheme seem legitimate—such as by dropping well-known names, such as FedEx or UPS, to deliver the products or using other well-known names to'compare their products with—these criminals develop a legitimate front that the consumer can believe in. Like online fraudsters creating a whole e-commerce site to seem legitimate, telemarketing fraudsters use a seemingly legitimate pitch. If the consumer falls for the scheme, the fraudster can continue contacting him for more money because they already have his trust.

Available consumer information is but a mouse click away in the online world. Legitimate and illegitimate telemarketers can easily purchase databases of consumer contact and preference information. Calling a consumer whose preferences are already known makes committing the fraud easier. Various telemarketing schemes can be used after the fraudster has your contact information. Several of these are as follows:

- **Charity schemes**—Fraudulent telemarketers take advantage of people's sense of community and desire to help others by pretending to be from a charitable organization. Some of these organizations even donate some of the money to a real charity so as not to be completely illegal.

- **Credit repair**—Marketers can obtain credit information on people and then try to sell them a service to repair their credit for an upfront fee. They even tell victims that they can get them a new credit card.

- **Cross-Border schemes**—Telemarketers go after victims in other countries. The schemes used are typically advance-fee loan schemes, investment schemes, lottery schemes, and prize-promotion schemes. This reduces the risk of the fraudster getting caught. As with online fraud, the cooperation between countries is lacking for prosecuting telemarketer fraud.

- **Investment and business opportunity schemes**—These schemes involve investing in such items as gemstones or rare coins that are sent in sealed containers that have nothing in them. They also convince the consumer that a failed or closed company is still in business, and the consumer invests money in the stock. Selling franchises that are either fake or of very poor investment value is another method of fraud.

- **Magazine promotion schemes**—Magazine subscriptions, although they seem very cheap, can be a money-making scheme for illegal telemarketers. A telemarketer contacts a victim and tells him he has won a prize but must subscribe to the magazine to claim it. The victim spends money on the subscription, which he might or might not get.

Resources

Few government organizations deal specifically with telemarketing fraud. The Federal Trade Commission's Consumer Response Center maintains numbers consumers can call with questions or complaints about all types of consumer fraud, including telemarketing fraud. The Consumer Response Center numbers are 202-382-4357 and 202-326-3128. The National Fraud Information Center (NFIC) does take calls from consumers about fraud and assistance in combating telemarketing fraud; it can be reached at 800-876-7060. The government does not really become as involved as it does with online fraud. As a consumer, you can request to be put on a list that telemarketers can't call. The Federal Trade Commission's Telemarketing Sales Rule requires that telemarketers comply with your request, and if they do not adhere to your request, they can be faced with civil litigation. Contact the Direct Marketing Association to request your name be put on the list at 212-768-7277 (New York) or 202-955-5030 (Washington, D.C.).

Summary

The threats individuals face through illegal means of compromising their personal information is greater today than it has ever been. The most obvious threat consumers face is from hackers. If you had asked a typical consumer 10 years ago what a hacker was, the odds of getting a clear answer would have been pretty slim. Today, though, consumers have been educated the hard way in understanding how the online world threatens them at the same time that it benefits them. With the increased functionality of the online community, hackers have numerous new access points to consumer information and methods of attacking consumers. The news stories of how thousands of credit cards get stolen or some inventive way a hacker stole and used someone's identity have brought awareness of technological crime into every household. A CIO KnowPulse poll of 450 chief information officers (CIOs) conducted in late 2001 found that most (88%) of the CIOs of major companies did not think existing security measures of government entities are skilled enough to handle cybercrime. Many believe better training and exclusive organizations dedicated to combating cybercrime are needed.

For consumers, the difficult threats to understand are how businesses can use the online world to illegally compromise your privacy. The legal means to exploit you on the Internet that were discussed in Chapter 4 might make it seem as if illegal access was not needed to your data, but businesses can further exploit you by taking advantage of technology and the lack of laws to find more inventive ways of using your information. The fraud capability that has developed with the Internet has expanded the reach of a small company that seeks to deceive people with some scam in a local community to anyone around the world. The ability of businesses to come and go on the Internet after they have collected consumer information and money is easy with the anonymity inherent in the online world.

The final serious threat consumers face that we have not really seen prior to the global economy is threats by governments that can target individuals, businesses, and governments. Anyone who is politically motivated or any government that needs a hidden weapon can use the Internet to target its enemies. How governments should secure their people in the online world is still open to debate. This is probably a problem that will not be solved anytime in the near future. The very question of governments taking an active role in protecting and policing cyberspace is still being debated. We have seen that both governments intervening and governments ignoring protecting the online community have drawbacks and can be damaging to consumers. Government monitoring and forceful compliance of security standards has privacy advocates up in arms, yet citizens need more protection than industry self-regulation has so far provided.

Collaboration between countries to track and capture cybercriminals has not happened, but we can see the need for it. It is also easy to see that too much control by the government can be stifling to the development of e-commerce. Where the middle ground is in government intervention when it comes to cybercrime is yet to be determined. But prosecution is necessary, and to have prosecution, we need practical, enforceable laws. We can't really say what exactly those laws should be in this book, but hopefully examining what is currently being done and what is proposed will shed some light on how the government should proceed.

The threats we face are because of a lack of understanding of the technologies being used by both professionals and consumers. A police squad to patrol cyberspace is necessary, but we do not have the right people trained and do not have cooperation between governments to build a unified force that can track attacks across the globe. Rapidly changing technology means constant learning and updates of knowledge, software, and hardware. The vision to see how technology will change the way we operate on a daily basis and anticipate future attacks is sadly lacking by individuals, businesses, and government.

III

Dangerous Territory: Protecting Your Privacy in the Online Environment

6

Understanding the Online Environment: Addresses, Domains, and Anonymity

T his chapter looks at the online environment itself. The Internet is probably the best medium for the delivery of public information to the online community. We'll examine the basics surrounding various Internet components such as IP addresses and DNS. A fundamental understanding of these technologies will help you see the connection between technology, how it is used, how it can be abused, and how it affects your privacy. This chapter also examines ways to remain anonymous on the Internet and a variety of methods and techniques to help you achieve anonymity.

Governmental efforts to protect consumer information have often been misdirected and have provided further compromises of user data and even more means of collecting user information. In early 2001, news leaked out about a Securities and Exchange Commission (SEC) plan to automate its monitoring of Internet chat rooms and message boards for fraudulent stock promotions and other get-rich-quick schemes. A large database of these postings would be created. The *Wall Street Journal* and the Associated Press published news about the new initiative, and the SEC's response was that the effort would merely automate surveillance techniques SEC agents were already using.

IP, Anyone?

Just as your street address is a pointer to you for the rest of the world, so is your Internet Protocol (IP) address. It is your identifier so that traffic can "find" you on the

Internet. Without a way of finding you on the Internet, you would not be able to receive e-mail or set up a home network. But, there is always a trade-off between usability and security in the online environment. Yes, if the world can find your Internet presence, they can attempt to gain information about you or hack into your computer systems. However, without a place in the online world, you'd be secure, but you wouldn't be able to perform many valuable functions.

As was mentioned in earlier chapters, home users have the ability to set up their own domain names and home networks and become miniature e-commerce sites. Within 5 minutes, we were able to register our book's Web site domain name, `www.privacydefended.com`, for a $70, two-year registration fee. The Domain Name System (DNS) consists of a directory, organized hierarchically, of all the domain names and their corresponding computers registered to particular companies and persons using the Internet. When you register a domain name, it is associated with the computer on the Internet you designate. We own this domain name and have set up our Web site and mail server. After you have your domain registered and set up, you can add machines to your network; for example, we could add `mail.privacydefended.com` or `ftpserver.privacydefended.com`. But, by setting up and registering your domain, you are required to give up information about yourself. The disadvantage is that this information is then made public to the rest of the world.

Anonymity becomes harder to maintain with each new function you use in the online environment. If you connect more than one system or set up a mini-network, you are making available more targets that can be attacked and hacked. When using services such as free e-mail or signing up for game sites and contests, you are making personal information available. Any Web site you use can potentially capture your browsing preferences and search requests. Without securing your system and using applications that can hide your identity, you are injecting personal information into the online world that will never go away. Data mining on the Internet is a full-time job for many corporations.

TCP/IP Addresses

The Transmission Control Protocol (TCP) and Internet Protocol (IP) were developed to enable computers to talk to each other over long-distance networks. IP is responsible for moving packets of data between nodes and systems, and TCP is responsible for verifying delivery from clients to servers. TCP/IP forms the basis of the Internet and is built into every common modern operating system (including all flavors of Unix, the Mac OS, and the latest versions of Windows). Every device connected to the Internet has an *IP address* associated with it. Think of an IP address as an unique identifier for every system connected to the Internet. IP addresses typically take the form of ###.###.###.###. An example is 192.168.1.100. Each one the of the four groups of numbers is a value between 0 and 255. This provides for numerous address that can be used by millions of computer systems.

Note

A computer on the Internet also can have more than one address or more than one domain name. An example of this is a scenario in which an Internet service provider (ISP) hosts Web sites for many home users. Because home users typically have small Web sites compared to corporations, it does not make sense to host each site on a separate computer. In all likelihood, the ISP probably uses a powerful machine configured to host many Web sites on one physical machine. This becomes a case in which multiple domains go back to one physical machine. The physical machine can have many domain/IP address combinations associated with it. But for our purposes, we will assume that given an IP address, there is a single machine with which it is associated.

To determine the IP address of your machine, use the following commands:

Operating System	Command
Windows 95 or 98	`winipcfg`
Windows NT or 2000	`ipconfig`
Unix-based systems	`ifconfig`

For example, in Windows 95 or 98, from the Start menu, select the Run option. Within the Run dialog box, type the command **winipcfg**.

If you are running a Windows NT or 2000 machine, open a DOS window by selecting Start, Programs, Accessories, Command Prompt. Within the DOS window, type the command **ipconfig**. The results are shown in Figure 6.1. Our IP address in this case is 10.1.1.101.

Figure 6.1   Finding the IP address on a Windows NT/2000 machine with `ipconfig`.

In this example, our IP address is 10.1.1.101, which is on our internal network. When you run these same commands, whether in Windows 98/NT/2000 or Unix, you will most likely see a different address. The second set of numbers, 255.255.255.0, is called a subnet mask. The *subnet mask* gives the machine further information on how the network is configured. The third set of numbers, 10.1.1.1, is the *default gateway*, which is the device on which traffic goes in and out of your network. In a mini-network environment, this usually is your home firewall machine. If you are using just one system to connect via a dial-up connection, this gateway typically is your machine's IP address. If you are using a DSL or cable modem, it is your ISP's gateway machine. Without a gateway IP address, you can't send traffic into and out of your system to the Internet.

Static and Dynamic Addresses

When the home user employs a modem to connect to the Internet via his ISP, a dynamic address is typically assigned to the machine for the duration of the connection. "Always-on" and broadband (cable modem or DSL) also have an IP address assigned to them, which is either dynamic or static. As the names imply, *static* addresses do not change, whereas *dynamic* addresses typically change each time the machine connects.

ISPs are assigned blocks of IP addresses that can be used by their customers. Typically, large ISPs, companies, and institutions have many addresses assigned or available to them. On the other hand, smaller ISPs and organizations have a fewer number of addresses available to them. Because IP addresses are finite in number (meaning you can't just create new addresses), they must be conserved.

A way to conserve addresses to the assign them on an as-needed basis. This applies directly to modem dial-up access. When a user connects to his ISP via modem, the ISP assigns an IP address from an available pool. The IP address is then associated with the user while the connection remains active (the *lease time*). After the user disconnects, the IP address is "released" and returned to the pool of available addresses. The next dial-up user can then be assigned that same address. This scheme of assigning IP addresses is referred to as the *Dynamic Host Configuration Protocol (DHCP)*. This enables the ISP to have more customers than IP addresses because the likelihood of all its customers dialing in at the same time is slim. DHCP is also used in many DSL and cable modem connections, as well as in corporate local area networks (LANs).

Static addresses, on the other hand, are directly configured on the machine itself. Statically addressed machines have the same IP address until they are specifically reconfigured to have a different address. Many cable modem companies assign you an IP address via DHCP, but after you get that address, it's in effect static. It does not change for months or even years. A home user with a cable modem connection typically can set up a Web server on a home machine with his theoretically static address and register that address when he registers a domain name. Then, he can have complete control over his home Web servers rather than hosting his personal Web page on his ISP's servers.

Even though DHCP can be used, that is not to say there is no record of who had a specific IP address at a specific point in time. ISPs normally keep logs of this type of information. In the early days, ISPs gave out this type of information without much hesitance; as long as the request seemed reasonable, the information was given out.

That is no longer the case. This type of data is no longer available for the asking; however, it is available with the proper legal authorization (court orders, subpoenas, and so on) to entities such as the government or law enforcement. An example of this is law enforcement requesting this type of data to aid in an investigation. One thing to keep in mind, though, is that the disclosure of your data is governed by the service agreement you agreed to when registering with your ISP. This information is usually in a term of services document or privacy policy document. The release, or non-release, of your data should be clearly described by the ISP.

To determine additional DHCP information, open a DOS window by selecting Start, Programs, Accessories, Command Prompt and then typing **`ipconfig /all`**. You see something similar to Figure 6.2.

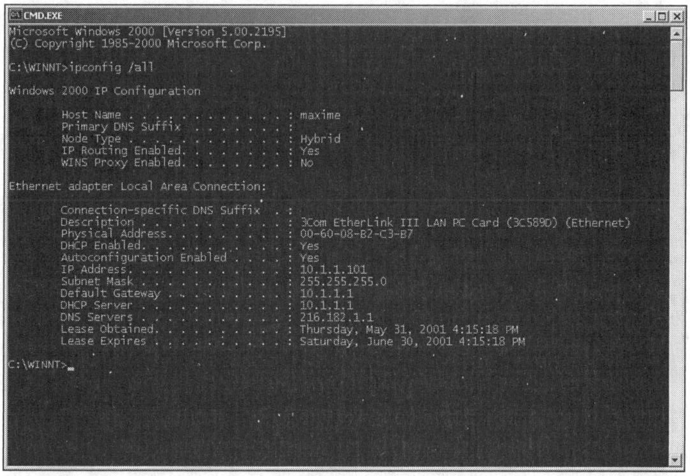

Figure 6.2   `ipconfig /all` output.

In this example, the command also gives you the address of the DHCP server and lease times associated with this address. Whenever an address is given out via DHCP, it is actually assigned with varying lease times. The lease times of DHCP addresses are configured by the network or system administrator.

So how do static and dynamic addresses affect your privacy on the Internet? Well, if you have the same address all the time (static), a definitive correlation or link can be made between you and your IP address. A static IP can be beneficial if you want to set up a Web server and domain name for home use. An address provided by your ISP is usually associated with a name, such as `cco2-absha-home.com`, so after you have a permanent address, you can register a domain name to that static IP address. When you set up your Web server, instead of using the given name of `cco2-absha-home.com`, in the browser, you could use `www.privacydefended.com`, for example, which is much easier for people to remember. The downside to having static addresses is that your system is always associated with that one IP address.

On the other hand, with dynamic addresses, you can't be sure of the linking between an IP address and a particular user. Each time you log on, your IP address can potentially be different. This makes setting up an easily accessible home Web server or network more difficult, but it also makes it harder for an attacker to track you down.

After a link can be made between IP address and user, there is an erosion of privacy. Web surfing and usage of data can then be correlated and linked to a specific person. (Chapter 7, "Understanding the Online Environment: Web Surfing and Online Payment Systems," discusses cookies as a means of storing this type of data and this linkage of user and IP address.)

One of the easiest methods for a single Web site to monitor a particular user's surfing habits on that site is to search its Web server logs for traffic from a specific IP address. In the case of static addresses, the Web site will know that all traffic from that address comes from "User A." Assuming the Web site operator has logging turned on, she can know exactly what User A clicked, at what time, and in what order. In the IIS Web server log shown in Figure 6.3, IP address 10.1.1.101 is surfing to Web server 10.1.1.103. Note the first two fields of each log entry: the date and time fields. Each Web page access can be tracked, and the time the user spent on that page can be determined. If it is an e-commerce site where the user has to enter sensitive information (name, address, credit card number, delivery instructions, and so on), a definitive link can be created. Now, imagine if that information is then passed along or even sold to another party.

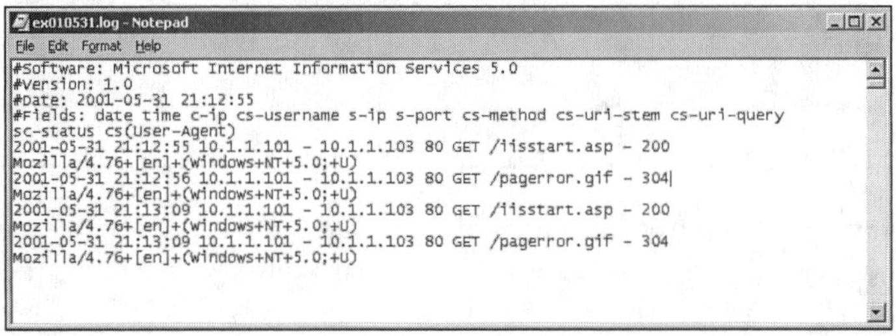


```
#Software: Microsoft Internet Information Services 5.0
#Version: 1.0
#Date: 2001-05-31 21:12:55
#Fields: date time c-ip cs-username s-ip s-port cs-method cs-uri-stem cs-uri-query
sc-status cs(User-Agent)
2001-05-31 21:12:55 10.1.1.101 - 10.1.1.103 80 GET /iisstart.asp - 200
Mozilla/4.76+[en]+(Windows+NT+5.0;+U)
2001-05-31 21:12:56 10.1.1.101 - 10.1.1.103 80 GET /pagerror.gif - 304
Mozilla/4.76+[en]+(Windows+NT+5.0;+U)
2001-05-31 21:13:09 10.1.1.101 - 10.1.1.103 80 GET /iisstart.asp - 200
Mozilla/4.76+[en]+(Windows+NT+5.0;+U)
2001-05-31 21:13:09 10.1.1.101 - 10.1.1.103 80 GET /pagerror.gif - 304
Mozilla/4.76+[en]+(Windows+NT+5.0;+U)
```

Figure 6.3 Web server log file.

Often, a user's IP address is sent to a third party when a Web site is visited. This usually happens when banner ad networks are involved. The exact amount of information related to a specific IP address varies greatly depending on the specific IP address (static versus dynamic) and the specific pieces of data being logged.

Your ISP's Security

The ISP is a wellspring of valuable information. After all, it arguably contains your most private data: 1) the link between your screen name/username and your real identity; 2) your payment information (typically, credit card data); and 3) access to your e-mail if you are using the ISP's e-mail service. Such information is usually held in computers in an ISP's office. Many users also have their personal Web sites hosted by the ISP.

For the reasons listed previously, ISPs have become a frequent target of hackers. Therefore, the security over the ISP's systems is just as important as, if not more important than, that of the individual's machine. An ISP should provide a secure location for its devices and machines, establish policies about confidentiality of customers' e-mails, and not use customer information for any other purposes. Internal threats are usually the most frequent sources of information compromise. ISPs should be privacy-aware and strive to offer privacy-enhancing capabilities to their customers. Some ISPs provide the store-and-forward function of data traffic and connectivity to the Internet, such as AT&T's Worldnet Service, whereas others such as AOL provide content and applications for consumers to use. The confidentiality of data or content contained in Web pages hosted by the ISP for its customers or e-mails in-transit is usually not the responsibility of the ISP. If you as the end user have taken all the appropriate steps to secure your systems, there might still be an element of exposure from the ISP if its systems are vulnerable.

When you evaluate the services of an ISP, consider its capability to secure itself. Frequently, that's easier said than done. ISPs are naturally reluctant to discuss their security breaches, so you'll have to rely on reputation and recommendations. Generically speaking, larger, more established ISPs have better security. That is not to say, though, that they will not experience security breaches, but they typically have more resources available to aid in the prevention and detection of such occurrences. They also might have more resources to devote to putting security policies and systems into effect. Smaller, mom-and-pop ISPs might not always have these resources available to them (for example, dedicated security staffs). On the other hand, the larger ISPs make for more attractive targets. However, regardless of the ISP chosen, it is important to at least note that a potential exposure point exists at the ISP level.

The Domain Name System

The Internet boom of recent years has contributed to thousands of domain name registrations at entities such as Network Solutions and Register.com. Prices for registering a domain name have fallen to as low as $20 per year. The abundance of choices available has made registering domain names a bit more confusing, but it is still a simple enough process for the average computer-savvy person. Domain names grew out of a need to translate the IP address scheme into a more understandable format. But before delving into the privacy issues associated with domain names, let's take a quick look at how it all works.

The Domain Name System enables the mapping of domain names and IP addresses. It also enables the easy conversion of system names (which are easy for humans to remember) to numerical IP addresses (which are required by machines but more difficult for humans to remember). An example is when a user types `http://www.privacydefended.com` in a Web browser. The machine must convert that text string to a numerical IP address (192.168.1.200) so that the request can be properly routed to the appropriate Web server. Therefore, a domain name is actually an alias for an IP address. Multiple domains can point to the same IP address, but a domain has only one IP address.

Registering a Domain

To claim domain names, you must register with a registrar. The bulk of domain name registrations made have been at Network Solutions (`http://www.networksolutions.com`), but a growing number of registrars are now appearing due to the ending of Network Solutions' monopoly over domain name registration. Register.com (`http://www.register.com`) is an example of another registrar. The Shared Registration System (SRS) prevents a domain registered at one registrar from being registered again at another registrar.

When a user decides to register a domain, she must provide data that might be considered sensitive, such as name, address, phone number, and e-mail address (see Figure 6.4). Additional information, such as who to contact for administrative, technical, and billing issues, also might be provided to the registrar. This information can either be fake or real. We'll look at why this is important after discussing the registration process.

Data supplied during domain registration is information most people are comfortable with disclosing to the registrar, but it is important to realize that this type of information is also available to the general public. So, even if you've chosen to have an unlisted phone number, for example, there is no such equivalent when it comes to domain name registrations. For home user registrations, people usually complete the application by providing their home addresses, as opposed to business registrations, where business addresses are provided.

DNS Information Retrieval

It's surprisingly easy for someone to retrieve your domain name information. There are multitudes of ways to retrieve this data via Web interfaces and programs. They all basically use the WHOIS program, which is essentially a database-like program that, when sent a domain name, responds with the corresponding registration data.

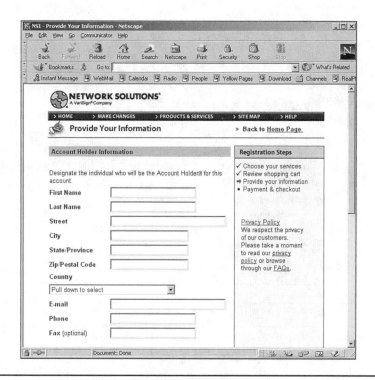

Figure 6.4   Network Solutions' domain name registration.

Because multiple registrars exist, a properly functioning WHOIS program first queries the shared domain registry to determine which registrar has reserved the domain. The program then queries that specific registrar's database for the correct domain information. Most—but not all—WHOIS programs do that automatically. As mentioned earlier, this information can be fake.

Several Web sites let you conveniently perform WHOIS queries:

- `http://www.networksolutions.com`
- `http://www.register.com`
- `http://www.betterwhois.com`

They all provide a convenient Web-based form in which the query can be made, as shown in Figure 6.5.

If the domain lookup you are performing involves domains that are not the typical .com, .net, and so on—for example, .co.uk (for an address in the United Kingdom)—you might have to query alternative databases. European-based queries should be directed to the Rèseaux IP Europèens Network Coordination Centre, commonly referred to as RIPE (`http://www.ripe.net`). Figure 6.6 shows the RIPE WHOIS domain name query Web site.

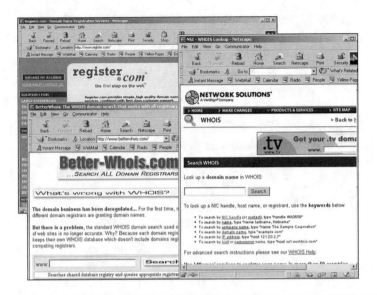

Figure 6.5   Registration sites.

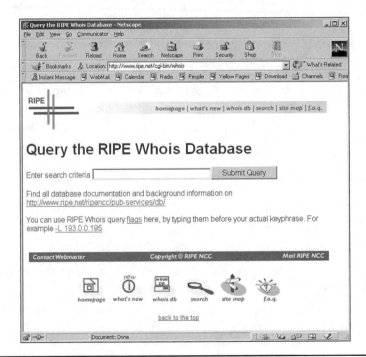

Figure 6.6   RIPE's WHOIS query Web site.

Asian-based queries should be directed to the Asia Pacific Network Information Centre, commonly referred to as APNIC (`http://www.apnic.net`). Figure 6.7 shows the APNIC WHOIS domain name query Web site.

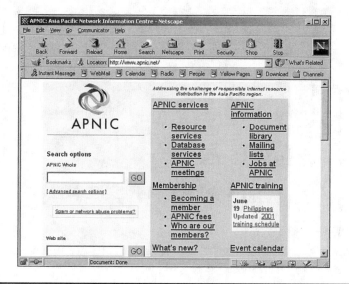

Figure 6.7   APNIC's WHOIS query site.

In addition, several other tools automatically query the appropriate database. Two such sites are Allwhois.com (`http://www.allwhois.com`), shown in Figure 6.8, and GeekTools (`http://www.geektools.com`), shown in Figure 6.9. Both are excellent sites from which to perform WHOIS queries.

The most convenient way to get WHOIS information is probably via the Web sites noted previously. However, the same information can be obtained by using any one of the many freeware, shareware, or commercial utilities that run on your PC. Most of the software download sites, such as Tucows (`http://www.tucows.com`), have these utilities available.

One of our favorites is Northwest Performance Software's NetScan Tools (`http://www.netscantools.com`), shown in Figure 6.10. The basic version is inexpensive, costing approximately $40. The application is actually a suite of utilities primarily aimed at the networking professional. Among many other things, it can perform WHOIS lookups, automatically querying the appropriate WHOIS database.

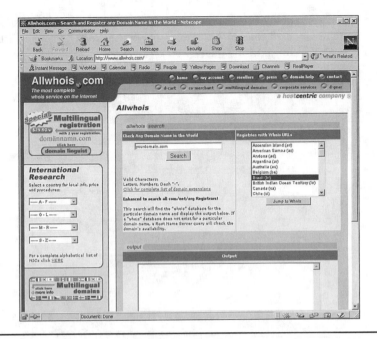

Figure 6.8   The Allwhois domain name query site.

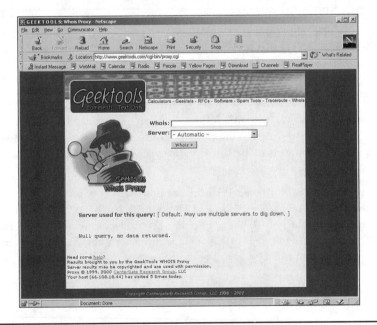

Figure 6.9   The Geektools domain name query site.

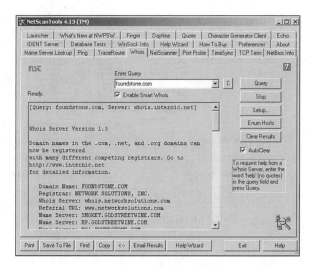

Figure 6.10   NetScan Tools' WHOIS query of foundstone.com.

Note that, so far, we have performed only WHOIS domain name lookups. You also can query a WHOIS database for information by means other than by domain. You can have it provide information about hosts, IP addresses, the registrant's name, and contact names. This is usually done by prepending the query with the appropriate query type, as shown in Figure 6.11, which shows the Network Solutions Web site. Table 6.1 lists the query types available on the Network Solutions WHOIS interface.

Figure 6.11   Advanced querying WHOIS information.

Table 6.1   **Query Types Available on the Network Solutions WHOIS Interface**

Query Type	What to Type	Type of Search
Handle	`handle WA3509`	Searches the database for information on the given *handle*—an identifier associated with each entity in the database. They typically appear next to a name in parentheses in all capital letters.
Name	`name lastname,` `firstname` or `name companyname`	Searches the database for information on the registered domain name. Multiple domain name listings are supplied if available.
Host	`host 121.23.2.7` or `host ns1.worldnic.com`	Searches the database for information on the given IP address or hostname.

All the queries can also be performed via a command-line WHOIS client in Unix. Windows-based operating systems do not come with a built-in WHOIS program. In Unix, the commands take the following form:

```
# whois "query-type search-text"@whois-server
```

where *query-type* can be the handle, name, host, mail, or domain (default); *search-text* is the text string the query should be made against; and *whois-server* is the registar's WHOIS server (for example, whois.networksolutions.com).

Here's an example:

```
[root@minimelin]# whois "domain foundstone.com"@whois.networksolutions.com
[whois.networksolutions.com]

Registrant:
Foundstone, Inc (FOUNDSTONE4-DOM)
   7 Century Drive
   Parsippany, NJ 07054
   US

Domain Name: FOUNDSTONE.COM

Administrative Contact, Billing Contact:
   McClure, Stuart (SM22550)  offsprung@HOME.COM
   26012 Marguerite Pkwy
   Suite H, #105
   Mission Viejo, CA 92692
   408-738-2852 (FAX) 949-367-1681
```

```
Record last updated on 06-Feb-2001.
Record expires on 10-Mar-2003.
Record created on 10-Mar-2000.
Database last updated on 25-Jun-2001 11:18:00 EDT.

Domain servers in listed order:

NS1.FOUNDSTONE.COM          206.135.57.173
```

Going in Reverse

Now that you have seen how IP addresses are used, let's try to go in reverse and see what data we can gather when the only information available is the IP address. A scenario where this might occur was illustrated earlier when you saw an IP address appearing in the Web server's log. A second scenario is when you see in your personal firewall logs only an IP address trying to contact your home system. If you find an IP address in your Web server log files or personal firewall log files, you can search for the owner using the IP and get contact information such as a phone number or e-mail address to learn more about the user(s) behind that IP address. (Recall the information you submitted when you registered your own domain name. Some of that information was contact phone number and e-mail address.) For corporate sites, finding this information is a frequent necessity to track down attackers who are launching exploits or port scans against your company firewall or Web server.

The administration and assignment of IP addresses in North America, South America, the Caribbean, and sub-Saharan Africa falls under the auspices of the American Registry for Internet Numbers (ARIN). RIPE and APNIC not only administer domain names for their respective countries, but they also provide IP registration services. By querying ARIN, you can begin to learn more about the IP address itself. Much like WHOIS searching, you can gather this information by using a Web interface over the Internet, using a Windows graphical client, or via the Unix command line.

The ARIN Web site (http://www.arin.net/whois) enables you to enter an IP address and determine the owner of it. Using ARIN, if we search for the owner of the IP address 216.182.6.84, we find it is owned by Tellurian Networks, as shown in Figure 6.12.

Note the range information that was returned in Figure 6.12. The IP address 216.182.6.84 falls in a range owned by Tellurian Networks: 216.182.0.0–216.182.63.255.

We can retrieve system owner information using NetScan Tools Pro (see Figure 6.13).

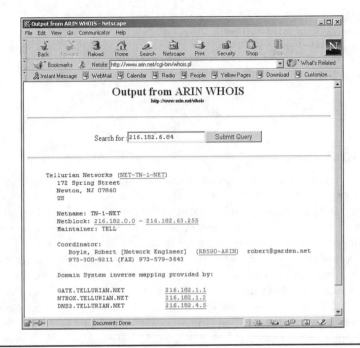

Figure 6.12   The Web interface to query ARIN via an IP address.

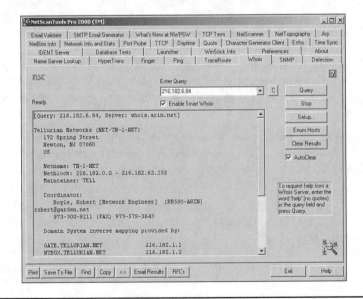

Figure 6.13   NetScan Tools—ARIN WHOIS information lookup for 216.182.6.84.

Using Unix, you can also determine the owner of an IP address with the built-in whois command. By specifying the IP address and specifying that site whois.arin.net, you can retrieve the contact information shown in the following code fragment. Note that in terms of syntax, it is almost identical to that of a whois query. However, instead of querying a WHOIS server like Network Solutions, we are querying ARIN (as indicated by the name after the @ symbol):

```
[root@minimelin]# whois "216.182.6.84"@whois.arin.net
[whois.arin.net]
Tellurian Networks (NET-TN-1-NET)
    172 Spring Street
    Newton, NJ 07860
    US
    Netname: TN-1-NET
    Netblock: 216.182.0.0 - 216.182.63.255
    Maintainer: TELL
    Coordinator:
       Boyle, Robert [Network Engineer]  (RB590-ARIN)  robert@garden.net
       973-300-9211 (FAX) 973-579-3643
    Domain System inverse mapping provided by:
    GATE.TELLURIAN.NET            216.182.1.1
    NTBOX.TELLURIAN.NET           216.182.1.2
    DNS3.TELLURIAN.NET            216.182.4.5
    Record last updated on 28-Feb-2001.
    Database last updated on 23-Jun-2001 23:00:43 EDT.
```

In most cases, it is unlikely that IP addresses can be traced all the way to an individual. You will usually find that registrations are traced to an ISP or a large corporation. After you try to contact the ISP, you will find it to be unresponsive, in another country, or incapable of tracking down the user because dynamic IP addresses are used.

Protecting Your Contact Information

After performing several of these searches, you can begin to see the wealth of information stored in these ARIN and WHOIS databases. As illustrated previously, an abundance of tools is available that can be used to gather this information. As you take a look at the data being requested and being displayed, you should come to the conclusion that you can at least hide this data a bit more. For example, when registering the domain name, a fictitious or innocuous name can be provided. Your mailing address can be a post office box, and e-mail addresses provided can be from one of the many available free e-mail sites on the Internet, such as Hotmail (http://www.hotmail.com) or Yahoo! (http://mail.yahoo.com).

Note
Be sure you log in to free e-mail accounts on a monthly basis at a minimum. Some of these free e-mail sites close down mail accounts if they remain inactive for long periods of time.

If you do not want others to know that information, employ techniques such as pseudonyms, post office boxes, and so on to help maintain your privacy.

Anonymity on the Internet

One of the goals of this book is to show that even though an element of privacy is lost when conducting activity on the Internet, you can also take some steps to maintain an element of anonymity. This next section looks at some of these steps, covering items such as anonymous surfing, anonymous remailers, and various shareware and commercial products that help maintain anonymity on the Internet. The majority of these tools are either free or low cost, making them attractive to the end user.

Anonymous Surfing

Anonymous Web surfing was developed to help protect consumers who give up private information, both knowingly and unknowingly. A variety of products available on the Internet enable anonymous surfing. Typically, these products enable you to visit Web sites without leaking information such as originating IP address, geographical location, browser type and operating system, installed plug-ins, screen height and width, local time zone, and previous site visited. To illustrate the amount of information you divulge when visiting a site, visit a "Privacy Analysis" page at `http://privacy.net/anonymizer`. The page shows you exactly how much information you are leaking when you are surfing the Web. Many Web sites log and compile this information with the hopes of better, more targeted marketing, or even with the hopes of selling to third parties such as marketing firms and advertisers.

Instead of surfing the Internet directly from your Web browsers, you can employ *surrogates* or *proxies* to perform that function for you. These are also referred to as *anonymizers*. The anonymizer surfs on your behalf: You request a page via the anonymizer, the anonymizer retrieves it, and then the anonymizer displays it on your machine (see Figure 6.14). The log entries on the visited Web server will be that of the anonymizer, not your IP address. Anonymizers also are a way around the use of cookies. *Cookies*, which track who is visiting a Web site, store information about your preferences on a particular site and can be used for targeted advertising.

The next section examines some of the more common anonymizers used today.

Anonymizer.com

`http://www.anonymizer.com`

One of the most popular anonymizers in use today is Anonymizer.com, shown in Figure 6.15. Users can surf the Internet for free by typing in the desired URL on the home page. They can then eliminate the pop-up banner ads and built-in delays by subscribing to the service (approximately $50/year). Other useful features available with the paid service are Safe Cookies and URL Encryption.

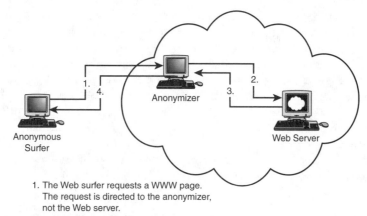

1. The Web surfer requests a WWW page. The request is directed to the anonymizer, not the Web server.

2. The anonymizer sends the Web page request to the WWW server. The WWW server does not know who is requesting the page.

3. The Web page is sent to the anonymizer.

4. The anonymizer forwards the page to the anonymous surfer.

Figure 6.14   Diagram of an anonymous surfer.

Figure 6.15   The initial Anonymizer.com home page.

Safe Cookies enables Anonymizer.com to accept, encrypt, and then present cookies to the end user. Cookies from the original Web site are encrypted so that they can't be disclosed to anyone watching network traffic. The cookie is also deleted at the end of the session so that no trace of visiting that Web site exists on the user's machine. Companies that read cookies for information about you will not be able to do so. Plus, browser exploits that allow an attacker to view your cookies can't be exploited with the use of technologies such as Safe Cookies. It also renders any type of vulnerability related to cookies ineffective because the cookies are encrypted and can be understood only by the Anonymizer.com system. However, one problem with using anonymizer sites and technology such as Safe Cookies is the speed of your connection and browsing, which can slow down noticeably.

URL Encryption enables the encryption of the URL you are visiting so that anyone watching network traffic will not be able to discern the Web site address. Most traffic on a network is sent in clear text, so anyone who is on your local network can watch the traffic coming into and out of your computer. For example, without this feature, an unencrypted Anonymizer.com URL looks like this:

```
http://anon.user.anonymizer.com/http://www.yahoo.com
```

However, with this feature enabled, the URL you are browsing would be unreadable to someone watching network traffic and would look something like this:

```
http://anon.user.anonymizer.com/cipher:KisUpoeYUa/=ecDjsj29Gleui4&qew
```

With this feature in effect, it's very difficult for your ISP, network administrator, or other people on your network to determine which sites you are visiting.

After you have submitted the Web site request, Anonymizer.com carries out your HTTP request, and you surf the Web site anonymously. Figure 6.16 shows the anonymous connection.

Zero Knowledge's Freedom 2.0

```
http://www.freedom.net
```

Another widely used product is Zero Knowledge's Freedom 2.0, a suite of features that help you protect your online security and privacy. The free services include a Personal Firewall, Form Filler, Cookie Manager, Ad Manager, and Keyword Alerting. The premium ($50) service of the software enables anonymous browsing and untraceable, encrypted e-mail. It captures messages you send and replaces the return addresses with your nym's (pseudonym's) return address. The message is encrypted and sent via the Freedom Network. If the recipient responds, the Freedom Network encrypts the message and routes it back to your true e-mail address. Freedom uses nyms to allow for different online identities. Each identity can be used while performing different online activities. For example, while in a sports-related chat room, you might adopt a sports nym, and when participating in a chat room related to online trading, you could use another nym.

Figure 6.16 Anonymous Web surfing.

The anonymous browsing feature of Freedom builds "private access routes through the Internet" to allow you to surf without being tracked. Freedom automatically sends data through a series of machines it refers to as the Freedom Network. The intermediary machines in this network do not know the original source or final destination of data packets they receive. They merely forward data along a series of machines in the Freedom Network. Similar to Anonymizer.com, the final Web server has no idea as to the original requestor of the Web page.

There are several drawbacks to Freedom, however, including

- Web browsing seems slightly slower.
- It doesn't work over an AOL connection.
- It doesn't work on machines not running Windows 9x.
- It won't work behind some firewalls.
- It is theoretically possible that your nym and your true identity are reconcilable.

Ponoi

http://www.ponoi.com

Ponoi is a relatively new service that also enables anonymous Web surfing, as well as secure password storage and secure file storage. Traffic to Web sites is encrypted such that users on the local network can't watch network traffic. Like other tools in this section, the Ponoi service enables you to surf the Internet without the destination knowing anything about you, and it prevents your ISP and local network administrator from knowing your surfing habits. Aside from the control panel window, shown in Figure 6.17, the service is pretty transparent. The Ponoi system is not an application you install on the local machine, but rather a service that is accessible from any machine on the Internet. At this point in time, it is compatible only with Microsoft's Internet Explorer.

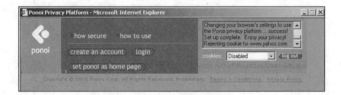

Figure 6.17   Ponoi control panel.

SafeWeb

http://www.safeweb.com

SafeWeb is another anonymous surfing service. Similar to the other services, SafeWeb contacts the destination Web server on your behalf. The service also replaces the URL address bar in your browser window and encrypts all traffic between you and the SafeWeb service (note the Netscape lock icon in Figure 6.18). If the Web site visited allows or calls for encrypted traffic, the same lock icon also appears in the SafeWeb address bar. Therefore, your traffic is not disclosed to your ISP or network administrator. SafeWeb's advanced security options also enable additional privacy settings. The ability to perform functions such as preventing pop-up windows and filtering cookies as well as disabling Java applets and certain types of plug-ins is also available. Figure 6.19 shows advanced configuration options within SafeWeb.

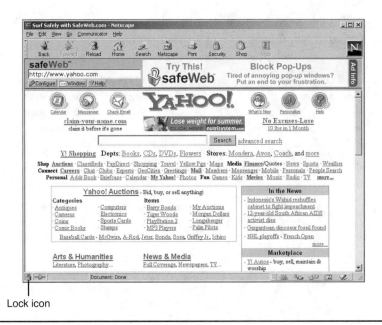

Lock icon

Figure 6.18   SafeWeb's browser window.

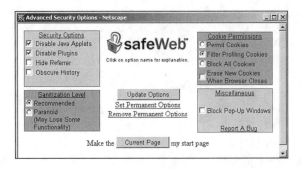

Figure 6.19   Advanced security options within SafeWeb.

Table 6.2 lists several anonymous services. For more information and a complete listing of services, see the site `http://webveil.com/matrix.html`.

Table 6.2   **Partial List of Anonymous Services**

Proxy Service/Application	Description
ORANGATANGO ■ Protocols: HTTP, HTTPS ■ Cookies: Managed remotely ■ Scripting: Filtering options ■ Encryption: SSL ■ Cost: Free; advertising supported	Now available as a beta service, the Orangatango VirtualBrowser is a new take on the Web-based proxy but does not bill itself as an anonymizer. Rather, it is a browser application delivered via the Web that provides some privacy functionality along with other features. No registration is required, but you can preserve data from session to session. It is competitive with SafeWeb in the handling of dynamic content and objects embedded in a Web page, but it offers much more than mere privacy protection. It has taken the Privacy Policy to the next rung, posting a nondisclosure agreement/privacy contract that could represent a new standard.
SAFEWEB ■ Protocols: HTTP, HTTPS ■ Cookies: Options ■ Scripting: Filtering options ■ Encryption: SSL ■ Cost: Free; advertising supported	Introduced in October 2000, this full-service, Web-based anonymous proxy service is straightforward but is much more versatile than a standard anonymizing proxy. It boasts the capability to render you anonymous without "breaking" dynamic or rich content such as DHTML, streaming media, Java applets, and animations like Flash. No registration is required; it's free.
FREEDOM ■ Protocols: HTTP, HTTPS ■ Cookies: Options include a cookie manager ■ Scripting: Allowed ■ Encryption: Yes ■ Cost: $49.99 for five 1-year tokens	A client application used to connect all your Web traffic through the Freedom network of servers. A free trial is no longer offered, but the purchase price provides you with five tokens; each token purchases one nym. The double-blind purchasing method of tokens attempts to separate the identity of the purchaser from the user of the tokens so that even Zero Knowledge has "zero knowledge" of who you are. Zero Knowledge honors a money-back guarantee if you're not satisfied. Service includes e-mail and newsgroup anonymity.

Table 6.2 **Continued**

Proxy Service/Application	Description
SiegeSurfer • Protocol: HTTP • Cookies: Option to block or allow • Scripting: Allowed • Encryption: Yes • Cost: Approximately $5 per month purchased in 3-, 6-, or 12-month increments. A one-year plan is discounted.	Completely Web-based anonymizing proxy. A free five-day trial version is offered with a registered e-mail address.

Anonymous Remailers

Just as you can "privatize" your Web surfing, you can privatize e-mail. Remailers enable you to send mail without revealing your true identity, much like sending a postcard in regular mail without a return address or meaningful postmark. These remailers used to be merely run as services on machines but now are also available via Web-based interfaces. It is also important to note that not all communication requires this amount of security. The appropriate degree of security depends on the sensitivity and volume of personal data communicated and how paranoid the consumer is about the e-mail she sends. The availability of remailer services can be sporadic at times. Remailers frequently go offline and come back up under different names and addresses.

How Do They Work?

Remailers typically accept a message and then strip out all identifying information related to the sender. Data such as e-mail ID and name is removed and replaced with dummy data (for example, the e-mail ID becomes anon123@anonymous.remailer.com). After identifying information is stripped out, the e-mail is then sent to the intended recipient with the anonymous remailer's information. The remailer informs the sender that the e-mail has been sent under the new identity (anon123@anonymous. remailer.com), and the recipient of the e-mail receives a message that has no discernable information as to its original sender. Identifying information can be given away in the body of the message, but that would be a blunder on the sender's part, not the remailer's.

Log information associated with the mail program itself is almost never kept. Frequently, these machines are located in foreign countries where U.S. law enforcement has no jurisdiction.

Pseudo-Anonymous Versus Truly Anonymous Remailers

The scenario described previously is actually that of a *pseudo-anonymous* remailer. After all, the operator of the remailer knows your true e-mail address. In cases like this, your privacy and security are only as good as the operator's capability to secure its systems against unauthorized disclosure. You are also relying on the operator's integrity to protect those records. The advantage of using this type of remailer is that it is convenient and easy to use. Usenet users frequently use pseudo-anonymous remailers to hide their true identities. (Usenet is a worldwide distributed discussion system that consists of a set of newsgroups that allow posting and reading of articles and files.) The following sections discuss two types of truly anonymous remailers.

Cypherpunk Remailers

Truly anonymous remailers do not contain your identity information at all. These operators could not divulge your identity because that information is not even kept on the remailer system! These *cypherpunk* remailers send messages without the anonymized return addresses, so there is no way for the recipient to reply to the message. Messages sent to the remailer are encrypted; the remailer then decrypts the message (which includes the destination address), strips off all identifying data, and then sends it to the final destination. Frequently, multiple remailers are used to provide a higher level of anonymity (see Figure 6.20). This *chaining* of remailers prevents even the remailers from knowing who the original sender is. These remailers accept messages that have been encrypted with its publicly available PGP key.

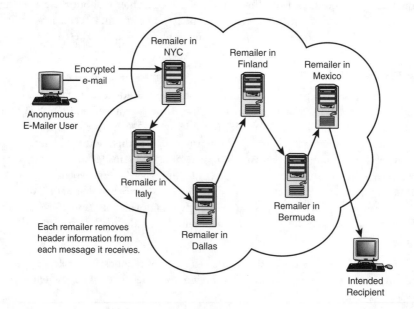

Figure 6.20   Anonymous chaining of remailers.

Cypherpunk remailer messages need to follow a specific format, as follows:

```
============
::
Anon-To: news.reporter@nbc.com">news.reporter@nbc.com
Latent-Time: +0:00

##
Subject: My Company Dumps Toxic Waste

I'm writing this anonymously because I don't want to lose my job.
My company has, for the past three years...
============
```

The previous message is cut and pasted into PGP and encrypted with the chosen remailer's key, say gretchen@neuropa.net. A PGP key allows only the receiving party to decrypt the message and read it:

```
============
-----BEGIN PGP MESSAGE-----

Version: PGP 2.6x
hQCMA8asoPEC0e2BAQP9GqR2aXN0stRq8eJW2QVubioR0gO7Ue0AOL/rFdnxXknC
YPpe2X2TKlcvd961+lhe9w2Y8vo3JcBYYBifTJRwmMjnXLagCU4Mhh0VZtk/QXMZ
/FLeJWi67qsb45a2mNw0/Q8eXHKfOQyHcmEQ7cg/bq4Xz6LusfxBHF8zsojVOgal
8RVRtr9drjBlOzJvWxaq7LrKidME6q0tM7pRiLN5dvVBon2NKlmpJI6vAFjyi8ma
f5Bg6Zor+PMxcm3EmuWbjLEiOu5USrTgU4OiaC7PHF9INxwXuKmdNz/JprgOc0c6
6s6Rvb0o6rsvlwqPKw==
=ICz/
-----END PGP MESSAGE-----
============
```

Finally, the user has to append a directive to the top of the encrypted message, making it look like this:

```
============
::
Encrypted: PGP

-----BEGIN PGP MESSAGE-----
Version: PGP 2.6x

hQCMA8asoPEC0e2BAQP9GqR2aXN0stRq8eJW2QVubioR0gO7Ue0AOL/rFdnxXknC
YPpe2X2TKlcvd961+lhe9w2Y8vo3JcBYYBifTJRwmMjnXLagCU4Mhh0VZtk/QXMZ
/FLeJWi67qsb45a2mNw0/Q8eXHKfOQyHcmEQ7cg/bq4Xz6LusfxBHF8zsojVOgal
8RVRtr9drjBlOzJvWxaq7LrKidME6q0tM7pRiLN5dvVBon2NKlmpJI6vAFjyi8ma
f5Bg6Zor+PMxcm3EmuWbjLEiOu5USrTgU4OiaC7PHF9INxwXuKmdNz/JprgOc0c6
6s6Rvb0o6rsvlwqPKw==
=ICz/
-----END PGP MESSAGE-----
============
```

The user then mails the encrypted message (double colons and all) *not* to the intended recipient but instead to the remailer's address: gretchen@neuropa.net. This arrives at the remailer, where it is eventually processed, decrypted, and mailed to news.reporter@nbc.com appearing to have come from "Anonymous" at nobody@neuropa.net. In this manner, a message is sent encrypted, so someone capturing traffic on your local network can't read it; all your personal e-mail information is removed, and the remailer then sends the anonymous message to the intended recipient.

Most remailers are not purely cypherpunks but will accept both cypherpunk and Mixmaster messages. Keep in mind, too, that there are currently only a few cypherpunk remailers that accept non-PGP messages, and their numbers are dwindling. PGP has become a de facto standard for encrypting messages and sharing encryption keys.

Mixmaster Remailers

Mixmaster remailers accept messages in a different format. A PGP key is not used, but instead, its own mix key is used. Here's an example of a mix key:

```
08daa0412580b473b0405a27b6eb72f6
258
AATLm+Il10etAgaOBsAMfggFXi2ghiyypIkZkqhh
W0Ef6LvDNLdPZ94Gu4QgPDD+q13JyRwmU/TvTgIk
SBGxv9dUH3J22BEg600vD91WOcFiq3ApjUuxS76T
Zf+lGTINOIs+zkAmrojqueQfHFxBE0rMembno8jg
VHlOpyeHRfJNIQAAAAAAAAAAAAAAAAAAAAAAAAAA
AAAAAAAAAAAAAAAAAAAAAAAAAAAAAAAAAAAAAAAA
AAAAAAAAAAAAAAAAAAAAAAAAAAAAAAAAAAAAAAAA
AAAAAAAAAAAAAAAAAAAAAAAAAAAAAAAAAAAAAAAA
AAAAAAAAAAAAAAAAAAAAAQAB
```

The messages themselves are encrypted multiple times and formatted so that they appear similar to other messages leaving the remailer. All the messages go through multiple remailers, and each remailer is responsible for decrypting the layered message and sending it to the next remailer for decryption. When the message reaches the recipient, it is impossible to determine the original sender, even if a remailer in the chain was compromised. The advantage Mixmaster remailers have is that they make traffic analysis more difficult. Every message entering and leaving a Mixmaster remailer is exactly the same size.

Anonymity Software Tools

Several utilities are available to help you maintain anonymity when bits of information are left on your computer. These tools are particularly useful when more than one person has access to the same machine. These utilities remove or clear the remnants of your Internet surfing. These include entries in the browser's history, cookies, and so on.

HistoryKill

HistoryKill (`http://www.swanksoft.com/historykill/index.html`), shown in Figure 6.21, can be used to clean up all the files and saved information that gets stored on your system during your browsing sessions. It runs on Windows NT, Windows 2000, Windows 9.x, and Windows Me. You can purchase it on the Web site and download it immediately. Several of the features of HistoryKill include

- Deletion of cached files, history, URLs
- Removal of cookies while you browse and after you end your session
- Removal of your AutoComplete history to hide search engine terms
- Removal of Windows Temp folder
- Deletion of recent files played in Windows Media Player
- Removal of Windows' `index.dat` file in the Temp folder
- PopUp Killer feature that stops windows and ads from popping up
- "Boss key" feature that immediately hides all Web browser windows

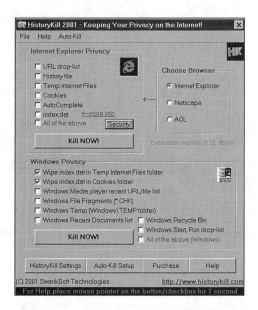

Figure 6.21 HistoryKill's main screen.

Complete Cleanup

Complete Cleanup (`http://www.softdd.com/cc_order.htm`), shown in Figure 6.22, is similar to HistoryKill in that it cleans up files and caches of data left on your system through browsing. This program run on Windows NT, Windows 2000, Windows 9.x, and Windows Me. You can purchase it from its Web site and download it immediately. This program performs the following functions:

- Identifies and removes cookies, cache files, Web history, and location URL history
- Views and deletes your temporary Internet files
- Cleans files on your system, including your recent documents list, temp files folder, and files you've run or searched on within Windows
- Cleans out Registry entries
- Secures file cleaning so undelete will not recover
- Works with Internet Explorer, Netscape, and AOL browsers
- Removes leftover entries from previous browser versions

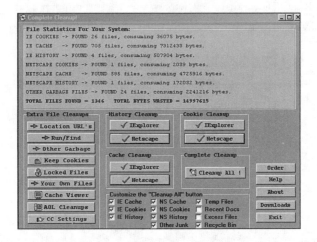

Figure 6.22   Complete Cleanup's main screen.

SurfSecret

SurfSecret, shown in Figure 6.23, is similar to HistoryKiller. One feature that SurfSecret has in addition to cleaning up cache files and images downloaded from Web sites is that it removes all visual evidence of SurfSecret on your desktop until a user-defined hot key is pressed. It can also prevent Java and ActiveX tracking of your browsing sessions. If you share a computer, all your surfing preferences are removed. You can purchase it from its Web site (http://www.surfsecret.com) and download it immediately. It runs on Windows 2000, Windows 9.x, and Windows Me. Several features of SurfSecret include

- Internet Explorer History is cleared.
- America Online cache and cookies are cleared out.
- Recycle bin is automatically emptied, and the Temp folder, `C:\TEMP`, is cleared out.
- The Start menu's Documents folder and the last Find/Run folder are cleared out.
- Advanced settings let you customize default directories.
- The Browser Close option is cleaned out.
- The File Shredder option mutilates files multiple times even after they are deleted.
- Several third-party applications can be cleaned.
- AutoComplete data is cleared from IE in Windows 95/98 (forms and password data).
- Support is available for Netscape 6.0 and Mozilla.
- Clear tracks in instant messaging software, such as AOL IM, MSN IM, and ICQ, are included.
- Clear unsecured Java applets hiding in your system prevent Java tracking.
- Clear hidden, unsecured ActiveX components prevent ActiveX tracking.

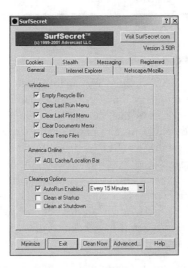

Figure 6.23   SurfSecret's main screen.

Anonymity 4 Proxy

Anonymity 4 Proxy (`http://www.inetprivacy.com/a4proxy/`), shown in Figure 6.24, is a local proxy server installed on your computer that includes a database with hundreds of anonymous public proxy servers. You can then use the software to connect to these proxy servers and surf the Web anonymously. The data you request comes to the proxy first, and then it is transmitted to you. The program lets you scan each server, check its response time, and confirm its anonymity. It runs on Windows 2000, Windows 9.x, and Windows Me.

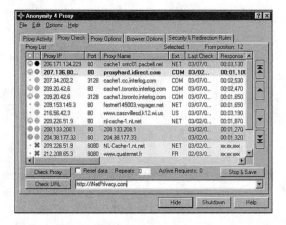

Figure 6.24   Anonymity 4 Proxy.

Current Trends

Anonymity, like privacy, is being defined as a right of the consumer. In the case of Rural/Metro v. Does, the company Rural/Metro Corporation issued a third-party subpoena to the online service provider Yahoo!. The subpoena required Yahoo! to reveal the identities of the defendants and portions of their online correspondence. The Electronic Frontier Foundation (EFF) is defending the defendants to promote the cause of Internet anonymity. Yahoo! was sued in 2000 for obeying such a subpoena without the Yahoo! user's consent. The EFF is one of many organizations that has been promoting the cause of anonymity. First Amendment rights of being able to speak anonymously on issues that otherwise would not become public are the heart of the case. These types of subpoena requests have been steadily growing and could potentially seriously affect user anonymity if companies are forced to turn over log files.

A new movement in anonymity is Controlled Nymity IP, or NymIP for short. The NymIP effort is designed to use open, public processes to implement anonymity, and its goal is to create a set of standardized protocols for pseudonymity and anonymity at the IP layer by first conducting research into Internet anonymity. The founding organization is Zero Knowledge. This is a very small effort in attempting to increase Internet anonymity.

The browser technologies can also be a help or hindrance to Web surfing anonymity. Microsoft's Internet Explorer 6 will provide users with new tools for privacy using a new standard protocol called the Platform for Privacy Preferences (P3P). The browser will automatically be capable of reading the privacy policies associated with cookies, which will be blocked or allowed through settings users select. The use of cookies or blocking of cookies is one way to restrict which types of data you are submitting to Web sites you surf. Netscape has not yet made such a commitment to include such functionality in its newest browser.

Peer-to-peer networking is being used to promote the cause of anonymity. One such network is Freenet, which connects member computers around the world to create information stores. Processes are anonymized and decentralized, and no single storage site of consumer information exists. Therefore, information can't be compromised in one location. Freenet makes it difficult for anyone to spy on the information you are viewing, publishing, or storing using peer-to-peer networking, and information can be encrypted to avoid monitoring of network traffic. Freenet protects freedom of speech by enabling anonymous and uncensored publication of material; this would avoid the subpoena-type situations being faced by Yahoo!

There have also been a number of steps in the wrong direction to keep consumer Internet activities anonymous. Infomediaries are firms that collect and analyze customer information. These outsourced data collection companies take over the role of collecting data from the Web site owner. One report by the Interhack Corporation (`http://web.interhack.com/`) specifically criticizes Toysrus.com and its Babiesrus.com site, as well as sportswear sites Lucy.com and Fusion.com, for using the infomediary Coremetrics. This company collects user activity data, but the Web sites did not specifically notify users of this outsourced activity. These Web site might be in violation of the Web sites' terms of agreement with privacy advocate TRUSTe. Coremetrics uses cookies to collect user information, which is collected for statistical analysis for marketing purposes. Because Coremetrics has more than 40 customer Web sites, this data can be correlated and better browsing patterns matched. But Coremetrics CEO Brett Hurt has said, "We are legally and contractually bound not to do multisite profiling." Privacy advocate Dave Farber, who sits on Coremetrics' advisory board, as well as on the EFF's board of trustees, says Coremetrics protects user privacy. The use of infomediaries is still vague, and anonymity of consumer information is still to be decided. Some companies, such as Zero Knowledge and SafeWeb, can also be considered infomediaries, but they attempt to bring information to you anonymously. This category is still being defined.

Summary

This chapter examined the fundamentals of how the architecture of the Internet itself affects our privacy. Internet components such as IP addresses, domain names, and Web surfing all allow for the leakage of various levels of private information. The amount and sensitivity of the information your ISP has about you illustrate how important it is for the ISP to maintain a high level of security and privacy over customer data. The role your ISP plays in your privacy is very important; its capability to disclose information about you and your activities is described in your terms of service or privacy policy document. Everyone should understand their ISPs' policies regarding disclosure of their private data.

Employing various tools and methods such as anonymous remailers and anonymous Web browsing can keep some of your information from public consumption. These types of programs and services help control disclosure of your private data, help prevent tracking of your online activities, and make it harder for attackers to find out information about your PC.

7

Understanding the Online Environment: Web Surfing and Online Payment Systems

Imagine the Internet as an ocean and your computer as the sailboat. Maybe you are sailing to reach a destination, or maybe you are just sailing for fun. Either way, you shouldn't sail onto the open waters of the Web without first learning about sailing technique, safety, and navigation. The Web, much like the ocean, has rough seas and the occasional pirate who wants to pillage your boat, or rather your PC. But if you learn the proper technique, learn proper safety precautions, and navigate your PC correctly, you'll arrive at your destination safe and sound. The next few sections of this chapter examine some of the Internet ventures that are more likely to be taken for granted, illustrating the threats associated with them and what you can do to prepare and protect yourself.

The Internet is a neutral entity, a medium for communications. In all of its complexity and simplicity, the Internet truly is one of the greatest achievements of the modern world—a creation destined to impact the next several hundred years. It is one of the last frontiers we have for sharing free thoughts and ideas. Protecting our thoughts and ideas from people who want to exploit or manipulate them is the goal of this chapter. Our current generation will be known in the future history books as the creators of the Internet. Every decision we make now regarding the Internet and the circulation of free, uncensored, and unexploited information will impact the evolution of the Internet and its place in our global society.

Note

If you want to learn more about what is happening in the world around you and about the advocates who are speaking for the masses to defend personal freedoms in the digital world, just visit the Electronic Frontier Foundation (EFF) at www.eff.org and the Electronic Privacy Information Center (EPIC) at www.epic.org.

This chapter focuses on online surfing (or sailing) activities. The most popular resources of the Internet are covered, including the World Wide Web. Some general discussions are included about just where all that personal information goes when you register on portals (Web sites that offer a broad range of services, such as e-mail, search engines, and shopping malls) and other sites, and some technical talk is included on what goes on under the hood of your Web browser. Be prepared for an awakening that will arm you with enough knowledge to make intelligent decisions in the online world, as well as references to keep you informed.

After discussing the networked flow of your personal information, cookies, and Web bugs (which are different from software bugs), we will get into a discussion of spyware and online shopping systems. Be prepared to learn and have some fun! Remember that you are in control of your own privacy because you control what personal information you give away.

Site and Portal Registrations

Sign up here! Come join us! Just provide a little bit of your personal information, read our privacy statement, and agree to our terms! It seems that nearly every Web site on the Internet wants you to be a part of its returning community of visitors. Granted, some sites do have good intentions of treating your information confidentially, but it is up to you to make the decision of who to trust and who not to trust.

As a general rule, you should provide the least amount of information possible when registering on a new site or portal. If it asks for more information than you want to provide, e-mail the Webmaster first and ask whether providing that information is necessary and how you can register by providing less information. If the site will not downgrade its requirements, consider not registering with that site, or just fill in arbitrary information for items you know the site does not need. For example, if you do not see a reason that a portal site needs your home address and occupational information, just fill in fictional information when you are asked for it.

The Web of Marketing

Many folks are unaware of the marketing strategies employed across the Internet, which exploit personal information in a network of collaboration. Maybe this is because these exploitations of privacy are overshadowed by the more widespread fears of someone stealing credit card or bank account numbers while users shop online.

However, the fact is that many sites are part of a vast information sharing chain, using your personal information as the prize. This prize is called *demographic information*, one of the most powerful means of analysis available to marketing groups. The information might be only a name and e-mail address, or it might be your entire profile, including your home address, occupation, and Social Security number. On portal sites, the profile can contain the URLs you've visited and any other information gained from your surfing activities within the portal. Maybe you like that idea because you want a personalized surfing experience, right? Something tailored just for you? Well, you're not the only one who likes that idea—there are many organizations out there who just thrive on it.

Consumer profiling and marketing organizations would love to get a hold of this information. In fact, they will even pay a portal to get it. Then, one of two things happens. Either the portal hands over its consumer database and that's the end of it, or the portal agrees to work on a long-term contract, allowing the marketing organization to track visitors with its own methods and store that information in its own database.

This might concern you for several reasons. This data about you can be aggregated between multiple sources. The aggregated data, which might or might not be accurate, can be used by some person or organization to form opinions about you, target specific ads to you, and possibly even discriminate against you.

What if this information is released publicly, or to other parties you would not want to have it? The risks are high when you realize that many people believe what they see, read, and hear without question. In a country whose culture is driven largely by media and the media's unfortunate, anxious moves to get out information that might or might not be accurate, the subjects of the information are usually guilty until proven innocent. You might be at risk of consequences that include embarrassment; harassment; questioning by employers; and relationship problems with family, co-workers, and friends.

The point here is not to scare you, but to make you think about the sites you register with. Read their privacy policies; ask other people about their experiences; ask the site operators whether you need something clarified. Do not blindly trust that your information will be kept secret by the site or portal. You have a right to know how your data is being handled and what will happen with it should the site ever go belly-up. You also have the right to know whether the site is allowing third parties to interact with and monitor its visitors.

Third-Party Content

When you visit a Web site, typically two parties are involved: You are the first party, and the Web site you are visiting is the second party. But third parties can also be involved. For example, sometimes an ad appears as an image on the Web site. The ad could be coming directly from the Web site you know you are visiting, or it could be loading from another company's Web site. In this case, the technical details are simple. Consider this: The HTML code that creates the Web site uses links to find all the images it loads. Most of the links point to the Web site you know you are visiting. However, there are times when the link points to another organization's Web site. Whenever a Web site loads content such as images or sounds from a third-party site, you are no longer just visiting the Web site you intended to. Now you have been subjected to third-party content, which is just the same as if you had visited that third-party Web site directly.

Third-party content can come in many forms. It can be images or sounds loaded into your browser, or it might be other active content, such as ActiveX or Java. What you should be concerned about is cookies and Web bugs that come from third parties. We will discuss these more in the next few sections.

Let's illustrate this with an example: I am going to visit my favorite portal Web site, `www.mifavorita.com`. After I open `www.mifavorita.com` in my Web browser, I log in and begin my surfing activities. I am actually doing some camping next weekend and need a new sleeping bag. So, I type three keywords in the portal's search engine: **buy sleeping bag**. Hold it a minute; before I even click Submit on this search page, I am being monitored by a third-party Web site. Not just one…but two! I didn't realize that a Web bug had been loaded in my browser by `www.bigmarketing.com` or that a cookie had been set on my machine by `www.bigads.com`. Wow! And, worse still, after I click the Submit button for this search, both of these third-party Web sites will learn my three keywords. They'll learn them because my favorite portal Web site is sharing them.

I click Submit, and the search page ends up returning a bunch of results, with an ad from a famous online camping store. Well, I guess that's not so bad. But wait a minute; think back now—didn't I log in to this portal with a username and password? And isn't all that information correlated with the initial registration information I gave `www.mifavorita.com` when I signed up—things like my age, sex, occupation, and home address? Hmmm…is there anyway these third-party sites could have that information as well? If so, then they could easily correlate my search keywords with my profile. Then they could keep this information in a database and keep collecting over time. But it doesn't end there, either, because they are tracking my clicks through this portal—every Web page I visit, every link I click.

How did these third parties get so deep inside `www.mifavorita.com`? Well, I am upset to know that my favorite Web site actually let them! Not just that, but the Webmasters at `www.mifavorita.com` had to actually add the HTML code to the site themselves. Well, let me take another look at the privacy policy of `www.mifavorita.com`. It says that they keep my personal information secure and do not disclose it except under a few certain circumstances where I agree to it. But what's this? Oh, they do mention that www.bigmarketing.com and www.bigads.com are third parties to their site. The policy says that they use cookies and other tracking methods to monitor how the site is used and provide www.mifavorita.com with important feedback. Okay, wait; there is another sentence that says these third-party sites do not collect personal information about me, but rather just track aggregate information. Well, it is actually rare that a site will even tell you third-party monitoring is occurring, so…I feel better…I guess. This is how most of your Web surfing will be, unfortunately.

Can You Trust Them?

Just because a site's privacy policy gives you a warm, comfortable feeling, it does not mean it will always be that way. Even if a Web site claims that the personal data you register with it will be used exclusively by the site and never disclosed to third parties, don't be so sure. In the era of failing dot.com companies, this promise is in jeopardy.

In May 2000, Toysmart, an online toy store with a TRUSTe (www.truste.com) seal of approval, filed for bankruptcy protection. With approval to display TRUSTe's seal, an online company such as Toysmart says it will abide by standards that include the following:

- **Disclosure**—The Web sites will post clear notices of what personal information is collected and who else might share it.
- **Choice**—Users can choose to opt in or opt out whether to allow other access to their personal information.
- **Access**—Users should be able to get to the information they provide to correct and update it.
- **Security**—Reasonable security must be in place.

In the course of the bankruptcy procedure, the business was forced to sell off its assets. One of its most valuable assets was the customer databases, which included names, addresses, shopping preferences, and credit card numbers. TRUSTe worked hard to keep Toysmart from selling its customer database because the TRUSTe seal would inevitably lose credibility and value if companies like Toysmart could break their TRUSTe contracts during bankruptcy. In a Massachusetts bankruptcy court, the FTC argued that Toysmart.com would be breaking its promise "to never release the data to third parties by selling its customer lists and databases." Toysmart would have sold its database if it could have, but continued resistance from the FTC made it hard. In the end, the FTC ruled that Toysmart would be violating consumer protection laws and privacy rights through deceptive practices in commerce.

The FTC's rulings were considered a good step forward for consumer privacy protection by many, but others saw the FTC rulings as weak because they did eventually mean that Toysmart would be paid by a third-party company to "delete" the information. TRUSTe does take steps to ensure that the privacy seals it certifies Web sites with are kept respectable and credible.

Contests and Freebies

In your surfing habits, you have probably come across a contest. So, you want to win that shiny new car? Maybe you just like that cool letter opener 3Com is giving away this week. There a thousands of contests going on each day; just check Iwon.com (www.iwon.com), and you will see more contests than you can shake a stick at. Just what do you think a company is doing with the registration information you provide to enter its contest?

Most Web sites know you as merely an IP address (keep this in mind because it becomes important later). The site owners might want to get more information about who is visiting and what they are interested in. By enticing you to enter a contest or pick up a freebie, they get to learn a lot more about you. You are no longer an IP address; you have graduated to a consumer profile.

Did you register your name, e-mail address, occupation, and home address with the site? Maybe there was a small survey you had to fill out. The organization is using its Web site to collect demographic information about its visitors.

So maybe you don't care that the organization wants this personal information; after all, you just want that cool flashlight. Well, there is more to it than that. The same web of marketing already discussed can weave its way into the contests and freebies you see on the Internet. The information you provide when registering can be used to build a profile on you or be added to an existing one. Your product interests are verified based on what you are registering for, and your e-mail and home addresses will probably be used to spam you with more ads and propaganda.

Precautions for Web Surfing

We have brought together a wealth of information to arm you with enough knowledge to protect your privacy and home computer systems in your Web surfing habits. Pass this information along, share your knowledge with friends and family, and seek others' advice when in doubt. The following list of precautions will be reiterated throughout this book, expanding into the details of each. Although we provide product names throughout to help you get going, we do not endorse any products mentioned. Remember that in the war to defend your privacy, it is up to you to keep your guard up! Here are some guidelines to help you do just that:

- **Be aware of home computers and networks**—Know who is using your computers and your home network. At work, do you share a computer with others? At home, does the family share the same computer or do the kids have their own? Do your friends or your children's friends use the computers, too? If you have a network set up at home, you should take some of the precautions described in Chapter 13, "Securing Your Home Network." Considerations include personal firewalls and folder sharing among others. If your Web surfing activities result in your PC being infected with a virus or compromised by an attacker, the next threat is spreading it across your network.

- **Understand your Web browser**—Learn about it, and read the help files and any documentation you can find on it. Search the Internet for information on the latest news surrounding your browser of choice. The two most popular Web browsers are discussed in this book, in their latest versions: Netscape Navigator 6.1 and Microsoft Internet Explorer (IE) 6.0. However, other good browsers do exist for many operating systems, including Opera and NeoPlanet. Take the time and learn the security features of your Web browser.

- **Be aware of Web security**—Secure Sockets Layer (SSL) is useful in protecting Internet banking, shopping, and other activities. SSL protects the communications between your Web browser and a Web site by ensuring that identities and exchanged information are protected with encryption. Understand, however, that SSL protects your information only while in transit! After that, information is sent to the server, where it can be stored in an unencrypted form, or much worse, in a completely unsecured manner. It can be sold by your trusted e-tailer to a third-party marketing agency. Stay abreast of the latest methods people and organizations are using to get your personal information—be it Web bugs, spyware programs you download, e-mail harvesting, or cookies for surveillance! At least by staying aware of the threats, you have a greater chance of recognizing them when they come.

- **Know the sites you are visiting**—Be wary of the content and amount of personal information you provide them. Read their privacy policies—do they make sense? Does this company have a good reputation? Before registering with it, look around for information about its business doings, and ask people who might know. Does the site you are visiting allow third parties to bug or advertise on its Web site?

- **Be selective about the personal information you give out**—Never give out personal information to strangers online in chat rooms or through e-mail messages. Teach your kids about this, too.

- **Control your cookies**—Pay attention to the cookies that sites put on your system. Use a cookie manager program that lets you easily control which sites you will and will not accept cookies from. The program should also let you block third-party cookies; luckily, the latest popular browsers (Netscape Navigator 6.1, Internet Explorer 6.0, and Opera 5) provide for this.

- **Use anonymizing techniques**—Keep a separate e-mail account for making newsgroup, chat room, or any other public Internet postings. Do not tie any personal information to this e-mail account that you do not want publicly available. Be prepared for this e-mail address to receive a lot of spam mail and junk mail (one and the same really). Do not put your e-mail address on Web pages or other Internet postings that make it an easy catch for Web bots or other Internet spiders (small automated programs that search the Web for information).

Cookies

This topic perhaps deserves its own chapter, but we will try to keep things concise here and cover all the important points. Most people reading this book have probably heard about cookies on the Internet, and we have mentioned them briefly throughout the book. We will cover the background on the good and bad uses of cookies (after all, they are not all bad) and then get into some of the technical details, as well as a discussion of how cookies are commonly used to monitor and exploit your Web surfing habits.

So, what are cookies? A *cookie* is a small amount of data stored in a file on your hard drive. When you visit a Web site, it creates a cookie for you and asks your Web browser to store it. The cookie identifies you to the Web site. Web sites pass out cookies like they are identification cards. Not much different from common ID cards you are used to, cookies store information unique to you, expire at a certain time, and are carried around with you.

When you revisit the Web site, the cookie is sent back to it. The Web site uses the cookie to determine who you are and when you last visited. It really depends on what the cookie stores in the first place. The Web site might store username and password information, your personal preferences for the Web site, items you are shopping for, or whatever else it wants to store.

Cookies can be great for convenience because they make your returning Web site visit exactly the way you want it. If you are visiting a site for weather information, you will be taken right to the local weather for your home town because the cookie provides your preference to the Web site. If you regularly log in to a site, a cookie might let you bypass the painstaking process by providing the Web site with your username and password.

The issue with privacy comes from several angles. Cookies can be used to easily track your movements across the Web. They are used by marketing agencies and other organizations to accumulate Internet user data. When cookies store personal information such as username and password or financial data, they become a security concern. After all, you do not want this information stored on a shared computer or transmitted across the Internet in a readable form.

It is important to realize that a cookie by itself is harmless. A cookie is merely a file that stores some data. It is the manner in which the cookie is used, and the motivation behind it, that can make a cookie become a privacy and security concern.

Cookies are created either by the Web site you are visiting or by another Web site you are not directly visiting. As discussed in the earlier section "Third-Party Content," there can be an important difference. *First-party cookies* are the ones you would expect because they come from the Web site you intended to visit. Although privacy concerns still exist, at least you are aware of them. *Third-party cookies*, on the other hand, are the ones you do not expect. These are the cookies placed on your computer by an intervening Web site that you did not directly visit. These raise a higher privacy concern because they are more commonly used for tracking and monitoring purposes and profile data collection.

RFC 2965

A cookie is actually an industry standard. That means the technical details and high level functionality of a cookie have been outlined and described in a document called a Request for Comments (RFC). RFCs have been around for years and have been used to define standards for most of the functionality that exists on the Internet today (such as TCP, IP, and HTTP).

Vendors, such as software companies, use these standards when they build software programs. By sticking to the standards, they can rest assured that their software will play nicely with other vendors' software. When a Web server, such as Apache, is built around the standard of HTTP and a Web browser, such as Netscape Navigator, is also built around the standard of HTTP, the two will be capable of interacting.

RFC 2965 defines the latest standard for cookies. The original standard defining cookies was 2109, dated February 1997. RFC 2965 is the latest version of this standard, dated October 2000, it and makes the previous RFC 2109 obsolete.

The standard is a fairly technical read; however, it also provides some high-level information that is easy to digest. For example, the standard says in plain English that neither a Web browser nor a Web server needs to use cookies, but if the Web server wants to use cookies, it might refuse to send data to a Web browser that does not accept cookies. Some important updates to the cookie standard are in RFC 2965. The curious can read it directly at RFC 2965, "HTTP State Management Mechanism" (`http://www.ietf.org/rfc/rfc2965.txt`).

As evident in the title, the purpose of the cookie is to provide Web sites a mechanism for managing the ongoing state between a Web client and the server. Traditionally, Web servers just answered client requests as they came in. In today's Internet, however, the level of interactivity between a client and server can be nearly unified. Everything from personalized portals to online banking and even virtual worlds now exist. The need for a server to manage its ongoing interaction with each client is necessary in many cases.

RFC 2965 provides guidelines for security and privacy protection, as well. The RFC suggests that at a minimum, a Web browser should provide the following cookie management capabilities:

- Complete disabling of the sending and saving of cookies
- Notification before a cookie is sent

- Notification that cookies are being used
- Capability to control the acceptance and sending of cookies based on the domain
- Capability to examine and delete the contents of a cookie

It is great to see that the creators of the cookie standard are looking out for our privacy and security. Unfortunately, it is up to the software implementers to take the advice of and stick to the standard.

Functionality

Now, let's look at some of the functionality cookies are used to provide. This includes the benevolent actions of providing session state and personal preferences and the privacy concerns of surveillance and information gathering.

This is not a full list, but it does represent much of the common functionality cookies provide for a user and a site.

Session State

When you first open a Web page in your browser, you have established a *session*. If the Web site is interactive in some way (for instance, a banking, an e-mail, or a credit card site), it might be designed to keep track of who and where you are within the site. This is known as *maintaining session state*. It is important to most Web sites so they don't mix you up with someone else while you're doing your online banking.

Persistent and Session Cookies

Basically, two types of cookies get stored on your hard drive. *Persistent* cookies are meant to be stored permanently by your Web browser. This is typical for sites at which you have personal preferences saved and for sites where you have saved a username and password. The Web browser will not delete persistent cookies—you have to manually do it yourself.

Session cookies, as the name implies, are cookies stored only for the duration of your current visit to the Web site. As soon as you close your Web browser, all the session cookies are deleted from your hard drive.

Personal Preferences

As you know, cookies can contain the data necessary to remind a Web site what your personal preferences are. Maybe when you log in, you want certain stock quotes to appear along with the weather for your home town. This makes the workload easier for the Web site because rather than storing your preferences in a database, the Web site can leave the task up to you. If the Web site had to store all that information itself, it might suffer performance problems, and visitors would complain about how slow the site is. As you might be starting to realize, cookies can contain nearly any piece of information a site wants them to keep.

Authentication

As stated, cookies can serve to authenticate you with a Web site. You might log in to a Web site that gives you the option of storing your credentials in a cookie. In this case, there is one thing you need to be concerned about: Is the site using encryption? The Web site's privacy policy should let you know what contents are in its cookies and whether those contents are encrypted. A cookie used for authentication needs to be encrypted when it is stored on your hard drive and when it is sent across the Internet (using SSL) between your browser and the site. If it is not encrypted, anybody who has (or who has gained) access to your computer can read the contents of the cookie and thus your login information.

In May 2000, Microsoft released a patch for Internet Explorer. The patch fixed a serious problem that affected Web surfers like you and me. The problem was that a specially designed Web site could read all the cookies stored on your computer by Internet Explorer. All that was needed in the Web site's HTML code was a special string of JavaScript that, after being executed by your browser, would send all your Internet Explorer–stored cookies to the malicious Web site. See the Microsoft Security Bulletin (MS00-033) at `http://www.microsoft.com/technet/security/bulletin/ms00-033.asp` for details and the patch.

Surveillance

We talk about surveillance tactics throughout this book. The fact is, cookies are great for surveillance. Just as they can provide session state to one site, they can be used to track your movements across the Web by another. A lot of surveillance is done by third-party marketing or advertising sites. They commonly place HTML code on other Web sites that ask your browser to download the third-party cookie. If a third-party entity is large enough, it can use cookies across many different domains and Web sites. By correlating the cookie data from across the range of sites, it can easily map out a user's Web surfing activity, possibly storing it in a database for profiling and trend analysis.

Demographic and Information Gathering

Demographic and information gathering usually goes hand in hand with surveillance. Many organizations are interested in gathering demographic information about you, including the town you live in, your occupation, your income, your age, your marital status, the number of kids you have, and what kind of car you drive. Basically, all this information is used to profile you into a category with similar people who can be identified, studied, and considered a target audience. When an advertising agency can combine demography with surveillance, it can get powerful results.

Cookie Ingredients

Cookies are stored in different places on your hard drive. Netscape Navigator stores all cookies in a single file called `cookies.txt` on the PC and `magiccookie` on the Mac. Internet Explorer stores each cookie in its own separate file, all in a directory named `cookies`, which can be stored either under the User Profile directory or the Windows System directory, depending on which version of the Windows operating system you are using.

Remember RFC 2965? Well, it also defines some guidelines for Web browsers as to the minimums they should support. Per this RFC, here are the minimums that any Web browser should support:

- At least 30 cookies
- At least 4096 bytes per cookie
- At least 20 cookies per unique host or domain name

Table 7.1 lists the RFC-specified data types that can exist in a cookie. The only mandatory requirement is the `Name=VALUE` data type; the rest are optional. The data types denoted with an ★ are the new ones, defined in RFC 2965. They are barely in use on the Internet because most sites still use the original data types defined in 1997's RFC 2109. Regardless, we provide them here for completeness.

Table 7.1   **A Cookie's Allowable Data Types**

Data Type	Description
`Name=VALUE`	A string value where *Name* describes some attribute, and *VALUE* is some data corresponding to that attribute. *Name* is also applied as the name of the cookie. This data type can be arbitrarily defined by the Web site creators and can represent anything they want. Also, as shown in the earlier example, the *VALUE* can contain multiple variables.
`Comment`	This optional field is designed for the Web site owners to document how they intend to use the data in the cookie. Because a cookie can contain private information, this field is important to alert you and let you decide whether to continue with your session.
`CommentURL`	This should be a URL value in the form of `http://www.cookiesite.com`. It follows the `Comment` data type to denote the Web site URL.
`Discard`	If this value is set, the Web browser is instructed to discard the cookie upon exit.

Table 7.1   **Continued**

Data Type	Description
Domain	This value contains the valid domain name for the cookie. The value should be proceeded by a dot. For example, if you get a cookie while visiting www.google.com, this Domain value would be .google.com— notice the dot preceding the domain name.
Max-Age	Specifies the lifetime of the cookie. After a cookie has reached its expiration date, as specified by Max-Age, the cookie is discarded by the Web browser.
Path	The Path value specifies the subset of URLs on the origin server for which the cookie is valid. As an example, when visiting www.google.com, the path set in the cookie might be a /. This says that the cookie is good for all subsets of the google.com domain, such as www.google.com/groups or www.google.com/help.
Port	Represents a port or list of ports allowed for the cookie to be returned to in the cookie request header.
Secure	When set, the Secure value communicates to the Web browser that the cookie should be secured. If set to Yes, the browser attempts to return the cookie to the Web server over a secure channel, such as SSL.
Version	Specifies the version number specification to which the cookie conforms. From the current RFC 2195, this value is set to 1.

The Name data type can be manipulated by Web site developers to describe nearly any type of information they want. The value Name can be any string name you choose with a certain string VALUE. Some examples include

```
ID                12345
HumanClickID      192.168.17.2-ACCEPT
BA12345           WebStatLastOrder=&WebStatFirstVisit=09/21/01 11:47:25
                  PM&WebStatVisitCount=0&WebStatUserID=001-00-3-10-6692-
                  7351&WebStatLastVisit=09/21/01 11:47:25
                  PM&LastPage=http://noscript&LastPage1=&LastPage2=&LastPa
                  ge3=&VisitEntry=http://noscript&VisitReferrer=&FirstDate
                  =09/21/01 11:47:25
                  PM&FirstPage=http://noscript&FirstReferrer=&PageDepth=0&
                  NumVisit=2&NumOrder=0&stats.bigads.com/S001-00-3-10-
                  6342-7351   1024   4025877728   39239082   958762368
                  29412947   *   wtl27915
                  WebStatLastOrder=&WebStatFirstVisit=09/21/01 11:49:15
                  PM&WebStatVisitCount=0&WebStatUserID=001-00-3-10-6342-
                  7351&WebStatLastVisit=09/21/01 11:49:15
                  PM&LastPage=http://noscript&LastPage1=&LastPage2=&LastPa
```

```
ge3=&VisitEntry=http://noscript&VisitReferrer=&FirstDate
=09/21/01 11:49:15
PM&FirstPage=http://noscript&FirstReferrer=&PageDepth=0&
NumVisit=2&NumOrder=0&
```

Whoa! That last cookie was loaded with information. Just look at all that stuff—everything from `WebStatUserID`, `WebStatFirstVisit`, and `WebStatLastVisit` to the current time and date to the `VisitReferrer`. Think these folks are tracking anything? Knowing data types in a cookie, let's take a look at an example. We will fill in the values from a harmless cookie set by `www.google.com`, whose purpose is to keep track of my preferences for the site (see Table 7.2).

Table 7.2   **Breakdown of a Sample Cookie from Google**

Data Type	Description
PREF	ID=4fbaf3da6b41b29:LD=en:NR=100:NW=1:TM=10006008:LM=1056222827
Comment	
CommentURL*	
Discard*	
Domain	.google.com
Expires	Sunday, January 17, 2038 11:19:22
Path	/
Port*	
Secure	No
Version	1

Google sets only one cookie on my system, and it is a persistent cookie. You can see that half of the data types are not even used, but that's okay because they are optional. Not to mention, the new data types defined in RFC 2195 are not widely implemented yet. Google is just using the data it needs, and no more, which actually might be considered a good practice. When you consider the volume and speed that Google must have to dish out cookies, you'd think that there must be some performance concerns. By streamlining their cookies, though, Google can deliver faster performance to visitors.

Getting back to Table 7.2, notice that `PREF` is the `Name` of the cookie, and it has a value of `ID=4fbaf3da6b41b29:LD=en:NR=100:NW=1:TM=10006008:LM=1056222827`. Because I know that I set my preferred language to English and the number of records I want displayed to be 100, I can make out those values in the string: `LD=en` and `NR=100`. However, I can't make out the other values. The rest of the data in the string—`ID`, `TM`, and `LM`—is probably used to identify me as a unique user. It is nearly impossible for anyone to know what the contents of a cookie represent, except for the people who created the cookie. Identifying unique visitors is a practice that Google states in its company's privacy policy at `http://www.google.com/privacy.html`. The remaining data types can be explained by the definitions in Table 7.1.

Take a look at Netscape's and Internet Explorer's displays of the cookie contents. Figure 7.1 shows the contents of a cookie in Netscape, and Figure 7.2 shows the contents of a cookie in Internet Explorer. In Netscape, you select Edit, Preferences, Privacy and Security, Cookies, View Stored Cookies, Netscape to display the contents of each cookie. This is a great breakdown of the contents. For the raw information, you could just open the `cookies.txt` file Netscape stores on your hard drive. In Internet Explorer, you must have the browser set up to prompt you before saving cookies. Set this up through Tools, Internet Options, Privacy, Advanced. After you are prompted that a Web site wants to save a cookie to your disk, click the More Info button to see the window displayed in Figure 7.2.

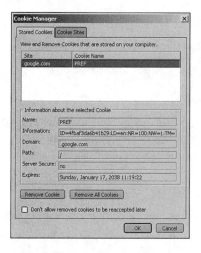

Figure 7.1   Netscape Navigator 6.1 cookie information.

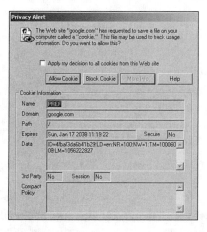

Figure 7.2   Internet Explorer 6.0 cookie information.

So, just where did this cookie come from and how was it created? Well, the first part is easy: This cookie came from www.google.com. It was created by some HTML code the Web site sent to my Web browser. The contents of the cookie are actually defined in the Web site HTML code. First, my Web browser sends a common HEAD or GET request that looks like this:

```
HEAD / HTTP/1.0
```

When the Web site receives this request, it returns the following HTML code to my Web browser:

```
HTTP/1.0 200 OK
Connection: close
Date: Sun, 23 Sep 2001 08:36:31 GMT
Server: GWS/1.11
Set-Cookie: PREF=ID=4fbaf3da6b41b29:LD=en:NR=100:NW=1:TM=10006008:LM=1056222827;
domain=.google.com; path=/; expires=Sun, 17-Jan-2038 11:19:15 GMT
Content-Type: text/html
Content-Length: 1494
Cache-Control: private
```

That is it, and the cookie is created. So now what? The next time I visit www.google.com, my Web browser is smart enough to find that a cookie already exists, and it offers the contents of the cookie to the site, before completing my request. And that completes the basic cycle of a cookie. To sum it up, the basic lifecycle of a cookie goes something like this:

1. I visit www.google.com because I want to do an Internet search.

2. www.google.com uses the Set-Cookie: HTML code to request that my Web browser create a cookie.

3. My Web browser saves the cookie to my hard drive, with the data created by www.google.com.

4. I leave www.google.com, and stop Web surfing for the day.

5. The next day, I open the same Web browser and go right to www.google.com.

6. This time, my Web browser finds an existing cookie and uses the Cookie: HTML code to notify the site with its contents.

7. www.google.com takes the cookie data my browser provides and decides whether to make any modifications.

8. If the site wants to modify the cookie, it just replaces it altogether; otherwise, things continue as normal.

In the year 2000, Marc Rotenberg, director of the Electronic Privacy Information Center, along with Jason Carlett, President of Junkbusters, sent a concise but alarming letter to congress. In it he urged Congress to investigate the use of cookies on federal Web sites operating under the Clinton administration. The result was a sincere, quick response by the U.S. government, which unfortunately did not follow through enough to address the cookie issue. The point became clear that this type of privacy, which was not the responsibility of the private sector industry, was no longer the responsibility of our government either.

Remember that you can control your cookies. A good suggestion is to set up your Web browser so it prompts you before a cookie is created. This gives you a great way to see when third-party sites are sending cookies your way. The simple thing about it is that the newest browsers make this easy and give you the option to apply your decision to the site in the future, so you are not continuously prompted. See the section "Cookie Management," later in this chapter, for more information on setting this up.

The Dangers of Cookies

We have looked closely at the privacy dangers of using cookies. The fact that your personal information can be shared between organizations to profile you and monitor your surfing habits is one thing. But the dangers extend into attacks that malicious folks can take directly on your cookies. Some examples are discussed in the following sections.

Cookie Spoofing

Cookies can be tricked, or mistakenly used, from site to site if the original creator did not take the design precautions necessary to guard against this. Say, for example, that you visit `http://friendly.site.com`, and it sets a cookie on your system. If the site specified the `Domain` data type as `.site.com`, rather than a more specific `.friendly.site.com`, your browser will offer that cookie to any page in the same domain, such as `http://malicious.site.com` or `http://unfriendly.site.com`, that you might visit. This is a common practice, unfortunately, and can lead to cookies leaking information that is not intended.

Cookie Sharing

Web browsers should be built to protect against cookies being shared between disparate domains. A malicious Web site, one with bad intentions for its visitors, might try to embed cookie information for a third-party site into a URL for the malicious site you are visiting. This sort of activity is discouraged by the RFC, and guidelines are set for Web browsers to protect against information cross-exchanging between different domains.

Cookies for Account Information

Per the specification, cookies are not designed or intended to store and provide authentication information, such as usernames and passwords. However, they are commonly used in this way. If the cookie is stored with such valuable information, an attacker can view or use this information. In addition, if a cookie that stores authentication information is not exchanged with the site over a secured channel, such as SSL, someone can intercept the cookie when you send it out on the network and learn your user credentials.

Note

When a Web site asks whether you want to save your username and password, the best choice is to say no. There is no good reason to store usernames and passwords on your computer for return Web site visits.

Cookie Management

Cookie management is the cure to the cookie problem. Software that gives you full control of your cookies should allow you to

- Completely disable the sending and saving of cookies.
- Control the acceptance and sending of cookies based on the domain.
- Get notification before a cookie is sent.
- Get notification that cookies are being used.
- Examine and delete the contents of a cookie.

This section discusses some tools that give you full control of your cookies. In addition to the third-party tools, the newest version of Netscape Navigator 6.1, Internet Explorer 6.0, and Opera 5.12 all provide for the best built-in cookie management to date.

Each Web browser manages cookies in its own way. Netscape Navigator stores all cookies in a file called `cookies.txt`, which you can open directly to get the raw cookie information. However, Netscape does provide you with an easy-to-use interface for getting at the raw cookie data. Internet Explorer, on the other hand, stores each cookie in its own text file, under a folder named appropriately enough, Cookies.

Some good advice for starting with cookie management is this: Reject all cookies by default. You can set up your software to reject all cookies by default and specify sites that you know you want to allow. Actually, though, there is a better way than this. The software discussed next can be set up to prompt you when a site wants to create a cookie. The prompt asks you whether you want to accept or reject the cookie being created. Better yet, you can opt to make your choice permanent for the site. If you later change your mind about the decision, you can simply go into the configuration and change things. Keep reading to find out how.

Netscape Navigator 6.1

Netscape has always included privacy controls for cookie management. Now, these controls have gotten even better. Netscape gives you per-site cookie control, but it might not be as obvious to new users. In general, Netscape gives you three simple options:

- Disable all cookies
- Enable all cookies
- Enable all cookies for the originating Web site only

The meaning of the last option might not be as obvious as the other two. When you select this, all foreign or third-party cookies are blocked. So, if you are visiting www.friendlysite.com, you will allow cookies from it but not allow cookies from www.meanmarketing.com that might be running through the site.

You can access the cookie controls by selecting Edit, Preferences, Privacy and Security, Cookies. You will see the screen shown in Figure 7.3.

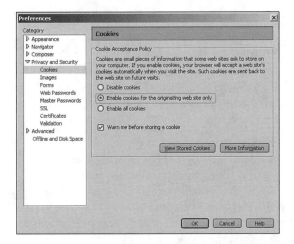

Figure 7.3 Cookie controls in Netscape 6.1.

Select the Warn Me Before Storing a Cookie option, in which case you will be prompted every time a new site wants to drop a cookie on your computer. The prompt enables you to accept or reject the cookie and permanently add the site to a list that can or cannot set cookies, so you are not prompted anymore when visiting this site. Leaving this option enabled lets you know the amount of cookies being created and about the third-party sites that often create them.

If you ever change your mind and want to change a site's status of being able to set cookies or not, simply click the View Stored Cookies button and then select the Cookie Sites tab, shown in Figure 7.4.

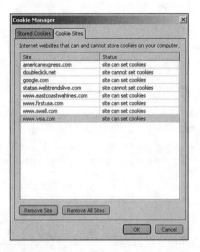

Figure 7.4   Netscape Controls over cookies per site.

You now have direct access to the cookies known by Netscape. Here you can see the raw cookie data and remove cookies from your system. You can also view and control the list of sites you have configured to allow or disallow cookies from.

If you ever select the Save Password option that pops up when you log in to a site (which you shouldn't do), Netscape 6 shows you all your displayed passwords. If you are sharing a computer, anyone can check all your saved passwords and copy them and do all kinds of malicious things with your ID and passwords to various sites. The password shows up in the Password Manager, as shown in Figure 7.5. Password Manager can be accessed by selecting Tasks, Privacy and Security, Password Manager. You also can remove passwords from the application.

Internet Explorer 6.0

Internet Explorer 6 has privacy controls for personal information and cookie management, as shown in Figure 7.6. (Select Tools, Internet Options and select the Privacy tab.) It even includes content controls that let you define allowable content that can be viewed on your computer. This is a great form of parental control for the kiddies' surfing experience. We suggest setting up Internet Explorer to prompt you before you create any cookies. This gives you full control over the choices.

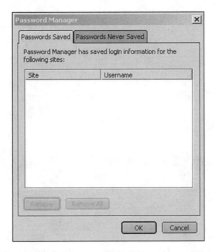

Figure 7.5   Netscape Password Manager.

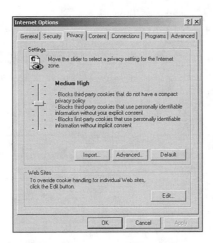

Figure 7.6   Internet Explorer 6 options for cookie management.

IE provides six settings—from Accept All Cookies to Block All Cookies. From this screen, though, you actually have an even greater range of options. Click the Advanced button to override the automatic cookie handling, and explicitly define how first-party cookies are handled, separately from third-party cookies. Your choices for each are as follows:

- Accept
- Block
- Prompt

If you select Prompt, you will probably get an education in the amount of cookies getting created, but you might also get annoyed very quickly as your surfing experience quickly turns into a constant window pop-up asking whether you want to allow this cookie. If you can bear with it through the beginning, this is actually your best option because you can apply each choice indefinitely. That is, after you are prompted about whether to accept or reject a cookie, as shown in Figure 7.7, you can choose to make your decision permanent for that site or domain. You can also click the More Info button to see the contents of the cookie.

Figure 7.7   Internet Explorer prompts you with a Privacy Alert about cookies.

In the Privacy Alert window, select the option to Apply My Decision to All Cookies from This Web Site, and your decision to allow or block will be permanently applied to that site and you will never be prompted about that site again. If you ever want to change your decision, you can simply do so by going back to the Privacy Configuration screen (refer to Figure 7.6) and clicking the Edit button in the Web Sites section. You will see a screen similar to Figure 7.8, where you can specify on a per-site basis when to allow and block cookies.

Figure 7.8   Internet Explorer gives you cookie control over specific Web sites.

So, if I know that I will be shopping at Amazon.com often, and I want them to keep my preferences active when I visit, I would add Amazon.com to the list and click Allow for its setting. And I could always add doubleclick.net with a setting to Block cookies from them.

You can see an alert about a site failing your cookie options in the right corner of IE. A little red graphic appears to let you know an alert was issued against the site you just visited (see Figure 7.9).

Figure 7.9   Privacy Alert icon.

You can double-click the icon and see the privacy report shown in Figure 7.10. This shows you the blocked cookies that fail your filter options.

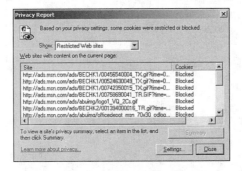

Figure 7.10   Privacy report.

This interface provides most of the flexibility you could want for managing cookies in IE. Netscape has offered these features for years, but Microsoft was slow to integrate complete cookie control into IE. With IE claiming nearly 80% of the Web browser market share, it is reassuring to see more complete cookie control being built into the browser. This surely means that Microsoft recognizes the importance of giving people more control over their Web browsing experience.

You also can control cookies on a per-zone basis in versions of IE prior to IE 6. Internet Explorer provides security zone settings, allowing you to put sites you trust in the Trusted Sites zone and put all non-specified sites in the Internet zone. Each zone has its own security settings, which you can get to by selecting Tools, Internet Options and selecting the Security tab. By clicking the Custom Level button, you can choose to allow, block, or prompt for session and persistent cookies. The new cookie controls in IE 6 provide for a much greater degree of control.

A couple other advanced settings are worth considering, too. You access the Advanced options by selecting Tools, Internet Options and selecting the Advanced tab in IE. Scroll down to the section on Security, and check the option for Empty Temporary Internet Files Folder when Browser Is Closed to clean up any information you might not want hanging around. Uncheck Enable Profile Assistant if you do not want to use this feature, which allows Web sites to ask IE to provide them your personally registered information. If you are not sure what information this is, select Tools, Internet Options; then select the Content tab, and select My Profile.

CookiePal

CookiePal, shown in Figure 7.11, is an awesome program from Kookaburra Software (www.kburra.com) that gives you a full range of cookie control not just for Web browsers, but for other programs as well. This tool is fun to use but runs only on Windows.

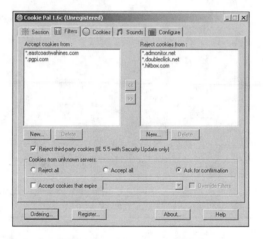

Figure 7.11   CookiePal filters.

CookiePal can be configured to accept and reject cookies from Web sites that you specify, through the Filters tab. You should check the Reject Third-Party Cookies option so you do not get unexpected cookies. You also should check the Ask for Confirmation option so you will be prompted when a site wants to create a cookie.

CookiePal shows you currently active session cookies, as well as stored persistent cookies, each in separate spaces. Plus, it gives you access to the details of each cookie, including the ability to delete them.

CookiePal, Internet Explorer, and Netscape Navigator are the few programs that let you view the detailed contents of each cookie. The CookiePal filters enable you to specify from which domains you will accept and reject cookies. You can also choose the important option to block third-party cookies. The configuration options continue by enabling you to control cookies that come from unknown servers or to control cookies based on their expiration dates.

By clicking the Modules button, you can specify the programs and Web browsers CookiePal should monitor for cookie use. You can specify programs other than Web browsers, such as Real Player, Windows Media Player, Eudora, and Outlook.

For full control of cookies through an easy-to-understand interface, check out CookiePal. It is available for a 30-day trial or low-cost purchase.

Web Bugs: Nasty Little Critters?

Web bugs are not the same as software bugs, which cause your programs to perform badly or crash. These are bugs in the sense of surveillance and monitoring tools. Unfortunately, monitoring on the Web does not stop with cookies. Several companies and advertising agencies use Web bugs to track and log the time and page a user has visited. Not only that, but by spreading Web bugs out over various pages and sites, a company can trace your movements across the Web. You can find further details about Web bugs from the man who has raised widespread public awareness about the phenomena, Richard Smith, at `http://www.privacyfoundation.org/resources/Webbug.asp`.

Smith has also made a Web bug detector available free of charge. It is called Bugnosis, and you can get it from `www.bugnosis.org`. However, it is available only as a plug-in for Internet Explorer at the moment and works only with Web surfing. But there are plans to make it available for e-mail Web bug detection, too.

That is right; Web bugs can operate through HTML-enabled e-mail, too. Why would someone do this? If someone is using Web bugs to track your movements across a Web site, isn't that enough for her? No way! If I am a big marketing company, I can save a lot of money by doing e-mail advertisements rather than commercial TV ones. I might find an e-mail harvester or third-party spammer that will send out an e-mail ad to a select group of consumers I have pulled from the database.

After you open or preview your HTML-enabled e-mail message, the Web bug is activated, letting the originator know you have read the e-mail. After it's installed, the Web bug is known as a small or invisible graphic on a Web page or in an e-mail message meant to monitor who is visiting the Web page or reading the e-mail message. Indeed, Web bugs have even proven to be usable in applications such as Microsoft Word. This is because Microsoft Word, like many of today's applications, supports HTML. Because HTML provides for the useful functions of hyperlinks and sharable formatting, it is commonly supported.

Web bugs are typically delivered via an HTML hyperlink. Just as every image that pops up in your Web browser is linked to the page, so is a Web bug. Notice how the

Web bugs in the following examples are delivered: 1) as an image using the `<img src>` HTML code, and 2) as a hyperlink using the `"http://somesite.com"` code. For example, the following is the HTML code of a Web bug we encountered recently on the home page of `http://www.us.buy.com`:

```
<img height="1" width="175" src="http://switch.avenuea.com/action/buy_homepage">
```

We know this is a Web bug because we are visiting Buy.com's Web site and an image is being loaded from a popular online marketing site, Avenuea.com. This Web bug is rather unassuming compared to the Web bug that Richard Smith encountered back in 1999 on `www.quicken.com`:

```
<img src="http://ad.doubleclick.net/ad/pixel.quicken/NEW"
width=1 height=1 border=0><IMG WIDTH=1 HEIGHT=1 border=0
SRC= "http://media.preferences.com/ping?ML_SD=IntuitTE
Intuit_1x1_RunOfSite_Any&db
afcr=4B31-C2FB-10E2C&event=reghome&group=register&time=
1999.10.27.20.5 6.37">
```

This is a more obvious Web bug because it includes a reference to HTTP twice in the code and because image size is 1×1 pixels (`width=1 height=1`).

Web bugs can come in several variations, each serving a different purpose. Sometimes the Web bug is used to extend the privacy invasion to another function. In this way, a Web bug can do the job itself, or it can be the carrier, actually passing control off to some other program that does the job of watching you. Consider some of the following Web bug uses:

- **Simple tracking**—A Web bug comes as a transparent GIF that sends information to a third party about a user's travels across the Web.
- **Executable bugs**—These might tell your browser to download and run a small program that can be used to scan your hard drive for personal information. The program might scan for files containing the word "financial" and then send that information back to the bugger. This is basically the concept of a Web bug providing a means for spyware to get on your system.
- **Script-based executable bugs**—These nasty bugs use scripting features of certain operating systems and browsers to grab files off your hard drive. It has even been reported that these can use PC-attached Webcams and recording devices that are plugged in and running on your computer. This brings new meaning to the word *spyware*.

That is some scary stuff. The time has come to definitely secure our PCs and be aware of what is going on out there. As was discussed earlier in this chapter, in the section "Precautions for Web Surfing," if you know your Web browsers, Web sites, and some basic security guidelines, you can have safe, enjoyable Internet experiences. Otherwise, prepare to be exploited.

We mentioned previously that Web bugs can sometimes provide a means for spyware to get on your system. That doesn't mean Web bugs are spyware, but they can be the delivery means for spyware. Spyware is usually a program on your computer that invades your privacy by sending personal information back to the program's inventor. By themselves, Web bugs can provide only the following information:

- The type of browser you use
- The time you accessed the Web bug
- The IP address of your computer
- The URL of the site from which you got the Web bug
- The URL of the Web bug image, which could be a third-party site
- An already saved cookie value

And it just keeps getting better. If the cookie contains valuable information about you, suddenly the third-party site that placed the Web bug has that information too. Imagine a site you have to log in to. You probably provided an e-mail address. Well, if you're hit with a Web bug through this site, that e-mail address can potentially be sent to the site that placed the Web bug. Not only that, but now that e-mail address can follow you around as you visit other sites, which means those other sites also have potential access to your e-mail address!

In February 2001, an Internet tracking and security company named Security Space released a report identifying large Web advertising networks, such as DoubleClick, LinkExchange, and Excite.com, as some of the top sites using Web bugs to track users across third-party Web pages.

Earlier in the same year, Intelytics, a company developing privacy-related software, scanned some 51 million Web pages with its privacy scanning tools. It found that 16 million of the pages had some type of Web bug set up from a third-party advertising agency. This all just proves that the activity is real, and growing.

Most people aren't concerned that their online activities are being tracked, but there is a larger picture to ponder. With all the useful profiling and tracking information the top organizations are capturing, you have to wonder just what potential that information gives them. They can, of course, correlate users' actions over time, distinguishing things such as what a user typically searches for to what types of sites a user frequents. They can also collect e-mail addresses and provide those addresses to third parties that might be interested. But you have to ask, what is the legal role of someone placing Web bugs across the Internet? What if he is able to determine that a household is frequently visiting sites about murder and bomb-making? Does he have a responsibility or right to turn that information over to law enforcement?

The next section includes descriptions of various programs to help you identify and block Web bugs, such as Bugnosis and WebWasher that give you some control over

Web bugs. Some Web-based solutions include proxies, such as www.Junkbusters.com, which let you surf the Internet behind its shield of protection.

Solutions: Web Surfing, Personal Information, Web Bugs, and More

This section discusses several programs you can use to control your Web surfing experience. You can control many things in addition to what we have addressed in this chapter, including pop-up widows, banner advertisements, and active content such as Java and ActiveX. First we cover Web browser settings because your Web browser is the most important piece of software you use, and it is important to understand its configuration options.

Web Browsers

The following sections discuss some of our recommended settings for both Netscape Navigator 6.1 and Internet Explorer 6.0. Although the best settings for you really depend on your needs and habits, this is a good reference point. We recommend reading through the documentation and help files that come with your Web browser to understand the full range of configuration options it provides. The recommendations we make provide security in exchange for convenience. It is up to you to decide the balance that you want. Today's Web browsers store personal information about you, store words you commonly type in forms and search engines, and try to enable features that allow for the most diverse and rich Web experience. You must understand the features of your browser to decide what to turn on and off and what personal information to make available.

Netscape Navigator 6.1

Netscape offers many options for adding security and privacy. You get to the main controls by selecting Edit, Preferences, Privacy and Security. Table 7.3 covers some of the subcategories under Privacy and Security and tells you whether each setting should be enabled or disabled.

Table 7.3   **Netscape Navigator 6.1 Privacy and Security Settings**

Privacy and Security Subcategory	Recommended Settings	Setting
Cookies	Enable Cookies for the Originating Web Site Only	Check
	Warn Me Before Storing a Cookie	Check
Forms	Save Form Data from Web Pages when Completing Forms	Uncheck

Table 7.3 **Continued**

Privacy and Security Subcategory	Recommended Settings	Setting
Web Passwords	Remember Passwords for Sites that Require Me to Log In	Uncheck
	Use Encryption when Storing Sensitive Data	Check
Master Password	Change Password—Add a Master Password	Select
	Netscape Will Ask for Your Master Password: Every Time It Is Needed	Check
SSL	Enable SSL Version 2	Uncheck
	Enable SSL Version 3	Check
	Enable TLS	Check
	All of the SSL Warnings	Check
Certificates	Client Certificate Selection: Ask Every Time	Check

In the SSL section, we choose to uncheck SSL Version 2 because SSL version 3 has been found to be more secure. Sometimes sites using SSL try to negotiate an SSL version with your Web browser. If SSL version 2 is offered in addition to version 3, oftentimes it becomes the negotiated choice. By unchecking the option to use version 2, you force a negotiation to use version 3 if it is provided. Be aware, though, that some sites can use only SSL version 2, in which case you would have to enable this option to negotiate.

Netscape offers other ways to get to some of its privacy controls. By selecting Tasks, Privacy and Security, you can access the Cookie Manager, Form Manager, and Password Manager. By selecting Tasks, Tools, you can access your History files, Java console, and JavaScript console.

Internet Explorer 6.0

A large number of configuration options are available for Internet Explorer. You can organize Web sites into one of four zones, each of which is set with certain configurations. Aside from zones, you have control over forms, personal profiles, cookies, and active content.

Security Zones

Four security zones exist in IE—Internet, Local Intranet, Trusted Sites, and Restricted Sites. By placing domains such as `google.com`, `amazon.com`, or `mifavorita.com` into these zones, you can organize and secure your Web surfing. Access the zones by selecting Tools, Internet Options, Security. The default configurations for most of these zones are fine, but we will customize the Internet zone to make it a bit more secure. By default, any site or domain you have not specified in another zone is considered a part of the Internet zone and is handled according to the Internet zone's configuration. For this reason, you need to tighten it up a bit more. If you have sites you frequent and trust content from, such as Amazon.com or Microsoft.com, you can specify them in the Trusted Sites zone by clicking the Sites button. If you know of sites that you should never trust, just specify them in the Restricted Sites zone. The Local Intranet zone is reserved for Web sites that exist inside your company's or home network. The default is that these sites would be trusted more than the Intranet zone but less than the Trusted Sites zone.

We are not covering all the options available for configuration—just the ones we want to change from default. By default, the Internet zone is set to Medium. Click the Custom Level button to get to the settings shown in Table 7.4.

Table 7.4 **Internet Zone Options**

Internet Zone Option	Recommended Setting
ActiveX Controls and Plug-ins: Run ActiveX Controls and Plug-ins	Prompt
ActiveX Controls and Plug-ins: Script ActiveX Controls Marked Safe for Scripting	Prompt
Scripting: Active Scripting	Prompt
Scripting: Scripting of Java Applets	Prompt
User Authentication: Logon	Anonymous Logon

Beyond zones, IE provides cookie control. The recommended settings for cookies, located under Tools, Internet Options, Privacy, are Advanced, Override Automatic Cookie Handling, and Prompt for Both First-Party Cookies and Third-Party Cookies.

IE also provides controls over content you store by and provide to Web sites. Access the Content controls by selecting Tools, Internet Options, Content. Click AutoComplete, and uncheck each option to Use AutoComplete for: Web Addresses, Forms, Usernames, and Passwords on Forms. To remove anything you might have had previously stored, click the Clear Forms and Clear Passwords buttons.

Under Tools, Internet Options, General, you can access controls for your history files, cache, and stored cookies. To clear these traces and any remnants of unwanted cookies or cache, click each button: Delete Cookies, Delete Files, and Clear History.

There are still some more advanced options you can configure. We cover only the options that we are changing from the default settings. Under Tools, Internet Options, Advanced, set the recommended options shown in Table 7.5.

Table 7.5   **Advanced Internet Explorer Options**

Advanced Option	Recommended Setting
Browsing: Enable Install on Demand (Internet Explorer)	Uncheck
Browsing: Enable Install on Demand (Other)	Uncheck
Security: Check for Server Certificate Revocation	Check
Security: Do Not Save Encrypted Pages to Disk	Check
Security: Enable Profile Assistant	Uncheck
Security: Use SSL 2.0	Uncheck
Security: Empty Temporary Internet Files Folder when Browser Is Closed	Check

Third-Party Software

Several packages are available that can assist you in tracking bugs and cookies. These help you understand what a Web site is trying to do to your machine and what information is being sent out to a third party. You can also stop information from being sent out with these programs.

Bugnosis

From Richard Smith and the team at www.bugnosis.org, Bugnosis is a plug-in available only for Internet Explorer. It gives you a visual and audio alert whenever a Web bug is encountered on a site you are visiting. It also gives you more information about the bug, including the complete URL and why it determined this was a bug.

In its current version, Bugnosis does not do anything about Web bugs, other than just letting you know that they exist. In Figure 7.12, you can see the flag Bugnosis gives you when it finds a Web bug, as when we visited eBay.

The next version is expected to actually let you block Web bugs. Even without this feature, though, Bugnosis is good for letting you see just how many Web bugs are out there and which of your favorite Web sites are using them.

AdSubtract

This is a wonderful program for sale at www.adsubtract.com that works for Internet Explorer, Netscape Navigator, Opera, and AOL browsers. AdSubtract is developed by Intermute, a leading company dedicated to providing solutions for letting Internet users protect their privacy. AdSubtract gives you a range of privacy controls, including

- Cookie management, with a color-coded listing of existing cookies on your system
- Ability to block referrers from tracking your movements across the Web
- Ability to block ads, images, Web bugs, Java applets, JavaScript, pop-ups, animations, autorefreshes, and sounds

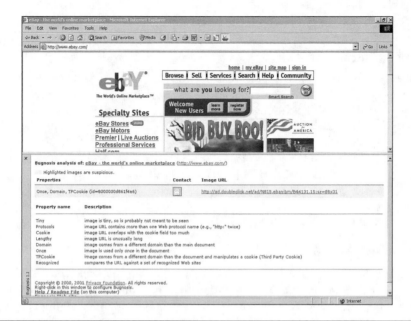

Figure 7.12   Bugnosis analysis of eBay Web bugs.

AdSubtract is thorough because it also keeps a log of everything it filters, as well as every HTTP request your Web browser makes to AdSubtract. This can be an interesting log to review to learn what is really going on behind the scenes because it shows you the raw HTTP traffic. It also includes a statistics screen that breaks down the numbers of different items blocked per site.

AdSubtract works by acting as a proxy, sitting between your Web browser and the Web site you are visiting. It intercepts requests from your Web browser to the site and then intercepts the data coming from the site you are visiting to your browser. The Filters screen can be seen in Figure 7.13.

FilterGate

FilterGate is marketed as a privacy filter for Windows, available for purchase from `http://www.adscience.co.uk/`. It consists of three main components—the Adult filter, Ad filter, and Privacy filter. The Adult filter provides controls to make surfing the Web safer for your children and includes protection from pornography, bad language, and violence. The Ad filter protects against all types of advertisements, including banners, pop-ups, music, and header ads.

The Privacy filter has configuration options that are easy to set up. You simply check a single box to turn on cookie protection, for example. It protects against Web bugs, advertising cookies, and referrers, and you just check a box to enable each option.

There is not much flexibility in configuring the options, which makes it easy for you, but it might not be as granular as you need. For greater cookie control, you will need another tool.

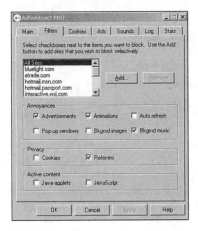

Figure 7.13   AdSubtract filter options.

FilterGate has some bells and whistles, though, including an easy update feature that downloads the latest FilterGate database of ads and other objects that should be blocked.

WebWasher

WebWasher, shown in Figure 7.14, is another tool with a wide range of surfing controls. It is available from the German company Webwasher.com AG at `http://www.Webwasher.com/`, and it actually runs on Windows, Linux, and Macintosh. Its features allow for control of many of the same things as the other programs, including ad control, banners, pop-ups, scripts, and animations.

More related to privacy, WebWasher has filters for the following:

- Web bugs
- Referrers
- Cookies
- Prefix removal

The Prefix removal feature is unique and useful. It disables a site's capability for tracking your movements across it if the site uses a common method that essentially amounts to a link containing two references to HTTP in a single link, as was demonstrated in the section "Web Bugs: Nasty Little Creatures?" For example, consider a link in your Web browser with the following HTML code:

```
http://search.com/track?url=http://realurl.com
```

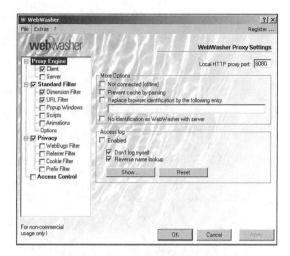

Figure 7.14   WebWasher configuration.

WebWasher safely converts this link into `http://realurl.com`, removing search.com's capability to track your click on the link. As with most programs that provide a lot of Web surfing control functionality, however, there are usually stripped-down controls on cookie management. You get the basics for cookie management, but you might need to supplement the program with CookiePal or an alternative if you want more cookie control.

You can configure WebWasher for use with a proxy server, or even run WebWasher as its own proxy. Be careful with this setting, though! If you run WebWasher as its own server proxy, and you are not behind a firewall, other computers can use your computer as a proxy, cloaking themselves with your IP address and appearing to be coming from your computer.

Spyware

This chapter wouldn't be complete without a mention of spyware. *Spyware* can be defined as any program that monitors or accesses your personal information without your permission and sends it back to the program's inventor. Spyware is usually some program you downloaded as shareware. It can be an MP3 player, a cool backgammon game, or anything else. Spyware can also come to you over a Web site that installs and runs programs on your computer that you really have no clue about. The next time you get a message from your Web browser asking whether you will allow the Web site to install and run software, think twice.

Here are several ways that a spyware program can operate:

- The program can search your computer for stored information, such as your name, address, phone number, and IP address, and then secretly send this information out to someone on the Internet.

- The spyware can monitor your every keystroke, storing every word you type in a file and sending the file out to someone on the Internet.

- The spyware can monitor and log your Web surfing habits, logging which sites you frequently visit, what music you download, or what products you shop for, and then send this information to someone on the Internet.

- The spyware can search your hard drive for all files containing the word "financial" and send them to someone on the Internet.

There really is no limit to just what a spyware program can do on your computer. Depending on the people who created the spyware, the functions and intentions are limitless.

Spyware usually gets installed by you. It does not typically just come along and install itself. There might be a shareware program you really want to test, in which case you download and install it. The next thing you know, the program is doing things you never expected it to do, such as accessing personal information on your computer and sending it back to the software company.

Spyware Cases in the News

In 2000 and 2001, several cases of spyware usage were revealed to the public. In fact, the realizations of just what type of spying the major software companies are doing has initiated legislative movements.

Recent real-world examples of spyware activities include

- AOL and Netscape's SmartDownload utility
- RealNetworks Real Download
- NetZip Download Demon
- Egames.com inclusion of "marketing-friendly" spyware in its demos

SmartDownload Utility

In July 2001, a federal judge ruled that the AOL/Netscape spyware case would move through the court system. Originally filed in July 2000, this lawsuit concerns how AOL's Netscape division used the SmartDownload utility as a form of spyware (see `http://www.newsbytes.com/news/01/167714.html`). The widely used software was used to assign a unique ID to each user and then monitor and log the files the user downloaded using the utility. What this information was used for is unclear. Specifically, the

SmartDownload utility captured the following information and sent it back to AOL/Netscape computers:

- The user's computer's name and IP address
- The complete URL of the file downloaded (for example, `http://www.somesite.com/somefile.zip`)
- The time and date of the transfer

Going one step further, if you were a registered user of the NetCenter portal, your personal information was also sent! Your personal NetCenter logon ID and personal e-mail address were also sent!

Since the initiation of this lawsuit, the spyware functions of SmartDownload have been removed.

These types of activities are becoming increasingly common in software distributed on the Internet. Many companies want to know exactly what people are doing online, be it for marketing reasons or other reasons. The SmartDownload case was similar to the RealNetworks Real Download utility and the NetZip Download Demon, which monitor and report user's downloading activities. Steve Gibson takes much credit for identifying these spyware activities and bringing them to public attention. You can read his reports and full details of his findings at `http://grc.com/downloaders.htm`.

Solutions for Spyware

The Gibson Research Center from Steve Gibson is responsible for creating one of the early spyware detection programs. Named OptOut, this program was available for download from `http://grc.com/optout.htm`. Although its development has been discontinued in the wake of Ad-aware, a spyware detection program from Germany, the Web site is still a valuable reference for spyware information.

Ad-aware (discussed next) is currently one of the best programs available for detecting spyware on your computer. More important than detection, however, is prevention. Prevention of spyware starts with you. By following the recommendations in this chapter and paying closer attention to your Web surfing habits, you can avoid a lot of the spyware that wants to find its way to your computer.

Similar programs for spyware detection can be found at the following sites:

- `http://www.spychecker.com`—Offers a search engine for known spyware programs
- `http://www.spychecker.com/radiateremover.html`—Offers the Aureate/Radiate DLL file remover
- `http://www.zonelabs.com/`—Offers the ZoneAlarm personal firewall, which blocks all outgoing Internet connections by default

Ad-aware by Lavasoft

Available from `http://www.lavasoftusa.com/`, Ad-aware has gained much attention as the spyware-detection tool of choice. Designed by a German company, Ad-aware has support for many languages across the world. This program is completely free to users everywhere, but it can be registered for a small fee to enable even more options. The registration fee is a good gesture to ensure that Lavasoft keeps developing the Ad-aware program.

Download Ad-aware from `http://www.lavasoftusa.com/aaw.html`, and review the latest features and tutorials. After you have it installed, using it is a breeze. Just launch the program through its shortcut in your Start, Programs, Ad Aware Group, and you will see a screen similar to Figure 7.15.

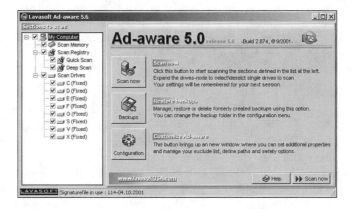

Figure 7.15   The Ad-aware program interface is simple to use.

Ad-aware scans three components of your computer for the existence of spyware:

- Memory
- Registry
- Hard drives

Ad-aware scans each of these with a click of the Scan Now button. You are notified which spyware is found at the end of all scanning. When notified, you have a few options, including removing the spyware from your computer. Ad-aware provides the option to back up before deleting spyware, in case you later realize that you really need the software even though it is spyware. Ad-aware updates its list of known spyware when you use the RefUpdate program; then, when scanning, it uses this list of spyware "signatures" to identify spyware on your computer.

Shopping on the Internet

The Internet's explosive growth in recent years has largely been fueled by e-commerce and e-tailers. The term *e-commerce* is taken from the phrase *electronic commerce*. Shopping done over an electronic medium such as the Internet can be called e-commerce, just as an online retail store can be called an *e-tailer*, short for *electronic retailer*. Nearly anything can be bought online, from jewelry, books, and music to groceries, movies, and cars. The auction craze has also boomed. eBay has lead the way, with many other popular sites like Amazon following right behind. On auction sites, consumers can sell or buy anything from knick knacks to rare paintings.

Shopping on the Internet has many benefits. Using your home computer is much more convenient than driving, finding parking, and standing in line at a retail store. Using the Internet, you can browse through multiple stores, search for the best prices, and buy nearly anything imaginable from anywhere in the world, anytime of day. Even if you decide that you must purchase from a traditional retail store, you can use the Internet to get your research done before ever getting in your car. Indeed, the benefits of shopping on the Internet are great, yet many people are still reluctant to dive in and make their first purchase.

The problem most people have with shopping online is that they do not want to give out their credit card information. The fears of credit card fraud are valid; however, most people forget that they are just as valid with traditional shopping. Many of the online shopping dangers are the same as traditional shopping dangers. Just as your credit card number can be stolen by Web site employees, it can be stolen by a store employee, as well. In the online world, however, an e-commerce site stores many credit card numbers in a single database. This database can be a juicy target for criminal hackers active in credit card fraud.

Recent years have proven that the hackers of organized crime are going after the big catch. They are not after individual home computers and individual transactions. The organized criminal hackers are after a company's database, where thousands of credit card numbers and transactions might be stored.

The FBI and Secret Service were involved in what the SANS Institute for security research and education (`http://www.sans.org/newlook/alerts/NTE-bank.htm`) called "the largest criminal Internet attack to date." During 2000 and 2001, more than 40 sites in 20 states were attacked and more than one million credit card numbers were stolen. The criminal hacker organizations were announced as being from Russia and the Ukraine. These groups were able to exploit vulnerabilities in the Microsoft Windows NT operating system as well as the Microsoft Internet Information Server (IIS) software. (IIS is the software that powers many Web sites on the Internet, providing the capability to host Web sites and interact with client Web browsers.) These vulnerabilities were publicly known for almost two years, and Microsoft had released patches to fix the problems years before these incidents. The problem was not necessarily that the Microsoft software was vulnerable; the problem was that the companies running the hacked Web sites did not take the necessary steps to secure their computer systems, and thus all the personal information and credit card numbers that resided on them. This was a harsh lesson of poor security that affected many of these companies in more ways than one. Not only were reputations damaged, but in many cases, the hacker organizations blackmailed the companies into "buying" security services that would fix their weak security problems.

This example demonstrates how hackers will target company databases. After the credit card information is obtained, it can be sold in the black market, traded across the Internet, publicly posted, or used for blackmail. The problem is that this type of activity is more common than most people realize. Many companies do not turn to law enforcement after they have been hacked for fear of media exposure and the negative effect on business. There is also a problem when the hackers are overseas because tracking them down and prosecuting them can be difficult or impossible. Such was the case with Babygear.com in September 2000, when its site was broken into by a hacker in Yugoslavia. The hacker grabbed credit card numbers stored in an unencrypted database.

Most people do not even know that their credit card numbers are floating around on the Internet. It typically takes a series of suspicious transactions on a credit card bill to alert someone to credit card fraud. The notice might come in other forms as well. If the credit card company gets wind of the Web site break-in, it might initiate a call to customers with the jeopardized accounts.

The rash of online credit card theft and fraud has raised security concerns to a whole new level. Many e-commerce sites across the Internet are doing more to stay ahead of the risks and protect the consumer as well as the company from unwanted exposure. Although e-commerce has created a whole new world of business for companies and consumers alike, there is great determination to keep Internet shopping safe and beneficial.

Internet shopping can save some people a lot of time and money, and the benefits are more than enough for most people to risk the dangers. In fact, Internet shopping is for the most part safe, having come a long way in the past few years. Many popular e-commerce sites have gone to great lengths to add security measures that make shopping very safe for online consumers. It is important, however, that consumers understand these measures, so they can be conscious of when the security is in place and when it is not. In general, the following traditional security measures can make shopping safe for online consumers:

- Transactions are encrypted with SSL.
- Consumer information is kept private or anonymous.
- Credit card and other sensitive information is not sent through e-mail.

Many credit card companies have taken steps to ensure security of credit card numbers and individual transactions. This has created a new generation of electronic money and several means for using it to shop online. This chapter more closely examines some of the latest options for secure online shopping available to consumers. Internet-based companies have emerged to address the needs for consumer privacy and anonymity, and credit card companies have created new means of making secure online payments.

Online Payment Systems

Several companies have risen to facilitate the secure and sometimes anonymous exchange of money online. Some of these companies are Citi Platinum Select, CyberCash, eCharge, iPin, MilliCent, PayPal, Qpass, RocketCash, and WISP. The following sections discuss a few of these companies and their payment systems. Some of these online payment systems offer different levels of security through anonymity, fraud protection, and insurance. Most of the emerging e-commerce payment solutions try to minimize security risk to private data that would compromise an individual's privacy.

eCharge

eCharge is like an online credit card. Instead of carrying around a plastic credit card, you use its service as online credit. eCharge exercises security throughout its own corporate networks and throughout its payment systems. It offers the eCharge Net Account in two methods. You can use it like a credit card, purchasing on credit and paying later. Or you can use it like a debit card, where you simply add money to the account whenever you want and use it until it runs out.

The catch is that the Web site you are shopping at must have support for the eCharge payment system. Most likely, you will see this option under a heading such as Choose Payment Method, where you would also find credit cards and checks. The great thing is that, if the Web site does support eCharge, you do not have to enter any personal information such as name and address, so you get a certain level of online anonymity by using eCharge.

hyperWALLET

hyperWALLET.com is like your wallet on the Internet. When you go to the bank or ATM to take out some cash, you put that cash into your wallet until you need to spend it.

When you get a hyperWALLET ID, you go to your participating online bank to transfer money into your hyperWALLET. Within two days, you can then use the cash to "beam" anyone with an e-mail address to pay for anything as long as that person is also enabled with hyperWALLET. The key to the security of the system is the minimal amount of private information required to open a wallet—just an e-mail address and a password. The only possibly unsecure information required is your mother's maiden name, which can lead to identity theft if other security measures fail.

PayPal

PayPal (`http://www.pay-pal-infocenter.com/`) allows both businesses and individuals to send and request money, as well as sell and shop for goods. To send money, the buyer gives PayPal the seller's e-mail address and payment amount. When the seller gets an e-mail with the subject "You've Got Cash!", she is given a link to `www.PayPal.com`.

The request money can be used for auction payments and donations for charity. If you are an online merchant, you can send a bill to the buyer through PayPal and have the customer pay you by sending the money through PayPal. Then, you can ship the goods with payment in full.

PayPal uses encryption to encode credit card information into what is called *cipher text*, or unreadable text. A secret key converts the plain text of any sensitive information into indecipherable strings of numbers or characters. (See Chapter 12, "Securing Your Standalone PC: Viruses, Chat, and Encryption," for a more thorough discussion of encryption.) Encryption provides a secure communication channel even if a user's computer is not secure. Only the holder of a corresponding PayPal key can decipher or decrypt the cipher text.

PayPal.com has both a Buyer Protection Guarantee and Seller Protection Guarantee. If a buyer does not receive goods purchased from a verified seller, she is entitled to a full refund and protected for up to $5,000 per year for fraudulent transactions. If a verified seller finds himself accepting an order from either a stolen credit card or false claims of non-shipment, he is not held liable for charge backs.

A *verified member* is one who has added and confirmed a bank account at PayPal.com. PayPal.com claims the verification process to be secure and easy for the online merchant to have additional proof of a user's identity in addition to authentication methods.

PayPal.com suggests additional measures for merchants to prevent fraud, including telephoning the buyer. PayPal advises not shipping to post office boxes; being wary of requests for expensive fast delivery; and checking for authenticity of the buyer's mailing address, ZIP code, and phone number.

Verisign/Cybercash

The Verisign company is being called an Internet trust services provider. This is because Verisign offers a full circle of security services focused on Internet authentication and payment services. Verisign's payment services are targeted primarily at online merchants by offering SSL and certificates for encryption and authentication and full payment processing systems run by Verisign. An online merchant could enable her Web site just by connecting to Verisign's system.

Recently, Verisign acquired Cybercash, which offered merchant and reseller services similar to Verisign's. Cybercash had full payment systems already built and secured that online merchants could just connect to and use as their own, and the company offered sophisticated payment systems that could get an e-commerce business processing online transactions in no time.

Disposable Credit Cards and Debit Cards

Many credit card companies offer disposable credit cards to pay for small purchases. These cards are similar to prepaid phone cards that can be bought at a convenience store. Disposable credit cards are not connected with your personal information, offering you a certain level of anonymity while shopping. You buy them without registering any personal information and use them as long as they have a cash value.

Debit cards are similar to bank debit or ATM cards. With a debit card, you put money into an account and shop with the debit card using money from that account. You can add money to the account at any time. Typically, debit cards do not offer complete anonymity because you set up an account using personal information.

MasterCard ecount

MasterCard offers a debit card to consumers, called ecount. Although this does not provide anonymity for the online shopper, it does provide a secure payment method. There is no chance of credit card fraud, and the value of the card is only as much as you put toward it.

Visa Cash

Visa Cash is a chip-based card that can be used in the brick-and-mortar world or on the Internet. Visa Cash cards can be disposable or reloadable, offering anonymity to the consumer. *Disposable* cards get assigned a predetermined value, and when that value is used, the card is discarded. However, new cards can be purchased. *Reloadable* cards do not have predefined values and can be reloaded at special terminals and ATMs. Used up that $100? Just slip the card into your ATM and reload it.

InternetCash

As of March 2001, people can buy InternetCash cards at convenience stores, at retail outlets, or on the Internet at http://www.internetcash.com. Similar to phone cards, these are available in various denominations up to $100. When you log on to www.internetcash.com, you activate your card and create a personal PIN—the site doesn't ask for any private information about you.

American Express

Following American Express and its launch of the disposable credit card in 2000, MBNA Corporation—which includes MBNA American Bank—announced similar services using software by Orbiscom Technology. Similar to the American Express disposable credit card, the bank software creates disposable credit card numbers.

Similar to American Express's disposable card, online shoppers download software that generates a one-time-only number to use in shopping on a Web site. Only the customer and the bank know the actual credit card number, decreasing the likelihood of either misuse or fraud.

American Express initiated an online version of the disposable credit card number for its members to make a one-time purchase on the Internet. After installing software that only American Express card holders can download, the user makes purchases online when a Private Payments box pops up at the top of the screen asking for the customer's name and ID. The box then displays a one-time-use credit card number along with an expiration date.

Discover Card has also entered the disposable one-time-use credit card picture with a different twist: A user can create the number while on the e-tailer's Web site, and it can be used at that site one or more times.

Shop Smart

As with most online activities, security and privacy do not come from a single product. They come from having a knowledge of the threats and a sense of how to be safe.

There are a variety of ways you can get robbed online. Giving your money to shady companies or people, sending credit card payments through e-mail, and shopping at Web sites that have been hacked are just a few of the common things that lead to credit card fraud and robbery.

I know someone who was robbed while purchasing an auction item through Amazon.com. The buyer was purchasing a new Sony Playstation II from a seller whose profile was new to Amazon. After mailing the seller a check for $350, the buyer never heard anything or saw anything. Weeks passed, and the buyer's frustration turned into the realization that he had been robbed. Amazon.com was very responsive to the buyer's e-mails and concerns. Luckily, its policy covers theft through auctions on its Web site. If the buyer would have paid through the Amazon.com payment system, he would have been covered and reimbursed for the entire purchase amount. However, because he paid with a money order, Amazon.com paid up to only about $250.

Many of the threats associated with online shopping are the same as those associated with traditional shopping. Things such as credit card theft, buyer/seller disputes, and damaged product shipments can happen anywhere. If you decide not to shop online for these reasons, you are missing out on a whole new world of opportunity.

Online shopping has many benefits and can be lots of fun. As long as you make good decisions, your shopping experiences will be wonderful. This list of good practices will help you to make safe shopping decisions online:

- Shop with merchants you trust.
- Do research on the company and product before making any purchases.
- Look for signs of security from the Web site, such as SSL encryption and privacy assisting payment methods.
- Read the company's privacy and security policy.
- Use a payment system you feel comfortable with, such as an online payment company or disposable credit card.
- Keep a record of your transaction.
- Never send payment information through unencrypted e-mail.

Summary

The Internet started as a medium for free, unhindered communication. As an expanding network of ideas, thoughts, and Web sites grew, the Internet quickly brought people together from all over the world. Today, the Internet is faced with countless threats. It is being exploited by large companies to monitor and "understand" people's habits, and it is a money tree that everyone with a business mind wants a piece of.

As we reflect throughout this book, there is a struggle between the freedom the Internet brings and the dangers it delivers. Stay aware of what you and your family do in the online world. Learn to control your Web browser and make it work for you instead of against you. Watch which sites are making cookies for you, and block them if you know they are used exploitatively, such as for advertising, monitoring, and tracking. Keep your eye out for Web bugs, and e-mail the Web sites you visit if you think they are inappropriate. Be wary of the programs you download and install. Some organizations want to watch what you are doing online, but it is your right not to let them. Shop smart online. Read a company's privacy policy. Is the company exercising good security practices? Does it use SSL and ask for minimal personal information? In the battle over your privacy online, it is up to *you* to protect yourself.

8

E-mail Security

Electronic mail, or e-mail, is one of the most used resources on the Internet. It's up there with HTTP (Web surfing), and having access to both e-mail and HTTP is enough reason for most people to get their first computer. E-mail has been around since the earliest days of the Internet. During the dawn of the ARPAnet, predecessor of today's Internet, e-mail was built to facilitate electronic communication between people geographically dispersed, but connected by a network of computers. Today, e-mail serves much the same purpose, but in many more ways. E-mail is no longer a novelty item; it has become a common and almost necessary part of everyday life.

When you tell some folks that their e-mail is not private, they shrug it off and say, "I don't care." They might think that because they are law-abiding citizens, they have nothing to hide. Well, having nothing to hide is one thing, but allowing anyone to read your personal conversations is another. Sending e-mail today is like using post cards instead of letters. At least a letter is sealed in an envelope, so you and the recipient will know when someone has tampered with it. Would you send all your correspondence through the mail on a postcard?

It is important for you to understand that your e-mail is not private. It can be easily read by anybody, and anybody can send mail that appears to come from you. Not only that, but computers, or servers, are used to store e-mail and can be accessed by anybody responsible for the mail servers. These e-mail server system administrators have complete access to the e-mail that is stored on them. That means the computer administrators for your work and ISP e-mail accounts can read your e-mail whenever they want and forward them to other people. The capability of the U.S. government to monitor e-mail has existed for years. With public awareness of the FBI's DCS-1000 system (originally called Carnivore), the government's ability to monitor e-mail is becoming common knowledge. (DCS-1000 is an e-mail monitoring system that can filter e-mail based on keywords in the subject and body, or by e-mail address. DCS-1000 is discussed in more detail later in this chapter.)

Until recently, if U.S. law enforcement wanted to invade a person's privacy, it had to go through some legal hurdles. For a wiretap to be placed on phone lines or e-mail systems, a court order was required, as well as some monetary and labor investment. With the attacks against the U.S. on September 11, 2001, the laws quickly changed. The Combating Terrorism Act of 2001 expanded the FBI's wiretapping powers, giving it the ability to monitor e-mail in the U.S. for up to 48 hours without a judge's approval.

A common notion is that because of quantity, it would be too difficult for anyone to monitor or read a person's e-mail. After all, millions of e-mail messages are sent across the Internet every week. Some people question the government or anybody's ability to monitor millions of e-mail messages. The fact is, this is not as difficult as it first appears. Increasingly powerful computers are used to filter e-mail, searching for specific e-mail addresses or keywords in the subject and body. When a match is found, the e-mail is flagged so that a person can more closely analyze it.

You probably use e-mail on a daily basis. Maybe you are working out the details of a business contract, planning a political event, or just communicating with friends overseas. Those messages are nobody else's business. Our face-to-face conversations in the past were private. We could go into the park and have a personal talk with nobody eavesdropping on us. The Postal System is largely private because our letters are sealed to prevent tampering. We shouldn't allow the privacy of our electronic communications to be jeopardized either. Just because our thoughts, words, and ideas are more easily intercepted and read across electronic media rather than traditional media doesn't make it acceptable to do so.

Pretty Good Privacy (PGP) is the best means of e-mail privacy that is available. PGP is software you install that allows you to encrypt and decrypt messages between people so that nobody else can read them. It has been around for years and has proven itself in countries across the world. The trick is that you have to spend the time learning what it is and how to use it. After you figure out the system and share PGP with your friends and family, you will see just how fun it is to encode and decode messages.

The Mechanics of E-mail

Sometimes it seems that the Internet only exists to support the transmission of e-mail. In e-mail's brief history, it has grown as a hacker's creation for communication on the small ARPAnet into a neoteric communication method that spans the globe. It's a wonderful way to stay in touch with friends and family and to conduct business. The benefits of e-mail seem enormous, but, of course, dangers also exist.

This section covers e-mail software such as Eudora (`www.eduora.com`), Netscape Mail (`mail.netscape.com`), and Microsoft Outlook (`www.microsoft.com/outlook`); however, everything we say can also be applied to online mail services such as Yahoo! Mail and Hotmail. In the next few sections, we will have a closer look at some of the dangers of e-mail, followed by the measures you can take to protect against them. First, we need to mention POP3, IMAP4, and SMTP, the major e-mail protocols in use today:

- **POP3**—Post Office Protocol version 3. A set of communication standards that define how an e-mail client (such as Microsoft Outlook or Eudora) is to retrieve e-mail from a mail server.

- **IMAP4**—Internet Message Access Protocol version 4. A newer set of communication standards for retrieving e-mail from a mail server. Similar to POP3, IMAP supports more advanced features, including the ability to search through e-mail messages for keywords while they are still on the server.

- **SMTP**—Simple Mail Transport Protocol. A set of communication standards for sending e-mail. SMTP is used for sending e-mail from an e-mail client to a mail server. It is also used when one mail server sends mail to another mail server.

POP3 and IMAP4 are similar because they are both designed for retrieving mail. When you open up Outlook or Eudora and start downloading your e-mail, you are most likely using POP3 or IMAP4. When you send an e-mail message to a friend, you are using SMTP to get it there. We will focus on POP3 and SMTP in this chapter because they are the most widely used.

POP3 and SMTP are the protocol standards that define how e-mail travels through cyberspace. In short, these protocols are old and have undergone their share of security problems. Some security problems are inevitable, such as spoofing and spamming; however, you can take precautions to protect yourself against these and against the other attacks we have mentioned.

Most of the security problems surrounding POP3 and SMTP are due to their clear text nature and lack of strong authentication controls. Most e-mail travels across the Internet in clear text. That means it can be intercepted and read by anyone with the skills and intent. In regards to authentication, most e-mail systems use basic controls that do not prevent attackers from attempting to guess username and password combinations.

Corporate E-mail Systems

Many medium- or large-sized companies and organizations have internal mail systems that might differ from the ones we just mentioned. Lotus Notes, Novell GroupWise, and Microsoft Exchange are examples of popular corporate e-mail systems. These e-mail systems typically operate using their own set of protocols that can be used for e-mail exchange within the organization. Security and privacy are typically provided to each e-mail message as it is sent between people. That is, a snooper who is capturing e-mail from the network cannot easily read it.

Strong authentication exists in each of these systems, making it difficult for unauthorized people to access your mailbox. Encryption exists to protect the e-mail messages as they travel across the network. These features are often a configuration of the e-mail system, which can be enabled or disabled. If you work for an organization that uses a popular e-mail system such as Lotus Notes, GroupWise, or Microsoft Exchange, you can rest assured that your e-mail message is kept more secure and private than it would be otherwise.

The rest of this chapter will focus on the Internet-based protocols of POP3 and SMTP and the privacy problems associated with them. POP3 and SMTP are the e-mail protocols you most often use when sending and receiving e-mail through your ISP.

How E-mail Works

E-mail is one of the oldest resources that is still used on the Internet. In fact, it is considered by some to be the most used resource on the Internet. E-mail lets people communicate using text, graphics, sounds, and video. E-mail is sent from one electronic mailbox to another. E-mail traffic on the Internet can be likened to a busy interstate that never sleeps. If you were to peek into the backbone of the Internet, you would see a large amount of e-mail passing back and forth.

From its earliest history between 1972 and 1980, the Internet's builders loved e-mail. Ray Tomlinson is credited with the creation of e-mail. One of the Internet's earliest pioneers, Tomlinson first created a small e-mail system that only worked for a single computer. Mail could only be sent between people who shared that computer. This is much like a town whose post office does not exchange postal mail with other towns, a rare find these days. In the infancy stages of the Internet, sharing information across a network of computers was a developing idea. In fact, sharing information was one of the goals. The idea of interconnecting computers across an electronic network was fantastic and magical. Tomlinson realized that interconnected e-mail had a place on the Internet, so he moved it from a single computer system to a system that could operate and exchange mail across the electronic network. During this time, Tomlinson determined that the @ symbol would be used to separate the person's name from the computer on which their mailbox was stored. Little did he know that @ would become the symbol of a legacy.

Viewed from a high level, e-mail actually works quite simply. In fact, it can virtually be compared to the postal service we have been using for years. When referring to the "e-mail system," we can visualize the interconnected mailboxes across the entire Internet, from Australia to the U.S. We can also use "e-mail system" to refer to a local exchange of e-mail between an e-mail user and the e-mail server, quite similar to the local postal service where you go to drop off and pick up mail. The core components of an e-mail system include the following:

- The e-mail address
- The mailbox
- The e-mail server
- The e-mail client
- The protocols (POP3 and SMTP)
- The network

These components are responsible for the e-mail communications that take place every day. The *e-mail address* is comparable to your home address. It is the unique address that identifies your mailbox's exact coordinates on the Internet. The *mailbox* can be equated to your post office box number at the post office. It is the storage place where mail is delivered and mail is sent. The *e-mail server* is like the post office. It houses many peoples' mailboxes, and it provides a central place for mail exchange. Sticking to the post office analogy, the *e-mail client* is you, the person who picks up and delivers mail to your PO box, and the person who reads and trashes mail. In reality, the e-mail client is the software on your computer that retrieves your incoming e-mail from the e-mail server and sends outgoing e-mail to the server for its delivery.

The *protocols* are the agreed-upon methods for exchanging mail. The protocols define how e-mail clients talk to e-mail servers and how e-mail servers talk to each other. The Post Office's standard means of retrieving, delivering, and storing postal mail are no different. The POP3 protocol defines how mail is to be retrieved from an e-mail server by the e-mail client. The SMTP protocol defines how mail is to be delivered across the network.

The *network* is the fabric that ties everything together. It is similar to the streets, buildings, mailmen, and trucks that the Post Office has. The difference is that this network is electronic, made up of IP addresses, computers, and the Internet. Of course, e-mail would be useless without the people who use it and make it all possible.

Let's tie all this together into some examples that describe from a high level what happens when you both retrieve an e-mail message and send one.

Retrieving an E-mail Message with POP3

This is how e-mail gets from its destination to you:

1. Start the e-mail client and establish a connection to the mail server. You power on your computer and open your e-mail program, be it Outlook, Eudora, or

even Web-based e-mail such as Hotmail. The e-mail client establishes a connection to your e-mail server, typically on TCP port 110, the port for POP3. If your e-mail address is `cindy@company12345.com`, your mail server might have a name of `mail.company12345.com`. After a connection is established, the e-mail client is prepared to retrieve mail.

2. The e-mail client uses POP3 to retrieve mail from the server. Your e-mail client contacts the e-mail server using the POP3 protocol. It knows how to find the e-mail server because you configured it ahead of time by specifying `mail.cyberspace.com` as the name of the server. The POP3 protocol defines commands such as `USER`, `PASS`, `LIST`, `RETR`, and `DELE`. POP3 is a simple protocol with few commands and minimal security:

   - The e-mail client uses the `USER` command to tell the server your username.
   - The `PASS` command sends the server your password.
   - After the server accepts your `USER` and `PASS`, the e-mail client is ready for the next step.
   - `LIST` tells the server to return a numbered list of all your e-mail messages.
   - The `RETR` command is used to retrieve your e-mail messages one by one.
   - A few other commands, such as `DELE`, tell the e-mail server to delete a message.

3. After all the e-mail has been `RETR`ieved, the e-mail client closes the connection with the server.

That is the process of retrieving e-mail, in a nutshell. With all of your e-mail downloaded to the e-mail client, it is available to be read, deleted, or responded to offline. POP3 e-mail has a large security problem because everything is sent over the network in plain, readable text. Nothing is encrypted with POP3 mail. Your username and password are sent in plain text, so that anybody snooping on the network can read it. If you are on a cable modem connection, all your neighbors can see your e-mail message as it crosses the network if they are looking for it. Each e-mail message you retrieve is also sent to you in plain text, so a snooper can read those e-mails as your retrieve them.

Sending an E-mail Message with SMTP

This is how e-mail gets from you to its destination:

1. Start the e-mail client and establish a connection to the mail server. Again, open your e-mail client (unless you still had it open from earlier), and this time choose to compose a new mail message. Type in the To field the e-mail address of your intended recipient, such as `friend@electronic.com`. Then click the Send button.

2. The e-mail client sends your e-mail from the server using SMTP. The e-mail client connects to your mail server using the SMTP protocol to communicate with it. The SMTP protocol contains more functionality than the POP3 protocol, and more commands as well. Again, however, minimal security is offered with SMTP:

   - The HELO command is used to set up the connection.

   - The MAIL FROM: command is used to send the e-mail server the e-mail address that you want this message to appear to be coming from.

   - The RCPT TO: command is used to tell the e-mail server the e-mail address for the delivery destination.

   - The DATA command is used to fill in all the important information, such as the subject, the message, and the formatting features of this e-mail address. If you are sending attachments, the e-mail client tells the server what type of attachment it is.

   - The e-mail client denotes the end of the e-mail message using some special character such as a single period on its own line. This notifies the e-mail server that the message is finished.

3. The e-mail server takes over. The e-mail message is queued for delivery. The server examines the header of the message, which contains the destination e-mail address of friend@company6789.com. The e-mail server uses the Internet Domain Name System (DNS) to look up this domain name company6789.com and find its e-mail server name and IP address. After it finds that the mail server is mail.company6789.com, it sends the message out on the public Internet, to be routed to its destination.

4. The destination mail server receives the e-mail message. After the message is received, the mail server, mail.electronic.com, reviews the headers to find that the e-mail message is addressed to friend@company6789.com. The mail server identifies that "friend" has a mailbox here, and puts the e-mail message in "friend's" mailbox. Sitting in "friend's" mailbox, the message is waiting retrieval via POP3.

SMTP is also a clear text protocol. That means that the e-mail messages are sent across the network in plain readable text. If a snooper on the network were to intercept the message, he would be able to read it and even modify it.

The Dangers of E-mail

E-mail was first thought of by Internet pioneers as a way to communicate, criticize, argue, and joke around. Its potential was quickly realized, as e-mail spread worldwide among the earliest Internet users as a medium for sharing ideas, collaborating on emerging privacy issues, and communicating in general. The fascination of e-mail quickly turned from a hacker's toy to an important means of information exchange. In fact, e-mail is one of the driving forces behind the growth of the Internet. Its quick, worldwide spread did not require too many changes to the core protocols. The security shortcomings of POP3 and SMTP were considered an acceptable risk by those responsible for setting up e-mail systems, and the risks were largely unknown to the vast public, who uses e-mail without fully understanding it. Today, the security short-comings of e-mail have manifested themselves into several obvious dangers. Let's look at the major dangers that face e-mail users:

- E-mail can be intercepted by a man-in-the-middle attack, where an unexpected third person reads and possibly modifies e-mail sent between two legitimate parties.

- E-mail can threaten your privacy when government agencies or intercepting ISPs monitor and read the e-mail messages (as in the case of DCS-1000).

- E-mail can be exploited by attackers who spoof (masquerade as) someone else's identity to gain information from trusting recipients.

- E-mail can be exploited by spammers or advertising agencies by using a shotgun delivery approach to send a widespread message or sales pitch in bulk.

- E-mail can be used to deliver threats to networks and computers, in the form of viruses, worms, and Trojans.

Man-in-the-Middle Attacks and Surveillance

A man-in-the-middle attack takes place when someone intercepts communications between two people. If Alice and Bob are communicating through e-mail, a man in the middle can, unbeknownst to them, intercept and either read or modify their e-mail. The concept is not at all different from a wiretap on a telephone. If someone places a wiretap on your telephone line, he can listen in on your phone conversations and record them. Wiretaps can even be taken a step further. Telephone conversations can be intercepted and modified before the receiving party gets it, creating misinfor-mation. These same concepts can be applied to e-mail communications. Surveillance is just an outcome of the wiretap. If your e-mail can be intercepted, it can be monitored over time.

After the tragic events of September 11, 2001, the issue of wiretapping was quickly brought to the attention of the U.S. Congress. The arguments before this time were that people's privacy should be considered more important than wiretapping. In the past, law enforcement had to go through rigorous legal channels of gaining permission to set a wiretap. Of course, they could wiretap without permission, but the informa-tion they gained would not be usable in court. In the week following September 11, the Senate passed laws to allow law enforcement more freedom in wiretapping com-munications. In the heat of the moment, this seemed like a good idea. Many Americans agreed that giving up some privacy was a fair return for increased security.

Note

Stop for a minute to consider the different places that people can intercept and read your e-mail. Many people do not realize just how insecure traditional e-mail is. After you realize that nearly anybody can read your e-mail messages, you will probably be anxious to use encryption methods such as PGP.

- In a small office environment, it is typically trivial for a co-worker to read e-mail you are sending and receiving.

- In a home network or when using a cable modem, other people in your house and neighborhood can easily read your e-mail.

- When you use a public computer such as at an Internet café or at the library, it is trivial for people to see your e-mail.

Don't be scared to use e-mail because of its insecure nature. You can take several actions to secure your e-mail in each of these settings. The strongest and most common approach is to use PGP or a PGP-enabled e-mail service, such as LokMail or HushMail.

DCS-1000

The laws that were passed after September 11 applied to nearly all communications, including e-mail. The FBI has long possessed a controversial e-mail-capturing system they call DCS-1000 (originally called Carnivore). The DCS-1000 system is a computer that is installed on a network to monitor all e-mail traffic going across the network. It is designed to filter all of this e-mail traffic, so that it only captures and stores what is relevant. That is, if the FBI wants to collect e-mail communications between `criminal@badguys.com` and `terrorist@evil.net`, it would configure DCS-1000 to filter all traffic, looking for these e-mail addresses. When it finds these e-mail addresses, it can capture an entire e-mail message and store it so that FBI agents can later look through it. This is a basic description of DCS-1000. It actually has a range of powerful functionality, including the ability to filter for keywords in e-mail subject lines. For more details, visit the FBI's Web site at `http://www.fbi.gov/congress/congress00/kerr090600.htm`. Many ISPs are now cooperating with the FBI because of the terrorist attacks. In the past, ISPs were reluctant to hand over user data.

The point here is not to scare you about DCS-1000—the media has already done a good job of that! DCS-1000 can actually serve as a useful tool in fighting crime and terrorism. The point is that you should be aware that your e-mail messages are susceptible to monitoring. Your e-mail is not private. Many tools similar to DCS-1000 exist, and the FBI is *not* the only group using them.

That's where e-mail encryption through tools such as PGP comes in handy. PGP can give you back your privacy. We will discuss in the following sections how you can use PGP to encrypt your e-mail.

Caution

Because of these security concerns, you should never send sensitive information via e-mail. You should not use e-mail to send payment information such as credit card numbers or bank accounts. Remember that unless you protect your e-mail with something such as PGP, your e-mail is readable by nearly anyone.

Where Does E-mail Go, and Who Can Access It?

Some people might wonder what happens to their e-mail after they click Send. The section "How E-mail Works" illustrated the process of how e-mail gets from point A to point B, but what happens to it at point B? The e-mail is stored on a server somewhere until the recipient retrieves it. The people who own and manage the e-mail server might choose to do a few different things with the e-mail that passes through:

- Archive all e-mail messages
- Journal all e-mail messages
- Back up the e-mail server
- Administer the e-mail server

The fact is, the administrator who manages the e-mail server has complete access and control to all the e-mail that is created on, sent to, or retrieved from the server.

Archiving all e-mail messages means that the administrator keeps a copy of every e-mail message that passes through the server. An administrator might do this for legal or business reasons, but the effect is that people's e-mail messages can be stored for weeks or years.

Journaling all e-mail messages means that the administrator keeps traces of all the e-mail messages that are passing through. This means that he keeps the header information, such as who sent the message, who the recipient was, and what the subject line read. With journaling, the message body and contents are not usually kept. Just like archiving, the journaling records can be stored for weeks or years, depending on how the administrator has it set up.

Most e-mail systems are backed up. If the server crashes, the administrator wants to be able to get it up and running as quickly as possible, hopefully with all the data and e-mail in tact. This typically means that all e-mail on the server is copied over to a tape, CD-ROM, or some other removable storage media. The tape or CD-ROM stores all of the e-mail and can be used to quickly restore the e-mail to the server. Any removable storage media can be kept for months or years. This means that just because you have deleted an e-mail message, it might not really be deleted everywhere. It might be stored as part of a backup for years.

E-mail servers must be maintained, or *administered*. This is the basic process of tending to the server to keep it running and updated. The administrators have total control over the e-mail server. They can typically access anybody's mailbox and read the e-mail. They might actually do this if a legal or business reason arises. However, known cases have existed in which bad-intentioned administrators have read other people's e-mail for no lawful reason.

In all these cases, the best means of protection you have is once again encryption. Using PGP, you can protect your e-mail from prying eyes, even if it is stored for years. We talk all about PGP in the second half of this chapter.

Spoofing and Spamming

Spoofing and spamming are two completely separate e-mail phenomena. When someone *spoofs* an e-mail message, he is making it appear to be coming from an e-mail address that you trust. For example, I can send you an e-mail message that looks like it was sent by `yourmom@isp12345.com`. You would probably not even question the authenticity of this e-mail message; you would trust it just as if it were your mother who sent it. By masquerading as a trusted person, I can trick you into giving out sensitive information. This tactic is similar to when somebody calls you up under a disguised voice, trying to trick you into saying or doing something. People do not commonly question the authenticity of an e-mail message. Most people see the e-mail address that its from and assume that person really composed the message.

The problem is that it takes little skill for someone to forge an e-mail message. I can make any e-mail message look like it is coming from an e-mail address of my choice. The only real way to defend against spoofing is to use digital signatures. (These are discussed in more detail in Chapter 9, "Securing Digital Transactions or SSL and Digital Certification.")

Authenticity of an e-mail message is only secured in one real way. By digitally signing an e-mail message using PGP or some other digital certificate, a person is sealing the message and providing a level of assurance that he is the one who sent it. Digital signatures prove almost beyond a doubt that the e-mail message is authentic and from the person it appears to be from. If someone tampers with a signed message and tries to forge its contents, the signature becomes invalid and the recipient is notified.

Authenticity is not a new problem to the Web or to e-mail. Knowing that information is truly coming from the expected source is a problem that has largely been solved. PGP has provided a means for proving authenticity in e-mail messages and allowing you to identify spoofed, or forged, messages.

Spam is the junk e-mail you get. Spam is also known as unsolicited e-mail because it comes unwanted and unexpected. However, most spam is commercial in nature, bringing a sales pitch or other advertising propaganda. For this reason, spam is most commonly used to refer to unsolicited commercial e-mail (UCE). However, many people consider unsolicited mail of any content, sent by itself or in bulk, to contribute to the overall spam problem. Spam can come as an e-mail advertisement for a low-cost Web site development company, a flame war between two people on your same mailing list, or a chain letter reminding you to spread peace on Earth.

People get spammed because their e-mail address has been "harvested" (collected). It happens if someone surfs the World Wide Web and accesses as many newsgroups as he can to collect every e-mail address he comes across. If he is smart, he might create an automated program that will do this for him. Indeed, such programs exist; some call them *Web bots*, and their job is to find and collect as many e-mail addresses as possible.

If you want to avoid spam, you have to be selective about when you use your e-mail address and where you give it out. You shouldn't put your e-mail address in every message board and newsgroup posting, or on every Web site you visit. Purists will tell you that you shouldn't even put your e-mail address on your own personal Web site, at least not in obvious form. To avoid acquiring more spam over the course of your online lifetime, be conscious about where you use your e-mail address, and consider the following guidelines:

- **Keep two separate e-mail accounts**—Keep a public e-mail address and a private one. Use the private address for communications between people close to you, and never post it online. Use the public e-mail address for other communications, and be prepared to receive a lot of spam mail for the account.

- **Use your public e-mail address for public postings**—When building your personal Web site or participating in newsgroups, message boards, or chat rooms, use your public e-mail address. You can expect that no matter where you display your e-mail address online, it is just a matter of time before the e-mail harvesters get it.

- **Never respond to spam, and never visit hyperlinks that a spam message might contain**—Most spam today comes as HTML-enabled e-mail, and many e-mail clients will launch the HTML code unless you have this option disabled. When image hyperlinks are launched in HTML code, a message might be sent to the spammer indicating that you read the e-mail message and that your e-mail address is valid. When you respond to a spam message, you are also telling the spammer that your e-mail address is valid. Valid e-mail addresses are valuable to spammers, who collect many bogus e-mail addresses through their harvesting techniques. A collection of valid e-mail addresses is more valuable than bogus ones.

- **Use third-party spam filters or ones built into your e-mail client**—Spam filters are designed to catch the junk or spam mail and automatically move or delete it. Although the filters are not 100% effective, they can manage to cut down on the majority of spam that you get.

By following the first three tips, you can minimize the amount of spam you receive. Spam filters, on the other hand, are designed to help you deal with the spam that you *do* get.

Spam Filtering

Most e-mail clients today, including Outlook and Eudora, have robust spam filtering capabilities. They provide the ability to filter e-mail messages based on e-mail address, subject, keywords in the body, and more. Some ISPs even provide filtering for their customers. By using the granular level of filtering provided in these e-mail clients, you can manage the majority of your spam mail by automatically deleting it or by moving it to a junk-mail folder.

In Outlook XP, you can get to the spam filter by selecting Tools, Organize. This brings up the window shown in Figure 8.1 from which you can set up a rule for the e-mail message you have selected. Similar features can be found in Outlook Express by selecting Tools, Message Rules, Mail.

Figure 8.1   By selecting Tools, Organize in Outlook, you can control your spam mail.

Outlook also gives you detailed control of your messages. If you cannot do what you want with the Organize Wizard, try selecting Tools, Rules. This is where you can find the most detailed control of e-mail, in an easy-to-follow display, similar to Figure 8.2. These filters are designed to help you fully control how your e-mail is handled. You can define filters to search for curse words in the subject or body of a message and automatically move the message to a specified folder. You can also define filters to search for messages that appear to be junk mail, and automatically move them to a folder for review or delete them. The purpose of these filters is to let you control spam and your e-mail in general.

In Eudora, you also have detailed control over your e-mail filters. By selecting Special, Make Filter, you can see a quick and easy-to-use screen for setting up a filter, as shown in Figure 8.3.

The filter defined in Figure 8.3 says to find incoming mail from spammer@somecompany.com and automatically delete the message.

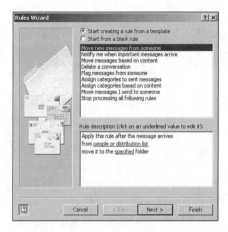

Figure 8.2   The Outlook Rules Wizard gives you comprehensive control over your e-mail.

Figure 8.3   Eudora provides an easy method of making filters to control e-mail.

When you are ready for maximum control over your filters, select Tools, Filters to make modifications. Eudora gives you a central place for managing the filters, with control over what is filtered (that is, e-mail address, keywords in subject or body, and so on), and what actions to take when an e-mail message matches a filter. For example, you can choose to automatically delete, play a sound, or move to another folder when a message matches a filter, as shown in Figure 8.4.

The slightly more advanced filter shown in Figure 8.4 tells Eudora to find incoming mail where either the sender's e-mail address is `spammer@somecompany.com`, or the subject contains the words "get rich." When Eudora finds a matching e-mail, it transfers it to the trash.

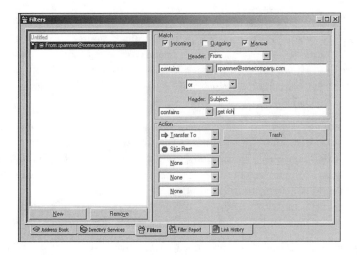

Figure 8.4   Eudora provides a more advanced method of controlling e-mail when you select Tools, Filters.

With the options available under Tools, Filters, you can control your e-mail in more ways than you ever thought possible.

Spam filters can also be set up on e-mail servers and at network gateways. System administrators can set the same filters to block spam before it ever reaches their mail servers. They can also set filters directly on the mail server to reject spam that comes to it.

Many of the online, Web-based e-mail systems such as Yahoo! Mail and Hotmail also offer spam filters. Many of these online e-mail services, including HushMail and LokMail, block spam before it ever arrives at your mailbox, leaving you with little to worry about. Look through the documentation and help files for your e-mail client of choice to figure out just what its options are for e-mail filters and spam control.

For more information on spam, visit `http://www.spamfree.org`, `http://www.cauce.org/`, and the Network Abuse Clearinghouse at `http://www.abuse.net/`.

Viruses, Trojans, and Worms

It is interesting to consider how fast time passes on the Internet. Just a few years ago, a difference was readily apparent between a virus, a Trojan, and a worm. Each had its place and caused its own mischief on a personal computer. Today, however, the lines have become blurred to the point of confusion, although it is quite common for a single program to represent characteristics of each. Today, viruses, Trojans, and worms have the potential to wreak havoc on the entire Internet infrastructure, bringing major Internet backbones and servers to their knees by overloading them with traffic.

What Is a Virus?

A *virus* is a piece of software that installs itself on your computer against your wishes. It typically has some sort of payload. Viruses are manmade and typically are created to bring destruction. Their payload might consist of such things as randomly deleting files on your hard drive, or making infinite copies of themselves until a computer's resources are overloaded and the system halts.

Viruses might piggyback on file attachments you get in e-mail. They rarely come as their own software, but more often come by another infected piece of software. The infected file attachment could be anything from a Microsoft Word document to an entertaining game program. The analogy can be likened to the flu bug. Most people get the flu bug by contact with infected people. The infected people might not even know that they are sick with the flu bug, although they are passing it around. The flu bug started somewhere, and then kept replicating, much as a computer virus does.

The common characteristic that represents a virus is that it replicates itself. The replication is usually local to the computer that is infected. The virus might infect memory on the computer, or might infect individual files on the computer. The virus might also infect the Master Boot Record (MBR), which is responsible for booting up the computer. Mass infection makes an infected computer difficult to clean.

What Is a Trojan?

A *Trojan* is also a piece of software that installs itself on your computer against your wishes. Trojans get their name from the ancient myth that the Greeks used a Trojan horse to gain access to the city of Troy. By fooling the people of Troy into believing that this huge wooden horse was a gift that would only bring good, the Greeks tricked the people into opening their gates and letting their guard down. The Trojan horse was filled with Greek soldiers. At night, when the people of Troy slept, the Greek soldiers who were hiding inside the Trojan horse quietly exited and either killed or captured everyone in Troy.

Software programs that install Trojans do not appear obvious. They come as e-mail attachments, like those funny executables that get passed around during the Christmas holidays, running a program that shows Santa riding his sleigh. The Trojan can be a secret piece of code that tags along and is launched with the executable. After the Trojan is launched, it installs on your machine. A Trojan also delivers a payload. In fact, it might look very much like the payload of a virus. Sometimes, the Trojans open backdoors in your computer. *Backdoors* are openings that allow control of your computer.

A hacker across the Internet, for example, might create a Trojan that e-mails him after it is installed on your machine. The e-mail contains the IP address of your computer, and the Trojan opens a backdoor for the hacker to connect to your computer. The hacker might connect using some special software, or just the built-in networking functions of the operating system. Typically, the connection will carry whatever privileges you were logged in with at the time the Trojan was installed. If you were logged in as an administrator with full control of your computer, the Trojan and the hacker gain the same level of control. Trojans do not replicate themselves like viruses do. A Trojan's main characteristic is that it comes disguised as a benevolent program.

What Is a Worm?

A *worm* is basically like a virus, in that it replicates itself many times over. However, worms replicate themselves over networks, whereas viruses remain local to the machine. A worm can spread over a network in many ways. It can spread by distributing itself through e-mail when someone launches it from an attachment. It can spread through JavaScript on a Web site, or it can spread itself by scanning for vulnerable computers and infecting them. The worm might be designed to exploit a specific application that is running on a computer.

This was recently the case with the Code Red and Nimda worms. Appearing in the wild in September 2001, the Nimda (Admin spelled backwards) worm displayed characteristics of a virus, Trojan, and worm. Nimda would arrive in a person's e-mail box as an e-mail message with an attachment named README.EXE. If the e-mail user tried to open this attachment, the Nimda worm would start infecting his computer and start looking for ways to spread itself. Nimda had virus characteristics because it would modify and create files on the computer and change the computer's configuration. It also had Trojan characteristics in that it would arrive as some benign e-mail attachment and would pollute trusted files on the computer, such as RICHED32.DLL, a file used to open Microsoft Word documents. Its worm characteristics were also advanced, because it could spread itself in multiple ways. Nimda would attempt to find and infect vulnerable Microsoft Web servers and spread between them. It would also modify (Trojan) the Web server's home page so that other users who trusted and visited the site with Internet Explorer would download and install the worm on their own computer. Then, of course, it would spread itself through e-mail messages, using its own e-mail engine instead of the e-mail client (Eudora or Outlook) that delivered it.

Viruses, Trojans, and worms are often referred to as malicious software because they are essentially programs that have an ill intention. Most of the malicious software activity in 2000 and 2001 was by sophisticated programs. These programs represented characteristics from each of the categories of virus, Trojan, and worm, similar to the Nimda worm. The programs' propagation through e-mail was the worm-like activity, whereas the infection of computers was the virus-like activity. In most cases, the Trojan characteristic was simply that the software came disguised as a non-harmful file. Several people have even released so-called good worms, which find bad worms and fix the problems caused by those bad worms, but this is fighting fire with fire.

The media has not been shy about informing people of the dangers of e-mail. Many of the most popular viruses and worms of 2000 and 2001 got a fair bit of television coverage. These included the ILOVEYOU virus and the Code Red worm.

Malicious Software Solutions

In the end, it is up to each person to be aware of the dangers and to practice a few basic security measures to prevent being infected by a virus or spreading a worm. These malicious software programs are still growing in frequency and power. The following list represents some of the best practices that each person can follow to stay virus-free:

- **Do not open or forward e-mail attachments from untrusted sources**— Also, you shouldn't open or forward ones that arrive unexpectedly.

- **Use antivirus software**—AV software is discussed in Chapter 12, "Securing Your Standalone PC: Viruses, Chat, and Encryption."

- **Learn your e-mail program's security features and exercise them**— E-mail clients such as Outlook XP now prevent the execution of attachments by default.

  Disable processing of HTML in your e-mail client. Outlook XP processes HTML-enabled e-mail by default. However, it provides a means to minimize the risks. In Outlook XP, select Tools, Options and then select the Security tab. You see the dialog box shown in Figure 8.5. This dialog box presents you with the same zones that are used to configure security in Internet Explorer. Set the Zone to Restricted sites, and click Zone Settings to get more detailed with the configuration. Doing so applies strict security controls to e-mail that is composed in HTML. For instance, by default, Java and JavaScript content are disabled.

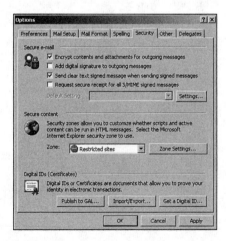

Figure 8.5   Outlook XP e-mail security options: Select Tools, Options, Security.

Eudora comes with HTML e-mail enabled by default. However, by default, it enhances security by disabling the processing of any active content such as Java, JavaScript, VBScript, and ActiveX controls. This is a configurable option displayed as Allow Executables in HTML Content, located under Tools, Options, Viewing Mail (see Figure 8.6). Be sure this check box is unchecked for tighter security.

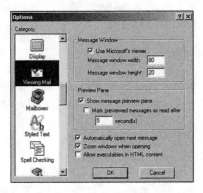

Figure 8.6   Eudora's options for securing HTML e-mail: Select Tools, Options, Viewing Mail.

- **Delete suspicious e-mail.**
- **Keep your e-mail client software up to date and pay attention to security alerts**—You can get the latest security news and updates for Eudora from http://www.eudora.com/security.html. The latest security alerts and patches for Outlook can be found at Microsoft's site (http://www.microsoft.com). Microsoft has a search engine for searching security vulnerabilities and patches for all Microsoft products. The search is done by product and version: http://www.microsoft.com/technet/treeview/default.asp?url=/technet/security/current.asp.

Pretty Good Privacy: Encrypted, Sealed, and Signed E-mail

A bumper sticker out there says, "My child reads your honor student's e-mail." What a message! It seems true today that the majority of people using their computers do not realize in the least just how easy it is for someone else to read their e-mail. If the password can't be guessed, other means can be taken to read the message. Encryption is the strongest defense in keeping e-mail private. If you think it is an invasion of your privacy that the people in your office, at your house, and even your government can all read your e-mail, we want you to realize that there is something you can do about it. Pretty Good Privacy (PGP) software is free. It was created and has been actively developed since 1991. PGP Freeware is the best publicly available and free program for securing e-mail. Commercial and corporate versions of PGP are available from Network Associates at www.pgp.com. Network Associates recently put the PGP product line up for sale; it's uncertain who the next owner will be.

If you have a reason to keep your e-mail private or secure, you need software to encrypt it. *Encryption* is the process of taking a readable message and turning it into unreadable gibberish. If someone else gets the encrypted message, he will not be able to read it unless he decrypts it first. It seems easy enough to click a button to have your e-mail encrypted, but how is the e-mail supposed to be decrypted and read? Asking someone to just click a button to decrypt wouldn't be very secure. After all, the purpose of encryption is to make it difficult for some unintended recipient to read the message. *Public key cryptography* is the answer. It provides a system of secure communications and secure exchange of keys.

Public key cryptography is the model on which PGP operates. Whitfield Diffie and Martin Hellman introduced the concept of public key cryptography in 1975. We discuss the concepts of encryption and cryptography more in Chapter 12. The next few paragraphs will rely on some of those concepts.

Cryptography is the process of communicating in secret codes or writings. For secret codes to be useful between two people, one person must know the code to encrypt and the other must know the code to decrypt. With PGP and public key cryptography, a *public key* is used to encrypt a message, whereas a corresponding *private key* is used to decrypt it. To use PGP, Bob generates a private/public key pair. Bob keeps the private key, and the public key is distributed to Alice and anybody else who wants to send Bob a secure e-mail message.

The keys (both private and public) are really just very large numbers. To Bob, they appear as two separate files: secring.skr for the private key and pubring.pkr for the public key. The public key is used to encrypt a message, and no other key but its corresponding private key can be used to decrypt that message.

PGP works through what is known as a *Web of Trust*. Because Alice relies on the validity of Bob's public key to send him an encrypted message, she wants to be sure that the public key is up-to-date and authentic. Determining the authenticity and validity of a public key is important because it is possible for a man-in-the-middle to create a public key in Bob's name. Therefore, Alice uses a trusted source to find Bob's public key. One place to find Bob's public key is to query a public key server. These are machines on the Internet whose purpose is to serve as a repository or database of public keys. People can submit their public key to the server so that other people can find and use it. Although the public key servers are great ways to find public keys for

people, they are not always considered to be trusted sources. Try visiting each of the
following sites in your Web browser to see how they differ:

- `ldap://keyserver.pgp.com`
- `http://pgpkeys.mit.edu:11371`
- `ldap://europe.keys.pgp.com:11371`

Notice that two of the servers use Lightweight Directory Access Protocol (LDAP)
instead of HTTP (note the preceding `ldap://`). LDAP is a standard that provides for
database access across the Internet. PGP Freeware comes with a search facility that
searches these servers for any e-mail address or name you type in. To search for public
keys of anyone you know, just select Server, Search from the PGPKeys window.

Alice might also find Bob's key by getting it from a friend who has it, or directly from
Bob. A valid and authentic key will be *signed* by someone that Alice trusts and by Bob.
By having a valid *digital signature* from someone that Alice knows and trusts, Bob's
public key can be considered legitimate.

The PGP Web of Trust is distributed among the user community. It's up to the users
to decide how trustworthy the public keys are. This is unlike many popular Public Key
Infrastructure (PKI) systems, where public keys are maintained and secured by a
Central Authority (CA). In a PKI system, users can rely on a trusted CA to store and
manage many people's public keys. Although PGP has traditionally operated on a distributed Web of Trust, PKI systems are also being used for PGP public keys. As we will
see later in this chapter, online Web-based e-mail services such as HushMail represent
a trusted CA that manages multiple PGP keys.

The PGP Web of Trust is based on a social structure that assumes that chains of trust
can be made through anyone—friends, family, employers, anyone. PGP is basically a
distributed way of doing things, as opposed to a tree-like or hierarchical way of doing
things that PKI provides. In both cases, a certificate is associated with each person's
key. The certificate contains information such as the person's name, e-mail address, and
public key. To be considered valid, the certificate is digitally signed with the public key
of a trusted person. When the public key is passed along, the next person considers it
valid when it is signed by someone whose public key is already trusted. This process
continues on and on, so that public keys are exchanged between people who trust
them as valid.

The traditional distributed nature of PGP is different from the hierarchical structure of
PKI. The PKI systems were originally developed to provide the industry with a secure
method of doing e-commerce and other electronic exchanges. In a PKI system, many
people trust a few *root* systems that have central authority to manage and distribute
keys. Certificates can be distributed to individuals, to Web sites, and even to other
smaller authorities underneath the root authorities. Whereas PGP operates using private and public key pairs, traditional PKI systems use something similar, but termed
Digital Certificate. Under the hood of these two systems, you will find different methods of key exchange and encryption.

As PGP has developed into the OpenPGP standard over the years, more PKI systems are actually being built to support the PGP infrastructure. In fact, many companies are investing in OpenPGP-based PKI solutions for secure communications across the enterprise. Because OpenPGP is based on open-source industry-standard protocols, it can be freely developed by different people whose products all interact with each other.

PGP Past, Present, and Future

PGP was first developed and released by Phil Zimmermann in 1991. Its impetus was the 1991 Senate Bill 266, an anti-crime bill stating that all encryption software must have a backdoor that allows the government to decrypt any message. This is the ultimate portrayal of the Orwellian Big Brother watching and listening to the public's every word. The believers felt that privacy was the glue that held society together. Without privacy, people are not themselves.

In the pgpguide.lst file of the original PGP version 1.0, Phil R. Zimmermann (PRZ) says:

> "The 17 Apr 1991 New York Times reports on an unsettling U.S. Senate proposal that is part of a counterterrorism bill. If this nonbinding resolution became real law, it would force manufacturers of secure communications equipment to insert special 'trap doors' in their products, so that the Government can read anyone's encrypted messages. It reads: 'It is the sense of Congress that providers of electronic communications services and manufacturers of electronic communications service equipment shall ensure that communications systems permit the Government to obtain the plain text contents of voice, data, and other communications when appropriately authorized by law.'"

Ten years later, following the September 11 terrorist attacks, the same proposal was made in Congress. This time the motion was made for a globally supported ban on encryption products that do not include backdoors for government access. This motion was separate from the bill that gave the FBI more wiretapping rights.

PGP was spawned by PRZ as an effort to protect private e-mail communications in the increasingly watched electronic medium of wires and computers. When PRZ was first developed, it spread PGP 1.0 to a few friends. Some people uploaded it to bulletin board systems (BBSs), where it could be accessible to more people. The goal was to get PGP to the public and in use before the government's draconian cryptography laws would jeopardize personal communications altogether. Luckily for us, it worked. Shortly after its first release, PGP had leaked out of the U.S. and into the computers of people across the world. PGP was in global use.

With its popularity came some of the first threats from government organizations that accused PGP of breaking patent laws. Although noting that no valid laws were broken, PRZ eventually stopped development and distribution of PGP at version 2.6, to prevent getting sued by a company called Public Key Partners. Other people quickly got involved in the active development of PGP. More controversy arose from the U.S. Government actions, which seemed to take aim at stopping more spread of PGP, accusing PRZ of violating export and other laws. The PGP buzz spread with all of the controversies, and newbies around the world started installing PGP to see what it was all about.

From about 1993 to 1996, PRZ was the target of criminal investigation by the FBI for the accusations that PGP was illegally exported from the U.S., and it broke several patent laws. Contrary to these criminal charges, PGP spread to become the most widely used e-mail encryption software in the world. When the charges against PRZ were dropped in 1996, he founded his own company PGP, Inc., where he could continue development of this monumental privacy-protecting software. Shortly after, at the end of 1997, Network Associates (NAI), a large security software company, acquired PGP, Inc. and rights to the PGP software.

PGP software became the cornerstone of NAI's product line. Although part of the deal with PRZ was that NAI must continue offering a freeware version of PGP, NAI expanded the original software to create a commercial version of PGP. Over the years, NAI has grown the PGP suite of products to include a line of privacy and security-related products such as PGP Corporate Desktop, which comprises the PGP e-mail plug-ins; PGP encrypted disk; Firewall; Intrusion Detection System; and PGP VPN. The NAI product line has also been expanded to included PGP-enabled programs for security of wireless devices.

PRZ worked directly with NAI until February of 2001, at which point he decided to leave and pursue goals he felt were not been achieved at NAI. (His official letter to the public can be found at `http://www.pgpi.org/files/PRZquitsNAI.txt`.) Releases of PGP freeware up through version 6.5.8 had included the full, open source code, so that anybody could see that the software operated as expected, without backdoors which would allow government or others to gain secret access. After this release, NAI decided to only release portions of the source code for PGP Freeware, an action that drew troubled reaction among the user community. Never before had the PGP Freeware source code been kept hidden from public view.

By leaving NAI's PGP development team, PRZ has been able to focus on the future of PGP. With that said, the future of PGP is both active and bright. Notably, several movements are ongoing to keep an open source version of PGP and to develop new products using the nearly finalized OpenPGP standard as it is defined in the IETF RFC 2440. An RFC (Request for Comments) is a longstanding document that describes the technical and high-level details for a technology. The RFC is intended to serve as a reference document. If different vendors or software developers base their products off of the guidelines in the RFC, their products will operate and play nicely with each other. If different products play nicely with each other, the consumers will get more use out of them, being able to share and communicate with people from all around the Internet. These products range from entire corporate enterprise PGP solutions to end user programs similar to PGP Freeware. Although NAI holds the trademark and source code to PGP, PRZ is dedicated to furthering the use of PGP solutions among companies and the public. Some of the activities that PRZ is directly involved in include the following:

- **The OpenPGP Consortium (http://openpgp.org)**—This working group is dedicated to defining the non-proprietary OpenPGP standard, educating the public, and promoting its public use by product developers and consumers.
- **HushMail (http://www.hush.com)**—This Web-based e-mail service is operating on the OpenPGP standard. HushMail is available free for personal use. It also offers paid corporate services.
- **Veridis (http://www.veridis.com)**—This company is dedicated to making e-mail security available to everyone on the Internet through its OpenPGP-compliant products.

June 2001 marked the 10-year anniversary of PGP software. Its use has continued to grow worldwide, respected and appreciated by many consumers, businesspeople, and even government employees. Over the years, PRZ has received numerous technical and humanitarian awards for his work on PGP. Check out http://www.philzimmermann.com/ for more details.

Legal Use of PGP

Currently, PGP is legal to use inside the U.S. as well as many other countries. Millions of people are legally using PGP inside the U.S. and around the world. Many U.S. laws surround cryptography, primarily related to the export of strong encryption. In general, PGP software should not be exported from the U.S. If you live in a country other than the U.S., check for laws related to restrictions on cryptography and the use of PGP inside your country. Notably, countries including France, Russia, Iran, Iraq, and China have more restricted laws relating to the personal and commercial use of cryptography within their countries. To get started finding out the laws related to your country or other countries, visit Bert-Jaap Koops's home page on "Crypto Law Survey" at http://cwis.kub.nl/~frw/people/koops/lawsurvy.htm.

Installing PGP

This section walks you through getting PGP installed and working on a Windows computer. The version you choose depends on the country in which you live. Different distribution sites are available for different countries. In addition, commercial versions of PGP are available, but not as freeware. Although the commercial versions do have their advantages, such as professional technical support, we will be discussing the PGP freeware version here, specifically version 7.0.3. Table 8.1 lists some of the main distribution sites for PGP Freeware and commercial versions.

Table 8.1   **Distribution Sites for PGP**

Site URL	Description
`http://www.pgp.com`	This is the official Network Associates site for commercial versions of PGP inside of the U.S. As the main point of PGP freeware distribution, this site has the latest version before anyone else does.
`http://web.mit.edu/network/pgp.html`	This is the Massachusetts Institute of Technology (MIT) site for information and distribution of PGP Freeware versions inside of the U.S. The distributions here are typically a version or so behind the official NAI release.
`http://www.pgpinternational.com`	This is the Network Associates European site for commercial versions of PGP.
`http://www.pgpi.org`	This is the International PGP home page. This is the main site for PGP FAQs, documentation, source code, and freeware versions for distribution outside of the U.S. Many foreign language translations of the software and documentation are available.

Note

Refer to the documentation and FAQs on these distribution sites for the latest installation instructions and answers to questions or problems you might be having with the installation and use of PGP freeware.

Download the PGP Freeware version of your choice. The latest version is PGP Freeware 7.0.3 available from `http://www.pgp.com/products/freeware/default.asp`. The MIT distribution site has version 6.5.8. After downloading the PGP freeware version of your choice, follow the steps in the next sections to get PGP installed and running on your Windows computer.

Before beginning the setup of PGP, you need to decide which e-mail address you will use with it. Although you can have PGP keys for multiple e-mail addresses, the following tutorial will only use one. Decide on an e-mail address, and decide on a good passphrase to use with PGP. Your passphrase is just like a password, but it is used to sign and decrypt e-mail messages. The passphrase can be as strong or as weak as you want. If you want a strong passphrase, plan on using a sentence that you will not forget.

PGP Setup: Step 1

The first step involves file installation:

1. Unzip the PGP distribution to a folder on your computer. (C:\TMP is a good place.)

2. The setup files are extracted to a subfolder that is probably named PGPfw703. Launch the executable file that has been extracted, probably named PGPFreeware 7.0.3.exe.

3. The PGP setup begins. If you have any other programs open, such as Windows Explorer, you are asked to close them before continuing with the install. After you agree to the end-user license agreement, you have a chance to view the Readme file. This file contains the most current information and installation instructions for the version of PGP freeware that you downloaded. Please read it.

4. Setup asks you if you already have keyrings or if you are a new user, as shown in Figure 8.7. These instructions assume that you are a new user, so select the option No, I'm a New User.

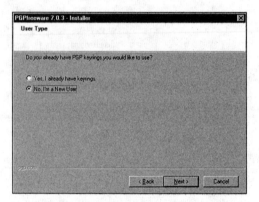

Figure 8.7   Setting up new PGP keys.

5. Setup then asks you the location to install the files. Unless you are running low on disk space or have a preference in mind, you should just stick with the default installation location.

6. Setup then asks which components you want to install, as shown in Figure 8.8. Select at a minimum PGP Key Management, PGP Documentation, and the PGP Plug-in for the e-mail client you use.

7. Setup continues and installs the files onto your computer.

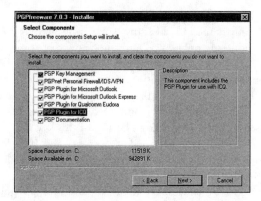

Figure 8.8   PGP installer components.

PGP Setup: Step 2

With the file installation process over, it is time to set up your PGP private and public keys. Remember that your private key is the one you want to keep to yourself. Nobody else should ever get it. Your public key is the one you want to give to everybody else. Using your public key, people can send you encrypted e-mail:

1. The PGP Key Generation Wizard appears. Click Next after you read the dialogue.

2. You are asked to enter your name and an e-mail address for the private/public key pair. The name and e-mail address you enter here are viewable by everybody, and are used to identify the private and public keys. Be sure to enter them exactly as you want them to appear. See Figure 8.9 for an example of how your name and e-mail address appear to other users. These are my keys for when I set up chris@privacydefended.com and specified my name as Chris Weber.

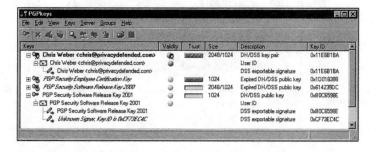

Figure 8.9   Your name and e-mail address appear to others exactly as you have entered them.

Referring to Figure 8.9, you can see my name highlighted in bold letters. Directly under my name in bold is my name again with an icon of an envelope beside it, indicating my public key. Directly below that is my digital signature, indicated by the icon of a pencil and my name and e-mail address yet again. In the next column over, titled Validity, you see two circles, one with the icon of a person on it. The green indicates that this key is valid because it is signed by someone I trust (myself), and the icon represents that this is a private/public key pair, as opposed to just a public key. The size of this key is 2048 for the Diffie-Hellman portion (the key used to encrypt), and 1024 for the DSS portion (the key used for signing). The Key ID represents a unique identifying number for this key. Key IDs are useful for distinguishing between keys that have the same username and e-mail address. Yes, I can have multiple public keys for the same e-mail address.

3. After you have entered your name and e-mail address for this key pair, click Next to be prompted to enter a passphrase.

4. Enter your passphrase to be used for your private/public key pair. You will use this passphrase each time you decrypt messages sent to you, and sign messages you send to others.

5. Your passphrase and a randomly generated number are used to create your private/public key pair, as shown in Figure 8.10. Depending on the speed of your computer, this can take anywhere from one minute to several minutes to complete.

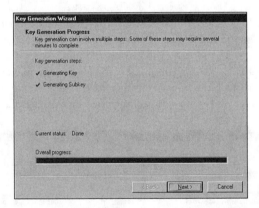

Figure 8.10   Passphrase is used with a randomly generated number to create your key pair.

6. That's it! You are asked to reboot your computer for the installation phase to complete.

PGP freeware is now installed on your computer and ready for use. The following section describes some of the basics of using PGP freeware to send secure e-mail.

E-mail Solutions

This section gives you some freely available solutions for regaining privacy in your communications. First, we discuss PGP and walk you through sending a signed and encrypted e-mail message. Then we discuss some Web-based e-mail solutions such as Yahoo! Mail, HushMail, and LokMail. Of these, both HushMail and LokMail are based on the OpenPGP standards.

Imagine for a minute that Alice is a biologist. She has been working with her colleague Bob on a new vaccination for a rare disease. They want to keep their communications private until their testing is finished. Otherwise, the media or someone else might exploit their work and misrepresent it. After Alice and Bob have each installed PGP software and generated their own private/public key pairs, they are in business and are almost ready to exchange secure e-mail.

They must follow seven basic steps to send and receive PGP encrypted and signed e-mail:

1. Alice creates her message for Bob using her favorite e-mail program.
2. Alice encrypts the message with Bob's public key before sending it.
3. Alice sends the message to Bob using SMTP.
4. The e-mail message travels across the Internet from Alice's e-mail server to Bob's e-mail server.
5. Bob receives the message using his favorite e-mail program.
6. Bob decrypts Alice's message with his own private key.
7. Bob reads the message.

At step 4, the message is traveling across the Internet, where it would normally be vulnerable to a man-in-the-middle attack. Because the message is encrypted and digitally signed, no one can modify or read it, except Bob, the intended recipient.

Let's expand upon steps 2 and 6 a little bit, taking a closer look at the technical details of when the message is encrypted (step 2) and decrypted (step 6).

Step 2

1. The message is sealed using either the MD5 or SHA-1 hashing algorithm. Recall that using a hashing algorithm (discussed in Chapter 12) on the message is just like sealing an envelope. If the seal is broken, the receiver knows that the message has been read or modified.
2. Alice signs the message with her private key (RSA, DSS).

3. The message is compressed, making it smaller.

4. The message is encrypted with a random session key and algorithm such as IDEA, CAST, or 3DES, using Bob's public key with DSS and Diffie-Hellman.

Step 6

1. The message is decompressed, returning to its normal size.

2. The seal is examined for tampering, using a hashing algorithm such as MD5 or SHA-1.

3. Bob verifies Alice's digital signature using her public key.

The previous steps summarize the big picture of how PGP works. If you can understand these steps, you have a good grasp of the PGP concepts. Now let's move on to a practical example of using PGP from Outlook XP. Although each program is a little bit different, this process will be nearly the same for any e-mail client, including Outlook Express and Eudora. In the following few steps, you are going to add the PGP public key for pgp@privacydefended.com to your key ring and send a new message to that address that is both signed and encrypted. Let's get started.

PGP E-mail Setup: Step 1

We have already discussed getting PGP freeware installed and working on your computer. We will just outline the four steps here:

1. Install PGP software.

2. Generate a public and private key pair.

3. Exchange public keys with people you plan to swap secure e-mail with.

Caution

Never give out your private key!

4. Upload your PGP public key to a PGP key server. (You do not have to, but if you do, people will be able to easily find your public key.)

Learn Your PGP Keyring

After PGP is installed on your system, you should get familiar with your keyring. This is just like the keyring that holds your house and car keys, except that the PGP Keyring holds all of your friends' and correspondents' PGP public keys, as well as your very own private/public key combination. You can access the PGP Keyring by selecting Start, Programs, PGP, PGPKeys. You will see a screen like Figure 8.9 from earlier. At first, only a few entries are available for the default public keys that come installed with PGP, but as you add more friends' and associates' public keys to the list, you will see their names fill up your key ring. Within the PGPKeys interface, you can manage keys, export them and mail them to others, search key servers for public keys, and more.

Caution

When you export a key from your key ring, you can e-mail it to other people. Be careful never to export your private key! You should only be exporting your public key to send to others. If you send someone your private key, that person will be able to impersonate you and open messages encrypted to you.

If you use Eudora, Outlook, Outlook Express, or Lotus Notes for your e-mail client, PGP provides a plug-in for you. A plug-in is like an extension to a program. After you install PGP, it extends Outlook or Eudora with direct support for PGP. From within the e-mail client, you can now use the PGP functionality. That is, you can directly sign and encrypt your messages from within an e-mail message.

PGP E-mail Setup: Step 2

Before youcan send someone a PGP-encrypted e-mail, you have to have his PGP public key on your key ring. If you do not have anybody in mind already, you can use our PGP public key for pgp@privacydefended.com:

1. Use your Web browser to visit http://pgpkeys.mit.edu:11371. (Make sure you put in the colon and 11371 just as shown.) This site exists just for PGP public keys. In its database, millions of people have uploaded their PGP public keys, which anyone can download and view. If you cannot reach this site, try http://keyserver.pgp.com instead.

2. Search for PGP@privacydefended.com by typing it in the search or lookup form.

3. Our PGP public key will be returned.

4. Use the mouse to highlight and copy all of the text inside your browser. Windows users can click inside the browser and then press Ctrl+A (Select All) followed by Ctrl+C (Copy) to copy everything.

5. Open your PGP key ring by selecting Start, Programs, PGP, PGPKeys.

6. Select Edit, Paste. You see the Select key(s) window, as shown in Figure 8.11. Click Import to add this public key to your key ring.

Figure 8.11   Importing the PGP public key for pgp@privacydefended.com.

That's it! Move on to step 3 to compose a secure message.

PGP E-mail Setup: Step 3

Now that you have some PGP public keys on your key ring, you are ready to send secure e-mail. Remember: You can only send secure e-mail to people whose public keys you have. You can use whichever e-mail program you normally use in the following steps—that is, provided it is one that PGP supports, and you have installed PGP with the e-mail plug-ins for it. In our example, we are using Microsoft Outlook XP. However, users of older versions of Outlook can follow along, and even users of Eudora will follow similar steps:

1. Open Outlook and start a new message.
2. Enter pgp@privacydefended.com for the e-mail address you are mailing to.
3. Type the subject and message body as you normally would.
4. Encrypt and sign the message using PGP. You can do this in one of two ways using the PGP plug-ins, as shown in Figure 8.12:
    - Click the PGP icons for Encrypt Message Before Sending and Sign Message Before Sending.
    - Select PGP, Encrypt on Send or PGP, Sign on Send.

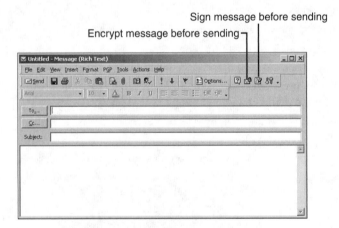

Figure 8.12   PGP e-mail plug-ins are accessible from either the menu bar or the icon buttons.

5. After you have composed the message and selected to both Encrypt and Sign the message, you are ready to send it.
6. To perform the digital signature, you will be asked to enter your secret passphrase.

That's it! You have successfully sent a secure e-mail message. If you go into your Sent Items folder and try to open the message, you will notice that not even you can read the contents! That is because you encrypted it with our PGP public key, which makes it readable only by us.

PGP is valuable only if you use it. Ask your friends to set themselves up with PGP, and start exchanging secure e-mail with as many people as you can. PGP might seem complicated at first because of all the functionality it has, but it becomes simple to use after you are familiar with the basics.

If you are wondering what this message looks like to someone who was not intended to see it, take a look at Figure 8.13. The message is encrypted and appears as unreadable gibberish to anybody but the person or persons for whom it was intended.

Figure 8.13   PGP e-mail is encrypted and unreadable to anybody but the intended recipients.

You can rest assured that if you are encrypting with a valid and trustworthy public key, your e-mail message will be unreadable garbage to anybody other than the people you want reading it. This will be the case whether you use your own installed copy of PGP Freeware or an online e-mail service that supports OpenPGP, such as HushMail and LokMail.

Secure Web-Based E-mail Solutions: Yahoo!/Zixit Mail, HushMail, and LokMail

Although they do not all use PGP, many online e-mail providers are offering Web-based e-mail with security. You can sign up for a free e-mail account and you only need a Web browser to check, send, and manage your e-mail. Many people have used Hotmail, Yahoo! mail, or some similar type of Web-based e-mail service before. Adding secure e-mail to these services is a recent trend, and will no doubt continue.

Yahoo!, LokMail, and HushMail each work differently. Yahoo! provides its e-mail security through a third-party organization. E-mail messages can be sent encrypted to any e-mail address on the Internet. The recipient of the Yahoo! message must go to http://www.SecureDelivery.com to read the encrypted message.

This is in contrast to LokMail, which can only encrypt messages to people who have PGP set up either on their computer or through some Web-based e-mail service (such as LokMail). Based on the OpenPGP standard, the advantages of using LokMail include security throughout the entire e-mail process, from composing to sending to receiving. More than that, LokMail offers you LokVault, which is PGP encrypted storage space for your files. The other advantage is that it allows you to manage a PGP keyring and send e-mail between anybody who uses PGP. You must have somebody's PGP public key on your keyring before you can send that person encrypted e-mail. LokMail is a wonderful and advanced system whose main disadvantage is perhaps that it is more difficult to use. You have a password for logging into your mail account, and another password for encrypting/decrypting with PGP.

HushMail is also based on the OpenPGP standard. HushMail is simple to use because no PGP keyring is required to manage, and you only need to remember one password. The same password used for logging into your mail account is the one you use to encrypt and decrypt e-mail. Encrypted e-mail messages can only be sent between HushMail users. In this way, the HushMail system acts like its own central authority for managing people's PGP keys. You can trust the validity of the keys more because they are centrally managed, but you can not send e-mail to other PGP users outside of the HushMail network. This is true at least in the free, current version of HushMail.

Table 8.2 lists some of the features of each.

Table 8.2   **Web-Based E-mail Services**

Web-Based E-mail Service	Characteristics
Yahoo!/Zixit Mail http://mail.yahoo.com	Free. Requests personal information for account setup. Easy for sender to use, but not necessarily receiver. Inconvenient for receiver to use because he has to check mail from the Web site, rather than having it delivered to his mailbox.

Table 8.2 **Continued**

Web-Based E-mail Service	Characteristics
	Exchange secure mail with any e-mail address on the Internet.
LokMail `http://www.lokmail.com`	Free.
	More difficult to use than HushMail.
	No sponsor advertising.
	No personal information requested for account setup.
	Easy for sender and receiver to use.
	E-mail is sent directly to the receiver's mailbox.
	Uses OpenPGP as the method of encryption.
	Full-blown Web-based e-mail system that allows you to manage e-mail, folders, and PGP keyring, and exchange unsecured mail with anybody on the Internet.
	Exchange secure e-mail only with people using PGP or PGP-enabled systems, such as LokMail.
	Digitally sign e-mail messages (to anybody) using OpenPGP.
	LokVault—encrypted and secure storage for your files.
HushMail `http://www.hushmail.com`	Free.
	Simplest to use.
	Advertising by sponsors.
	No personal information is required for setup.
	Easy for sender and receiver to use.
	E-mail sent directly to the receiver's mailbox.
	Uses OpenPGP as the method of encryption.
	Full-blown Web-based e-mail system; you can manage e-mail and folders and even have new mail notifications sent to another e-mail account of yours.
	Exchange secure e-mail only with other HushMail users.
	Digitally sign e-mail messages (to anybody) using OpenPGP.

Yahoo! Mail

`http://mail.yahoo.com`

Yahoo! has joined forces with `Zixit.com`, formerly `SecureDelivery.com`, to bring secure e-mail to its user community. When you sign up for a free Yahoo! e-mail account, you are asked for personal information such as your name, zip code, and occupation. Of course, no checking takes place to see if the information that you register is true. As a Yahoo! mail user, the steps for creating and sending a secure, encrypted e-mail message to someone are as follows:

1. Bob composes a message and selects the Send via free `SecureDelivery.com` option, as shown in Figure 8.14.

Figure 8.14   Yahoo! mail enables you to encrypt mail by clicking Send Via Free `SecureDelivery.com` before sending your message.

2. Alice receives a message from `SecureDelivery.com`, inviting her to the site to set up a secret passphrase.

3. Alice goes to the `SecureDelivery.com` Web site and sets up her passphrase.

4. Alice is e-mailed a confirmation request inviting her back to the Web site.

5. At the `SecureDelivery.com` Web site, Alice accepts her passphrase and reads the secure message that Bob sent.

6. Bob gets a Message Pickup Receipt, indicating that Alice has read the message.

After Alice has read the message from the `SecureDelivery.com` Web site, she has the option to reply using the same level of security. The same process will repeat, but this time Bob will be the one receiving the secure message.

Security is achieved by keeping the encrypted e-mail on the `SecureDelivery.com` e-mail servers; however, the extra steps of having to log into this Web site cannot be ignored. Alice must visit this Web site to view the mail, but after she is in, she can also send secure messages to Bob.

HushMail

`http://www.hushmail.com`

HushMail provides an effective solution in what is perhaps the most simple to use OpenPGP Web-based e-mail system available. If you just want to get up and running with secure e-mail, without having a bunch of advanced options to figure out, use HushMail. Through a completely Web-based interface, you can exchange secure e-mail with other HushMail users, and even send non-encrypted e-mail to non-HushMail users. As of October 2001, HushMail began offering HushMail Professional, a software application that integrates with Microsoft Outlook, to allow for secure HushMail usage directly from your Outlook e-mail client. In this section, we will be referring only to the features of the HushMail Web-based e-mail system available from `http://www.hushmail.com`.

Setting up a HushMail account is simple and does not require you to enter personal information. You sign up by entering the username of your choice (such as `privacydefended@hushmail.com`) and your chosen password. As usual, be sure *not* to forget your password or you will be unable to open encrypted messages. The HushMail support staff cannot retrieve messages encrypted for you if you forget your password.

The HushMail user interface is friendly and familiar. As shown in Figure 8.15, buttons are available for checking mail, composing mail, and managing your contacts, preferences, and folders.

Sending and reading e-mail is simple. To send it, click the Compose button to start a new message. As shown in Figure 8.16, your options are limited, making the decisions easy. You choose to encrypt or sign the e-mail message, and then you send it. If the person you are e-mailing is a member of the HushMail.com network, your message goes through as soon as you click Send. If the recipient is not a member, you will get an error saying that the message cannot be encrypted. Remember: With the HushMail system, messages can only be encrypted between HushMail users. The HushMail people store and manage all of the PGP keys. You can still send messages to people who don't use HushMail, but you can't encrypt them.

Part of the simplistic allure of HushMail is that you do not have to bother with multiple passwords. Although some people find separate passwords to bring added security, others find them to bring headaches. HushMail requires only one password, and after you have entered it the first time, you do not need to continue typing it in every time you want to sign a message or read an encrypted one.

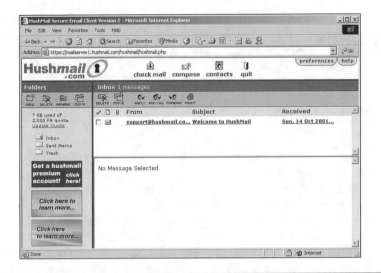

Figure 8.15   The HushMail interface.

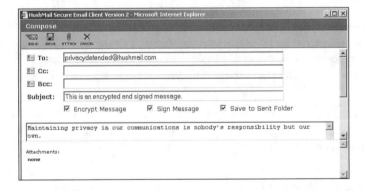

Figure 8.16   Composing a secure e-mail message is simple using HushMail.

Web-Based PGP by LokMail: A Tutorial

http://www.lok.com

LokMail works differently, providing perhaps one of the most advanced and usable secure e-mail experiences. LokMail provides more advanced functionality than HushMail, and it is not for the faint of heart. If you are looking for an advanced secure e-mail solution, and you are willing to spend some time figuring things out, use LokMail; otherwise, try out HushMail which provides an easier-to-use secure e-mail system, without many of the advanced features. LokMail uses OpenPGP security at the core of its system. LokMail operates over a secure SSL-enabled channel. You can notice this in the URL address bar, where `https://` precedes the address. Everything you send between your browser and LokMail is encrypted and secured.

By using LokMail, you get two main features:

- LokMail OpenPGP encrypted and signed e-mail
- LokVault OpenPGP secure file storage

LokMail gives you the benefit of easily exchanging secure e-mail with people who use PGP (or LokMail). It provides a rich Web-based e-mail experience, offering you full control of e-mail, folders, and preferences. You get the LokVault, which is basically just secure storage space for your files. One of the best parts is that you have a PGP Keyring built right in for you.

Setting up and using LokMail is simple and free, and possibly one of the easiest Web-based e-mail systems to get started with in under a minute. Currently, LokMail version 2 works only with Internet Explorer and versions of Netscape prior to 6.0. LokMail does not ask for personal information when you are setting up a free account.

Follow these steps to set up LokMail:

1. Sign up at `www.lok.com` by clicking the REGISTER button.
2. At the LokMail signup screen, you are asked to enter four items. Make sure you read the few paragraphs describing the requirements for setting up each of the following because minimum and maximum lengths are allowed for each:
   - **Your full name**—The name that will be associated with your PGP public key
   - **Your desired e-mail username**
   - **Your password**—Used to access and use the e-mail account
   - **Your passphrase**—For using the PGP encryption built into LokMail

That's it. After you make it through steps 1 and 2, you are ready to start using your new LokMail account.

When you finish signing up with LokMail, you are given a chance to e-mail your new public key to somebody. Take this opportunity to e-mail a friend, so that he can respond by sending you a secured message.

Sending e-mail with LokMail is fun and secure. It is important to note that not only do you have a password for access to LokMail, but you have a separate passphrase for use with PGP. Do not forget either of these. Before we walk through setting up secure e-mail with LokMail and PGP, realize that you can also send e-mail unsecured to anybody on the Internet. Just click Compose and off you go. LokMail is a full-blown Web-based e-mail client, allowing you to send and receive your choice of unsecured or secured messages.

When you first log in to LokMail, you are given a chance to configure your options, as shown in Figure 8.17. Take a minute to see what your options are, and customize LokMail to suite your needs.

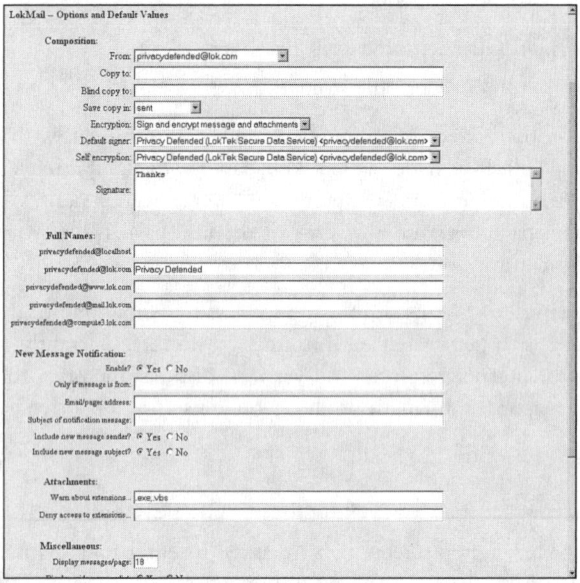

Figure 8.17   The LokMail configuration.

You have options for things like the following:

- Display name
- Message signature
- E-mail or pager notifications for new e-mail
- Warn/deny access to certain file attachment extensions (.exe and .vbs are good ones to include here)
- Miscellaneous options related to your LokMail preferences

To send secure e-mail to somebody, you first need to get that person's PGP public key from a public key server and add it to your key ring. For starters, you can use our PGP public key, created just for this exercise. Follow these steps to find our PGP public key and add it to your key ring in LokMail. You must first have completed the previous steps to set up your LokMail account:

1. Use your Web browser to visit http://pgpkeys.mit.edu:11371. (Make sure you put in the colon and 11371 just as shown.) This site exists just for PGP public keys. In its database, millions of people have uploaded their PGP public keys,

which can be searched, downloaded, and viewed publicly. If you cannot reach this site, try `http://keyserver.pgp.com` instead.

2. Search for `PGP@privacydefended.com` by typing it in the search or lookup form.

3. Our PGP public key will be returned, as shown in Figure 8.18.

Figure 8.18   Your PGP public key for `pgp@privacydefended.com` e-mail address.

4. Use the mouse to highlight and copy all of the text starting from the words *Public Key Server*. Windows users can click inside the browser and then press Ctrl+A and then Ctrl+C to copy everything.

5. Now, open a separate Web browser window and go to `http://www.lok.com`.

6. Log in using your username and password, and select Key Ring, Add Key, as shown in Figure 8.19.

Figure 8.19   Add a public key to your LokMail key ring by selecting Key Ring, Add Key.

7. Paste our public key for `pgp@privacydefended.com` into the form, and click Execute. If you get a message saying that the public key is invalid, you have

copied the wrong text. Just try again, this time copying all of the text that appears in your browser.

That's it! You have added the first public key to your keyring.

If you select Key Ring on the LokMail menu, you should see a screen similar to Figure 8.20. You will see our PGP public key and your own keys for your e-mail address and your private key.

Figure 8.20   LokMail provides a PGP keyring for you to store people's public keys.

Note

Other people must have your PGP public key to securely e-mail you. You can send it to them via e-mail by clicking KEY RING and then clicking the link with your e-mail address located under the Public Keys section. Type the e-mail address for a friend or someone you know who uses PGP, and select Send Key.

The grueling part is over. From now on, you are ready to exchange secure e-mail. You just need to add new people's public keys to your KEY RING when you are ready to mail them. Follow the next few steps to send an encrypted and signed e-mail to pgp@privacydefended.com:

1. Select LokMail, Compose.
2. You will see a screen similar to Figure 8.21, where you can create and send your e-mail.

Figure 8.21   Composing an e-mail message at `www.lok.com`.

3. Compose your e-mail normally, addressing it to `pgp@privacydefended.com`.

4. Select Sign and Encrypt Message and Attachments from the Encryption drop-down menu, and select Send Message Now from the other drop-down menu.

5. You are asked to enter your passphrase so the message can be signed. Remember that your passphrase is specific to PGP and separate from your login password.

That's it! Your e-mail message is signed, encrypted, and securely sent on its way to `pgp@privacydefended.com`. Try to get one of your friends to send you a PGP encrypted message using your PGP public key.

LokVault

Lok Technologiesalso provides you a place to securely store your files. LokVault is integrated with the LokMail service. Just click LOKVAULT on the Links menu to access the secure storage area. From here, you can create folders and upload files, as shown in Figure 8.22. Your files are encrypted either with a password of your choice or by using your public key. The free account comes with 25MB of storage space, but if you need more, you can upgrade to a Premium Service that is bound to give you or your company what you need.

Figure 8.22   LokVault access.

Think of LokVault like Windows Explorer. You create folders on your computer in which to store files. LokVault is no different, except that your files are encrypted and stored securely on the LokMail servers instead of your hard drive.

For more information regarding LokMail, and to see tutorials on using it, visit `https://admin0.lok.com/support/`.

Looking for More E-mail Solutions?

If you are running out of allowed storage space for your e-mail, try upgrading to one of the commercial accounts on HushMail or LokMail. Both systems offer more enhanced e-mail functionality and storage space for a small yearly or monthly fee. Additionally, both HushMail and LokMail offer total, secure e-mail solutions for entire companies. If you have a small or even a large business, these companies can solve your e-mail decisions by providing you with a complete e-mail solution for your workforce.

With HushMail and LokMail you can rest assured that your e-mail communications are private. Without your PGP password, nobody else can read your e-mail, not even the people who own the mail servers.

For more information on the corporate services that these two companies provide, visit their business Web sites at `http://www.hush.com` and `http://www.loktechnology.com/`.

Alternatives to PGP

Although this chapter has focused on PGP, you should realize that other options are available to you. As we mentioned, systems that are similar to PGP exist, operating on a Public Key Infrastructure (PKI). Whereas PGP operates on a Web of Trust, the commercial PKI-based systems operate through Certificate Authorities (CAs).

The PGP Web of Trust distributes the responsibility of maintaining valid and legitimate public keys among the community of PGP users. This has advantages such as the freedom to change keys at will and the freedom to set up and use keys. The disadvantages of the Web of Trust model include the security problems that exist with distributed key management. It is not always easy to tell whether a person's public key is valid and current. Sometimes it takes an experienced PGP user to be able to look at a key and tell whether it is legitimate. An important point to remember is that just because a PGP public key is signed doesn't mean it is valid.

The commercial PKI-based systems take away these disadvantages and bring new ones. The CAs take on the responsibility of managing all public keys and ensuring that they are valid and current. This centralization adds more security to the exchange of public keys in some people's minds.

Several companies exist as central Certificate Authorities to offer, sell, and manage the digital certificates and infrastructure for individuals and companies to communicate securely. Some of the largest include the following:

- Verisign Digital IDs (`http://www.verisign.com/products/e-mail/index.html`)
- Thawte Personal Certificates (`http://www.thawte.com/getinfo/products/personal/contents.html`)

PGP and commercial PKI have traditionally represented two similar concepts that use two different systems to manage key exchange and secure communications. However, the creation of the OpenPGP Consortium is changing this, and the future will most likely see more PKI solutions based on the OpenPGP standard. In fact, PKI and PGP go hand in hand, as they always have.

Summary

The concept of Defense in Depth means that not only must your operating system be secure, but the applications and data that go into and out of your network must also be secure. E-mail is a critical part of any business. It is becoming a critical part of the home user's lifestyle as well.

If you ask anyone for their e-mail address, the odds he will have one to give you. E-mail addresses are like phone numbers—just about everyone has one. Like caller ID and call blocking, your e-mail now comes with some security options that you should take advantage of when going online. You probably don't want someone listening in on your phone conversation, so why would you want someone to read your e-mail if it is not intended for them?

Today's e-mail systems have become robust and somewhat complex. The needs for security and privacy of information have driven the development of PGP and other secure mail alternatives. If you are not using some form of encryption on your private e-mails, you are asking someone to read all about your life. Secure e-mail options are available freely, and you should implement one as soon as possible.

IV

Ground Zero: Securing Your PC Against a Hostile World

9

Securing Your Internet Transactions with SSL and Digital Certificates

Fear still keeps many people from making a purchase online. The fear might be that their credit card information will be stolen or their shopping habits will be monitored. The problem is that the fear is real. The explosive growth of the Internet over the past 10 years has created widespread dependence on communication protocols, which were not developed for privacy and security. The communication protocols of the Internet, known as Transmission Control Protocol/Internet Protocol (TCP/IP), were designed to allow computers to share information, not hide it from each other. TCP/IP can basically be thought of as the language of the Internet. Whereas people in the U.S. speak English, computers on the Internet speak TCP/IP.

TCP/IP makes the World Wide Web possible. It enables us to send e-mail, surf Web pages, and chat on instant messengers. Because all these types of Internet communications depend on TCP/IP to operate, they all suffer from its inherent problems. Computers talk to each other (using TCP/IP) across the Internet much like people talk across phone lines. Anybody can put a wiretap on your telephone and listen to your conversations, just like anybody can intercept your computer transmissions (e-mail, Web surfing, and chats) and read them. The thing is, people can do even more malicious things with computers. Not only can they eavesdrop on you, but they also can change the information that you send and receive, appear as trusted parties to you (a trusted Web site or trusted e-mail), and even impersonate your identity. Although these risks and fears are valid, means are available to minimize them.

Secure Sockets Layer (SSL) provides protection from some of these problems. It still operates using TCP/IP, but it adds layers of protection to the information exchange. You can think of SSL like armor protecting your information from prying eyes. It does more than that, however. By using *digital certificates*, you can validate the identity of people or Web sites with whom you communicate, and they also can validate yours. Digital certificates are like passports or drivers licenses. They serve as identification cards on the Internet.

The Internet is cyberspace, a place where people travel with no identity. Trust is the only proof you have that someone is who he says he is. That is part of the beauty of the Internet. The Internet transcends all human boundaries of race, religion, culture, and belief and presents people as complete equals.

The rise of e-commerce has led much of the push to bind identities to people. Digital certificates are supposed to provide trusted documents of identity to any entity on the Internet, be it an organization, a Web server, or a person such as you or me. Pretty Good Privacy (PGP) is one method of providing this type of identity. Unlike PGP, however, where the decision to trust an identity is ultimately left up to you, the popular systems of digital certificates today are based on a centralized administration of trust authorities. Instead of making the decision yourself to trust somebody, you are forced to rely on a central authority to make the decision for you. As we will explain in this chapter, using digital certificates has several advantages, but it also has several problems.

What Is SSL?

Proving identity and securing the exchange of information has been an ongoing goal of the Internet community. Now that the Internet community includes not only people like you and me, but also companies, governments, and criminals, it is more important than ever to have these reassurances. SSL is the Secure Sockets Layer set of protocols. In general, it is a standard way to achieve a good level of security between a Web browser and a Web site. Actually, SSL can protect more than just Web surfing activity, but we will cover that as we go along.

SSL has reached version 3 in its development. SSL version 1 was quickly replaced with version 2 several years ago. When several security problems were discovered with version 2 of SSL, the developers at Netscape created version 3. SSL v3.0 is considered the strongest yet, and it is the focus of this chapter. Today, Netscape is not the only company that is developing SSL-enabled products. Several companies are making SSL their own way; free, open-source versions of the software are available for anybody to use. For all these different SSL-enabled products to work together, they must follow a standard set of guidelines.

SSL is designed to create a secure channel, or tunnel, between a Web browser and the Web server. The secure tunnel is just for you and the Web server, so that any information you exchange is protected within the secure tunnel. The information exchange is protected because it is nearly impossible for anybody else to see or modify the information while it is in transit. Even better, SSL can provide protection for many types of communications, not just Web surfing. In fact, SSL can be used to secure e-mail, file uploads/downloads using File Transfer Protocol (FTP), and even Internet Relay Chat (IRC). SSL is wonderful because of its flexibility in protecting so many types of digital communications.

When you use an SSL connection, you are assured that it is difficult for snoopers or thieves to see the information you exchange. The fact is, it is quite simple for anyone to read the information you are transmitting across the Internet. Unless something special is being done to protect that information, it travels from your computer to its destination in a clear, readable format. The path that information travels across the Internet can be likened to a simple telephone conversation. When you pick up your phone to call someone across the country, your voice is traveling across miles of wires that are connected by central telephone offices that stretch across the country. Your voice passes through each central office, where it is given a signal boost that carries it to the next central office, again and again until your voice reaches the person on the other end of the phone. Computer information travels a similar path across the Internet, moving from router to router until it reaches its destination. Just as a wiretap can be used to listen in on your telephone conversation, similar techniques can be used to listen in on all your computer transmissions.

Client/Server Design

SSL connections require two parties. On one hand is your SSL-enabled Web browser. On the other hand is the SSL-enabled Web site you are visiting. That's it. You are the client, and the Web site is the server. For SSL to work, both parties must support it, and both parties can negotiate the terms of using it.

Public Key and Symmetric Key Cryptography

Encryption is discussed more in Chapter 12, "Securing Your Standalone PC: Viruses, Chat, and Encryption," so it will be only lightly covered in this chapter. SSL uses both public key and symmetric key cryptography. Public key cryptography is when encryption is based on two different keys. In the example of an SSL-enabled Web site, the server has a public key that is widely distributed to anybody who wants to encrypt communications with the Web server. The server also has a private key, which it can use to decrypt those communications. If a server or Web site wants to set up an SSL connection, it gives you its public encryption key. You then use the server's public key to encrypt data for the server, but you cannot decrypt the data. Only the server can decrypt the data with its private key.

Public key cryptography is only used to exchange symmetric encryption keys that will be used for the majority of the SSL session. They are called symmetric encryption keys because each party uses the same key to encrypt and decrypt data. It's comparable to several people in your family sharing copies of the same house key for locking and unlocking the front door. The main problem with symmetric keys is that they must be exchanged securely—after all, you don't want somebody eavesdropping on your key exchange to get his own copy of the key. To solve this, SSL uses public key cryptography to securely exchange the symmetric keys. Consider the following example:

1. Bob connects to his favorite Web site using `https://` to signify an SSL connection.

2. The Web site gives Bob its digital certificate and public key.

3. Bob's Web browser generates a symmetric key and sends it to the Web site encrypted with the Web site's public key.

4. The Web site decrypts the symmetric key with its private key and starts using the symmetric key for the rest of the SSL session.

These four steps provide a broad outline, intended to describe only how public key cryptography is used to exchange the symmetric keys. It is extremely important that the public keys are also securely exchanged. If they are not securely exchanged, man-in-the-middle attacks are likely. In this case, an attacker could intercept the public key in transit from the Web site to the Web browser and modify it to the attacker's liking. The Web browser would receive the modified public key and, not knowing the difference, would use it to encrypt the transmission of the secret key. The attacker then would intercept the transmission of the secret key and be able to easily decode it, after which the attacker could decode the rest of the SSL session. The designers of SSL have thought of these and other tricks and have taken steps to ensure that the public keys are securely exchanged.

Server–Side Digital Certificates

When visiting an SSL-enabled Web site, you are typically using the server's digital certificate to establish the SSL session. That is, the server's certificate is the trusted source for authentication of the server's identity and public keys that are used for encryption. It is less often the case that a client-side certificate is used. A client-side certificate is one that you possess and that your Web browser uses in the SSL connection. When both client- and server-side certificates are used, both sides have complete trust and both parties know each other's identities.

Although we are focusing on SSL's use for Web surfing, SSL can actually be used in many more places. It's true that SSL has been optimized to work over HTTP, the protocol of the World Wide Web. However, it also can be used with nearly any other protocol that operates above the TCP/IP layer. In other words, SSL can be used to secure the authentication and delivery of e-mail using the POP3 and SMTP protocols (see Chapter 8, "E-mail Security"). When combined with SSL, these e-mail protocols can be referred to in short as POP3/SSL and SMTP/SSL. As discussed in Chapter 8, the

POP3 and SMTP e-mail protocols by themselves generally are not secure. Although they can provide for authentication using a username and password, those credentials are sent over the network in clear text. If you use a cable modem, anyone else on your block can read your credentials and even your e-mail messages. However, if you add the security of SSL to these protocols, your authentication credentials can be protected as well as your e-mail messages. Public key cryptography and encryption keep your e-mail account and messages safe from prying eyes.

Why Do We Use SSL?

Most communication between computers across the Internet is done using the TCP/IP protocols we have been discussing throughout the book. TCP/IP makes it possible for information to get from one computer to its final destination, be it an e-mail message, Web page request, or online chat. TCP/IP moves the data from the source computer to the destination across the networks of intermediary computers that make up the Internet. TCP/IP has gained worldwide acceptance because of its flexibility and simplicity. Any computer can be designed to talk the TCP/IP language and participate on the Internet.

Picture the information moving from your computer to its destination. Maybe you are surfing a Web site or sending an e-mail message. Either way, the information that you are sending is vulnerable to manipulation when it passes through each of the intermediary computers on the way to its destination. TCP/IP by itself does not provide protection of the data or information that it carries. That means that your Web surfing, e-mail, and other Internet communications are open to attack unless they use SSL. Three fundamental security and privacy issues exist within the Internet infrastructure:

- **Eavesdropping**—Anyone can intercept and read the information you send across the Internet. It doesn't matter if you are sending e-mail, surfing a Web site, or chatting on an instant messenger—these all involve sending data between two computers across the Internet. Someone could secretly learn your credit card or bank account number or listen to your personal and confidential conversations.

- **Tampering**—Communications across the Internet can be secretly intercepted and modified or changed before they reach their destination. As an example, someone could potentially change an e-mail message you send before it reaches your intended recipient, or even change an order you are placing at an e-commerce site.

- **Impersonation**—Impersonation has two sides. First, someone can pretend to be you on the Internet. That person might masquerade with your identity by sending e-mail messages appearing to come from you, or by surfing Internet sites with your credentials. Second, a Web site might appear to be a legitimate business, when in fact it is a scam set up to collect personal information or credit card numbers from people.

All three of these issues have long existed on the Internet, and SSL v3.0 provides a set of protocols that address each of them.

We need privacy and security. In an ever-increasing digital world of information sharing, stealing, and exploitation, people need assurance that they can do something to protect themselves. Four critical concepts can be applied to online security and privacy, each of which is provided by SSL:

- **Authentication**—Authentication of each party (the client and the server) is done before a trusted secure channel is set up.
- **Integrity**—Integrity of the secure channel is maintained so that any tampering can be detected.
- **Confidentiality**—Confidentiality of the transactions is achieved by encrypting the data.
- **Non-repudiation**—This is the ability to prove that the sender actually sent the message.

Remember that you can use SSL for more than just Web surfing, including e-mail and even FTP. SSL applies *authentication* to digital transactions, be they online shopping or e-mail, to ensure that the parties involved are really whom they say they are. Authentication provides the means to fight back against the threats of *impersonation*. SSL provides *integrity* of the digital transactions so that any *tampering* with them can be detected. If someone were to change a transaction while it was in transit, the receiving party would be alerted through the use of SSL. SSL also provides *confidentiality* of the transactions through the use of encryption technology that makes the transaction unreadable to anybody but the intended parties. If an *eavesdropper* attempts to intercept and read the message or transaction, he will see only unreadable gibberish that encryption created. Only the intended parties can decrypt and read the contents of the transaction. SSL provides *nonrepudiation* when the sender digitally signs a message or transaction. Because only the sender's secret key can be used to sign a message, the message is considered beyond a doubt to have originated from the sender. Additionally, when the message is signed, it is also sealed so that any tampering can be detected. A signed message is proof that the apparent sender actually delivered it.

If you don't fully understand these concepts, keep reading through the next sections to get an example of SSL in action.

A Brief History of SSL

SSL was originally developed as a strategic business move by Netscape Communications, now a subsidiary of AOL Time Warner. Netscape wanted to gain a competitive advantage through the use of security. Netscape was in the midst of partnering to open up an online shopping mall and portal site. The use of SSL would give Netscape an advantage over other e-commerce sites that were not cryptographically enabled.

The first version of SSL was 1.0, but the protocol was not publicly released until version 2.0, which shipped with Netscape Navigator 1 and 2. Of course, a Web browser by itself cannot set up an SSL connection. A computer must be at the other end as well. Netscape also integrated SSL support into its Web servers so that the browser and server together could set up the secure SSL tunnel. At the time, Netscape had the market covered because it was the only one with both SSL-enabled browsers and servers.

Several shortcomings were found in SSL v2.0. In response, Microsoft created a similar protocol named PCT, which was designed to overcome the shortcomings of SSL v2.0 and give Microsoft its own advantage in the cryptographically enabled browser market. Aware of the advances made by PCT, Netscape worked to release SSL version 3.0, which has become the most popular cryptographic protocol for Web browsers and Web servers in use today. The SSL v3.0 protocol has become the basis for the Internet Engineering Task Force (IETF), the formal group that governs standards for use across the Internet to use in their secure protocol development.

SSL Technically Speaking

Think of your computer in layers. A house or building is built in phases, which also can be thought of as layers. The first layer is preparing the land. The next layer is building the foundation to support the house. On top of that, the framework of the house is built, and after that, at the outermost layers, are your plumbing, electrical, walls, and siding. A computer works in layers as well. The bottommost layer is the foundation, which includes the hardware devices such as the motherboard, processor, and memory. The next layer is the operating system, which runs on top of the hardware. Above the operating system is the application layer, which includes the programs and software you use, such as word processors, Web browsers, and e-mail programs.

TCP/IP is the set of protocols that computers use to communicate. Essentially, it's the language that computers use to speak with each other. For a computer to speak TCP/IP, it must have some software that makes it possible. TCP/IP runs at a layer just above or at the operating system layer, and SSL operates at a layer just above TCP/IP. In other words, SSL depends on TCP/IP to run. Just as SSL uses the TCP/IP layer to do its work, the higher layers can also use SSL to do their work. This is why some of the most popular protocols on the Internet can run using SSL, including HTTP, POP3, and SMTP.

Now that we know SSL operates on top of TCP/IP, the set of protocols through which computers on the Internet communicate, let's look at just how SSL works, in more detail.

Note

To use SSL, you must have an SSL-enabled Web browser and you must interact with an SSL-enabled Web site, or server. Most major browsers, including Internet Explorer, Netscape, and Opera, are SSL-enabled.

SSL is considered a suite of protocols because it actually uses many different standards of key exchange, authentication, and encryption together to get its job done. SSL consists of two main subprotocols: the SSL record protocol and the SSL handshake protocol. The SSL record protocol provides the foundation by defining the format in which data will be transmitted. The SSL handshake protocol uses the record protocol to set up the SSL channel. The SSL handshake protocol is where the server authentication process and the optional client authentication process are done.

How SSL Works in a Typical Transaction

Cryptography is central to the function of SSL. In general, you can picture an SSL session as a tunnel between your Web browser and the Web server. The tunnel provides a protected path for all the transactions that are sent between the browser and server. Information that is exchanged cannot be tampered with or read by anybody but you and the Web server. The tunnel exists solely for your session with the Web server. After the tunnel has been created, your information exchanges are safe. When the tunnel is destroyed, you are once again open to the basic threats of the Internet described earlier. The Web server or the Web browser typically destroys the SSL tunnels when the need for protection is over or the session is finished because you leave the site.

This is how SSL works:

1. You visit a Web site (the server) that is SSL-enabled by using the `https://` prefix.

2. The server sends its digital certificate to you, and your Web browser verifies the authenticity of the certificate by querying the signing Certificate Authority. If the CA is unknown or is not listed in your browser's database of CAs, the Web browser alerts you and asks whether you want to accept it. If the certificate is not accepted or does not exist, the SSL session cannot be established, and the connection is stopped.

3. Your Web browser then takes the information in the server's certificate and computes what is called a *premaster secret*. This premaster secret then is encrypted with the server's public key and sent to the server.

4. When the client's premaster secret is accepted, the server continues the secure key exchange. Optionally, if the server wants to authenticate you, it asks your Web browser to send over your client certificate, which it attempts to validate against a signing CA.

5. The server uses its private key to decrypt the premaster secret and then takes some steps to compute the *master secret*. (Your Web browser actually does the same thing, performing a series of steps with the premaster secret, to derive a master secret. This master secret is the same for your Web browser and the server.)

6. Your Web browser and the server both use the master secret to generate session keys. The session keys are used for the encryption and decryption of further communications to prevent eavesdropping. They are also used to help detect any tampering with the communications.

7. Your Web browser and the server let each other know that they have the session keys and continue using them. The handshake process has completed, and an SSL tunnel has been successfully set up.

Key Lengths and Encryption Strength

It is possible for several different ciphers to be used in an SSL transaction. In fact, SSL uses a combination of symmetric and public key ciphers to do its job (see Chapter 12 for a discussion of encryption). The main encryption that is provided by the tunnel is done using symmetric key cryptography. Both the browser and server share a secret key that can be used to encrypt and decrypt the information. This secret key is exchanged securely using public key cryptography.

Symmetric key cryptography is the process by which two or moreparties share the same encryption key. It's like when you share the same house key with people in your family. Only one key locks and unlocks the front door, but each member of the family has a copy of it. SSL uses symmetric key cryptography for one reason: performance. Good performance is critical to a Web server that serves up pages to thousands of visitors. For the server to handle the extra load of encrypting and decrypting information, it needs to streamline the process. Symmetric key cryptography provides a server the most secure method of encryption, combined with moderate decreases in performance. This is as opposed to public key cryptography, which tends to have a higher performance cost. Public key cryptography requires more work on the server's part. It's inevitable that performance will suffer; after all, it takes time and processing power to make the calculations that encrypt and decrypt information.

SSL is offered to Web browsers in U.S. domestic and exportable versions. Because the U.S. has export laws associated with cryptography technology, SSL-enabled software that leaves the country is limited by certain restrictions. The restrictions basically lessen the strength of the encryption. The U.S. government might not want to provide the rest of the world with strong encryption algorithms and software, so it chooses to restrict the encryption strength in exported software.

Within the U.S., the strength of SSL ciphers that can be used has no restrictions. This means that the public keys and symmetric keys can be any key. Most commonly, the public keys are either 1024 or 2048 bits, and the symmetric keys are 128 bits.

Table 9.1 lists some of the encryption laws in the U.S. It shows that the U.S. government imposes limitations on public keys and secret keys used inside the U.S. and exported from the U.S.

Table 9.1 **Laws Regarding Key Strength Usable in and Exportable from the U.S.**

In the U.S.	Exporting from the U.S.
Public keys are not limited by law.	Public keys are limited to 512 bits.
Secret keys are not limited by law.	Secret keys are limited to 40 bits.

In general, the strength of the encryption is comparable to the size of the keys used: The larger the key, the stronger the encryption. The U.S. government does not allow keys stronger than 40 bits to be exported for good reason. With the right equipment, it only takes a few hours for 40-bit keys to be cracked. It can take nearly forever to crack a 128-bit key, even with many powerful computers working together.

You might be wondering why a public key is exportable up to 512 bits. The reason is because public keys are generally not as strong as symmetric keys. In fact, a 384-bit public key is nearly equivalent in strength to a 40-bit symmetric key. Although a 512-bit key is extremely strong and nearly impossible to crack, the keys are not used to provide the main SSL encryption. The public keys are only used to set up encryption long enough for the symmetric keys to be securely exchanged. After the symmetric keys are exchanged, they are used to carry out encryption of the transactions during the SSL session.

Tip

Go to http://verisign.netscape.com/advisor to learn the encryption strength your Web browser is capable of providing.

Configuring Your Web Browser for SSL

Most common browsers today, including Netscape, Opera, and Internet Explorer, support both versions 2.0 and 3.0 of SSL. In general, you will want to choose SSL v3.0 over SSL v2.0 because it is a stronger and more secure version. Because the SSL version you use is negotiated between your browser and the server, we recommend disabling SSL v2.0 in your browser and only enabling SSL v3.0. This ensures that negotiations settle on using SSL v3.0; however, it might cause problems at sites that do not support SSL v3.0. If you cannot establish an SSL v3.0 connection with a particular site, you will have to enable SSL v2.0 support in your browser, accepting and understanding that it has known security issues. Let's have a look at the configuration options that Netscape Navigator v.6.1 and Internet Explorer v6.0 offer you.

Netscape Navigator

Netscape Navigator gives you much control over its SSL configurations. Select Edit, Preferences in Netscape, and then select Privacy and Security and then SSL from the

Category list on the left, as shown in Figure 9.1. Options are available for enabling and disabling versions of SSL, as well as the different ciphers you want it to use.

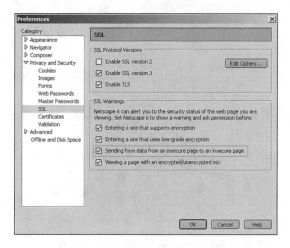

Figure 9.1   Netscape offers detailed control over its SSL configurations.

With Netscape Navigator v6.1, you can enable SSL version 2 and version 3, as well as TLS, which is another protocol that is similar to SSL v3.0. In general, most sites support SSL over TLS, but TLS is becoming more popular. Take a look at the SSL warning messages that Netscape gives you. These come across as pop-up windows while you are using your browser. If, for instance, you select the warning option for Entering a Site That Uses Low-Grade Encryption, you will be alerted whenever you visit an SSL site that uses 40-bit keys.

By clicking the Edit Ciphers button, you can configure just which ciphers you want Netscape to support, as shown in Figure 9.2.

Most likely, you will not need to modify the cipher settings for SSL. However, should the need arise, you do have the ability under Netscape. For example, you might decide one day that you want Netscape to use only the strongest encryption available. In this case, you could disable the use of any 40-bit keys and enable only the use of 128-bit keys. Of course, you might run into problems if the Web site you are visiting can't support 128-bit keys, but at least you know you can do it.

Netscape gives you two ways to see that you have an SSL session established with a site. You not only have `https://` as the prefix for `www.amazon.com`, but you also see a padlock icon in the bottom-right corner of the Netscape browser window, as shown in Figure 9.3. (If SSL were not enabled, the padlock would appear unlocked instead of locked.)

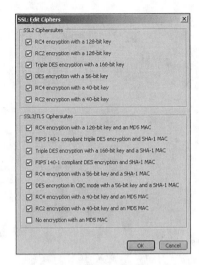

Figure 9.2   Netscape gives you complete control over the ciphers it uses for SSL encryption.

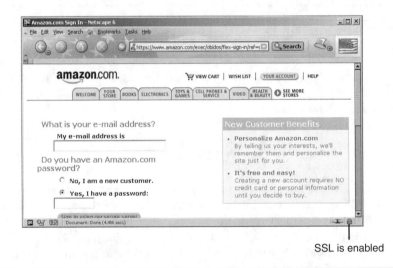

Figure 9.3   Netscape displays an icon indicating that SSL is enabled.

You can view the information about the security of this session in two more ways. You can either double-click on the padlock icon to bring up the page information, or you can select View, Page Info. The Page Info window is shown in Figure 9.4.

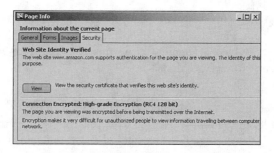

Figure 9.4   Security information details.

By clicking on the Security tab, you can see what the encryption strength is of your SSL session; in this case, it is RC4 128-bit, which is very strong. You can also click the View button to have a closer look at the site's digital certificate. (You'll read more about digital certificates later.)

Internet Explorer

Internet Explorer does not give you quite the level of control that Netscape gives. In fact, you only get control over the versions of SSL you want to support, and a limited amount of warning messages. Controls for SSL are thrown in under the Advanced configuration options, shown in Figure 9.5. You get there by selecting Tools, Internet Options, and then selecting the Advanced tab.

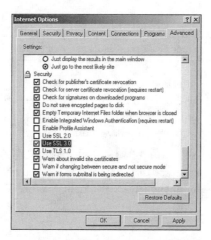

Figure 9.5   Configuring Internet Explorer for SSL support.

With Internet Explorer 6.0, you can enable or disable support for SSL 2.0, SSL 3.0, and TLS 1.0. It is a good idea to enable support for SSL 3.0 and TLS 1.0 while disabling support for SSL 2.0. Your options for warnings are limited to Warn If Changing Between Secure and Not Secure Mode.

Internet Explorer displays a padlock icon similar to Netscape. When you establish an SSL session, you see a padlock in the bottom-right corner of the window, as shown in Figure 9.6. If you hover the mouse over the icon, you will see the message SSL Secure (128 bit) or 40 bit depending on the strength of encryption you are using.

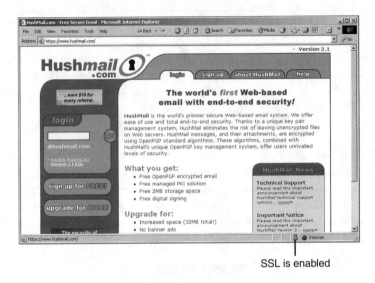

SSL is enabled

Figure 9.6   Internet Explorer displays a padlock icon when an SSL session is established.

Double-clicking on the padlock icon brings up the Web site's digital certificate. If you want more details about the encryption strength being used, select File, Properties. You will see a screen similar to Figure 9.7, which tells you the key size and encryption ciphers that are used for your current SSL session.

In the Properties dialog box, it is revealed that www.hushmail.com is using SSL 3.0 for the encrypted session. You also see that the encryption strength is 128 bit, which is very strong encryption. The public key exchange that was used to exchange the secret keys was 1024 bit.

Figure 9.7   Internet Explorer gives you more details about the SSL session when you select File, Properties.

SSL Doesn't Protect Everything

Remember the tunnel that SSL sets up to protect your transactions? It is important to understand that the tunnel is the *only* protection that SSL gives you. Although the tunnel is safe and secure, the computers at each end of it might not be. *SSL only protects information in transit*. After your credit card or any other information has made it across the Internet, it sits on a server in a database. SSL cannot protect the database or the server from being attacked. The server still needs the basic kind of protections that we discuss throughout this book. Firewalls, antivirus software, the latest operating system patches, and good security awareness are some of the fundamental protections that are needed.

Your personal computer needs similar protection. After you have performed a credit card transaction, your Web browser might cache a local copy of the receipt page that displays all of your personal information, including address, credit card number, and purchase details. If you are not aware that this page has been stored on your computer, you might fail to properly remove or secure it. If your computer is not protected with some of the basic security controls we discuss throughout this book, it might be an easy target for an attacker.

Attacks on SSL

One of the many functions of SSL is providing for encrypted communications. Many attacks on SSL are designed to break the encryption by discovering the secret key used. Remember that SSL uses symmetric key cryptography to provide encryption. This basically means that the client and server each share the same secret key that is used to both encrypt and decrypt the communications. If an attacker can discover this secret, he can decrypt the communications.

The way that this symmetric key is generated is important. In a basic sense, combining a random number with some mathematical computation might generate the secret key. The computation will remain the same and should produce a secret key that cannot be easily deduced. Because an attacker will most likely know what the computation is because it is part of the software and public knowledge, he will be more interested in finding out what the randomly generated number is. If he can figure out what the random number is, he can simply run it through the same computation to get the secret key.

As mentioned earlier, another attack is the man-in-the-middle attack. Although several different attacks are performed from this perspective, one of the simplest is for the attacker to impersonate both parties. The attacker tries to get into a position where he appears to you as the trusted party and appears to the trusted party as you. The attacker might then try to intercept communications during the early stages, when you are just starting to set up the SSL connection. He will present to you a fraudulent certificate for your trusted party that you might accept as valid. If he can get you to set up an SSL connection through him, he will have access to all of the information you are sending to the trusted party.

What Are Digital Certificates?

A digital certificate is supposed to be the computerized equivalent of a passport. It proves a person's identity online and provides a means of legally valid signatures in some cases. In today's society, you might have many forms of identification, including a passport, driver's license, membership card, or similar type of ID card. Just as you can have many ID cards for many different purposes, you can have many digital certificates to serve you. A certificate is used to identify a person or a thing. It is a digital document, which is really a file stored on a computer that can be used to identify a person, server, or company. A server that is running a Web site usually has a digital certificate for your Web browser to authenticate the server and verify its identity. The digital certificate also contains the server's public key for use in establishing encryption.

The concept of digital certificates has been around since before the earliest days of the Internet. VeriSign made an early attempt at issuing digital certificates, thus marking its place as an identity authority on the Internet. Early on, VeriSign was primarily concerned with issuing certificates to identify Web servers for use in SSL connections.

Since then, certificates have spread into use by government, businesses, and netizens (citizens of the Internet community).

The most popular systems of digital certificates today are based on three things:

- Public Key Infrastructure
- X.509
- Certificate Authorities

Public Key Infrastructure (PKI) is a system of creating, maintaining, distributing, and validating digital certificates. As a model of trust, the PKI system of X.509-based digital certificates can be thought of as a pyramid. At the top of the pyramid is the Root Certificate Authority. This Root Authority has ultimate responsibility for validating the trustworthiness of all certificates that it issues, as well as certificates issued by other Certificate Authorities beneath it. The Certificate Authorities, including the root, are also the central directories of certificates. They are the actual entities responsible for carrying out the goals of the PKI: creating, maintaining, distributing, and validating digital certificates.

A PKI does not have to refer to a system that uses CAs as the trusted authorities. In fact, the OpenPGP system can be considered a PKI in which responsibility for validating certificates is distributed among the people who use the system. Within a close group of friends, it might be easy to maintain trustworthy public keys. On a larger scale, trustworthy public keys and certificates depend on their acceptance within the Web of Trust (described more in Chapter 8).

When you hear people talk about digital IDs, digital certificates, and the like, they are usually referring to what is known as X.509. The many names all point to a single set of recommended practices known worldwide as the X.509 standard. X.509 is a recommended standard to which most digital certificates conform. The X.509 recommended standard has been actively developed by the International Telecommunications Union (ITU). The ITU, established in 1965, consists of members from countries across the world who have a mission that includes developing international telecommunications standards. Because the X.509 standard has not been officially approved beyond just a recommendation, companies and organizations use it as a framework but modify it to suit their needs. For this reason, the X.509-based digital certificates in use worldwide across the Internet do not all contain the same types of information.

Note

The industry has moved forward with version 3 of the X.509 standard. Although this is officially referred to as X.509 v3, we call it X.509 throughout this chapter.

PKIs are still maturing, and no agreed-upon PKI system or standards for PKI operations currently exist. Industry standards are still developing. Companies, individuals, and governments alike might choose to set up PKI systems in different ways. Many states have been developing legal frameworks for the use of digital signatures, most of which have been based on Utah legislation from 1995. Drafts have been written of a federal PKI system to dish out the passport equivalent of digital certificates.

Some people think that PKI and digital certificates are the answer to most of the Internet's security problems. Even the domain name system (DNS) can be secured using certificates. DNS is the protocol that translates host names (www.privacydefended.com) into IP addresses (172.16.2.100). The DNS serves as the phonebook of the Internet; you look up a name, and DNS gives you the number. The fact is, you use the DNS (or rather your software does) every time you surf to a Web site, send an e-mail, or do anything that involves traveling across cyberspace. Securing the DNS is just one example of digital certificates' answer to Internet security problems. Of course, digital certificates are used in SSL, e-mail, and other transactions requiring a high level of trust.

On the other hand, many people see the whole PKI, Certificate Authority, and X.509-based certificates as a complex solution that carries its own bag of problems. How will something riddled with loop holes, security problems, and arguable standards give us trustworthy solutions and answers? Some of the problems surrounding the use of digital certificates are discussed in the later section of this chapter, "Problems with Certificates."

The Purpose of Digital Certificates

As mentioned previously, a digital certificate is supposed to serve as a valid identification for a certain entity, be it a company, a Web site, or an individual. Besides performing the role of an Internet passport, a digital certificate can provide some core security functions:

- Identification
- Encryption
- Authentication

Identification is achieved because a certificate is issued from a central authority that signs the certificate, essentially saying "Yes, this certificate has been verified as belonging to Bob." Bob's certificate represents him on the Internet, and he can use it when exchanging e-mail with his mother, so she knows that it was really Bob who sent the e-mail, and not some imposter.

Bob's certificate can also be used for encryption. The certificate carries Bob's public key with it so that people can send him encrypted and private e-mail. If Alice wanted to send Bob a private e-mail message, she would find Bob's certificate either from a CA or from another trusted source, and encrypt her e-mail message with Bob's public key (contained in the certificate) before sending it. When Bob receives the message, he decrypts it with his private key. This functionality is based on the concept of public key cryptography, which is discussed more in Chapters 8 and 12. It is no different from the encryption and privacy that PGP provides.

Bob's certificate can also be used to authenticate him. If Bob needs access to a Web site that contains confidential company information, that Web site might require that Bob present his digital certificate. After Bob presents the certificate, the Web site validates the trustworthiness of the certificate by checking with a Certificate Authority that issued it.

Digital certificates carry a tangible value these days: legal nonrepudiation. For example, they can be used to sign a lease online safely and legally.

What Is in a Digital Certificate?

All this talk of PKI, X.509, and CAs can seem like nonsense until you have seen something tangible. The certificates are typically files that are stored on your computer, one of which is a public file that you can share with other people. Let's get inside an X.509 certificate and see what kind of information it contains.

We will look at one of the digital certificates for Foundstone, Inc., which has been issued by Thawte Consulting. By visiting the Foundstone Web site at `https://www.foundstone.com` with Internet Explorer 6.0, our Web browser downloads the Web site's digital certificate and validates its authenticity with the issuing CA, Thawte Consulting. Keep in mind that this process is the same for any Web browser, and the contents of the X.509 certificate which we are about to discuss will be the same whether viewed through Netscape Navigator, Opera, or any other Web browser. Although each Web browser might present the contents in different ways, it cannot change the contents.

After we have loaded the page for `https://www.foundstone.com`, we can select File, Properties in Internet Explorer 6.0 and then click the Certificates button. We will see the General properties of the certificate, as shown in Figure 9.8. These General properties summarize some of the contents of the certificate, which we will see in more detail under the Details tab. The main things we are concerned with are presented here under the General tab. We know that the certificate is valid, or else it would appear with a red circle and slash over the certificate symbol, denoting that it could not be validated. We see that the certificate has been issued by Thawte Server CA, which happens to be one of the CA certificates that comes bundled with Internet Explorer and Netscape Navigator (see the later section "The Almighty Certificate Authority"). Because Thawte Server CA is one of the CA roots that we trust, our Web browser was able to automatically query the CA to validate the Foundstone certificate. The process was transparent to us; the decision of trust was left to Internet Explorer more so than it was to us. We see also the valid timeframe for this certificate, which is from 8/15/2001 to 8/21/2002. It is quite typical for server or Web site certificates (and even personal certificates) to be valid for one to two years. By expiring certificates and renewing them, the owner takes less of a risk that the certificate will get lost, be stolen, or otherwise be compromised by an attacker.

Figure 9.8   The General tab of this certificate shows a summary of important certificate properties.

If we want to see more details about this certificate, we can click the Details tab, shown in Figure 9.9. This displays what can be considered the raw X.509 properties. This is best explained when you consider the basic structure of an X.509 certificate. Table 9.2 describes some of the core fields with which you might be concerned.

Figure 9.9   Some of the raw information stored in the certificate can be viewed.

Table 9.2 **A Basic Description of What Makes Up an X.509 Digital Certificate**

X.509 Field Name	Description
Version	This is the version of X.509 certificate that is being used.
Serial number	The CA that issued the certificate is responsible for giving it a serial number to distinguish it from other certificates that the CA creates.
Issuer	This is the name of the CA, or other entity, that signed this certificate. In our example, the issuer is Thawte Server CA. Anybody who wants to use this certificate must trust the entity that signed it. Root CAs sign their own certificates, essentially telling you "Here, this certificate is mine, I signed it, trust me."
Valid from and Valid to	Certificates are valid for finite periods of time. The strength of the private key that is used to sign the certificate and the amount of money a subscriber pays for the certificate are some of the factors that determine a certificate's lifetime. A validity period is described by the date when a certificate becomes valid and the date it is valid to.
Subject	The subject gives the name of the subscriber to which the certificate has been issued. In our example, Foundstone is the subject. The subject name is intended to be unique across the Internet by breaking the name into components such as the following: CN—The subject's common name OU—The subject's organizational unit O—The subject's organization C—The subject's country
Subject public key	This is the subject's public key.

X.509 certificate can contain more fields, such as the Certificate Revocation List. However, the major pieces of information have been described here.

The path that the certificate took when it was originally created is also of interest. By selecting the Certification Path tab, shown in Figure 9.10, we can see who the issuing CA is for the certificate, and any other CAs or entities that might have signed it before it arrived at your Web browser. In our example, we only have one signing CA, which happens to be the same CA that issued the certificate. Thawte Server CA is at the top of the list because it is the first CA to have signed this certificate. A CA signs a certificate with its own private key to mark it with a seal of trust. That seal can be traced back to the CA, and is actually what you are checking on when you validate a certificate.

Figure 9.10   The path that a certificate took before arriving at your Web browser.

What Are Digital Signatures?

A digital signature does not involve taking your handwritten signature and scanning it into your computer; however, it is similar. A digital signature is unique to you, like a fingerprint or a handwritten signature is. A digital signature is a seal put on a digital piece of information (such as a file or an e-mail message). As an example, a digital signature can be attached to an electronic transaction (such as an e-mail) to let the recipient of the transaction know with a high degree of certainty that it was really you who sent it. Let's take a look at what makes digital signatures work.

Digital signatures are a byproduct of public key cryptography. We have been discussing public key cryptography as it relates to PGP, SSL, and digital certificates. In all cases, public key cryptography remains the same. It allows security and privacy of information exchanges by allowing you to possess two keys: a public key and a private key. Bob distributes the public key to anybody who will be communicating with him, such as Alice, and he keeps the private key to himself. Alice, in turn, uses the public key to encrypt data that is destined for Bob. When Bob gets the encrypted data, only he can decrypt it by using his private key. Nobody else has his private key, and security is maintained because the public key does not jeopardize the private key.

A digital signature is made by first producing a one-way *hash* (a unique identifier, similar to a fingerprint) of the original data and then encrypting that hash with the private key. Let's make sense of this sentence now. Remember that this process is the same whether using PGP or an X.509-based digital certificate. Bob wants to send Alice a signed e-mail message so that she knows with a high degree of certainty that it was really sent by Bob. Bob composes his e-mail message, clicks the Sign the Message button, and clicks Send. The following steps happen next:

1. The contents of the message are calculated with a mathematical equation to produce a unique hash (see the Chapter 12 section "Hashing Algorithms"). This unique hash is like a fingerprint for the message. If a single letter in Bob's message were to be changed, a recalculated hash would be completely different from the original.

2. This unique hash is then encrypted with Bob's private key. This keeps the hash private and secure while it is being delivered. It is encrypted in such a way that only Bob's public key will be able to decrypt it. This "encrypted hash" is essentially the digital signature.

3. Alice receives the message and her e-mail software recognizes that a digital signature is associated with it. Because the message is from Bob, her software uses his public key to decrypt the digital signature and reveal the original, unique hash. Her software then performs the same calculation on the message to produce a new hash. The new hash is compared against the original hash. If the two match, it is determined that the message is authentic (really sent by Bob) and it has not been tampered with along the way. If the messages do not match, then either the message has been tampered with and modified, or the message might have been created with a private key that doesn't correspond to Bob's public key.

Although encryption and decryption solve the problem of privacy by preventing outsiders from reading data sent to you, they do not by themselves address the problem that the data can be modified in transit, or that the data is actually from who you think it is from. That is where digital signatures step in. These little fingerprints actually solve two major security problems:

- Tamper detection
- Identification and authenticity

Digital signatures are comparable to handwritten signatures. Handwritten signatures are used to validate credit card purchases, contract agreements, and many other documents. They provide a high degree of non-repudiation. That is, after you have signed a document, it is difficult for you to deny having signed it later. The same holds true for digital signatures. Provided that your private key is not lost, stolen, or compromised, a digital signature can be considered as unique and legally binding (in some cases) as your handwritten signature.

Why would you want to use digital certificates and signatures? Here are some reasons:

- To build trusted relationships online
- To prove your identity online
- To verify other people's identity online
- To prove that messages exchanged have not been tampered with
- To keep communications private and unreadable by eavesdroppers
- To protect yourself and your family

The Almighty Certificate Authority

A certificate cannot certify itself. That is, by itself, a certificate cannot be trusted. Some entity has to mark the certificate as valid with a trusted seal of approval. The PKI model includes a CA, which essentially signs and validates a given certificate as being trustworthy. The CA is at the top of the PKI pyramid. The CA can be a company like VeriSign, Entrust, or Thawte who manages digital certificates for public Internet citizens. It can also be a government organization like the U.S. Postal Service, or a private company like the one you work for that wants to use certificates for employee identification purposes. Sometimes, a CA can even be an individual like you or me.

We are focusing on CAs that serve the public Internet community, even though any CA serves the same purposes. Many CAs can exist in a single country, and each can operate independently of the other. In many cases, a chain is formed where a large root CA is responsible for establishing a chain of trust between smaller CAs.

CAs have a huge responsibility. When all is said and done, anybody who uses this centralized system of X.509-based certificates is putting his trust in the CA. The CA takes all responsibility for the creating, distributing, revoking, redistributing, validating, and binding of the attributes of a certificate to a real identity. You, on the other hand, trust the CA to do a good job at it. After all, every time a certificate is used, it must be verified and validated with a CA that issued it or signed it.

Certificate Revocation List

One big job the CAs have is managing the Certificate Revocation List (CRL). Because certificates can be stolen, lost, cracked, or compromised in other ways, they cannot always be trusted. Those certificates that can no longer be trusted are put into the CRL. It is your job to check the Certificate Authority's CRL when you are validating a particular certificate.

For the most part, CAs operate independently of one another. Each CA's main jobs are to manage the directory of certificates and the authentication services that are associated with them. The X.509 PKI system, which revolves around the CA (as opposed to a PKI based on something more grassroots and distributed, like PGP), actually involves three parties:

- Certificate Authority
- Subscriber
- User

The CA issues certificates to the subscribers in a way that the users can verify the certificates. A subscriber registers with a CA when he wants his own certificate. The subscriber could be a company, an individual, or some other real-world entity. Consider for a minute that Alice is the subscriber.

Alice goes to the Web site of a major CA such as VeriSign or Thawte. She registers to get a personal digital certificate that she can use for identification and secure e-mail. The CA processes her order, charges her a yearly fee, and gives her a certificate that expires in two years. As the subscriber, Alice has just created an online identity that anybody else can use to communicate with her.

Bob is a user who doesn't even own a digital certificate. Alice has given Bob her public digital certificate (as a computer file) because she intends to exchange secure e-mail with him in the future. Alice later sends an e-mail message to Bob and signs it with her digital certificate's public key. As a user, Bob queries the CA that issued Alice's certificate and public key. Because Bob's software is set up to trust the CA that issued Alice's certificate, it trusts the CA's response saying that Alice's certificate is valid. That's it. Alice sent a signed message to Bob, and Bob verified that it was authentic and valid.

Different Levels of Certificates

The CA will issue different levels, or classes, of certificates that indicate what role the certificate can serve. Some general-purpose roles of a certificate include the following:

- Server authentication and SSL
- Client authentication and SSL
- Secure e-mail
- Software code signing

In the case of server (running a Web site, for example) or client authentication and SSL, a digital certificate can serve multiple purposes. When you browse to an SSL-enabled Web site, that Web site gives your Web browser its digital certificate. Your browser verifies that it trusts that certificate if it is issued or signed by one of the CAs that are preinstalled into your browser. If the certificate is issued or signed by an unknown CA, your browser alerts you and asks you to make the choice of whether to accept it. If it is accepted, the server might ask your Web browser for your digital certificate. The process is similar; the server attempts to validate your certificate before continuing. When the certificates are validated, your browser and the server trust each other, having authenticated each other's identity. The next step is to use the public keys that are stored in the certificates to set up an encrypted SSL channel.

The validation process can be the same for e-mail and code signing. If you receive a signed e-mail message from your boss, your e-mail client attempts to validate the signature based on the CAs in the chain of trust. Additionally, the certificates can be used to send encrypted, private e-mail, similar to PGP. When a Web site asks your browser to download and install software on your computer, it might present a digital signature for that software. Your browser then goes through the process of validating that signature with a trusted CA before it decides to trust and install the software. If you have your browser configured securely, you will be made aware of the process.

The Root Certificates

The CA, or root authority, has a root certificate, which is distributed to clients, like you. The CA uses the root certificate to sign certificates that it issues or trusts. These root certificates are preinstalled into popular Web browsers such as Internet Explorer and Netscape Navigator. In fact, with Windows 2000 and XP, these certificates are pre-installed into the operating system as well. By storing these root certificates, your Web browser implicitly trusts any certificates that are issued by that CA. For example, let's take a look at Netscape Navigator 6.1's trusted root certificate list. To view the list of trusted certificate authorities that Netscape bundles with its browser, select Edit, Preferences, Privacy and Security, Manage Certificates. In the Certificate Manager dialog box, select the Authorities tab to see a screen similar to Figure 9.11.

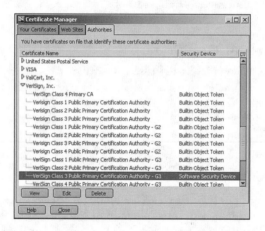

Figure 9.11   The list of trusted CAs bundled with Netscape Navigator 6.1.

In this window is the list of all CA root certificates with which Netscape Navigator 6.1 comes bundled. It is important to be aware of this list because it essentially takes the responsibility of validating a certificate out of your hands. The Web browser validates a given certificate if a CA in this list issues it. This might seem in violation of the function of X.509 PKI and the digital certificate architecture, which is supposed to leave the choice of whether to trust a certificate up to the end user. However, you really do have control over the decision of which certificates you will trust, which we cover in the next section.

Click the triangle symbol next to VeriSign, Inc. to see their root certificates that have been bundled with Netscape. Then click the VeriSign Class 3 Public Primary Certification Authority and click the View button. You are shown the details of this certificate, including its X.509 properties. If you click the Edit button, you see the Edit Certificate Trust window, shown in Figure 9.12.

Figure 9.12   Click Edit to view the functions for which this certificate authority is trusted.

In this window, you can edit the settings for which you want certificates issued or signed by this authority to be trusted. As an example, if you visit a Web site that holds a certificate issued by VeriSign Class 3 Public Primary Certification Authority, you trust the identity of that Web site because it can be verified with that CA. Likewise, you trust e-mail messages that are signed with a certificate from this CA, and you trust software, or code, that is digitally signed with a certificate from this CA. In the Edit Certificate Trust window, you can modify the things that explicitly define to Netscape what certificates issued or signed by this CA should be allowed to identify.

Let's take a look at how Internet Explorer manages the same certificate. In IE 6.0, select Tools, Internet Options. Select the Content tab and click the Certificates button. Then select the Trusted Root Certification Authorities tab to see the list of CAs that come bundled with IE (see Figure 9.13). Notice that Netscape and IE each come with some of the same but also some different CAs. Who is making the decisions to bundle which CAs? Not you.

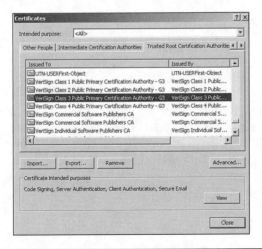

Figure 9.13   Internet Explorer's location for managing Trusted Root CAs.

Select VeriSign Class 3 Public Primary Certification Authority and click View to see the contents of the X.509-based certificate. Click the Advanced button to see the functions that certificates issued by this CA can fulfill, as shown in Figure 9.14. Whereas Netscape refers to these as the Trust Settings, Internet Explorer refers to them as the Certificate Purposes.

Figure 9.14   Internet Explorer offers similar options to Netscape for you to define what a given certificate's purpose is.

Remember how we mentioned that the same root authorities preinstalled into Internet Explorer are also preinstalled into the Windows 2000 and Windows XP operating systems? Let's take a look at just where those root certificates are stored and how you can view them. Microsoft has provided an interface for managing certificates on your computer, and it is accessible through the Microsoft Management Console (MMC). Select Start, Run, type MMC, and click OK. A rather empty-looking MMC is displayed. We actually have to add the Certificates snap-in to get to the certificates. Select Console, Add/Remove Snap-in, and the Snap-In Manager pops up. Under the Standalone tab, click the Add button. Highlight the Certificates snap-in and click Add. For the option that says This Snap-In Will Always Manage Certificates For, select My User Account, and click Finish. Click Close and OK to finish up. You see a screen similar to Figure 9.15. By expanding Trusted Root Certification Authorities and then Certificates, you can see all of the same CA root certificates that are used with Internet Explorer. From here, you can manage all of these and other certificates. You can add, delete, and modify the "intended purposes" of each certificate, as shown in the figure.

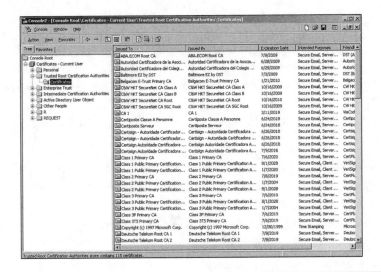

Figure 9.15   Windows 2000 provides a Certificate Manager interface.

Problems with Certificates

In today's typical PKI, CA distribution of X.509-based certificates, several known problems exist. First, perhaps calling them certificates is a misnomer. As the definition implies, a certificate is a document testifying that its subject matter is true and authentic, officially and under the law. As in a Certificate of Birth or Certificate of Deposit, the contents are deemed true, authorized, and sealed; their truth should not be questionable. As the name implies, you would think a digital certificate serving to prove identity and validity would also be considered true beyond a doubt. However, that is not the case, and most CAs even have a disclaimer saying that they are ultimately not responsible for the contents or validity of a certificate. In the end, you are solely responsible for trusting a given certificate. Why then do you choose to trust in a CA when you could do the same thing on your own in a distributed system such as PGP?

Certificates can be faked, stolen, or filled with invalid information. In early 2001, VeriSign was tricked into issuing two digital certificates under the identity of Microsoft. The certificates were issued to people claiming to be from Microsoft. They used the certificates to sign software that would be downloaded into people's Web browsers over the Internet. Because your Web browser trusts all digital certificates signed by VeriSign by default, your browser would immediately download and run the software of these malicious people. The attackers could have the software do anything they wanted, from wiping out your computer to spying on your activities for months to come.

What happens when somebody steals your digital certificate from your computer? After all, it is most likely just a file, and it is up to you to protect and secure it. A thief might get to it in any one of many ways. He could trick you into e-mailing it to him, hack into your computer the old-fashioned way, or set up an evil Web site. The evil Web site might exploit some new vulnerability in your Web browser that lets it read files directly off of your computer. Thanks be to buggy software!

CAs have a big job just managing CRLs. The following problems are typical with CRLs:

- Somebody wants to revoke her certificate but hasn't done it yet.
- The CRL is not always checked, just like SSL does not check the CRL to validate whether a certificate has been terminated.
- Interims of lag time exist between updates. Certificate Authorities typically update their CRLs on a periodic schedule, such as every six hours.

Perhaps, for example, Alice's computer has been broken into. She has no idea if the thief has gotten a hold of her digital certificate but it is entirely possible. She might not think to revoke her certificate, or if she does consider it, she might not know how. The time between when her certificate is compromised and when she actually revokes it from her CA is a dangerous time. This is basically like the time between when somebody has stolen your credit card and you call to have it cancelled. By the time you call to have the card cancelled, the thief could have already maxed it out. Luckily, the law has credit card fraud protection. Unfortunately, you don't have that kind of protection with digital certificates.

When people validate a certificate, they do not always check a CRL to see if it has been revoked. For instance, if you visit an SSL Web site that has a certificate that is signed by multiple CAs, you might go straight to the root CA to validate it. If one of those signing CAs has the certificate on a CRL, you will not know unless you check it, in which case you might establish the SSL session with a bogus certificate.

CRLs cannot be constantly updated. They are typically updated periodically, which could mean once every four hours or once a day. If you tell your CA that you need to revoke your digital certificate, a lag time will occur before your CA updates its CRL for the world to see. During this lag time, people who send you encrypted e-mail can still use your digital certificate's public key. If someone has jeopardized your certificate, he might have access to the e-mail that is being sent to you during this time.

Many privacy concerns are associated with digital certificates in the PKI and CA model of their use. Why don't you just replace all of your loosely scattered ID cards, keys, usernames, and passwords with a single digital certificate? It might make life a lot easier. What if a nationwide (or even worldwide) CA could sign your certificate? As soon as you went online, you could be validated against that CA, which would determine the Internet resources available to you and your privileges with them.

If every Web site you visited, every media file you downloaded, and every e-mail you sent had your digital signature associated with it, that nationwide CA would be able to track your every move through cyberspace. Sure, it would not be as easy to do as it is to imagine, but it is possible. If, over the next few years, you find yourself being asked more and more to provide a digital signature for your daily online transactions, you have a right to be suspicious.

Privacy can be maintained as long as the use of digital signatures is kept optional and voluntary. If it becomes compulsory or mandated, the world of privacy is threatened immediately. Just as the inventory in a grocery store can be tracked as it moves through each register's bar code readers, your life online (and even in the offline world) can be tracked.

In the end, security measures such as digital certificates are just speed bumps on the criminal highway. They make things more difficult, but with time methods of circumventing security are usually found. It can't be guaranteed that the holder of a digital certificate is the actual owner of it. Therefore, you should not blindly trust an e-mail message that is signed by someone who you trust because the CA said the signature is valid. In the end, it is up to each person to decide who is to be trusted.

This can also be illustrated using SSL and digital certificates. Perhaps Bob is visiting `https://www.privacydefended.com`, or at least, he thinks he is. Some imposter has set up a server to impersonate `www.privacydefended.com` and has stolen the authentication certificate so that he can use it on his phony Web site. Bob will never know the difference, and visiting this phony `www.privacydefended.com` Web site, he will probably let his Web browser make the trust decision for him. This type of activity is possible today, where people or computers can steal each other's online identity just by stealing each other's digital certificates.

It is important to realize that a CA can only verify that a particular certificate or signature is valid. A CA cannot verify if the certificate has been stolen, or if a signature has been made by someone other than the original owner of the certificate. This is where our trust in CAs breaks down, and why a distributed system such as PGP's Web of Trust can seem more secure. With the PGP system, you determine the trust based on who signed a public key and when it was signed. I will be more likely to trust a PGP public key signed yesterday by one of my friends who is extremely knowledgeable about technology than I will to trust a public key signed more than a year ago by someone I barely know.

Summary

SSL provides a means of protecting Internet users from having people eavesdrop on their communications, tamper with their data in transit, or impersonate the identity of an entity whom they trust. SSL has evolved to version 3 over the years, and is being matched by a similar, industry standard protocol called Transaction Layer Security

(TLS). In conjunction with digital certificates, which, if trusted, can be used to prove identity online, SSL can provide a high level of privacy and security.

You hear many terms today such as smart cards, smart chips, digital IDs, and so on, and you see the drive to provide better methods of identity for people. In most cases, people are referring to X.509-based digital certificates, although PGP certificates can provide similar functionality.

The fact is that PGP and X.509-based certificates differ in a couple of important ways. First, PGP certificates are distributed and validated (signed) by individuals. No centralized authority appears to take responsibility for the validity of a given certificate or public key. Instead, individuals share in the responsibility of distributing their own public keys and vouching for the authenticity of other peoples. In addition, the PGP Web of Trust provides a fault-tolerant system. Because you can't depend on a centralized hub to verify the validity of certificates, a single point of failure doesn't exist. The PGP Web of Trust will continue to operate no matter how many hits it takes—no Central Authority is available to call the shots.

On the other hand, although X.509-based systems might seem to provide total administration of their directory of certificates, they might actually be providing a false sense of security. If a given CA's last words to you are that it cannot be 100% certain of the true validity of the certificates for which it is vouching, why are you paying them money and vesting your trust in them? If the responsibility of determining whether somebody's certificate is valid ends up being your own in the end, why don't you just use a distributed grassroots system like PGP instead? Aside from the problems that surround X.509-based certificate systems with Central Authorities, many people find convenience and a high degree of certainty worth a certain level of risk.

The choice of which identification system to use is your own for the moment. What if it were mandated at some point that everyone must file under a Certificate Authority and place all trust in it? What if everything you did on the Internet could be tied to your digital certificate so that the root CA in your country knew of every Web site you visited, every media file you downloaded, and every time you logged into an instant messenger? That would certainly be an invasion of privacy, and a major shift in what defines trust. Currently, many organizations across the world offer proposals for systems to address some of the major problems associated with X.509-based PKI systems. Look for systems named PKIX, SDSI, MetaCertificates, SPKI, and OpenPGP, and you will see some of the alternatives that people around the world are offering. A fine balance exists between the ability to identify yourself and the ability to keep your business private, and it is up to each of us to determine the morality of it all in a system that works.

10

Understanding Your PC Operating System and Its Security Features

An essential step in protecting and defending your privacy in the online environment is understanding the security features that are available via the computer's operating system. Having a secure system will help prevent successful attacks against your system. The operating systems and computers we will be discussing all contain basic security features, but it is often left to the consumer to configure and enable those features. Although this book and its recommendations are geared toward the home user, many of the security issues we will discuss can also be applied in the office environment, subject to your company's security policies. For example, policies that govern the use of encryption in your organization might already be in place. Obviously, those procedures should be followed first. Good security habits followed in the work environment should be carried over to your personal home computers.

This chapter focuses on Windows 95/98, Windows NT, Windows 2000, and general Unix (Linux) security, but these same principles can be applied to all types of operating systems.

How do attackers select and gain knowledge about your computer or network? In the case of the casual home user, the selection of a victim system is more likely by chance. Attackers can easily identify networks and their ownership by performing the address and domain lookups described in Chapter 6, "Understanding the Online Environment: Addresses, Domains, and Anonymity." For example, large providers of cable modem and DSL services such as Road Runner, Mindspring, and AOL have IP network address blocks that someone can look up. This makes it easy for the attacker to specifically target the home user's machine. Using the same methods, the attacker can also target other entities, such as ISPs that cater to small businesses. After an attacker has identified your presence on the Internet (your IP address), the process known as footprinting begins.

Footprinting Analysis

Footprinting is the process by which an attacker tries to learn as much as he can about the target. Think of it as reconnaissance. An intelligent attacker would try to learn as much as he could so that a more focused and direct attack could be made against the target. For example, if he discovers that the target is running Windows 98, it would be useless to try attacks that only work against Windows 2000 machines. Being able to complete the footprinting process in a quick and accurate manner is an indication of a skilled attacker. The footprinting process typically involves the following basic steps:

1. Host identification
2. Open ports
3. Running services and their versions
4. Operating system identification

Host Identification

Host identification is the act of determining whether a host is actually present at an IP address. A home machine might be configured with a static address, but if the machine isn't powered on, the host identification process would indicate that no host resides at that IP address. Therefore, the goal of this step is to determine if a live machine exists at the given IP address. The most basic way to determine if an address has a live machine behind it is to *ping* it. Ping is actually an acronym for Packet INternet Groper. It is named after the sound that a sonar makes, inspired by the principle of echo location. Ping utilizes Internet Control Message Protocol (ICMP), which allows for the generation of error messages, test packets, and informational messages related to IP. When you ping a machine, a packet of data is sent to the supplied IP address. If you receive a response, some sort of device is alive at that address. If not, the machine is either turned off or unreachable because of network congestion or because of some network filtering or security device. Filtering rules or security devices such as firewalls can protect a computer from being found by dropping incoming ping packets. The `ping` command is available by default on almost all of the common operating systems that one might find in a home environment. On a Windows-based computer, we can issue the `ping` command against a known IP address or name to see if it is alive, as shown in Listing 10.1.

Listing 10.1   **Pinging IP Address 192.168.4.1**

```
C:\>ping 192.168.4.1

Pinging 192.168.4.1 with 32 bytes of data:

Reply from 192.168.4.1: bytes=32 time<10ms TTL=64
Reply from 192.168.4.1: bytes=32 time<10ms TTL=64
Reply from 192.168.4.1: bytes=32 time<10ms TTL=64
Reply from 192.168.4.1: bytes=32 time<10ms TTL=64

Ping statistics for 192.168.4.1:
    Packets: Sent = 4, Received = 4, Lost = 0 (0% loss),
Approximate round trip times in milli-seconds:
    Minimum = 0ms, Maximum =  0ms, Average =  0ms
```

In Listing 10.1, we see four replies from the computer located at IP address 192.168.4.1. We now know that this computer is alive and available for further investigation. In Listing 10.2, we ping the address 192.168.4.4.

Listing 10.2   **Pinging IP Address 192.168.4.4**

```
C:\>ping 192.168.4.4

Pinging 192.168.4.4 with 32 bytes of data:

Request timed out.
Request timed out.
Request timed out.
Request timed out.

Ping statistics for 192.168.4.4:
    Packets: Sent = 4, Received = 0, Lost = 4 (100% loss),
Approximate round trip times in milli-seconds:
    Minimum = 0ms, Maximum =  0ms, Average =  0ms
```

In this listing, we receive a `Request timed out` message from the `ping` command. This indicates that in all likelihood, no live machine is at that address. Note that some firewalls and hosts can be configured not to respond to pings, so this method of determining live hosts is not always accurate. In the case of the typical home user, however, this is rarely done. As we will see in Chapter 11, "Securing Your Standalone PC: Broadband Connections," many products are available to protect the home user's computer with additional features that the operating system does not have.

If we did not know the IP address of the computer, but knew its name, we could ping the computer by name to determine if it were alive. A real address on the Internet that we can use is Yahoo! In Listing 10.3, we ping the Yahoo! Web site to see whether it is alive.

Listing 10.3   **Pinging Yahoo! (*www.yahoo.com*)**

```
C:\>ping www.yahoo.com

Pinging www.yahoo.akadns.net [64.58.76.225] with 32 bytes of data:

Reply from 64.58.76.225: bytes=32 time=90ms TTL=241
Reply from 64.58.76.225: bytes=32 time=91ms TTL=241
Reply from 64.58.76.225: bytes=32 time=90ms TTL=241
Reply from 64.58.76.225: bytes=32 time=80ms TTL=241

Ping statistics for 64.58.76.225:
    Packets: Sent = 4, Received = 4, Lost = 0 (0% loss),
Approximate round trip times in milli-seconds:
    Minimum = 80ms, Maximum =  91ms, Average =  87ms
```

Listing 10.3 shows us that the DNS server translates the name www.yahoo.com into an
IP address (64.58.76.225). When the computer knows the IP address, it can ping the
address; in this case, we see that the address is alive.

Ping is an extremely useful utility. The basic function of determining if a computer is
alive is valuable in troubleshooting your Internet connection. If you have ever dialed
up your ISP, tried to surf the Internet, and found that nothing was happening, you
could easily open a DOS window and ping an address such as Yahoo! or Netscape.
The odds of Yahoo! or Netscape being unavailable are slim. If you are not getting a
response from these addresses, you can tell that traffic is not going out from or coming
back into your computer, and you can begin your search for the problem with some
valuable information. If you are trying to surf your favorite Web site but nothing is
coming up in the browser window, you can ping the Web site address to see if it is
alive.

An example of a computer that is alive but does not respond to a ping request is
Microsoft. We know that their main Web site, www.microsoft.com, is alive because we
can bring it up in a Web browser. However, if we try to ping it, as in Listing 10.4, we
get the Request timed out response. Microsoft uses filtering rules to block ping
requests.

Listing 10.4   **Pinging Microsoft with Filter Rules in Place**

```
C:\>ping www.microsoft.com

Pinging www.microsoft.akadns.net [207.46.197.102] with 32 bytes of data:

Request timed out.
Request timed out.
Request timed out.
Request timed out.

Ping statistics for 207.46.197.102:
    Packets: Sent = 4, Received = 0, Lost = 4 (100% loss),
Approximate round trip times in milli-seconds:
    Minimum = 0ms, Maximum =  0ms, Average =  0ms
```

Open Ports

When a live host is discovered, the next step is to determine what ports are open on the machine. A *port* is a software characteristic of the machine, not a physical one. Every network-based service provided by a computer (Web, mail, FTP, and so on) runs on a specific port number. If a host that is connected to the network is performing some sort of function that requires network interaction, open ports will exist on the host. For example, telnet servers listen at port 23, and Web servers listen on port 80. Although services have assigned numbers, no rule prevents Web servers from using a different port number. By examining open ports on a machine, we can determine what services are probably running.

One of the easiest tools to use in determining open ports is Fscan available from Foundstone (http://www.foundstone.com). Fscan works on all flavors of Microsoft Windows and is freely available. Listing 10.5 shows a port scan of a machine located at IP address 192.168.4.2.

Listing 10.5   **Port Scan of IP Address 192.168.4.2**

```
C:\>fscan 192.168.4.2
FScan v1.12 - Command line port scanner.
Copyright 2000 (c) by Foundstone, Inc.
http://www.foundstone.com

No ports provided - using default lists:
TCP: 21,25,43,53,70,79,80,110,111,113,115,119,135,139,389,443,1080,1433
UDP: 49,53,69,135,137,138,161,162,513,514,515,520,31337,32780

 Scan started at Mon Aug 20 07:40:27 2001

 192.168.4.2        21/tcp
 192.168.4.2        25/tcp
 192.168.4.2        80/tcp
 192.168.4.2        135/tcp
 192.168.4.2        139/tcp
 192.168.4.2        443/tcp
 192.168.4.2        135/udp
 192.168.4.2        137/udp
 192.168.4.2        138/udp

 Scan finished at Mon Aug 20 07:40:29 2001
 Time taken: 32 ports in 2.674 secs (11.97 ports/sec)
```

In this case, we see that 192.168.4.2 is alive and that it has Transmission Control Protocol (TCP) ports 21, 25, 80, 135, 139, and 443 open. It also shows that User Datagram Protocol (UDP) ports 135, 137, and 138 are open. Ports can either be open on the TCP or UDP protocol. Each protocol provides various services and running functions that can be contacted. The majority of services we will be dealing with are TCP based. TCP is the most common transport layer protocol used on Ethernet and the Internet. TCP is a more robust communication protocol that allows for reliable connection, whereas UDP is a connectionless protocol without transmission guarantees.

Running Services and Their Versions

After the attacker has determined open ports numbers, he needs to associate them with actual services. Two methods of identifying a service are by the port number and by the actual banner information that can be retrieved using a port scan. We can match up ports to typical information that is usually found on that port. For example, we know that in most cases, a Web server runs on port 80. If we see this port open in our port scan, we can gain further information by grabbing the banner. We can also use Fscan to grab banners, as shown in Listing 10.6.

Listing 10.6   **Banner Grabbing with Fscan**

```
C:\fscan -b 192.168.4.2
FScan v1.12 - Command line port scanner.
Copyright 2000 (c) by Foundstone, Inc.
http://www.foundstone.com

No ports provided - using default lists:
TCP: 21,25,43,53,70,79,80,110,111,113,115,119,135,139,389,443,1080,1433
UDP: 49,53,69,135,137,138,161,162,513,514,515,520,31337,32780

 Scan started at Sun Sep 16 13:07:24 2001

192.168.4.2        139/tcp
  [83][00][00][01][8F]
192.168.4.2         80/tcp
   HTTP/1.1 400 Bad Request[0D][0A]Server: Microsoft-IIS/5.0[0D][0A] Date: Sun,
   16 Sep 2001 20:07:25 GMT[0D][0A] Content-Type: text/html[0D][0A]
   Content-Length:
192.168.4.2         21/tcp
   220 kraa Microsoft FTP Service (Version 5.0).[0D][0A]
192.168.4.2        135/tcp
192.168.4.2        443/tcp
192.168.4.2        135/udp
192.168.4.2        137/udp
192.168.4.2        138/udp
192.168.4.2        520/udp

 Scan finished at Sun Sep 16 13:07:31 2001
 Time taken: 32 ports in 7.321 secs (4.37 ports/sec)
```

We see that the banner for the Web server running on port 80 says Microsoft-IIS/5.0. In most cases, that will be an accurate determination that the Web server is running Microsoft IIS 5.0. It is possible for a knowledgeable system administrator to change the banner to say something else, giving false output, but most consumers and businesses do not do this. This same analysis can be performed for all open ports found and all banner information available. Table 10.1 lists common ports and their service names that you will find on many systems that can be a potential problem.

Table 10.1 **Common Ports and the Services They Run**

Port	Description	Port	Description
TCP Ports		1313	bmc_patroldb
11	SYSTAT	1352	Lotus Notes
15	Unassigned (was netstat)	1433	MS-SQL-S
21	FTP	1494	Citrix-ICA
22	SSH	1498	Sybase
23	Telnet	1524	Ingres
25	SMTP	1541	RDS2
43	nickname	1542	gridgen-elmd
53	DNS	1723	PPTP
66	Oracle SQL*NET	2000	Callbook
79	Finger	2001	Dc
80	HTTP	2003	GNU Finger
88	Kerberos	2049	SUN NFS
109	POP2	2301	Compaq HTTP
110	POP3	2447	OpenView
111	sunrpc/rpcbind	2766	Compaq
118	SQLServ	2998	iss.net
119	NNTP	3268	msft-gc
135	EPMAP	3300	SAP
139	NETBIOS	3306	MYSQL
143	IMAP2	3389	Remote Display MS
150	SQL-NET	4045	NFS - lockd
156	SQLServ	5631	PCAnywhere
256	RAP	5632	PCAnywhere
389	LDAP	5800	VNC
396	NetWare-IP	6000	X-Windows
427	Svrloc	10000	Netscape Administration
443	HTTPS		Server
455	Creativepartnr	32771	WinRoute
465	SMTPS	UDP Ports	
512	print / exec	53	DNS
513	Login	69	TFTP
514	Shell	135	EPMAP
515	Printer	137	NETBIOS
524	NCP	161	SNMP
593	HTTP-RPC-EPMAP	256	RAP
1024	Reserved	500	ISAKMP
1080	Socks	2049	SUN NFS

Operating System Identification

After the attacker has determined the running services and ports on a machine, he needs to identify the operating system. Identification of the operating system allows for a more surgical attack. The simplest form of operating system identification is banner grabbing. Banner grabbing is merely viewing the message that appears when connecting to a service. A banner might give the attacker information on the operating system, type of host, and version of the application running on it. As shown in Listing 10.6, we can determine that the operating system is a Microsoft flavor. Another example of operating system identification via banner grabbing can be seen using FTP banners. Listing 10.7 shows an FTP banner.

Listing 10.7   **FTP Banner**

```
220 server1 FTP server (Version wu-2.6.0(1) Mon Feb 28 10:30:36EST 2000) ready.
```

By looking at the banners, we can surmise that this particular server is running wu-ftp version 2.6. We can also guess that this is a Unix machine because that is the typical platform on which wu-ftp runs. FTP runs on port 21. Other ports can be used to identify the operating system. The Telnet function usually has banner information that can let you know what the target system is running. In Listing 10.8, we see that one system is running Red Hat Linux and the other is a Cisco device. The mail port also gives us information, as shown in this listing.

Listing 10.8   **Identifying Banner Information**

```
Telnet on a Red Hat Linux machine (port 23):
    Red Hat Linux release 6.2 (Zoot)
    Kernel 2.3.99-pre9 on an i686
    login:

A telnet login for Cisco devices (port 23):
    User Access Verification
    Username: ...

A mail prompt running on port 25:
    220 server2 ESMTP Sendmail AIX4.2/UCB 8.7; Tue,
      24 Jul 2001 13:27:03-0500 (CDT)
```

This last machine in the example is running Sendmail, a popular mail program on the Unix platform. Notice that according to the banner, the operating system is AIX (IBM's version of Unix). After these pieces of information are gathered, the attacker should have a pretty good sense of what he is up against. At this point, the question in his mind becomes: Are any vulnerabilities associated with the services that are running on these machines?

Vulnerability Information and Resources

The Internet is probably the best place to turn to for vulnerability information. A hacker will find an open port on your computer and research all the possible vulnerabilities that are associated with that open port. Hundreds of Web sites, mailing lists, and other forums discuss computer vulnerabilities. Table 10.2 highlights some of these resources. Regardless of your existing security experience, you should consult these resources on a regular basis to stay abreast of the latest security developments.

Table 10.2   **Security Web Sites and Mailing Lists**

Web Site	Location	Description
Security Focus	http://www.securityfocus.com	Security site containing news tools, mailing lists, and a wide variety of security-related resources
Technotronic	http://www.technotronic.com/	Security site containing news, tools, mailing lists, and a wide variety of security-related resources
Nomad Mobile Research Center	http://www.nmrc.org/	Good information in several areas of hacking; includes tools
Packetstorm	http://packetstormsecurity.org	Security site containing news, tools, mailing lists, and a wide variety of security-related resources
Bugtraq	http://www.securityfocus.com	The premier list for discussion and announcements related to new vulnerabilities: what they are, how to exploit them, and how to fix them
Forensics	http://www.securityfocus.com	Discussion list on computer forensics—technical and policy-related issues
Incidents	http://www.securityfocus.com	Discussion list on computer incidents—information on new attack methods, signs of intrusions, information on new worms, Trojan horses, and viruses
Pen-test	http://www.securityfocus.com	Discussion list for penetration testing—tools, methods, techniques, and network auditing
NT Bugtraq	http://www.ntbugtraq.com	Focused discussion list for Windows-related problems

Based on the results of the footprinting analysis and the results of vulnerability research using the resources mentioned in the previous two tables, the attacker might have a means of breaking into the system. For example, during the port scans shown in Listing 10.7, the attacker determines that one of the FTP services running is wu-ftp 2.6. After doing research on a site like `www.securityfocus.com`, the attacker then learns that vulnerability is associated with that version of wu-ftp. At this point in time, he might have a possible entry point into the system.

The good thing about all this is that countermeasures are usually associated with all of these vulnerabilities. The appropriate vendor involved has addressed most vulnerabilities. Along with the vulnerability and exploit information, practically all of the resources listed in Table 10.2 also address the defensive side so that users can protect themselves. Later in this chapter, we will look at how Microsoft addresses vulnerabilities with its product update features.

How does this affect your privacy? Your ability to secure your machine directly affects your ability to maintain your privacy. Today's machines are vast repositories of personal data. Everything from your Quicken files to personal e-mail on your hard drive has a wealth of information about you. Leaving a machine unsecured is practically akin to inviting intruders. The rest of this chapter will discuss the basic security features found in common operating systems.

Physical Security

An important item to keep in mind at this point is the need for physical security. Imagine the following scenario: You return home from work one day and see that a break-in has occurred. Not only are several valuable items missing, but your home computer has disappeared as well. Most people immediately begin thinking about their data that was lost. But wait, backups were religiously made according to a schedule. But where are those backups? In most cases, they were probably left unsecured next to the computer. Businesses often spend a great deal of money addressing these issues on a larger scale with off-site backup and recovery processes, and as an individual, these same issues should be addressed, although on a smaller scale.

Think about all the data that resides on the computer that was stolen from your home. Do you keep your family budget on the computer? Do you use TurboTax, Quicken, Microsoft Money, or any other personal finance or tax software? Do you keep personal letters and correspondence on the machine? Does your computer contain files of historical or sentimental value? All of this information is potentially disclosed to that third party. It's come to the point where the data is more valuable and important than the computer. A PC can be purchased for less than $1,000 today, but the cost of losing the data can easily exceed several times that amount. Not so long ago, it was the other way around.

Our example, albeit a bit of scare tactic, illustrates the importance of *physical* security. All of the information noted in the previous scenario—the family budgets, tax and financial data—can also be stolen or disclosed over a network, which relates to *logical* security. As long as the machine is connected to some sort of network, an office local area network (LAN), to the Internet via an ISP account or through your cable modem, it's possible that an unauthorized person can access that data through logical means.

One of the most obvious, but frequently ignored steps of computer security is that of the physical realm. Computer security experts often say, "If I have physical access to the machine, all bets are off." These experts are referring to the ease of breaking into a computer that is sitting in front of you, as opposed to connecting to the same machine over the Internet. One of the easiest methods of accessing a computer through physical means is by using a floppy disk, which can bypass any login user ID and password scheme being used. Someone with a floppy and physical access can do anything from access the data to format the hard drive. That is when you hope that all of your personal files are encrypted! (We talk more about encryption in Chapter 12, "Securing Your Standalone PC: Viruses, Chat, and Encryption.") Although it is unlikely that a home user actually situates his home computer in a secure room (do you store your computer in a vault?), the house must be secure from unwanted entry and access to your computer.

One of the easiest things a physical intruder can do is open up the computer and remove its hard drive. The hard drive, which contains all your data, is about the size of an average paperback novel. That hard drive can then be loaded and read in any of a number of ways. All the data can be copied to another hard drive. If you were the target of corporate espionage, and your home computer had company data on it (many of us work at home these days), someone could break into your house, copy the hard drive, and replace it without your even knowing it. True, this is unlikely, but it is possible. The bottom line is that computer security starts at the physical layer.

BIOS and the Bootup Process

Because a computer is typically not physically secured or locked up at all times, such as in an office environment, we will look at several other ways to protect the unattended computer.

When a computer is powered on, the initial actions it takes are based on its basic input/output system (BIOS) settings. BIOS is the fundamental set of instructions for that individual computer. Every PC has BIOS settings. Whether the PC is running Windows 95/98, NT, or 2000, BIOS settings govern the basic operation of the computer. The BIOS performs such functions as memory and hardware checks. The BIOS also provides a place for the user to configure the date and time, hardware setup, order of boot devices (that is, whether the computer boot from the floppy drive or the CD-ROM drive first), and power management. The settings we will be focusing on are the security options within the BIOS settings.

How Do You Get to and Configure the BIOS Security Settings?

When you turn on your computer and it goes through the boot process, pay attention to the messages that appear on the screen. One message usually says something to the effect of Press the Del key to enter Setup. On some machines, it might be the Esc, F1, or F2 key. The key to press differs for BIOS manufacturers. Machine manufacturers (Dell, Gateway, IBM, Compaq, and so on) select and install a BIOS for each one of their computers. Different models produced by the same manufacturer might use different BIOSes. Sometimes the word "Setup" is used, and at other times, it might say "Diagnostics." In any case, a similar message usually pops up. If you don't see a message like that, try holding down the Delete, Esc, or any of the function keys to enter the BIOS settings. Typically, a user has a few seconds to press the proper key sequence to enter the BIOS setup. If no key is pressed, or if the improper key sequence is pressed, the computer continues to boot from the hard drive.

When you are in the setup screen, look for a Security Options area. In this configuration area, you should be able to set different passwords. If a security setting can be made, a System or Boot-Up password can usually be set. This password controls access to the system at bootup. To continue the boot process and boot from the hard drive, a password must be entered. This helps prevent unauthorized users from walking up to the machine, turning it on and then being able to access the hard drive or operating system. With this option set, the user of the system is required to enter a password during bootup. Other security settings that can be found in the BIOS include disk access password (prevents access to the hard drive), setup password (controls access to BIOS), and various user-level passwords. These options will vary from BIOS manufacturer to BIOS manufacturer.

Assigning a BIOS password to your machine helps prevent unauthorized access at the console. Even with physical access to the computer, an intruder will have a hard time accessing your data. If the boot sequence did not have the floppy drive listed first, an intruder with a bootable floppy could not access your data if you had a BIOS password set at boot time.

Computer Backups

Computer backups, if performed properly, contain all your data from your computer. Creating backups of machines on a regular basis is typically a tedious task. If the user even performs this valuable function, little thought is usually given to where those backup tapes should be stored or secured. Backup tapes should be afforded the same level of security given to the physical machine—if not more. If those tapes fell into the evil hands of a hacker, they could be used to create an exact copy of the machine as it existed at the time of backup. Even if the data on the tapes were old, the tape would still contain much relevant data related to the user: account numbers, usernames, password files, Quicken financial information, and so on. Think about how often you change all the data on your hard drive. It's probably not very often in most cases. Old copies of your data will contain private, relevant information about you. Thought and planning should be given not only to how you perform your backups, but also to how they are stored and secured. Many backup programs mandate using a password to restore the information, which is an added security feature.

Many operating systems have built in backup utilities. Figures 10.1, 10.2, and 10.3 show the backup programs that come built-in with Windows 98, Windows NT, and Windows 2000, respectively.

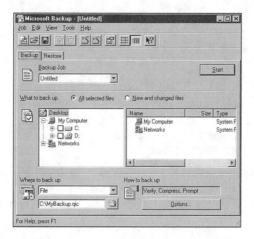

Figure 10.1   Windows 98 backup program.

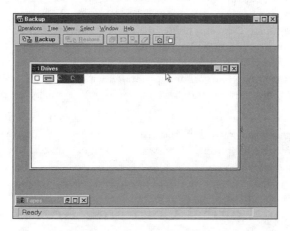

Figure 10.2   Windows NT backup program.

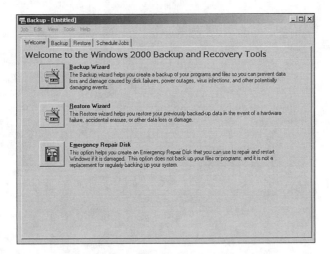

Figure 10.3   Windows 2000 backup program.

To access the backup program in Windows 98, select Start, Programs, Accessories, System Tools, Backup. In Windows NT, select Start, Programs, Administrative Tools, Backup. In Windows 2000, select Start, Run. In the Run box, type **ntbackup**.

The backup medium can be a Zip drive, a writable CD-ROM drive, another networked computer with a large hard drive, or a tape backup device. Some backup software packages allow for the use of encryption. During the backup process, the data being written to the backup medium is stored in an encrypted form. If the encrypted backup tapes fall into the wrong hands, the data on the backups remains incomprehensible. The legitimate user who knows the proper password can decrypt the data during the data recovery process. Although weak encryption schemes can be cracked, the typical user can get by with basic encryption schemes because the odds of someone sophisticated getting your backup tapes are rather slim. To crack encryption schemes, sophisticated software and powerful hardware are usually necessary.

Backup media is just as important as the original data on your computer. Store your backups in a secure place away from the machine. To keep that information secure, you will need to use encryption and passwords to add extra layers of protection on your personal information.

Controlling Logical Computer Access

Physical security is not the only area that home users need to worry about. Controlling *logical* computer access is the key issue faced by home users with always-on connections. This section deals with access controls and examines how the various operating systems provide for these controls. The majority of these controls are easy to implement and require just a few changes to the operating system's base configuration. We show you how to do all that.

Windows 9x was never really intended to be a secure operating system. Even though you can use passwords for your desktop, a simple test can show you how insecure it really is. When confronted with the login prompt, shown in Figure 10.4, if you simply press the Esc key or click the Cancel button, Windows boots normally, even without a password being entered! The reality of the situation is that the only thing that the Windows login password protects is your individualized settings. Operating system security in a Windows 9x environment is next to nothing. We'll now take a look at some other security issues faced by Windows 9x.

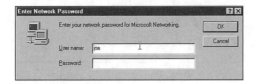

Figure 10.4   Windows 9x login screen.

Do not rely on Windows 95/98 security. It cannot really be called security because anyone can bypass it and have access to your information.

Windows 95/98 File Sharing

By default, Windows 95 and 98 come with file sharing turned on. Assuming this is your Internet connected machine, this feature allows you to share files with other users on the Internet. File sharing is a mechanism that gives other PCs access to your PC's directories and printers. File sharing is the principle behind such services as Napster and Gnutella. Users share files on their computer that anyone can have access to. Quite often, people turn on this feature and inadvertently allow remote access to the contents of their entire hard drive. Unintentional access to printers can allow malicious people to waste resources such as paper and toner by sending large print jobs to your printer. You can disable this feature by selecting Start, Settings, Control Panel, Network and then clicking the File and Print Sharing button (see Figure 10.5). The options for File and Print sharing should be turned off. The Client for Microsoft Networks should also be removed.

Sharing your locally attached printer might not be wise. For cable modem users, this sharing can be especially dangerous. If that feature has been enabled, an unauthorized user can identify and connect to that printer by merely clicking Network Neighborhood. At that point, the person can send print jobs to that printer. The damage can be anything from printing an innocent note saying "I hacked your printer!" to sending a 1,000-page print job using up the printer's toner and paper.

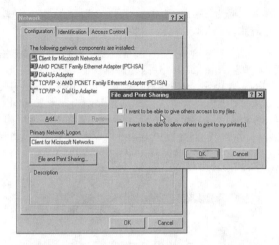

Figure 10.5 Configuration of shared devices.

If you need the functionality of multiple people having access to the same files on a computer, a server operating system such as Windows 2000 Server should be installed. Even Windows 2000 Professional can act as a server, and it has more robust security features than Windows 9x. These operating systems allow the functionality but give you much greater control over who can do what with those files. They also protect against individual PCs being compromised.

PWL Files

Windows 95 network procedures contain built-in password caching and store the passwords in a file called *username*`.pwl`, where *username* is the name of the user whose passwords it contains. Windows creates this file so that passwords can be *cached*. Typically, caches contain information so that you don't have to retype it. Passwords are frequently cached—you type them once at login time and then your computer remembers them. Whenever you require access to a password-protected resource, the password is read from the cache and you are not prompted each time. Therefore, whenever you connect to another domain and use your dial-up networking dialer, your password might be cached in this file. Also, if you check Save Password (see Figure 10.6), your password is really being stored in your password list (PWL) file.

The PWL is actually a database file. It contains information representing the resource name, type, and an encrypted version of the actual password. These PWL files are stored in `C:\Windows` with a filename of `username.pwl`. Using a tool called pwledit, we can actually view the password cache. Pwledit is available on the installation Windows 98 CD-ROM under `\tools\reskit\netadmin\pwledit`. On the Windows 95 CD-ROM, it can be found in the `\admin\apptools\pwledit` folder. The Pwledit program allows for the removal of individual resources from the computer, as shown in Figure 10.7.

Figure 10.6 Dial-up networking passwords are stored in PWL files.

Figure 10.7 Pwledit program.

Shortly after the release of Windows 95, a program called Glide surfaced on the Internet. This program decrypted the contents of the PWL file and reduced the security of Windows 95 significantly. Using Glide and similar programs such as Cain, shown in Figure 10.8, you can launch attacks against passwords in an attempt to decrypt them. (Both Glide and Cain can be found on the Packetstorm Web site http://packetstormsecurity.org.) Dictionary-based password attacks could then be set against these PWL files. In its most basic form, a dictionary-based attack takes a word, encrypts it, and compares it to the encrypted version. In our case, it is compared to the entry in the PWL file. If the encrypted version matches, you have found the password.

How do you protect yourself from this type of password decryption? The most basic thing to do is disable password caching by adding the following Registry key using the regedit command. The Registry controls many Windows functions and stores information about the system. To use the regedit command; select Start, Run; type

regedit in the Run box; and click OK. Then find the HKEY_LOCAL_MACHINE\
SOFTWARE\Microsoft\Windows\CurrentVersion\Policies\Network\DisablePwdCaching
key and set the value of DisablePwdCaching to "1", as shown in Figure 10.9. Keys
store values that can allow the computer to perform certain functions. Double-clicking
the DisablePwdCaching value allows you to set its value.

Figure 10.8   Using Cain to decrypt passwords.

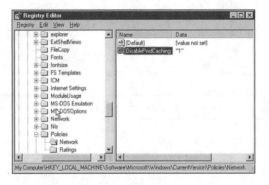

Figure 10.9   Use regedit to set a Registry value.

After setting the system to stop caching passwords, you must remove all the PWL files
from the system so they will not be created again. Disabling password caching and
never making use of Save Password features protects your passwords from being discovered should some attacker gain access to your computer.

Note

Additional information can be found in the following Microsoft article: http://support.microsoft.
com/support/kb/articles/q140/5/57.asp.

Patches and Updates

Without a doubt, one of the easiest and most prudent steps to take to secure your computer is to make sure it is up-to-date with its patches. Your best protection is to remain current with patches and updates. The vast majority of hacks and security vulnerabilities can be easily prevented if the operating system is kept up-to-date with the latest patches and upgrades. The customary method for releasing vulnerability information is to first notify the software manufacturer and allow them time to create a patch or fix. The vulnerability is usually made public when the manufacturer has a patch or fix available. Therefore, by merely applying patches and fixes as soon as they become available, one can remain relatively secure.

Microsoft and other vendors release patches, but it is up to you to download them. You can use Microsoft Windows Update (`http://windowsupdate.microsoft.com`) or visit the Microsoft Security Web page (`http://www.microsoft.com/security`). Windows Update, shown in Figure 10.10, is a Web site that helps you determine the upgrade state of your computer. It analyzes your machine and informs you if you are missing any patches or upgrades. After you select your desired upgrades or fixes and reboot, your machine becomes up-to-date. The packages are categorized as Critical Updates, Recommended Updates, Device Drivers, and Picks of the Month. Obviously, the Critical Updates should always be applied because they usually contain security updates.

Figure 10.10   The Windows Update site.

Visit the Microsoft Windows Update Web site (`http://windowsupdate.microsoft.com`) on a regular basis to check for upgrades, patches, and product updates. Keeping up-to-date on Microsoft operating systems by visiting the Windows Update Web site is a security requirement for every Windows user. Microsoft has made available this site to automatically notify you of a new patch that you need. It also has links to various programs you need.

User Accounts and File Security

As mentioned earlier, when you "log on" to your Windows 95/98 computer, you might be asked for a username and password. This username and password is only used to identify you to other Windows 95/98 machines. It does not in any way protect files on your local computer. Among other things, the identification is made so that you can retrieve personalized settings made by the user, such as restoring the desktop with the right color scheme. This means that other users who access your computer, including people who might be accessing it from the Internet, can do everything you can do, including reading, deleting files, and so on.

If file security is important to you, an alternative is to change to an operating system that supports the concept of user passwords and user-level security. Many such operating systems are available, and quite often they can be implemented with no loss of functionality. Another alternative is to make use of encryption software such as PGP or Jetico BestCrypt (see Chapter 12). If you use encryption, even if the attacker has access to your physical machine, the data still remains unreadable.

Security Resources: Share-Level and User-Level

In most cases, the home user who has one PC and broadband (DSL or cable modem) access to the Internet does not require file and print sharing. With some home networks, however, it might be necessary to have that feature turned on. In scenarios like this, where file and print sharing must be turned on, it is essential to turn on share-level security. This requires the use of passwords and user authentication before using shared resources. With share-level security, one can restrict access to a shared directory or printer by either defining it as read-only or by assigning a password to it.

To share a directory or printer with share-level security, in Windows Explorer, right-click the icon for the directory or printer you want to share, and select Properties. You see the Properties dialog box, shown in Figure 10.11. Select the Sharing tab and enter a share name. Specify whether you want the user to have read-only or full access to the resource. Selecting Read-Only or Full requires you to enter a single password, whereas Depends on Password requires you enter two passwords—one that allows read-only access and on that allows for full access to the resource.

By right-clicking a folder or printer and selecting Sharing you can control access to a resource. It is also possible to specify user-level security for each resource. If user-level security is employed, each resource will have a list of users and groups that can access that resource. To share a directory or printer with user-level security, in Explorer, right-click the resource and select Sharing. In the resource's properties, click Add. Then click a user or group and assign access rights as required.

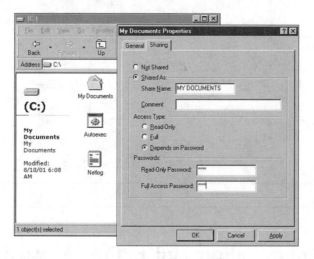

Figure 10.11   File sharing.

To better secure your files and printers, set passwords on shared directories and printers to control access. Even better, do not share resources unless you absolutely have to. Hackers can easily scan Internet-accessible systems for open shares and copy data. An example of a piece of software that performs that function is Legion, shown in Figure 10.12. After you input an IP address range, Legion looks for open shares in that range. Another product that looks for open file shares is Shed (shown in Figure 10.13) from Robin Keir (www.keir.net). Tools such as these are easy to use and are freely available on the Internet.

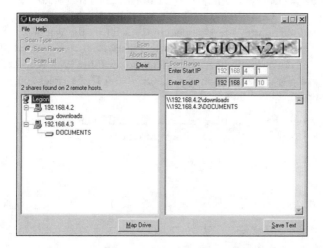

Figure 10.12   Legion share checker.

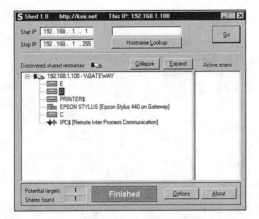

Figure 10.13   Shed share checker.

Using Policy Editor and Enforcing Password Security

You can restrict what users are allowed to do from the desktop and what they are allowed to configure using the Policy Editor (poledit). Also, system policies can be used to centrally configure network settings, such as the network client configuration options and the ability to install or configure File and Print Sharing services. Policies can be used to customize certain parts of the desktop, such as Network Neighborhood or the Programs folder.

As a consumer, you might be concerned about your children having access to certain programs and need to restrict what they can do on the computer. The Policy Editor does not come installed by default. You must install it by using Add/Remove Programs in the Control Panel. Under the Windows Setup tab, select Have Disk and install the Policy Editor located at \tools\reskit\netadmin\poledit on the Windows 98 CD-ROM. After you have installed the Policy Editor, select Start, Run and type **poledit** in the Run window to launch the Policy Editor. Then select File, Open Registry. You can then select Local Computer, as shown in Figure 10.14. This enables you to make settings for a standalone machine.

Navigating through the expandable tree, you can make policy settings by checking or unchecking the appropriate boxes, as shown in Figure 10.15.

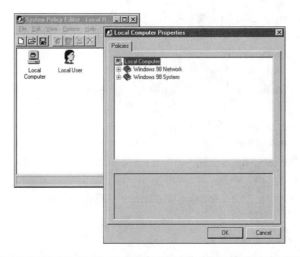

Figure 10.14   Using Poledit.

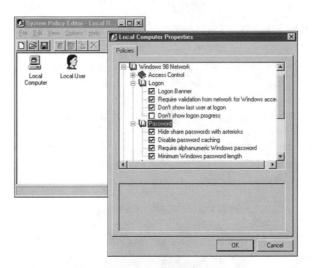

Figure 10.15   Individual policy keys.

System policy settings can be used to enforce good security practices, such as the following:

- **Require Validation from Network for Windows Access**—This specifies that a server validates each logon before access to Windows is allowed.
- **Minimum Windows Logon Password Length**—This controls the minimum number of characters accepted for a Windows 95 logon password.

- **Require Alphanumeric Windows Logon Password**—This forces a Windows 95 logon password to be a combination of numbers and letters.
- **Hide Share Passwords with Asterisks**—This causes asterisks to replace characters that users type when accessing a shared resource.
- **Disable Passwords Control Panel**—This prevents access to the Passwords option in Control Panel.
- **Hide Change Passwords Page**—This hides the Properties dialog box in the Passwords option in the Control Panel.
- **Disable Password Caching**—This prevents saving of passwords for share-level resources, applications, or NetWare passwords.
- **Disable Caching of Domain Password**—This prevents the caching of the network password.

Install the Policy Editor to set these Registry settings. Using these settings further restricts access to your computer from intruders. These settings can also enforce better security practices by home users who share a computer.

Password-Protecting the Screensaver

This is a basic security step that is often circumvented or unused by many users. Make sure all of your machines have this feature enabled to prevent an unauthorized user from taking advantage of an unlocked console. Figure 10.16 shows the password feature of the screensaver. To activate the screensaver, right-click the Desktop background, select Properties, and then select the Screen Saver tab. An idle (inactive) time of 15 minutes or so is a good configuration setting for this security feature. By merely performing this step, many simple "hacks" of unattended workstations can be prevented. The intruder would see the locked screen and simply move on the next machine.

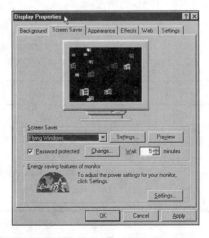

Figure 10.16   Screensaver password.

Always use a password-protected workstation or lock your keyboard when you leave the machine's console. It's easy for someone to walk by your computer and access you data if the screen is not locked, especially in a work environment. (At home, you might trust your kids, although they could inadvertently delete information if they had access to the data.)

Windows NT Professional and Windows NT Server are much more robust in terms of security features and capabilities. Although these features are available, the default installation of Windows NT can be considered insecure. It is left to you, the user, to enable and configure many of the security options.

Security principles such as locking unattended workstations and safeguarding backup media can be applied to any operating system. Screensaver passwords and backups to the system apply to just about all operating systems.

Service Packs

One of the easiest ways to eliminate many of the existing and known vulnerabilities and bugs associated with Windows NT is through the application of service packs. Service packs are applied directly to an existing system. They usually take into account all of the previous patches and hot fixes and then apply them en masse to the existing operating system. Service packs are released after a number of hot fixes and patches have been released. A service pack is Microsoft's way of making it easier for the end user to update her system. It is absolutely critical to remain up-to-date on service packs. Applying the latest service pack is the easiest and most efficient way for keeping your Microsoft-based system up-to-date.

A recently released free utility from Microsoft is also available to help an end user determine whether a system is up to date with patches. Microsoft Network Security Hotfix Checker (hfnetchk), found through the Web site www.microsoft.com/technet, is a command-line tool that checks the patch status of a given machine. It runs on both Windows NT and Windows 2000. This utility should be run on a periodic basis to determine if a machine is current on its patches and hotfixes. Listing 10.9 shows some sample hfnetchk output. If you do not patch the system with these updates, you will continue to be vulnerable to attacks against the operating system.

Listing 10.9   **Sample hfnetchk Output**

```
C:\>hfnetchk -a b
Microsoft Network Security Hotfix Checker, 3.1
Developed for Microsoft by Shavlik Technologies, LLC
info@shavlik.com (www.shavlik.com)
  ** Attempting to download the XML from http://download.microsoft.com/download/
     xml/security/1.0/NT5/
EN-US/mssecure.cab. **
  ** File was successfully downloaded. **
  ** Attempting to load C:\bin\mssecure.xml. **
Using XML data version = 1.0.1.142  Last modified on 8/30/2001.
```

Listing 10.9 **Continued**

```
Scanning MACHINEA

.........................................................................

Done scanning MACHINEA

----------------------------

MAXIME

----------------------------

Windows 2000 SP2

                    Patch NOT Found MS00-077    Q299796
                    Patch NOT Found MS00-079    Q276471
                    Patch NOT Found MS01-007    Q285851
                    Patch NOT Found MS01-013    Q285156
                    WARNING         MS01-022    Q296441
                    Patch NOT Found MS01-025    Q296185
                    Patch NOT Found MS01-031    Q299553
                    Patch NOT Found MS01-037    Q302755
                    Patch Found     MS01-041    Q298012
                    Patch Found     MS01-043    Q303984
                    Patch NOT Found MS01-046    Q252795
      Internet Information Services 5.0
                    Patch NOT Found MS01-004    Q285985
                    Patch NOT Found MS01-025    Q296185
                    Patch Found     MS01-026    Q293826
                    Patch Found     MS01-033    Q300972
                    Patch Found     MS01-044    Q301625
      Internet Explorer 5.5 SP1
                    Patch NOT Found MS00-093    Q279328
                    Patch NOT Found MS01-012    Q283908
                    Patch NOT Found MS01-015    Q286045
                    Patch NOT Found MS01-015    Q286043
                    Patch Found     MS01-020    Q290108
                    Patch Found     MS01-027    Q299618
```

In this example, we see that this machine is missing several patches related to Windows 2000, IIS 5.0, and Internet Explorer 5.5. The far-right column contains the Microsoft Knowledge Base identifiers. More information on each security patch can be obtained at http://www.microsoft.com/technet/security/current.asp. Each bulletin has a link to the specific patch that can be downloaded.

Windows NT Passwords

Windows NT's password scheme and feature set are completely different from that of Windows 9x. The first thing to ensure is that every user has his own account with his own password. In other words, do not allow the use of shared "group" accounts or allow users to share their passwords. Family members should each have their own account rather than sharing the Administrator account if they all use the same computer. If accounts are shared, it's impossible to track who was using the computer and possibly doing something he shouldn't do. In addition, people can cause a lot of damage with the Administrator account if they do not know what they are doing.

The passwords chosen should also be non-dictionary words (that is, one should not be able to find the word in any dictionary). This is because hackers can launch attacks against NT machines, trying every word in the dictionary until the legitimate password is discovered. Adding punctuation marks and numbers to passwords makes them even more difficult to guess. Other password settings can be enabled, such as maximum password age and minimum password length.

Account lockout is another feature that must be set. This feature locks out an account whenever more than the specified number of allowable attempts are made. This prevents an unauthorized user from continually guessing at an account's password. With a recommended setting of 5 or lower, a user is only allowed 5 chances before requiring system administrator intervention.

Table 10.3 shows basic password features that should be enabled.

Table 10.3   **NT Password Recommendations**

Password Feature	Recommendation
Shared passwords or group accounts	No
Password length	Minimum of seven characters
Password composition	Non-dictionary
	Use punctuation marks and numbers (alphanumeric characters)
Password expiration	Every 45 days
Account lockout	Five attempts

Set the password policy to use minimum-length passwords and enforce password changes. These changes are made in the Account Policy settings area of User Manager, as shown in Figure 10.17. In Windows NT, select Start, Programs, Administrative Tools, User Manager and navigate to the Policies option. User Manager is a tool that administrators use to manage users, accounts, and policies for the system. One can set the audit capabilities, account options, and user rights policies in this utility.

Using User Manager, you can pull up the list of all users on the system, as shown in Figure 10.18. Through this feature, you can add, delete, or modify user accounts.

Choosing Good Passwords

Many attacks against computer systems involve password guessing. Users with poorly chosen passwords are susceptible to these attacks. Poorly chosen passwords include words that can be found in any standard dictionary. Dictionary-based words are considered to be bad passwords because one method of attack employed by crackers against systems involves using every word in a dictionary against a login prompt. If a user has chosen one of these words, the cracker gains access.

To minimize the chances of this occurring, it is advised that users select passwords that do not appear in dictionaries. These passwords should contain characters like spaces, numbers, punctuation, and other alphanumeric characters (1234567890-=~!@#$%^&*()_+,./<>?). A strong password contains several of these characters in various positions of the password.

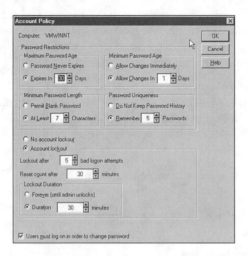

Figure 10.17   NT password settings.

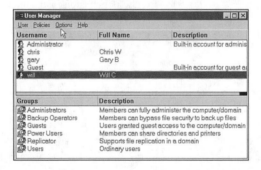

Figure 10.18   User Manager for password settings, users and groups, and policy settings.

One key to having good passwords that is a mainstay in corporate environments is the use of password testing utilities. One common utility that is used is L0phtCrack (www.atstake.com). L0phtcrack, like other password guessers, takes a password, encrypts it, and compares it to the encrypted password on the system. If the two match, the password is guessed. You can download L0phtcrack and test your own system passwords. We will discuss L0phtCrack in more detail in Chapter 13, "Securing Your Home Network."

The Windows NT Audit Policy

The other item to keep in mind regarding passwords is to periodically review the NT audit logs for suspicious activity. The logs might help identify attempts or even unusual activity on your machine. Of course, to actually view login data, logging must be turned on. By default, logging is not turned on in Windows NT. By using User Manager's Policies option, you can set the audit policy for the machine. Figure 10.19 shows some suggested audit settings you can use to track what is happening on and to your computer. At a bare minimum, account logons and logoffs should be audited. Even when logging is enabled, NT won't warn you about suspicious behavior. You have to check the logs on a periodic basis. A common mistake is to audit too many things. If the log grows too large, you'll be less likely to pay close attention to it. That usually means potential security breaches might go unnoticed. Consider auditing only login failures and file access failures if you have security set up on directories and files. These are good indicators that trouble is brewing. If someone attempts to log in with a bad password or access a restricted file, this will be considered a failure and be written to the log. If you get in the habit of analyzing your security log at least every morning, if not more, you'll be better armed.

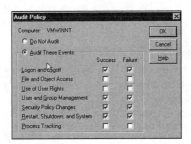

Figure 10.19 Suggested NT audit settings.

Auditing and logging are perhaps the most often neglected aspects of computer security. When properly set, logs can be an extremely valuable source of information, both for security-related events and general system administrative problems. Without logs, you cannot adequately investigate computer incidents. Even when audit logs are generated and events are logged, that data serves no purpose if no one actually monitors those logs. The logs could easily be filled with many traces of unauthorized activity, but NT will not notify you.

In many organizations, logs often go unchecked simply due to the sheer volume of data and the mundane nature of the task. Lucky for us, many freely available tools exist on the Internet to make it easier to extract data from the NT event logs. Using a utility such as NTLast from Foundstone, Inc. (`http://www.foundstone.com`), you can easily parse the NT event log and pull out logon information. Using the `-f` option of NTLast, it is easy to view all failed login attempts to a particular machine, as shown in Listing 10.10.

Listing 10.10   **NTLast Output**

```
C:\WINNT>ntlast  -f
StrangeUser    GHOST         GHOST         Fri Aug 03 01:01:56pm 2001
StrangeUser    GHOST         GHOST         Fri Aug 03 01:01:53pm 2001
StrangeUser    GHOST         GHOST         Fri Aug 03 01:01:49pm 2001
Mark           \\PC01        PC01          Thu Aug 02 04:27:14pm 2001
Joe            \\PC01        PC01          Thu Aug 02 04:27:14pm 2001
Administrator  \\PC14        PC14          Wed Jul 25 12:04:27pm 2001
Administrator  \\PC14        PC14          Wed Jul 25 12:02:30pm 2001
Administrator  \\PC12        PC12          Wed Jul 25 10:40:47am 2001
Administrator  \\PC12        PC12          Wed Jul 25 10:40:47am 2001
```

In this example, we see that StrangeUser tried unsuccessfully to log in three times on Friday, August 3, at 1:01 in the afternoon from a machine called GHOST. If this isn't someone we know, it bears investigation.

Turn on auditing and review your logs on a periodic basis. You will be able to see if you are being attacked in some cases. Although auditing is not as robust as using third-party software to detect attacks, it is a free start.

Users and Groups

If multiple users will use your system, it might make sense to organize them into groups. This way, security rights can be granted in a logical and repeatable fashion. Granting rights to individual accounts can become cumbersome and can be difficult to administer. Logically created groups make it easier to assign and maintain permission settings. You can create and administer groups in the NT User Manager program by double-clicking them. Figure 10.20 shows the User Manager Group Creation program.

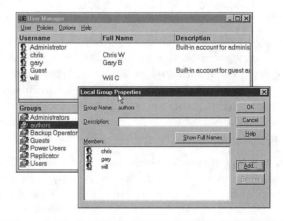

Figure 10.20   User Manager Group Creation process.

Aftergroups have been created, we can use them to help us maintain security and access control lists. Access control lists define access to programs, files, and functionality. We can create groups based on user functions and roles and assign them accordingly. Instead of granting permissions to many individuals, we can grant them once and remove them easily by making use of groups. Make use of groups to ease administration of access control lists.

NTFS File and Directory Settings

A feature of Windows NT and Windows 2000 is the availability of a new type of file system, NTFS. NTFS has built-in security options that allow you to protect your files. Unlike the Windows 95/98 FAT file system, you can now set security over files and directories on your machine using the NTFS file system. By default, any new folders created on an NTFS volume extend full control to file permissions for the group Everyone. By default, every user on your system is a member of the Everyone group. Any subdirectories or file additions inherit these settings. As new directories and files are created, the permissions should be reviewed and set accordingly.

Sharing Folders

By right-clicking a shared folder and selecting Properties, you see a window that allows you to configure its properties: General, Sharing, and Security (see Figure 10.21). (Note that not all of these options appeared when we were looking at Windows 9x.) Under the Sharing tab, you can configure various permission settings by clicking the Permissions button (see Figure 10.22). Sharing folders allows remote access to folders on your hard drive by other computers on the network. Specific users or groups can be granted Full Control, Read-Only, or Change access to the folder. NT gives you much greater control for securing folder shares. Now instead of simple password protection provided in Windows 9x, you have user-level security that requires a username and password for access. You also have the ability to specify what actions a user can perform on this share - such as Read, Write, or Full Control. Under the Security tab, shown in Figure 10.23, Permissions, Auditing, and Ownership of the folder can be set.

Not only can you set share permissions, but you can also set various security properties for the shared resource. These directory permission settings allow you to better control access to data on the machine. In fact, the settings can be made so that they become pretty granular (specific). You also have the ability to audit the directory, flagging specific folders and files for suspicious activity. If you have administrative privileges, you can grant ownership of the resource to other users so that they can manage its security. Figures 10.24 and 10.25 show the granular permission settings that are available. You access these dialog boxes through the Security tab of the shared resource's Properties dialog box.

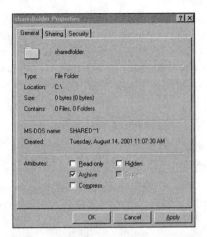

Figure 10.21   General permissions on files and folders.

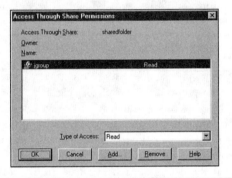

Figure 10.22   Sharing permissions.

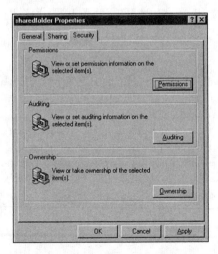

Figure 10.23   Security options.

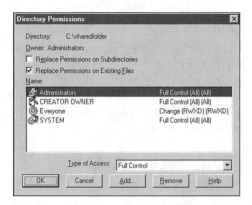

Figure 10.24   Directory permissions.

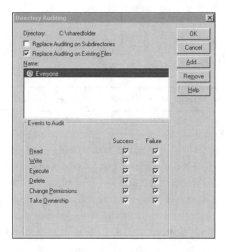

Figure 10.25   Directory auditing.

Note

If you are using both Sharing permissions and NTFS permissions together, the more restrictive security permission will be applied to anyone accessing your share from over the network.

The Windows NT Registry

The Windows Registry is a repository of information about all aspects of the computer—software, hardware, peripherals, applications, operating system, and users. The Registry brings together information that was previously held in files like autoexec.bat, config.sys, and the various .INI files. Information in the Registry is spread over several *hives* (files) and can be edited using a utility call Regedit. You can start Regedit by selecting Start, Run and typing **regedit** in the Run window. Regedit has an Explorer-like interface, with the tree to the left and the data to the right, as shown in Figure 10.26. Data in the Registry is organized in a key/value pairing. You can think of keys and subkeys like folders and subfolders, much like a file system structure. The final data structure along the tree is known as a *value*. By double-clicking the value in the right pane, you can update it.

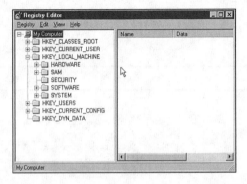

Figure 10.26   Regedit and its Explorer-like interface.

The Registry stores a tremendous amount of information about the user, system, and computer. Accordingly, it should also be protected with the same amount of vigilance. Windows NT's Registry is by default more secure than that of Windows 95/98 (information is stored in the file's system.dat and user.dat files). You can assign key security to the Registry as you would to a disk volume. This blocks general outside access, and you can even assign administrative rights to users or groups that do have Registry access. The Registry corresponds to the system files listed in Table 10.4.

Table 10.4 **Registry Paths**

Hive Registry Path	**Hive File Path**
HKEY_LOCAL_MACHINE\SYSTEM	\winnt\system32\config\system
HKEY_LOCAL_MACHINE\SAM	\winnt\system32\config\sam
HKEY_LOCAL_MACHINE\SECURITY	\winnt\system32\config\security
HKEY_LOCAL_MACHINE\SOFTWARE	\winnt\system32\config\software
HKEY_LOCAL_MACHINE\HARDWARE	Volatile hive
HKEY_LOCAL_MACHINE\SYSTEM\Clone	Volatile hive
HKEY_USERS\UserProfile	Profile, usually under \winnt\profiles\usere
HKEY_USERS\DEFAULT	\winnt\system32\config\default

Even with appropriately set Registry access settings, you would have other problems. For example, at one point, hackers discovered a major security hole within the NT Registry. This problem revolved around security keys that assign specific programs or services to run automatically after the server boots. Under a default Windows NT Server installation, all users have access to these keys, making it relatively simple for hackers to run one of their own programs every time a server boots. A hacker program that adds an account, copies data somewhere, or even formats the drive can be added to the Registry to run when the server boots up. Table 10.5 shows some security Registry settings that can be used to add more security features to a default installation of Windows NT.

Table 10.5 **Registry Security Settings**

Function	**Key**	**Value**
Remote Registry Access	`HKLM\CurrentControlSet\Control\` `SecurePipeServes\Winreg`	1

Legal Notice 1	`HKLM\SOFTWARE\Microsoft\`
	`WindowsNT\Current Version\`
	`Winlogin\LegalNoticeCaption`
		"Legal Notice for All Users"

Legal Notice 2	`HKLM\SOFTWARE\Microsoft\`
	`WindowsNT\Current Version\`
	`Winlogin\LegalNoticeCaption`
		"Warning: This system is to be used by authorized individuals only. By using this system you consent to be monitored for law enforcement and other purposes. Unauthorized use of this computer might be subject to criminal prosecution and penalties."

Last User Name	`HKLM\SOFTWARE\Microsoft\`
	`Windows NT\Current Version\`
	`Winlogin\DontDisplayLastUserName`
		1

Protect Event Logs	`HKLM\System\CurrentControlSet\`
	`Services\EventLog\Logname\`
	`RestrictGuestAccess`
		1

Secure Print Drivers	`HKLM\System\CurrentControlSet\`
	`Control\Print\Providers\`
	`LanManPrintServices\Servers`
		1

Restrict Anonymous Login	`HKLM\System\CurrentControlSet\`
	`Control\LSAName\`
	`RestrictAnonymous`
		1

Restrict Scheduled Commands 1	`HKLM\System\CurrentControlSet\` `Control\LSA\Submit Control`	1

Table 10.5 **Continued**

Function	Key	Value
Restrict Anonymous Registry Access	HKLM\System\CurrentControlSet\ Services\LanManServer\Parameters \NullSessionPipes	\<Configure with authorized names\>
Restrict Scheduled Commands 2	HKLM\System\CurrentControlSet\ Services\Schedule	\<Restrict to administrators\>
Clear the Page File at Shutdown	HKLM\SYSTEM\CurrentControlSet\ Control\Session Manager\Memory Management\ ClearPageFileAtShutdown	1
Disable Default Shares	HKLM\SYSTEM\CurrentControlSet\ Services\LanManServer\ Parameters\AutoShareWks	0

As with Windows NT, Windows 2000 is an improvement over its predecessor. Many of the Microsoft security features described in earlier sections of this chapter can also be applied to Windows 2000. For example, the password, auditing, and NTFS recommendations from the Windows NT section should all be applied to Windows 2000 computers. In Windows 2000, accessing the password and audit setting is a bit different. To set these parameters, select Start, Control Panel, Administrative Tools, Local Security Settings. From there, you can change password, account lockout, and audit policies through the Account Policies and Local Policies options. You can select the same parameters we use in Windows NT.

Encrypting File Systems

Windows 2000 includes the ability to encrypt data directly on partitions that are formatted with the NTFS file system. NTFS is the usual file system type for Windows NT and 2000. This feature of the Windows 2000 operating system is known as the Encrypting File System (EFS). Setting an attribute in the object's Properties dialog box can encrypt files and folders. After the data is encrypted, no other user can use it.

Users should employ EFS to protect file information, particularly on laptops, so that a malicious individual cannot read confidential files even if he or she steals the computer. From the Explorer list of files and directories, right-click the folder name and select Properties to see the Properties dialog box, shown in Figure 10.27. Click the Advanced button to see the dialog box shown in Figure 10.28, in which you can set encryption. The default configuration of EFS allows users to start encrypting files with no extra effort; data is automatically encrypted in folders marked for encryption. EFS automatically generates a public-key pair and file encryption certificate for file encryption the first time a user encrypts a file.

Figure 10.27   The Properties dialog box in Explorer.

Figure 10.28   The Advanced Attributes dialog box for setting encryption.

You don't need to manually decrypt a file to open and use it. EFS automatically detects that an encrypted file is being accessed and automatically locates the file encryption key from the system's key store when the valid user logs in.

File and Directory Settings

The file and directory properties, such as permission settings and sharing, are similar to those of Windows NT. You can configure property settings for Web Sharing, normal file sharing, and security options. Web Sharing is an option that should not be used in normal circumstances. It allows the user to share contents of the folder as part of a Web site. If the ability to share folders is required, make use of Microsoft's IIS Web server. A new feature of folder sharing is the ability to set access based on how users access the folder over the network. The security configuration options mirror those of

Windows NT. Figures 10.29 and 10.30 show how you can select permissions on shared folders. To access these Properties dialog boxes, you can right-click a file or directory through Explorer.

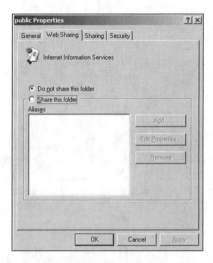

Figure 10.29   Web Sharing a folder.

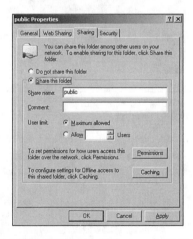

Figure 10.30   Granular permissions on a shared folder or file.

Lockdown Steps

You can take many steps to further increase the security of the operating system. In a home environment, implementing more security features will have less of an impact than might be possible in an office networked environment. In an office, many computers need to communicate with each other, and too many internal restrictions can lead to administrative problems. Many of the security measures can also be applied in the NT environment:

- **Rename the Administrator account**—For a sophisticated attacker, a renamed Administrator account does pose a serious obstacle. However, as we have mentioned, many attackers are unskilled, or they are just script kiddies who use publicly available tools for attacks and don't really understand the underlying principles of how exploits work. Simple steps such as renaming the Administrator account can easily fool tools.

- **Create a fake administrator account**—If you rename the Administrator account and then create an account called Administrator that has no privileges, an attacker will go after the fake Administrator account. Attackers usually launch brute force attacks against the Administrator account.

- **Disable the guest account**—The Guest account is a default account in Windows 2000. It should be disabled because all attackers know the account exists and can be a source of possible brute force attacks.

- **Replace the "Everyone" group**—The "Everyone" group gives anyone who gets into your network access to data that is assigned to the Everyone group. The group Authenticated Users should be used for file share access.

- **Disable unnecessary services**—By default, Windows has many services installed that might not be necessary to the function of your home system. In an office network environment, more services such as Terminal Server or DNS Server might be needed. For your home, however, you can turn off many services. To turn off services, you can access the service listing by selecting Start, Settings, Control Panel, Administrative Tools, Services. You see the window shown in Figure 10.31. You can double-click a service and stop it and change the startup option to Manual or Disabled at startup. Several services that can be disabled include Distributed Link Tracking Client, Distributed Transaction Coordinator, Alerter, Internet Connection Sharing, Fax Service, Net Logon, Remote Access Connection Manager, Remote Registry Service, Run As Service, Simple Main Transport Protocol, Simple TCP/IP Services, SNMP Service, SNMP Trap Service, and Telnet.

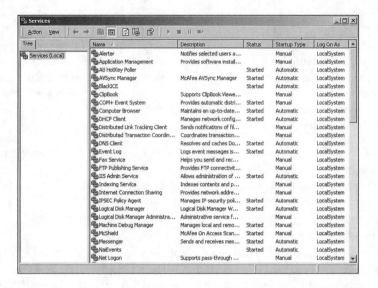

Figure 10.31   Service listing.

Local Security Policy

Microsoft has provided a central interface for managing many of the security and auditing features of Windows. Settings that required Registry access in Windows NT can be managed through an informational GUI in Windows 2000. To start up the Local Security Policy interface, select Start, Run and type **secpol.msc** in the Run box. You can also launch it by selecting Start, Programs, Administrative Tools, Local Security Policy. From this GUI, you control the password policies for your computer, as well as the auditing policies. A section on Security Options also exists (see Figure 10.32). These settings can be tuned to significantly increase security on your computer; however, they do require an advanced understanding to manipulate.

Port Restrictions

Earlier in the chapter, we discussed the possible threats that open ports pose to the security of the system. When an attacker has the ability to contact an open port, he can launch an attack against the system if a known vulnerability exists. Because your home system is not behind a corporate firewall, you need some protection against attackers looking for open ports. Chapter 11 discusses third-party personal firewalls available to the home user; even without a third-party package, however, Windows 2000 comes with some built-in port filtering capability.

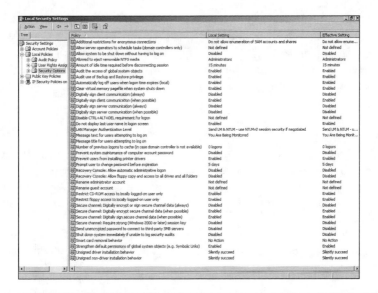

Figure 10.32   Local security settings—security options parameters.

You can find a list of open ports on your local system at `%systemroot%\drivers\etc\`
`services`. Port restrictions can be implemented using the TCP/IP Security console
located in the TCP/IP properties. Select Start, Settings, Control Panel, Network and
Dial Up Connections, Local Area Connection, Internet Protocol (TCP/IP). Click the
Properties button, and then click the Advanced button. On the Options tab, choose
TCP/IP filtering. You see the dialog box shown in Figure 10.33. To allow only TCP
and ICMP connections, configure the UDP Ports and IP Protocols to Permit Only
and leave the IP Protocols box blank.

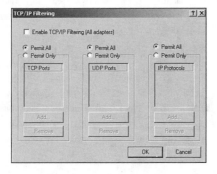

Figure 10.33   TCP/IP filtering.

Port filtering can be difficult with the Advanced TCP/IP settings. You have to set these filters on each network adapter you have, which can vary from 1 to 3 in many computers—even home systems. This type of filtering is basic and is not meant to replace firewall filtering. A better filter built into Windows 2000 is IP Security Policy (IPSec), which is discussed next.

IPSec

You will also see the "IP Security Policies" section in your Local Security Policy. IPSec is an advanced topic that requires knowledge of some important networking and security concepts. In brief, the IPSec standards are newly built into the Windows 2000 and Windows XP operating systems. Although TCP/IP filtering on the network adapter is one method of restricting port access, it can be cumbersome and difficult to manage because you have to enable all ports that you want to use. TCP/IP filtering does not scale well to ranges of ports that are needed, and it can be difficult to understand.

IPSec is a combination of protocol standards that protect IP communications between two computers. You know that TCP/IP is the language that computers use to communicate with each other across the Internet. TCP/IP is an old set of protocols that was never prepared to deal with all of the evildoers on the Internet. It is inherently insecure and easily taken advantage of by attackers and criminals.

IPSec is a new set of standards that is just starting to be implemented in computers across the Internet. It has been widely tested and proven secure, gaining industry-wide respect. IPSec provides three important security protections to communications between computers:

- **Confidentiality**—Communication is encrypted so that third parties cannot intercept and read the data being transferred.
- **Authentication**—Communicating computers authenticate with each other to prove their identities. This way, you can be sure that you are talking to the right computer, and not some hijacked host.
- **Integrity**—Communications are protected packet by packet. If one packet is tampered with while in transit, the system is alerted and the packet is dropped.

To set up IPSec policies, select Start, Settings, Control Panel, Administrative Tools, Local Security Settings, IPSec Policy on Local Machine. Select Action, Create IP Security Policy. Give the policy a descriptive name for what you want to do and walk through the wizard, selecting the default options. When you reach the Rules tab, shown in Figure 10.34, you can set up filtering rules.

You can then add a rule. Select the defaults, including applying the rule to all network connections. Two existing policies exist: All ICMP Traffic and All IP Traffic. You will see these when you start to create an IPSec rule. These are too broad for our needs, so we need to add specific rules. Click Add to create a name for your filter. In this case, we will name it Net Filter, as shown in Figure 10.35.

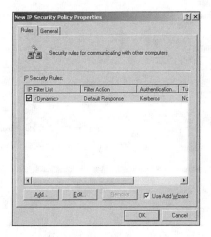

Figure 10.34 IPSec Rules tab.

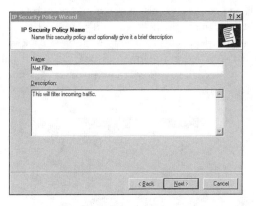

Figure 10.35 New filter rule.

At this screen, we then click Add. In the Source Port field, we select Any IP Address, and in the Destination Port field, we select My IP Address. The Protocol Type is TCP, and the To This Port option is set to 139. When this is complete, edit the new filter by double-clicking it and then clearing the Mirrored check box. What we have just done is set up filters that will block anyone (Any IP Address) on the Internet from connecting to port 139 on our machine (My IP Address). We will then redo this process to filter out ports 445, 137, and 138 for TCP and 139 and 445 for UDP. These ports are default Windows ports that can be used to retrieve information about your system and attempt connections to your system over the Internet. When complete, our filter rule should look like Figure 10.36.

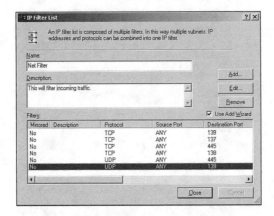

Figure 10.36   Filter rule.

When you have finished the filter list, click Close. Then select the filter you created and click Next. This will get you to the filter action screen. By default, you cannot block traffic, so click Add, and then click Next on the first page. Type a name (`Block`), and click Next. The action you want to select on the next page is Block. Click Next and then Finish. When your action is defined, click Finish. After you associate the Block action with your Net Filter, you will have enabled your filter, as shown in Figure 10.37.

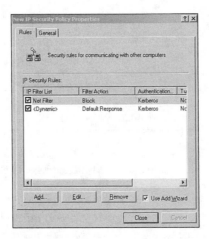

Figure 10.37   Enabled filtering rule.

IPSec can be granular and robust, but it is easy to set up filters incorrectly. Like corporate system administrators who implement expensive firewalls incorrectly, you can make the same mistakes inadvertently and allow an intruder to bypass your filtering rules. If you want to learn more about IPSec and the security services it can provide, start by reading the documentation that Microsoft has provided in the help files. Be prepared for a head spinning blast of information.

After you have installed your Windows operating system, you should put together a checklist of security measures you need to take to secure it and keep it secure. Table 10.6 is a good start to follow in creating your security checklist.

Table 10.6 **Checklist for Securing Your Windows-Based PC**

Step	Windows 95/98	Windows NT	Windows 2000
Address physical security concerns.	X	X	X
Use a BIOS or bootup password.	X	X	X
Perform backups and secure media properly.	X	X	X
Apply Windows updates (windowsupdate.Microsoft.com).	X	X	X
Disable file and print sharing.	X		
Use user and group accounts.	X	X	X
Use Policy Editor to enforce password security.	X		
Password-protect the screensaver.	X	X	X
Set audit policy.		X	X
Set password characteristics.		X	X
Set security for sensitive files and shares (NTFS permissions).		X	X
Set Registry keys.		X	X
Use the Encrypting File System (EFS).			X
Disable unnecessary services, applications, utilities, and programs (IIS, FTP, SMTP, and so on).	X	X	X
Use virus scanning software and keep it up-to-date.	X	X	X
Run hfnetchk.exe on a regular basis to see if machine is up-to-date on patches.		X	X
Use local security settings to enforce password restrictions.		X	X
Use NTFS for disk volumes.		X	X

Unix/Linux

The growing popularity of Unix and particularly Linux has led to its appearance in many home-based machines. Many computer enthusiasts have installed this operating system on their machines and found that it can be both highly secure and highly complex. Many of the steps one takes to secure a Unix machine have analogous steps in the Microsoft world.

The basic steps of physically securing the machine remain the same. Regardless of the operating system, the same steps taken to physically secure a machine, its BIOS, and backups remain the same. Linux comes with file permission and directory setting as well as screensaver password protection. Years ago, Unix/Linux was more command-line driven. However, in today's flavors of Linux, graphical interfaces are common and emulate many of the Windows features. We can use many methods to implement basic security in a Linux installation. As with Windows, these steps need constant vigilance and update to keep the operating system secure over time. Linux is not as user friendly as Windows. For any questions you have on a command or function, you can invoke the man command. man, which stands for manual, can be invoked on any command by typing **man *commandname***. man is your friend in the Linux world.

File System Security

To check what files are on your system and what the permissions are on those files, we can display a list similar to the dir command used in DOS. To display it, type the command **ls -la**. You see the following output:

```
   |----1----|-2--|---3----|----4-----|--5--|-----6------|---7-----|
1.  drwxrwxr-x 24 root    users      1024  Jun  20 01:10  .
2.  drwxr-xr-x 22 root    root       1024  Jun  20 01:12  ..
3.  drwxr-xr-x  3 root    root       1024  Jul  01 01:40  Mail
4.  -rw-rw-r--  1 john    operator  43244  Jul  01 01:11  file
5.  drwxrwsr-x 17 john    operator   1024  Jul  01 02:48  Test
```

Each field has a function:

- **Field one**—The first nine positions from the right describe the user, group, and other permissions. Each group of three letters specifies read access, write access, execute access, directory, symbolic link, or another type of special file. (These are discussed more in a moment.)
- **Field two**—This is the number of hard links to this file or directory.
- **Field three**—This is the owner of the file or directory.
- **Field four**—This is the group to which the file belongs.
- **Field five**—This is the size of the file.
- **Field six**—This is the modification time.
- **Field seven**—This is the filename.

File permissions can allow or disallow access to files and directors to individuals, groups of individuals, or everyone on the system based on where the permission flags are set. The first group of three relates to the user, the second group of three relates to the group to which the user belongs, and the third group belongs to all users on the system. The meaning of each permission is listed in Table 10.7.

Table 10.7   **File Permissions**

Letter	Permission	Description
r	Read	Can be opened to read the contents
w	Write	Can be modified, including appending and deleting
x	Execute	Can execute the file if it is a program or shell script
s	Special Permission	Runs with another user's permission
t	Special Permission	Save text attribute

Note

The setuid and setgid programs can be dangerous. They have been the target of hacker "buffer overflow" exploits.

Note

The Save Text attribute (t, also known as the *sticky bit*) is set on directories so that a user might only delete files that the user owns or has been granted explicit permission.

Changing File and Directory Permissions

The chmod command sets the file and directory permissions. The owner of the file or directory can make these changes, as well as the system administrator. The two modes of operation are *absolute mode,* which works by explicitly specifying the permissions using an octal value, such as 444 or 446, and *symbolic mode,* which works by using combinations of letters and symbols to add or remove permissions, such as wrx or rx.

Table 10.8 shows what each octal value means.

Table 10.8   **Octal Values**

Value	Permissions	Description
0	- - -	No permission
1	- - x	Execute only
2	- w -	Write only
3	- w x	Write and execute
4	r - -	Read only
5	r - x	Read and execute
6	r w -	Read and write
7	r w x	Read, write, and execute

The following is an example of changes to files using chmod. When you use the chmod 755 files command, all users on the system are given read and execute access to the files directory.

```
bill@host$ ls -ld files
    drwxr-x---  1 john     files     1024 Jun 10 00:10 files
bill@host$ chmod 755 files
bill@host$ ls -ld files
    drwxr-xr-x  1 john     files     1024 Jun 10 00:10 files
```

Symbolic mode can also be used to change the file permissions. In the following example, the permissions Read and Execute will be changed on the file Files and will be applied to everyone in the Group and everyone else on the system Other. The permissions Read and Execult will be removed from the file Files:

```
bill@host$ ls -l files
    drwxr-xr-x  2 john     john      1024 Jun  10 01:10 files
bill@host$ chmod go-rx files
bill@host$ ls -l files
    drwx------  2 john     john      1024 Jun  10 01:10 files
```

Changing File/Group Ownership

The administrator or owner of a file can change the permissions on the file with chown and chgrp to change the group owner. When ownership has been changed to someone else, the original owner cannot change the file unless the new owner allows change permission on the file. The following example demonstrates chown usage:

```
bill@host$ ls -l fileowner
-r--r--r--  1 bill     sysadmin    424 Jun 10 02:10 file
bill@host$ chown joe file
bill@host$ ls -l file
-r--r--r--  1 joe      sysadmin    424 Jun 10 02:10 file
```

After the chown command is run, Bill no longer owns the file; Joe does.

You also can change ownership of files recursively by using the chown -r option. When you use the -r option, the chown command descends through the directory and any subdirectories below that one, changing the ownership.

Use chgrp to change the group ownership in a similar fashion, as in the following example:

```
root@host# ls -l file
    -r--r--r--  1 root     admin      424 Jun 20 02:10 file
root@host# chgrp newgroup file
root@host# ls -l file
    -r--r--r--  1 root     newgroup       424 Jun 20 02:10 file
```

After the chgrp command is run, the admin group no longer owns the file; newgroup does.

Umask Settings

The umask commandcan be used to determine the default file creation mode of files. When you create a new file, it has the permissions of the umask settings until you manually change the umask or the file permissions after it is created. Typically, umask settings include 022, 027, and 077 and are usually set in the /etc/profile file. Settings 022 and 027 restrict read, write, and execute access to the owner of the file, and setting 077 gives everyone read access. The umask can be used in the following manner:

```
root#host umask 033
```

Be sure to make root's umask to at least 022, which restricts access to the file to the root account. A user's default umask setting can also be set individually in his startup scripts. Servers that spawn files using weak umask permissions can create files with excessive permissions that hackers know how to target.

Monitoring Files with Special Permissions

You must monitor and check unauthorized access to significant files on the system, such as setuid or setgid files, password files, world-writable files, group-writable files, configuration files, unowned files, and startup files. Users with permission to use the superuser account must also be monitored. These are users who are in the "wheel" group. Because this account can do anything, restricting access to those who need it is very important. Use the following command to find all setuid and setgid programs:

```
root@host# find / -type f -perm +6000 -ls
```

To check for world-writable files, you can use this command:

```
root@host# find / -perm -2 ! -type l -ls
```

To check for unowned files, use this command:

```
root@myhost# find / -nouser -o -nogroup
```

Host Security

Even if you don't allow anyone else access to your computer, you should secure your local system from local attack. If an attacker were to somehow gain local access, whether through physical access to your computer or through some remote connection such as with Telnet, he could take advantage of local weaknesses to gain superuser privileges. Privilege escalation is the goal of an attacker after he has user access locally to the system. You can take several steps to secure the local file system to make it difficult for an intruder who has command-line access locally. The following sections discuss a number of steps that you can take to secure the system.

Remove Unnecessary Applications

Linux installations come with many packages that are probably unnecessary, such as programming compilers and utilities if you are not a programmer. Games can also be considered unnecessary. As we mentioned in Windows operating systems, you should remove all unnecessary programs. Linux flavors have different methods of installing and uninstalling programs, such as /bin/rpm in Red Hat Linux and /bin/dpkg in Debian Linux. During the initial system installation, do not install unnecessary services.

Using Your System Accounting Data

In Linux, the system log files in /var/log, /var/run/utmp, and /var/log/wtmp should be restricted to the superuser only (root). These files can have permissions of 644 without affecting the system. Numerous programs can read through these files and give you valuable information. A couple of these are Chklastlog and Log Analysis. You can find many of these programs on Packetstorm (`http://packetstormsecurity.org`).

System Updates

It's important to apply patches and updates to Linux just like it is to Microsoft products. New versions of the Linux operating system and the applications are made available rather frequently and should be applied to the system. Several flavors of Linux now have automated features that can check for updates at the vendor Web site, much like the Microsoft Update feature.

User Accounts

Any user you set up on the system should be restricted in what privileges they are assigned, and the passwords they use must be strong. You should periodically review login times of your users and remove inactive accounts. You should also check for invalid login attempts to the user and root accounts; this could be a sign of an attacker attempting brute force access to the system.

Root Account

The superuser accounts (equivalent to the Administrator account in Windows NT/2000) should always be logged into from a user account. Create a user account, which you log into first, and then use the su command to become root. Review the logs of root access, for valid as well as invalid login attempts. Only one root account should exist on the system. The root account should be restricted so that you cannot log in directly. You can do this with /etc/securetty. Because root controls the entire system, be careful with how you use the account and the security of the password. You can use a program such as sudo to give normal users limited access to root functions, thereby limiting the need for multiple people having access to the root password.

Services

As with Windows, running services can pose a threat to the system. The more services you have running, the more points of access that an intruder can have into the system. Services are started from the /etc/rc* startup files: /etc/inetd.conf and /etc/xinetd.conf. All services that are not required should be disabled. To disable running services from /etc/inetd.conf and /etc/xinetd.conf, you can comment out the line in the file or remove the lines that start the services. You should check your /etc/rc.d/rcN.d, where N is your system's run level for started services. The files in /etc/rc.d/rcN.d are actually symbolic links to the directory /etc/rc.d/init.d. Renaming the files in the init.d directory can prevent the services from starting. Disable a service for a particular run level by renaming the appropriate file with a lowercase *s* instead of an uppercase *S*.

Remote Access

If you require services to be running for specific sites or functions, you can use a program such as TCP Wrappers to restrict access. TCP Wrappers is used to restrict access between sites for various functions, such as Telnet or FTP. For example, if you want only people from a specific machine or domain to access your system or access only Telnet on your system, you can use TCP Wrappers. It is also possible to deny or allow incoming connections using TCP Wrappers. By placing a machine's name or address in the /etc/hosts.allow and /etc/host.deny files, you can restrict access accordingly. You should disable or restrict any host or function that is not necessary for remote connection by making the appropriate entry in the /etc/hosts.deny file. A tcp_wrapper (/usr/sbin/tcpd) is invoked from /sbin/inetd instead of the real service. It then checks the host that is requesting the service and either executes the real server or denies access from that host based on restrictions of /etc/hosts.allow and /etc/hosts.deny.

Linux systems can connect to each other without password authentication through the use of /etc/hosts.equiv and /.rhosts files. Use TCP wrappers instead to allow access between remote Linux systems, and never allow unauthenticated access between systems. Network File System (NFS) is a widely used file sharing protocol that allows servers running the nfsd and mountd services to export entire file systems. The /etc/exports configuration file can be used to share file systems much the same way that directories can be shared in Windows. This should be restricted to specific systems when file sharing is required. You can check for shared file systems with the /usr/sbin/showmount -e *host* command. Never export the root file system. You can restrict other people from checking for your exported file systems by disabling the portmapper service (TCP and UDP port 111) and restricting access to these ports with filtering software such as firewalls.

Password Security

Like Windows, Linux has complex password features. Linux passwords are stronger than Windows password encryption. Different encryption algorithms such as DES and Blowfish can be used to encrypt Linux password files. This encrypted password is typically stored in /etc/passwd and /etc/shadow. The /etc/shadow file is used to keep the encrypted password from normal users on the system. If a user were to obtain the encrypted password file, he could potentially crack the password. The password you type is encrypted when you log in and is compared to the one stored in the password file. Although the encryption is stronger in Linux, a password can still be guessed/cracked using such programs as Crack and John the Ripper. Password cracking programs try every word in the dictionary, with variations, and then encrypt that word and compare it to the encrypted password on the system. A weak password can be guessed using these programs, which is why stronger passwords that have alphanumeric characters and special characters are necessary. Red Hat Linux has a unified authentication scheme called PAM (password authentication module) that allows you to change your authentication methods without recompiling. If you use the default password scheme in Linux and are dissatisfied with the security measures, you can use PAM to increase your password security without recompiling the operating system kernel and rebooting the system.

SSL, HTTPS, S-HTTP, S/MIME, and SSH

Services that are used to connect to systems such as Telnet, FTP, and Sendmail are considered insecure services because data is transported in an unencrypted format. Data can be captured as it crosses the wire. Much like the message portion of a postcard, which anybody can read, these cleartext protocols are vulnerable to anyone who decides to monitor that traffic. Several of these services can be replaced with secure, encrypted versions, such as SSL, S-HTTP, HTTPS, S/MIME, and SSH:

- **Secure Sockets Layer (SSL) and HTTPS**—SSL is an encryption method that supports several different encryption protocols for client and server authentication. SSL operates at the transport layer. Data transferred over SSL is encrypted and is used in many online shopping applications. If you are going to run an e-commerce site on your Linux server, you will have to use SSL to encrypt information. HTTPS is the protocol that uses SSL.

- **S-HTTP**—S-HTTP is a security protocol utilized by Internet applications. It was designed to provide confidentiality, authentication, integrity, and nonrepudiation and to support multiple key-management implementations. It encrypts information. It is not as widely used as SSL.

- **Secure Multipurpose Internet Mail Extension (S/MIME)**—S/MIME is used to encrypt electronic mail and other types of messages. This open standard is being implemented more often as Internet commerce expands.

- **SSH**—SSH (secure shell) is the de facto communication program used for login to remote systems. It provides encryption of the entire process and can replace such services as Telnet, rsh, and rlogin. It uses public-key cryptography to encrypt communications between two hosts and for authentication.

Other Tips for Your Home PC

Both Windows- and Linux-based operating systems come with a whole host of functions that we will not try to cover in detail in this book. Numerous books are available on every detail of the operating system. You can take a few steps in addition to those already mentioned to will help in your operating system security.

Server Software

Never run unnecessary servers on your machines. A server is a program that will allow others to access data on your machine. Examples are Web servers or FTP servers. If you run a Web site on your home computer through the functionality provided by your ISP, you allow people to interact directly with your computer. Most of these servers allow you to restrict access to certain directories. However, some servers are easily configured incorrectly. Others have bugs that can be exploited to bypass the access restrictions. If you have to run a server, make sure you read the manual and configure it properly. As an example, if you install Windows 2000 Server, it also automatically installs the IIS Web server, an FTP server, and an SMTP server (mail function). You must go into Internet Information Services Manager to turn these services off manually if you do not really want them running (see Figure 10.38). You can get to the Internet Information Services Manager by selecting the Administrative Tools option from the Control Panel.

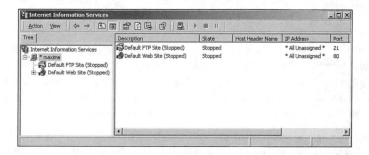

Figure 10.38   Using the Internet Information Services Manager utility to administer Web, FTP, and Mail servers.

Remote-Control Programs

Use remote-control programs on home computers with caution. Programs such as PC Anywhere, Microsoft's Terminal Server, Carbon Copy, and Virtual Network Computing (VNC) should be paid special attention because they provide console-equivalent access to machines. By using this type of software, a user can connect to your machine remotely and have full control over it. It's easy to misconfigure such software to allow unauthorized individuals who find the open connection to take control of your computer remotely. Therefore, password authentication to access the computer via this class of software is absolutely required. Many of these programs also have built-in encryption functions that can add another layer of security. If the software allows it, set options that allow encryption of traffic as it travels from the host machine to the remote machine. You might also set options that allow access only from specific IP addresses.

Virus Scanning

Antivirus software is a must on every personal computer. We'll address this subject in more detail in Chapter 12, but suffice it to say, every personal computer should be running an up-to-date antivirus software package. Many of these programs have automated capabilities that can go to the vendor Web site and update the software with new virus signatures without your intervention.

E-mail Attachments

Most e-mail readers allow you to send and receive binary files as attachments. Be careful if you receive an attachment. Make sure you know where the e-mail came from. If you receive an attachment and do not recognize the sender's address, exercise caution. Lately, e-mail attachments contain malicious code that spreads across the Internet. The "I Love You", Melissa, and Anna Kournikova viruses are all dangerous viruses. Viruses can range from the annoying to the destructive. The viruses just listed did not destroy data, but they did create a tremendous annoyance to mail and systems administrators, overloading servers and some network connections. If an e-mail recipient of the virus opened (double-clicked) the infected attachment, the virus automatically sent the message to contacts in the user's address book. When those recipients opened their e-mail, the same actions occurred, causing an avalanche of e-mail.

Never double-click an attachment to open it unless you trust the sender or already know that it has been scanned by an up-to-date virus checker. (Picture attachments are usually harmless.) Save the attachment, start the image viewer, and load the attachment. This prevents you from opening an executable that disguises itself as an image. Even if you receive an executable from a familiar source, it is still worthwhile to run it through a virus checker first. Many virus programs have the capability to scan e-mail attachments for infection and quarantine the e-mail if it is infected. The sender might not know that his system is infected by a virus and is sending out e-mail on the virus' behalf.

Deleting Files

Most of us know that when we delete a file by pressing the Delete key or dragging it to the Recycle Bin, the file isn't really deleted yet. What about when the Recycle Bin is emptied? Is the file really gone then? What about when a hard drive is reformatted? The answer is no in all cases. Measures can be taken to retrieve the supposedly deleted data. Delete commands usually only remove the pointers that tell the computer where on the physical hard drive the data is stored. When the pointer for a particular file no longer exists, the file is thought to be deleted, even though the data still resides on the disk. All of that data can still be recovered from the disk. Software programs such as Norton Utilities UnErase and various computer forensics products such as Encase allow for the recovery of these "deleted" files. If the deleted data was not overwritten by new data, the chances of recovering those lost files are excellent.

To completely wipe deleted files from your hard drive, make use of utilities such as PGPtools, Norton Utilities Wipeinfo, Shredder, and BC Wipe. Because a deleted file is not really deleted and can be recovered, you need some additional help to completely delete a file and make it unrecoverable. These utilities tackle this problem by over-writing the hard drive's data portion. This cleaning process overwrites all parts of the hard drive multiple times so that it is next to impossible that data can be recovered.

One example of a program used to really delete a file is PGPtools. Using PGPtools (www.pgp.com), we can securely delete or "wipe" a file. You open the Wipe utility and specify the appropriate filename in the dialog box (see Figure 10.39). PGPtools deletes the file by not only removing its pointer, but also by overwriting the data on the hard drive. This easy-to-use utility should be employed when you need to really delete a sensitive file.

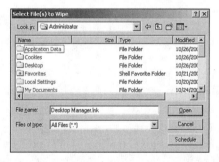

Figure 10.39   Securely delete (wipe) a file by using PGPtools' Wipe utility.

Another interesting utility available in PGPtools is FreeSpace Wipe. It does what its name implies—it overwrites freespace so that preexisting data is overwritten. When you open the FreeSpace Wipe utility in PGPtools, a wizard appears, guiding you through the process, as shown in Figure 10.40. The wizard prompts you for informa-tion such as the drive to be wiped and the number of passes that it should make. The more passes that the utility makes, the less likely that the file can be recovered. For most purposes, a setting of 5 is adequate. Department of Defense standards for secure deletion of files require multiple writes, implying that there is technology that can read data if only one pass is made.

Figure 10.40 Using PGPtools FreeSpace Wipe to overwrite freespace.

If you ever need to dispose of your computer equipment or computer disks, make sure you take the appropriate steps to clean the storage media. You might have heard the press lately about failing dot.coms that auctioned off their computer equipment without deleting, much less cleansing, the data that was present on their hard drives. These computers contained information such as social security numbers of employees, salary information, termination letters, and meeting minutes from executive and board meetings. Actually, it is not surprising that cleansing hard drives is not a priority when it comes to closing down a business. However, given the fact that employee and customer data was present and unsecured, greater care should have been taken.

Electronic Eavesdropping

An individual (or, more likely, an organization) can thwart most of the logical access controls described so far with access to sophisticated (expensive) electronic eavesdropping equipment. Eavesdropping is the interception of radio frequency interference (RFI) and electromagnetic interference (EMI) emitted by the various computer equipment in use (screens, keyboards, cables). All electronic equipment emits these faint signals, which, if interpreted correctly, reveal the information being processed. An example of EMI is the use of older household appliances while watching TV or listening to the radio. Whenever these appliances were turned on, they emitted interference, which, in turn, affected the image on the TV screen. These emanations can theoretically be captured and analyzed. Although there might be no interest in capturing emanations from a toaster, one could certainly find interesting information when capturing emanations from a computer monitor or printer.

This type of technology is also thought to be possible because of the existence of Transient Electromagnetic Pulse Emanation Standard (TEMPEST) standards and TEMPEST-related certifications. TEMPEST typically refers to a set of standards for limiting RFI and EMI "leakage" from computer equipment. It's also used to describe the process of preventing those emanations.

Realistically, you are only at risk for TEMPEST-based attacks if the data you are processing is of extremely high value. The resources required to purchase and develop this technology remain out of reach for most people and organizations. Only governments are thought to be able to carry out TEMPEST-based attacks. A mini-industry has developed around TEMPEST hardware and consulting.

Keystroke Logging

Another interesting item to be aware of is the use of keystroke loggers. Keystroke loggers take every key pressed on the keyboard and record it in a log. This is particularly useful when someone wants to discover a password. As a user types a password, the keystrokes are recorded in the log, which can later be retrieved and analyzed. Hackers commonly use software-based keyboard loggers after they have broken into a machine. Alternatively, if physical security is breached, a hardware-based keystroke logger can be installed. This kind of device is installed between the keyboard cable and the computer. Unless the keyboard cable is checked frequently for the existence of such a device, the detection of a hardware-based keystroke logger remains low. These devices are widely available, however. They can be purchased for less than $200, as opposed to TEMPEST equipment, which falls in the millions of dollars (if it's available at all).

The detection of software-based keystroke loggers can be fairly easy if a thorough search of a computer is performed, although some loggers conceal themselves quite well. Detection of hardware-based loggers is much easier, obviously, but can be difficult based on where and how the computer equipment is situated.

An example of a software-based keystroke logger is Invisible KeyLogger Stealth (IKS), manufactured by Amecisco (`http://www.amecisco.com`). IKS is shown in Figure 10.41. After it is installed, it captures every keystroke typed at the console, including the password you type after pressing Ctrl+Alt+Delete. Keystrokes are saved to a file on the hard drive. In the case of IKS, a special viewer is required to view the file.

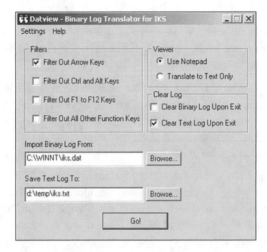

Figure 10.41   Keystroke capturing.

Summary

In this chapter, we looked at several of the major operating systems used in the home environment. We also looked at some of the basic steps you can take to secure those systems. Keeping your home system secure can essentially be addressed by performing two major actions.

First, you must take the initial installation and configuration of the machine and secure it properly. Just because a machine has been bought at a store and has the operating system preloaded doesn't mean it is also properly secured. You must take the basic steps of configuring and double-checking the initial configuration of your new machine. Manufacturers often ship their machines or software with poor default settings. An example might be preinstalled software that does not include adequate password settings or no passwords at all to control access. There is no way to really hold manufacturers accountable for weak security. No cases have been successfully tried against a manufacturer for weak security in its product. Because users can't force good security on a manufacturer other than by not buying a product, the speed at which the manufacturer changes a product is directly related to consumers' purchases.

Second, you must remain up-to-date and knowledgeable about your systems. When new viruses or new system vulnerabilities are made public, it is imperative that you apply the appropriate countermeasures. The security industry has been good about posting information related to newly discovered vulnerabilities. You can find detailed analyses on the new vulnerabilities with information on how to determine if you are infected, how to purge your system of the vulnerability or virus, and how to prevent your system from being infected in the first place.

You can usually find this type of information in various Internet mailing lists and newsgroups that are devoted to security. The speed with which you apply the appropriate patches and fixes is also critical. Many of the recent security issues (Code Red, SirCam, Nimda) have propagated with extreme speed. If your system is not patched early on, chances are fairly high that your system can become infected or compromised.

You can remain fairly secure if you learn all you can about your system and the latest threats to it and take the appropriate steps to secure your machine. If you become unsure about the security of your system, it is best to remove its network connection first and then investigate. In later chapters, we will discuss in some detail how you can track what was done to your system during an attack and what you can do to additionally secure your system.

11

Securing Your Standalone PC: Broadband Connections

As we saw in Chapter 10, "Understanding Your PC Operating System and Its Security Features," many security features are inherent in each operating system, to greater or lesser degrees. Utilizing these security options is a definite necessity, but you might want additional security functions as well. As we have been continuously discussing, the easy access that consumers have to the Internet makes for an easy target. Internet service providers (ISPs) do not provide security features with the broadband connections they sell (Digital Subscriber Line [DSL], cable modem, and satellite); it is up to individuals to protect themselves. The term *broadband* usually refers to a connection that can carry at least 384Kbps from the Internet to your PC. In practical terms, we use it to describe connections through cable modems, DSL, satellite, and wireless connectivity from service providers. Much like the pioneers who settled the West in the United States, today's consumers are settling new territory in cyberspace. With new frontiers come new dangers. The dangers discussed in Chapter 5, "Illegal Threats to Individual Privacy," must be addressed if people are to keep their home connections secure.

Another danger to keep in mind is the advent of wireless technology. This new method of connecting to the Internet has its own dangers. You must realize that whether you are at home, at the office, or traveling with your wireless laptop, the Internet provides threats from all directions. With a connection to the Internet, you are a target for attack. As we have seen with worms and viruses in the news, threats come from more directions than just hackers. Personal firewalls are effective weapons against those who would invade your personal domain via your Internet connections. (Firewalls are discussed in more detail later in this chapter.)

The home user connects in most cases via high-speed access using DSL or cable modem, and to an increasingly lesser degree, dial-up. Satellite and wireless connectivity are also available, but these are minor and we will not concentrate on them. We will focus on connectivity via cable modem and DSL because that is the spreading technology. However, the security features we will discuss can be applied to any system no matter the connectivity type.

In the corporate environment, any company that does not have a firewall in place is asking to be hacked. Firewalls provide inbound and outbound security controls that attempt to secure the complex applications that are needed in business. The corporate environment has already been educated about the need for firewalls. Now that consumers have such extensive and complex access to the Internet, they must be educated about the needs for personal firewalls. As we have discussed in earlier chapters, consumers are now a target for attack both from a technical standpoint and from a personal information standpoint. Your home computer is a treasure trove for the right attacker, and you need to protect it diligently.

In this chapter, we will discuss several different personal firewalls that can be used to protect your PC and your private information. Several different scenarios will be examined for ways that firewalls can be configured and when to use different features. DSL, cable, and dial-up connections each provide different pros and cons for Internet connectivity and firewall use. The type of connection and type of software that is best for you is debatable, but we will endeavor to provide you with practical advice that will assist you in making a choice by walking through the setup of several firewalls and showing you how that can benefit you by increasing your home security.

Threats Recapped

As we discussed in Chapter 5, many attackers on the Internet want to compromise your home systems for various reasons. Your job is to be your own system administrator as well as security officer. You must protect and defend your home computer on a daily basis. The "why" behind being attacked over your broadband connection is easy to understand. First, the speed of your connection allows quick attacks. Second, because you are always connected, attacks can go on for days. If you were on vacation for a week and left your computer on, you could have a week of unnoticed attacks by a determined intruder. Third, automated programs such as worms can hammer away at your connection without human intervention. We have seen the damage that worms like SirCam, ILOVEYOU, Melissa, and others have caused against corporations. Just imagine what has happened to home users who have not reported anything to the authorities. Fourth, if you have a large hard drive, it can be used as a storage point for pirated software, or *warez*. Because you are always on, hackers from around the world can connect to your compromised machine and drop off and pick up files. Fifth, a good hacker never attacks his final target directly from his own system. He uses multiple hops along the way to cover his tracks, and your system can be one of those hops. Last, your personal information is a gold mine—everything from your bank statements to your Quicken files can be used to cause trouble. With all the information that is on your PC, someone could easily steal your identify.

The built-in features of both Windows and Linux make it easy to compromise an unprotected system. Even if you lock down the operating system, the applications you run such as Internet Explorer or Microsoft Outlook pose threats to the system that cannot be ignored. Malicious software such as some of the spyware products we mentioned can slide under your security precautions. All these problems lead to the need for additional security features that are not inherent in the operating system.

Today's Internet connections are tens or hundreds of times faster than those available five to ten years ago. A malicious attacker can mount a powerful attack with a DSL or cable modem because of the fast, unfiltered access that these connections provide. As technology advances, so will the capability of the attacker. As consumers, we must implement the right tools to combat these growing threats.

Cable Access

Cable access is becoming more widespread than DSL connection. With the failure of several of the smaller DSL providers such as Flashcomm, it's easy to see why consumers turn to the cable companies. Providers who just provide DSL service have had a harder time than companies that provide a mix of services, such as cable companies. It's hard to state specific reasons why a number of DSL providers have failed.

The coaxial cable connection you have coming into your home provides the Internet connection through the same line as your cable TV and is easy to bundle with your cable service. It is not even necessary to have cable TV reception to have Internet access. Cable service is an always-on connectivity. Many ISPs offer DSL, but to get cable access, you must go through the cable companies.

Cable access reaches about 40–50% percent of the United States. Cable coverage is steadily increasing, but more heavily populated markets get coverage first. It's simple to check if your cable company provides access. Just call them or go to their Web site and you will easily be able to check whether your street gets cable access. The monthly fee that your cable company will charge can vary anywhere from $20 to $70 typically, plus the cost of rental of the cable modem or purchase of the cable modem and setup fee.

Cable speeds can reach up to 5Mbps, but with shared access on your local neighborhood network, you most likely won't get speeds faster than 2Mbps. Your cable company can't guarantee the fastest speed. Your cable connection is similar to your office connection. When more people are in the office and sharing the network, you will typically get slower connectivity to the Internet. If you have seen some of the DSL commercials on TV, they tout faster speeds than cable modems because they don't have the same type of bandwidth sharing that cable modems have. If all your neighbors simultaneously download some MPEG files from Napster or the latest movie trailer, you will see a definite decrease in speed.

To get that connection through your cable company, you are limited in your choice. If your cable provider does not have it, you can't really go to other cable companies who do not provide access in your neighborhood. Legally, you have more options if your current cable provider does not provide you access. In June of 2000, in the case of AT&T Corp. versus City of Portland, the court ruled that cable modem access as telecommunications access has subjected the cable industry to the same open access requirements applicable to telephone company-provided broadband service.

Limitations

The dangers of cable connectivity come from more than just the hackers. The sales pitch says that you can get super-fast connectivity for $30–$40 a month. Well, that's sort of true. You do get faster access than dial-up, but the rate can vary, as we just mentioned. Also, more people on your local network can slow down your connection speed. The costs of the modem, whether you purchase or rent it, can be somewhere between $150–$200. You also must pay a setup fee and wait for the cable guy to show up to install it. In most cases, self-installation is not a viable option.

The cable company does not provide direct security over your cable connection. If someone using their system uses the connection to hack and someone complains, the cable company does sometimes notify the user to desist hacking activities. Because you are on a local area network (LAN), it is possible for your neighbors to sniff (capture) your traffic and perhaps watch what you are doing if you allow access to your computer or do not use encryption over your e-mail and other Internet functions.

One good and bad feature of cable access is the static IP address that is provided. This can be helpful if you want to set up a Web server, but it can make you a target over time to an attacker because the attacker can always reach you via the same IP address.

An always-on cable connection can be "mostly-on." Like DSL and dial-up, the connection can have outages sometimes, or your computer can have a problem that requires a reboot. Cable will be up more than DSL in most cases.

Digital Subscriber Line

A Digital Subscriber Line (DSL) connection uses existing copper telephone lines to connect homes and small businesses. Because the DSL line can carry voice and data, you do not lose access to your phone line when using your computer. DSL's always-on technology (well sort of) provides high-speed access comparable to cable modem access. Speeds typically range from 512Kbps to 1.544Mbps for downloads and slower for uploads, around 128Kbps. (The change in speed holds true for cable modems also; upload speeds are typically slower than download speeds.)

Consumers can have dynamic or static IP addresses for DSL. A *static* address remains the same over time, whereas a *dynamic* address can change every time you log in. In some cases, you pay extra for a static address. Many small businesses purchase static IP addresses because you can buy faster connections and still pay less than it would cost for a full or fractional T1 connection for a business. For the consumer, this means that you have several choices for using DSL, if it is available in your neighborhood.

Setting up a home DSL is an easy self-installation process. Like the cable modem, you have to purchase or rent a DSL modem, connect it to your phone line and your computer, install some software, and you should be ready to go.

DSL-only providers around the U.S. and larger companies such as the phone companies are slowly providing more DSL coverage. ISPs resell the DSL service of the major providers. To get DSL, you must live within two to three miles of the local phone company's switching facility. This can be a problem for people living in the middle of nowhere. Being further away from the telephone facility can have the effect of slowing down your connection speed. Cable modem access is far easier to get than DSL because the cable companies have a wider range of coverage, although this is changing. With the failures of DSL companies such as Covad, people are having even more trouble connecting through DSL because few competing DSL providers exist in the same market. If one DSL provider goes out of business, there might not be another in the same market to provide service.

DSL is obviously better than dial-up access and Integrated Services Digital Network (ISDN) connections, which max out at about 128Kbps. Because you are not sharing a network with others in your community, you don't have to fear sniffing of your traffic on the LAN as you would when using a cable modem. Also, the lack of sharing means that your connection speed won't degrade when other people in your area go online.

DSL comes in several flavors. Sometimes you can actually get a choice of what type of DSL service you get, and other times you have only one option, as is periodically the case in choosing cable access. One option is Asymmetric Digital Subscriber Line (ADSL), which provides fast download rates up to 1.544Mbps and upload rates from 128Kbps to 512Kbps. Symmetric Digital Subscriber Line (SDSL) has both fast upload and download rates, and is used more in businesses. Another option is Universal ADSL, which does not require a splitter to separate voice and data traffic. The following are other forms of DSL that you probably won't see:

- ISDN DSL (IDSL), which is a version of ISDN
- High-bit-rate Digital Subscriber Line (HDSL), which is fast and symmetrical
- Rate-Adaptive Digital Subscriber Line (RADSL), which determines DSL connection speed by how fast data can travel on your individual phone line

Cable and DSL rates are rather similar. The monthly fees can range from $30 to $150 depending on the speed you choose and the type of DSL connection you have, the rental charge of the DSL modem, and the setup fee. You can typically get DSL through your phone company, but you don't have a choice of provider. With a local ISP, you probably will be given a choice or providers. National providers also have service that you can use. An example of such a provider is DSL.com. The hit to the DSL market has caused failures of some national companies, one of which was Flashcomm. Going out of business can seriously affect your service!

Limitations

Like cablemodems, DSL does have its drawbacks. One main drawback for the consumer can be cost. It's easy to run up a high monthly fee if you choose a fast connection speed rather than the basic DSL packages. Another potential problem is connection slowdowns. Although it's not as easy to slow down the speed, electromagnetic noise and distance from the telecommunications facility can affect the DSL modem. In many cases, the IP address you get will be dynamic unless you request and possibly pay for a static address. This can be good because you won't be a static target for hackers, but you could have a hard time setting up a Web server address. And as with every other type of connection that consumers get, few DSL companies take responsibility for helping you secure your computer against attacks. Although some providers do take some measures to protect you, such as by warning you against hacking and providing information on security, it is still up to you to secure your system. Only recently have some providers, such as EarthLink, begun adding security software such as personal firewalls to their connectivity. Rather than just providing you an account and access, they help you secure your PC by providing some additional software.

Dial-Up ISPs

Although dial-up connections are currently the majority, they are becoming increasingly less used as cable modem and DSL access make it into homes. Dial-up connections are modem-based and max out at 56Kbps speeds. They are much slower than broadband connections.

You can still find a few ISPs that provide free dial-up connections (although the number of them has significantly decreased in the past year). Free dial-up providers make money by forcing you to view ads and doing such things as selling your personal information to marketing companies. (One of the most well-known was NetZero, but it now charges for access.) Dial-up accounts come with free Web hosting and disk space (although both cable modems and DSL have this feature also in some cases).

Dial-up connections are available just about everywhere in the U.S. Even if you don't have a local ISP, you can contact one of the major telephone companies, such as

AT&T, and sign up with them. They probably will have a local connection number for you to dial in to. For home users who travel a lot and need a local number to call to avoid long-distance charges, a national provider is a good choice.

Most dial-up connections offer unlimited connection for $10–$20 a month. The most poplar service is America Online. The maximum speed of basic dial-up service is around 56Kbps. Setup is generally very simple—much easier than DSL and cable setup—with little or no setup fee involved. All you need is a modem attached to your computer.

Limitations

The limitations that we all face with dial-up lines are the connectivity speeds. You are lucky if you get a full 56Kbps. If you are a road warrior, you know that most hotel dial-up connectivity ranges from about 14Kbps to 50Kbps. A number of firewall products can cause connectivity problems with dial-up lines and affect your connection to the Internet. With the multimedia content of the Internet, dial-up connections are becoming increasingly more limiting. If you want to listen to music over the Internet, view videos, or watch the latest movie trailer, a high-speed connection is almost a requirement. Most Web sites are so graphics-intensive that slow dial-up connections make Web surfing a long and slow process. Downloading the latest AOL update or the latest release of a Web browser can take hours on a dial-up connection but take only minutes on a broadband connection.

DSL Versus Cable Versus Dial-Up

In many cases, you really won't have a choice between purchasing DSL or cable access. You are probably limited to one or the other type of connection for now because coverage isn't complete across the U.S. for both cable and DSL access, although each month sees more access spreading across the country. Dial-up connections are available everywhere, but we should be moving to broadband connections. The speed of broadband connection is the main reason most consumers make the switch to DSL, cable, or wireless. Some points used for comparison are as follows:

- **Security**—Both static and dynamic IP addresses are vulnerable to attack. DSL and cable services can assign either a static or a dynamic IP address to you. Dial-up access provides dynamic IP addresses. We will discuss security additions you can make to the operating system security measures covered in Chapter 10 as well as antivirus software you can use. Several DSL providers, one of which is Verizon, provide blocking of some traffic to your IP address. By blocking some ports, they are providing some security to you.

  Cable access does lose out to DSL and dial-up when it comes to snooping on your neighbors or your neighbors snooping on your traffic. Because you are in a LAN, a unique security issue with cable is that the line is shared with others in your area, which makes it easy for a neighbor to snoop around your computer.

All three types of connectivity are subject to denial-of-service attacks. A remote attacker can easily send traffic to your connection and slow it down or knock you off the network if you do not have good firewalls in place.

- **Cost**—The relative costs of DSL and cable services are comparable. Both have varying monthly fee, setup fees, and cost of owning or renting the devices. DSL does provide a good inexpensive solution (only a couple hundred dollars a month) for small businesses that cannot afford a T1 connection but need an always-on connection. Dial-up is inexpensive compared to the other two services. Note, however, that some dial-up plans have limited hours if you choose the cheapest package.

- **Availability**—Cable access is spreading faster than DSL access. Some of the major DSL providers have gone out of business or are in financial trouble. But with the regional telephone providers such as Verizon and SBC providing DSL access, both are viable options in just about all large markets. Many small town or out-of-the-way residences will not have available to them either cable or DSL service. Dial-up access is everywhere.

- **Network reliability**—Being able to get online is important. Nothing can be more annoying than a busy signal. As some of you AOL members might know, getting online can be a problem with some dial-up services. With DSL and cable, it's rather rare that you will have a network outage. Many dial-up providers can have busy signals at peak usage hours, whereas both DSL and cable modem will almost always give you access.

- **Support**—If you have ever dealt with your cable company or phone company, you will probably have a few choice words to say about their support services. Fortunately, the Internet parts of their business are somewhat better. No reliable statistics are available on the service levels, but from experience with dealing with both types of providers, the support is average. Average service is better than what you normally get from cable and telephone companies, however. Cable and phone companies usually provide 24/7 technical support with their own support number. The only challenge you will face with support is having the company go out of business. Again, this is more of a problem with DSL providers. Several failed DSL providers include Northpoint, Flashcom, Zyan, and Jato Communications. Support for dial-up connectivity is usually 24/7 as well. Because it is simple to set up, troubleshooting a problem is simple in most cases.

Personal Firewalls

The purpose of a firewall is to filter inbound and outbound traffic to your computer or network. Information is sent through the Internet in packets of data, and these packets have sources and destinations. You become vulnerable to attack when you have no protections from all the various types of packets that are being sent to your computer. On the Internet, connections are made to open ports on your computer. As we discussed in Chapter 10, when you have an open port that anyone can reach on the Internet, you are potentially vulnerable to an attack. Your broadband cable or DSL connection leaves you wide open day or night to attack. Even your dial-up account leaves you open to attack, but the limited time you are connected via dial-up access and the slow speed make dial-up accounts less of a target.

A basic firewall architecture is shown in Figure 11.1.

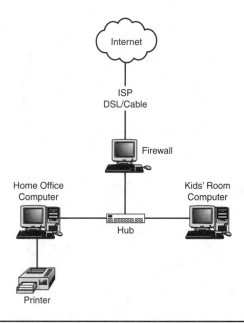

Figure 11.1   Basic firewall architecture.

Your IP address is the defining point of who you are on the Internet. Your computer's IP address is like your house address. If someone knows your IP address, he can find you. When a person knows your IP address, he can perform port scans. A port scan checks for open points of connectivity on your connected computer. Port scans are like open windows and doors in your house. If you don't lock them, anyone can come into the house. Figure 11.2 is a refresher of what an IP address looks like. In this case, our IP address is 192.168.1.5.

Figure 11.2   An IP address of 192.168.1.5.

The average consumer is not a specific target of a hacker. Many hackers and even more script kiddies target people blindly. It would be the same as a burglar just walking down your street trying every door until he found one that was open so he could break in.

Firewall software is used to set rules or filter what kinds of data packets can be sent into the computer and leave the computer. *Rules* or *filters*—two interchangeable terms—are used to allow or deny certain types of data into and out of a system using a filtering device such as a firewall. Data packets contain everything from IP address information to port information. The firewall is your first line of defense against hostile attacks. Whatever filters you set up are used to allow or deny packets. If you are running a Web server, you probably only want Web traffic to port 80. You can set up your firewall rules to allow only that port and block all other access from the Internet. Perhaps you are also running a mail server (port 25) on your Web server, but you only want specific people on the Internet to access that mail server. In that case, you can restrict, by IP address, who can connect to check mail on your server.

If a packet is sent that matches the rules you define, then it is allowed through to the open port. If the rules you set up deny access to the requesting packet, the data can be rejected or just dropped. If the data is rejected, the computer that is sending the packet can know that the data was denied. If your filter drops the packet, the data will appear to have gone into a void without confirmation that it reached its destination.

An application gateway, often called a *proxy*, acts like a customs officer for data. Anything you send or receive stops first at the firewall, which filters packets based on IP addresses and content, as well as the specific functions of an application. For instance, if you're running an FTP program, the proxy could permit file uploads but block other FTP functions, such as viewing or deleting files. You could also set the firewall to ignore all traffic for FTP services but allow all packets that are generated during Web browsing.

As was discussed in Chapter 7, "Understanding the Online Environment: Web Surfing and Online Payment Systems," spyware programs that you inadvertently install on your computer can send traffic out from your computer to some malicious site on the Internet. You also could have installed a Trojan horse program by mistake that tries to contact some malicious site on the Internet and send out your personal files from your hard drive. With the use of a firewall, you can restrict outbound access from your computer. That way, if the malicious program were trying to make a connection to a port on a remote machine, you could have restrictive filter rules that control what data is allowed out of your machine. Another key feature of firewalls making connections to remote sites is that when a valid connection is established, the firewall can keep the connection open and secure so you can have faith that only valid connections are open on your system.

A key feature of firewalls is network address translation (NAT). NAT translates a single, Internet-routable IP address into many non-routable addresses on the LAN.

Therefore, if you have several machines at home and have only one IP address from your ISP, you can set up a home LAN with non-routable addresses, such as 192.168.1.x. That way, your one firewall machine that is running NAT can protect all your computers. Several firewall products perform NAT, but others do not.

Firewalls can be categorized into several basic categories as follows:

- **Packet filters**—Examine every packet for IP address
- **Circuit-level**—Allow communication only with approved systems
- **Stateful inspection**—Check the configuration of approved packets and allow/deny traffic

This chapter covers the various functions of different firewalls in action. Every firewall has advantages and disadvantages, which we will discuss in some detail later in this chapter.

Why Firewalls Are Necessary

The following list presents the benefits that a personal firewall brings to the operating system:

- Enhances the native operating system security features
- Protects the operating system and network resources from attack
- Protects the system from Trojans, worms, and virus
- Watches inbound and outbound traffic
- Monitors connectivity to the system
- Allows secure remote connections and enable encryption
- Tracks potential attackers back to originating source of the attack
- Secures data from compromise

Note

The personal firewalls we will focus on for this chapter are all Windows based. That is not to say that Linux is not worth mentioning, but most of our readers are Windows users, and the complexities that Linux brings could fill a separate book. Suffice it to say, Linux has built-in firewall capabilities; perhaps we will cover them in more detail in the next edition of this book.

By being your own system administrator, you are forced to learn the ins and outs of security. Firewall technology can be difficult to grasp, implement, and maintain. These challenges should not discourage you from implementing a personal firewall. A personal firewall is a necessity.

Each of the firewalls we will discuss has some different features and works slightly differently. Like anything you buy, you will look for features that are important to you. Some of the features you should consider when making a choice include the following:

- Ability to defend against attacks
- Interaction with virus scanners or built-in virus scanning capabilities
- Ability to stop denial-of-service attacks
- Reporting capabilities of attacks and activity on and against your system
- Ability to track intruder footprints
- Ability to track an attacker back to their source
- Ease of use
- Ease of implementation and maintenance
- Cost versus features
- Support services of the vendor
- Whether you want a hardware- or software-based firewall

The proper time to install a firewall is when you first install the operating system. If you are like most of corporate America, security comes after everything else has been done. Before installing the firewall, you should perform a through virus scan of your system to ensure that no virus is waiting in the background. A firewall will be ineffective if the virus acts as a valid application and you do not even know to check for it or design filters to find it. When you check for viruses, be sure you have the system logged off the Internet and then install your firewall. Apply your filter's rules before putting it back on the Internet. We will go through some basic steps to test the security of your firewall rules.

Problems with Firewalls

The trouble with Tribbles (*Star Trek* reference for those who don't watch the show) and firewalls is that if you leave them unattended, all sorts of problems can occur. First, if you don't get the firewall that suits your needs, you will either have more features than you can deal with and comfortably configure or you will not have enough features to protect you. For example, if you need virus scanning and choose a firewall that has *some* virus scanning capability, but is not as fully functional as a robust standalone virus scanner, you might have a false sense of security and be infected.

With all the features in many firewalls, people have a tendency to implement them and hope the filters they have set up do the job. This is asking for trouble. The hacker community is constantly coming up with new attacks, and firewall vendors always seek to update their products to meet the new attacks. If you are not vigilant in updating your firewall version or the filters you have designed, you might leave yourself open for the latest attack.

Another great problem with firewalls, the same problem that corporations with expensive products face, is how to read the log files and determine if you are being attacked or if an attacker successfully circumvented your filter rules. When you begin playing with these firewalls, you will see that reading the information that spews out is not easy to understand and definitely not easy to keep up with. Configuration of the reporting and filter rules to give you the necessary information is an important step in setting up any of these products.

Understanding the role of the product in your home is essential in a good implementation. If you have just one home machine, then perhaps a simple firewall will work. But if you have several computers at home, you will need to protect all of them. In such a case, you will need a more robust firewall that can act as a DHCP server and route traffic from multiple machines and enable different filtering rules for each machine if necessary.

Product Review

The firewall products we have selected to detail in the following sections were chosen to show a variety of different variations on how firewalls are built, implemented, and used and represent what is currently popular in the marketplace. These are described in Table 11.1. Many firewalls are on the market. Table 11.2 shows several products you might want to consider after you better understand firewalls and how they can be used. By no means is this a complete list of firewall products available to you.

Table 11.1   **Software Firewall Products**

Product	Cost	Operating System	Web Site
BlackICE Defender 2.5	$39.95	Windows 95, 98, Me, 2000, or NT 4.0	www.networkice.com
Norton Personal Firewall 2002	$49.95	Windows 95, 98, Me, 2000, NT 4.0, or XP	www.symantec.com
ZoneAlarm Pro	$39.95	Windows 95, 98, Me, 2000, NT 4.0, or XP	www.zonealarm.com
Sygate Personal Firewall	Free	Windows 95, 98, Me, 2000, or NT 4.0	www.sygate.com
Tiny Software Personal Firewall	Free	Windows 95, 98, Me, 2000, or NT 4.0	www.tinysoftware.com
Tiny Software WinRoute Pro	$149	Windows 95, 98, Me, 2000, or NT 4.0	www.tinysoftware.com

Table 11.2   **Other Firewalls for Consideration**

Product	Web Site
PC Viper Personal Firewall	www.pcviper.com
Biodata's Sphinxwall Firewall	www.sphinxwall.com
Neowatch 2.4	www.neoworx.com
F-Secure Distributed Firewall	www.datafellows.com
VirusMD Personal Firewall	www.virudmd.com
Conseal PC	www.candc1.com
PrivacyWare	www.privacyware.com
McAfee Personal Firewall	www.mcafee.com

Firewall Appliances

Small hardware appliances (devices that are separate from your computer) that you can connect and configure are available on the market, although they're not as popular with home users as software products are. Appliances enable remote management of small remote offices or home offices and are used to protect several computers. Setting up hardware appliances is easier than setting up software products, but hardware appliances tend to be more costly. As for feature sets, these generally tend to be similar to software firewalls. Although we will not go into any great detail about these more expensive hardware appliances, you should keep them in mind after you have learned a bit more about the capabilities of firewalls. Several hardware firewalls include the following:

- **Watchguard SOHO**—The small office/home office (SOHO) uses stateful inspection and NAT. One feature, LiveSecurity, is a subscription that provides software updates, technical support, and some training. This makes for a painless process in updating the features of the firewall. The SOHO also has a remote management feature and is frequently used in corporate environments to connect small home offices to the central corporate office, forming a virtual private network (VPN).

- **D-Link Systems DI-704**—The DI-704 comes with a built-in hub or switch. This cuts down on the cost of buying a hub or switch to set up your internal network. It is not a robust appliance like the SOHO and has no VPN capability, Remote Authentication Dial-In User Service (RADIUS) capability, or encrypted remote management.

- **SonicWall SOHO2**—The SOHO2 is on the expensive side of small appliances, retailing for about $495 for a 10-user model. It includes NAT, Web proxy, antivirus protection, multiple user IDs, RADIUS, DHCP server and client services, Web-content filtering, VPN, an intrusion detection mechanism, digital certificate authentication, centralized policy management, and customizable firewall protection.

- **Linksy's BEFSR11**—This model, similar to the DI-704, is cheaper than a SOHO2, but it does not have VPN capability, support for centralized policy management, built-in antivirus or Web-content filtering support, or Java and cookie filtering capabilities. It uses packet filtering to protect the system, and it has an easy-to-understand user interface.

- **SNAPgear PRO**—SNAPgear focuses on providing PPTP and IPsec VPN capabilities. Its price competes with the SOHO2 and the Watchguard SOHO. It has a second serial port that can be used to simultaneously support a dial-up/ISDN WAN and dial-in RAS connection and supports RADIUS/TACACS+ authentication and encryption. This is a robust Linux-based firewall.

Appliances do not really fit the needs of consumers in many cases. Remote management, VPN, and authentication to RADIUS servers is not really high on the priority list for home users. Many of these acronyms are beyond the scope of this book and are not necessary for the time being to the security of your home. The robust user interfaces that most software products have and the cost of the software products makes them a better choice for the home user, which is why we chose to concentrate on the software firewalls.

What to Block

The most difficult part of implementing a personal firewall is knowing what to block. The simplest answer is that you should block all unsolicited incoming traffic. This means that unless you are browsing a Web site or making a purchase over an SSL-enabled Web site, you should block incoming traffic you have not initiated. In both Windows- and Linux-based systems, a number of ports are open by default that can be dangerous to your system. In addition, several ports exist that are really of no consequence, and it does not really matter whether you block them.

For the typical home setup, in which you have perhaps one or two machines and are not running server software such as your own Web site or mail server, blocking incoming traffic using firewall software is easy. If you're running applications that can open ports on your system, such as PCAnywhere or Winroute Web Administration, you must be aware of what these third-party applications open on your system. Several of the ports you really need to be concerned about (whether you run Windows or Linux) and ensure that your firewall software blocks if you are not running server software include

- FTP (21)
- Telnet (23)
- Mail (25)
- DNS (53)
- Finger (79)

- Web (80)
- Sunrpc (111)
- Auth (113)
- SNMP (161)
- EPMAP (135)
- NetBIOS-NS (137)
- NetBIOS-SSN (139)
- Microsoft DS (445) TCP, (445) UDP
- R-Services (511-515)

Firewall Implementations

The products discussed next were tested against two criteria. The first criterion was out-of-the-box implementation of the firewall. The process of implementation and the default filter settings were analyzed in all products. For the second criterion, we walked through the details of how to set up filter rules in each product and then performed a comparison of how each was configured and what needs were best suited to these products. After each product was set up with the correct filter rules, we performed a mini-test to see how well the rules held up against a basic attack.

BlackICE Defender

BlackICE Defender is one of the simplest yet most powerful personal firewalls on the market. If you are looking for a product to set up a demilitarized zone (DMZ), perform NAT, and perform internal routing, then this is not the product for you. If you have one system that needs to be locked down inside of 3 minutes, and you want it to function without much interaction, then this is the product for you. BlackICE Defender can make your system secure with the basic functionality it has, and it's alerting feature lets you know when someone is trying to attack your system.

BlackICE Defender's four basic security settings say it all: Trusting, Cautious, Nervous, and Paranoid. These options range from blocking just about everything to letting whatever traffic you want through. The Paranoid setting blocks programs such as ICQ, IRC file transfers, NetMeeting, and PCAnywhere, whereas the Cautious setting blocks only unsolicited network traffic. You can allow application functions but block access to the operating system.

The program's alerting features block traffic when they detect an attack; trace the attacking IP address, NetBIOS name, DNS information, and MAC address; and place the attacker in a block list that denies all access from that attacker. This information can give you a lot of data about who is attacking you in case you want to try to contact the attacker's ISP to complain about the attack. The intruder log includes what BlackICE thinks is the severity level, a short description of the type of attack, and the intruder's name and IP address. If you click on the attack type, BlackICE provides a description of what the attack means, which is more than many firewalls will do. BlackICE has an "AdvICE" database of information about attacks that is very helpful.

When BlackICE runs, it stays in the system tray. If you have the attack indicators set, you will see a flashing yellow or red icon depending on the severity of the attack. You can do more investigation of the attack by clicking on the icon and seeing details about the attack. BlackICE has a nice sort feature to check attacks and attackers.

The default installation level is Cautious. This setting automatically starts protecting your computer by blocking unsolicited traffic. The other settings perform the following functions:

- **Paranoid**—This is the most restrictive setting. It blocks just about every piece of inbound unwanted traffic. The problem is that it might also block some traffic you want, such as Web traffic or applications like ICQ.

- **Nervous**—This setting blocks all unsolicited inbound traffic, but it allows more traffic such as Web content, ICQ-type programs, and streaming media to function without a problem.

- **Trusting**—All ports remain open and unblocked, so no filtering protects you. This is probably a good setting to use if you have a laptop that you use at work or if you are running it on a computer that is already behind another firewall.

BlackICE's latest incarnation, version 2.5, has added port filter rules that enable you to allow specific ports or deny specific ports, no matter which setting you have turned on. BlackICE is slowly adding features that will increase its feature set, but its basic functionality and ease of use, coupled with its alerting capability, make it a great consumer choice.

Caution

Although BlackICE has some great features, it's not the most robust of firewalls. With the addition of the port filtering options, it is making progress to compete with products such as WinRoute, but it has a way to go. The "AdvICE" data is helpful, but sometimes it reports an attack that doesn't correspond to the actual attack. The signature of the attack is not quite identified correctly. Basic information is reported in the interface, but to get a log history, you have to turn on logging. After logs are written, it's not that easy. Other products are available from NetworkIce and from third parties that allow you to better manage log files, but these do not come installed with BlackICE Defender. If you stay with the Cautious level, you will be protected, but some ports might be open to attack. Attackers can use ping to see if you are alive even if you use the Paranoid level. Although the Paranoid level will stop just about all inbound traffic, outbound traffic is not monitored. If a Trojan horse compromises your system and data is sent out from your machine automatically by the malicious program, BlackICE wouldn't be able to tell you. Finally, to get even more details about port blocking, you must use the advanced firewall settings to allow certain ports through or block ports depending on what security level you are using. No password is available to restrict access to modification of the filter rules. Be careful who can access your computer.

Installation

BlackICE is one of the few firewall products that does not require a reboot after installation. After you have downloaded and installed the software, it automatically begins blocking traffic. You can check for the latest update of the software with the Tools, Download Update option. If an update is available, you can download it and execute the update, all without rebooting the system.

Configuration

1. The default installation of BlackICE is set to the Cautious level, as shown in Figure 11.3. This level blocks some unwanted inbound traffic and has Auto Blocking enabled. Packet logging is not enabled, but Evidence logging is. The Alert indicator goes off with a flashing icon when an attack is detected in the system tray.

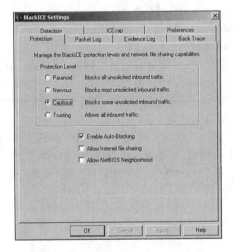

Figure 11.3   Default BlackICE settings.

2. You can change the configuration of the security levels through the Tools, Edit BlackICE Settings option. The Cautious level that is the default protects against basic attacks and allows free access to outbound Internet resources. The Paranoid level is the most secure, but it can block certain traffic that you might actually want. When this type of blocking occurs, you can set up specific rules to allow certain ports to have access to your computer.

3. Logging of Evidence is enabled by default, but regular packet logging is not. You can turn on packet logging through the Tools, Edit BlackICE Settings, Packet Log option, as shown in Figure 11.4. The problem with this option is that all packets are logged, not just selected traffic. In addition, you will need a separate program to view the log files. They are not readily viewed with a basic program such a text editor. Windows Network Monitor can view these programs or

other third-party programs. Network Ice has additional programs that can be used to analyze the logs in the BlackICE installation directory. You can set the log size and number of logs to create. After the number of log sets is created, they will start overwriting each other.

Figure 11.4   Logging enabled.

4. With the basic configuration options, you can begin blocking traffic. Detailed traffic blocking can be accomplished with the Tools, Advanced Firewall Settings. Through this option, you can filter by IP address, as shown in Figure 11.5, or by port number, as shown in Figure 11.6. These settings trust the IP address 192.168.1.5, block port 139, and allow ports 20 and 21.

Figure 11.5   IP address filter.

Figure 11.6   Port filter.

5. An attack will set off the alert function, which can be audible beeping or a flashing BlackICE icon in the system tray. The attacker's IP address and domain name (if a lookup on the IP address is possible) will be shown in the Attacks and Intruders windows, as shown in Figure 11.7. By right-clicking on the attacker, you can set up blocking or trusting of the IP address for a period of time.

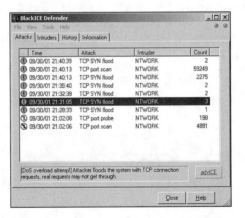

Figure 11.7   Intruder detection.

Default Installation Port Scan Results

After BlackICE is installed, the basic security options enable a good deal of security. Unsolicited traffic is blocked, and Auto-Blocking can further block an intruder. The

Alert function notifies you when an attacker is attempting to probe or break into your system. A port scan of the default installation is shown in Figure 11.8.

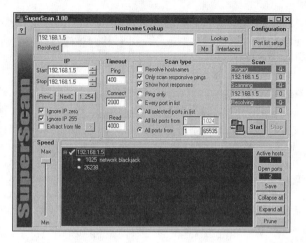

Figure 11.8   Port scan results.

Enhanced Filtering Options

1. To further restrict access, set the security level to Paranoid, as shown in Figure 11.9.

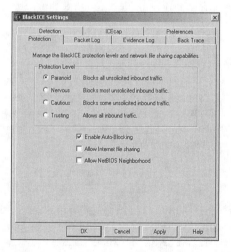

Figure 11.9   Paranoid option.

2. The Paranoid level might block some traffic you want, such as Java or ActiveX, but with the Advanced Firewall Options, you can enable specific ports and IP addresses.

3. Logging is always beneficial, even if you don't review the log files on a daily basis. Enable Packet Logging from Edit BlackICE Setting, Packet Log. Review your log files frequently.

ZoneAlarm Pro

ZoneAlarm Pro is the paid version of the firewall from ZoneLabs. The free version is ZoneAlarm. We will look at the robust Pro version to compare it with the other products we are reviewing. Like some of the other products we tested, Pro provides a wide range of firewall capabilities to block attacks from hackers on the Internet who are seeking to pillage your broadband connection. From the ZoneAlarm Web site (www.zonealarm.com), you can download a fully working evaluation version for 30 days, or you can purchase it, of course. The Pro version is about 3.2MB in size.

The installation process is simple and provides a helpful walkthrough wizard that sets up most of the filter rules for you. By selecting all the default options, you will be ready to go as soon as the wizard is complete. During the wizard process, you can set a password to protect the application. The nice thing is that no reboot is required.

Pro has a built-in networking capability so you can set up a DMZ and have your internal computers, such as your kid's PC, protected by your Pro firewall. It has three configuration options: low, medium, or high. The easy-to-understand user interface allows you to navigate the functions easily. ZoneLabs has a comprehensive support Web site. Technical support is also available through technicians.

> **Caution**
>
> You don't have much to worry about with Pro. The default installation is secure. The one problem is that you have to know what programs you need to allow access to the Internet, such as Netscape, Mail, and Internet Explorer. When someone port scans your system, the number of alerts can be daunting; you have to understand what is a legitimate connection and what is not. Unlike some of the other programs, you cannot set up your own filter rules without first having a program execute and attempt to perform some function that Pro does not already know about.

Installation

After you have downloaded the installation program and run through the install process, Pro starts a wizard that walks you through the setup procedure. Using the default install directory should be fine for most operating system implementations. Pro runs at startup by default whenever you reboot your machine.

Configuration

1. Most of the wizard screens are informational, as in Figure 11.10. The nine wizard screens explain a bit about firewalls and Pro.

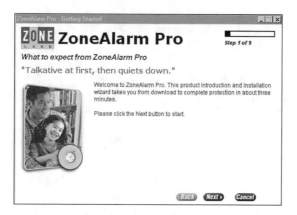

Figure 11.10   ZoneAlarm Wizard.

2. One of the configurations you can select is setting up a password, as shown in Figure 11.11.

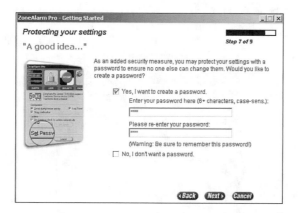

Figure 11.11   Password protection.

3. The next configuration option you can select is to enable ICS/NAT network. If you are not running a network, use the default option, as shown in Figure 11.12. If the computer on which you are installing Pro is going to be a gateway

firewall to protect the rest of your computers, give the computer IP address as the gateway. This computer will then route data into and out of your network. If another computer on your network is the gateway, select the third option and put in the IP address of your other gateway computer.

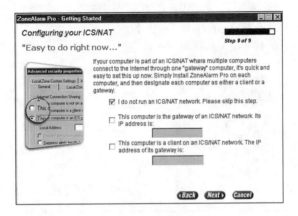

Figure 11.12 ICS/NAT configuration.

4. After you finish the walkthrough wizard, Pro is up and running and protecting your computer with the High security level, as shown in Figure 11.13. This level blocks just about all unsolicited traffic. Security zones are already defined that you can modify: Local, Restricted, and Internet.

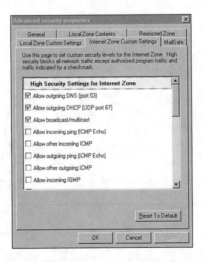

Figure 11.13 Custom zone settings.

5. Selecting the Advanced option under the Security tab allows you to customize each zone, as shown in Figure 11.14. For example, by default, the Internet Zone blocks ICMP (ping). You can allow your system to respond to ICMP requests by selecting the Allow Incoming Ping and Allow Outgoing Ping requests. If you see constant attacks from one IP address or network, you can add that IP address or network to the Restricted Zone to block traffic from that hostile source.

Figure 11.14   Security settings.

6. If an attack or a port scan is launched against your computer, the default setup options will block it and pop up an alert, as shown in Figure 11.15.

Figure 11.15   Alert pop-up.

7. To further research the attacks and alerts that your system shows, you can select the Alerts tab, as shown in Figure 11.16. You can change the log file location, disable the pop-up alerts, and request more information about an alert from the ZoneLabs Web site. Using the Advanced option, you can change the Alerts that are flagged, change log parameters, and prevent your IP address information from being sent to ZoneLabs Analyzer.

Figure 11.16 Alerts configuration.

8. If you are going to step away from your computer, you can stop all Internet traffic with Lock functionality, as shown in Figure 11.17.

9. You can also restrict each program that you use to access the Internet, as shown in Figure 11.18. In the default setting, when a program runs, Pro asks you if you want to let it have access. After you enable a program, you can use the Programs tab to change options on each program. These options might include allowing or denying access in the Local and Internet Zone, allowing the program to function if the Lock is on, and specifying ports that the program can access.

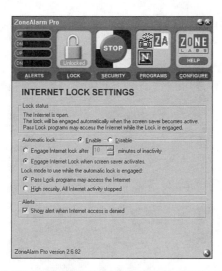

Figure 11.17   Internet Lock settings.

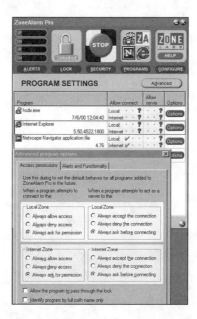

Figure 11.18   Program settings and zone restrictions.

10. Pro runs automatically at startup. The Configure tab allows you to change this option, change the password, and check for updates, as shown in Figure 11.19.

Figure 11.19   Application Configuration option.

Default Installation Port Scan Results

The tight restrictions that are enabled by default with Pro block just about all outside connections that are not specifically allowed. When a port scan is performed, it does not return results, as shown in Figure 11.20.

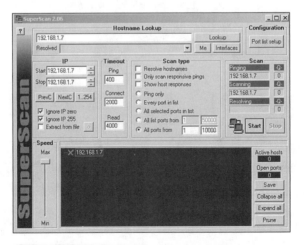

Figure 11.20   Port scan output.

Enhanced Filtering Options

The default options of Pro (security level High) are extremely secure. You can block almost all traffic, and you can disable ping. You can add a password to the system during the configuration to keep anyone else from modifying your rules. You don't need much else to make the program more secure, but keep it functional.

Norton Personal Firewall

Personal Firewall 2002 is part of Norton's Internet Security 2002 suite. Although it is somewhat geared toward businesses, home users can also use it. The product comes with antivirus built-in, which is a nice feature. Like the other products already discussed, Personal Firewall 2002 has logging capability of attacks. It shows the attacker's IP address. During the initial setup, you can have configurations set up for the programs you have on your system that might need further restrictions.

The Norton product goes a step beyond the other firewalls already discussed by allowing you some control over cookies. This cuts down on the need for a separate program such as CookiePal. With the addition of a password feature, only the home administrator can change these types of settings; therefore, you can control all changes to the filter rules. Some additional features that are privacy geared include the ability to protect specific information such as your credit card numbers, your Social Security number, and your e-mail address.

The varying security levels (Minimal, Medium, High), Internet access, and privacy options can be adjusted separately, giving more granularity to the controls. The Minimal selection allows the firewall to block only known malicious applications; the Medium selection blocks most malicious applications; and the High selection allows only approved programs to function.

The Security category offers a rule-based, interactive-learning firewall capability that automatically generates rules based on the programs the user uses to connect to the Internet. Both inbound and outbound access can be filtered. Like the other products already discussed, Norton Firewall 2002 has logging capabilities.

Caution

By default, Norton Personal Firewall (NPF) is not enabled. You are asked to enable it after you have installed and rebooted your system. The default installation still leaves two important ports open: 135 and 139. These are two key ports in Windows systems. You must enable further port filters to restrict these ports.

Installation

Purchasing NPF 2002 saves a setup file to your hard drive. The full 15MB program is downloaded to your computer after you execute this setup file. After you have downloaded NPF, the installation procedures are simple. You do not need to reboot the

computer when you are finished with installation. NPF is not enabled after the installation is complete and before the configuration starts. You must configure the program
to have it start blocking.

Configuration

Configuration is a simple process, as it is with many of the other products. A wizard
provides a basic walkthrough for you to set up the configuration. Follow these steps:

1. When installation is complete and you reboot, the configuration wizard has
   some basic configurations already set. You can check the preset configuration
   level, which is Medium, as shown in Figure 11.21.

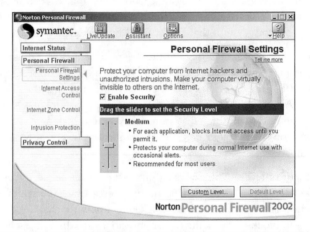

Figure 11.21   The default security level is Medium.

2. The next action you can take is to set up Privacy Controls, as shown in
   Figure 11.22. You can set up the program to block access to information such as
   e-mail, bank account information, credit card information, and so on.

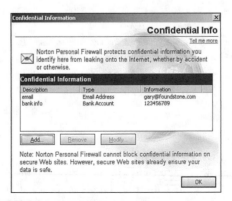

Figure 11.22   Privacy controls set during configuration.

3. The next configuration option can automatically set up rules for the applications that connect to the Internet, and you can allow or deny access to these applications. NPF can look for applications such as Netscape and e-mail, as shown in Figure 11.23.

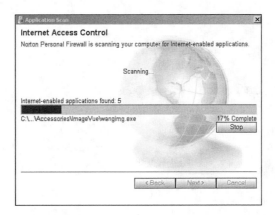

Figure 11.23   Scanning for applications.

4. The next step is to set up detailed network configuration. The Trusted Zone allows access to systems you trust, and the Restricted Zone blocks access to systems you do not trust. Our system is on a 192.168.x.x address and becomes part of the Trusted Zone.

5. The next configuration screen is where you select Current Status to enable the firewall rules, as shown in Figure 11.24. After the rules are enabled, they start blocking traffic. Through this screen, by default, the Intrusion Protection section enables Detect Port Scan Attempts and Enable Autoblock.

6. The Reporting option shows that the reporting level is set to Minimal. This can be increased to Medium or High to enable more logging information.

7. The Alert tracking is automatically enabled in the next configuration option.

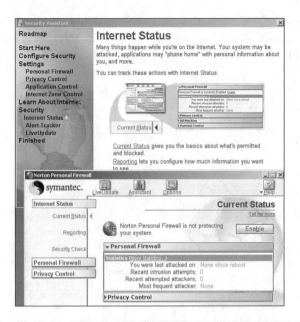

Figure 11.24   Enable Norton filter rules.

Default Installation Port Scan Results

The default installation of NPF, with its security setting set to Medium, blocks ICMP. No port will show up in the port scan output unless you have enabled the ports in NPF prior to this point. The output of the port scan against a default install is shown in Figure 11.25.

After the actual configuration wizard walk-through is complete, the port scan of the default settings changes to show the output (see Figure 11.26).

As you can see from this output, most of the ports are blocked, but an attacker still sees some key ports with the default options. To restrict the ports that are visible, it's necessary to manually change the filtering options.

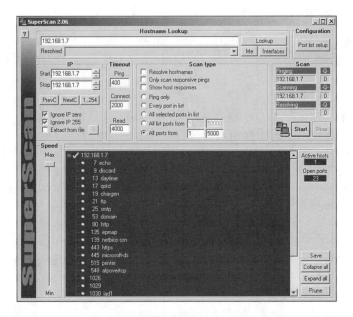

Figure 11.25 Port scan output.

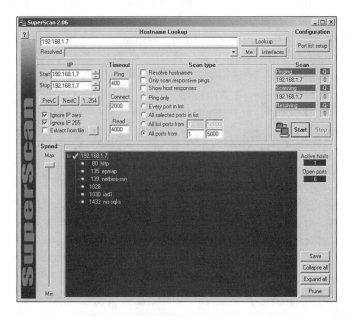

Figure 11.26 Port scan output after the configuration wizard is complete.

Enhanced Filtering Options

As with most firewall products, you can increase the default security options with enhanced features. By increasing the security features, you further restrict access to your computer. Follow these steps:

1. Increase the Reporting level from Minimum to Medium.

2. The Trusted Network enables trusts for the network your machine is on. If there are other machines on your network that you do not own or control, you do not want to automatically trust them. Remove the network from the Trusted Zone and only add single IP addresses.

3. Enter information such as e-mail addresses in the Privacy Controls options. You do not have to enter the full information of your credit card or social security number. Partial numbers can be used to block information.

4. Use the Medium Level for cookie checking under the Privacy Control, Custom Level option.

5. Under the Personal Firewall, Configure option, enable more granular controls such as the following:

    - Disable Default Inbound ICMP
    - Disable Default Inbound NetBIOS Name
    - Disable Default Inbound NetBIOS
    - Disable Default Inbound Bootp
    - Disable Default Outbound Bootp (see Figure 11.27)

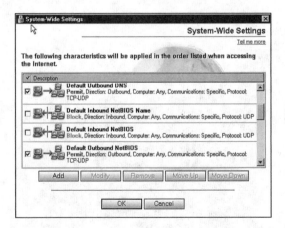

Figure 11.27   System-wide filter rules can be modified.

6. Modify the Personal Firewall Settings, Custom Level option to enable the
Medium setting for Java Applet Security and ActiveX Control Security, as shown
in Figure 11.28.

Figure 11.28 Custom security settings.

Sygate Personal Firewall

Sygate Personal Firewall (SPF) 4.2 is a robust firewall product. It has an easy-to-
understand user interface that is intuitive and simple. The display window shows activity and traffic patterns as they occur. The custom rule configuration makes it easy to
set up new rules and increase the filtering capabilities that come built into the standard
installation. One key feature is the ability to test the rule set using the Sygate Web site.

Like the security setting of other programs, the SPF offers three security settings:
Normal, Block All, and Allow All. Normal is the recommended mode of operation,
allowing setting of security rules and protection. Block All stops all traffic, and Allow
All disables all filtering options. With the Test function, you can use the Sygate Web
site to test your filter rules.

Ports and IP addresses can specify granular access. When an attack is launched that is
blocked by the ruleset, SPF can send an e-mail to you. Detailed logging shows attacker
information such as time, date, remote IP, remote port, local IP, and local port. You can
backtrace the attack information that is logged to gain more information about the
attacker. An example might be performing a trace to see where the attacker is coming
from, or performing a WHOIS lookup on the owner of the IP address.

Caution

Several problems are apparent with this product. The first is that password protection is not forced by
default; you must manually configure the password. Secondly, having the application ask you every time
you need access to some function can be quite cumbersome. And third, the Sygate Test feature worked
only once in about three tries as we tested this product.

Installation and Configuration

Sygate installation is packaged and simple. A reboot is required when the install is complete. A default installation has security features turned on. All traffic in and out of the system is checked, and you can allow or deny access. Do the following:

1. Install the setup file and reboot the computer. If you are connected to the Internet when you restart the computer, the machine might attempt to broadcast to the Internet for some reason, such as checking for a DNS server. In our example, as soon as we rebooted, the computer started broadcasting information. Sygate picked it up immediately, before we got to set up rules and security settings (see Figure 11.29). You have the option of remembering your answer to allow or deny the function to occur.

Figure 11.29   Detection of activity at program start.

2. After you have rebooted, you can start the Sygate administration program from the Start menu, as shown in Figure 11.30.

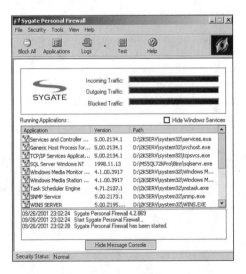

Figure 11.30   Administration screen.

3. From the Tools menu, you can check all applications. You can modify each process to allow or deny granular access to and from ports using the Advanced button, as shown in Figure 11.31. Each service has the Access methods of Allow, Ask, or Block. The system can use these options to let the service function, ask your permission, or always block access. Right-clicking on the service allows the access method to be changed or even removed.

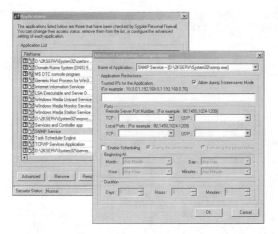

Figure 11.31 Setting up port rules.

4. Through the Tools, Options menu, you can set a password to secure access to the program, run the program at startup, and set up e-mail notification and log settings (see Figure 11.32).

Figure 11.32 Setting up logging.

5. When you have the system up and running, you can set up the Advanced Rules through the Tools, Advanced Rules option. You can set up specific rules, as in Figure 11.33, to fine-tune your access to the Internet and provide a good defense against attackers. In this example, we have set up two rules. The first one blocks ports 80, 20, and 21 (Web and FTP) from the IP address 192.168.1.1. The second one blocks ICMP (ping) from IP address 24.7.48.70.

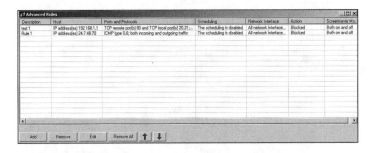

Figure 11.33   Advanced filter rule setup.

6. After you have set up the rules you need, you can start watching your log files for hacker activity. The default settings are enough to stop many attacks. Pinging the system from a remote computer is enough to issue a warning to the screen. You can see log file captures of traffic in Figure 11.34. Several types of logs are being captured in a readable format: Security, System, Traffic, and Packet. In the Log window, you can select an IP address and perform a Backtrace, which attempts to find more information on the attacking IP address by using WHOIS. (We discussed WHOIS in Chapter 6, "Understanding the Online Environment: Addresses, Domains, and Anonymity.") You can save the log with the File, Export function.

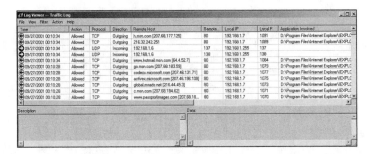

Figure 11.34   Log output.

Default Installation Port Scan Results

The default installation of Sygate is pretty secure in that it asks you if you want to allow any kind of access to your system. The port scan of the default installation, shown in Figure 11.35, immediately pops up an alert on the computer. The default installation does not show open ports if you deny access when the alert pops up. The default option also disallows ICMP, which will block a ping to your system.

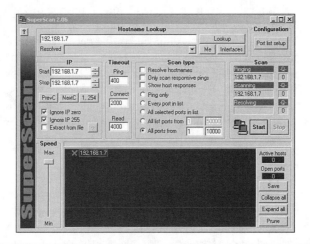

Figure 11.35   Default port scan results.

Enhanced Filtering Options

Several enhanced options can be turned on to make the Sygate firewall more secure. Several of these include

- **Sygate Personal Firewall**—This is not enabled by default. Enable it to start on system startup by selecting Tools, Automatically Start Service.

- **A password**—This can be enabled on the application through Tools, Options, Set Password.

- **E-mail notification**—If you are away from your computer and want to be notified when an attack occurs, use this option, under Tools, Options, E-mail Notification.

- **Sygate Web site**—Click Tools, Test Your System Security to use this site to check your security settings.

- **Granular rules**—Use Tools, Advanced Rule Settings to define granular rules that might be needed, such as allowing ICQ or blocking a specific type of traffic.

Tiny Software Personal Firewall

Tiny Software Personal Firewall (TPF) is a scaled-down version of the WinRoute Pro/Lite model. After it is installed, it sits in the system tray. Temporary logging information is in the main window, but information is saved to a file.

Installation of TPF is simple. It is not as robust as Norton or McAfee, but it does the job. The default installation is in AskMe First mode. When allowing incoming and outgoing connections for the first time, TPF asks you permission. Installing with network connections open does not close the connections. Only when the operation is complete does TPF ask you to apply a filter rule to the network process. The Firewall Administration function allows you to configure more granular access controls. Granular access includes filtering by port and IP address. When you allow connections, a feature of TPF allows you see open connections in the Status window. When you are attacked and access is blocked based on your ruleset, an alert window displays. Support for TPF comes in the form of online manuals and FAQs and a toll-free phone number.

Caution

TPF has several disadvantages. A key feature that is missing is the ability to allow specific ports or ranges from the security levels. This can hamper you if you want maximum security but want to allow one key port to be open. TPF comes with logging capabilities like the other programs, but the logs do not show the information. When you create a Filter rule in the Advanced dialog box, you must close the dialog box and reopen it for the new filter rule to appear. Although the filter rules can alert you to an attack, if you specify during rule creation to apply the rule to all further instances of the attack, you will not be alerted again that the attack has occurred. You can be under constant attack and not know it, even if your filter rules are blocking attacks. An intruder might eventually get by your rules if you are unaware that you are in danger. A View option is not available for you to see all the attacks, as so many of the firewall products have. You must check the log files to see information on attacks.

Installation

After you have installed TPF and rebooted your computer, TFP immediately begins asking you if you want to permit or deny inbound/outbound connections. Figure 11.36 shows an obscure alert message during system startup. This is helpful because the system is being secured even before you configure the firewall. The problem with this, as with Sygate, is that you probably don't know what all the services are. To understand some of these low-level communications, you might need to do some research. As a basic rule, you should probably allow the connections you don't understand, although this really isn't a secure option. Research all the alerts you receive that you do not understand, and then go back and disable them if they are not necessary. You don't want to break the system when you're trying to secure it.

Figure 11.36 Pop-up alert message during system startup.

Configuration

1. The firewall is enabled by default with the Ask level. Like Sygate, it has two other levels: Cut Me Off, which disables all network activity, and Don't Bother Me, which removes all firewall filters.

2. The Filter Rules tab, shown in Figure 11.37, shows all the default rules. These can be added, deleted, or modified to enable more granular filter rules.

Figure 11.37 Advanced port filter ruleset.

3. Like its big brother WinRoute Pro, TPF has a password protection, remote administration capability and can be run automatically when the system starts as a service. These options can be set through the Miscellaneous tab, shown in Figure 11.38.

Figure 11.38   Password and remote administration capability.

4. Setting up password protection requires you to enter the password to administer the program, as in Figure 11.39. If you want to administer another computer running TFP, place the IP address in the Host box and make the connection.

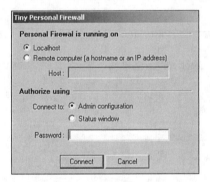

Figure 11.39   Administration Login dialog box.

5. When a rule does not match the list of already defined rules, TFP asks you if you want to have it created. Rather than your having to set up all the details of the new rule, TFP automatically generates the new rule for you.

6. You can obtain a list of listen ports and connection to other IP addresses from your system by right-clicking the icon in the system tray and selecting Status Window. The results are shown in Figure 11.40.

Figure 11.40   Status window.

Default Installation Port Scan Results

The default installation blocks many ports, but not all of them. During the scanning, TFP pops up alerts on the screen with messages about certain services being contacted, which can then be denied. But after the scan is complete, some ports are still found and reported to the port scanner, as shown in Figure 11.41.

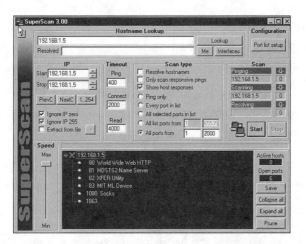

Figure 11.41   Default setup port scan results.

Enhanced Filtering Options

The enhanced filter options available in TPF are not as numerous as in some of the other products. Several changes that can be made include

- Modify the filter rules not to ask each time a frequently accessed service such as ICMP is contacted. For new filter rules that are generated the first time FTP sees the traffic, this can be set; however, for already defined rules, this can only be set when the filter is activated by incoming or outgoing traffic.

- As soon as you start up the program, set a password and do not enable remote administration unless you require it.
- Perform a port scan of your system after you have completed the installation and determine what ports are still visible. Setup Filter rules through the Advanced option to block those ports that you do not want available to an attacker.

WinRoute Pro

WinRoute Pro is a bit out of the league of the other firewall products. Although it is not geared specifically at the home user market as is WinRoute Lite and Tiny Personal Firewall, it is easy enough for a home user to understand eventually. WinRoute Pro can be used to set up a complex home network to filter just about any kind of traffic you need. It does require a good understanding of networking, but we will go through some basic setup options to get you going.

WinRoute Pro has some complex features. One of its main features is the remote administration capability. With password protection and administration via a Web page, corporate administrators can modify rules remotely. Because it is a networking firewall, multiple users can be set up, DMZ and NAT can be used, and individual rules can be applied to protocols, IP addresses, and ports. Incoming and outgoing data can be filtered, monitored, and logged. All pieces—such as TCP, UDP, ICMP, ARP packets, DNS requests, and time information—can be logged.

With the firewall features comes built-in server capabilities. WinRoute Pro has Mail, DHCP, Proxy, and DNS capability. With all these capabilities, your main gateway machine can run these services and protect all your computers behind the firewall. Port mapping can be set up to forward packets to specific machines and ports. All these features can be turned on or off by clicking on the icon in the system tray and stating or stopping the program.

The support that is provided by Tiny Software through its Web site and documentation gives troubleshooting information and example information for setting up the firewall. Tech support is also available for any questions.

Caution

WinRoute Pro is not for the faint of heart when it comes to networking. It is a robust and detail-oriented program that can be used to build an extensive internal and external network. By default, it has no filter set. It is up to you to define each rule by port and protocol. You need in-depth knowledge to operate the program.

Installation

WinRoute Pro 4.1 is easy to install and runs on several flavors of Windows. The complexity of the program is matched by its capability. WinRoute has a simple installation procedure. After you run the setup program, you are required to reboot. When you install, no rules are active, as shown in Figure 11.42. WinRoute starts by default. If you want to manually start WinRoute (not recommended), you can disable automatic startup by right-clicking on the icon in the system tray and selecting Startup Preferences. You can then uncheck the two options for automatic startup.

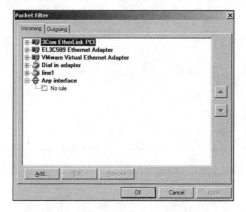

Figure 11.42   Rules screen.

Configuration

1. After you reboot and enter the license key, you are ready to configure one of the most robust personal firewalls. Because no rules are installed by default, the servers are running (mail, proxy, and DNS), and remote administration capabilities are enabled, you want to set a password on the account. If you do not set a password on the Admin account, anyone can port scan your system, see the remote administration ports are open, and modify your filter rules. You can set a password through the Settings, User Accounts, Edit option. Add your own password where the *s are, as in Figure 11.43. Through this option, you can also set up other users, although for home users, you probably don't want to do this. In a corporate environment, you might want to do this.

2. When the password is set, turn off the servers that are running—such as Mail and Proxy—if you do not need them. You can disable these servers through Settings, Mail Server and Settings, Proxy Server (runs on port 3128 by default) option. The DHCP server is disabled by default. You can leave the DNS Forwarding settings as they are. Figure 11.44 shows how you can enable or disable these servers.

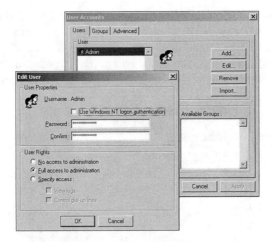

Figure 11.43   Password protection.

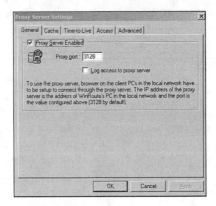

Figure 11.44   Proxy server screen.

3. After you have disabled the server from running, disable the remote administration capabilities if you will not be performing remote functions. Don't run services that are not absolutely necessary. An attacker can contact the remote administration port if it is open and attempt to gain access. You can disable the remote function through Settings, Advanced, Remote Administration, as shown in Figure 11.45.

4. You can turn on some built-in security options. To select them, choose Settings, Security Options. Instead of using the packet filter rules manually, you can select Drop ICMP packet to deny pinging of your system by attackers, drop packets that don't have a NAT destination, set up logging of NAT, and report to the display window, as shown in Figure 11.46.

Figure 11.45   Remote administration screen.

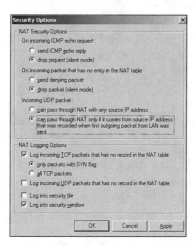

Figure 11.46   Security Options screen.

5. When the basic options are set, you can begin setting up the packet filter rules by selecting Settings, Advanced, Packet Filter. Without these rules, WinRoute is no good to you. From here, you can set rules for inbound and outbound traffic. You can select the specific interface you want to apply to the rule or apply it to all interfaces. If you are using the system that is running the WinRoute program as your gateway and you have another interface to your internal network, you might want different rules on each interface. (If you are not sure what an interface is, it's the network card. Most systems will typically have just one network card unless you have an internal DMZ setup that is protected by your firewall). You can set up a rule to block ICMP (ping) to the system, but that allows you to ping other systems. In other words, you can tell if someone else is connected to the Internet, but that person can't tell if you are alive, as shown in Figure 11.47. This example denies any address from replying to a ping request with the

Echo Request selected. The error message "Unreachable" is denied from going back to the attacker. (This can give you away because error messages can let you know a system is alive.) The packet is "dropped" into nonexistence and logged into the display window. You could also log to a file, of course.

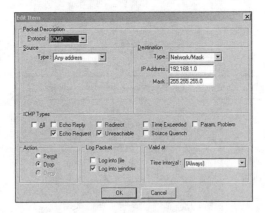

Figure 11.47   Rule to block ICMP (ping).

Another example of a filter rule is shown in Figure 11.48. In this example, a filter is set on a TCP protocol. Any address that tries to make a connection to Port 139 (a dangerous port in Windows) on the host is "dropped" and logged into the display window and written to the log file. In this case, "drop" is used instead of "deny" because a "deny" rule cannot let someone know that a port is active. A "drop" rule sends the packet into nowhere and does not give the attacker any information.

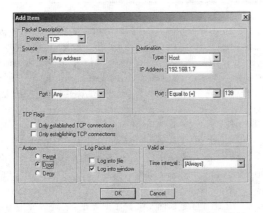

Figure 11.48   Filter rule to block port 139.

> **Note**
>
> Learning all the intricacies of setting up filter rules will take you some time. A good principle to follow is just to allow the certain ports you need, such as Web (80) and SSL (443) for credit card transactions, FTP (20,21), and other programs you use. If you allow these ports and block everything else, you should be able to stop most attacks, especially denial of service attacks. The supporting documentation on the Tiny Software site is helpful in understanding filter rules. The site also provides some good examples of setting up a home network.

6. The filter rules, with logging enabled, will send information to the display window and the log files if you check those log boxes when setting up rules. To check the files, open the Security window by selecting View, Logs, Security Logs to see what activity is taking place on your system (see Figure 11.49).

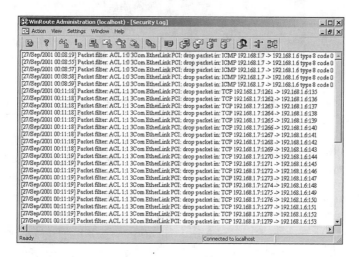

Figure 11.49   Logging output.

Default Installation Port Scan Results

The default installation of WinRoute Pro does not apply firewall rules. This basically means your system is just as open to attack as if you had no firewall installed. A port scan of the system with a default installation returns the results shown in Figure 11.50 with SuperScan.

As you can see, many ports are open, including the Web-Admin port, 3129. If you have not password-enabled WinRoute, anyone who sees this port with a port scanner can connect to your system and administer your firewall! This is a very bad thing.

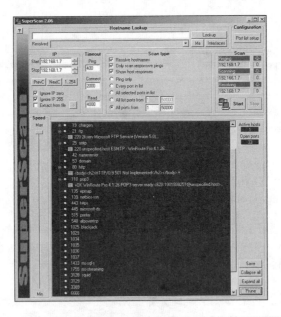

Figure 11.50   Default WinRoute port scan results.

Enhanced Filtering Options

To use WinRoute securely, you can do a few things immediately:

- **Add a password to the Admin account**—Do this by selecting Settings, Accounts. Select the Admin account and Edit it.

- **Disable or restrict Remote Administration capability**—From Settings, Advanced, Remote Administration, uncheck Enable Remote Administration over Network or select Allow Access From and put in an IP address where you allow connectivity, such as from your work computer or work firewall IP address. In this same screen, uncheck Enable Web-Admin Interface on Port or select Require User Authentication. In most cases, you will want to just disable these options.

- **Disable the mail server**—From the Settings, Mail Server option, uncheck the Mail Server Enabled option.

- **Disable the proxy server**—From the Settings, Proxy Server Option, uncheck Proxy Server Option. This is not a security weakness, just a usability issue.

- **Enable the option DHCP Server Enabled**—If you will be using this WinRoute computer as a DHCP server, do this under Settings, DHCP. Then, set up your Internet IP address range by selecting New Scope (see Figure 11.51). A typical setting for your internal home network can be a range from 192.168.1.2

to 192.168.1.10, a Mask of 255.255.255.0, a Default Gateway of 192.168.1.1, a DNS Server that is the same as your ISP's DNS server, and a Lease Time of 60 days.

Figure 11.51   WinRoute DHCP settings.

- **Set several ICMP options**—Do this by using Settings, Advanced, Security Options. However, you can make things more granular by using the Packet Filter rules.
- **Set up several packet filter rules to allow basic functionality**—These rules can be set through Settings, Advanced, Packet Filter. From here, select the Network Adapter or Any Interface on the Incoming tab to apply the rules. These rules can be set as shown in Table 11.3.

Table 11.3   **WinRoute Rules**

Protocol	Source	Destination	Action	Log Packet	Other Options
ICMP	Any	Host: Your External IP Address	Drop	Window	ICMP Type = Echo Request, Redirect, Unreachable Time Exceeded
ICMP	Any	Any	Permit		ICMP Type = Echo Reply
UDP	Any, Port = 53	Any, Port = Any	Permit		
UDP	Any, Port = Any	Any, Port = Any	Drop		
TCP	Any, Port = Any	Any, Port = Between (IN) 135-139	Drop	Window, File	

Table 11.3 **Continued**

Protocol	Source	Destination	Action	Log Packet	Other Options
TCP	Any, Port = Any	Any, Port = 445	Drop	Window, File	
UDP	Any, Port = Any	Any, Port = 445	Drop	Window, File	
TCP	Any, Port = Any	Any, Port = Any	Permit	Window	TCP Flags = Only Established TCP Connections
IP	Any	Any	Drop		

These rules, as shown in Figure 11.52, allow you to ping systems. However, they do not allow anyone to ping your system. You can resolve names of Web sites on the Internet and log any attempted access to blocked Windows ports such as 135–139 and 445 (key weaknesses in Windows). These rules allow you to perform various functions on the Internet but block all incoming connections by anyone else to your system. If you run SuperScan against your system now, you will see that it does not show any ports open, or even that the system is alive. If the attacker does not know you are alive and cannot see any open ports, he can't attack you. You can, of course, get more granular and set up more rules to run your own Web server or FTP server. It will take a bit of time to explore all the great functionality of WinRoute Pro.

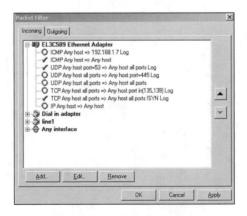

Figure 11.52 WinRoute rules.

Comparison Chart

Although each firewall product can protect your computer and perhaps your home network, each has special functions that you might find more useful. Table 11.4 shows a brief description of the pros and cons of each program that was discussed in detail, and a basic conclusion about how each program performs.

Table 11.4   **Product Comparison**

Product	Pros	Cons	Conclusion
BlackICE Defender 2.5	Easy setup and installation	No remote management	This is a good basic program. The alerting capability is just right—not too annoying and glaring in the middle of your screen, but enough to get your attention. The port filtering addition has increased its value exponentially. For basic functionality that you can just plug in and forget about, this is a great choice.
	Visible and audible alert function	No capability to set up an internal protected network	
	Added port filtering capability	False positive alerts	
	Trace attacker IP address	No password protection	
	Real-time alerting	Additional programs needed to enhance functionality	
	Easy to understand		
	Lot of information available about attacks	Remote administration capability not available	
		Cannot filter outgoing data	
Norton Personal Firewall	Automatically configures Internet applications for access	Filtering is not enabled by default	The privacy checking gives Norton a unique feature that the other products do not have. The test feature can be useful. The update capability allows
	Privacy controls are unique	Trusts entire local network by default	

Table 11.4   **Continued**

Product	Pros	Cons	Conclusion
	Antivirus software built in	Default security level is set to minimal	Symantec to upgrade the product with minimal effort on the user's part. The reporting capability is rather poor. The information about attacks is not readily available, but is sorted in a manner that can be useful.
	Auto update feature	Difficult to get attack data	
	Online Security testing site from Symantec.com to check rules	Remote administration capability not available	
	Autoblock feature	No password protection	
	Easy-to-understand interface		
	Ability to block cookies and active content		
	Ability to set up specific port rules that are not already defined		
Tiny Personal Firewall	Part of the ICSA Certified WinRoute Pro	No explanation of the attack	Tiny Personal is a good free product. The Remote capability, although useful to administrators, will probably not see much use by home users. The lack of information on attacks and the inability to do lookups on attacker addresses can limit the usefulness of the product. Although the product is robust and has
	Logs can be sent to a syslog server	No ability to remove ports or port ranges from the firewall's scrutiny	
	Very compact		
	Provides MD5 checksums of programs	Reboot required after install	
	Easy to understand	No advanced filtering (Java/ JavaScript pop-up windows, and so on)	
	Remote control capability		

Table 11.4 **Continued**

Product	Pros	Cons	Conclusion
	Password protection	Web-based support is confusing to locate	the ability to filter ports and IP addresses, it is not easily understood, and the interface to the port filtering is not intuitive.
	Inexpensive		
	Runs at startup by default	No reporting mechanism to display attack information on screen in real time	
	Asks if you want to allow applications and connections to occur		
		Cannot backtrack attacker to his IP address	
	Ability to stop all traffic immediately Granular port rules can be set up		
Sygate Personal Firewall	Powerful configuration options	Test site doesn't always function	Sygate Personal Firewall is a comprehensive firewall that has just about all the necessary features. The interface is easy to understand and displays information in an easy-to-read format. The logs of attacks can be readily viewed, and information on the attacker is easy to retrieve. The e-mail notification is a good feature not found in many of the other products. The
	E-mail notification	Remote administration capability not available	
	Lists all services running and the ports that are listening	Pop-up alerts can be hard to understand if the incoming traffic is low-level and cryptic	
	Backtrace ability can track an attacker's IP and WHOIS information		
	Detailed list of security log information		

Table 11.4   **Continued**

Product	Pros	Cons	Conclusion
	System log show system functions, startup, and shutdown		out of the box security is very good for the new user.
	Ability to stop all traffic immediately		
	Sygate Web site has test function to test your filter rules		
	Password protection available		
	Ability to enable or disable all system services		
WinRoute Pro	ICSA Certified	Complex configuration requires network knowledge	For the home user who has a good bit of networking knowledge and wants to set up a good home networked environment, WinRoute Pro is the best option. The ease of setting up rules can allow the novice to quickly grasp networking rules, and the help files are easy to understand. By far one of the best detailed firewall products on the
	Can monitor all outgoing traffic and ports used	No default filter rules installed	
	Easy to set up DMZ network	No blocking at startup with defined rules	
		No explanation of attack	
		More expensive than other products	

Table 11.4 **Continued**

Product	Pros	Cons	Conclusion
		No built-in auto update feature	market. You do have to have a good understanding of detailed filter rules to use this product correctly.
		Cannot backtrack attacker to his IP address	
Zone Alarm Pro	Strict default configuration	Remote administration capability not available	With simple network settings and a great interface, this adds up to a powerful Internet security package. The addition of more advanced configuration options would be useful and would complete the already impressive feature set of this package. Even without this feature, ZoneAlarm proves to be a valuable product.
	Runs at startup by default	Alerts might not be readily understood if the traffic is not intuitive	
	Ability to block incoming and outgoing traffic		
	Easy-to-understand user interface		
	Ability to stop all traffic immediately		
	Ability to block application attacks such as worms and Java		
	Ability to check for certain e-mail attacks		
	Password protection		

Feature Comparison

Table 11.5 compares several features of the firewall products discussed in this chapter.

Table 11.5   **Feature Comparison**

Product	Alerting	Logging	Password Protection	Remote Management	Predefined Security Levels	Ease of Use
BlackICE Defender	Yes	Yes	No	No	Yes	Easy
Norton Personal Firewall	Yes	Yes	No	No	Yes	Easy
ZoneAlarm Pro	Yes	Yes	Yes	No	Yes	Medium
Sygate Personal Firewall	Yes	Yes	Yes	No	Yes	Medium
Tiny Personal Firewall	Yes	Yes	Yes	Yes	Yes	Easy
WinRoute	No	Yes	Yes	Yes	No	Hard

Summary

The use of broadband connections gives attacker 24×7×365 access to your home network connection. The comparison between cable, DSL, and eventually satellite and wireless access will shift back and fourth over the coming years as to which is better, but their common goal is to keep you "always on" the Internet. Each has its good and bad points. Service might change as providers enter and leave markets, but eventually just about everyone will have access to broadband connection.

The need for dial-up connectivity will not disappear for years to come, but we see broadband taking more of the market from dial-up connectivity. The limitations of dial-up are one of its best security features. Hackers do not spend their time attacking dial-up connections when fast broadband connections are available. With more people using such connections each day, the target for hackers grows exponentially.

You must protect your broadband connections like never before. You have fast connections—sometimes as fast as a small company. Believing you won't be a target is an invitation to be hacked. The availability of personal firewalls makes it very easy to protect your home broadband connections. The several products we discussed should give you an idea of what you can use in your home environment. Whether you choose a free, cheap, or expensive firewall, just pick one and protect yourself.

Securing Your Standalone PC: Viruses, Chat, and Encryption

Using applications on your PC poses threats that are separate from blatant attacks by hackers or marketing companies. The data on your computer, which is full of useful things about you, can be a target for destruction by automated attacks. The operating system is one form of protection, and firewalls are another, but when an intruder or automated attack gets past these defenses, you might also need to rely on virus scanning and encryption.

The home user market is the latest testing ground for the virus writers. In the past, it was rather hard to spread a virus quickly because the Internet connections were just not available. With the advent of broadband connections and the use of multiple technologies that allow you to share files and applications, it has become extremely easy for a virus to infect hundreds of thousands of computers in a matter of hours. You, acting as your own system administrator, have to take responsibility for virus scanning at home and keeping up-to-date with the latest releases of the software just as corporate system administrators have been doing for years.

Sharing of files, which could possibly be infected with a virus, can happen in a number of different ways. One popular method of sharing information is through Chat type services such as Instant Messenger, ICQ, and Yahoo! Messenger. Everything from viruses to denial of service attacks can be launched over these types of Internet applications. Many people assume that security is built into these types of applications, but just the opposite is true. Security was the least required feature in these sharing types of applications until recently.

After an intruder has access to your system, whether it's through a virus that can steal a file and mail it to the attacker or through the file upload capabilities built into the messenger/chat programs, your last line of defense becomes encryption. If an intruder breaches all of your security measures, encryption is the last and possibly strongest defense you can hope to have. With good encryption in place, even if you become hacked and all your files are stolen, you would not have to worry about the data being read by the attacker.

Virus Infections

If you have heard any technology news story in the past few years, you have heard about virus attacks. Computer viruses are digital attacks against your computer, your Palm Pilot, and eventually every piece of Internet-related technology you have. Some simple viruses even use cell phone e-mail capability to propagate themselves. A virus is a self-replicating program that can attach itself to files or applications to do some function that the user didn't intend. A virus can harm your system by wiping out files and causing substantial destruction.

Just as you can catch a biological virus that can affect your health in many ways, your computer can receive a virus through several means, some of which include e-mail, downloads, infected floppy disks, and browsing a Web site. A virus can be triggered when you execute some attachment in an e-mail or execute some piece of code on your hard drive. People don't usually execute a virus intentionally, so virus writers have to hide them behind files or rename them to somehow make the virus seem benign. The networked world makes it so much easier to transfer a virus and cause widespread destruction. The Code Red worm in the third quarter of 2001 caused more than 1.2 billion dollars in damage.

The terms *virus* and *worm* have become almost interchangeable. Both cause damage and spread from computer to computer, propagating themselves. The main difference is that a virus remains local to a single computer, depending on humans to spread it by floppy disk or intentionally sent e-mail. Worms, in contrast, replicate themselves automatically across a network, spreading through various ways, which might also include e-mail. The difference is that worms do not require human intervention to spread through e-mail. When a worm is launched, it takes the liberty of searching your contact list and mailing itself to every e-mail address it finds. Recent worms have been as destructive as viruses. Along this same vein are Trojan horse programs. These usually hide themselves as some other program. They can actually perform the functions of that other program, but in the background, they can do something completely different, such as allow a hacker a backdoor into your computer that you do not know about. A stealthy virus or worm can hide itself for months and then execute on some specific day. The sophistication of these types of attacks is growing, and the Internet now helps them spread them worldwide in a matter of hours.

The reasons people write viruses are about as varied as the reasons people hack. The reasons are numerous, but unlike hacking, which was born of a desire to fix things and be creative with technology solutions, viruses have always been created for evil purposes.

Virus Categories

Although many types of viruses exist, they basically fall into the following categories:

- **Boot sector virus**—This type of virus modifies the boot sector of the computer. Boot sector viruses hide in the first sector of a disk. The virus is loaded into memory before any operating system files are loaded.

- **File virus**—This virus operates in memory and infects executable files with the following extensions: *.COM, *.EXE, *.DRV, *.DLL, *.BIN, *.OVL, and *.SYS. When the file is executed, the virus copies itself to other executables and remains in memory.

- **Macro virus**—Many applications have macros, and this type of virus takes advantage of the macro program languages to execute malicious code.

- **Polymorphic virus**—This is a sophisticated virus that can change itself and try to bypass virus scanners.

- **Stealth virus**—This virus can hide itself and make infected files seem safe. This type of virus is usually caught easily.

- **Multipartite virus**—This virus can infect system sectors or files. This type of virus is difficult to develop.

- **Script virus**—This virus can take advantage of programming languages such as Visual Basic or JavaScript and take advantage of the user through applications, attachments, or a Web site.

Software Solutions

The number of viruses has grown over the years to more than 40,000. Each day, we see news stories about a new virus. Within the past several years, viruses have become increasingly more dangerous and destructive. You might recall several of the more popular and destructive viruses such as Melissa, ILOVEYOU, SirCam, Code Red, and Nimda. The reason these spread so quickly and around the world is because of e-mail and Internet access. By taking advantage of vulnerable Web servers and e-mail systems, a virus can spread around the world in a matter of hours.

The business of virus scanning is booming because of such destructive attacks. Virus scanners have to do much more today because of the various methods of attacks that a virus has available. The days of just spreading a virus by sharing an infected disk are long past. Every method of connecting to the Internet can be a potential method of contracting a virus, such as receiving an e-mail, browsing a Web site with Java/ActiveX applications, or downloading a shareware program. With the many forms of virus attack, the virus scanners have become very sophisticated. They can monitor every file in or out of the computer, by whatever means you are connected to the Internet or however else a file can get on your computer, such as through a floppy or CD-ROM.

There are as many antivirus vendors as there are firewall vendors (we saw a number of firewall vendors in Chapter 11, "Securing Your Standalone PC: Broadband Connections"). As we have seen, viruses come out on an almost daily basis. The vendors must keep updated with the latest attack and find a detection method as soon as the virus hits the public. The easiest way of getting the update to you is through built-in update capabilities, in which the virus scanner retrieves updates from the vendor's Web site. Any virus software worth anything will have such a feature. If you had to go out and find the patch to download from the vendor every time you thought you needed to update the virus software, you would get annoyed very quickly.

Software Operation

A virus scanner can find a virus through two methods: looking for a known signature of how a virus operates (it's already been detected and analyzed) and looking for virus-like qualities in unknown viruses. Known viruses have a signature that identifies them to the scanner. Unknown viruses will have some qualities of other viruses that the scanner can use to guess that it is a virus. This type of guessing can lead to the scanner thinking that a valid program or file is a virus when it is not. Just about all scanners provide options of quarantining the file, deleting it, or letting it pass through, so this type of heuristic checking isn't so bad.

Each vendor has an extensive information section on its Web site so that you can research known viruses and get any update information you might need. When one virus comes out, you can usually guess that another will follow that is similar and easier to detect after the type of activity it performs is known and a signature for the virus is defined. One such example is the Code Red virus/worm. When Code Red finished its run and was detected, another couple variants came out such as Code Red II and Code Blue.

Most software has two modes of operation to detect viruses: on-demand and on-access. The on-demand model allows you to selectively determine when and what to scan. This means you can choose to scan once a week and perhaps only scan a part of your hard drive, or just scan your e-mail. You manually determine when and what should be scanned. The on-access model means that the scanner is running in the background; any time a file is accessed through e-mail or downloaded, it can be scanned. The scanner can be running patiently in the background at all times, continuously scanning your system for viruses. Both can work in conjunction to keep you secure.

Several popular products do a good job of protecting your system. They are listed in Table 12.1.

Table 12.1   **Virus Scanners**

Product	Web Site	Cost	Key Features
F-Secure Anti-Virus (available for Windows Me, Windows 2000, Windows NT 4.0, Windows 95/98, and Linux)	www.datafellows.com	$125	Multiple scanning engines operating together (F-Prot, AVP, and F-Secure Orion Scanning Engine)
			E-mail scanning
			Automated installation and updates
			Policy-based management for security settings
			Daily updates to antivirus signatures
			Fully integrated with all F-Secure Workstation Suite applications
			Command-line scanning capability
			Includes the F-Secure Firewall
Panda Antivirus Platinum (available for	www.pandasoftware.com	$29.95	Detects various forms of viruses

Table 12.1 **Continued**

Product	Web Site	Cost	Key Features
Windows Me, Windows 2000, Windows NT 4.0, and Windows 95/98)			Auto-update capability for signatures
			Checks e-mail, Java, ActiveX, and Internet downloads
			24/7 technical support
			Multiplatform support
			Daily virus update
			Fix technology for damaged files
			Checks for unknown viruses
Norton Anti-virus 2002, Norton Anti-virus for Macintosh (available for Windows Me, Windows 2000, Windows NT 4.0, Windows 95/98, and Windows XP)	www.symantec.com	$49.95	Automatically detects virus signatures
			Blocks e-mail viruses and scans both inbound and outbound e-mails
			Integrates with Windows Explorer
			Security site to perform remote checking of the computer
			Scans for Java and ActiveX
			Sends infected files to Symantec

Table 12.1 **Continued**

Product	Web Site	Cost	Key Features
McAfee VirusScan 6.0 (available for Windows Me, Windows 2000, Windows NT 4.0, Windows 95/98, and Windows XP)	www.macfee.com	$39.95	Scans both known and unknown viruses
			Content scanning looks at e-mail, downloads, Java, and ActiveX
			Easy-to-understand user interface
			Incorporates well with other McAfee products
			Extensive virus information on the Web site
			Wide range of platform support
			On-demand and on-access scanning
			Incremental virus updates
			Password protection
			Automatic updates
			Paid technical support available
Pc-cillin (available for Windows Me, Windows 2000, Windows NT 4.0, Windows 95/9, and Windows XP)	www.antivirus.com	$29.95	Automatic updates
			Microsoft Outlook and Eudora e-mail scanning
			Web URL filtering

Table 12.1   **Continued**

Product	Web Site	Cost	Key Features
			Download file scanning
			Password protection
			E-mail virus to Symantec support
			Version available for Palm OS
			Certified for Windows
			ICSA Certification
			Free online virus scan
			Business hours technical support by phone and e-mail support

When using any of these products, keep several key features in mind:

- **Speed**—How fast does the product scan your entire system and scan downloaded files? A virus scanner can have an impact on your computer's performance.

- **Accuracy**—How often will the scanner miss a virus? This is the most important aspect. You really don't have to worry about known viruses with signatures already defined, but it's the ones that are unknown that your scanner can miss that are the major problem.

- **Update**—How often does the vendor update the virus signatures? When you see a news story on Monday morning about a new virus spreading like wildfire, you don't want to have to wait until Tuesday to get a signature for that virus. The vendor should be responsive to new viruses and be tracking viruses that don't make the news stories with equal vigilance. Updates are a key feature in a scanner. The program should be able to automatically go out and get updates from the vendor's Web site.

- **Interface**—Does the product integrate well with your system and perform in the background? You do not want to have to interact every five minutes with the running software. You should be able to configure it and let it do its thing without your intervention in most cases. The user interface should be intuitive and easy to use. The worst thing about an interface is that it can make it hard for you to understand how to update the signatures and configure the scanning options.

- **Trial period**—Most vendors offer a trial period for the software. Download some different programs and try them out to see which one you like best. Important: *Do not* run multiple antivirus programs simultaneously because doing so will likely crash your computer. Install a program, try it, and then uninstall it before trying another program.

A Server-Side Strategy for Home

Most home users install a virus scanner on each of their home computers. Your firewall computer, the kids' computer, and your home office computer each run their own client-side scanner. Detection and disinfection can occur separately on each computer. This can be a problem if each home user can shut off the virus scanner because it introduces a weakness in your environment. Therefore, if you are running your own small networking kingdom at home, perhaps running your own firewall, e-mail, and Web server with other computers in your home network, you might want to consider a server-side antivirus scanner. With this type of strategy, the server can scan all the incoming e-mail and files through the firewall, and the other users cannot change virus scanner configuration options. The downside is that server-side strategy can be much more expensive than just client-side software.

If server-side were your only virus strategy, you would have a problem protecting each individual computer from viruses that might get past the server. Combining both types of virus scanning, server-side and client-side, will give you thorough coverage.

Virus Detection and Disinfection

After the scanners are installed and functioning, they should automatically find most viruses. In a typical scenario, a message alert box will pop-up giving you the following options:

- **Try to clean the infected file**—This option tries to remove the virus and salvage your file.

- **Delete the file**—This option removes the virus from your computer.

- **Quarantine the file**—This option allows you to separate the virus from the rest of your files and come back and do something with the infected file later.

- **Do nothing with the file and continue operation**—This should be the last option you ever choose.

False positive results could exist if the virus scanner thinks a file is a virus when it clearly is not, such as if you have a UNIX file on your Windows computer or a piece of hacking software such as Back Orifice.

Caution

The explosive growth of viruses and worms has expanded the virus scanner market. Numerous vendors exist in the field. Although most of the products do a credible job of virus scanning, some are limited and some are exceptionally good. The several that are mentioned in Table 12.1 are some of the market leaders. The vendors are proactive in releasing a new virus signature as soon as a virus becomes known and they make attempts to educate consumers. Keep in mind that these products will not work 100% of the time, however. Once in a while you will get a virus, worm, or Trojan that is not caught by the scanner. Do not rely on just one piece of security to protect your whole environment. As we have mentioned already, security encompasses many tools and practices, and virus scanning is just one of those tools.

The final responsibility falls on each person. After all of your computer defenses fall through, you have to rely on good decisions for protection. Keep in mind some of the best practices, which might seem like common sense:

- Do not download and run software from untrusted sources.

- Do not open e-mail attachments from untrusted or unexpected sources.

Privacy and Instant Messaging

Instant messaging (IM) enables users to send messages to each other in near–real-time. IM is typically used while online on computers, but it is also sometimes used on other wireless devices, such as PDAs and cell phones. Even though each brand and version of IM software offers unique features, the basic premise—online chat—remains the same. These applications enable the user to set up lists of people with whom they chat, also known as *buddy lists*. When you log in to your IM software, your machine contacts the central server and checks to see which of your buddies are online. You can chat with multiple people at one time.

Instant messaging (IM) has grown significantly over the past several years. It has been spreading informally through networks of friends and colleagues. After one user is signed up with the service, he convinces and persuades other potential users to do the same. Not only have teenagers adopted this form of quick communication, but employees have also increased use of this technology in the businesses realm (although IM usually doesn't have an organization's IT group's approval or support). Employees have adopted this as an alternative form of communication with colleagues, vendors, and other parties. The immediacy and ease of use has helped the popularity and acceptance of this technology as a new form of communication.

The market leader for IM is America Online (AOL), which controls the top three IM clients: ICQ, AOL's native instant messaging, and its AOL Instant Messenger (AIM), which comes bundled with software such as Netscape's browser. Microsoft's MSN Messenger is second in terms of IM, and a number of others fill out the rest of the pie chart. In the next section, we'll take a look at these various IM clients and review the different configuration options that you can set when using this software.

As with the case of almost all types of technologies, the benefits of IM arrive with privacy and security risks. The problem with this technology is that it is inherently insecure. In the early days of IM, the software itself was vulnerable to several cracks and exploits. The latest versions of IM software have addressed many of the software programming problems, but plenty of security issues still exist. We'll now take a look at these various security issues and see how they can be addressed in AOL Instant Messaging, Microsoft MSN Messenger, ICQ, and Yahoo! Messenger. We will be looking at always-on broadcasting, leakage of personal information, IM logging, and clear text protocol.

Always-On Broadcasting

One thing that comes on by default on IM software settings is the "I am logged on!" broadcasting function. This is pretty ironic given the fact that users have taken steps to secure and "hide" their machine (not responding to pings is one example we discussed in an earlier chapter). IM software does the opposite—it is ready to answer with the "I am logged in!" type of message for anyone who asks. When this feature is turned on, people can learn more about you, such as your IP address and when you are logged in. It is as if people can check a bulletin board to see whether you are on your computer and see where you are (your IP address). Coupled with profile-type information supplied by many users, this can lead to a loss of personal information.

In AIM, this broadcasting feature can be configured by selecting My AIM, Edit Options, Edit Profiles. Then select the Privacy category option to get to the configuration window shown in Figure 12.1.

You can set options for who can contact you, prevent other users from seeing how long you've been logged on, and control how much another user can find out about you if he knows your e-mail ID.

In MSN Messenger, you can configure the privacy feature by selecting Tools, Options and selecting the Privacy tab, as shown in Figure 12.2.

MSN Messenger enables you to control who can see your online status and also allows you to view the list of users who have you on their contact (buddy) lists.

In ICQ, you can control the privacy feature by right-clicking the ICQ icon in the system tray and selecting the Status option. Your choices will be Available/Connect, Free for Chat, Away, N/A (Extended Away), Occupied (Urgent Msgs), DND (Do Not Disturb), Privacy (Invisible), and Offline/Disconnect. The recommend option for remaining stealthy is Privacy.

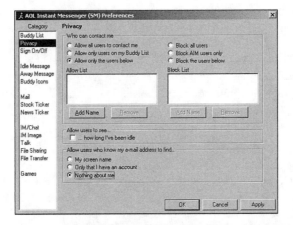

Figure 12.1 AIM privacy configuration.

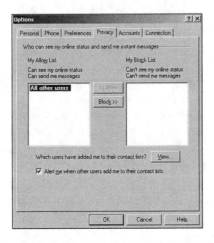

Figure 12.2 MSN Messenger privacy settings.

You can choose additional settings by opening the ICQ panel and clicking Security and Privacy. A security configuration window appears, as shown in Figure 12.3. It has various tabs available for indicating status to other users. By going to the Invisible and Visible tabs, you can control your ICQ visibility to other online users.

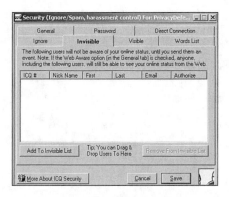

Figure 12.3   ICQ security and privacy.

You also can configure Yahoo! Messenger to show you as "invisible." Select Login, Preferences and then choose the General category, as shown in Figure 12.4. At the bottom of the window, check the Login as Invisible (Others Cannot See Me Online) option. Selecting the Privacy category, shown in Figure 12.5, also allows you to set additional options. You can choose to ignore instant messages from people who do not appear on your list and not allow users to see you online and contact you when they see your ID on Yahoo! sites. You also can select Invisible mode by selecting Login, Change My Status. That setting allows you to appear invisible to other users and to set additional Privacy options.

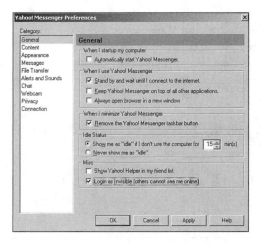

Figure 12.4   Yahoo! Messenger General options.

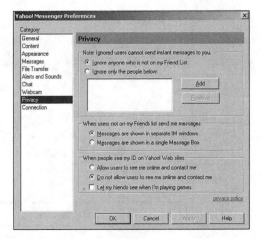

Figure 12.5 Yahoo! Messenger Privacy options.

Releasing Personal Information

Every IM client enables you to complete a profile for your IM identity. It enables you to specify varying types of demographic information (age, sex, address, contact) and data on interests and hobbies. You can choose to release as little or as much information as you feel comfortable with. We recommend giving out as little information as possible.

AIM has pretty strong capabilities to prevent other users from seeing profile data. As you begin to edit your profile, it displays a warning reminding you that the data you input is not private and can be seen by all AIM members, as shown in Figure 12.6. You can also control whether users can search for you and if you are available for chatting, as shown in Figures 12.7 and 12.8.

Figure 12.6 IM warning message about member profiles.

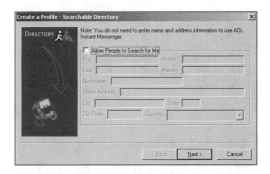

Figure 12.7   Privacy profile in AIM.

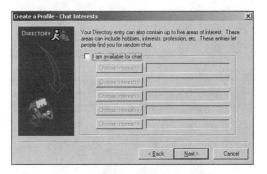

Figure 12.8   Chatting preferences in AIM.

MSN Messenger enables you to configure your Profile information by making updates on its Member Directory Web page. By selecting Tools, Options and clicking the Edit Profile button, you are brought to a Web site where you can control what information is released to the public, as shown in Figure 12.9. Note that *all* information is optional. Once again, use your judgment, but realize that less information is better.

The setting of ICQ profile information is also purely voluntary, and even warns you with a message shown in Figure 12.10. By selecting View, Change My Details, a window appears allowing you to contribute information—everything from your interests and hobbies all the way to submitting a picture of yourself, as shown in Figure 12.11. Once again, the information you submit is purely voluntary; like AIM, ICQ provides you with a gentle reminder that information is viewable by others. Enter information as you feel appropriate.

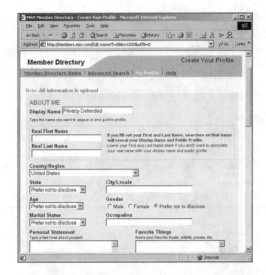

Figure 12.9   Editing your MSN optional profile.

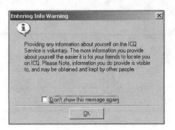

Figure 12.10   Information warning message.

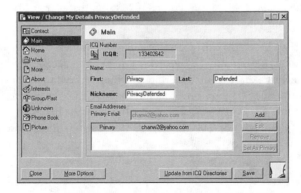

Figure 12.11   ICQ user profile.

Much like MSN Messenger service, Yahoo! allows you to update your profile information by visiting a Web site. By selecting Login, Account Info, you are brought to a Web site where you can edit your information as well as select whether other Yahoo! users see your online status, as shown in Figure 12.12.

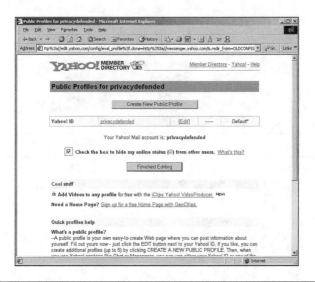

Figure 12.12   Yahoo! Messenger online profile.

IM Logging

Log files save the contents of IM discussions, including sensitive, private ones. This content is only as secure as the PC on which it resides. In one case, thousands of confidential messages from IM logs were posted to the Internet. IM communications between the CEO of an Internet company and his top executives were all posted on the Web. In this case, the logging feature of ICQ worked as designed, storing all incoming and outgoing messages in a log on the machine. That machine was apparently compromised and the bandits made off with the log. This feature is not shared by the MSN Messenger service, Yahoo! Messenger, or AOL Instant Messenger (AIM) for Windows. AIM for Macs have this feature as well, but it is turned off by default.

You can access the ICQ log by clicking the ICQ button (the MyICQ button in ICQ 2000) and selecting Message Archive. From this window, shown in Figure 12.13, you can delete individual messages and URLs. If you want to disable this logging altogether, click the ICQ button and choose Preferences & Security, Preferences. Click the Accept tab. At the bottom of the window, check the box labeled Do Not Log Event History. Future messages will not be logged. (In ICQ 2000, select Preferences, Events, General to find the Do Not Log Event History check box, as shown in Figure 12.14.)

Figure 12.13   Deleting messages in the ICQ message archive.

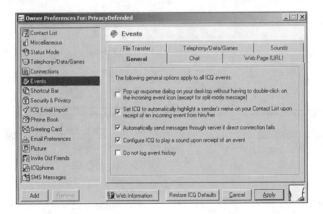

Figure 12.14   Disabling ICQ event logging.

Centralized Logging

Your PC is not the only place where message logs are kept. Most common IM applications send data through a central server where all communications are recorded and stored. The messages remain there until logs are purged or maybe even until an attacker steals them. These logs can also be subpoenaed by law enforcement. This was the case during the investigation of the World Trade Center attacks of September 11, 2001. The FBI approached AOL and Mindspring for their IM and e-mail logs during its investigation. Being cooperative, AOL handed the FBI AIM log files for the several days surrounding the events.

Yahoo! Messenger has logging off by default. You can check its current configuration by selecting Login, Preferences, Messages. Make sure that the Enable Archiving box is not checked. If you do decide to archive messages and chat, you can also configure the expiration period for messages.

Clear Text Protocol

Because the majority of instant messages are sent over a public network without encryption (cleartext), it is easy for someone using a sniffer to eavesdrop on the chat in real time. Some of these IM packages also allow for file sharing, and as such, viruses like Trojan horses and worms can be readily sent and spread. All information being exchanged via IM clients travels over public networks and is relatively easy to intercept. Because the IM protocol uses a specific port and is constructed in a specific way, sniffers can be programmed to eavesdrop on this type of communication.

Even the ICQ and AIM user agreements tell users not to use their applications for anything that is sensitive or mission-critical. MSN Messenger hasn't had the same security problems, but it is subject to its own liabilities. MSN Messenger relies on the Passport protocol for authentication, and it has had problems in the past. It is subject to compromise if a user's password is disclosed. In summary, all major IM software carries security risks, and they must be used with the appropriate security and privacy considerations. IM was never intended to be a form of secure communication.

Secure IM

Because the demand for IM has been large and because its security weaknesses are well established, a couple of startup organizations are developing secure instant messaging solutions. Startups like Bantu, Ikimbo, FaceTime Communications, Jabber, Mercury Prime, Odigo, QuickSilver Messenger, WiredRed, and 2way have raised millions of dollars in venture capital in the pursuit of a secure IM solution. Most of the companies listed are really developing IM applications for businesses rather than the home or casual user. At this time, this crowded field has no clear leader. One problem facing many of the new products is that the existing products are so popular that new products, even better ones, have trouble being accepted. After an installed base of users exists for a particular product, getting people to switch is difficult.

Home Encryption

Encryption is a safe harbor. It is one of those things that you use sparingly. The Electronic Frontier Foundation (www.eff.org) lists using encryption as one of the steps to protecting your online privacy. It is the innermost layer of protection in your strategy of Defense in Depth. *Defense in Depth* is the concept of providing multiple layers of protection. In the Middle Ages when a threat to your personal security was an advancing army, your outer castle walls were intended to be your first lines of defense, and armed watch guards protecting your inner treasure were your last lines of defense. These days, the more realistic threats are teenage hackers with Internet connections. For personal data, your last line of defense is encryption.

Figure 12.15 illustrates the concept of Defense in Depth, an idea that is reiterated throughout this book. When you apply security at different layers, you are building a Defense in Depth. The concept can be illustrated with concentric circles, each representing a different layer of defense. Notice the hacker outside of the area of defense. The hacker must contend with three layers before getting to the confidential files:

- **Firewall**—Outermost layer of defense
- **Operating system security**—Second layer of defense
- **File encryption**—Last layer of defense

Figure 12.15 Defense in Depth.

The outermost layer of defense is the firewall, which monitors all network traffic and blocks unauthorized traffic. If the hacker gets past the firewall, he must deal with the next layer of defense, the operating system security. The operating system security might include a username and password login. After logging in and gaining access to the operating system, the hacker would look for the encrypted file. Encryption is the last layer of defense here. The hacker cannot open the file or see its contents without first breaking the encryption that protects it.

In an ideal world, all of your personal information would be secured with encryption. Actually, in an ideal world, there would be no need for security because everyone would just get along. In the real world, however, encryption is one of the greatest security controls.

Why would you want to use encryption at home? Here are some reasons:

- Protect communications from eavesdropping
- Protect sensitive files from unwanted exposure
- Protect sensitive files from access by attackers
- Available software makes encryption easy

Do you have personal files related to financials, medical records, or something else you would rather keep private? Maybe you run a small business, and keep a copy of payroll information or other employee records on your computer at home. No? Have you ever e-mailed yourself at home a copy of your company's confidential information for review at home? Where is that file now? For these reasons, you want to use encryption. The problem is that just as *you* have access to encryption tools, so do the attackers. This is the dark side to encryption. Just as any powerful tool can be used for good purposes, in the wrong hands, it can be used to foster evil.

Why would a hacker use encryption? Here's why:

- Hide hacking tools.
- Secure communications with other hackers.
- Keep stolen files safe from prying eyes.
- Personal security. Yes, most hackers practice good security!

In this section, we will not delve too deeply into the technical bits and bytes of encryption (well, maybe a little), but instead try to encourage you to take an interest in security of private and confidential information through the use of encryption. If you become aware of the threats facing you in the online world, the means you have of defending against those threats, and the desire to protect yourself, security will become a pleasure rather than a burden.

That is not to say that security does not come with a price. The monetary cost of the software is typically minimal, if not free. The time required to learn and use the software is where many people give up. This chapter is intended to help explain the fundamentals of what the threats are and what the encryption software is doing to counter those threats. It will be easier to get started using these applications if you understand the concepts of what it is they are actually doing. Then all you have to do is figure out the cool tweaks and buttons that make the different software applications customizable.

Remember: Adding security to your life does not typically make things more convenient. Consider your home or car security system. You have locks for your doors and perhaps an alarm system. If you are coming home from work, you have to go through two security boundaries just to get to the couch. First, you unlock your door, and then you disarm the alarm. Is that convenient? Is it necessary? Either way, it adds the layers of protection that deter most criminals, and might even lower your insurance rates.

What Is Encryption?

Simply speaking, encryption is a product of cryptography. Encryption is the process of taking some plain text information and converting it to *cipher text* by using a secure key such as a password. The following example shows some plain text and its corresponding cipher text after it is encrypted:

Plain Text   I would like to keep my private files safe.

Cipher Text   jbUVBsE1odz3t/ZnAzlerFV9DmwHZClC9Pf

Cipher text appears as unreadable gibberish, and can only be decrypted back to plain text by someone who knows the secret key, or password, that was originally used to encrypt it. Get ready to speak a bit of the crypto language:

- **Cryptography**—The art and science of creating and using secure codes
- **Cryptanalysis**—The art and science of breaking other people's codes
- **Cryptology**—The study of codes, includes creating, using, and breaking them
- **Cipher**—The mathematical function or algorithm used to encrypt and decrypt messages
- **Plain text**—A message in human-readable form
- **Cipher text**—An encrypted message in non-readable form
- **Encryption**—Using a cipher to transform a plain text message to cipher text
- **Decryption**—Using a cipher to transform a cipher text message to plain text

Encryption techniques date back thousands of years. Ancient Babylonian merchants used intaglio to identify themselves during trade and transactions. Intaglio is a stone carving of images and some writing. The Babylonian merchants used this more as a form of identification than encryption, representing themselves much as a digital signature can be used today.

Some people use foreign languages to hide messages from people who do not speak the language. And some people create their own personal systems of words or symbols to communicate secretly with friends. Does anyone remember pig Latin?

The popular Caesar cipher was said to be used in Roman times by Julius Caesar, who wanted a secure means of communicating with friends via written letters. This very simple cipher involved shifting the plain text letter three places forward in the alphabet. In this way, an A would be replaced with a D, a B replaced with an E, and so on.

Table 12.2 illustrates this form of encryption, showing first the plain text, with its corresponding cipher text.

Table 12.2 **Caesar Cipher**

Plain text	A	B	C	D	E	F	G	H	I
(Caesar) cipher text	D	E	F	G	H	I	J	K	L
Plain text	J	K	L	M	N	O	P	Q	R
(Caesar) cipher text	M	N	O	P	Q	R	S	T	U
Plain text	S	T	U	V	W	X	Y	Z	
(Caesar) cipher text	V	W	X	Y	Z	A	B	C	

The Caesarcipher is only secure as long as an attacker does not know or guess the method employed.

Ciphers and cryptology techniques have come a long way since the days of the Roman Empire. World War II brought a sort of revolution in cryptology, fostering the development of increasingly sophisticated secret-key codes. The secret-key idea is a few steps beyond the ancient techniques like the Caesar cipher—the key can be changed for each message.

For years, encryption technologies were used primarily in military and other government offices. With the explosion of the Internet and online transactions, encryption has become a necessary part of securing confidential information. Encryption has reached and is widely used in the public domain.

This is because encryption has many practical uses in the online world. For most computer users today, including family, students, and businessmen, the practical uses for encryption include the following:

- Securing communications between computers
- Securing files and information that is stored on computers
- Securely exchanging files with other people
- Securing e-mail messages

By understanding what encryption is, a person can gauge where and when it is useful. It is also important to understand what encryption is not, and where its limitations are.

What Encryption Is Not

Encryption is not the single solution to solve all computer security risks. As we have described throughout this book, security is not a single product. Security is a process, an active mindset, and typically involves using a number of different products to build layers of defense. Encryption is one of the innermost layers of defense. After an intruder has defeated your firewalls and access controls that serve as outer defensive layers (discussed in Chapter 10 and 11), he still must crack your encryption defenses to get the information he is after.

Think of where the encryption is being provided. Maybe your online bank account uses Secure Socket Layers (SSL) to encrypt the traffic that is sent between your Web browser and the bank's Web server. An attacker who intercepts that traffic would have a hard time cracking the codes to gain the plain text information that you are sending the Web server. Your personal bank account information would be secure from prying eyes as it travels across the Internet when its encrypted. However, the next layer to be concerned about is how that Web server handles the data you send to it. Does the Web server insecurely pass the data to a database on another computer that doesn't use encryption? Does that Web server keep a copy of your transaction unencrypted on its local file system? If either of these questions can be answered with an affirmative "Yes," you realize that the security risks still exist, beyond the SSL tunnel.

When you hear a news story about how a hacker broke into an online company and stole credit card numbers, it is sometimes because the company was not using encryption on its database. When people make purchases, the data is sent over encrypted channels using SSL, but sometimes it is stored in an unencrypted format on the company's servers, thus negating all previous security measures.

Figure 12.16 depicts this scenario. This is another illustration of the Defense in Depth concept, which we all hope that our banks are actively practicing. This figure shows a basic secure transaction. From your computer, you make a purchase online from a Web site, and your transaction is sent over a secure channel using SSL to the Web server. Hackers can't take advantage of this connection to steal data. But when the information is stored on the company's database in an unencrypted format, a hacker who breaks into the company can copy all the unencrypted information, such as credit card numbers. Defense in depth means having security at all levels.

Next, we'll look at the specific threats that encryption tends to defend against, and then we will look a little more closely at the types of encryption systems that are available and some common attacks against them.

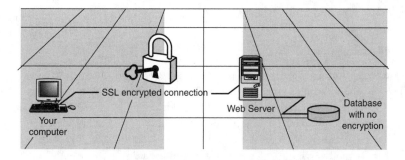

Figure 12.16   A basic secure transaction.

Threats

Theseare the threats that encryption can help protect against:

- Disclosure of data due to laptop thefts
- Accidental access to information or files
- Intentional, motivated access
- E-mail lack of security
- Online purchase information transmitted to merchants

Studies show that thousands of laptops are stolen each year. The thief's motivation can range from selling the laptop for quick cash to actually reading through the files for useful information. Consider that most peoples' laptops contain e-mail messages, work-related files, contact information, financials (Quicken or Microsoft Money), passwords, and lots of Web browsing information including bank account cookies or other online shopping cookies. With a stolen laptop, most thieves have enough information to steal or masquerade as a person's identity. Surely, someone will think that this catch is more valuable than stealing a credit card! Currently, a laptop can be replaced for less than $3,000. But the cost of lost or stolen data can be much higher. Although encryption cannot prevent a thief from physically stealing your laptop, it can make it difficult or impossible to get any useful information off of it.

Accidental or intentional access to computer files can come in many forms. If you share a computer with others, they may stumble across files unexpectedly. Other things you have to be careful of include how your computer might "leak" information. Concerns for Windows users include these sources of information leakage or hidden files:

- Swap file
- Temp files

- Delete does not really delete a file
- Clipboard
- Volatile memory

Windows keeps information and documents everywhere, not just where you expect them to be. The temp files created when you are working in Microsoft Office will not be cleaned up if the program crashes. When you delete a file, you are merely "unlinking" it from the file system. The file is still there, but it is not readily viewable anymore. The Department of Defense (publication: DoD 5200.28-STD) actually defined a method for securely "wiping" files from a computer hard disk. By using these techniques with PGPtools, as described in Chapter 10, "Understanding Your PC Operating System and Its Security Features," files can be more thoroughly removed from a system.

Intentional access to your personal computer files can also come in many forms. An attacker might gain physical access to your computer and just browse your file system for what he wants. In addition, he might use malicious software such as viruses and e-mail worms to jeopardize your privacy. Consider the June 2001 outbreak of the SirCam worm—it grabbed random files from your hard disk and e-mailed them to everyone in your Outlook address book. How funny would it be for your boss to get a copy of that new job contract you are working out with a competing company? What if SirCam e-mailed one of your employees a spreadsheet file of payroll information? That would not be very amusing!

We described some of the e-mail insecurities in Chapter 8, "E-mail Security." The fact that e-mail is sent unencrypted, traveling through many gateways toward its destination, with no guarantee that it will be received with the message you intended, is inherent in standard e-mail unless you do something about it. Encryption and digital certificates can save the day. Refer to Chapter 8 for a discussion of e-mail encryption using PGP.

Transmission of information to online merchants is an everyday activity if you buy goods, pay bills, or carry out just about any type of transaction. That data can be sent in the clear, so someone can capture what you send or encrypt. Encrypted data restricts access to your information to sources who can decrypt it. Online transactions would not be popular unless the data being sent back and forth was encrypted for your protection.

Encryption Systems

Most encryption systems consist of a lock and key. The lock is the encryption of your files, or data in transit, and the key is some password, ID, or certificate that only you possess. The security of the key is important and typically is left up to you, the user, to protect.

That brings us to the question of what makes encryption strong. It might seem that the algorithm or cipher determines the strength of the encryption system. This is partially true because a good algorithm is important. However, the strength of the encryption system should not depend on the *secrecy* of its algorithm. In fact, a strong algorithm is typically one that is widely known, and has been widely studied and attacked by knowledgeable cryptanalysts. In other words, no problems should exist with making an encryption algorithm public. In fact, it is considered good practice when developers release their encryption algorithms for public scrutiny. This shows that they are willing to accept any criticism to make their algorithm stronger.

When encryption algorithms are not made public, they are strongly questioned and often cracked. A clear example of this happened in 1999, when the CSS (Content Scrambling System) was developed to encrypt DVD movies. The hope of its creators was that CSS would prevent people from copying DVDs and reselling them on the black market. However, by depending on an encryption scheme that was kept largely private, their plans were quickly foiled when they released CSS-protected DVDs. Some young hackers from Norway quickly reverse engineered the encryption and created DeCSS, a software program to undo the protection of CSS. When DeCSS was made publicly available on the *2600 Magazine* Web site, a legal controversy quickly ensued.

What determines the strength of encryption? The strength of a cryptosystem is largely dependent on the size and security of its keys. The key should be at least 64 bits (128 bit is preferable) for symmetric key systems, and larger for public key systems (these are discussed in the next section).

The security of the secret key is what really determines the strength of the system in the end. The type of secret key used depends on the software program being used. Some programs will store the secret key in a file. Others will just use a password for the key. Others still will use a combination of a secret key file and a password. This is where the human factor plays a large role. The ability for a human to keep his password and secret key well protected is critical. Exercise the following precautions to keep your secret key safe:

- Do not write down passwords.
- Keep the secret key file in a protected location on the hard drive.
- Do not distribute the password or secret key to anybody else.

Symmetric Versus Public Key Cryptography

Two common types of encryption algorithms are in use today. The one you choose depends on your needs because each is well suited for different scenarios.

With *symmetric key algorithms,* the same key that is used to encrypt a message is the key used to decrypt it. Think of it as having just one house key but two people in the house who need to lock and unlock the door. You both have to share that one key. Symmetric key systems are designed to be fast and easy to implement. They have been around longer than public key systems, and it is evident when you realize just how many more symmetric key algorithms exist than public key algorithms.

An inherent problem exists with symmetric key systems, however. If you and I want to encrypt/decrypt the same electronic document, for example, a secure exchange of the secret key is required. Do I e-mail it to you? Snail mail it? Hand deliver it? Tell it to you over the telephone? Unless I hand deliver it to you, I am making the transfer vulnerable to a man-in-the-middle attack and jeopardizing our secret. A man-in-the-middle attack means that someone can intercept the key, copy it, and pass on the original communications to the intended person. If I mailed the key or password to you via the postal service, someone could get the letter, open it, read the key, seal it again, and send it on its way to you without either of us knowing. With symmetric keys, it is up to both of us to keep it safe from prying eyes. Using the same house lock example, if you lock the door and I come home and need to unlock the door, we would need to exchange the key securely for me to unlock the door. Leaving the key under the doormat for me to use is an insecure key exchange. Getting the key to the other person securely is the main problem.

Public key algorithms attempt to solve the problems of secure key exchange. In 1976, Whitfield Diffie and Martin Hellman at Stanford University proposed a public key encryption system that was made practical by Ron Rivest, Adi Shamir, and Leonard Adleman at the Massachusetts Institute of Technology. The technology was known as RSA (after the first letters of the creators' last names). In a public key cryptosystem, a public key is used to encrypt the data, and a private, or secret key, is used to decrypt it. The public key is so named because it can be made publicly available without jeopardizing the security of the system or the private key. The private key, also referred to as a *secret key*, is so named because it is meant to stay secret, or private, to the person who uses it. For a full description and illustration of public key cryptography, refer to the Chapter 8 section on PGP.

The terminology with these two encryption systems can be confusing. People often refer to the symmetric key algorithms as either the private key or the secret key algorithm. You will notice some overlap in terms when discussing public systems; however, rest assured that the two cryptosystems are completely different. The concept of the secret key, however, is more or less the same between them. The secret key is the magic wand used to encrypt and decrypt data.

Again, in a public key cryptosystem, the public key encrypts the data, and the private key decrypts it. Why would anybody want such a system? The system has many real-world advantages over the symmetric systems. For the majority of us who want an easy-to-manage means of sending and receiving encrypted files and e-mail, public key systems are great. Additionally, public key systems have another advantage over symmetric key systems—they allow for the creation of digital signatures.

Perhaps Alice wants to send Bob some private information. It could be financial information, a Christmas shopping list, or an e-mail message. Alice wants to make sure that the data is encrypted and that the data maintains its integrity without being modified in transit. First, Alice would obtain Bob's public key. She would obtain that key from a public server or directly from Bob, and she would use that key to encrypt the file. Remember that encrypting this file with Bob's public key means it is encrypted until Bob gets it. At this point, no one else can decrypt it, not even Alice. Only Bob with his secret private key can decrypt this message. Assuming that no one else has Bob's private key, Alice is now sure that up until the point when Bob decrypts the message, no one else can read or tamper with the original message. If the message were tampered with, Bob's private key would not be able to decrypt the message.

How can Bob be sure that it is really Alice who created the original message? After all, anyone can obtain Bob's public key from a key server and send him a message. Digital signatures address this issue of authenticity. In our example, Alice would "sign" her message by encrypting the message (or just some text) with her private key. Now Bob must not only decrypt the message with his private key, but he must also decrypt Alice's digital signature with her public key. That proves that the message really came from Alice. Because Alice's public key decrypted the message, only Alice could have encrypted the message. Note that up to this point, anyone can decrypt this portion of the message because anyone can get Alice's public key. However, the only person who can decrypt the rest of the message is Bob with his private key. This is a simple but elegant method of providing authenticity, integrity, and secrecy.

Attacks Against Encryption

People who want to crack encryption systems have options ranging from brute-force key guessing to finding a weakness in the encryption software. Different attacks can exist for symmetric key and public key.

Several methods of cracking encryption include the following:

- Password guessing
- Finding and stealing private keys
- Exploiting flaws in encryption software
- Exploiting flaws in the operating system
- Publicly known versus secret techniques

Password guessing is simple to do and works fairly often. In a cryptosystem that uses a password for the secret key, you need to plan extra hard to create a strong password that will not be forgotten. Consider that many people use the same password for everything—ISP access, e-mail, bank account, and so on. You, of course, are not one of these people, right?

Many ciphers today have encryption strength comparable to their key size in bits. Therefore, bigger key sizes can translate to stronger encryption. The most effective attacks are not done by people who are trying to crack the encryption, but instead by people who are trying to exploit weaknesses in the implementations of the encryption software you choose. People will try to exploit mistakes you might have made in the way you operate your computer and encryption software. For example, you should not leave copies of your secret key file in multiple places on your computer. The main benefit of having a secret key is that you need to secure only a single key. Only one key needs to be protected and secured on your system. You can even keep it on a floppy disk for further security. Some other key mechanisms require multiple keys, which are harder to keep track of.

Securing Files on the System

Several programs come with their own security features for file encryption. Sometimes the encryption is strong, and other times it is weak. As an example, Microsoft Office allows you to password-protect files. This protection is supposed to prevent people from opening the file unless they know the password. (However, there have been cracking tools to get around password protection on these files.) As shown in Figure 12.17, Microsoft Word XP offers password protection of Word documents. You can access this through Word by selecting Tools, Options, Security.

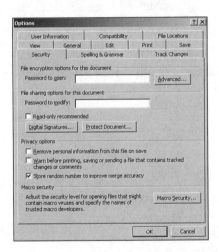

Figure 12.17   Microsoft Word XP security features.

Word enables you to set separate passwords for opening the file and modifying it. By setting a "password to open," Word encrypts the document with an encryption method that you choose. The default is the standard Office 97/2000 compatible encryption, which is easily cracked with tools that are available on the Internet. Luckily, the new version of Microsoft Office XP comes equipped with stronger encryption options for programs such as Word and Excel. If you want strong encryption, click the Advanced button in the dialog box shown in Figure 12.17, and select one of the RC4 encryption types, such as RC4, Microsoft Enhanced Cryptographic Provider, v1.

It is good to know about the encryption features in various programs. However, using individual programs such as Word and Excel to encrypt files can quickly become cumbersome and hard to manage when many files with different passwords are stored all over your hard drive. You can solve this problem by using programs that are geared specifically toward file encryption.

In this section, we will walk through installing and using a low-cost and easy-to-use software program that allows you to encrypt files on your computer. Table 12.3 lists several of these programs. These are third-party programs that you can add to your system. As we discussed in Chapter 10, Windows 2000 has native encryption capability with EFS. These third-party programs work by allowing you to create what can be referred to as an *encrypted disk*. The encrypted disk is a storage place for files of your choice. Any files that you store in the encrypted disk will be secured with professional strength encryption. You will only be able to read or use these files when you unlock the encryption and *mount* the encrypted disk.

Table 12.3 **Encryption Products**

Product	Available From
Jetico BestCrypt	www.jetico.com
PGP Freeware	www.pgpi.com

Differentsoftware implementations provide you with various means of encrypting files on your system. Although the algorithms and encryption systems we discuss here are pretty standard, a software vendor's implementation of them will have a unique touch, good or bad.

In the following walkthroughs, we will use Jetico BestCrypt, which can be downloaded from www.jetico.sci.fi as a 30-day fully functional evaluation. You can purchase it for a low price if you really like it.

However, we want to at least mention PGP Freeware version 6.0.2i in this section. We mention an older version of PGP Freeware for a simple reason. It is the last version of PGP Freeware to come with the PGP Disk functionality that allows you to create mountable encrypted disks, free of charge. You can still download this version from http://www.pgpi.org/products/pgpdisk/. If you want the latest version of PGP Disk, you can purchase it from Network Associates at www.pgp.com.

It is our opinion that Jetico BestCrypt is one of the most user-friendly programs that are available for file encryption. The user interface and menus are easily understandable, and the documentation is clear and concise. We chose this program as a usable and powerful introduction for people with little or no experience using file encryption software. This is not to say that BestCrypt is only for beginners. On the contrary, its simplicity and power make it usable for anybody, beginner to advanced. Jetico also makes the widely used BCWipe software, a popular deletion program that securely removes files from your computer so they cannot be recovered.

BestCrypt is completely transparent to your other programs. The files that you encrypt with BestCrypt will operate normally after they are decrypted. If you use BestCrypt to store Word or Excel files, the files will work just as they did before when they were decrypted.

Caution

Back up your system before installing and using encryption software. There's an irony. You're getting ready to protect your hard drive with encryption, and you've probably just copied all your data to a backup media (tape, CD, other) in an unencrypted form.

Take a step back and look at your file system for a minute. File systems are structured like trees, with a core root directory from which all other directories and files branch off. On Windows systems, this root directory is C:\, whereas on Unix systems, the root directory is known as /. Branching off the root, you might have some files, but you will definitely have some directories, also referred to as *folders*. Branching out further, you have subdirectories; files exist in the various directories and subdirectories on your computer. The main purpose of a directory is to act as a container for storing files.

Let's get started. We are using Windows 98 to demonstrate the installation and use of BestCrypt; however, the software does run on all Win32 operating systems, including Windows 95, 98, Me, NT, 2000, and XP, as well as Linux. Download the trial version of BestCrypt to your computer. After double-clicking the downloaded file, the installation begins. Click Next to get through the next few screens, until you get to the Choose Destination Location screen, shown in Figure 12.18. If this location has enough disk space for the installation (about 2MB), click Next to continue.

Another option during installation will appear, asking if you want to install BCWipe. BCWipe is a popular disk wiping utility, a secure alternative to the built-in Delete function of Windows. By using BCWipe to delete your files, you ensure that they are securely removed from your file system, making them impossible to recover. This is similar to using a paper shredder in an office where confidential documents need to be shredded rather than just tossed in the trash. It is your choice whether to install this.

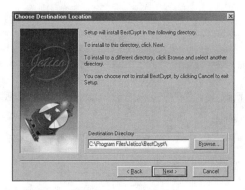

Figure 12.18   Installation of BestCrypt.

Moving on, the installation will begin and end in less than a minute. Few files are required to install BestCrypt, and they are all fairly small. BestCrypt will require you to restart your computer for some of its changes to take place. Go ahead and restart before continuing.

You should now have a program group of shortcuts for BestCrypt in your Start, Programs menu. Open the BestCrypt Control Panel shortcut icon, shown in Figure 12.19.

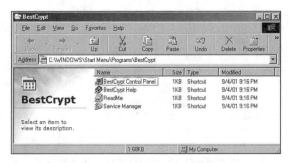

Figure 12.19   BestCrypt shortcuts.

The BestCrypt Control Panel opens, appearing similar to the Windows Explorer program. Consider the way that BestCrypt works for a moment. The program allows you to create a file (BestCrypt-file.jbc) and mount it as a disk drive that is encrypted. The file is known as a *container* in BestCrypt. After you have created this container, you can mount it as a disk, and it will appear in Windows Explorer as another partition, just as the C:\ or D:\ partition you currently have.

Now for the fun part—we will walk through the setup of your first encrypted disk! From this point on, we will use the terms *encrypted disk* and *container* interchangeably when referring to the encrypted disk. Figure 12.20 illustrates the BestCrypt interface for creating and managing the encrypted disk—the BestCrypt Control Panel.

Figure 12.20 BestCrypt Control Panel.

In the BestCrypt Control Panel, you can see all of your normal Windows partitions. In our example, Figure 12.20 shows four disk partitions. A C:\ partition is labeled WIN98, a D:\ partition is labeled WINSWAP, an E:\ partition is labeled XOLR, and an F:\ partition is labeled SHAREMOUNT. Your configuration will be different from ours, so you will not see exactly what we have shown. The important thing to realize is that the BestCrypt Control Panel gives you a central place to create and manage your encrypted containers.

Select the partition on your computer in which you want to store the encrypted disk. This might be the C:\ partition, or any other one you decide. You will notice that the disk must be created on the root of your partition, and not in a subfolder. With your chosen partition selected, choose Container, New. You see the New Container window, shown in Figure 12.21.

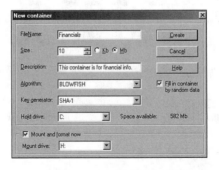

Figure 12.21 Creating a new container.

This is the core part, where you define your new encrypted disk. In our example, we decided to make this the Financials container, where we plan to store our Quicken files and other financial information. We are storing the container on the C:\ partition, but could just have easily stored it on any partition. Remember that BestCrypt is transparent to other applications. That means that after we have opened our encrypted container, files on it will be accessible to applications like Quicken, without any changes. Let's explain each of your choices here:

- **Filename**—This is where you name the file as it will be stored on your hard drive. The filename will end up having a .jbc file extension appended to it.

- **Size**—Specify the size you want your container to be. First make sure you have enough free space on your disk for it, and remember that this is the maximum size for your container.

- **Description**—This is your personal description to help you in identifying this disk. If you end up having more than one of these containers, the description will help you to distinguish between them. For example, you might have one container with a description of Personal Finances and another with Client Information.

- **Algorithm**—Select the algorithm you want to use for the encryption. Unless you have some specific needs, the default choice of BLOWFISH will suit you fine.

- **Key Generator**—Choose the algorithm that will be used to transform your password into the pseudo-random binary encryption key. The default choice of SHA-1 is fine.

- **Hold Drive**—Your container will be stored as a file on this drive.

In addition to these main choices, you have the following two options as well:

- Mount and Format Now
- Fill In Container by Random Data

Select the Mount and Format Now option. You need to mount and format your encrypted disk prior to using it. The drive letter choice you have is the drive letter as it will appear on your computer, through Windows Explorer, for example. The other option, Fill In Container by Random Data, is also a good option to check; doing so only adds to the security of your encrypted disk.

With all of your options filled in, you can proceed by clicking the Create button. Figure 12.22 shows the Enter Password screen, where you are prompted to enter your secret password. Notice that you have to enter the password twice, for confirmation. The password is extremely important; it is your only means for decrypting this disk and accessing the files stored on it. If you forget this password, you will lose access to all of the files stored on your encrypted disk.

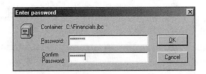

Figure 12.22   Enter your secret password.

Use a good password—something with a combination of letters and numbers is best. Do not use a single dictionary type of word or other easily guessed word. You can type a phrase or sentence if you want, or even the first letter from each word of a sentence that you will remember. (See the section "Password Examples" for further information.) Commit this password to memory and do not write it down. If you absolutely must write it down, store it securely in a safety deposit box, or equivalent.

Caution

Remember that this password controls access to the files in your container. If you forget this password, you will not be able to access these files, and they will essentially be lost.

Now you are asked to press random keys on your keyboard. This *seed value generation* is used to pseudo-randomize the seed to be used for the encryption. The encryption algorithm uses the seed to scramble the data. It is better to have the seed be as random as possible so that the encryption cannot be easily guessed. The OK button will not activate until you have typed in enough keys to fill up the progress indicator.

After you click OK, the encrypted disk container is created and the Format window appears. Select the File System with which to format this encrypted disk and click Start. If you're unsure, select the FAT file system, unless you are running Windows NT or 2000, in which case you can select NTFS. The NTFS file system was introduced with Windows NT several years ago. Its primary advantage over the FAT file system is that it provides file level security. With NTFS, you can specify which users have access to which files. Under some operating systems, you will not be able to choose a File System format. That is okay; you can proceed normally because BestCrypt knows which file system you need.

That's it! Now a warning box appears before you format, reminding you that all information on this disk will be erased. (That's okay because this new encrypted disk has no data yet.) Your container is created and you have a new encrypted disk with which to work. You will see the new encrypted disk appear in the BestCrypt Control Panel, as in Figure 12.23.

You can now move existing files to the container, or start using it as the storage location of new files that you create. It would probably be best, however, if you just played around with the new container for a week or so, to get familiar with it.

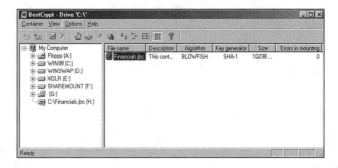

Figure 12.23   The BestCrypt Control Panel displays our newly created container.

Mounting and Dismounting

From this point on, you will need to access the container by *mounting* it, and release access of the disk by *dismounting* it. The next time you shut down your computer, the container will be dismounted for you, and the next time you boot up, the disk will need to be mounted before you can use it. This is where your password comes in handy—you cannot mount without it.

BestCrypt gives you a few different ways of mounting and dismounting the encrypted disk. You can do so through the BestCrypt Control Panel, through Windows Explorer by double-clicking the .jbc file, or by right-clicking the system tray icon for BestCrypt.

Be sure to use your container over the next few days. Play around with it, and try mounting and dismounting it. Try adding, modifying, and deleting files stored in it. When you are comfortable with the way it works, you can transfer over any personal or confidential files that you want to keep encrypted and secured.

Product Comparison: Personal File Encryption

There are several good file encryption programs are on the market today. This section discusses and compares some of the popular ones for personal use. For a business setting or a multiuser environment that requires centralized administration, several products exist that will not be discussed here, such as F-secure's FileCrypto and RSA's Keon system. If you're looking for a solution to fit a medium-sized office environment, have a look at systems like these.

Table 12.4 lists some of the highlights of each product discussed.

Table 12.4   **Encryption Products**

Product	URL	Pros	Cons	Operating Systems	Price
PGP Freeware	`www.pgpi.com`	Full-featured functionality	Difficult for novice users	Windows, Linux, Macintosh	Free for personal, noncommercial use
Encryption Plus Folders	`http://www.pcguardian.com/software/folders.html`	User account management, password recovery	Clumsy interface	Windows	Freeware version or $49.95
Scramdisk	`http://www.scramdisk.clara.net/`	On-the-fly encryption, stenography, share encrypted folders with others	Complex interface	Windows	$20
Jetico BestCrypt	`http://www.jetico.sci.fi/home.htm`	Simple to use and effective	Basic functionality	Windows, Linux	$89.95 for Windows

PGP

PGP is a wonderful product that has been around for many years. Its creator, Phil Zimmerman, first released it as a freeware product in 1991. Ten years later, it has undergone several rewrites through a team of devoted professionals, who want the value of PGP to be accessible to everyone worldwide. The freeware version of PGP is still available to the public, courtesy of Network Associates, who now owns the rights to PGP software. Network Associates also sells it as a commercial product, called PGP Desktop Security. The commercial version of PGP includes the PGPdisk software, whereas the freeware version does not. PGPdisk is the software similar to Jetico BestCrypt. It allows you to keep multiple files encrypted in a virtual disk, which appears to the operating system as any other partition. You actually can still obtain the last PGP freeware version, PGP 6.0.2i, to have included the PGPdisk software. Get it from `http://www.pgpi.org/products/` for both Windows and the MacOS.

The current free version, PGP Freeware v6.5.8, runs on Windows, Macintosh, Linux, Solaris, HP-UX, and AIX. It is available for personal, non-commercial use from `www.pgpi.com` or the MIT distribution site at `http://web.mit.edu/network/pgp.html`. The interface for PGP is somewhat difficult to use because of its many features.

However, wizards exist to help simplify the process for new users. The features vary across operating systems. We will focus on the Windows version here:

- **Secure e-mail**—You can do the following with this feature:
    - Exchange encrypted e-mail with other people who use PGP.
    - Have support for Outlook, Outlook Express, Eudora, Lotus Notes, and Claris E-mailer.
    - Digitally sign e-mail messages to ensure the identity of the sender.
- **Secure files**—You can do the following:
    - Encrypt and decrypt individual confidential files on your computer.
- **Key ring**—This feature enables you to do the following:
    - Consolidate all of your friends' and associates' public keys into a single key ring.
    - Search public PGP key servers such as `http://pgpkeys.mit.edu:11371/` directly from the PGP software application.
- **PGPnet**—This feature does the following:
    - Can be configured for use between PGPnet-enabled computers, as well as several standard VPN servers
    - Provides an encrypted tunnel that secures all TCP/IP traffic sent between two computers
- **Self-Decrypting archives**—This feature enables you to do the following:
    - Encrypt individual or multiple files into a single, encrypted file that anybody—even non-PGP users—can decrypt with just a passphrase.

The commercial version of PGP is available from Network Associates at `www.pgp.com`. It represents a suite of the preceding features, plus PGPdisk, a firewall, an intrusion detection system, and a plug-in for ICQ. With the commercial product, you get the benefit of support from Network Associates.

PGP freeware uses industry-standard algorithms of CAST, IDEA, 3DES, Twofish, Rijndael, RSA, and Diffie-Hellman.

BestCrypt

Jetico (`www.jetico.sci.fi`) is a company based in Finland that provides well-known security products such as BestCrypt and BCWipe worldwide. As we saw in the section "Securing Files on the System," BestCrypt provides a great method for easy and strong file encryption. The interface is intuitive and easy to use. It works by creating a container on your computer. You access the container with your password, and the Windows operating system sees it as another hard drive partition. You put files that you want to be encrypted into the container. When you open the container with your password, all files are accessible and require no further decryption. When you close the container, all files are encrypted and secured as a single file.

BestCrypt monitors access to the container files. The container files have a .jbc file extension. BestCrypt prevents you from accidentally deleting a container file. You must explicitly delete the file through the BestCrypt interface as long as the software is active on your computer.

BestCrypt provides strong encryption algorithms: Blowfish, Twofish, GOST, and DES. The key generator it provides is a hashing algorithm, either SHA-1 or GOST.

Similar to other software, BestCrypt is completely transparent to the applications you use. Transparency means that your other programs such as Quicken or Microsoft Word operate normally, and you access files in your container just as you would normally access any file. If you store Microsoft Word files in your container, Word is not affected in any way. Your files are kept confidential, and you can still use them as you normally do.

BestCrypt is inexpensive and well worth the price. The interface is easy to understand and the documentation is clear and concise, making BestCrypt extremely user friendly.

The latest version of BestCrypt is v7.0. It has some notable new features, including the following:

- Swap file encryption
- Centralized, network-wide BestCrypt management
- Multiple passwords per container, which enables multiple people to share a single container without sharing passwords

Caution
If you lose your password, you will lose access to your encrypted files. Period.

Encryption Plus Folders

Encryption Plus is also simple to install. It uses the Blowfish block cipher.

To start using encryption, you create a folder on your hard drive that will be the encrypted folder, or you can use one that already exists. Through the EP interface, you select the folder you want to encrypt by clicking the Protected Folders button, and then selecting the folder. You can alternatively unprotect the folder at any time through the same interface.

Encryption Plus transparently protects data with on-the-fly encryption. Whereas other programs offer on-the-fly encryption by decrypting on demand entire files, EP decrypts only the portion of the file that is in use, which adds extra security.

EP operates completely transparently to your other programs. Microsoft Word for example, is unaffected when you are accessing a file stored in an Encryption Plus protected folder.

EP also includes a password-protected screensaver for unattended computer security. EP includes a password recovery feature, which is unique. When you first enter your password, you are given the option to create three personal questions and answers. EP will keep these safe, and if you should forget the password you used, you can answer these three questions to retrieve it.

With the licensed version of EP, you can create multiple users and share encrypted folders between users that you specify. This sharing does not work across the network, but is simply local to the computer.

EP prevents users from accidentally deleting the protected folders by locking the folders when the Windows operating system is loaded. EP allows for encrypted folders to be transferred to removable media devices such as floppy drives or zip drives; be aware, however, that it cannot protect files on removable media from being deleted.

Tip

Encryption Plus Folders includes a password recovery feature. If you forget your password, you will be able to recover your files by answering the personal questions that you set up for recovery purposes.

Scramdisk

Scramdisk is similar to BestCrypt. It uses the container concept to provide a single file that is opened by a password. This container file is seen by the operating system as another drive partition. That is, after the container is open, the container appears as another drive letter in Windows.

Scramdisk provides for many industry standard encryption algorithms, including 3DES, IDEA, MISTY1, Blowfish, TEA, and Square, as well as a proprietary algorithm called Summer, which is fast algorithm intended for low security needs. We will, however, always recommend using widely tested industry standard algorithms over proprietary algorithms.

Scramdisk provides some unique functionality. Not only can you encrypt with the container concept similar to BestCrypt, but you can also hide your encrypted disks inside of picture or sound files. This practice is known as *steganography*. Steganography hides messages inside harmless looking files, such as images. Unless you know to look for the message, it is transparent to you. Scramdisk allows you to use up to four different passwords to protect a container. The container is really a file on your hard drive with a .svl extension.

Scramdisk also includes a wiping utility to securely wipe files from your disk. This wiping technique is similar to the functions that are built into BCWipe and PGP. It is an alternative to simply using Delete in Windows, which doesn't actually remove the file from the disk, but rather unlinks it.

The interface for Scramdisk is a bit difficult to navigate at first, but knowing the concepts of how the program works makes it easier. In addition to creating, mounting, and dismounting protected container files, Scramdisk provides some additional functionality, including access to Windows Disk Defragmenter, ScanDisk, and volume labels.

Another cool feature, in addition to steganography, is the ability to create an SFK file. You can distribute this file to other users, and it acts as a key to unlock your protected containers. By using this file, other people can unlock your containers, without knowing your password. Your passwords are kept safe, and your encrypted files can be shared.

Caution

If you lose your password, you will lose access to your encrypted files. Period.

Encryption Algorithms

Encryption algorithms, or *ciphers,* are core components of any cryptosystem. These are the mathematical functions that combine plain text and a secret key to produce cipher text.

This section describes some of the common encryption algorithms publicly in use today. Keep in mind that this is not a complete list, but rather a sampling of some popular ciphers. Recall the two different encryption systems: symmetric and public key (or asymmetric). Each uses a different set of algorithms to do its job.

Symmetric key encryption algorithms can operate in one of two modes: block ciphers and stream ciphers. *Block ciphers* apply encryption to a certain block of data, measured in bits. For example, a typical block cipher like Digital Encryption Standard (DES) encrypts data in 64-bit blocks. What do you do with data that cannot be evenly broken down into 64-bit blocks? In this case, the extra bits needed to fill up a block are added to the plain text. This process is called *padding,* and it involves adding random data to the plain text to achieve a 64-bit block.

Consider the following sentence:

This sentence does not add up.

Your computer sees this sentence as a string of 30 bytes. Because a byte has 8 bits, this sentence contains 240 bits. 240 bits are not evenly divisible by 64, so the DES algorithm needs to pad an extra 16 bits of random data to this string, making it a total of 256 bits, which can be divided into four blocks of 64 bits. A block cipher might then apply encryption to each block separately, using a different seed for each, or the same, depending on the implementation.

Stream ciphers are the other major mode of symmetric key algorithms. In this case, the data can be encrypted byte by byte. The stream cipher is obtained from a pseudo-random number generator (PRNG) to produce a pseudo-random stream of bits. This bit stream is combined with the plain text to create the cipher text. Notice that the stream ciphers do not work on blocks of data as the block ciphers do. The stream cipher is considered faster, working on a bit by bit or byte by byte stream of data, depending on the implementation.

The concept of a stream cipher can be hard to understand. Let's try to illustrate. Remember invisible ink pens? As you wrote, each word was hidden, invisible to prying eyes. This is nearly the same thing as stream cipher encryption. Imagine that as your data is sent across the network, it is being encrypted one word at a time.

The AES Project

In 1997, the U.S. National Institute of Standards and Technology (NIST) opened a worldwide competition aimed at deciding a replacement algorithm for DES. Known as the Advanced Encryption Standard (AES), the project decided its winner in November of 2000: the Rijndael cipher. This was an important event for NIST because DES had become outdated, and a new encryption standard was needed for government use. The contest also helped to raise encryption awareness globally, and it brought together developers worldwide.

Symmetric Key Algorithms: Block Ciphers

Listed here are some popular block ciphers. DES is mentioned because it is still widely used today, even though it has been proven insecure by the power of modern hardware to crack it. Each block cipher is unique, using different algorithms, key lengths, and block sizes to do its job. The important thing to note is that these are each widely used, and primarily considered secure with the exception of DES.

DES

The Digital Encryption Standard was developed at IBM Thomas J. Watson Labs in the 1970s. It was soon after adopted by NIST as the standard encryption algorithm to be used for unclassified, low-security files. DES encrypts in 64-bit blocks by using a 56-bit key for encryption. DES was a good solution for many years, but with the power of technology increasing with Moore's Law (computing power doubles every 12–18 months), the DES encryption algorithm has been proven insecure, cracked by Distributed.Net and Electronic Frontier Foundation in a record 22 hours in January of 1999. It is believed that DES can be cracked even more quickly today. Refer to `http://www.eff.org/Privacy/Crypto_misc/DESCracker/HTML/` `19990119_deschallenge3.html` for full details.

3DES (Triple DES)

3DES is DES three times over. Created by IBM and the National Security Agency (NSA), it makes three passes on the plain text, encrypting each pass with a new 56-bit key, making for a total of 168-bit key encryption. It, like DES, applies encryption in 64-bit blocks. This algorithm has proved highly secure, with no publicly known compromises to date. Although it is three times DES, the end result is only about twice as secure as DES.

Blowfish

Bruce Schneier and the team at Counterpane Labs invented this popular encryption algorithm. It allows for a variable length key of up to 448 bits. This algorithm is unpatented and available for public use. Blowfish is considered a highly secure and highly optimized algorithm, with no major attacks against it to date.

CAST

Designed by Carlisle Adams and Stafford Taveres, CAST is also confidently considered highly secure. The CAST algorithm is patented by Entrust Technologies, but released to the public for free use. This cipher has 128- and 256-bit versions.

IDEA

Another block algorithm that is considered highly secure is IDEA, developed in Zurich, Switzerland by Xuejia Lai and James Massey. IDEA uses a 128-bit key and is designed to be resistant to certain popular attacks (differential cryptanalysis) on symmetric key encryption systems.

RC2, RC5, and RC6

RC2 is a block cipher that was originally created by Ronald Rivest of RSA Data Security. RC5 was the successor to RC2, attempting to overcome the discovered security weaknesses of the algorithm. David Wagner, John Kelsey, and Bruce Schneier found weaknesses in both RC2 and RC5. RC6 is the latest from Ronald Rivest. It was an AES submission, and it works on 128-bit blocks.

Rijndael

Two Belgium cryptographers, Joan Daemen and Vincent Rijmen, developed Rijndael. The creators have graciously decided to never patent this algorithm. It uses a variable length block and key length. When people refer to the current AES algorithm, they are referring to Rijndael.

Twofish

Also designed by the team at Counterpane Labs, Twofish was originally an AES submission. A 256-bit block cipher, it is considered highly secure, and is being considered by the NIST as a replacement for the current AES.

These are just some of the choices you have for block ciphers. The one you should choose depends on your needs. If you have a high security concern, you should not choose DES because it only suffices for low security. CAST and Blowfish are great choices. Both are considered relatively fast and extremely secure. Block ciphers are important because these are what you will use most often when encrypting files on your computer.

Symmetric Key Algorithms: Stream Ciphers

Stream ciphers are popular in Web browsers and SSL connections. They are commonly used to help set up secure channels between a Web browser and an online shopping site. Stream ciphers are considered faster than block ciphers. They encrypt data byte by byte, as opposed to a block cipher, which encrypts data in chunks of multiple bytes.

RC4

Another breed of algorithm from Ronald Rivest, RC4 can be found in popular Web browser implementations including Internet Explorer and Netscape Navigator. RC4 is a variable key length stream cipher operating in bytes.

SEAL

The Software optimized Encryption Algorithm was originally designed by Rogaway and Coppersmith in 1993. It is a fast stream cipher for 32-bit machines. Operating systems such as Windows 95, 98, Me, 2000, and XP are considered 32-bit operating systems because they are capable of processing data 32 bits at a time.

Public Key Algorithms

Public key algorithms are largely used for sending secure e-mail messages with programs such as PGP. Web browsers and Web sites can also use them to set up secure SSL channels. Public key systems operate using two keys. They can serve two purposes: 1) encryption of information; and 2) digital signatures. For encryption, the public key is used to encrypt the information, whereas the private key is used to decrypt it. For digital signatures, the owner uses his private key to encrypt a portion of text, whereas the recipient uses the owner's public key to decrypt and verify the signature.

Diffie-Hellman Key Exchange

The Diffie-Hellman key exchange is a popular method for exchanging secret keys over an insecure medium such as the Internet. It was developed by W. Diffie and M.E. Hellman around 1976. These pioneers of public key cryptography knew that it would be essential for two people to securely exchange a secret key over an insecure network. The Diffie-Hellman key exchange is not perfect because it is vulnerable to a man-in-the-middle attack; however, it is widely agreed to be a good method for secret key exchange.

RSA

RSA can be used for both encrypting data and as the foundation of a digital signature. Originally developed by Ronald Rivest, Adi Shamir, and Leonard Adleman, RSA is well known worldwide. Public experts in mathematics and cryptography have tested RSA, and it has proven secure. However, attacks have been proposed against it, and certain implementations were found to be weak. RSA key sizes can be any length, although 1024 bits is common. RSA can be computationally slow on a small PC.

DSS

The NSA created the Digital Signature Standard, and NIST adopted it. It is based on the Digital Signature Algorithm (DSA), which allows for keys of any length. As specified by NIST, DSS should use keys of either 521-bit or 1024-bit sizes. Although DSA can be used for encryption, the standard calls for DSS to be used only for digital signatures.

Hashing Algorithms

We have not mentioned the hashing algorithms up until this point because they do not provide encryption in and of themselves; rather, they aid the encryption process. These are known as message digest functions. They can have several purposes:

- Create encryption keys for use with symmetric key ciphers
- Provide proof that files are authentic and unaltered
- Aid in the creation of digital signatures

Basically, a message digest function looks at a file bit by bit and equates it to a single large number of 128 or 256 bits in length, which basically serves as an ID for the file. Technically, this single large number is called a *message digest*, *hash*, or *fingerprint*. If you run the same message digest against the same file at any point in time, you will get the same digest. If a single bit in the file changes, the entire digest changes. In this way, you can detect when a file has been modified or tampered with.

Why should anybody do this? Using hashing algorithms to create a message digest is beneficial in several instances:

- To give Web site visitors a way to determine if downloaded files are authentic
- To ID personal files and later determine whether they have been modified
- To create a semi-random number used by an encryption algorithm

For example, consider that Bob shares a computer at work with Alice. Bob is going on vacation for two weeks. He has some important client files stored on the computer. Upon return, Bob wants to be able to determine whether Alice has modified any of his client files. By creating a message digest for these files before he leaves for vacation, he creates a file fingerprint. When he returns from vacation, he can create a message digest again. If the files have not been modified, the file fingerprint will be the same as when he left. If the fingerprint is different, he will know that somebody modified the file.

The following sections detail a few message digest functions that are in use today.

MD5

Message Digest 5 (MD5) was created by Ronald Rivest. It produces a 128-bit message digest. Although attacks have been proposed against MD5, it is still widely used and generally considered secure. It is not quite as secure as SHA-1 because of its smaller digest size, but its size actually makes it faster to use.

SHA-1

The Secure Hash Algorithm (SHA) is a standard developed by NIST. SHA-1, a 1994 revision to SHA, is used today to produce a 160-bit message digest. SHA-1 is slower to use than MD5, but it is stronger because of the larger digest size.

HMAC

Hash function-based Message Authentication Code (HMAC) is actually something applied to one of the functions such as MD5 or SHA-1. HMAC is a protection mechanism that takes the digest one step further by actually protecting the integrity of the digest. If an attacker tries to modify your message digest, HMAC knows that the digest has been tampered with. HMAC is a technique that uses the message digest function (MD5 or SHA-1) in conjunction with a secret key to produce a checksum on the message digest.

MD5SUM.EXE Walkthrough

It is good to get your feet wet with hashing algorithms, so we will go through an example. As stated, hashing algorithms provide a great way to get the fingerprints of a file. Using these fingerprints, you can easily tell if the file has been tampered with or modified. MD5SUM.EXE is a Windows program for generating the fingerprint. You first run MD5SUM.EXE with any file as input, and the fingerprint of the file is output to you. You can also feed the file fingerprint to MD5SUM.EXE as input, and get output that tells you if the file has been modified.

Why would you want to use MD5SUM.EXE? Here's why:

- It can create a baseline of fingerprints for important files on your computer.
- Several Web sites are offering their MD5 fingerprints for files that you download. By running MD5SUM.EXE against their file and fingerprint, you can determine whether the file has been hacked or modified.

It is important to realize that these hashing algorithms are used to create an ID or fingerprint for a file. They do not contain data from the original file or alter the original file. Let's stop and run some MD5 digests of our own to see how this works:

1. Download MD5SUM.EXE for Windows and save it to `C:\md5sum.exe`. The program is openly licensed under the GNU license agreement, so different versions exist all over the place. One place you can get it is `http://unxutils.sourceforge.net/`, but you will have to load the `UnxUtils.zip` and extract it from there.

2. Open Notepad (select Start, Run, Notepad) and enter the following text: **This is a test of MD5 message digests.**

3. Save the file as `C:\md5test.txt`.

4. Open a command prompt (select Start, Run and type **command** or **cmd**).

5. At the command prompt, type **md5sum.exe md5test.txt > md5test.md5**.

   After you press Enter, a new file named `md5test.md5` is created, containing the message digest and a reference to the original filename.

6. Now verify the file integrity by typing the following command at the prompt: **md5sum.exe -cv md5test.md5**. `md5sum.exe` returns with a message saying that the file is okay, as in Figure 12.24.

Figure 12.24   Using `md5sum.exe` to verify a file's integrity.

7. Now open `md5test.txt` in Notepad again, and delete the word `is` so that you only have the following: `This a test of MD5 message digests.`

8. Repeat step 6 to see how the modified file will fail the fingerprint check, as shown in Figure 12.25.

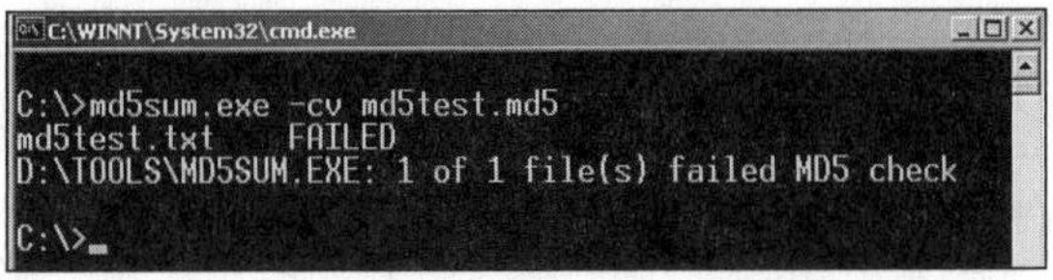

```
C:\>md5sum.exe -cv md5test.md5
md5test.txt     FAILED
D:\TOOLS\MD5SUM.EXE: 1 of 1 file(s) failed MD5 check

C:\>_
```

Figure 12.25 Using md5sum on a modified file returns a failure.

Success! In essence, you have succeeded in using md5sum.exe to verify a file's integrity. The next time you download a file from the Internet, grab its MD5 message digest if it is provided, and check its integrity.

9. If you want, go ahead and add the word is back to the sentence. Run the check again, and you will see that your MD5 sum returns OK.

Today, many sites are using message digest to protect you from downloading the wrong version of a file. Because the fingerprint IDs the file, you can determine whether the file you downloaded is the original. This protects you against such things as forgeries, viruses, or transmission errors.

Let's look at the message digest. The message digest, or fingerprint, is a string of letters and numbers. It appears as unreadable gibberish, but serves to identify the file. You might think of it as a serial number, which also often appears as a string of unreadable text. Tables 12.5 and 12.6 demonstrate the input to the MD5 function and the digest or fingerprint of those results. Each row of text in the column on the left was typed into a separate text file using Windows Notepad. The text in the second column shows the corresponding message digest produced from the original text. These tables show how different the message digest is for each text file.

Table 12.5 **MD5 Digest 1**

MD5 Function Applied to the Following Text	Message Digest
This is a test of the MD5 function.	162135972a0371739a6e33e820ef0971
This is another test of the MD5 function.	d288caebe9951d53e06a4ea08b6aa82a
This is a third test of the MD5 function.	7f1979a409067cdb62b951bac57bf91c

Table 12.6 **MD5 Digest 2**

MD5 Function Applied to the Following Text	Message Digest
This is a test of the MD5 function.	162135972a0371739a6e33e820ef0971
This is the last test.	0749f091848d6f995bd368e068624f12

Take a look at the first example in Table 12.6. Notice that the same text file produces the same message digest. This is a natural outcome of the message digest function. What is important is that two different text files (or any files for that matter!) do not produce the same digest. If they do, you have a *collision* of digests. Collisions do happen, but for a message digest function to be secure, it must be computationally improbable for a collision to occur.

For example, if you produce the same message digest for your Microsoft Money financial file as you do for your top secret business plan file written in Microsoft Word, you have a collision. When this happens, you no longer have a unique fingerprint for each file, so the message digest is more or less invalid. This is a rare occurrence, but it's possible.

Password Examples

Strong passwords, or passphrases, are hard to guess and hard to crack with brute force. They should not be common words or dictionary words. Strong passwords should incorporate letters, numbers, and special characters such as !@#$%^&*(into the single passphrase.

Here are some strong password examples:

- `/<7h1s+1s+pr3tty+s7r0ng>/`
- `j09nny15@m^H0#$3`
- `the^will!never@guess#m^password$because%it&is*so(strong)`

Here are some weak password examples:

- `surfing`
- `12345`
- `password`

Maintaining strong passwords also is a result of how they are handled. Things that might seem obvious include the following:

- Be sure nobody is looking when you type your password.
- Do not write the password down. (If you must, then store it in a safety deposit box or equivalent.)
- Do not reuse passwords across systems. Keep them unique.
- Passwords should be easy to memorize for you, but hard to guess.
- In the case of encryption, passwords should be long.

The Dark Side of Encryption

The unspeakable events that occurred on September 11, 2001 in the U.S. led to a war on terrorism. In the back of the picture sits the war on encryption.

Many in the U.S. government and other organizations argue that all domestic encryption products should include backdoors that would give certain government agents the ability to decrypt. Indeed, the arguments continue. Encryption should not hinder law enforcement and military's ability to maintain good intelligence. On the other hand, clear reason tells us that this is in direct opposition to encryption's purpose of maintaining personal security and privacy. It also seems contradictory to the basic American values of freedom and privacy.

In a speech on the tragic events, U.S. Senator Judd Gregg encouraged international, global requirements prohibiting encryption products built without backdoors for government access. Arguing that these laws are necessary to combat terrorism and other criminals who use encryption to make their communications unintelligible to outsiders, some citizens agree with Gregg. Indeed, some of these same groups think that many tools people use to protect privacy online, such as anonymizers, should also be banned.

On the flip side, many citizens oppose this view, arguing that a free society has the right to privacy through encryption that has not been backdoored. Taking this right away conjures many unpleasant thoughts and stirs stories of George Orwell's book *1984*. Indeed, many would think such laws would only trample on individual privacy for law-abiding citizens, when criminals and wealthy terrorists would just get their own non-backdoored encryption software anyway. If the effort were not worldwide, the U.S. would outlaw encryption without backdoors, whereas other countries would still make encryption products that were not backdoored. These products could easily be obtained and used by criminals and terrorists, and possibly even smuggled into the United States.

A *Wired* article by Declan McCullagh describes some of these events, quoting leaders on both sides of the argument, and encouraging readers to think clearly about the issues at hand. Read the article, "Congress Mulls Stiff Crypto Laws," at `http://www.wired.com/news/politics/0,1283,46816,00.html`.

Indeed, terrorists and criminals can use encryption technology to scramble their communications. However, normal people also use encryption to protect personal information and confidential transactions. Just as any tool can be used to build or destroy, protect or endanger, encryption is no different. It is up to us to protect the value of encryption and its use in our society for securing our information and transactions.

Summary

Operating systems and firewalls can protect your PC's data, but after an intruder or automated attack gets past these defenses, you must fall back on virus scanning and encryption. It's somewhat simple for a virus to get by a firewall or the built-in security features of the operating system. If someone sends you a file over e-mail or on a floppy disk or allows you to download through the ICQ File option, a firewall can do nothing to stop an attack because you are allowing such connectivity.

Virus scanning is a must-have in today's environment. We can't say you shouldn't share files via the chat/messenger programs, open files in e-mail attachments, or download a file from your favorite Web site. Security shouldn't make it impractical for you to use the Internet. What you must do, however, is take the necessary precautions to enable you to have some comfort level in the functions you perform on the Internet. Your personal information is stored on your hard drives, and that data is valuable to you and to the attacker.

Encryption is strong protection for your personal and confidential files and information. For encryption to be effective, it must be used with a goal in mind and knowledge of the encryption system and software being used. Keys are extremely important. They must be protected with care. If the key is a digital file, it must be secured on the computer, and not duplicated or given out. With password-based keys, the password must be strong and kept secret. Encryption is your last line of defense if an attacker gets past your firewalls and a virus gets past your scanners. Make sure you are using strong encryption over the data you value the most.

13

Securing Your Home Network

The home network, in which computers in different rooms of your house communicate and share the same network, has become a reality. Several years ago, if you asked most people about their home network, you would probably have gotten a blank stare in return. With the advancement of technology and the ease of use of technologies such as e-mail (ask almost anyone for an e-mail address these days and you will see that he has one), broadband connections, and wireless devices, you have the ability to quickly comprehend how technology can benefit your life. The learning curve is not steep for these tools that the corporate machine gives us every other day. Home networking is probably one of the more complex ideas, but it is still easy enough to implement.

If you don't have a home network, perhaps by the end of this chapter you will see the benefits and ease of installation of home networking. However, as we have mentioned throughout the book, with every new technology out there, the potential for attackers to gain access to your personal information and invade your life is real. The same holds true for your home network. What you must know to connect to the Internet securely are the tools and techniques that corporations use on a daily basis to protect their own vast networks. Although you do not have the millions of dollars that companies have to implement network security tools, you can do many free and inexpensive things to protect your own vast network.

To get you operational, we will go through some of the basic concepts related to networking. You should have a basic understanding of what the terms are and why you will be implementing what we discuss. After we have laid out how your home network will operate, we will go through the steps you need to take to protect your entire network. With more computers connected to the Internet, your potential points of attack increase. We touched briefly on networks when discussing firewalls in Chapter 10, "Understanding Your PC Operating System and Its Security Features." In this chapter, we will go into detail on how firewalls work in a networked environment and how you can test their effectiveness.

The growth of high-speed Internet access coupled with the spread of Windows-based home computers has made the need for security more real than ever. Because of this, Microsoft is working to address the inherent insecurities of its operating systems. In the past, Microsoft's answer has been to educate the public through its Web site and provide patches whenever a new OS or application vulnerability was discovered. This approach has proved futile, however, considering the wake of recent Internet worms and past Distributed Denial of Service (DDoS) attacks. With public concern growing, Microsoft has responded by saying it will make future default installations more secure than past ones. Regardless of who is promising security, it is important to realize that no one solution will solve all of these problems. In the end, it is up to each of us to take the steps necessary to secure our own systems, part of which includes protecting our home networks from Internet attacks with the use of firewalls.

The Growth of Home Networking

The Yankee Group estimated that the number of home networks will grow at approximately 95% to reach about 10 million homes by 2003. The major growth factor is broadband connectivity. When you only had access to dial-up, you were lucky just to be able to surf the Internet and have Web pages come up every few minutes. Imagine what your connection speed would have been like had you shared that one modem connection with several other computers in your home.

Home networking is all about sharing your access with other computers in your home. You might have a computer in the home office, one in the kid's room, and another in the family room. Broadband Internet access brings speed and reliability to all these computers at the same time, all for one low cost and ease of configurability. The Internet is becoming increasingly multimedia based, and speed and bandwidth are required. Broadband access provides these things.

The majority of home network access will be over DSL and cable modem, although wireless networking is starting to catch on and will continue to eat up its share of the market. Wireless networking does not require Ethernet cables or any other form of cabling to connect computers over a network and makes connectivity very simple in homes and offices. The Yankee Group estimates that by 2003, an estimated 5 million broadband homes will have gateways set up for routing home traffic to the Internet.

Home networks can easily be wired using existing telephone lines for DSL or through existing cable connection for cable modems. The cost, outside of the ISP connection fee and monthly charges, can be rather cheap. As mentioned in Chapter 11, "Securing Your Standalone PC: Broadband Connections," the costs are minimal and the technology is easy to implement. To network a few computers in the home through your broadband connection requires only a couple of network cards, some cables, and networking software. A Frost & Sullivan report, "U.S. Home Networking Markets," says the growth in the home networking space will continue to grow because of inexpensive and easy-to-understand products.

Broadband Connectivity

The debate over which is better, DSL or cable modem, still rages on. (These topics are discussed more in Chapter 11.) However, this debate should not stop you from taking whatever broadband connection is available to you and using it to set up your network. For many companies, DSL provides good connectivity that can't be found in the business community by cable modem. For home users, cable modem access is easy to set up and run and is in many places that DSL is not provided. The distance problems that many users face with DSL are not a problem with cable modem. The security measures of each technology have something to be desired. Each is susceptible to attack, and it's up to you to keep your network secure.

Cable modem service does have more security problems initially than DSL. Because you are already connected to a network environment that includes your neighborhood when you use cable modem, you have all the problems that are associated with local network access. We will cover these problems later in the chapter. Windows Network Neighborhood can show you all the computers on your local area network (LAN) if they do not have security measures in place.

Because DSL is akin to dial-up, you are not sharing a LAN when you make a connection. Because of this problem, some cable modem providers assist users with security and provide software to help protect their connections. Most cable modems today also implement the Data Over Cable Service Interface Specification (DOCSIS). DOCSIS includes support for cable network security features, including authentication and packet filtering.

The always-on connectivity of DSL and cable modem connectivity is a blessing and a curse. You can stay logged into the Net indefinitely, but this makes you available to attack indefinitely. The static IP provided by both DSL and cable modems can be a permanent address that can be used to find you. Although it's possible that you will be assigned an IP address via DHCP, if you are online for a day, that one IP address will be used by your computer for that whole day, and it can be attacked throughout the day using that same IP address.

Attacks on your home network over your broadband connections, whether DSL or cable modem, are constant. As you will see when you have your personal firewalls set up and logging enabled, attackers are constantly attempting to penetrate your environment and take control of your computer, steal information, or just wreak havoc. Typically, vulnerable applications include e-mail, Web, instant messaging, multimedia applications, and operating system flaws.

LANs are subject to many problems, one of the most significant being "sniffing" of network traffic. Sniffing gives someone on the local network the ability to see and capture another user's traffic. When a computer on an Ethernet network sends a broadcast packet, every other host on the network automatically receives that packet. Microsoft Windows uses broadcast packets to find the hosts for the Network Neighborhood window. The Internet's Address Resolution Protocol (ARP) uses Ethernet broadcast to determine which computer on a LAN has a particular address.

Sniffing is prevalent in cable modem connections. Cable modems can alleviate this problem by implementing the DOCSIS 1.1 protocol to restrict ARP packets and packets that are not intended for your computer. DOCSIS 1.1 is capable of encrypting all information sent over the cable. These new security measures can help, but you still need further protection.

To protect your broadband connections, you can get hardware and software solutions, but they should be just one part of your overall home network strategy. As we mentioned, operating system security and encryption can keep your network secure. These steps in combination can provide a layered model of security, the Defense in Depth we have talked about, to keep your home network secure from the first attacks against the perimeter (your firewall) to the inner layer if an attacker should get to the actual data beyond the firewall.

We haven't covered wireless access such as satellite connectivity. This is an option, although it is not widely used and not worth in-depth discussion until it becomes used in more homes. Corporations are working through the problems of wireless network, which have different problems than wired networks. Even if you use a wired network connection and then implement wireless LAN in your home, you are opening yourself up for a different type of attack. The privacy problems that are associated with wireless will be covered in Chapter 14, "Securing Your Privacy Using Other Digital Devices."

The Need for Home Networks

The reasons for setting up your home network are varied. The one you are probably most concerned with is cost. Rather than having two or three DSL or cable connections in your home at two or three times the cost, you can share one connection, which is probably fast enough for everyone in your household. Other reasons for networking your home include the following:

- **Share the home's Internet connection between mom and dad's computer and that of their children**—Many families now have multiple computers and all want Internet connectivity. (This is probably the most common reason for networking.)

- **Share peripherals such as printers, CD-ROM burners, and scanners over the network**—You don't have to have one printer for each computer. Computers can share one printer over the network just as in an office environment.

- **Use network applications**—These include databases or financial applications over the network.

- **Share data over the network through folders or shared hard drives**—You no longer have to FTP files back and forth or copy them to floppy disks to share data.

- **Implement security on one gateway computer**—This can protect the rest of the environment.

- **Enable privacy of information by not having to share one computer to perform all Internet functions**—You don't want the kids using your computer in all likelihood.

- **Play games over the network**—Just about every major new PC game comes equipped with Internet capabilities. Most games, such as Half-Life, Quake, and Unreal Tournament, can be played by multiple users over a network.

You definitely should take advantage of all the benefits available to you through a home network. If you have at least two computers in your home, you can network. Saving money is as good a reason as any to design and implement your home network.

The cost of computers has also dropped significantly enough to make it feasible for many homes to have more than one computer. Software to run these computers has also dropped enough to enable you to network and secure your home. Physical hardware has never been cheaper. The ability for home users to implement both hardware and software has been made simple by new technologies. Where once it was easy to share a floppy disk between computers, now you can just as easily share a whole hard drive or folder. With this type of sharing, however, you must be concerned about security. The same way that a floppy could be stolen and all your data copied, so can that shared folder be accessed and copied over the network.

Problems with Home Networks

The major problem with home networking has been difficulty with implementation. Books have been geared toward the corporate environment. The home segment, which is still developing, has not been thoroughly addressed. This could be because the home user technology is still developing and changing so rapidly that it is hard to assist home users in designing their environment. The tools that are available to you today are easier to use, but they still require some assistance.

The second major problem faced by the home network is security. When you dialed up to the Internet with a simple phone connection, you were not online for days and your IP address always changed. You had some security through obscurity. This is no longer the case. All your personal information is available for attack 24×7 with broad-band connections. You have to figure out how to protect your home environment on a 24×7 basis now. Management of the operating system and the software needed to secure your network is somewhat difficult to manage and understand beyond the basic settings.

With a secure setup, you can connect to many corporate environments to tele-commute safely. The problem is setting up your connecting correctly and ensuring that your home network is safe and does not provide a risk to your office environment. Many people who work from home keep company-sensitive documents at home. Then they connect to work to do some function. For this type of scenario, you have to make sure your home environment is as secure as your office network. If your home network is compromised and the attacker gets your work documents, it would be the same as if the attacker broke into your company to steal the documents.

To network your home, you have a number of options from the firewalls, applications, hardware devices, and operating systems that you use. Each of these categories has numerous options available to you. Making them all work together can be a serious problem to designing and implementing your home network. We will attempt to sim-plify scenarios you can use to implement and secure your network.

Home Zombies and DDoS Attacks

DDoS attacks are a threat to the entire Internet infrastructure. In February 2000, sophisticated DDoS attacks affected several sites. These attacks were covertly planned and executed over a period of time. The attackers were groups of hackers, and the sites were large e-commerce sites. The attackers carefully planned an attack that used inse-cure home computer networks as *zombie* machines. The attackers used their own crafted code to control these zombie machines. When many zombies were under con-trol, the attackers were able to launch the attacks remotely.

The concept was simple and effective. First, the hackers distributed their code to inse-cure computer networks with high-speed Internet connections. Many of these systems were home networks. The code infiltrated the insecure system in one of several ways, either by a virus in an e-mail attachment or an infected Web site programmed to install the code on the victim's computers. After the code was installed, the infected computers sent out a message to the hacker, letting the hacker know that he had claimed another victim. The code gave the hackers the ability to control the infected machine. With thousands of victims under control, the hackers were able to launch the attack.

In unison, thousands of unprotected zombie systems were ordered to attack a Web site that the hacker specified. Because the attacks on the Web site were coming from thousands of zombie machines, the hackers could not be easily identified. In fact, the hackers never did any attacks from their own computers. Much like using a remote control to flip through channels on a television, the hackers controlled the zombie machines to do their bidding.

If you run your home network without protection, you take a greater risk of becoming a zombie to a hacker's DDoS attack. By using firewalls with outbound filtering rules to control the traffic that can leave your network (in addition to traffic that can enter your network), you are providing a much stronger level of security. If you do become a zombie, you are essentially responsible for the attacks. Take responsibility in the Internet community and do what you can to protect this type of attack from happening. The simplest defense is to use a good firewall that controls both incoming and outgoing traffic.

Network Design

The first thing to do is decide how to design your home network. We will make some assumptions in designing a network that you can use. The first is that you have at least two computers ready to network. The second is that you are using a broadband connection such as a cable modem. Whether you have a static IP address or dynamic address doesn't really matter—they are interchangeable. The third is that you have some personal firewall such as ZoneAlarm Pro or WinRoute Pro to protect your home network and be your gateway to the Internet. We will use a mix of Windows operating systems to give you different tastes of how networking can work with different operating systems. We will not cover Linux or MacOS in these scenarios. The last assumption we will make is that you know how to install a network interface card (NIC) and have one in each computer.

We might not leave you completely on your own with the NICs. What you really need to understand is that two basic type of cards exist, and they deal with speed. For speed, NICs can either send data at 10 megabits per second (Mbps) or 100Mbps. You probably want to get a 10/100 NIC, which can handle both speeds. The way the card fits in your computer is the other concern. NICs can either be PCI or ISA cards, depending on which slots you have available in your computer. Your computer specs should tell you what kinds of slots you have available. Most new computers have PCI slots available. The NICs come with the appropriate drivers on a CD-ROM that you will use to install them properly.

After you have the NIC cards installed, you need a hub. A *hub* is a small device with jacks for twisted pair plugs that can be used to connect computers in the network. You can connect multiple computers through a hub. You probably won't need more that two 4-port hubs. Again, you can buy these at any computer store. Several popular models include SMC, Netgear, Linksys, and Dlink. If you are going with 10/100 NIC, you will want to buy a hub that supports 10/100 transfer speeds. You also will need 10BASE-T Ethernet cables to connect all your devices. To know the length of the cables, you will have to measure the distance between computers. You can, of course, get rid of cables altogether and use wireless, but we won't go into those scenarios here. We will discuss the pros and cons of wireless in Chapter 14.

We discussed the various firewall products that you can use. Of the several products we discussed in detail, only a few of them can act as gateways for the rest of your network. Some, like BlackICE, can only protect one machine and are not really meant for networking computers together. For our discussion, we will use ZoneAlarm Pro and WinRoute Pro to demonstrate two products at different ends of the home networking spectrum that gives you the widest possible choices.

Design Diagram

Figure 13.1 is the basic diagram we will follow in setting up the home network environment. It's basic, but it shows all the necessary functionality you probably will need as you start your vast networking empire. One key feature we want in the network design is a gateway/firewall to protect the network. We also want a computer on the internal network for printer sharing that will reside on the internal IP address space of 192.168.1.x. We allow a Web server to run on a computer behind the firewall that allows all outbound traffic but blocks inbound traffic and restricts access to a shared folder with a password. This scenario can cover all your basic needs, from sharing information, protecting the network, and running your own Web site where you can share picture of the kids to running a small e-commerce Web site from home.

The network design is as follows:

- **Your cable modem/DSL connection is the first thing you must set up**—When you have your connection working correctly, you can begin setting up the rest of your network.

- **Your gateway machine is your first line of defense as well as your main system to perform routing and provide DHCP service for the rest of your network**—You do not have to use DHCP for your internal network. You can use a static internal address scheme if you want. You can run any other service such as a Web server on this machine or any other machine.

- **Your external NIC will be set with the IP address that your ISP provides, whether by DHCP or via a static IP address**—In our example, the external IP address that the ISP provides is 24.7.48.68. Our DNS address is 216.182.1.1. This allows us to resolve names such as www.microsoft.com to an IP address. Our firewall must have a gateway (24.7.48.1) to route traffic out to the Internet.

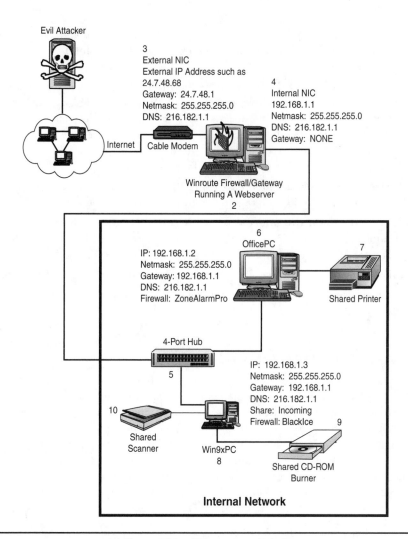

Figure 13.1   Home network design.

- **The second NIC in our firewall machine has the internal address for our home network (192.168.1.1)**—This is the gateway for the home network, which will route traffic out the external interface and out to the Internet. Because this internal address is the gateway for the Internet, it does not need a default gateway address. The DNS server address is 216.182.1.1.

- **The Ethernet cables must be connected to a hub**—This allows all the devices to talk to the one internal interface. If you were connecting multiple hubs together—for example, one hub from the second floor connects to a hub on the first floor of your house—you would have to use the uplink port on the main hub. In this case, we are only using one hub, so we do not have to worry about the uplink port on the hub.

- **Our computers and devices are on the internal network**—We can run anything on the internal network from ICQ to Web servers. This machine can get an IP address from the firewall, or we can assign it statically, such as 192.168.1.2. The gateway is 192.168.1.1, which is the internal interface of the firewall. The DNS server we use is the external IP address 216.182.1.1. Another option is running a DNS server on our firewall.

- **A shared printer is connected to our PC**—Because it is shared on the internal network, all PCs on the network can share one printer.

- **A second PC on the internal network is Win9xPC, which is assigned IP address 192.168.1.3**—It has the gateway address of 192.168.1.1 and DNS address of 216.182.1.1. It has a shared folder with a password.

- **Like a shared printer, we can share a CD-ROM burner off of this PC.**

- **We can also share a scanner**—Any device can be shared with other PCs on the internal network.

Firewall Configuration: WinRoute

To set up a robust home network environment, you will need a robust firewall. Most of the firewalls we detailed earlier in the book are meant to protect a single computer and not to defend an entire network. A firewall does more than just defend the network; it allows functionality and routing when it is configured properly. WinRoute is a great example of a small personal firewall that can be used to design your home network. We will use WinRoute to configure our network and set up our filtering rules. Although we cannot cover every possible firewall available to you, most firewalls that can be used to design a network and defend more than just one computer work on the same principles, which you should be familiar with by the end of this chapter.

As we have already mentioned, WinRoute can be used as a Dynamic Host Configuration Protocol (DHCP) server. DHCP assigns an IP address automatically to any computer in the internal network that requests an address from the pool of addresses defined by the DHCP server. The DHCP server assigns the netmask, default gateway, and DNS server as part of the configuration of the requesting computer. The benefit of using DHCP is that you can set up the configuration in place. All other computers are then automatically configured with the correct IP address information to allow them to route traffic to and from the Internet. The information can be set for a specific period of time, the lease time, such as a day, month, or year. Using a DHCP server, no two computers are assigned the same address; therefore, no conflict is created as is possible with manual configuration.

If your ISP used DHCP to provide your external IP address, you must enable the option Obtain an IP Address Automatically and Obtain DNS Server Address Automatically, as shown in Figure 13.2. Select Start, Settings, Control Panel, Network and Dial Up Connections in Windows 2000. In Windows 9x/Me, select Start, Settings, Control Panel, Network, TCP/IP *Adapter name*. If you are given a static address, you can enter it through this screen also.

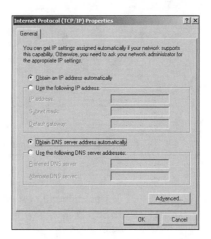

Figure 13.2   IP address setup.

To set up DHCP in WinRoute, perform the following actions:

1. From WinRoute, select Settings, DHCP and check the box DHCP Server Enabled, as shown in Figure 13.3.

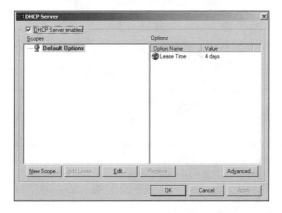

Figure 13.3   WinRoute DHCP Enabled.

2. Change the Default Options by clicking the Edit button. Set the default DNS server to whatever DNS server your ISP has assigned to you, as shown in Figure 13.4.

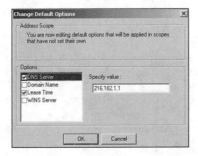

Figure 13.4 Default DNS server configuration.

3. Define a pool of addresses from which your internal network can choose by clicking the New Scope button. For this example, we will set up a pool of four IP addresses from 192.168.1.2–192.168.1.5, as shown in Figure 13.5. With this scope, you can have up to four machines in your home obtain an IP address from your DHCP server. If you have more machines, you can increase the scope to perhaps 192.168.1.2–192.168.1.10 to give you a pool of nine IP addresses.

Figure 13.5 DHCP scope of addresses.

4. When your DHCP server is configured, you can set up the external NIC. When you set up your cable modem/DSL, you set the external IP address of one of the two NICs in your firewall computer. To do this, select Settings, Interface Table. Select the external interface and click the Properties button. You see the dialog box shown in Figure 13.6. In our example, the external IP address is 24.7.48.68. In WinRoute, we have to enable Network Address Translation (NAT) on the external interface and disable NAT on the internal interface.

NAT allows the unroutable internal addresses, 192.168.1.x, to translate traffic to the real IP address that can be routed in the Internet, 24.7.48.68.

Figure 13.6 NAT enabled on external interface.

5. On the internal interface, the 192.168.1.1 address NIC, we have to turn off the NAT option by selecting the adapter and then clicking the Properties button. You see the dialog box shown in Figure 13.7.

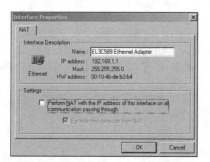

Figure 13.7 NAT disabled on internal interface.

6. DNS forwarding is turned on by default in a WinRoute installation, and you can leave it that way. You can check the status by selecting Settings, DNS Forwarder (see Figure 13.8). This enables your internal computer to perform DNS lookups. When you type a name into your browser window, such as www.foundstone.com, DNS enables this name to be translated to an IP address and your computer can find the Web site for which you are looking. Computers talk to each other with IP addresses rather than names. Names are a convenience for people. You can turn off the Hosts File option and DHCP Lease Table option if you have not set up a hosts file on your computer, which you probably will not do in a simple network design such as this. You could use a hosts file to

add your internal IP address and associated names, but this is really not necessary. Leave the cache option turned on to have the firewall remember repeated DNS queries for a faster response.

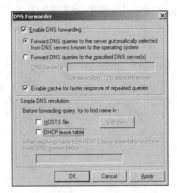

Figure 13.8 DNS Forwarder configuration.

7. To run a Web server on your firewall machine, you have to allow traffic to the Web server default port, 80. Because you are hosting the Web server, you have to allow traffic from any source. All rules allow or deny traffic, and you have to allow traffic to the Web server. You can log traffic if you need to, but watching all Web traffic probably is not feasible. Select Settings, Advanced, Packet Filter and select the external NIC. Enable the rules shown in Figure 13.9.

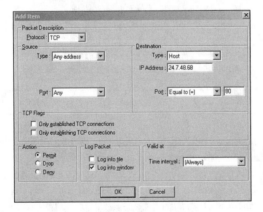

Figure 13.9 Enable Web server access.

Additional Internal Network Protection

The configuration of WinRoute is to protect your perimeter network. This is your first line of defense. As we have already mentioned, you need multiple layers of protection to keep your personal data and systems secure. Your internal computer can use some enhanced security measures. You can add more of this security, such as outbound filter rules, additional firewalls, virus scanners, and spyware checkers.

More Firewalls

We have already discussed the operating system security measures you can take to strengthen your system. You can run a personal firewall on each system. You might not want to run a full-blown WinRoute installation on each internal computer. You can use any of the other personal firewalls we have already discussed.

Because we have WinRoute or another firewall protecting the network and providing routing, you might want a simple product on the internal system to minimize your administration tasks. You might want to run a product such as BlackICE, which is easy to install and has security turned on by default (see Figure 13.10). A typical security installation of BlackICE includes checking the Nervous protection level, disabling Allow Internet File Sharing, and disabling Allow NetBIOS Neighborhood. You can set these options by selecting Tools, Edit Blackice Settings, Protection. Be aware that if you select Auto-Blocking, it could lead to problems. If your internal network machines send out traffic that BlackICE might misinterpret as an attack, valid internal addresses might be blocked. Because you are already on an internal network behind a firewall, you can probably do without Auto-Blocking turned on.

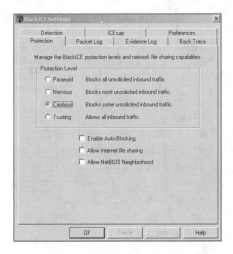

Figure 13.10   BlackICE settings.

You should run a virus scanner on all your internal and external computers. You never know when a virus will sneak into the network, and each machine should have its own virus protection. As we have mentioned earlier in the book, some of the personal firewalls such as those from Norton and McAfee have integrated virus scanners.

Outbound Filters

We have discussed all the inbound rules you can apply to protect someone from attacking your computer from the Internet. In the off-chance that an attacker makes it past your firewall into your internal network and compromises a computer, you probably want to block the attacker from using your computer as a launching point for Denial of Service attacks or using your computer to hack up other computers. This scenario has several problems. The first problem is identifying the attacker on your computer and knowing that he has compromised your system. The second problem you face is being a victim and having your computer become an attacking computer. The authorities can contact you if your computer is linked to an attack on another site.

One step you can take is to apply outbound firewall rules to stop suspicious traffic. From the gateway firewall machine, 192.168.1.1 in our example, we can apply filters on the outgoing traffic. What kind of filters do you want to see? If you only want to watch outgoing traffic, you can just set up a rule to log all traffic to a file (not recommended) or log to the Security window by selecting View, Log, Security Log.

You can set up any type of outbound filtering, just as you can with inbound filtering. You do have to be careful of what you filter because you can block legitimate traffic easily by blocking the wrong ports. In Figure 13.11, we are blocking outbound TCP connection to ports 135, 136, 137, 138, and 139. These are potentially dangerous ports in Windows systems. Blocking these ports prevents an attacker from using your compromised computer and making a "Net Use" connection to another machine to launch certain Windows-based attacks. These ports can easily be anything, such as blocking outgoing mail or outgoing Web browsing.

Another method of performing outbound filtering is with one of the other firewall products such as ZoneAlarm Pro, which monitors all processes and asks you if you want to allow the process to execute. As shown in Figure 13.12, we have ZoneAlarm Pro running on the Win9xPC (192.168.1.2) on the internal network. When we try to connect using FTP to the gateway firewall (192.168.1.1), ZoneAlarm Pro flags this outbound connection with an alert so that we know if someone other than us is making the outbound connection. We can allow or disallow the FTP process.

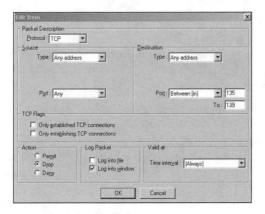

Figure 13.11   Blocking outgoing ports.

Figure 13.12   ZoneAlarm outbound connection alert.

File Sharing

File sharing was discussed earlier in this book. Briefly, file sharing allows other computers to connect to a folder on your computer and have read or write capability to the files in that folder. It is possible to share your entire hard drive, although you would never want to do this for every computer on the Internet. On the internal network, your firewall on the gateway machine should provide you with a reasonable level of comfort that no one on the Internet can access your shared files. This is assuming that the firewall filter rules protect your internal network from connection to your systems. As you see in our example, we are using addresses on our internal network that are nonroutable. Using nonroutable addresses belonging to network address spaces 192.168.x.x, 10.x.x.x, and 172.16.x.x will provide further protections because someone on the Internet can't attack a nonroutable address. Companies use these net-work addresses on their internal networks, and so should you. There aren't enough routable addresses for every machine in the world, so nonroutable addresses are used to solve this problem. These addresses allow someone to have only one valid IP address that can be reached on the Internet.

To password-protect your shared file by using Explorer, right-click on the folder you want to share and select Sharing. You see the dialog box shown in Figure 13.13. Give the folder a share name using the Shared As box and select Depends on Password. By password-protecting the shared folder using Read-Only Password and Full Access Password, you add further security on your internal system. You should always password-protect your shared folders.

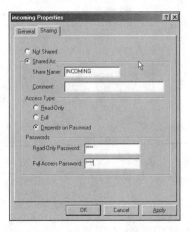

Figure 13.13   Password-protect a shared folder.

Many programs are available for testing your Web site for shared resources. The resource scanners look for shares such as folders or printers and show you what is available. (Remember: Do not scan other computers that do not belong to you.) We can see the output of one such program, Shed (`www.keir.net`), in Figure 13.14. We see that a folder share exists called INCOMING. We also see that IPC$ is shared. Interprocess communications (IPS), which handles exchanging messages between these processes on Windows systems, allows you to make connections between systems. An unprotected IPC$ connection can allow an attacker to make a connection to your sys-tem and have access to your system resources. It also gives an attacker the ability to extract information.

Another such program is NetBrute (`www.rawlogic.com/netbrute/`), which also shows shared resource information, as shown in Figure 13.15. NetBrute can also perform basic port scanning and check for weak passwords on a Web site that requires authenti-cation. Using this feature against a site that is not yours is an attempt to break into the site.

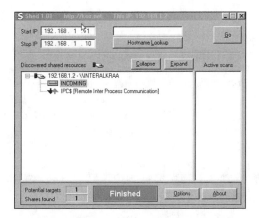

Figure 13.14   Shed shared resource scanner.

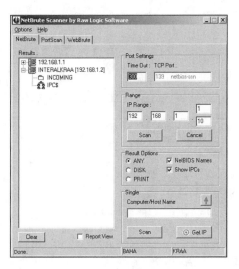

Figure 13.15   NetBrute shared resource scanner.

SpyWare Removal

Although virus scanners are a must-have for every computer, you might also want to install a spyware checking program on each computer. As has been mentioned, spyware uses your computer and connection to perform functions you have not explicitly allowed, such as streaming ads to your computer or sending information out from your computer. The gateway firewall of 192.168.1.1 in our example will not stop viruses or spyware outbound messages. Spyware uses common protocols that are allowed outbound to send information and collect the data, as we have previously discussed. To provide additional security, install a program such as Ad–aware (www.lavasoftusa.com/), shown in Figure 13.16, to check for spyware programs. Ad–aware scans memory, the registry, and hard drives for spyware components from a number of software products such as Alexa (through 5.0), Aureate (1.0, 2.0, and 3.0), Comet Cursor (through 3.0), Cydoor, Doubleclick, DSSAgent, EzUla, Expedioware, EverAd, Flyswat, Gator, Gratisware, HotBar, NewDotNet, OnFlow, TimeSink (through 5.0), Transponder, Web3000, and Webhancer. You can delete the suspicious programs as Ad–aware finds them.

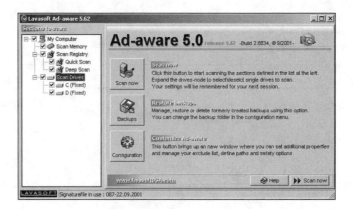

Figure 13.16   Spyware checking with Ad-aware.

Messaging Services

We have discussed the wide usage of instant messaging (IM) services such as ICQ, MSN Messenger, and others. Most of these services can work by default through a firewall, although you might have to change some configuration options. For example, in Yahoo! IM, you have to change the login preferences connection to No Network Detection. MSN Messenger can work using the WinRoute Proxy Server. You can enable proxy server by selecting Setting, Proxy for the default port 3128. The proxy server is used to access Web pages by a separate computer, so the site that is contacted is never contacted directly by the requesting machine. The proxy server makes all contact with the external site and protects the Internet computer from direct contact with the Web site. Some file transfer capabilities might be impacted when using a firewall. You have to enable some ports or set up port mapping to allow file transfers. It should be done on a case by case basis.

Secure Filter Rule Settings

In our sample network diagram in Figure 13.1, many filter rules should be set to enable access to and from the network securely. These filter settings are as follows:

1. Change the NAT security options in WinRoute by selecting Settings, Advanced, Security Options, as shown in Figure 13.17.

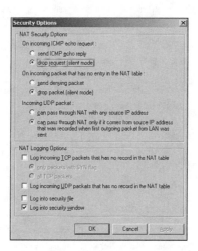

Figure 13.17 NAT security options.

2. Enable the rules shown in Table 13.1. The rules that restrict access to TCP 139, TCP 445, and UDP 445 are covered in other rules; however, you might want to enable blocking of these ports and logging to watch access on these ports because they are so critical to a Windows installation. The reason we log into the window is because it's unlikely you will watch your logs. Companies might monitor logs religiously, but most consumers do not have the time or inclination. You can watch activity in the window if you so choose. The reason we use drop instead of deny as the action is because a denied packet can send back denial information to the attacker, letting the attacker know that your system is alive and blocking certain ports. The last rule in our filter list, IP - Any - Any - Drop, is a catchall; it stops any traffic that is not specifically allowed by all previous rules. If you do not specifically allow something in the previous rules, the deny all rule will block all traffic. This might stop some functionality, but it will force you to specifically allow a function.

Table 13.1 **WinRoute Filter Rules**

Protocol	Source	Destination	ICMP Type	Action	Log
TCP	Any	Any, Port = 139		Drop	Log Window
TCP	Any	Any, Port = 445		Drop	Log Window
UDP	Any	Any, Port = 445		Drop	Log Window
UDP	Any, Port = 53	Any, Port > 1023		Permit	
TCP	Any	Host – IP ADDRESS, Port = 80		Permit	Log Window
ICMP	Any	Any	Echo Reply	Permit	Log Window
TCP	Any	Any, Port > 1023		Permit Established	
IP	Any	Any		Drop	Log Window

3. We disabled the proxy server by selecting Settings, Proxy Server and the mail server by selecting Settings, Main Server. Those servers were not necessary.

4. We disable remote administration by selecting Settings, Advanced, Remote Administration. It was not necessary. If you were to use the Web Administration option, ensure that you select the Require User Authentication option.

5. A password was added on the Admin account by selecting Settings, Accounts. Be sure you have a strong password that includes letters, numbers, and special characters.

Troubleshooting Potential Problems

Problems with even a basic network diagram can crop up in numerous places. The first thing to do when you have any kind of traffic routing problems is to check all connections. The simplest solution is sometimes making sure all hardware is plugged in and turned on. Check all the cables and make sure they are plugged in. Hardware can be a problem; if something is wrong with your cable modem, that will scrap your whole network. Your hub might have a bad port that will not route traffic. Ensure that all the hardware is functioning properly.

When you have determined that your hardware is functioning properly, your next step is to check your firewall rules. You can do this in several ways. One option is to turn on logging on all firewall rules and see what is happening to your traffic. You also can remove all the rules and then start adding one rule at a time to make sure that each is working properly. A third option is to allow all traffic through and ensure you are routing traffic and then start locking down each rule and determine where you break the network.

Windows 2000 and Windows XP come with built-in filtering capabilities. The operating system also can be a problem when it comes to filtering rules. If you enable some of the filtering capabilities in the OS and forget about them, your system could experience problems. If you are using other third-party firewalls on your internal systems, these can also cause a problem. You shouldn't run more than one firewall and antivirus scanner on each system. Software will most likely be the source of your problems.

The Ideal Firewall

This section would not be complete without at least a mention of one of the most secure operating system and firewall setups available to home users. Although WinRoute is an exceptional firewall running on Windows operating systems, some Unix-based alternatives are also available. OpenBSD is a free operating system that is available from www.openbsd.org. It is considered one of the most secure operating systems in existence. Using OpenBSD has a steep learning curve if you are only used to Windows systems. Plenty of help and documentation are available if you are serious about setting up an advanced and highly secure firewall system. Following is a quick list of what you will need:

- OpenBSD operating system (the latest version is 2.9)
- IPF and IPNAT software (comes with the operating system)
- Laptop with an Intel Pentium processor
- Two network cards
- Time and willingness to learn

A laptop makes a great firewall. It has its own built-in battery and its own monitor that you can use to see alerts from intrusion attempts. With OpenBSD installed on a laptop, you need two network cards to set up routing between your cable or DSL line and your internal home network. After your network cards are set up and you can ping computers both on the Internet and on your home network, you are ready to configure the IPF and IPNAT software. This software allows your home computers to share the Internet connection through IPNAT and sets up a secure firewall using IPF.

Computing with OpenBSD is perhaps more advanced than computing with Windows. We only recommend trying this setup if you are familiar with Unix operating systems or if you have the time and patience to learn. After you get things set up, you can rest assured that you have a secure firewall for your home network.

More detailed information on setting up OpenBSD firewalls can be found from www.bsdtoday.com and www.openbsd.org.

Traffic Analysis

After you have your network up and running, you can start performing functions. You must know what kind of traffic is running on your network. Perhaps your network is slow, or you are having problems getting out to the Internet. Traffic analysis is a tedious, complex process. Without going into excruciating detail and bits and bytes, you can do a few things to see what kind of traffic is flowing on your network (or not flowing, as the case might be).

All data travels in packets, as we have mentioned. Every message you send in e-mail or every Web page you browse breaks up the data into packets. Each packet carries some bit of information about the total message, such as the sender's IP address, the intended receiver's IP address, the number of packets in the message, and some data. Transmission Control Protocol/Internet Protocol (TCP/IP) is the backbone of the Internet.

Most packets are split into three parts:

- **Header**—The header contains instructions about the data carried by the packet, such as length of packet, synchronization (helps the packet match up to the network), packet number, protocol, destination address, and originating address.
- **Payload**—This is the data in the packet.
- **Trailer**—This contains information that tells the receiving device that it has reached the end of the packet.

You can use a protocol analyzer to see what is happening to your network and what is contained in each of these packets. These can be extremely complex programs that provide too much information even for seasoned administrators, although some basic bits of data can help you monitor your network. Your firewall can act as an analyzer by allowing you to see where traffic is going to and coming from. Companies use many expensive protocol analyzers, but you probably don't want to pay thousands of dollars. Analysis of traffic is probably beyond the scope of this book, but we'll touch on it to give you a taste of what traffic on the Internet looks like.

Vision

`http://www.foundstone.com`

Vision is a program that shows all running services, the ports they use, and the remote connections that they make, as shown in Figure 13.18. You would want to use a program like this for two main reasons. The first is to see what applications are actually running on your system, and the second is to map them to ports. If you want to know what port ICQ runs on, Vision can tell you. If you run ICQ and you are not making a connection to the ICQ server, maybe your firewall rules are too restrictive. You can tell what ports are being used by ICQ and check the log files of your firewall to see if you have blocked ICQ from going out to the Internet or blocked inbound ICQ traffic. Figure 13.18 shows that ICQ runs on ports 4445 and 4452, and an FTP connection (port 4426) is open to IP address 64.12.168.202.

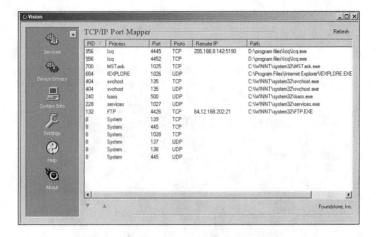

Figure 13.18   Vision port mapping output.

Windump

`http://netgroup-serv.polito.it/windump/`

Although the Vision output is readily understandable, it doesn't show the actual data that flows across the Internet when you perform a function that sends out or receives Internet traffic. Windump, which is a Windows port of the Unix program TCPDUMP, shows the actual bits and bytes of traffic flow. In the example shown in Figure 13.19, we see actual packets of data between the machines 2KSERV and kraa. This is how data travels, and this is a capture of that data. Other programs can decrypt the packets of data and make them readily available to the user.

Ethereal

`http://www.ethereal.com/`

Ethereal takes the packets of data that we saw in the Windump output and breaks them into an even more granular level. Ethereal also translates the data captured into readable information, as shown in Figure 13.20. Programs such as Windump and Ethereal capture or "sniff" data as it passes along the wire to which the PC is connected. In the top frame of the Ethereal output, we see packets of data and where they are coming from and going to. In the middle frame, we see a breakdown of the protocols being used, and in the bottom frame, we see a decryption of the actual packets of data into readable formats. If we had captured a basic e-mail session, we would have seen the user ID and user password. Because you are on a LAN with your neighbors, if you use unencrypted applications and transfer data unencrypted, anyone on the LAN can use such a network analyzer to capture all your traffic, which includes your data and your ID and passwords. DSL is not subject to this type of sniffing because it is essentially like a dial-up connection; you are not sharing a local area connection with anyone else.

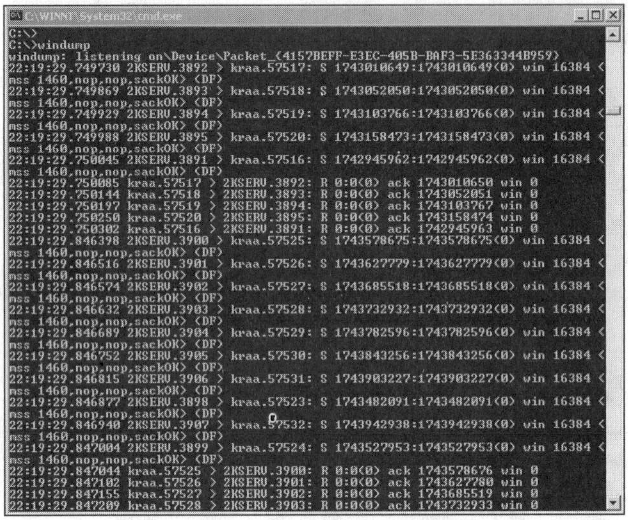

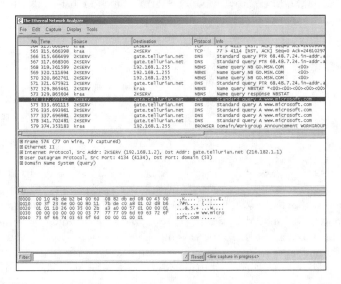

Figure 13.19   Windump output.

Figure 13.20   Output from Ethereal.

Why Test Network Security?

Every day, we see a news story of some hacker stealing credit card information, a new virus wreaking havoc in a matter of hours, or a company pilfering personal information and selling it to some marketing company. At one time you were just a spectator to hackers breaking into some company, but you have become a target. With your home network up and running, you need to protect yourself from the vandal hordes of cyberspace.

Like any large company that performs security testing of their own Internet sites, you must do the same. You might not have vast amounts of money to spend on consultants and expensive software, but the proliferation of the Internet provides the necessary tools and information that any consumer can use to protect himself. *Network penetration testing* is the process of imitating the steps a hacker would take to break into your site. You do the steps to find the weaknesses in your configurations before a real hacker does. When you have finished your network design, you can begin your testing to see how easily host systems can be compromised.

An attacker aiming at your system starts out with no knowledge of it. As we have been mentioning throughout the book, an attacker can gather that information about a system in several ways. The attacker begins by finding out as much information about your system as possible. He can launch attacks against vulnerable applications you might be running. These days, script kiddies are also lurking around and can find hacker software on the Internet—and no skill is involved in many cases. Script kiddies just launch attacks against a whole range of networks with an automated tool and hope for a hit. They can usually find a vulnerable system with the automated software.

Several sites are used by hackers and security specialists to upload and download new security and hacking tools. Some of the more popular ones include

- Security Focus (`http://www.securityfocus.com`)
- Packetstorm (`http://packetstormsecurity.org`)
- Technotronic (`http://www.technotronic.com`)
- NMRC (`http://www.nmrc.org`)
- Hackers.com (`http://www.hackers.com`)

Some basic attacks that are popular today include the following:

- Exploitation of vulnerabilities in vendor program applications, such as Outlook or Netscape
- Exploitation of Web vulnerabilities in the programming languages used by Web servers, such as PHP, CGI, and Java
- E-mail bombing, spamming, and relaying
- Exploitation of misconfigured services, such as FTP, Web, and mail

- Exploitation of named/BIND vulnerabilities
- Denial of Services (DoS) attacks
- Trojan horses, worms, and virus attacks
- Taking advantage of misconfiguration of firewalls and router filter rules
- Open connectivity to login prompts that are not necessary, using brute force attacks

The results of penetration testing of your own Internet connections present a list of possible holes in your network that need to be fixed before the attackers can find them. As you conduct tests of your site, you can check the log files and the logging capability to see if you have set them up correctly. You can determine how you will be alerted when you are attacked by the way you have configured your firewall and any intrusion detection systems you have installed. The results will help you determine what short-term fixes you must implement immediately and what you need to do over time to keep your site secure.

Caution

Testing your site security has many benefits, but the mistake that many people and companies make is that after they have completed that initial test of the environment and fixed any problems found, they do not do it again. Security is a continuous process, and a penetration test is only a snapshot in time of your security posture. A penetration test is aimed at the perimeter of your network. If your firewall is the only machine that can be attacked from the Internet and that is the only machine you secure, then you might be setting yourself up for future problems on your internal network. New vulnerabilities come out every day. A new vulnerability in the future might allow an attacker to get past your firewall and into your internal network. If all your internal systems have not been patched and secured, they will be easy targets for an attacker who makes it past the firewall. Checking your system for weaknesses or mis-configurations should be done once every two weeks for home users.

As has been discussed throughout the book, setting up firewalls and virus software is a must. To test your computer security stance, you can run port scanners to see which ports are open and close them or run vulnerability checking software to see whether any open ports you have are vulnerable to a known attack. There isn't a really great freeware vulnerability checker available. The best ones are commercial products that are very costly. Several products do some form of vulnerability checking for specific sets of checks, such as Web or Windows vulnerabilities. Several of these products that you might want to try include

- Nessus (http://www.nessus.org)

- SAINT (http://www.wwdsi.com/saint/)

- SARA (http://www-arc.com/sara/)

- Whisker (http://www.wiretrip.net)

- SATAN (http://www.fish.com/satan/)

- Cerberus (http://www.cerberus-infosec.co.uk/cis.shtml)

Making changes over time to your network or the firewall rules could affect the security of the network. A small change that you make could open up new weaknesses, and if you haven't retested, you could be vulnerable to attack. Also, because you are not a security expert, you probably don't keep up with the latest attacks and cannot devote your time to learning security and tracking attacks against your site. If you keep your network setup basic and your firewall rules simple with minimal changes, you will decrease the risk of allowing a new vulnerability in the network.

If you run your own Web sites and e-commerce applications, most penetration testing tools will not test application security. A hacker can attack you through the programming languages that your Web server uses and that a penetration testing tool will not find. You have to lock down the operating system and the applications you are running as well as implement firewall rules and perimeter security.

Security Testing Procedures

Security testing should follow a logical progression. The first thing to remember is that you can only conduct testing against your own site. If you start trying to break into other sites to test their security measures, you become a hacker and break the law, even if you mean no harm. Before you proceed, be sure you know exactly what your IP address is and only conduct your tests against that IP address.

The basic steps you need to take to conduct a security test of your environment include discovery, enumeration, vulnerability mapping, password cracking, and exploitation. We will go through the first four steps and leave a detailed discussion of exploitation to another book. Exploitation of vulnerabilities usually requires in-depth knowledge. Tools are available to tell you if a site is potentially vulnerable, but it is up to you to actively break into the site by taking advantage of that vulnerability. Our goal is to help you secure your site, not create a whole group of script kiddies who can just use tools without understanding what they do.

Discovery

The first step is discovering your site as a hacker would. This step is called *footprinting*. An attacker can find out the ISP that owns your IP address. He can find out the routes to your system and find out what the upstream routers are that protect you. An ISP typically owns and operates these. We went through how an attacker can find out information about you personally; he can find information about your system in the same way. The discovery phase is more relevant to attackers who are trying to find out as much information as possible about a company. For your home network, it's pretty simple to just ping your IP address and find out if you system is alive, or port scan the system to find services. When an attacker goes after a company such as Foundstone, he has to track down numerous network blocks and addresses, find subsidiaries that might have connections into the company, and spend a great deal of time and effort. This is not necessary for your home network in most cases.

If a hacker were to perform a full discovery of your IP address, he would identify domain names and associated networks of the target. In the case of large organizations, this can take hours. If the hacker is targeting a home user, finding the ISP takes a matter of minutes. A `whois` query is performed to identify your ISP's network (and therefore, you). After finding the ISP information, querying their DNS servers can glean more information. This isn't important in hacking home users unless that attacker wants to hack the ISP and then use that connectivity to hack the home user.

To begin discovery, the owner of the network is first discovered. Pretending we are the attacker, we see that our own IP address from our cable modem provider is 24.7.48.68. Taking this IP address and plugging it into Arin (`http://whois.arin.net/whois/index.html`), we discover the whole range of addresses that our ISP owns, as shown in Figure 13.21.

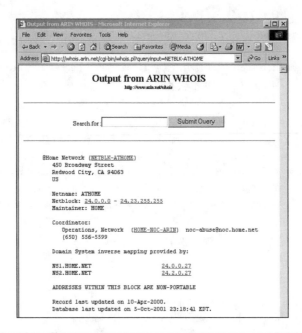

Figure 13.21   ARIN `whois` information.

From this information, we see that @Home Network owns the network block to which our IP address belongs. The first step is accomplished; the attacker has a block of addresses to target and discover if anyone is alive. The attacker knows we are on an @Home network.

Enumeration

After specific domain names, networks, and systems have been identified through discovery, an attacker then gains as much information as possible about each one. Your IP address is within the range that the ISP owns. When doing your own testing, you don't have to worry about other IP addresses.

The key difference between discovery and enumeration is the level of intrusiveness. Enumeration involves actively trying to obtain usernames, network share information, and application version information of running services (such as IIS 4.0, Apache 1.3.X, BIND 8.2.1). This information is obtainable by connecting to the various open ports and extracting data through mechanisms such as anonymous connections and banner grabbing. For example, you can glean an inordinate amount of information from an unsecured Windows NT/2000 system just by using a null session (also called an *anonymous* connection). You can perform this manually or with tools. In addition, usernames can be gleaned from many systems and used during the exploitation phase to circumvent security barriers if login prompts are available.

When you are ready to enumerate the service running, you have to identify each service running to map it back to vulnerability in the next section. When each live system is identified, the attacker then identifies each service running on the target system. A machine cannot be hacked unless it has a vulnerable service running. This scanning gathers operating system, service, and banner information. When each service is identified, the attacker can begin the exploitation.

To determine what ports you have open, we can use SuperScan as we have done before. A possible 65,535 TCP ports can be open. A port allows connection to the system. Different software runs on different ports. Software can also run on UDP ports, but these are not as dangerous as TCP open ports. We need to check *all* open ports. To test your system for open TCP ports, scan it with SuperScan, as shown in Figure 13.22 (use your IP address, not ours).

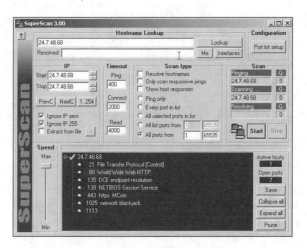

Figure 13.22 Open ports on IP address 24.7.48.68.

In Figure 13.22, we see several ports open: 21, 80, 135, 139, 443, 1025, and 1113. These ports are open with no firewall filters in place. Port 139 is dangerous in a Windows system. Much information can be retrieved from a Windows system using these ports, such as user accounts and system configuration information. An attacker will jump at the chance to pillage information from your system with these open ports. These ports allow a null session connection to be made to the system. All these open ports make the computer vulnerable from remote and local network attacks. If an attacker were to get to a machine within the local network, such as the Office PC in Figure 13.1, the attacker could compromise the system. As we discussed in Chapter 10, you can lock down the operating system better. An additional tool that is not built into the Windows operating system is the Microsoft Personal Security Advisor (http://www.microsoft.com/technet/mpsa). It can check your operating system settings for weaknesses, as shown in Figure 13.23.

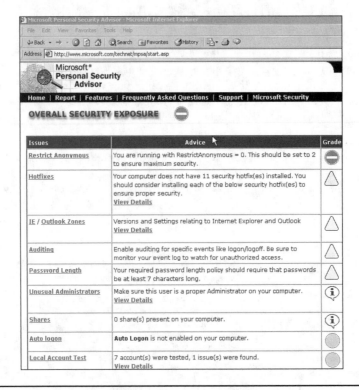

Figure 13.23   Microsoft Personal Security Advisor.

With SuperScan, we checked open TCP ports. We can check for open UDP ports with another product, such as AW Security Port Scanner (www.atelierweb.com), as shown in Figure 13.24. We see a number of open UDP ports that also need to be restricted.

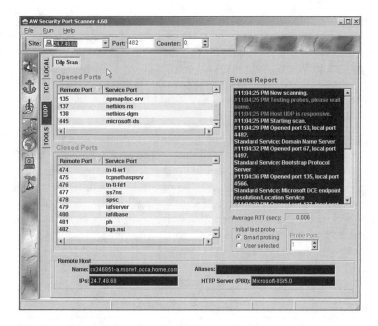

Figure 13.24   UDP port scan results.

When you see open ports on your system such as these, you have to look at the rules set in your firewall. Having too many open ports or extremely dangerous ports open can indicate that your filter rules are not correctly set. When we turn on the rules shown in Table 13.1, we see the results of another port scan in Figure 13.25.

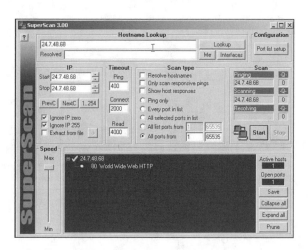

Figure 13.25   Port scan result with firewall rules enabled.

As we can see, the firewall rules we have implemented restrict access to the system and we see only one open port, 80 (Web). An attacker would see this port, and attacks would be restricted to the only open port available. Dropping ICMP packets will even hide your system from a typical port scan; if a system cannot be pinged (ping will tell you easily if the system is alive), the attacker would most likely not investigate an IP address, which has no response to ping. You would be invisible to most casual investigations by attackers.

If you do not want to run SuperScan or another port scanner against your Internet site, you can use a well-known site on the Internet to perform a port scan of your site. At Gibson Research Center's Shield Up site (`http://www.grc.com`), you can have Steve Gibsons' site port scan your site. Results of a port scan of our Internet connection, with firewall rules, are shown in Figure 13.26. By watching our firewall log output, we saw that only certain ports were tested. Be careful when using such sites; you want to check every port possible to see if anything is running, not just popular ports such as mail (25), Web (80) and FTP (21).

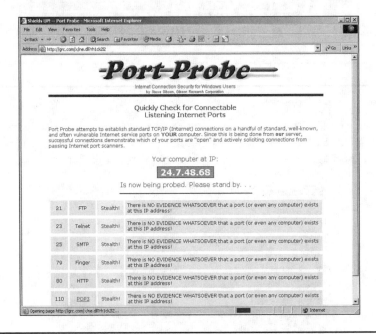

Figure 13.26   Gibson Research Center port probe.

Vulnerability Mapping

All the information in footprint analysis leads to specific targets with services running that might be vulnerable. If you were an attacker, you now have a detailed list of all devices that are alive and running services that are available. A smart attacker will look for specific vulnerabilities in the running services. The script kiddies will just launch vulnerability scanner programs against a range of IP addresses and hope for some results. With the sophistication of available tools, this shotgun approach will usually have some results. The attacker then launches attacks against the systems. You have to think the same way the attacker does. You must examine the open ports and vulnerabilities associated and lock down the ports that can be a problem.

The vulnerability mapping results in the following:

- Host name and IP address
- Services running on the system (that is, Microsoft IIS, MS SQL Server, FTP)
- Version of each service running
- Vulnerabilities associated with each service

In Figure 13.25, we saw that the Web port was open. Even with filter rules in place, as shown in Table 13.1, we can still test the security of the Web server because the Web port is open and traffic can be sent to the Web server. An attacker can use many Web security testing tools against your site when he sees a Web port open. One such program is Stealth HTTP Scanner (`www.nstalker.com`), shown in Figure 13.27. Running a security testing tool such as Stealth against your Web site alerts you to possible holes in your Web server.

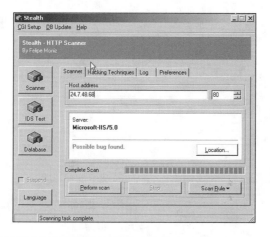

Figure 13.27   Web site security scan results.

Many home users run Web servers for various reasons. The problem that most people and companies face is that Web server security is not ingrained into the network design. The operating system has been the focus of security for so many years, and now we are seeing more application-level attacks. If the only port open on a network is 80, the attacker is forced to attack the Web application. A number of recent worms have specifically targeted Microsoft IIS Web server because, in many sites, that is the only source of attack.

Many programs in addition to Stealth can be used to test security. Microsoft has provided many of them on their Web site to assist with operating system and Web server security. Two such tools include the IIS Lockdown Tool (`http://www.microsoft.com/technet/security/tools/locktool.asp`) that allows you to configure an IIS 4.0 or 5.0 Web server securely, and URLScan (`http://www.microsoft.com/technet/security/urlscan.asp`) that only allows traffic that complies to a specified rule set. Further information such as IIS 4 and IIS 5 security checklists can be found on the Microsoft site at `www.microsoft.com/technet/security`.

It's easier than ever to learn how to hack and find programs that assist in compromising a system. There are those who write good programs that are used for hacking, and there are programs made for hacking. Some of the most popular sites for security resources include the following:

- **Packetstorm**—`http://packetstormsecurity.org`
- **Securityfocus**—`http://www.securityfocus.com`
- **Technotronic**—`http://www.technotronic.com`

Another program we can use that is free is LANguard (`www.gfisoftware.com`). This freeware program does a good job of performing simple checking against running services and open ports on the target system. Figure 13.28 shows the output of a LANguard scan against our system.

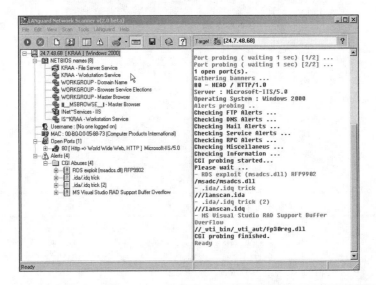

Figure 13.28   LANguard output of system security scan.

Because we are not hackers and don't need to be stealthy, we can use these types of programs even though they generate a log of file information, as shown in Figure 13.29. All the attacks against the firewall can be logged and reviewed.

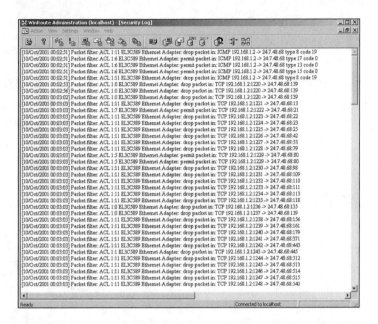

Figure 13.29   Log file output of LANguard security testing.

You can use numerous freeware and for-profit software programs to test your site security. Just perform a basic search for "network security," and any search engine will show you hundreds of sites.

Password Cracking

A key step you should take to test the security of your network is to see how strong your password is on all your servers. Password cracking is really aimed at Unix and Windows NT/2000/XP. We mentioned using the programs Glide and Cain in Chapter 6, "Understanding the Online Environment: Addresses, Domains, and Anonymity," to crack Windows 9x passwords. To test the security of your Windows NT/2000/XP password, one well-known tool you can use is called L0phtcrack (LC3) (www.atstake.com), shown in Figure 13.30.

In this password cracking output, we see that several passwords have been cracked (kraa = SECURITY, littlebilly = CHILDREN, www = INTERNET). We can see that two of the passwords are less than eight characters, and several passwords were not cracked. L0phtcrack can use a dictionary, the characters on the keyboard, or both to attempt to guess passwords.

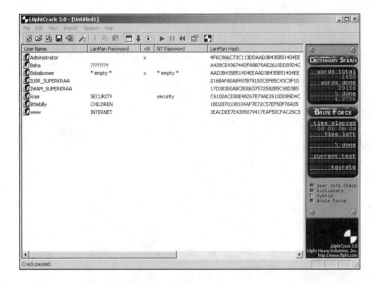

Figure 13.30   Password cracking.

In Windows NT/2000, the password is broken up into two sets of passwords, each seven characters long. Therefore, if you have a 10-character password, you in essence have two passwords—one of seven characters and the other of three characters. It is easy to crack a three character password. For example, if your password ended in the characters 123, L0phtcrack would easily guess this password. In Windows, a 7-character password is stronger than a 10-character password.

Weak passwords are the bane of just about every company and most user home systems. Brute force attacks (where the attacker just tries to guess usernames and passwords) are the most typical method of gaining entry to a system. If you can ensure that you have no weak passwords, you will eliminate half your system security weakness. A strong password uses special characters, numbers, and letters.

Exploitation

The exploitation phase begins after the target system's vulnerabilities are mapped. If you were an attacker, you would attempt to gain privileged access to a target system by exploiting the identified vulnerabilities. This might take the form of launching a password guessing attack using usernames collected during the enumeration phase or using exploit code targeted against the specific service running. Regardless of the method used, the goals of the test are user-level and privileged access. Because this is your own system, you just have to identify the vulnerabilities and patch them or enable rules to protect open ports rather than exploit the vulnerabilities. You are not a hacker, so don't start using this penetration methodology to attack your neighbors.

Security Checklist

Table 13.2 shows a basic checklist you can use to secure your home network system.

Table 13.2 **Security Checklist**

Action	Explanation
Use a virus scanner.	An easy way for you to become a victim, even if you have a strong perimeter network, good monitoring capabilities, and updated security patches, is to let a virus enter your network. A virus can use an application such as e-mail to get by your firewall and destroy the network from the inside.
Use a robust firewall.	A firewall that does not provide robust capabilities and allow you to network your entire home will be limiting and might even be vulnerable to certain attacks.
Restrict applications.	Don't run an application unless you are familiar with it. You have to be careful of what you download and execute on your home network.
Update the operating system and applications with patches.	Many security patches and updates to applications and operating systems are available. These should be applied religiously to ensure you are up-to-date.
Disable Java, JavaScript, and ActiveX.	These programs can be used for malicious purposes when you visit a Web site. Although too many valid reasons exist for using these programs to enhance a Web site, you should be cautious in allowing your browser to run them. You can disable these programs in each browser. In Internet Explorer, you can disable, enable, or prompt for action when encountering ActiveX and Java by selecting Tools, Internet Options, Security, Internet, Custom Level. In Netscape, you can change these options by selecting Edit, Preferences, Advanced.
Back up important data.	You should treat your data like a company would. Back up your files and keep them safe in case your system is compromised.
Test your security periodically.	Just because you ran a security test and checked your passwords once doesn't mean your system is secure. Testing your site by checking for open ports and vulnerable applications should be a continuous process.
Make a boot disk.	Have a bootable disk in case you have been compromised and need a clean boot of your system. A complete backup would be better; you can restore the entire system from a known safe backup if you get attacked. New in Windows 2000, you can create an emergency repair disk using the command NTBackup.

Table 13.2   **Continued**

Action	Explanation
Disable scripting in e-mail applications.	We have seen a number of viruses in the past year that use e-mail programs to execute code. Many e-mail applications have the ability to disable scripting and execution of programs from within the e-mail program. Check your e-mail program and see if this is possible.
Deny everything except what is explicitly allowed.	This rule means to deny everything unless you specifically allow access. Your first firewall rule is to deny all traffic. Then, open up traffic for specific functions you need the firewall to perform. If you don't need it, turn it off.

Summary

The home network is the next generation of home user activity. Now that a desktop or two is in just about every home, the home user is becoming more educated and sophisticated in the usage of networking technology. DSL, cable modems, and wireless connectivity are allowing faster connections that make sharing of one Internet connection in the household feasible. The days of struggling with a 28.8 or 56Kbps connection are slowly coming to a close.

Home networking technology is clearly necessary. You have to protect yourself and your entire environment; with great power comes great responsibility. You are now responsible for an entire network (which might only be two or three computers). Your always-on connectivity for your family means you have to have security procedures in place at all times.

Many personal firewalls are available on the market today that can protect your systems. A combination of different firewalls can help, but you want to keep your network design simple. The more complicated you make the system, the more problems can develop in the environment. Although many small personal firewalls might be sufficient to protect one computer, network technology does require some complex filtering rules. Think carefully about what you want to accomplish with a network and what your firewall should do for you.

A significant part of home network technology is setting up security measures to combat the hackers who will target your systems. You have to become knowledgeable in security testing and implementation procedures. You cannot rely on your ISP to help you because it won't. It's up to you to test your implementations before the bad guys do.

V

New Targets of Opportunity: Protecting Privacy Beyond the PC

14

Securing Your Privacy Using Other Digital Devices

In previous chapters, we have discussed technologies that focus on the Internet because therein lies the major source of threat to your personal privacy. However, as other technologies expand and grow that take advantage of the Internet and allow access to your personal data through other methods, you will be faced with new forms of attacks. Personal digital assistants, wireless technologies, and new protocols for sharing data have the potential to compromise your personal life the same as a hacker on the Internet can.

The use of digital devices over the past several years has grown tremendously. Businesspeople as well as students carry personal digital assistants (PDAs). People pulling out their PDAs at meetings to check schedules, make notes, or to beam (transmit) each other their contact information are common sights these days. Are PDAs secure? As we have stated earlier, the introduction of new technology also brings with it security and privacy risks. Devices such as PDAs are no exception. In this chapter, we take a look at several popular PDAs currently on the market. We examine their security risks and look at how to secure some of the devices.

The growth of wireless communications, in which data travels through the air as radio waves instead of through cables, has also been tremendous. Many schools and businesses now have wireless networks in place to help with the end user's connectivity and productivity. Wireless networking for the home user is also becoming more prevalent. Manufacturers are now producing and pricing wireless equipment so that it is attractive to the home user. As data travels through the air instead of through wires, additional risks and exposures to privacy and security are created. This chapter looks at wireless networks and devices and shows you some basic steps to take to keep your data secure and private.

PDAs

A PDA is a small, handheld computer that allows you to store and access data. Most PDAs work on either the Palm operating system, a Windows-based one, or on the RIM Blackberry device. Most PDAs allow you to do basic things such as store names, addresses, phone numbers, schedules, and appointments. The more sophisticated ones also run applications like word processors and spreadsheets. Some devices are even wireless, allowing remote access to things like e-mail, stock quotes, and news alerts.

Handhelds carry a wealth of sensitive data. Typically, a user's entire electronic phone book—complete with names, addresses, phone numbers, and e-mails—can be found on the device. The user's calendar—along with notes, comments, and to-do lists—are also all on that handheld. Medical doctors and others also use these devices to store sensitive information about other individuals. Doctors frequently store a patient's medical information as well as medical reference material on PDAs. Many users have come to completely rely on these pocket-sized devices. Those same small devices are relatively easy to lose and steal. How does one keep these devices from falling into the wrong hands? Even if they do fall into the wrong hands, what can be done to minimize the impact upon the user's privacy?

The greatest risk probably comes from the loss of the device. Any device the size of a handheld can easily fall out of a pocket or bag. If basic password protection is not set up on the device, all of its data is then disclosed to the individual who has taken possession of the device. It is more likely that your data will be stolen because your PDA was stolen. It is less likely that your data will be stolen as it travels through the air. The easy solution is to simply encrypt the data. As we have discussed in previous chapters, software encryption for personal computers has been around for years. But Pretty Good Privacy (PGP) is not available for the handheld device. Weaker encryption schemes that are used on PDAs can be decrypted.

Palm OS

The popularity of the family of PDAs produced by Palm Computing has led the Palm OS to be a widely accepted PDA platform. Many manufacturers (Palm Pilot, Sony, and Handspring Visor) have adopted the Palm OS for their systems. Although this might be changing as the Pocket PC (discussed later) rises in popularity, the Palm OS is still widely seen in the corporate environment. Palm also offers wireless connectivity built into its Palm VII and other models. Each of the other manufacturers just mentioned also provides the same wireless connectivity with the purchase of additional components and add-ons.

The Palm OS system, as shipped from the factory, is relatively insecure when compared to other computing devices such as the PC. It does provide basic security features with its Security Application. The Security Application allows users to mark records as "private." Records marked as such are invisible to users who do not have the appropriate password. The other feature of the Security Application is that it allows the user to "lock" the PDA so that only a user with knowledge of the password can unlock it. Although these security features might appear to be adequate, a few shortcomings still exist.

Another developing weakness of the Palm OS is its susceptibility to viruses. Like the Windows operating systems are vulnerable to various types of viruses, the Palm OS, with the ability of developers to write applications, allows hackers to write viruses for the Palm platform. Antiviruses such as Computer Associates, F-Secure, and Symantec provide virus protection for the Palm OS.

The most important weakness is that data is not encrypted on the device. We have stressed the importance of encrypting data on a hard drive. It is even more important to encrypt the data on a handheld because of the handheld's physical dimensions and the ease with which it can be misplaced or stolen. Although it is possible to encrypt data on a handheld, most people do not. Marking records or data as "private" only sets an internal flag in the device about whether to display the record. When the flag is set to "private," the application won't display it without the appropriate password. However, this assumes that the application will actually pay attention to these flags. Rouge applications installed by an attacker or unauthorized individual need not adhere to these markings.

Another shortcoming of the Palm OS is that the user must explicitly lock the device. Operating systems such as Unix and Windows 2000 require login passwords. With the Palm OS, the user must explicitly lock the device so that a password is required before it can be turned on. If you don't lock the device, someone could turn it on without using a password.

Certicom's movianCrypt

Certicom's movianCrypt (`http://www.certicom.com`) product extends the basic functionality provided by the Palm OS. It locks and encrypts all of the data that is on the device to help achieve stronger security. movianCrypt functions by placing itself between Palm's data storage area and the applications that access it. Data is encrypted as it is stored by movianCrypt. Data is decrypted only as it is accessed by applications that need it. A login system protects data if the device is lost or stolen. movianCrypt encrypts all data in user databases on the device. This includes the Address Book, Memo Pad, and third-party applications.

movianCrypt functions as shown in Figure 14.1. It inserts itself between Palm applications and user database. All data is encrypted before it is stored, and data is decrypted only when it is needed. You can relate this to SSL encryption that we discussed in previous chapters. All data is encrypted between the database and the application.

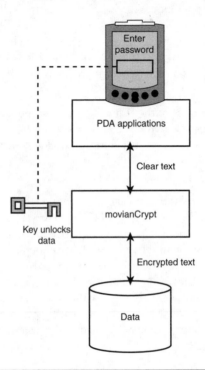

Figure 14.1   movianCrypt security measure.

Encryption settings are also configurable on an application basis. For example, it's unnecessary to encrypt large databases such as maps and restaurant listings. movianCrypt allows you to avoid unnecessary encryption of these large databases that are not sensitive.

F-Secure's FileCrypto

F-Secure produces a similar product, FileCrypto (http://www.fsecure.com), shown in Figure 14.2. It, too, provides for encryption of data that is stored on the device. It automatically encrypts the data of all record-based applications when the device is shut off. Data is decrypted when the files are opened.

The difference between FileCrypto and movianCrypt and the many products that are available via shareware is the fact that these encrypt data on the device and don't just require passwords to turn the device on.

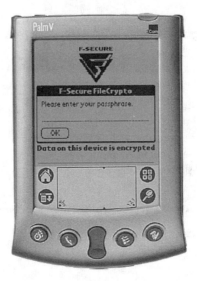

Figure 14.2   F-Secure's FileCrypto can provide additional security for Palm devices.

Pocket PC/Windows CE

As the popularity of PDAs increases, many corporate professionals are turning to the Windows CE-based Pocket PC. Manufacturers such as Casio, Hewlett Packard, and Compaq are now producing these devices. These devices are more than a calendar and address book. Like the Palm OS, the Windows CE PDA operating system allows developers to write applications and hardware vendors to make devices that use this operating system. These devices are application compatible—they run versions of Microsoft Office that are similar in features and functionality to their desktop counterparts.

Pocket PCs also offer a power-on password capability that locks the device until you enter your chosen password. Turning this feature on requires some navigation. Go to the Settings command, click the Personal tab, and select Password. Enter a password and check Require Password When Device Is Turned On.

Windows CE handheld PDAs have a system-level password application that can be accessed via the Control Panel. The application requires a user to enter a password when turning on the device. To advance past the first screen—which can include owner contact information to help with the return of lost devices—the proper password must be entered. Without the password, the only way a thief can use a protected Windows CE device is to remove the primary and backup batteries. But if this happens, all the data on the device is also erased!

To set the password on a Windows CE device, select Start, Settings, Control Panel, Password or Start, Settings, Password depending on your PDA and version of software. You are then asked to enter a password twice to confirm it. From there, you can click on a box to enable power-on password protection. After the password is set up, you can change or reset it at any time by re-entering the existing password.

In terms of third-party software, F-Secure also produces a version of FileCrypto for the PocketPC. Microsoft recommends a variety of third-party products in the white paper "Pocket PC Security," available at its Web site (`http://www.microsoft.com/MOBILE/enterprise/papers/security.asp`). Several security products available for the Pocket PC include those shown in Table 14.1.

Table 14.1   **Microsoft Recommended Third-Party Products for Pocket PC Security**

Company	Product	Web Site
DATA ENCRYPTION		
Applian Technologies	PocketLock	www.applian.com
Application Development Studio	PassKey	www.appstudio.com
SoftWinter	seNTry 2020	www.softwinter.com
Softwarebüro Müller	The Safe	www.sbm.nu
V-One	SmartPass for CE	www.v-one.com
Paragon Software	CryptoGrapher for Windows CE	www.penreader.com
ANTIVIRUS		
McAfee	VirusScan for Pocket PC	www.mcafee.com
Computer Associates	InoculateIT for CE	www.cai.com/innoculateit.htm
ACCESS RIGHTS AND AUTHENTICATION		
Applied Biometrics	Pocket PCPINprint from Applied Biometrics	www.appliedbiometrics.net
CIC/A2000	Sign-On for Pocket PC	www.a2000d.com
		www.audata.co.uk

Viruses, Trojan Horses, and Malware

Ask consumers about virus protection for their computers and most will know that they should be running some form of virus protection. Even if they aren't running a virus checker, they know about antivirus products from Symantec or McAfee. But ask

PDA users about virus protection for their handheld devices and most will not even know of the existence of handheld-based viruses, let alone what software is available for them.

Malware is programs or files developed for the purpose of doing harm. They can include computer viruses, worms, and Trojan horses that can attack computers and PDAs. Currently, the main Palm viruses are Liberties A and B and Phage (discussed in the next sections)—and the likelihood of hackers writing new strains of malicious code is always there. Fortunately, Central Command (`http://www.centralcommand.com`) produces AntiVirus eXpert for Palm and AntiVirus eXpert for Windows CE. Trend Micro (`http://www.trendmicro.com`) also produces PC-cillin for Wireless 2.0, which prevents a known virus from entry through possible points such as beaming, syncing, e-mailing, and downloading. F-Secure (`http://www.fsecure.com`) also produces antivirus solutions for Palm OS, Pocket PC, and Symbian OS. Other virus vendors are expanding their capabilities to detect and protect devices other than computers from viruses.

A virus or Trojan horse (malicious code that tricks a computer user into thinking that he is using a legitimate piece of software) can be installed to a PDA device in a number of ways:

- The most common way for a virus or Trojan horse to be introduced onto a PDA is during a hotsync operation. You synchronize data between your PDA and desktop through the hotsync process, which was first used with Palm Pilots. During this operation, a virus or Trojan horse is simply downloaded from the PC.

- Using the device's infrared (IR) capabilities, a malicious program could potentially communicate with another infected device. The devices could essentially communicate with each other without the victim noticing. The data is then beamed to the attacker's device.

- When the PDA is connected to a network, it might be possible to connect to it from another device on the same network. Malicious code can then be used to open ports, allowing for remote access.

- Users who can receive e-mail can also receive attachments that contain Trojan horses. This is analogous to receiving and activating a virus by executing an e-mail attachment.

In a sense, PDAs have become a victim of their own popularity. As their use increases, so does the likelihood of individuals writing malware and methods and devices from which to receive that malware. The security of Palm OS can be compared to older versions of operating systems. They are vulnerable to attacks simply because they do not possess the requisite security features. Much like the way Windows 95 did not require a login, when a PDA does not require a login, any person who picks up the device can turn it on and peruse its contents.

Now that Palm has seen its first signs of Trojan horses and viruses, it will not be long before more destructive viruses start infecting this computing platform. The only real defense is that the virus-scanning software that we currently have can perform multiple tasks by scanning any programs that might be transferred from the PC to the PDA. The same rules regarding desktop antivirus software apply here also: This will work only if the PC that is transferring the files has updated and working virus-scanning software that specifically checks for PDA software. As these devices continue to become more widely used, some speculate that these types of problems might continue to escalate. With increasing usage of PDAs in the business community, IT personnel should be aware of how rapidly these viruses can be passed among the organization and take the proper precautions to minimize the risks.

Although viruses, worms, and Trojan horses can infect many devices, the spread of such malware would not be nearly as fast as a PC-based virus. By their design, PDAs are not meant to be always connected to a network, constantly hotsyncing, beaming, or receiving e-mail (although we do not know what the future will hold for such devices).

The number of PDA users is much lower than the number of PC users. However, if PDA-to-PDA communication ever becomes more prevalent, this situation might change and we might see an increase in the amount of PDA-based viruses.

Even with these documented viruses, the antivirus software vendors downplay the threat of viruses in the handheld environment. The threat level is considered to be low at this point in time. However, it is always a good idea to be aware of the existence of these threats.

The following sections discuss the two most common Palm viruses.

Liberty Crack

One of the first pieces of malicious software aimed at handheld devices was Liberty Crack. In reality, it was actually a Trojan horse. The program he is using looks like the real thing, but it is also doing something else in the background. In this specific scenario, a malicious program that was designed to break the software piracy prevention features of the Liberty Game Boy emulator had the potential to delete all of the programs stored on the PDA. Liberty Crack spread after it was posted to a Palm developer's chat room. Instead of paying a small fee for the actual Liberty software, users would download Liberty Crack, thinking that they were getting a Game Boy emulator. They would then pass it along to other users via the IR port. Then, anyone who had executed this program wiped out the contents of their PDAs. Luckily, data could be restored to the infected device by simply resyncing the device to the desktop. Liberty Crack is assumed to be one of the first known viruses/malware designed to attack the PDA.

Phage

The first actual virus, as opposed to a Trojan horse, to hit the Palm OS was Phage. Phage infects programs that have been added to Palm PDAs either through syncing with your PC or loading files by disc. When infected, files become corrupted, causing them to lock up and be inoperable. The only way to rectify the problem is to delete the program. A dark gray box appearing on Palm and your program terminating might be an indication that you have been Phaged. This virus has no real means of replicating itself, so the risk of spreading it to other Palm users is pretty low. Since the Phage virus has been released, F-Secure and other vendors have released patches to detect this malicious code.

Mobile Phones

The expanded functionality of all mobile devices has also seemed to make them susceptible to all forms of attacks. Smart phones, which are cell phones that have some of the functionality of PDAs, can also be vulnerable to viruses. In June of 2000, Timofonica, a variant of the LoveLetter virus, spammed thousands of mobile phone owners in Spain. The virus routed mails through an Internet-to-cellular gateway. Virus hunters found themselves confronted with what might have been the first attempt to infect mobile phones. Somebody calling himself Timofonica—*timo* is Spanish for prank—sent a Short Messaging Service (SMS) message to a small number of subscribers to Spanish giant Telefonica's mobile phone network telling them that the company was ripping them off. Timofonica was relatively benign: Mobile phones can't run executable programs yet, so the virus couldn't replicate itself. However, many took this as a sign that mobile phones too, can be become targets of attack. Up to this point, mobile phones had been virus free.

Timofonica was a Visual Basic (.vbs) worm that used the Windows scripting host to infect the PC. For each address that Timofonica found in Microsoft Outlook, the worm then generated a random e-mail address for cellular phone users of MoviStar.net, a Spanish wireless e-mail provider. If the user clicked on the attached .vbs file, it became infected, and the worm then destroyed the user's CMOS settings the next time the machine rebooted. The majority of text in the e-mail message was in Spanish; however, the second part of the text was various links to Web sites that listed Spain's telecommunication policies. Although administrators are not sure where the worm originated, it is assumed that it was created in protest against the phone monopoly in Spain.

In Japan, an attack on NTT DoCoMo's I-mode phone system came in the form of a relationship quiz that was coded for this specific phone system. Users would receive this e-mail quiz on their phone. The questions were worded and designed so that most people would be dialing "110" on their phones when they responded to the quiz. "110" is equivalent to 911 here in the United States. Japanese police report that there were hundreds of these calls. Although no data or financial loss resulted, Japanese emergency services could have slowed down or been obstructed.

Today's cell phones might be reasonably safe, but tomorrow's smarter phones will be more vulnerable. As is the case with most new technologies, additional features and functionalities usually imply additional security vulnerabilities, not to mention bugs. In the not-too-distant future, your smart mobile phone might be used for everything from being an electronic wallet to functioning as a digital ID. In all likelihood, the more powerful and versatile a phone becomes, the less secure it will be. And the sheer number of people who will be using mobile devices means that the potential to create havoc, for thrills or financial gain, will be enormous.

The other area of concern is ensuring that transactions made over mobile phones cannot be intercepted. Much like we discussed regarding clear text transmission of data in computer cables, the ability to sniff this kind of traffic is also of concern. This issue must be addressed if the general public is going to accept wire mobile commerce. Although some phones require PIN codes and built-in protocols for activation, full-fledged wireless commerce requires a higher level of certainty. Use of strong encryption to guarantee confidentiality and digital signatures to ensure authenticity will be required. This form of encryption relies on a public key and a private key for a transaction to be completed. The private key identifies the consumer wanting to buy an item from an Internet retailer, whereas the public key holds the identity of a business like Amazon.com. The private key can also be used to create and verify a digital signature. Some analysts say it will be several years before transactions can be made in a trusted and relatively secure manner. Until then, most people aren't too concerned about Timofonica-type viruses that don't directly affect the mobile phone.

Disposable Phones

Disposable cell phones are becoming their own small industry. These types of phones are developed outside the U.S. and are slowing making their way into the U.S. market. From a privacy perspective, these types of phones can increase anonymity somewhat when making calls, but for this very reason, U.S. authorities are struggling to determine how law enforcement would be affected.

U.S. Attorney General John Ashcroft and FBI Director Robert Mueller cite disposable phones as potential roadblocks in the war on terrorism. Disposable cell phones come preloaded with a finite number of calling minutes, like a calling card. These slimmed down versions of phones are relatively inexpensive, such as $10–$30. They allow anyone to quickly and perhaps anonymously make phones calls, and the FBI relates this ability to terrorists using the technology for evil purposes.

Law enforcement's ability to eavesdrop on any phone conversation even without a wiretap warrant signed by a judge is being debated in the wake of the terrorist attacks on the U.S. The anonymity of the phones is still in question, and how they will affect or protect privacy is yet to be determined.

Bluetooth

Bluetooth is the solution to short-range wireless requirements. This low-cost radio solution provides links between mobile computers, mobile phones, other portable handheld devices, and connectivity to the Internet. The Bluetooth Special Interest Group (SIG) is a group of companies that include 3Com, Agere, Ericsson, IBM, Intel, Microsoft, Motorola, Nokia, Toshiba, and more than 2,000 others who strive to drive development of the technology and make marketable products using Bluetooth technology and specifications.

Intel, Nokia, Ericcson, Toshiba, and IBM founded Bluetooth in May 1998. It started out as a way to create a wireless technology that would enable data transfer between mobile devices such as cell phones, portable digital assistants (PDAs), and cars. Bluetooth uses common, unlicensed frequencies of radio spectrum and operates in the 2.4GHz range, providing short-range (10cm to 10m) communication between devices.

Bluetooth might be added to different technologies such as these:

- Mobile phones
- Digital cordless phones
- Notebook and desktop PCs
- Handheld PCs
- Digital still cameras
- Output equipment
- Automotive
- Home networking

Bluetooth has not cornered the wireless market, and it won't with the rise in popularity of the 802.11 wireless standard. This standard has become the de facto standard based on business usage and increased home usage of wireless networks. Bluetooth's place is now in the small mobile devices that need to share information over small distances.

Large companies such as Microsoft are incorporating Bluetooth in products that do not need to compete with the wireless standard of 802.11. Although the 802.11 standard allows connections of wireless devices over greater distances, Bluetooth was designed from the ground up for low-power wireless devices and for mobile devices that do not need the wireless technologies available for PCs and Internet connections. Microsoft has built-in support for Bluetooth in the Pocket PC. Siemens and Socket Communications are both creating Bluetooth products around the software built into Windows CE. TDK Systems announced a Bluetooth-enabled device for the Palm m500 series of handhelds that will allow users to access e-mail or the Internet. ICE International in Norway has made a device based on Bluetooth technology that can automatically turn off other people's cell phones. Sony and Ericsson have a joint venture to build wireless connectivity to an earpiece and the cell phone based on Bluetooth technology. Although Bluetooth has not taken over the wireless world, it has found a niche.

One company in the UK, Netario, has already launched a Bluetooth network in Manchester. This public-access Bluetooth wireless network offers users 400Kbps wireless Internet access. Netario plans for more such sites in the UK. Bluetooth can operate at a maximum throughput of 723 kilobits per second (Kbps), and various companies are planning rollouts in such places as airports, hotels, and conference centers. All the Internet connection sites in airports currently use wired networks for access.

In the U.S., the terrorist attacks on September 11, 2001, have prompted the Federal Communications Commission to consider requiring police and telecommunications carriers to be capable of locating cell phone callers inside large structures. Bluetooth technology can possibly be used for this function. This capability to locate people via cell phones worries many privacy advocates because it can be used for legitimate law enforcement purposes but also for malicious purposes.

The question of the security of Bluetooth communications has already been raised. The 802.11b wireless standard has already been proven vulnerable to hackers. Bluetooth security is not as well understood and has not faced serious hacker challenges yet. As Bluetooth becomes more popular and made available to the general public, we can expect successful hacker attacks to occur. No technology so far has been proven invulnerable to attack.

Research In Motion's Blackberry

Research In Motion's (RIM's) Blackberry is another device that has gained tremendous acceptance in the past few years. Blackberry is a wireless e-mail solution for mobile individuals. When in a coverage area, it provides a constant link between the desktop and the Blackberry handheld. The system, which consists of server/desktop software and the physical device, can monitor the user's Inbox for new mail. It can work with such e-mail software as Microsoft Outlook, Lotus Notes, and Eudora, as well as several other products. When new mail is received, the message is relayed to the device. The relaying is performed over the Internet and a wireless network. The system also works in reverse. The device can be used to create a message and have it forwarded to the Internet. A copy of that message is then placed in the user's desktop e-mail Outbox.

Users have various features on their handheld devices to protect their data. Every user should set an individual password on the device. This password is analogous to the login password—it prevents someone who happens to pick up the device from reading the contents of the Blackberry. The device usually contains e-mails and contact information that is almost always private. The password helps ensure that only the owner can view its contents. Selecting Options, Security can set this password. On that screen, you can set the password and the security timeout, which is the amount of time before the device locks itself and requires the user to enter the appropriate password so that the device can be used again. The device does reject some weak passwords. For example, passwords that are comprised of identical characters or those that are in a sequence (1234) are rejected. While the device is locked, it cannot be accessed without the password—you can't even access the device through its synchronization facility on the serial port. The user has 10 chances to log in. If the password is entered wrong 10 times, all e-mail and settings on the device are deleted and no information is available. The rightful owner would have to reinitialize the device and connect to his e-mail system through a setup process to gain access to e-mail and other functions such as a calendar and contact lists.

The Blackberry has also taken into account the security of data while it travels through the air. Data sent between the device, desktop, or corporate e-mail server is sent encrypted. A shared key exists between the desktop and the device. The key is first exchanged when the device is connected to the desktop via the serial connection. That is assurance of an authenticated connection. Information transferred between the desktop and device is not decrypted. This allows the data to remain private even when it passes through the service provider's network. Although Blackberry uses this security, it is not an open standard and has not been subject to thorough analysis like open applications and protocols are. Users are cautioned in the use of any proprietary device and technology.

As Blackberry devices increase functionality such as Internet browsing access and voice capabilities, the potential for hacker attacks and virus attacks also increase. One thing to keep in mind at this point is that, as with all systems, security is only as strong as the weakest link. In this case, it is more likely that the desktop is vulnerable rather than the Blackberry device. If the operating system is not configured or is improperly configured, e-mail and everything else on it is susceptible to disclosure and attack, including all the information the Blackberry synchronizes to the desktop.

Backup and Other Options

One basic configuration step to take on your PDA is to enter your contact information in the Owner fields of the device. On a Palm, you can find these fields under Preferences, and on a Pocket PC, you can find them under the Personal tab. Making this kind of information available makes it much easier to return the device if it should become lost. If the person who finds it doesn't even have contact information for the device, the chances of it being returned to its rightful owner are close to zero. Having your name and phone number appear on the screen should be enough information for someone to reach you. Alternatively, if your PDA is stored in a case, you might even tape your business card to the case. That way, even if the person doesn't know how to turn the device on, he will at least see some kind of contact information.

Pocket PC has a feature that allows you to display owner information when the device is turned on, even if you have activated password protection. Although Palm owner information is stored in Preferences, if you turn on the password lock-out feature, a Palm device displays owner information along with a password request when activated.

Every time you synchronize your PDA, the data is backed up to your PC. However, several applications offer supplemental backup to protect your data even more securely.

BackUpBuddy, BackupPro, and JackBack are all software backup tools for backing up applications and data on a Palm-based device. But only BackUpBuddy works with a standard Palm. The other two require a Palm-based device with removable Flash memory, such as a Handspring Visor with Flash Module, a Sony Clie with Memory Stick, or a TRGPro Palm device with CompactFlash.

Like the Visor, TRGPro, and Clie, all Pocket PCs come with a removable memory slot—either CompactFlash or, in the case of Casio, Multimedia Cards. You can use this expandability to add memory and features and to back up your PDA when you're not near a PC.

The Wireless Threat

The use of wireless technology has become increasingly popular due to its flexibility and recent affordability over traditional methods to access hard-wired LANs. Analysts from all the leading research organizations agree that the market potential of wireless networking is huge and will continue to grow as the technology matures. The popularity of wireless networking is quickly spreading. Both individuals and organizations are finding benefits in their ease of installation and ease of use. As seen in multiple times throughout this book, technological advancement does not come without a price. This technology has security and privacy risks like all the others, however. Wireless networking has flaws from a security and privacy perspective that place your data at risk. Unfortunately, due to the ease of deploying these wireless networks and the relative newness of the technology, many IT professionals and network engineers do not realize the risks associated with operating a wireless network.

Wireless is not a perfect technology, and security is part of the imperfection. Hackers have attacked the method of communications and found weaknesses that can be used to capture data, access corporate networks, and wreak havoc without having to be physically on a network. Another threat comes from the government. After the terrorist attacks in the U.S. in September 2001, the FBI has been given more leeway to use DCS1000 (Carnivore) to monitor e-mail and Internet communications. Prior to the attack, the Cellular Telecommunications and Internet Association (CTIA) warned in a letter to the Federal Communications Commission that the FBI might start using DCS1000. This surveillance now includes wireless technology, which is even easier to spy on.

The Benefits of Wireless Technology

Today's information systems, which include m-commerce (mobile commerce), are being exposed to a demand for increased flexibility and mobility. The introduction of wireless technologies will aid users of information systems in many ways:

- **They allow for increased efficiency and roaming ability**—Users are no longer tied to specific locations. They can move about the home or facility while always maintaining their network connection.

- **It is easier to share and transfer information**—Users no longer have to return to their desks or computers to send a file or e-mail. They can take immediate action because of network connectivity. This should lead to an increase in productivity.

- **In some cases, building a network using wireless technology is cost-effective**—If a temporary network is needed, a wireless network would be easy to set up and take down. This reduces infrastructure costs. Wireless technologies allow for the easy implementation of LANs without the associated expense of physically installing and running wires throughout a home or facility. This is especially important if the area is difficult to reach or not physically suited for wiring. These savings are also available to homeowners who are unwilling to retrofit their homes with network cabling. With an access point installed in a strategic location, a user can have Internet access from practically every room.

Wireless networks offer great freedom and flexibility to both home and business users. Traditionally, adding users or computers to a network required wiring to be pulled throughout a building and installed by a hired professional. Now, with its relatively low cost and ease of installation, practically any home or small office can have a wireless LAN. With this technology, data travels through the air, giving the user the ability to connect in locations that were once deemed inconvenient. (However, this newly found freedom is not without its costs, as discussed in the section "Disadvantages of Wireless.")

How Does Wireless Work?

A wireless LAN is a collection of two or more devices connected via open air for the purpose of sharing data. A wireless network can be put together in many ways. 802.11 wireless local area networks (WLANs) typically communicate between stations and access points (APs) using radio waves such that line-of-sight communication (an unobstructed path) between the access point and the wireless station is not required. The most widely accepted and common standard for wireless networking is the IEEE 802.11b protocol. Other standards such as Bluetooth also exist, but 802.11b is enjoying the most commercial success.

New technology that is being developed for wireless access uses the new 802.11a wireless standard. 802.11a is faster than 802.11b, which has data-transfer rates of 54Mbps. Intel, along with Proxim and Enterasys Networks, plans to release products based on 802.11a. Companies such as Cisco Systems and Agere Systems (3Com and Symbol) dominate the market with 802.11b technology, but that should change over the next year as 802.11a technology makes it to the market place. The two wireless standards are not compatible, but they both have security flaws in common.

Access Points

An access point (AP) is a piece of hardware that acts as a bridge between the wireless "network cloud" and the wired network. A wireless network that is installed with access points allows the user to roam about while maintaining his connectivity (see Figure 14.3). When a user travels outside of the AP's range, connectivity to the network is lost. Organizations frequently put up multiple APs so that people can roam about the premises and maintain connectivity. Figure 14.3 shows just one way an access point is used in a wireless LAN.

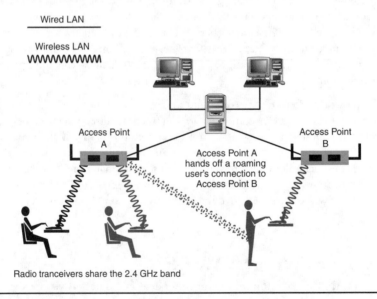

Figure 14.3   Example of a wireless LAN using access points.

In terms of hardware, wireless LAN cards are installed in client workstations, laptops, or PDAs that allow the clients to communicate through the access point to the wired network and its resources.

Ad Hoc Network

A wirelessnetwork composed only of stations without access points can be considered an ad hoc network (see Figure 14.4). This type of network can be used anywhere. Few requirements are necessary for this setup to work. An ad hoc network could potentially be the most dangerous of all wireless networks. Because this type of network is going to be set up on-the-fly when two people want to share data, it is more probable that less consideration is going to be placed on security. The user might set it up "just to get the job done" and forget, for example, that he is broadcasting traffic with his wireless network card.

Figure 14.4   An ad hoc wireless network.

Basic Security Features

Obviously, one of the most important considerations when using a wireless LAN is security. An identifier called the Service Set ID (SSID), which is simply a network "name" (alphanumeric characters), is sometimes considered secret. The SSID can typically be found by "sniffing" the network. Sniffing for wireless traffic is just like sniffing on a wired network, but the medium is different. Whereas with traditional network sniffing you are catching data on a wire, in wireless sniffing, you are catching data that is going through the air as radio waves.

Note that no physical network exists to control or protect. With wireless networks, it is much more difficult to control and protect the air that your data is flowing through. The very nature of this type of network lends little to securing a network.

The next level of security is typically Wired Equivalent Privacy (WEP), which is essentially encryption. The principal goal of WEP is to defend the confidentiality of data from eavesdroppers. Another objective is to guard against modification of data. WEP depends on a secret key shared between the communicating parties (mobile station and AP) to protect the data portion of a transmitted frame in each direction. With WEP, although the data portion of the packet might be encrypted, the SSID network name and the MAC addresses are broadcast in the clear.

Disadvantages of Wireless

One of the most obvious problems with wireless is the fact that you cannot easily control where the waves carrying your data will stop. The waves do not simply stop when they reach a wall or the boundary of a business; rather, they keep traveling into parking lots and other businesses in an expanding circle from the broadcast point. It's impossible to limit the wireless network to specific rooms in a building. With this type of network, you gain the ability to have connectivity in more places, but you lose the ability to tightly control where those waves can go.

This introduces the risk of unintended parties eavesdropping on network traffic from parking areas, streets, alleys, or any other place where a laptop can be set up to intercept the signals. Although 802.11b standards specify that the range of a broadcast is only 150–300 feet, in reality, the signal travels much farther. Beyond these distances, signals are weakened to the point that normal wireless cards cannot detect them with their small antennas. However, high-gain antennas can be used to amplify, detect, and analyze these weak signals far beyond the 300-foot range (vertically as well as horizontally). This is a serious consideration in multistory apartment buildings and offices. Even though your access point is set up in your 3rd floor apartment, its waves can potentially reach an apartment that is much higher.

Gaining access to a wireless network can be as simple as sitting in the parking lot of the intended target and monitoring the person's wireless communications. It is easy to sit in a parked car or van outside a company's main entrance and simply sniff for wireless traffic. In another frightening scenario, the person standing in your lobby might be checking his PDA for his next appointment, or he could be accessing your most sensitive data with his wireless connectivity network card. As mentioned, the normal range limit of 802.11b is approximately 300 feet, but signals can be both transmitted and intercepted from several miles away by using directional antennas. Although interception from several miles away takes much more sophisticated equipment, it is not out of the realm of possibility.

At this point, encryption is the easy fix. Who cares if someone is able to sniff your encrypted data? After all, it is all encrypted. However, serious concerns over security have been expressed about 802.11b and WEP. Vulnerabilities have been discovered that have cast doubt on the security of WLANS, even with using WEP. However, these concerns don't seem to be stopping the sales or popularity of 802.11b; the number of wireless devices is expected to grow at a high rate.

In the corporate realm, even if proper precautions are taken to ensure a secure wireless network environment, the risk of a user purchasing his own wireless AP or base station and installing it on the network without the IT staff knowing of its existence is still a concern. These are commonly referred to as rogue APs. Rogue APs lend themselves nicely to being installed by the individual user. Wireless devices are small and simple to install. A user can easily plug an AP into a network hub and set it beside his desk.

How Your Security and Privacy Are at Risk

The hardware to monitor wireless communications is readily available and inexpensive. As we have mentioned previously, high gain and directional antennas can be purchased to increase one's ability to capture and analyze traffic. When wireless standards emerge and the technology becomes more widespread, wireless hacking has the potential to become as prevalent as it is on wired networks today.

One of the biggest threats to corporate intranets is attack through people's PCs at home. The price on this kind of hardware has dropped to levels where it is being found in home networking scenarios. We have discussed the issue of securing home PCs and personal firewalls. All of those points can be applied in the scenario of wireless networks. Here, home users with wireless networks might be opening up their home network—and possibly their connection to their employer—to unauthorized users. Think of it as another access point that needs to be protected. Most of today's home wireless networking products are weak on the security side. Most only require the equivalent of an SSID. After the SSID is installed, the network is up and running. Most home users are not aware of the security risks that they might be imposing on their company's intranet.

What Kinds of Attacks Are Out There?

With wireless signals clearly not limited by walls or legal boundaries, wireless networks lend themselves to a host of attack possibilities and risks. These can include any or all of the topics discussed next.

Insertion Attacks

This type of attack involves unauthorized laptops or other devices being positioned in the wireless cloud to gain access to an existing network. Laptops or PDAs can be configured to attempt access to networks simply by installing wireless network cards and setting up near the victim's network. If password authentication is not enabled on the network, any user can simply join the network and use its resources.

Another type of insertion attack is the deployment of rogue access points. The rogue APs can entice other wireless clients (the ones that are supposed to be on the wireless network) to join to it rather than the legitimate one. From that point, the AP can monitor traffic going to and from the unsuspecting client. In addition, access points that are not authorized by the network administrators in corporate environments have the potential to be improperly configured and vulnerable to outside attack. For example, the rogue AP might not be set up to only send encrypted data. This presents the risk of the interception of login IDs and passwords for future attacks on the network. The risk can then be magnified if the rogue APs are deployed behind the corporate firewall.

Denial of Service

The 2.4GHz frequency range, in which 802.11b operates, is shared with other wireless devices such as cordless telephones, baby monitors, and Bluetooth-based devices. All of these devices can degrade and interrupt the wireless signals. It is also possible that an attacker can flood the frequency with artificial noise and disrupt the network's normal operation.

Client-to-Client Attacks

Just because a machine is on a wireless network does not make it immune to attack from machines that are on the wired segment. The same security principles discussed earlier in this book (port filtering, turning off unnecessary services, and so on) apply to machines here as well. Whether a machine is wired or wireless should not come into play when you are configuring and securing the hosts. Machines that are vulnerable when they are connected via a wire will still be vulnerable if they are wireless.

Brute Force Password Attacks

Even when password authentication is implemented on wireless network access points, unauthorized access is still possible through the use of brute force dictionary attacks. Password cracking applications can test passwords in an attempt to break in to a network access point.

Wired Equivalent Privacy Weaknesses

Wired Equivalent Privacy (WEP), the built-in security mechanism of 802.11b, has some known flaws in the encryption algorithms used to secure its transmissions. The details about these flaws can be found at the following locations:

- Security of the WEP algorithm (`http://www.isaac.cs.berkeley.edu/isaac/wep-faq.html`)
- Using the Fluhrer, Mantin, and Shamir attack to break WEP (`http://www.cs.rice.edu/~astubble/wep/wep_attack.html`)

The flaws described in the papers referenced show the following:

- Statistical analysis can be performed as a passive attack to decrypt traffic.
- Based on known plain text, new traffic can be entered from unauthorized wireless clients.
- After capturing data and traffic, a dictionary attack can be launched such that there is real-time automated decryption of all traffic.

Their analysis also demonstrated that these attacks were conducted with common, off-the-shelf equipment. The interesting thing to note also is that the attacks applied equally well to both 40-bit as well as 128-bit versions of WEP. Even though using WEP carries with it some vulnerabilities, using WEP is better than nothing at all. At the very least, WEP stops the casual sniffer.

Misconfiguration

Just as earlier versions of the Unix operating systems were insecure out of the box, many wireless networking hardware components also come insecure out of the box. Although security features are available on the product, in many cases, the default settings for them are frequently turned off to allow the network to be up and running as soon as possible. The last thing the manufacturer wants is criticism that its product is hard to install. By turning off security controls, installation is that much easier. Users then frequently leave the equipment alone, unaware that existing security issues must be addressed.

Sniffing, Interception, and Monitoring

Much in the same way that an attacker can sniff network traffic on a wire, an attacker can also passively intercept wireless network traffic. Then, through packet analysis, he might be able to determine login IDs and passwords and collect other sensitive data using wireless packet sniffers. The ease with which intruders can penetrate a wireless network is now being made easier with the release of several software applications that allow intruders to passively collect data for real-time or later analysis. This kind of analysis can compromise the network.

Examples of wireless sniffing software include Airopeek, AirSnort, NetStumbler, and WEPCrack. AirSnort is an application that utilizes known WEP flaws to extract the WEP key and allows for unauthorized network access. NetStumbler is a wireless sniffer that logs an extensive amount of information about any wireless network it happens to encounter. NetStumbler is able to grab information such as MAC address of the access point, network name, SSID, manufacturer, channel in use, signal strength, and whether WEP is enabled. An intruder wanting to attack a target wireless network can make use of all of this information.

Another new and interesting phenomenon is *war driving*, also known as *drive-by hacking*. This is when the hacker drives around with portable laptop equipment with wireless sniffing hardware and software. The hacker can then discover various wireless network clouds as they drive around town. More often than not, at least in the early days of WLAN technology, a hacker would come across unencrypted and unprotected networks. Hackers have been using portable wireless devices with great success to find insecure wireless APs.

How Can You Protect Yourself?

Despite the risks and vulnerabilities that are associated with wireless networking, certain circumstances do demand their use. As with everything we do, we can take steps to minimize the risks and make hacking into a WLAN a more difficult exercise for potential intruders.

If the use of wireless technology is in the corporate environment, be sure it include it in all of the overall network security policy, procedures, and best practices. Wireless networks need to be treated under the same rules as wired networks. Extra care should be taken in implementing wireless networks because, as we saw, they are even more vulnerable than wired ones.

Be sure to include your wireless networks in the next security vulnerability assessment you perform on your wired networks. A vulnerability assessment can help to identify any weak points that intruders could exploit. This includes poorly configured components, weak or missing passwords, unauthorized access points, and the absence of strong encryption protocols.

Treat your wireless network like the Internet; in other words, remember that it is untrusted. Some situations might even warrant a firewall in place between your wireless network and your wired network. That way, a successful break-in on the wireless network can't easily penetrate to your entire network.

Changing Default Settings

Just like we need to change default settings and passwords on PCs, we also need to change them on APs. The SSID on many APs does not get changed. Because the SSID is broadcast to provide clients a list of networks to be accessed, that information is also available to let potential intruders identify the network they want to attack.

If the SSID is set to the default manufacturer setting, it is frequently a sign that the additional configuration settings (such as passwords) are at their defaults as well. When an administrator has taken steps to change one default setting, he has probably changed others as well.

Good security policy is to disable SSID broadcasting entirely. If a network listing is a requirement for network users, then changing the SSID to something other than the default that does not identify the company or location is a must. Be sure to change all other default settings as well to reduce the risk of a successful attack.

Simply using encryption keys and SSIDs is not the optimal solution. If someone were to leave a company on bad terms but keep his wireless network card, he could drive up to the outside of the building and capture all of the network data that he wants to. One possible solution to this is the use of MAC address filters. APs would only allow connectivity for MAC addresses that are in its filter. In many cases, this is not particularly useful because of the administrative headaches associated with it. If you are administering a network of many wireless cards that turn over from one employee to another, keeping track of ownership and MAC addresses could be daunting task. This is, in most cases, the limit of today's wireless infrastructure.

Strong passwords should also be used on your access points. You should perform periodic checks to see if the password is being stored on your clients. You can do this by performing keyword searches for your password. Some passwords are stored in cleartext in the Windows Registry and are vulnerable to discovery if a client is compromised. Take steps to correct this if possible. Every client needs to know the password to communicate through an access point, so this gives you many points for a potential loss of security. Change the password on your access points regularly. Another tip is not to use the same password on all devices. If a password is compromised on one machine and you use different passwords across all machines, the attacker would not be able to log into all your machines with the same password. Having different passwords requires users to log on again as they move around, and it provides an extra layer of security.

Some access points and clients use Simple Network Management Protocol (SNMP) agents that are shipped from the vendor with weak or widely known passwords for both read and write access. If you are running SNMP agents, be sure to use strong passwords in place of the defaults.

Enabling WEP

One line of defense against hackers is encryption. As mentioned previously, WEP is disabled by default on many wireless network devices. Despite WEP's known flaws, enabling it is better protection than nothing at all. It adds an additional barrier against the casual war driver or curious sniffer. A program that is available for cracking WEP keys is Airsnort (http://airsnort.sourceforge.net/). This Linux-based program passively monitors wireless transmission and computes the encryption key when enough packets have been captured.

Using VPNs

Virtual Private Networks (VPNs) should be used to augment what 802.11b provides in the way of encryption and authentication. VPNs normally make use of encryption, user authentication protocols, and tunneling to allow secure end-to-end communications across the Internet (third-party network). In this case, your wireless network would be considered the third-party network. IP Security (IPSec) protocols are often used in conjunction with VPNs to provide secure communications. IPSec is attractive because it can encrypt or authenticate traffic at the IP layer, thus making it transparent to the end users. (That is, no training is necessary, and it doesn't affect other applications.)

Access Point Placement

The physical placement of the AP is also important. Consideration should be given to placing the equipment toward the center of the building or house to minimize the strength of wireless signals emanating to the outside world. However, this depends on the physical structure and layout of each building or house in question. Avoid placing equipment near windows, which allow the signal to travel farther and possibly reach unintended receivers. As with your normal wired home or office network, test the security of your wireless network. Use one of the packet sniffing products and walk around your house as if you were a stranger and see if you can break into your wireless network, get a connection, or capture traffic. Some access points allow you to control access based on the MAC address of the NIC.

Proactive Network Sniffing

Just as you would perform periodic vulnerability assessments against your network to gauge its security, you might also want to deploy network sniffers on a regular basis for the purpose of monitoring your wireless network. This action help to identify rogue APs that might be providing unauthorized access to the network. As an additional precaution, it is also good practice to take measurements external to a facility in areas that an intruder might be likely to attempt an attack. It is helpful to know just how far wireless network signals are traveling outside the intended boundaries of a building.

You can use several products to sniff wireless traffic, including Netstumbler (`http://www.netstumbler.com/`), Airopeek (`http://www.wildpackets.com`) and IBM Wireless Security Auditor (`http://www.research.ibm.com/gsal/wsa/`). Netstumbler and Airopeek are Windows utilities for 802.11b wireless LAN discovery, and WSA is a research prototype of an 802.11 wireless LAN security auditor, running on Linux on an iPAQ PDA.

Sample Wireless Products

Table 14.2 lists wireless products.

Table 14.2 **Wireless Products**

Access Point/ Gateway	Wire Ports WAN	Wire Ports LAN	Wire Ports Other	Encryption Level
2Wire HomePortal 100W 877-349-3304 www.2wire.com	1	1, 10Base-T	USB, phone-line jack	64-bit
3Com Home Wireless Gateway 888-638-3266 www.3com.com	1	3, 10/100	None	40-bit

Table 14.2 **Continued**

Access Point/ Gateway	Wire Ports WAN	Wire Ports LAN	Wire Ports Other	Encryption Level
Agere Systems Orinoco RG-1000 Gateway 866-674-6626 www.orinocowireless.com	11	1, 10Base-T1	Phone-line jack for built-in modem	64- or 128-bit
Buffalo Technology WLAR-L11-L AirStation 800-508-1110 www.buffalotech.com	1	4, 10/100	None	40-bit
D-Link DI-713 949-790-5290 www.dlink.com	1	3, 10/100	Serial	40-bit
Farallon NetLine Wireless Broadband Gateway 800-613-4954 www.farallon.com	1	1, 10/100	None	64- or 128-bit
Linksys BEFW11S4 EtherFast Wireless AP 800-546-5797 www.linksys.com	1	4, 10/100	10/100 uplink4	40-, 64-, or 128-bit
MaxGate UGate-3300 800-284-8985 www.maxgate.net	1	1, 10/100	Parallel	None
Netgear Phoneline 10X PE102 and RT3145 800-638-4327 www.netgear.com	None	1, 10/100	Phone-line jack	None
SOHOware NetBlaster II Hub 800-621-1118 www.sohoware.com	None	1, 10/100	None	40-bit
Xircom Wireless Ethernet Access Point 800-438-4526 www.xircom.com	None	1, 10/100	None	40-bit

Summary

PDAs and wireless devices have certainly made lives more convenient. But as we have frequently seen in this book, with the benefits come risks to security and privacy. Those small Palm and handheld devices are easy to misplace and are susceptible to being stolen. Encryption is a must. Users should be encrypting sensitive data on any computer that is connected to the Internet, as well as handhelds, smart phones, and anything else that is not physically nailed down in the office. Encryption is one good way to keep the secrets and private information from walking out the door.

Wireless networking is an appealing technology. It is important, however, to note that we need to treat the potential of intrusion and data theft from wireless networks as seriously as we would a wired network. Many of the same precautions and security measures used in the wired world are also applicable in a wireless environment. Outside of the transportation medium (air versus copper), there is no real difference. The deployment of firewalls, VPNs, encryption, and hardware security, as well as the development of comprehensive security policies and regular network monitoring, are all part of an effective wireless security program. As more applications, such as purchasing and corporate communications, are pushed to wireless devices, maintaining privacy, message integrity, identity, and trust will become paramount. Wireless technology for home users is still a growing field. Because home wireless technology is still relatively new, some of its components are still immature in terms of security. The user of home wireless networking technology should be extra vigilant in watching and maintaining his security.

VI

Fighting Back: What to Do if Your Privacy Is Compromised

15
Parental Controls

We have seen how easy it is for a hacker, a company, or a government to invade your privacy. You can take many steps to protect your information and your computer. What about protecting others in your household? If you are running a home network or even just have one machine that everyone shares, you really need to be concerned about who is using the Internet. If others in your house can compromise your information by modifying your computer and protection methods, you might as well have no protections in place. Your kids can be particularly dangerous to your home connectivity through inadvertent changes they make or threats to themselves by how they use the Internet.

Kids use the Internet for various reasons, including doing homework, e-mailing friends, chatting with friends and teachers, and playing games. With all this Internet activity, you should know by now that a danger to children exists. Their Internet usage is valuable to marketing companies, they can be targets of hackers, and more importantly, they can be targets of cyber stalkers. The Internet has brought forth new challenges for parents in protecting their children.

In many cases, children know more about computer usage than their parents. How are you going to protect them when they probably understand Internet surfing better than you do? You do not know everything about drugs and alcohol, but you know that your children need protection from them. The same holds true for the online environment.

Although the benefits of being online are numerous, all the features we described in protecting your privacy and being anonymous can be used for evil purposes. If someone in a chat room is trying to lure a child into meeting him, the anonymous mechanisms we discussed can be used to hide the stalker's identity and make it hard to track him down. Online access can be used in many inappropriate ways when it comes to children. You must understand that different levels of protection might be needed to protect your child's Internet access.

We have discussed all the threats you face in the online world. Your kids face the same threats plus another—you! Yes, you, too, can become a threat to your children's privacy. A fine line exists between protecting their access and invading their privacy. How much privacy you think your children need is completely subjective. We will not attempt to tell you how much control over them you should have. The security measures we will talk about are subjective. The final decisions are yours.

The following are what you should hope to accomplish as a parent when it comes to the online security of your children:

- Understand how to prevent access to inappropriate materials.
- Define online guidelines for your kids to follow.
- Know who your kids are communicating with online.
- Know how your kids are using the Internet.
- Understand what kind of parental controls are available to you.
- Know how and when to let your kids use the Internet at home.
- Monitor online usage.
- Educate children in the dangers of various tools available in the online world.

Benefits to Children

The reasons for your children using the Internet and being online are pretty obvious. To keep up with the world, both in everyday events and in education, the online community offers a wealth of information. One of the greatest benefits of the online world is not having to buy a whole bookcase of encyclopedias that your kids will never read! Just about anything your children want to know is somewhere on the Internet.

Many schools have incorporated Internet activity into their teaching curriculum and require students to do research using the Internet. Access is not just from your home anymore, either; many libraries and schools provide free access. The use of online tools such as Web designing and research have fostered a creative culture in which children can educate themselves.

The ability to communicate with people around the world whom you do not know is also a great benefit. The days of searching for a pen pal in another country are over. It's easy for children to find a pen pal online who has the same interests as they do by surfing the same Web sites or chatting in the same AOL chat room. The ability to share information has made it practical to use online services and resources.

Taking away Internet access because of the potential dangers is not the solution to all the threats you and your children face in the online world. Denying Internet access would be the same as denying them use of the post office, newspapers, television, radio, and just about every other form of communication you can think of. Education is a driving force behind children using the Internet, and your responsibility is to make sure they use it safely.

Threats to Children

As we have already discussed, the dangers that children face in their online activities are much the same as what you face. Both legal and illegal threats can compromise their personal information and even cause their computers to be hacked. The security software and measures needed to protect computer and home networks should be applied to any computer that your children use. The problem you face in protecting children is how they use technologies such as chat and e-mail, as well as why they are targets of attack. The technologies that are available to children have opened them up to new threats that they have never been faced with in the past.

E-mail

Kids face e-mail threats through viruses, worms, Trojan horses, and spam on a constant basis. Because they are children, these threats can be more powerful. Imagine if your child's e-mail address went onto an adult spam list. Your child would start receiving all sorts of inappropriate e-mails. What if your child's e-mail account got a virus and the virus detection software didn't catch it? Would your child know that the computer was infected when it started acting strange? Even if the virus detection software caught it, would your child know that he should delete or quarantine the e-mail?

E-mail has evolved into the de-facto form of communication on the Internet. Your kids might have multiple e-mail addresses you don't even know about. Free e-mail from sites such as LokMail, Yahoo!, Hotmail, and Eudora is easy to add to the AOL e-mail account you set up for them. Anyone could be communicating with your kids via e-mail without your even knowing it. Receiving spam e-mail is a way of life on the Internet; it could be harmless such as junk about a discount on purchasing toys, or it could be dangerous such as pornographic material. It's hard to get off spam e-mail lists.

As a communications vehicle, e-mail is private and anything could be exchanged with someone, such as pictures that you do not know about. Strangers could be e-mailing your children and you wouldn't know about it. Such e-mails could be links to Web sites that a stranger or even a marketing company wants them to visit, or they could be more nefarious such as setting up a meeting with some stranger.

Your kids probably wouldn't look into the security measures many popular e-mail programs have, such as the ability to block some spam or deny e-mail from certain addresses. Encryption of e-mail is probably something that your kids would never consider either. Your filter and security mechanisms need constant attention, and this is something most children will not know about or be concerned about.

You can take many steps to protect your children from e-mail threats:

- Ensure that you have virus scanner software running. A virus scanner ensures that your system is protected from viruses that can enter your system through e-mail, file downloads, or Web browsing. Educate your kids on what it does and how to use it when an alert pops up.

- Be sure your kids know not to click anything in e-mail. This includes an attachment that hasn't been virus scanned, and especially anything from someone they don't know.

- If your kids are young, monitor what e-mails they are sending and receiving.

- Try to limit their access to e-mail accounts you know about. Also, have them use e-mail only when you can monitor them.

- Remove their e-mail accounts from spam lists as soon as you detect spam mail in their Inboxes.

- Apply filtering rules to block spam e-mail as much as possible.

- Disable functionality in mail that allows scripts to run or HTML to be used in e-mail.

Chat

Chat rooms can be an entertaining place for children. They can talk to people with their same interests and hobbies and still not have to go anywhere to meet them. However, chat rooms have gotten a bad reputation of being a place for cyber stalkers and child molesters because of the very reason they have become popular. It's easy for someone of evil intent to be in a chat room and gain the confidence of a young person, eventually trying to convince the child to meet in person.

Chat rooms are public places, and anyone can be anonymous in them. The person your children might be chatting with could have fabricated his entire life—you can't really validate who he says he is. Gaining the confidence of children is easy. The same warning you give your children about not talking to someone on the street doesn't really apply to the online world. Everyone is a stranger and caution should be used, especially when it comes to children. Strangers can easily convince children to give away personal information such as their real full names and where they live. Because they are behind a computer and not in person meeting a stranger, kids might feel more secure in talking about their life and giving away personal data.

Following are some rules you should institute with chat room usage:

- *Never* **let your child meet someone in person without your full knowledge and consent**—Chaperone the meeting in a public place.
- **Allow your child to use only chat rooms that are moderated for language and content.**
- **Educate your child on the dangers of giving out personal information.**
- **Educate your children on the potential dangers**—These include kidnapping if they agree to meet someone or give out personal information about themselves. This can be scary for the child, but it's better to discuss it than have it happen.
- **Constantly remind your children of the dangers of the online world**—Repetition is needed to educate children. The National Center for Missing and Exploited Children has reported that one in five Internet users under 17 received an online sexual solicitation or approach during the past year. Also, 1 in 33 received an aggressive sexual solicitation for offline meetings.

Newsgroups

Newsgroups, forums, and message boards are the new pinup boards on the Internet. People can post anything from messages to software programs in these venues. Thousands of newsgroups, forums, and message boards on all sorts of topics are available. These are the same as Web sites in a way; if someone has an interest, a place on the Internet exists for it to reside. Most groups are not aimed at children. The odds of your child finding a "good" group site versus a "bad" group site are pretty small. Groups are often used to share pirated and pornographic material. Software tools make it easy to scan newsgroups for whatever interests you, and rarely will kids find a newsgroup that they should be viewing.

Newsgroups, forums, and message boards are interactive. You can read and post messages there, and so could a child. Your child could easily post a message with personal information or even a picture that anyone could view. This information can be dispersed beyond the limited number of people that are in chat rooms.

You can take the following steps to protect your kids from newsgroups:

- Use blocking software to restrict access to newsgroups with questionable material.
- Do not install software to read newsgroups. Newsgroups are usually unfiltered, and just about any type of material can be downloaded, from pirated software to pornographic material.

- Block ports that are used by newsgroup access.
- Monitor what Web sites, forums, and message boards your children use.
- Educate your children on the dangers of reading and posting messages to news-groups.

Web Surfing

Web surfing probably poses the largest threat to children. Content is so varied that it's hard to monitor what children are doing online; even the blocking software cannot keep up with the questionable material. Every bit of information you or a child would want to know is available.

As we have discussed, Web sites collect information about you through obvious methods such as online questions, surveys, and registrations and through not so obvious methods such as Web bugs and cookies. This information about you is valuable, and information about the habits and preferences of children is also worthy of collection. It's easy for you to miss what information your child is entering on a registration form or what information is collected with spyware, Web bugs, and cookies.

Another major threat that you are faced with that has sprung up in the past year or two is the easy ability for anyone to set up a personal Web site. Most e-mail accounts you set up allow you to set up a personal Web page free. The process is so simple that you don't need Web design skills; sites provide wizards and walk-throughs to set up the site within minutes. The danger of setting up a Web site is that your kids can put up anything they want, from pictures of themselves to home phone numbers and addresses.

Be sure your kids don't post personal information, photos, or anything else that could identify them. Also, be sure that nothing on the site could get your child into trouble at school or with the law, or might be harmful or offensive to other people. Kids frequently want to post pictures of themselves for their friends to see, but sexual deviants could just as easily view their pictures and information.

Web browsing is probably the hardest thing to protect, but some steps you can take include the following:

- Monitor what your kids put up on their personal Web page.
- Use blocking software to filter dangerous Web sites.
- Use antivirus software to check all downloaded files.
- Disable or filter scripting languages such as Java or ActiveX. Java and ActiveX can allow malicious code to be run on your computer when you surf a Web site. This code could harm your computer or capture information about your computer.

- Disable or erase cookies with built-in Web browser features or third-party software.

- Educate your child on the dangers of Web surfing, giving away personal information through Web sites, and downloading questionable software.

Instant Messaging

Instant messaging (IM) is fast becoming as ingrained in Internet usage as e-mail. (You can find more about IM in Chapter 12, "Securing Your Standalone PC: Viruses, Chat, and Encryption.") Many sites, including AOL, Yahoo!, and ICQ, provide IM. Cell phones and other mobile devices are even getting IM capability. Like chat rooms and newsgroups, you can interact with others in small groups or on a one-on-one basis. The same threats posed by chat rooms are prevalent in IM contact. Someone can find your child's IM name, send messages, and begin a dialog to gain your child's confidence. IM contact does not have the monitoring capability of chat room or newsgroups. This form of communication can be controlled only through your vigilance and third-party blocking software.

You can take several steps to restrict IM access:

- Remove IM software from your computer.
- Check on your child when he is online to see what programs he is using.
- Use blocking software to restrict IM software.
- Use firewall filter rules to block the common ports used by IM software if it uses a port other that 80 (http).

Privacy Loss

Being online in your home provides some comfort and security to children. They aren't encountering the people they are chatting with or e-mailing, so they aren't easily scared by the things that strangers say to them or ask them. This level of comfort can be detrimental to their privacy. Every bit of technology used has the potential to disclose information about the user. Chatting with someone might also let the user disclose personal information that should not be given to a stranger. By now, most people and children are educated enough to know that they should not talk to strangers or give out personal information over the phone to just anyone who calls. This same type of education needs to happen in the online world. We have discussed all the technological methods of disclosing information. Education of what to say on the Internet is up to the parent. It's also important to warn children not to give out information because not only can it hurt them, but it can also hurt anyone else they talk about, such as friends and family.

Not only do you have to worry about your kids giving away information about you and your family in your home, but you also have to worry about public access your kids might have to the Internet. The information that kids might view in Web browsers can be cached, and passwords they store can be saved to the computer in a public space. In public places such as libraries or cyber cafes, you have no way of monitoring what your child does on the Internet.

Through the use of technology and Web sites that children surf, companies collect information for marketing purposes. More dangerous reasons could also be for luring a child into being kidnapped or other equally dangerous activities. This information can be collected in numerous ways, such as registering for contests, filling out forms in exchange for prizes, or downloading a game. All these methods lead to a loss of privacy.

Online Fighting

Online fighting might seem absurd, but it happens. Fighting could occur in a chat room, message board, or newsgroup. People can get into verbal wars that spill over into the real world. Children can be exposed to these verbal duels that can get vicious. If a child gets involved directly in fighting with someone, it could be even worse. Because you are just writing, subtle hints as to the turn the conversation is taking are sometimes not available, and you can easily get into a dispute with someone. Disputes can lead to cyber stalking and hacking attacks against your system.

The best thing you can tell your child about online fighting is not to get involved. The same way you don't want your kids fighting at school, you don't want them fighting online. Children will face more dangers online than they will face in a school fight. Education is your only real defense against your child fighting online unless you want to read everything they write online. They have to know that nothing they read or people they deal with online require anger or verbal abuse.

Breaking Laws

With all the powerful tools available to kids, it can be easy for them to break the law knowingly or unknowingly. They can be the ones starting the fights or putting out a virus or worm that causes damage to other systems. Many of the news stories we read in the popular press these days seem to involve teenagers. The case involved a person going by the name Mafiaboy who launched denial of service attacks against major Web sites such as Yahoo! This person was recently sentenced to jail time for his attacks, and he is only a teenager.

Internet crime is being taken seriously these days with laws in many countries being passed to prosecute anyone, including minors, for hacking. Kids can post harassing or threatening e-mails and newsgroup messages the same as an adult. Just because children are minors doesn't mean they're protected. Making threats against people is being taken more seriously. If your child sends a threatening e-mail to the president of the United States, that e-mail will be investigated.

Posting inappropriate messages can lead to problems for you and your child. It could be something as simple as insulting a schoolmate to something as damaging as slandering a public figure, such as a musician. If you work for a publicly traded company and discuss company business at home and your child posts some sensitive information, that could be a serious problem for you. You need to educate your children on what is appropriate to post to the Internet via any means, such as chat rooms, personal Web sites, or forum boards.

Threat Response

The best thing we can suggest for you to do in regards to your children's safety on the Internet is to know what they are doing. In the same manner that you want to know who they hang out with, whose house they go to after school, and what TV shows and movies they watch, you must be fully aware of everything they do on the Internet. Not talking to them about it is the same as not discussing the evils of substance abuse.

The second best thing to do is to implement technology to secure the threats faced by your children. Monitoring and blocking software are available for content filtering and use of software. As we saw with some of the personal firewalls, you can block traffic as well as limit access to running programs. Inherent controls built into the major browsers and third-party software such as Cyber Snoop and Net Nanny are available to help you protect your kids.

Implementing Controls

As we have seen, your Web browser is a major source of problems your kids can face online. Surfing Web sites has become a popular pastime. Just about any information you want can be found in a Web site. In three of the major browsers, we will look at controls that parents can use to help protect their children. Following are the three browsers we will look at:

- Netscape 6.1 (www.netscape.com)
- Internet Explorer 6.1 (www.microsoft.com)
- Opera 5.12 (www.opera.com)

Netscape 6.1

You can enable several controls to protect the privacy of your children when they (and you!) are surfing online. We have discussed some of the controls earlier, and this will rehash what they are. The following granular controls can be implemented.

Disable cookies by selecting Edit, Preferences, Privacy and Security, Cookies, as shown in Figure 15.1.

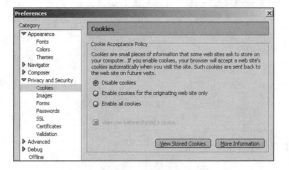

Figure 15.1   Disabling cookies.

Disable saving form information such as name and address by selecting Edit, Preferences, Privacy and Security, Forms and then unchecking the check box, as shown in Figure 15.2.

Figure 15.2   Disable caching of form information.

Disable storing Web site passwords and enable encryption on any stored information by selecting Edit, Preferences, Privacy and Security, Passwords. Uncheck the Remember Passwords box and check the Use Encryption box, as shown in Figure 15.3.

Enable SSL and SSL warnings for data being encrypted or not being encrypted when it is sent through forms by selecting Edit, Preferences, Privacy and Security, SSL, as shown in Figure 15.4. This will tell you when the information you transmit over the Internet is encrypted and safe from capture by malicious attackers. TLS is based on SSL and provides privacy and data integrity between two communicating applications.

Disable Java and JavaScript by selecting Edit, Preferences, Advanced, as shown in Figure 15.5; remember, however, that doing so can cause some Web site functionality to be disabled that you might want. By disabling Java and JavaScript, you reduce the risk that a malicious script on a Web site will steal information from your computer or perform some function on your computer that you do not allow when you surf a Web site.

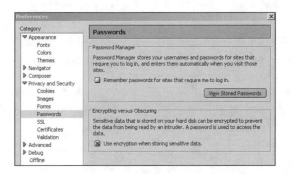

Figure 15.3   Do not save passwords, but do use encryption.

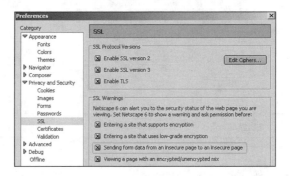

Figure 15.4   SSL enabled with warnings turned on.

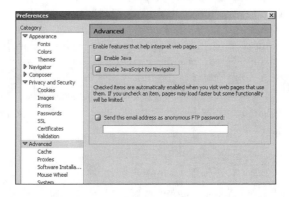

Figure 15.5   Disable Java and JavaScript.

Internet Explorer 6.1

Much like Netscape, Internet Explorer has many built-in controls, as we have discussed previously. Some additional controls that you can implement can limit the data
saved and sent to others on the Internet.

Limit the temporary files stored on the computer by selecting Tools, Internet Options,
General, Settings, as shown in Figure 15.6. If you store a lot of temporary files on your
computer and your computer gets compromised, the attacker can see where you have
been surfing and build a profile of all your preferences. Someone else who shares your
computer in your home would also be able to see where you have been surfing, and
that might be personal information.

Figure 15.6   Reduce the cache size of the browser.

You can enable the history of sites visited to see what sites your child has surfed by
selecting Tools, Internet Options, General. You also can specify how long you want to
keep a history of Web site use.

Internet Explorer has some additional controls over programming languages other
than Java and JavaScript. With the controls under Tools, Internet Options, General,
Security, Custom Settings, as shown in Figure 15.7, you can disable more functions
that could be harmful to your child's Web surfing. Under this option, you should select
Disable or ask for the browser to prompt the user for input. Programming languages
that can interact with your computer through Web sites can do anything they want to
your computer because programming languages are very powerful and can take advantage of any information you give them. Some of the options you should set include
the following:

- Download Signed ActiveX Controls—Enable
- Download Unsigned ActiveX Controls—Disable
- Initialize and Script ActiveX Controls Not Marked as Safe—Disable
- Run ActiveX Controls and Plug-Ins—Disable

- Script ActiveX Controls Marked Safe for Scripting—Enable
- Java Permissions—Disable
- Installation of Desktop Items—Prompt
- Launching Programs and Files in an IFRAME—Disable
- Software Channel Permissions—High Safety
- Submit Unencrypted Form Data—Disable
- Userdata Persistence—Disable
- Active Scripting—Disable
- Scripting of Java Applets—Disable

Figure 15.7   Disable ActiveX and Java functionality.

You can enable more security over the use of cookies by selecting Tools, Internet Options, General, Privacy, as shown in Figure 15.8. You can set the option to High to block most cookies or Advanced to block all cookies.

Figure 15.8   Disable most cookies with the High setting.

A unique feature to Internet Explorer is its Content Advisor. This function checks the content of Web sites for such things as nudity, foul language, sexual activity, and violence. It performs some of the functionality of third-party software. You can set these options by selecting Tools, Internet Options, Content – Enable, Ratings, as shown in Figure 15.9. These settings are termed the Recreational Software Advisory Council (RSACi) ratings. You can set the four settings (Language, Nudity, Sex, and Violence) to the highest level for the most protection. As mentioned earlier, these might block access to sites that *you* want to visit.

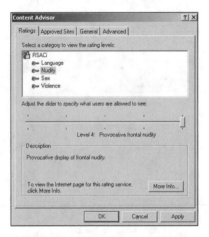

Figure 15.9   Content Advisor settings, set to the highest level.

You can add sites that you do not want blocked by selecting Tools, Internet Options, Content, General. You also can password-protect the Content Advisor so that your kids cannot change the content-checking options.

Additional security controls dealing with certificates and SSL authentication can be set by selecting Tools, Internet Options, Content, Advanced, as shown in Figure 15.10. You can select the check boxes to enable these security measures.

Opera 5.12

One of the main features of the Opera browser is its speed. The other functionality, such as the Content Advisor from Internet Explorer, is not present; however, you can still set many security options.

By selecting File, Preferences, History and Cache, you set up the cache to save the browsing that your child has been doing online so that you can go through the saved cache and see what sites were viewed, as shown in Figure 15.11.

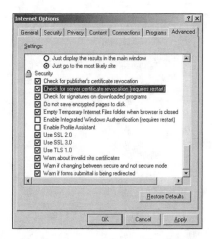

Figure 15.10   Advanced security settings for SSL and certificates.

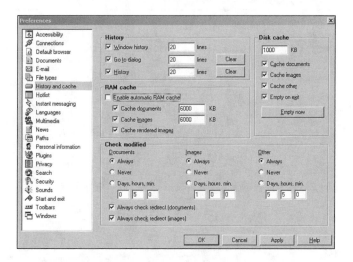

Figure 15.11   Setting the history and cache size.

To protect your child from sending form data inadvertently, keep the Personal Information form blank, as shown in Figure 15.12. This option can be set through File, Preferences, Personal Information.

You can increase the security options for cookies by selecting File, Preferences, Privacy, as shown in Figure 15.13. You can block all cookies or accept cookies only from the server to which you are connecting. On exiting, you can have the browser throw away cookies and display warning messages.

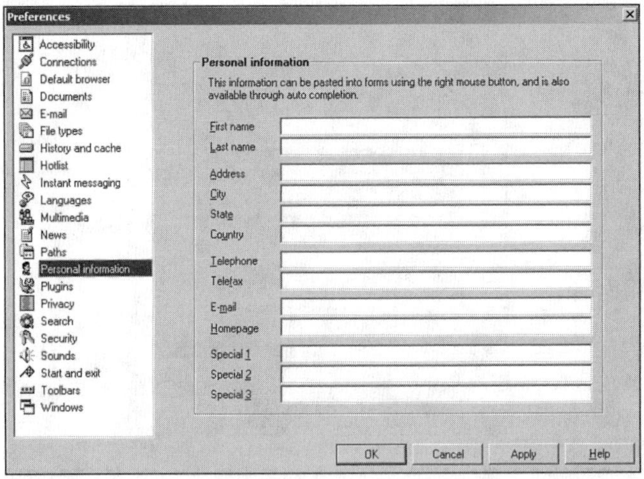

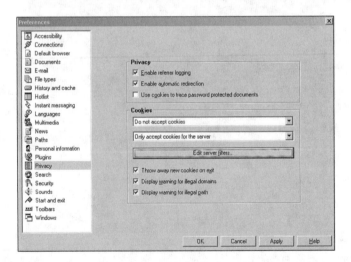

Figure 15.12 Blank personal information form.

Figure 15.13 Disable cookies.

Opera has the capability to password-protect the security features that you have set.
You do not want your kids to change your security options after you have set them.
Through File, Preferences, Security, you can set a password as well as enable and con-
figure SSL and certificates, as shown in Figure 15.14. You can use the setting shown in
Figure 15.14 to set up your security.

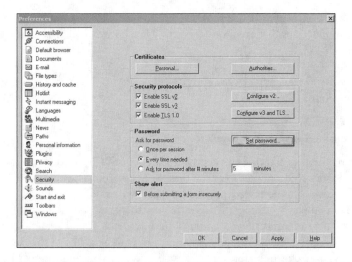

Figure 15.14   SSL, certificates, and password setting.

Third-Party Products

Many commercial software packages are available to help you control your child's access to the Internet. It's up to you to decide how valuable they are and how much they invade your child's privacy. These programs can do everything from monitor access to block access. Keep in mind, however, that these programs are by no means comprehensive or perfect in blocking all traffic you think is dangerous. Another problem with these programs is that they might block legitimate access to sites such as medical sites. Filtering rules based on content or key words is subjective. The software might block something that you consider to be allowable for your child to watch. It all boils down to your educating your children on what is appropriate.

Several third-party programs include the following:

- Cyber Snoop (`www.pearlsw.com`)
- Net Nanny (`www.netnanny.com`)
- Cyber Patrol (`www.cyberpatrol.com`)
- CYBERSitter (`www.cybersitter.com`)
- Internet WatchDog (`http://www.algorithm.com/algorithm/projects.html`)
- SurfWatch (`www.surfwatch.com`)

We will walk though Net Nanny in detail to describe some of the functionality available in these types of programs. The functionality between these programs might vary a bit, but the basic premise is that they attempt to block access to questionable material. The main functions that are monitored and blocked by these programs include the following:

- Web surfing
- Chat rooms
- Newsgroups
- Personal information dissemination

The main methods of filtering use keyword searches of Web site content and domain name for questionable keywords. If they find these keywords, they block the Web site from being viewed. Some programs have human intervention in the selection process. The filtering company puts together a list of sites that they add to their software to block. This is a continuous process because the Internet is always changing and new sites are always being added. You also have the ability to add sites to the list of blocked sites, but as you can imagine, for every site you find that you think should be blocked, there are probably 100 others that you and the software do not know about.

Net Nanny

Net Nanny is one of the more popular tools for monitoring what your kids do on the Internet. It has a broad range of features, which include filtering harmful Web sites, restricting access to the Internet, monitoring activity, and safeguarding personal information. You install it on the machine you want to protect and give each user an account. Each account can have different levels of restrictions and access. Net Nanny can control Web sites, chat rooms, and newsgroups. The ability to control every site your child visits can be a blessing and a curse. You will see which sites your child visits, but this requires a lot of attention and inspection on your part, which can be time-consuming and even annoying. Net Nanny has a feature to keep personal information such as names, addresses, phone numbers, e-mail addresses, and credit card numbers from being sent out from your computer. Logs of all activity can be viewed to see what your child has actually done online.

To configure and operate Net Nanny, you can use the following steps:

1. After installing Net Nanny and rebooting, you have to set up users in Net Nanny for it to perform any type of filtering. On each machine to which you give your children access, you need a program to perform filtering. You give the administrator a password and then set up users in Net Nanny, up to 12. You can set these options under the User Settings tab. In Figure 15.15, we are setting up a user called Bobby. Bobby can set up his password, or we can set it for him. Then we use the Add button to enable him.

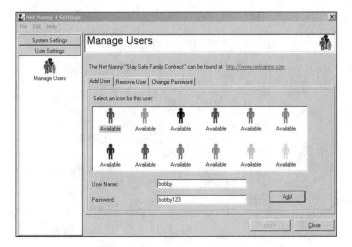

Figure 15.15   User creation.

2. The filters are set through System Settings, List Violations, as shown in Figure 15.16. For each function, Web Sites, Words and Phrases, Newsgroups, and Chat, you can set up the program to show a warning message, block access, and shut down the program.

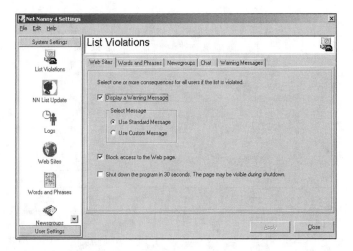

Figure 15.16   Setting up the filters in Net Nanny.

3. You can update the Net Nanny list of sites automatically through several different options under System Settings, NN List Update, as shown in Figure 15.17.

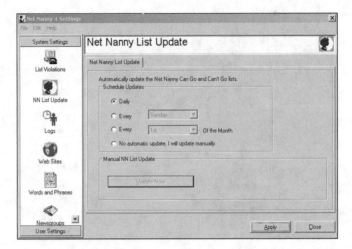

Figure 15.17   Update the list of sites to block.

4. You can set up logging to log everything that is violated in the activity log and set up the chat log separately by selecting System Settings, Logs. Logging all activity and all chat activity is probably a waste of time. Logging just the violations is a better idea, as shown in Figure 15.18.

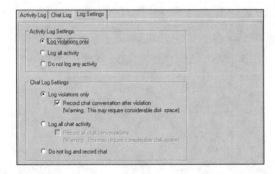

Figure 15.18   Set up logging of violations.

5. Blocking Web sites is the major task of Net Nanny and the other monitoring programs. The list of blocked sites can be quite extensive. In Net Nanny, you can set up the sites that are inherent to Net Nanny as well as add your own sites that you want to block, as shown in Figure 15.19, by selecting System Settings, Web Sites. In addition, you can exclude sites from the blocking program if you feel they are safe. When you update the list of sites, you will have to come back and check what changes have been made, which sites you might want to allow, or which additional sites you want to block.

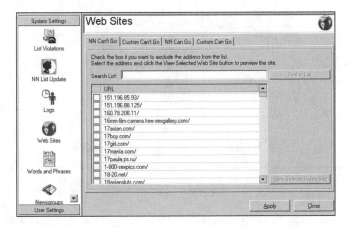

Figure 15.19   Set up Web sites that you want to block or allow.

6. The next major filter option that you can use is blocking sites based on words and phrases. A built-in list is available that you can modify through System Settings, Words and Phrases, as shown in Figure 15.20. This list is quite extensive. You can add or delete words. If you have ever tried to perform a Web search, you know how difficult it is to find the things that match your search criteria. This same problem exists with blocking based on words and phrases. These programs will miss certain sites and block some legitimate ones.

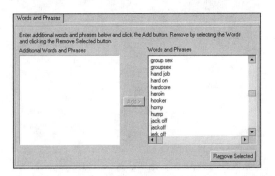

Figure 15.20   Setting up blocking by words and phrases.

7. You can block newsgroups through System Settings, Newsgroups, as shown in Figure 15.21. As with Web sites, many questionable newsgroups exist that you might want to block, but Net Nanny does not provide a list by default. You have to go out and find the groups you want to block and add them to the program.

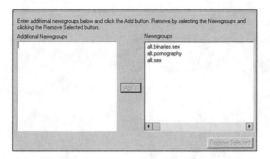

Figure 15.21 Set up newsgroup blocking.

8. Chat rooms can also be monitored and blocked using Net Nanny. The same problem exists with blocking chat rooms as exists with Web sites and newsgroups, but to a greater degree. Chat rooms can exist as Internet relay chat (IRC) channels, which is what Net Nanny blocks, but they can also exist within Web sites or even as standalone programs such as ICQ and Yahoo! Messenger. These all allow chat and use different ports; you should know that they are not checked thoroughly by Net Nanny or any of the other monitoring programs in granular detail. Figure 15.22 shows the chat restrictions you can set. Like the newsgroups, you have to come up with the list of chats to block on your own. Literally thousands of chat rooms exist on IRC alone.

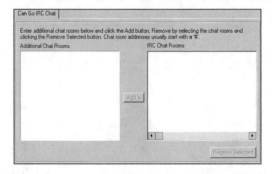

Figure 15.22 Setting up chat blocking.

9. A nice feature of the Net Nanny is the ability to stop personal information from being sent out from your system. You can do this by selecting System Settings, Personal Information, as shown in Figure 15.23. If you store all your sensitive information in one place—such as name, address, and credit card information—and your security becomes compromised, an attacker can get all your information from one place.

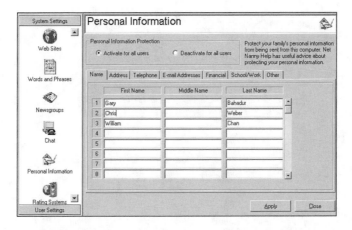

Figure 15.23   Controlling personal information from leaving your system.

10. The last significant feature of Net Nanny is the ability to use several rating sys-
    tems that sites voluntarily follow to rate their sites. You can set the rating options
    by selecting System Settings, Rating Systems, as shown in Figure 15.24. The
    problem is that Net Nanny uses two rating systems, and Web sites don't really
    use either of them yet. It's pretty useless to go by the ratings because not very
    many sites use RASCi or SafeSurf ratings. Until some rating system becomes a
    standard or is enforced through laws, these systems will not do you much good.

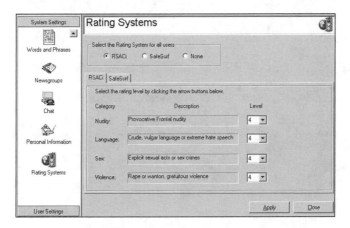

Figure 15.24   Selecting a rating system to use.

11. When you have completed your settings selection, you can apply the rules to
    each user, as shown in Figure 15.25. Select System Settings, Rating Systems.

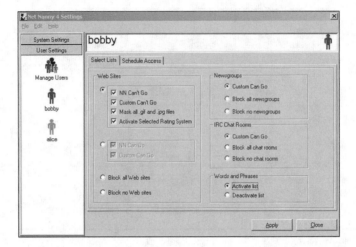

Figure 15.25   Applying settings to each user.

When you have Net Nanny in place, it begins blocking based on whatever rules you set up for each user. In the case of the user Bobby that we set up, trying to surf a Web site looking for "porn" blocked access and displayed the error message shown in Figure 15.26.

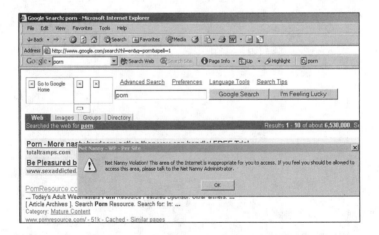

Figure 15.26   Warning message when a filter is activated.

You can check the log messages to see what kinds of violations occurred by selecting System Settings, Logs, as shown in Figure 15.27. In this figure, we see three violations by the user Bobby.

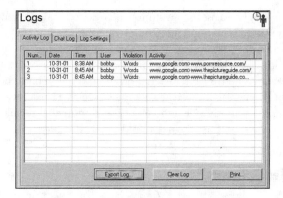

Figure 15.27   Check the log for violations.

What do all these security settings mean for your child's protection? Not much really. So many things cannot be blocked by these types of filter programs that you might as well not have them. For simple blocking schemes for young children, these types of programs do provide some value. For your older children, however, many of whom know more about the Internet and navigating through different programs and functionality than you do, these programs will just be a challenge to overcome.

If it is difficult to monitor and block your child's access to Internet resources, what do you do? Our answer is education. Without teaching them the proper usage of the Internet and technology, you are leaving them open to the evil influences that they will encounter in cyberspace. The Internet has both good and bad qualities; it's your job to educate your children in how to properly navigate cyberspace securely.

Government Involvement

Several laws are in the works or already in place that attempt to protect children in their online usage. The problem with these laws comes down to enforcement. The technologies needed for companies to follow the laws are not yet in place. Laws around the world are changing every day because of the changes brought on by the Internet.

Communications Decency Act

The U.S. Communications Decency Act (CDA) of 1996 prohibited and punished the dissemination of material considered "indecent" or "patently offensive as measured by contemporary community standards." These general terms were not described and could be interpreted in various manners. The CDA was so broad that it could affect all online services and have damaging effects to a wide range of service providers.

In 1997, the CDA was ruled as unconstitutional. The Electronic Privacy Information Center (EPIC) applauded the Supreme Court's Internet speech decision as "the first landmark decision of the 21st Century." This decision advocated the free speech of the Internet. Although this decision was a victory for free speech, it was a blow to keeping children from viewing questionable material on the Internet. Throughout the battle over this law, EPIC argued that the CDA compromised free speech rights and personal privacy. By having to verify the age and identity of all potential recipients of "indecent" material, everyone on the Internet would lose anonymity.

Federal Trade Commission

The Federal Trade Commission (www.ftc.gov) has a hand in various parts of Internet security. One of their Web sites is dedicated to the protection of kids (http://www.ftc.gov/bcp/conline/edcams/kidzprivacy/kidz.htm). The FTC has enforcement capabilities for some laws involving personal privacy.

The FTC has enforcement responsibilities for the Children's Online Privacy Protection Act (COPPA, discussed next). Sites that collect personal identifying information from a child who does not correspond to the COPPA are within the jurisdiction of the FTC.

COPPA

COPPA applies to the online collection of personal information from children under 13. Rules exist regarding privacy and security of personal data. The rules seek verifiable consent from parents for information that is collected from minors.

Any site that collects information from children under 13 must have *actual knowledge* that it is collecting personal information from children and must comply with the COPPA. The COPPA also has fallen under the scrutiny of organizations that protect privacy by saying it is unconstitutional.

The FTC is involved in the COPPA when it comes to determining if a Web site is directed at minors by checking visual or audio content, the age of models on the site, language and advertising, and enforcement and punishment. The FTC will consider who owns and controls the information that is collected on the site and how that information is used. The notice to parents must contain the same information included on the notice on the Web site. Different methods might be used to notify parents of the collection policies being used but all must comply with COPPA. The problem COPPA has caused for many Web sites is that the technology is not in place to easily follow the requirements of the law. The FTC is considering giving sites an extension of two more years to comply with the portion regarding parental consent via e-mail.

Rating Systems

Rating systems are the early stages of development for Internet content. Parental control software such as Net Nanny has been around for several years; yet it has still not quite figured out how to really control children's access to the Internet. Rating systems are trying to become like the movie ratings and give parents some guide to what a site contains. Taking this to the next level, software can be developed that can read the rating for each site and notify the user or even implement filtering rules based on the rating of the site. Several rating systems are being developed and are already in use, but their effect so far on the Internet and in the minds of consumers has been minimal.

The problem with rating and labeling systems is that they are subjective. Who decides how a site is rated? The site operators can rate it whatever way they want. Many sites don't even care to use the ratings. Non-rated sites are currently the majority. If you are an operator of a site that has some questionable material, you might want to rate it low for inappropriate content to get more hits.

Ratings systems for the Internet are much like rating systems for movies. Kids get in to see R rates movies or can rent them at home and get by the rating systems. Parents might not agree with the rating and allow their children to watch an R-rated movie anyway. The choice is up to you to allow your children to access material on the Internet and educate them about what is proper cyberspace behavior. No rating system will be as good a judge as you will be for your children.

Platform for Internet Content Selection

The Platform for Internet Content Selection (PICS) is a set of technical specifications developed by the World Wide Web Consortium to allow different companies to develop parental control programs to use the same specifications. The same specifications would allow products to function together to take actions such as searching, monitoring, warning, and blocking based on labels. PICS is not a product or service; rather, it is a method of allowing products to be developed that share the same standard.

A *filtering product* could be PICS compatible by reading labels from other rating services such as the Internet Content Rating Association (ICRA, discussed next) as long as the ratings were in a PICS-readable format. PICS filtering capabilities are built into Microsoft Internet Explorer and Netscape Navigator as well as other browsers. The Internet Explorer PICS implementation can read any rating service, and Netscape PICS implementation can read only RSACi and SafeSurf labels.

Internet Content Rating Association

The Internet Content Rating Association (http://www.icra.org) (ICRA) is an independent, non-profit organization that has developed a rating system for Internet content much like the ratings you see on movies. This rating system is aimed at protecting children. The RSACi rating service, which was the forerunner to ICRA, is already built into Internet Explorer 6.1, as we have already mentioned. The Content Advisor in IE 6.1 does not fully comply yet with the ICRA system.

The three most trafficked Internet destinations, AOL, MSN and Yahoo!, have begun using the ICRA rating system with the goal of protecting children and maintaining freedom of speech. Content providers are supposed to voluntarily label their sites to meet the criteria of the labeling system. A tool called ICRA *filter* is under development to help implement the labeling system. It is expected to be released in March 2002. The tool operates independently of the browser and supports "block" lists and "allow" lists.

SafeSurf

Another rating system worth mentioning is SafeSurf. Like ICRA, it uses the PICS standard to read labels from a Web site, but it has a more detailed and granular mechanism for labeling and controlling content. It describes both content and how that content is presented to the viewer. Like other rating systems, it is voluntary. The numerous levels and categories break up content by purpose and context of how the material is presented.

Summary

Parental controls such as the software we have discussed and the monitoring of e-mails, chat sessions, Web sites, and whatever else that you think might be necessary to protect your children can seem a bit excessive. Like anything you do, exercise moderation. For younger children, it is definitely necessary to monitor how they use the Internet and with whom they communicate.

For older children, education about the proper uses for the Internet and the dangers and pitfalls they face is probably your best solution. Technology solutions are just not comprehensive enough and cannot match the creativity and content of the Internet. It's just as easy to block a medical site as it is to block porn sites. Half the kids out there know more about the Internet and how to get around the weak controls of third-party software that are used to restrict access.

Although monitoring software has its place, your ability to track everything your kids do and watch log files on a daily basis is limited. Like system administrators for large companies, you will quickly become swamped with network administration and become frustrated. Focused logging and monitoring is needed if you plan to go down this path with your children's access.

The rating systems might be onto something good. Although they are nowhere near a perfect solution, they can provide a valid guideline for parents to site content. Like the movie rating system, everyone understands the ratings and the consumer is able to glean some valuable information.

The best advice we can give you regarding your children's access is to educate them about the dangers and proper usage, just as you would anything else they will encounter in life.

16

Guarding Your System Against Hacking

The risks and solutions we have discussed throughout this book so far make the Internet such an interesting place. With viruses, hackers, crackers, marketing companies, and script kiddies on the Internet, having the ability to respond to an intrusion on your computer or home network is more important and timely than it would have been in the past. With always-on connectivity, the risk of an actual break-in to your computer has skyrocketed. A breach in security could result in stolen credit card information, destruction of personal files and data, or use of your computer in a hacking crime, among many possible dangers.

We have been through many steps for securing your systems and data. Security is just a point in time, however. Just because one day you completed a full security test of your computer and found no vulnerabilities doesn't mean that tomorrow you won't be vulnerable again.

Keeping up to date with security measures can be quite difficult, but if you plan to be on the Internet, you must be secure. Being attacked is a foregone conclusion. The odds of your computer being compromised increase everyday as you install new services and applications and make your computer ever more versatile. Implementing a firewall, virus scanners, encryption, and everything else we have discussed should keep you secure if done correctly, and any modifications to your system are tested and patches to programs, applications, and operating systems are applied as needed. You might make a mistake in the implementation, or the software might have a problem that allows your computer to become vulnerable even with all this security in place. Thinking toward the future in case you are hacked makes sense. If you are prepared for an attack and a compromise, you will be able to fix your system quickly with the least amount of panic and problems.

Planning your security procedures is as important for home users as it is for any large organization. Whether you are just trying to protect a home computer or an entire home network, you will have to plan how to go about monitoring your systems and how you want to respond to attacks or break-ins. The first step in Internet security is to create an Internet security plan. The plan should establish which traffic into the system is acceptable and which traffic is prohibited. The plan should also define what types of activities are allowed, such as file transfers and Telnet, among others. The activities allowed should be consistent with the types of services that the company wants to provide to customers. The plan should also detail the setup of the firewall, which will be discussed later.

We have already discussed methods of protecting your computer systems with such things as the following:

- **Firewalls**—These can be hardware- or software-based protection methods. They filter out unwanted traffic and protect your internal systems, log traffic, and allow any function you want to have operate in a relatively secure manner. Although a firewall is a good solution to your perimeter security, it can be bypassed or even broken to allow an attacker access to your network because of software bugs or configuration implementation problems.

- **Virus scanners**—When you allow traffic into your computer or network, whether via e-mail, file transfer, or another method, you are opening yourself up to attacks via viruses, Trojan horses, or worms. These insidious attacks against your network can delete data, change system configurations, or destroy files. With virus scanners in place, you can stop most virus attacks, whether they come via e-mail, a file you download, or a Web site you browse. A virus scanner is as important in protecting your computer as a firewall.

- **Encryption**—Beyond firewalls and virus scanners, your last line of defense is encryption. Having all your information encrypted when it is stored on your computer and when it is traveling across the network can protect your data. An attacker will not be able to read personal files or e-mail if it is encrypted. If you store information or send it in the clear, however, an attacker can capture that information and read everything about you. Encryption of data stored locally and sent over the Internet solves this problem.

Many companies implement these protections and still get hacked. Don't feel bad if you get hacked—just be prepared.

What Is a System Compromise?

We have discussed why you are attacked. You can be a target because of monetary gain by the attacker, the usefulness of your system to hide tracks and be used in further attacks, or for fun or malicious purposes. The end result of a successful attack is that the attacker has compromised your system security and has control of your computer, network, or applications. If an attacker is just going after data in an application, such as all your financial information in Quicken files, he doesn't need complete control of the system as long as he obtains the data.

Hackers, crackers, script kiddies or just about anyone on the Internet can launch an attack against your system in an attempt to compromise your computer. Anyone can be a threat. It doesn't matter who takes control of your computer because of a security weakness. The result is that you can be compromised, all your data can be stolen, and all your files can be destroyed at will by an attacker.

A compromised system can be used for launching more attacks, for testing, or as a playground for the attacker. It could be used to store pirated software and share such software with other hackers, or used to capture traffic on the local network. If you are using a cable modem, the attacker can use captured software such as Ethereal to monitor traffic of your neighbors.

A system compromise means that the attacker got past any firewalls or operating system security measures you have in place. Your system might be comprised for any number of reasons. After you are successfully attacked, the only things you can do are to identify that you have been compromised, find out what the attacker did to your system, find out how the attacker got control of your computer, fix the problems, and attempt to clean up any mess he made on your system or home network. Recovering from a system compromise is difficult, as we will discuss in another section.

What Is Intrusion Detection?

An *intrusion detection system (IDS)* is an additional protection measure to firewalls, virus scanners, and encryption that helps ward off computer intrusions. IDS systems can be software and hardware devices used to detect an attack. Attacks can take many forms, as we have discussed. You can be attacked through applications such as Netscape, Internet Explorer, Eudora, or Microsoft Outlook. You can be attacked via the operating system, regardless of whether it is Unix-, Windows-, or Mac-based. You also can be attacked via the network through denial-of-service (DoS) attacks or attacks against protocols.

IDS products are used to monitor your connection to try to determine whether someone is launching an attack against you. Everything from a simple port scan to a full attack against your Web server can be detected by the IDS system. A flag is raised when you are being attacked. Some IDS systems just monitor and alert you of an attack, whereas others try to block the attack. As we mentioned when discussing BlackICE, some firewalls alert you of attacks, acting as an IDS.

Capabilities differ greatly between IDS systems. Because the more complicated IDS programs are too expensive for most home users, selecting a firewall that has IDS capabilities, such as BlackICE or ZoneAlarm, can be a key buying feature. Buying a personal firewall with IDS-like capabilities makes more sense for Windows users because free or inexpensive solutions for Windows are very limited. Unix users, on the other hand, have a wider selection of free IDS applications.

Software and hardware designed to detect attackers can pick up many levels of intrusions. IDSs still will not be capable of detecting certain things, such as information about to which ISP your IP address belongs. If someone is checking up on your ISP to find what blocks of IP addresses it owns, you will not know. Public information doesn't really affect your system until the attackers begin to ping your system to see if it is alive. These non-invasive techniques are used for reconnaissance and mapping out potential targets.

Another non-invasive form of reconnaissance is taking advantage of the legitimate services that you have running. If you run a Web site from home or have a mail server running, an attacker can use these legitimate services to find out information about your system. Information can be extracted without setting off any alarms, and normal traffic to your computer systems will not seem out of the ordinary. As we have already mentioned, an attacker can only take advantage of a running service or program that is on your system. If you are running a Web server, an attacker could launch Web server attacks against your machine. It's simple to get the pertinent information from your system through legitimate requests, as we have already mentioned.

As a refresher, when launching an attack, the attacker must know what services you are running to take advantage of the service. For example, if a Web server is running, the attacker wants to know what type of operating system and version of the Web server are being used. The attacker can simply connect to the Web server with a program such as netcat (nc) and get the information shown in Figure 16.1 without setting off IDS alarms.

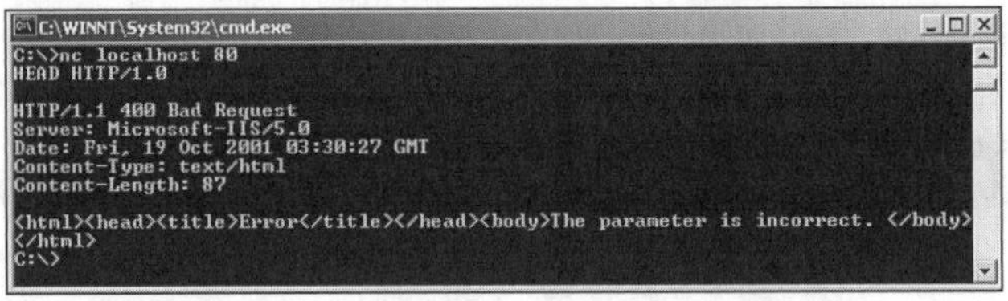

Figure 16.1   Non-invasive information gathering.

The job of the IDS is to pick up traffic that is outside the normal scope of system operations. Although simply browsing your Web site *does not* set off an IDS, launching an attack such as IIS traversal attacks *does* set off a correctly configured IDS. IDS configurations are much like firewall configurations. You set up a number of filter rules to look for certain types of traffic. A normal IDS is not meant to block traffic, but to watch traffic and report back to you on what is occurring against your system. Newer breeds of IDSs such as Entercept (www.entercept.com) can actually stop traffic like a firewall. If attacks match the signatures that Entercept knows, Entercept stops that traffic. The following code shows an example of the Entercept IDS output from an attack, which Entercept detects and blocks. The action taken by the product is Prevent, which stops the attack from doing any actual damage:

```
IIS Directory Traversal and Code Execution

This event indicates that a Directory Transversal attack was attempted against
Microsoft's Internet Information Server (IIS) through a request made to the web
server using cmd.exe.

Directory Traversal is a method of escaping the IIS webroot
directory, thus allowing access to normally-protected files or permit
execution of arbitrary code on the target host.

<a href="http://www.cve.mitre.org/cgi-bin/cvename.cgi?name=CVE-2000-0884"
target=_blank>CVE reference: CVE-2000-0884</a>


Reported by entercept.
Console: IDSConsle

Security Level: High
Application: IIS
Recording Time: 10/10/2001 11:52:48 AM
Incident Time: 10/10/2001 11:52:03 AM
Source: Exp3
User Name: WORKGROUP\TestUser
Process: C:\WINNT\System32\inetsrv\inetinfo.exe
Reaction: Prevent
Agent Type: Windows NT/2000 Web Server
Event Id: 28685

Workstation Name: Local
raw data: GET /scripts/..%255c../winnt/system32/cmd.exe?/c+dir HTTP/1.0

Host: www

Connection: close


server: www:192.168.1.1:80
local file: C:\inetpub\scripts\..%5c..\winnt\system32\cmd.exe
```

```
Web Server Type: Microsoft-IIS/5.0
source: 192.168.1.20
method: GET
raw url: GET /scripts/..%255c../winnt/system32/cmd.exe?/c+dir HTTP/1.0
query: /c+dir
URL: /scripts/../../winnt/system32/cmd.exe
```

Note

Products that have extensive IDS capabilities, such as blocking and firewall capabilities, are very complex and expensive and are not meant for the consumer. Personal firewalls are implementing this type of functionality slowly but surely, and consumers are slowly reaping the benefits of the large commercial programs.

When an attack is launched that fits the filters that an IDS defines, a flag is raised in the form of screen alerts, e-mail alerts, pager alerts, or any other form of alerting mechanism that is defined. Some firewalls can act as IDS because they provide alerting mechanisms such as onscreen pop-up alerts. BlackICE's alerting mechanisms show up as a small flashing icon in the system tray and show the attacks in the window, as seen in Figure 16.2. In this example, we see two attacks focusing on HTTP and FTP. As we mentioned, the newer personal firewalls can alert you and block attacks, as BlackICE does in this case.

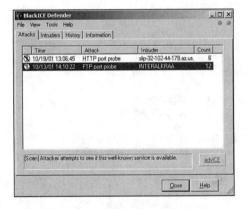

Figure 16.2   BlackICE alert window.

Another of the personal firewalls we tested had good alert pop-up capabilities. ZoneAlarm Pro's alerts are shown in Figure 16.3.

In the corporate environment, firewalls and IDSs are designed to protect the confidentiality, integrity, and availability of data. Firewalls have expanded their capabilities into the IDS arena, and as we have seen with some of the personal firewalls, they can act as IDSs. For your personal information and systems at home, you need strong protection and detection. Confidentiality means protecting your data from unauthorized disclosure. Integrity of your data means that no one was able to access your information and modify it in any way without your permission. You would not want someone accessing your Quicken or TurboTax files and making modifications to your entries. Availability means that you will always have access to your information. You would not want a hacker accessing and destroying your TurboTax files so that you couldn't access your data on April 14.

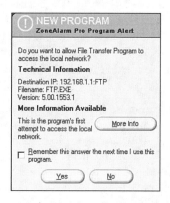

Figure 16.3   ZoneAlarm Pro alert pop-up.

Note

Here are two very good resources for Windows and Unix-based IDSs:

- Michael Sobirey's Intrusion Detection Systems page (`http://www-rnks.informatik.`
  `tu-cottbus.de/~sobirey/ids.html`)

- Coast Intrusion Detection page (`http://www.cerias.purdue.edu/coast/`
  `intrusion-detection/ids.html`)

Benefits of IDS

The main reason to use either a standalone IDS or a firewall that has IDS capabilities is to detect attacks against your system and alert you to the attack. In the same fashion as a virus scanner checking your system for incoming files or data with a virus and alerting you, so does the IDS. The new IDSs take a proactive stance toward attacks and block them in many cases.

The security measures we have discussed, from locking down your operating system to removing services and applications that you do not need, can still leave some vulnerabilities in your system.

To really get the most out of your IDS, you should first understand the potential problems in your environment, as discussed in Chapter 13, "Securing Your Home Network." By knowing where you are potentially vulnerable, from both the services you have running and applications that are installed, you can use the IDS to shore up those weaknesses. The IDS can block or just let you know when you are being attacked. Just because the IDS flags an attack doesn't mean that the attacker got through the firewall and filter rules you set up. Like the logging capabilities we discussed with firewalls, when an attack flags the IDS filter rules, it alerts you. Knowing your system helps you understand the alerts much better. If you see a Web attack being reported by your IDS and you know that you do not have a Web server running, then you have nothing to worry about. Let the attacker fire away—you won't be compromised if you do not have the Web server or a Web application running.

In the event that your system does get compromised, an IDS can continue to log activity and record the actual break-in. This can be valuable for two reasons. First, if you want to try to track down and prosecute the attacker, you have log files that can be used in a legal case. Second, you can use the log files of the break-in to see how the attacker launched the attacks and potentially what he did to take over your system. You can use this information to patch the holes in your environment so that other attackers cannot use the same hole. If you reinstall the operating system or application, you can be sure not to implement the same vulnerability again. This is, of course, dependent on the attacker not wiping out all your log files or destroying your system!

IDSs can be a great learning experience. If you are interested in seeing what kinds of attacks are launched against your system every day, you can watch all the traffic being logged by the IDS. One project that has been successful in identifying how attackers operate and has logged attacks for analysis is the Honeynet Project (`http://project.honeynet.org`). This project tracks how an attacker launches attacks against his own test system, or *honeypots*. Many companies also use honeypots to learn more about how hackers operate without sacrificing a real production system. The goals of the Honeynet Project as stated on the Web site are as follows:

- **Raise awareness**—The first goal is to raise awareness of the threats and vulnerabilities that exist on the Internet today. We raise awareness by demonstrating real systems that were compromised in the wild by the blackhat community. Many people believe it can't happen to them. We hope to change their mind.

- **Teach and inform**—For those in the community who are already aware and concerned, we hope to give you the information to better secure and defend your resources. Historically, intelligence about attackers has been limited to the tools they use. The Project intends to provide additional information, such as their motives in attacking, their methods for communication, the times they attack, and their actions after compromising a system.

- **Gather intelligence**—The third goal is to provide the technology and methods of intelligence gathering. Organizations, such as universities, might be interested in developing their own ability to research threats or adversaries.

Home users can benefit from the lessons learned from the Honeynet Project. Your IDS can monitor attacks, and you can use this data to learn more about incidents and what to look for when you see traffic coming to your network. A great benefit of knowing what traffic is being sent to your site is that you can know when a new form of attack is being launched. That gives you time to ensure that you have the correct security measures in place. For example, if a new worm such as Code Red IV comes out, you will see the traffic being recorded and hopefully stopped by your IDS. You can then check your operating system and applications to ensure you are not vulnerable in the event that the attacks makes it past your IDS or firewall.

Problems with IDS

As we have already mentioned in the logging capabilities of firewalls, too much logging can be just as useless as no logging. One of the main functions of an IDS is to log data. Logging data helps you analyze what attacks are being launched and how your protective measures handle attacks. If you log every bit of data, it's impossible to review it all in a timely fashion. Too much useless data can hide the important bits of information about real, deadly attacks. A consistent attack by a determined intruder can be hidden in mountains of data from script kiddies who don't know any better and are just port scanning at random. You would be subject to data overload and get no benefit from all the attacks you have logged.

Another failure of IDSs is their inability to learn of new attacks in some cases. As we have mentioned, new attacks come out on a daily basis. If the firewall you are using is not versatile enough, a new attack can bypass the filter rules of your IDS without it recognizing it as a new form of attack. For example, many Web attacks use port 80 (http). If your IDS cannot distinguish between normal Web surfing traffic and an attack against the operating system through port 80, you will not know that your Web server is under attack.

Finally, if you set up alerting to let you know when just about anything sets off your IDS filter rules, you will be inundated with alerts and begin to ignore them. By ignoring them, you will probably miss the real alert of a dangerous attack. If you hear a car alarm going off in any big city, what are the odds that you will be concerned and check on your car? The odds are low because these alarms go off all the time and everyone thinks they are no big deal. The same can happen to your IDS alerts if you send out alerts for every little thing that happens on your network. The following code shows some of the numerous log messages that can be written to a file. In this case, we see WinRoute log file information. If you don't know what all these messages mean, you might ignore them or turn logging off altogether. Here's the code:

```
[21/Oct/2001 11:45:52] Packet filter: ACL 1:7 FE575 Ethernet Adapter:
permit packet in: TCP 217.6.114.250:80 -> 10.1.176.234:1326
[21/Oct/2001 11:45:52] Packet filter: ACL 1:7 FE575 Ethernet Adapter:
permit packet in: TCP 217.6.114.250:80 -> 10.1.176.234:1326
```

```
[21/Oct/2001 11:45:52] Packet filter: ACL 1:7 FE575 Ethernet Adapter:
permit packet in: TCP 217.6.114.250:80 -> 10.1.176.234:1326
[21/Oct/2001 11:45:53] Packet filter: ACL 1:7 FE575 Ethernet Adapter:
permit packet in: TCP 217.6.114.250:80 -> 10.1.176.234:1326
[21/Oct/2001 11:45:53] Packet filter: ACL 1:7 FE575 Ethernet Adapter:
permit packet in: TCP 217.6.114.250:80 -> 10.1.176.234:1326
[21/Oct/2001 11:45:53] Packet filter: ACL 1:7 FE575 Ethernet Adapter:
permit packet in: TCP 217.6.114.250:80 -> 10.1.176.234:1326
[21/Oct/2001 11:45:53] Packet filter: ACL 1:7 FE575 Ethernet Adapter:
permit packet in: TCP 217.6.114.250:80 -> 10.1.176.234:1326
[21/Oct/2001 11:46:10] Packet filter: ACL 1:6 FE575 Ethernet Adapter:
permit packet in: ICMP 216.115.102.79 -> 10.1.176.234 type 0 code 0
[21/Oct/2001 11:46:11] Packet filter: ACL 1:6 FE575 Ethernet Adapter:
permit packet in: ICMP 216.115.102.79 -> 10.1.176.234 type 0 code 0
[21/Oct/2001 11:46:12] Packet filter: ACL 1:6 FE575 Ethernet Adapter:
permit packet in: ICMP 216.115.102.79 -> 10.1.176.234 type 0 code 0
[21/Oct/2001 11:46:13] Packet filter: ACL 1:6 FE575 Ethernet Adapter:
permit packet in: ICMP 216.115.102.79 -> 10.1.176.234 type 0 code 0
[21/Oct/2001 11:50:03] Packet filter: ACL 1:3 FE575 Ethernet Adapter:
drop packet in: UDP 10.1.176.234:137 -> 10.1.176.255:137
[21/Oct/2001 11:50:04] Packet filter: ACL 1:3 FE575 Ethernet Adapter:
drop packet in: UDP 10.1.176.234:137 -> 10.1.176.255:137
[21/Oct/2001 11:50:05] Packet filter: ACL 1:3 FE575 Ethernet Adapter:
drop packet in: UDP 10.1.176.234:137 -> 10.1.176.255:137
[21/Oct/2001 12:01:40] Packet filter: ACL 1:3 FE575 Ethernet Adapter:
drop packet in: UDP 10.1.176.234:137 -> 10.1.176.255:137
[21/Oct/2001 12:01:40] Packet filter: ACL 1:3 FE575 Ethernet Adapter:
drop packet in: UDP 10.1.176.234:137 -> 10.1.176.255:137
[21/Oct/2001 12:01:41] Packet filter: ACL 1:3 FE575 Ethernet Adapter:
drop packet in: UDP 10.1.176.234:137 -> 10.1.176.255:137
[21/Oct/2001 12:01:48] Packet filter: ACL 1:7 FE575 Ethernet Adapter:
permit packet in: TCP 216.239.39.101:80 -> 10.1.176.234:1330
[21/Oct/2001 12:01:48] Packet filter: ACL 1:7 FE575 Ethernet Adapter:
permit packet in: TCP 216.239.39.101:80 -> 10.1.176.234:1330
[21/Oct/2001 12:01:48] Packet filter: ACL 1:7 FE575 Ethernet Adapter:
permit packet in: TCP 216.239.39.101:80 -> 10.1.176.234:1330
[21/Oct/2001 12:01:48] Packet filter: ACL 1:7 FE575 Ethernet Adapter:
permit packet in: TCP 216.239.39.101:80 -> 10.1.176.234:1330
[21/Oct/2001 12:01:48] Packet filter: ACL 1:7 FE575 Ethernet Adapter:
permit packet in: TCP 216.239.39.101:80 -> 10.1.176.234:1330
[21/Oct/2001 12:01:48] Packet filter: ACL 1:7 FE575 Ethernet Adapter:
permit packet in: TCP 216.239.39.101:80 -> 10.1.176.234:1330
[21/Oct/2001 12:01:48] Packet filter: ACL 1:7 FE575 Ethernet Adapter:
permit packet in: TCP 216.239.39.101:80 -> 10.1.176.234:1330
[21/Oct/2001 12:01:59] Packet filter: ACL 1:7 FE575 Ethernet Adapter:
permit packet in: TCP 216.239.39.101:80 -> 10.1.176.234:1330
[21/Oct/2001 12:02:06] Packet filter: ACL 1:3 FE575 Ethernet Adapter:
drop packet in: UDP 10.1.176.234:137 -> 10.1.176.255:137
```

Why Not to Use IDS

For your home network of probably two to five computers, you are probably the only one administering security to it if you are reading this book. We assume that you are not sitting at home all day watching your firewall and IDS log files. (If you are, get out and go for a walk!) Because watching your home network logs and alerts is not your full-time job, you do not want to be flooded with data and scared every few minutes that you are being hacked.

Most of the attacks you will face are going to be by script kiddies with automated scanners. Unless the scanner does the hacking for them, most of them wouldn't know what to do with a sophisticated vulnerability. You will be constantly port scanned and checked for every exploit that is coded up by an automated vulnerability scanner. If you are running Windows, you really don't care if you are scanned for Linux vulnerabilities.

An IDS is not always necessary for the home environment. If you have just the logging and minimal alerting setup in your firewalls, you can have a decent comfort level. Security monitoring is useless if you don't actually check your logs, watch what is happening, and review files constantly. Most home users will not do this; therefore, practically speaking, implement the firewalls securely with good filtering rules and you probably won't need another form of IDS.

Intrusion Response

When the IDS detects an attack, you can usually set up some form of alert. A response can be anything from disconnecting your system to alerting you to blocking the attack. Your IDS can do several things as a result:

- Alert through a sound
- Send information to a log utility such as syslogd or NT Event logs
- Send an e-mail
- Send a page
- Automatically block the attack
- Save the attack information (timestamp, intruder IP address, victim IP address/port, protocol information)
- Look up information on the attacking IP address
- Launch a counterhack program (very bad idea)
- Terminate the TCP session

Log Analysis

Your logs are the source of all information about attacks against your system. If you are filtering traffic and monitoring just messages and alerts that are a high risk, your IDS will provide more benefits than if you tried to monitor everything. One thing to keep in mind is that you must ensure that your logs are on a secured machine that is not vulnerable. Your logs will be worthless if the computer on which your logs are stored gets hacked. Even if the attacker does not erase the log files, you cannot trust them because the intruder can erase parts of an IDS log file to hide his activity. Programs called rootkits are available on Linux- and Windows-based systems that are used to replace key programs and hide the activity of an intruder. If your IDS is compromised, the odds are that a knowledgeable intruder will install a rootkit to hide his activities. The rootkits will clean out entries of the attack from log files or remove log files completely if the files are on the system that was compromised.

If your log files are wiped out, you wouldn't know how the intruder got in, when he got in, or if Trojan horses and backdoors were installed for later access into the system. Several common Unix rootkits are lrk5, knark, and torn kit. One for Windows NT is Rootkit. Both can be found at www.rootkit.com or packetstorm.decepticons.org. The NT Rootkit can do the following:

- Hide processes (that is, keep them from being listed)
- Hide files
- Hide Registry entries
- Intercept keystrokes typed at the system console
- Issue a debug interrupt, causing a blue screen of death (BSOD)
- Redirect EXE files

As we have discussed with your data, log file information should be backed up regularly. In corporate environments, IDS logs are usually stored on a secure log server. Because you probably won't be dedicating a computer to be a log server, you should just back up the log files in whatever means you use to back up your normal applications and data. If you are compromised and your log is erased or modified, at least you will have some data you can sift through to see if the attacker had done anything previously to your system.

When reviewing your log files, looking for certain types of attacks is important. It's easy to tell a port scan from a concerted attack against your Web server. Attacks are launched against specific ports, and you can tell what type of attack is being launched by the port being used. An attack in which all ports are being contacted is indicative of a port scan. Seeing your FTP port being contacted repeatedly indicates someone trying to take advantage of your FTP server.

Collecting Evidence

Your log files are the best evidence you can collect to track attacks against your system and use for prosecution in the off-chance that you get authorities to track, capture, and prosecute an attacker. Yes, that does sound like no one cares about your computer, but the reality of home system compromise is that no government agency cares enough to help you. It's up to you to protect yourself and stop the attackers. In that case, you probably don't have to worry much about collecting evidence of an attack for legal prosecution, but you should know the basics behind collecting evidence like corporations do for prosecution.

Collecting all log traffic and attack signatures is a time-consuming and tedious process. You have to save all the data to some form of backup media and be thorough over a lengthy period of time for the evidence to be worthwhile. The main reason you as a home user should collect evidence of attacks is to educate yourself about how people view your presence on the Internet. By educating yourself about attacks, you can prevent future attacks and modify your firewall filter rules to protect yourself. If you know where you are potentially vulnerable, you can fix holes before they become a real problem. Watching what happens in your evidence logs will help you determine the current flavor of attacks that are being used.

If you choose to collect attack data and compromise evidence, you will be collecting data both before and after a compromise. It's easy to understand why you want to collect data before you are compromised. All that attack data will help you stop future attacks and make sure you are not vulnerable currently. What happens when you have been compromised? Do you take your computer off the network? Do you let it keep running and give the hacker continued access to your system? First, if you pull the computer off the network, you might lose the opportunity to see where the attacker is connecting from, what data he is transmitting, or why he is using your system. To see where he is making a connection, you can use a program such a Vision (`www.foundstone.com`). In Figure 16.4, we see that several remote IP addresses are listed. If an attacker compromised your system and made a remote connection to another server, such as to FTP files from your computer, you would see it listed.

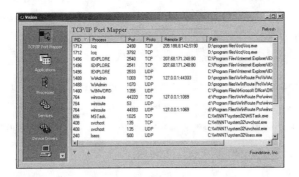

Figure 16.4   Vision detection of remote IP address.

If you wanted more detail, you could use a sniffer program to capture traffic in and out of your network. You could watch exactly what data was being transferred back and forth by the intruder. The problem with that is that you would run the risk of alerting the intruder that you knew of his presence; the intruder has full control of your system and watches the processes running just as you do. If the intruder sensed you, he might then wipe all traces of the attack or destroy all your files.

It is a risky venture to leave the system up and running after you have been compromised. Do the benefits of watching the intruder outweigh the risk that he will destroy your files or get all the information he wants from your system before you stop him? On the other hand, if you immediately disconnect the system from the network, you run the risk of losing valuable logging information. You might not be able to determine where the intruder connected from. If he hacked up some other system to get to yours, you could possibly find the ISP he belongs to and notify the ISP or the owners of the hacked system. By disconnecting immediately, you run the risk of not being able to track down the attacker.

As we have already said, the benefits of collecting data as a consumer are miniscule. You probably won't be able to prosecute anyone. The most you can do is notify the ISP of the hacker and his activities. If some company or university has been hacked and is being used as a launching pad, you can notify them that you are being attacked by one of their systems. Because many good attackers do not use their own system from which to hack, you probably won't be able to trace them back. Script kiddies use their own cable or DSL connections, so it's easy to notify their ISP of suspicious activity. The evidence you collect could be used in criminal prosecution if you collected it correctly and you were able to get law enforcement to track the attacker.

You can collect several types of evidence:

- **Real evidence**—These are actual logs of hacker activity that are not modified by you in any way that can be shown. This is the only evidence that really will hold up in a hacking case.
- **Testimonial evidence**—A witness provides this type of testimony. This is perceived reality (what they think happened), and the witness must testify.
- **Hearsay**—Someone who is not a direct witness provides this testimony. It is not reliable in court.

Five guidelines exist for collecting electronic evidence:

- **Admissible**—This evidence must be good enough to be used in court.
- **Authentic**—The evidence must relate directly to the incident.
- **Complete**—You have to show both the activity of the hacker and the activity of others on the system or network to prove it wasn't someone else doing the hacking.

- **Reliable**—The method you use to collect and analyze the data must be reliable so that the authenticity and veracity of the data is not in doubt.

- **Believable**—The data you provide must be understandable by a jury. If the jury cannot understand what the evidence shows, then you cannot prove anything.

Because many functions are performed by a running system, in the applications, in the operating system, and in memory, evidence and logging can change by the second. If you are serious about collecting evidence of a break-in, you have to collect all the information from applications, the operating system, and what is in memory. This is by no means an easy feat. You must minimize any chance of corrupting data; you can do this by shutting off the computer or disconnecting the system from the network. You should keep a copy of all your evidence, and it should remain untouched. All the actions you take from the moment you determine that a break-in has occurred should also be logged and recorded. The time of events is important as well. If you need to reconstruct events or chain actions by the attacker together, you need an accurate timeline. If you are working on a system that is currently compromised, you have to be quick about collecting evidence. You don't know what the attacker will do next, and you probably don't want more of your data to be accessed than has been already.

Detecting a Compromise

The easiest method of detecting an attack and a compromise of your system is by setting up alert capabilities of your firewall and IDS. Because firewalls and IDSs have similar functions, you can probably get by with one rather than having both in place. The several firewalls we reviewed have IDS-like capabilities, from the pop-up alert windows of ZoneAlarm Pro and Norton Personal Firewall to the flashing icon of BlackICE Defender.

Many commercial IDSs are available, but home users won't have much selection for Windows-based operating systems. The Unix environment offers many IDS products because Unix programs tend to be free and open source. Free solutions are more readily available to Unix users. One of the most popular is Snort (www.snort.org). Snort runs on both Unix and Windows systems, but it does require some in-depth knowledge. In addition, it requires a great deal of time in setting it up and understanding the reports.

Each IDS/firewall has different methods of displaying attack information and using filter capabilities to block and report attacks. Attacks and intrusions can be detected by the following methods:

- **Anomaly detection**—Statistical anomalies can be used to detect traffic that is out of the ordinary or does not follow a known pattern. If the traffic of the system is monitored and recorded, data such as CPU utilization, disk activity, user logins, file activity, transactions, and variation from the baseline can be seen as an anomaly and perhaps an attack. Although this type of detection cannot specifically tell you if a hacker is targeting your Web server with a file traversal attack, it can tell you that someone is launching an attack that goes beyond simple Web browsing of your Web site. All the traffic that is sent to the system is monitored. When invalid data or data that is not normally seen by the IDS is found, alerts are activated that notify you of an attack.

- **Signature recognition**—Sophisticated IDSs usually use a signature-based detection model. Because most attacks are known rather quickly and most attacks fall into known categories of attacks, such as Web attacks, DOS attacks, or buffer overflow attacks, looking for the known pattern of attack can be used to detect and stop the attack. Some of these systems have a database of signatures that they can use to detect attacks. When the attack from the database of signatures is seen, alerts notify you of an attack. This type of pattern matching is used for known attacks.

What to Detect

Intrusion detection looks for attacks against the system or network, but it also checks the system on which it is running for compromised data and programs. When an attacker compromises a system, he can insert Trojan horses, backdoors, and rootkits to cause further mischief.

Trojan horse utilities hide hacker activities from the system administrator. Trojan horse files can have the same size and time/date stamp of the file they are replacing to make detection difficult. The use of cryptographic checksums can help determine if a Trojan horse has replaced the real file on your system. The MD5 checksum can be used to compare your binary files to known checksums of good binary files. You can find it at `ftp://ftp.cerias.purdue.edu/pub/tools/unix/crypto/md5/`.

Backdoors allow the hacker to enter the system at a later time. Backdoors listen on a TCP or UDP port and allow an attacker remote access to the system so that he does not have to continuously hack up your system to gain entry. Backdoors can open TCP or UDP ports that can look like legitimate ports or can open on unused high-numbered ports. Popular backdoor Windows programs are BackOrifice (`www.bo2k.com`) and NetBus (`http://packetstormsecurity.org/`). After an attacker compromises a system and installs a program such as BackOrifice, he can use it to remotely control the compromised system. Figure 16.5 shows how the attacker can configure BackOrifice to control the victim's machine.

In Figure 16.6, we see some of the configuration options of NetBus. BackOrifice and NetBus allow an attacker who has compromised your system to take control of your desktop. Most virus scanners will detect these programs.

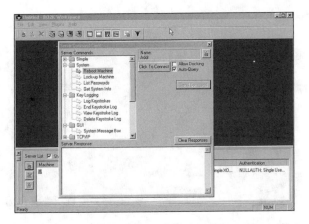

Figure 16.5   BackOrifice configuration.

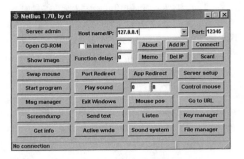

Figure 16.6   NetBus configuration window.

Rootkits are a combination of Trojan horses and backdoors. Rootkits can include log-wiping utilities that hide the steps taken by attackers from files such as utmp, wtmp, messages, and syslog in Unix and the event logs in Windows systems. Additionally, packet sniffers that can log all traffic on the compromised system's network and other utilities that can allow the attacker to perform other functions on your system can be part of a rootkit. With rootkits, you can't trust any binary file you have on your system. If you want to check for a backdoor that might be running on a high-numbered open port, you can use one of several third-party programs as well as the built-in netstat command. In Figure 16.7, we see the listening ports on our system using netstat -an in a DOS window. Many ports are open that are standard in our system, such as 135, 445, and some others; however, this example contains a port numbered 6666, which seems suspicious. This might be worth investigating to see what program is running.

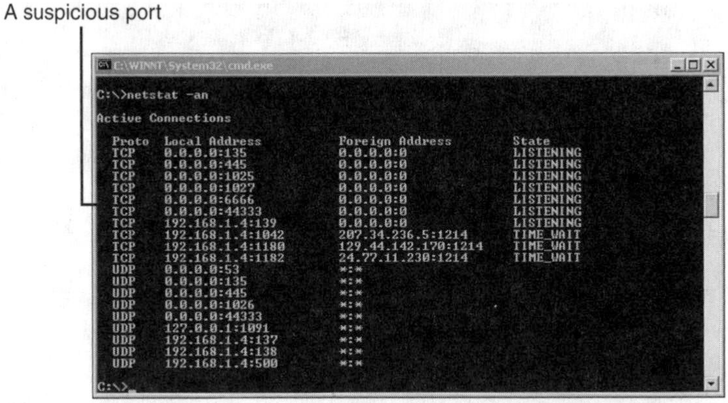

A suspicious port

Figure 16.7   Listening ports are shown using `netstat -an` with a suspicious port 6666.

IDSs and firewalls are good at detecting denial-of-service attacks, but stopping them is hard to do. Because DoS attacks can target everything from applications running to consuming network bandwidth to deny service, it's hard to stop all different forms of DoS attacks. Patches for operating systems and applications can stop many of these attacks, but they change so frequently that detecting them and attempting to block the attack is all that a consumer or a company can do.

Many ISPs implement filtering rules on their routers to help prevent DoS attacks. Consumers have no access to ISP routers, so this is out of your control. You can, however, disable any unused or unneeded network services, check your typical system utilization such as CPU and hard disk space for unidentified changes, back up your system in case a DoS attack destroys data, and adhere to good security measures. Your system can be compromised and used in distributed denial-of-service attacks. These attacks use multiple computers to attack a victim, thereby increasing the flood of data sent to the victim to easily overwhelm the computer and cause damage.

Traffic Monitoring

IDSs are somewhat synonymous with traffic monitoring. To detect an attack, an IDS looks at packets of data sent to the system or network. The computer that is running the IDS is put in promiscuous mode, which allows it to watch all traffic into and out of the system. Not all machines on the network need to be running an IDS. Ethereal, which we have already discussed, can be used to monitor all traffic and data, but it is not specifically designed as an IDS. IDS can capture every bit of data such as IDs and passwords that are used across the network. The firewall products we used can monitor traffic but cannot examine each packet of data and tell you exactly what is in them, such as what the ID and password that are being sent across the network contains.

Snort (www.snort.org), which is an IDS available for both Windows and Linux, provides traffic monitoring capabilities. It is a freeware program that is rather difficult to set up and understand. It does provide alerts via the screen or e-mails (you can choose the configuration). Unlike the firewall products that have IDS capabilities such as alerts, logging, and e-mail, Snort is not used to block traffic. It just detects attacks and reports on them.

Using WinRoute Pro, we can see how the firewall, along with blocking and filtering capability, can record to a log file and provide valuable attacker information. (Earlier, in the section "Problems with IDS," you saw that all attack data that is blocked or allowed by your firewall filter rules can be sent to a file.) Figure 16.8 shows how the attacks that are blocked by the filter rules can be sent to the screen. WinRoute doesn't have an alert capability, so you must check the files and screen for attack information. This type of firewall cannot provide sophisticated IDS capability to block traffic based on anomaly detection or signature detection.

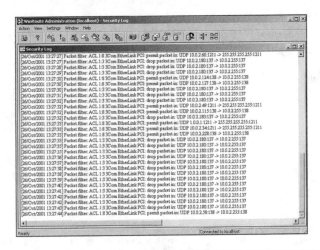

Figure 16.8   WinRoute screen data.

Another firewall product we used that has good alerting capabilities when the filter rules are violated is BlackICE Defender. Again, this product cannot check for any attack that does not specifically block by the filter rules. If you allow the Web server port to be open on your system, the firewall allows any Web attacks that are launched by an attacker that go over port 80 (http). Full-blown IDSs such as Snort do alert you to the attack. Many IDSs will not block traffic; in many cases, they just monitor and alert you to the traffic. A program such as Entercept blocks unknown attacks, but the average consumer cannot afford this corporate IDS product because it costs in the thousands of dollars.

Signs of a Compromise

Beyond reviewing your log files and looking for alerts from your IDS, you can check for other signs to see if your system has been compromised. Table 16.1 shows what you can look for.

Table 16.1   **Signs of a Compromise**

What to Check For	Description
Examine inherent log files.	Built-in logging capabilities exist in Windows- and Unix-based operating systems. Using Event Viewer in Windows NT/2000, you can see connections, errors, and security messages. Log files such as /var/log/ secure, /var/log/maillog, /var/log/messages, and var/log/httpd/access_log in Unix systems can provide valuable connection and security information.
Examine application logs.	Applications such as Web servers, FTP servers, and mail servers, among other,s have the capability to log access and errors in many instances. These can provide valuable intruder attempt information.
Evaluate your accounts.	You should know all the accounts that are valid on your system. If you see a new account that you did not create—especially one with privileged access—you should investigate it. You can use the User Manager tool in Windows NT/2000 to check the password file in Unix systems. You should also check accounts periodically that you do know about to make sure that they have not been given extra privileges. This could be indicative of an intruder gaining access to a valid account and escalating its privileges.
Check running processes and applications.	Intruders frequently start new services or install and run applications such as packet capture software. You should know what services you have running and if a new service or application is running that you have not started or don't know about. You can check services through the Services program in Windows NT/2000 (select Start, Control Panel, Services), use netstat (a built-in command in Windows that you can access by selecting Start, Run and typing cmd), or use Task Manager (by pressing Ctrl+Alt+Delete) to see what applications and processes are running. In Unix, you can check all the startup scripts and use the netstat command or top to check running processes. When systems start, programs can be run automatically through startup files such as the Startup folder in Windows or the rc* scripts in

Table 16.1   **Continued**

What to Check For	Description
	Unix. These should be checked to make sure nothing is started that you don't know about. If you see open ports that are listening that seem odd, a hacker program could be waiting for a connection or could be a backdoor.
Check your binaries.	Using MD5 checksums, as we have already mentioned, is a method of checking to ensure that the executable programs have not been replaced with Trojan horses. Although using MD5 checksums is difficult, it is a good measure to use periodically. Several programs are available that can do this automatically, including Tripwire (`http://www.tripwire.com`) for both Windows and Unix.
Watch your antivirus.	Your antivirus software can be used to help stop Trojan horses, worms, and viruses that are aimed at your system for malicious hacker purposes.
Check your network adapter.	If your network adapter has been placed in promiscuous mode to capture traffic and you weren't the one who did that, it's a sure sign that you have been compromised and someone is capturing traffic on your network. Programs such as Antisniff (`http://www.securitysoftwaretech.com/antisniff/`) for Windows NT/2000 and `ifconfig` in Unix will also tell you if the adapter is capturing traffic.
Check for shared data.	In both Windows and Unix, files and folders of data can be shared out to everyone. Check to make sure your system isn't sharing data that you do not know about.
Check for scheduled tasks.	An attacker frequently sets up a process or program to run at some future date to give him access or perform some function when the victim will least expect it. You can check what jobs might be scheduled for later execution with the `at` command in Windows NT/2000 and the `cron` command in Unix.
Check for network connectivity disruptions.	If you notice that your connection keeps going down or is sluggish for no reason, you might be the target of a denial of service attack. You can check your log files for failed connections or check your IDS for repeated connections.
Watch for obvious signs.	If your mouse is moving by itself or applications are opening and closing by themselves, someone might have taken over your system with a remote control program such as BackOrifice or VNC.

Security Maintenance Measures

We have discussed numerous methods of protecting personal information, your computer systems, and your networks. As we have said, security is just a point in time. Just because you are secure today does not mean you are secure tomorrow. Stopping the attacker from ever gaining access to your system is the best method of securing your systems. It's difficult to clean up a system after it's been compromised.

To keep your systems up-to-date with the latest security patches, fixes, virus scanner signatures, and any other security measures you might have in place, you must follow constant security procedures. Like any company that takes security seriously, you have to be serious in your endeavors to keep vigilant about weaknesses in your environment. If you only check your security periodically or implement patches infrequently, you are asking to be compromised.

Risk is a determining factor in how much security you feel you need to have implemented. If you have just one computer system in place that you only use for Web surfing, you might not need to have a lot of security measures in place. If that computer was hacked and files destroyed, it really wouldn't affect you very much. You could just reinstall the operating system and be back up and running in no time. What if the computer was running your routing for the entire home network or you had important files and personal information on it, such as Quicken or TurboTax information? If your system were compromised in that case, you would have lost your connectivity for the entire home network or all your personal tax information. You might be willing to invest more security measures, time, and effort in securing this second system.

System Updates

The best thing you can possibly do is to keep up-to-date with patches for operating systems and applications from the vendors. This is a simple fix to most security problems you will find. Whenever security vulnerability is made known, the vendor usually makes a patch available through its Web site.

For Windows-based operating systems, Microsoft has update functionality available through its Web site to install patches and provide you with information on any new patches that are made available. One good Web site that aggregates the Microsoft patches is Stroud's CWSApps (http://cws.internet.com/mspacks.html). The Microsoft updates are also found at the following addresses:

- **Windows 95**—http://www.microsoft.com/windows95/
- **Windows 98**—http://www.microsoft.com/windows98/
- **Windows ME**—http://www.microsoft.com/windowsme/
- **Windows NT and 2000**—http://windowsupdate.microsoft.com/

The Unix vendors have even gotten into the practice of making security patches easy to find on their Web site and have automated parts of the update process. One vendor, RedHat (www.redhat.com), has made its updates simple to access by bundling them on its Web site in the same fashion as Microsoft. For each version, all the security updates are easy to find and download. These security updates can be found at

- **RedHat Linux**—http://www.redhat.com/apps/support/errata/

Virus Protection

Computer security can easily be compromised via a virus. A worm, virus, or Trojan can have a backdoor installed on your computer, which can then open a hole in your system to let an attacker in or even send out your critical files to an attacker. Virus software is probably the best at updating for new virus signatures. You should definitely run a virus scanner. Many of them have the capability to automatically update themselves periodically without any intervention from the user. They can also performing virus scanning in the background automatically.

One example of an auto update feature is shown in Figure 16.9. In McAfee Virus Scanner 6.0, a popular scanner, you can manually download virus updates or have the system look for updates automatically.

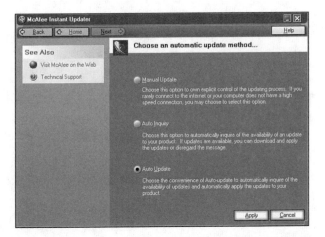

Figure 16.9   Automatic virus scanner update with McAfee.

Web Browsers

Web browsers are another form of constant attack. Because Web browsers are your gateway to the Internet and they are becoming more sophisticated every day, hackers are targeting them from both the application level and the programming level. The weaknesses in the browser applications can be used to exploit your computer. The programming languages such as Java and ActiveX can also be used to get you to execute malicious code that can compromise your computer. Web developers write code that your Web browser executes. Both Internet Explorer and Netscape have security measures that can be implemented from their Web sites:

- **Internet Explorer**—http://www.microsoft.com/windows/ie/downloads/critical/default.asp

- **Netscape**—http://home.netscape.com/computing/download/index.html

As we discussed earlier, the major browsers now have many built-in security features. These range from erasing cookies to removing stored Web site passwords. In Internet Explorer, you can change these options by selecting Tools, Internet Options. In Figure 16.10, we have selected the Security tab and then Custom Settings to disable such browser functions as unsafe ActiveX and prompting for allowing ActiveX plug-ins.

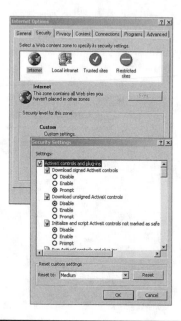

Figure 16.10   Internet Explorer security settings.

In Netscape, we can change the security options by selecting Edit, Preferences or Tasks, Privacy and Security. Through these options, you can change things such as cookie management (as shown in Figure 16.11), stored passwords, and SSL authentication.

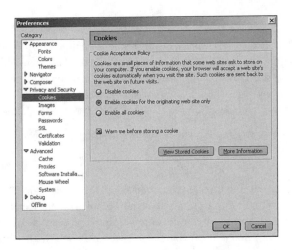

Figure 16.11   Netscape security management.

A new browser that is taking away some market share from Internet Explorer and Netscape is Opera (www.opera.com). Features such as improved speed, cross-platform capabilities, and security are making Opera quite popular. The browser supports SSL versions 2 and 3 and TLS 1 and has built-in support for full 128-bit encryption. Opera has several security and privacy options that you can change by selecting File, Preferences, as shown in Figure 16.12.

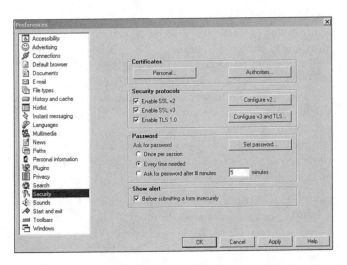

Figure 16.12   Opera security configuration.

E-mail

We covered e-mail extensively earlier in this book. E-mail, with its incorporation into just about everything we do these days, can be extremely dangerous. Viruses and worms can travel via e-mail attachments. Even the e-mail applications can cause a threat to your privacy. Data can be captured via e-mail, someone can forge e-mail in your name, and your e-mail can be intercepted on its way to its destination.

The best security you can implement is using encrypted e-mail. We discussed PGP and security options extensively. Keeping your virus scanner up-to-date and integrated with your e-mail system can stop e-mail–borne viruses.

E-mail bombing/spamming can be combined with e-mail "spoofing," which can mislead you or someone else into thinking that the e-mail was sent from you. An attacker can cause damage to your reputation if someone thinks you are e-mail bombing him or sending him spam e-mail. Spam is inevitable; yet, if people with whom you communicate know you use secure e-mail and your e-mail can be verified using your PGP public key, they will know that spoofed e-mail is not from you.

If you are the target of spam e-mail, you can configure your e-mail software to deny e-mail from the spam address. You can usually contact the spammer and request that you be removed from the spam list, but that's usually a futile effort. You can also track down the ISP of the spammer and send a message to their abuse-prevention e-mail address, letting them know someone on their network is a spammer.

Denial-of-Service Attacks

A denial-of-service attack prevents access to your system by flooding the network with traffic so you can't connect, disrupting connections between machines, targeting a particular service to deny access, or denying access to a specific account. If an attacker got on your system, he could stop services, destroy files and programs, or use up all disk space to deny service. When an attacker consumes all resources, uses up network bandwidth, or destroys the system, you lose the functionality of your system. A positive step for DoS attacks has been the sentencing of the attacker going by the name Mafiaboy in a Canadian court. This 17-year old launched DoS attacks against a number of sites in February 2000, and the U.S. FBI and Canadian authorities successfully prosecuted him in the fourth quarter of 2001.

For problems associated with applications and the operating system, patches are sometimes available to help prevent DoS attacks. In most bandwidth cases, you don't have much control over the attacks. Your ISP can put filtering rules in place on its router to deny some forms of attacks.

Penetration Testing

The value of testing your own security cannot be underestimated. As you continue to use the network, add services, add computers, or make modifications to the system, you increase potential to allow a new vulnerability into the network. Identifying the vulnerabilities in your network is not just a one-time event. You must continuously test your security stance. New vulnerabilities are always being made known, so you must know if you are vulnerable before the hackers do.

Your penetration tests should look at both your network vulnerabilities and the vulnerabilities in the operating system or applications from an internal perspective. If an attacker were to gain some form of user access to your system, you wouldn't want him using problems in the operating system or applications to escalate his privileges to administrator level before you could catch him in the act.

Defining Baseline Security Standards

Before you start playing on the Internet, take some time to follow some simple rules to protect yourself. Companies that set up an Internet presence usually take the time to secure each system that will be made available to the public. You need to do the same. Spend the initial time up front to follow a specific set of security procedures to get your system to a level of security with which you are comfortable. You will save yourself the grief of being hacked. Like the precautions you take when building a house, such as installing locks on all doors and windows, installing an alarm, and building a fence, you need the same type of baseline security measures in place before moving into cyberspace.

Operating Systems

No matter what operating systems or applications you run, you should enable security measures before getting on the Internet. Many companies have a process for securing a system according to a baseline set of security standards. If a computer does not meet these security standards or goes through the security measures, it does not access the Internet. This might be difficult for you because you have to connect to the Internet to download patches and fixes. The quicker you patch a new system, the smaller your window of exposure to an attack will be. Before you get online to get patches, install your firewall and antivirus software.

For all operating systems, strengthening the default security options is your first step in setting up your system. To do this, you should implement the patches and fixes made available through the vendor. Intruders frequently make use of the inherent vulnerabilities in operating systems to compromise a machine. Securing the operating system alone would solve half your security problems.

Most of you are probably using Microsoft operating systems. You can get service packs and hot fixes from Microsoft at the download center (`http://www.microsoft.com/downloads/`). Microsoft releases new service packs, hot fixes, and patches frequently. You can keep updated with Microsoft's notification service at `http://www.microsoft.com/technet/security/notify.asp`.

Each Linux vendor has some form of security patch and Web site related to securing the operating system that you must find.

Applications

Your applications (such as Web browsers), server programs (such as FTP, mail, and Web), and business productivity products (such as Microsoft Office) are also a source of vulnerabilities on your system. They can allow vulnerabilities in much the same fashion that the operating system can allow intruders to compromise the system.

Application vendors produce patches for programs just like the operating system vendors do. A good example of application updates can be found at the Microsoft support site for Microsoft Office updates (`http://office.microsoft.com/productupdates/`), shown in Figure 16.13. Each Microsoft Office application you run can be checked for updates, which frequently relate to security issues.

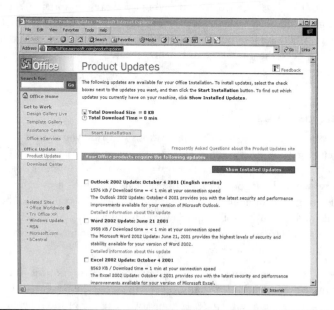

Figure 16.13   MS Office application update.

You should define a list of applications on your system and treat them as you would operating system fixes; check the applications periodically and ensure that no vulnerabilities are associated with them. Check the vendor Web sites for any fixes or patches that might be made available. This should, of course, be done as you install these applications and not months after installation. Setting up the system securely according to a baseline set of standards will go a long way toward keeping you secure.

Computer Virus Prevention

Virus scanners are much like normal applications in that they need to be installed and all patches and fixes updated immediately before going on the Internet. They also serve a much more important function. Like a firewall, virus scanners are strong protection for your system on the Internet. The scanner you use should be robust and should be able to scan your hard drive, the files you download, and e-mail attachments that you receive. A virus can get on your system in multiple ways, and the virus scanner must be able to stop all inbound paths that a virus might take.

When you set up your system, make sure you have a virus scanner running before you start downloading or installing any programs. The scanner can catch a Trojan horse or a virus that might come from a seemingly secure site. As we continuously mention, security is an ongoing process, and so is virus scanning. Your scanner should be set to scan your system in the background. You should plan how often you want to check for new updates to the virus scanner and to the virus signature it uses. Because a new virus comes out just about every other day, you want to do this pretty frequently. Some of the virus scanners have auto update capabilities that can take over much of the maintenance.

Two good sources of virus information include the following:

- **CERT**—http://www.cert.org/other_sources/viruses.html
- **AUSCERT**—http://www.auscert.org.au/Information/Sources/virus.html

Available Services

A well-known mantra for security in the corporate environment is to turn off any service that is not needed. You should apply this rule to your home network as well. On every computer in your home network, you should disable any service in the operating system or any application that is not needed by selecting Start, Control Panel, Services. Figure 16.14 shows the service listing in a Windows 2000 environment.

You can turn each service on or off by selecting the properties of each service. In Figure 16.15, we can see that the FTP service is stopped and disabled. By double-clicking each service, you have the option of stopping and disabling each service from running by selecting Control Panel, Services.

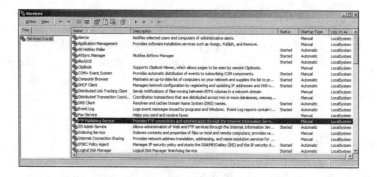

Figure 16.14   Service listing.

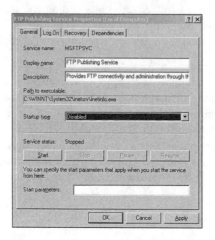

Figure 16.15   Starting or stopping a service.

In Unix systems, you can disable services through /etc/inetd.conf,
/etc/xinetd.conf, or the startup scripts. By disabling services that are not necessary,
you reduce your exposure risk. The more services you have running, the more you
have to track down patches and fixes for potential vulnerabilities in each service.

Accounts and Passwords

Accounts and passwords are the major weaknesses in any operating system. Just about
every company, no matter how large or small, has user accounts on its systems, and it's
guaranteed that several user accounts have weak passwords. The easiest and most common method for a hacker to gain access to your system is via a weak or default password. You should have strong passwords on every account on your system, both at the
application and operating system level. Many applications and operating systems come

with known default passwords or no passwords at all on built-in accounts such as the Administrator account in Windows NT/2000 systems. Good password controls should be in place such as these:

- Password aging
- Minimum password length
- Keeping passwords between accounts and people private
- Password uniqueness
    - Uppercase letters (A, B, C, ... Z)
    - Lowercase letters (a, b, c, ... z)
    - Numbers (0, 1, 2 ... 9)
    - Non-alphanumeric characters (punctuation symbols)
- Account lockout features
    - Number of failed logon attempts
    - How long to lock out an account

In Windows NT/2000, the program SYSKEY can be used to encrypt password data stored in the Registry.

Because the Administrator account is the default superuser, attackers know which account to target. You might want to consider renaming the Administrator account or removing privileges from the Administrator account and creating a new account with administrator privileges. A skillful attacker can find the real Administrator account if your firewall rules are not in place to deny queries to your system for such information, but it will fool most of the script kiddies and automated scanning programs. In Unix, the root account is the default superuser account. It should be treated with as much care as the Windows Administrator account. If an attacker were to gain access to your root account in Unix, he would be able to perform any function on your system that you can perform.

Summary

Guarding your personal data, your home network, and any other digital devices you might be using to connect to the rest of the world are becoming a full-time job. You are forced to learn new technologies often as new attacks against your privacy are made available. You have to constantly defend yourself and protect your information.

Security is an ongoing process. As soon as you connect in any way to the rest of the world, you will be a target for attack. We have discussed a number of technologies throughout the book to help you protect your technologies and your data. Being ever vigilant will keep the attackers at bay. Legal and illegal threats face you on a daily basis; never think otherwise in today's technological environment.

What we have striven for in this book is to educate consumers about the threats that have become serious problems over the past few years. With the advancement of technology and its ease of use, methods for attackers to compromise your security and information will progress on a daily basis. You have to be aware of what you are facing to combat these threats.

We hope this book has provided you with a solid foundation as a computer privacy and security reference for the home and workplace. With the knowledge of how your computer works, including the Internet, Web surfing, e-mail, virus protection, personal firewalls, networking, encryption and more, you will be able to take security of your personal information into your own hands today and in the future. Take back your privacy.

Security is a way of life.

VII

Appendixes

Personal Firewall Software

This appendix lists a number of software products that can assist you in protecting your system and networks against attackers. This is not a complete list of all such products, nor are these necessarily recommended products, but they are good resources for you to look into.

Product	Web Site
Biodata's Sphinxwall Firewall	http://www.sphinxwall.com/
Conseal Firewall	http://www.consealfirewall.com/
CyberwallPLUS-WS	http://www.network-1.com/products/plus-ws.html
eSafe Desktop	http://www.ealaddin.com/esafe/
Freedom	http://www.freedom.net
Internet Firewall 2000/IF2K	http://www.digitalrobotics.com
McAfee Firewall	http://www.mcafee.com/myapps/firewall/ov_firewall.asp
NAI's PGP Desktop	http://www.pgp.com/products/default.asp
Network Ice's BlackIce Defender	http://www.networkice.com
Norton Personal Firewall	http://www.symantec.com
PC Viper Personal Firewall	http://pcviper.com
Privacyware Personal Firewall	http://www.privacyware.com/
Sygate Personal Firewall Pro	http://www.sygate.com/products/default.htm
Terminet Personal Firewall	http://www.terminet.co.za/

Product	Web Site
Tiny Software's Tiny Personal Firewall	http://www.tinysoftware.com
Tiny Software's Winroute Pro	http://www.tinysoftware.com
VirusMD	http://www.virusmd.com
Zone Labs' ZoneAlarm	http://www.zonelabs.com
Zone Labs' ZoneAlarm Pro	http://www.zonelabs.com

B

Antivirus and Anti-Trojan Horse Software

This appendix lists a number of software products that can help you protect against viruses and Trojan horses. Tables B.1 and B.2 are not complete lists of all such products, nor are these necessarily recommended products, but they are a good resource for you to look into.

Table B.1 **Antivirus Software**

Product	Web Site
Alwil Software AVAST	http://www.anet.cz/alwil/alwil.htm
AVG AntiVirus	http://www.grisoft.com/html/us_index.html
Command Software AntiVirus	http://www.commandsoftware.com/index.cfm
Data Fellows F-Secure Anti-Virus	http://www.europe.f-secure.com/index.shtml
Dr Solomon's Antivirus	http://www.drsolomon.com/
ESET Software NOD32	http://www.nod32.com.au/
ETrust EZ Antivirus	http://my-etrust.com/products/info/Antivirus/2
Frisk F-Prot	http://www.frisk.is/f-prot/
Kaspersky Lab KAV	http://www.kaspersky.com/products.asp
McAfee VirusScan	http://www.mcafee.com/

Table B.1 **Continued**

Product	Web Site
Norman Virus Control	http://www.norman.com/
Norton Anti-Virus 2002	http://www.symantec.com/
Panda AntiVirus Platinum	http://www.pandasoftware.com/
Pica Software Virex	http://www.pica.com.au/Content_Pages/picavirex.html
Sophos Anti-Virus	http://www.sophos.com/
Trend PC-cillin 2000	http://www.antivirus.com/pc-cillin/

Table B.2 **Anti-Trojan Horse Software**

Product	Web Site
Agnitum Tauscan	http://www.agnitum.com/products/tauscan/
Anti-Trojan	http://www.anti-trojan.net/
AstonSoft PC DoorGuard	http://www.astonsoft.com/index.htm
Diamond Computer Trojan Defense Suite (TDS-3)	http://tds.diamondcs.com.au/
Privacy Software Corporation BOClean	http://www.nsclean.com/
SaferSite PestPatrol	http://www.safersite.com/
Software Oasis The Cleaner MooSoft	http://www.moosoft.com/

Parental Control Technology

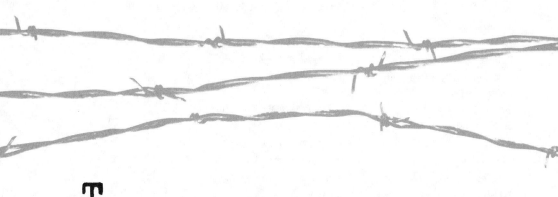

This appendix lists a number of software and services that can help parents monitor and control Internet access for their children. This is not a complete list, nor are these necessarily recommended products, but they are a good resource for you to look into (see Table C.1).

Table C.1 **Parental Control Software and Services**

Technology/Service	Web Site
Access Management Engine (AME)	http://www.bascom.com/
Alexa	http://www.alexa.com/
AltaVista Filtered Search Service	http://www.altavista.digital.com/
America Online Parental Controls	http://www.aol.com/
Bess	http://www.n2h2.com/
Bonus.com the SuperSite for Kids	http://www.bonus.com/
ChoiceView	http://www.cleanscreen.net/
Click and Browse Jr.	http://www.netwavelink.com/

Table C.1   **Continued**

Technology/Service	Web Site
Cyber Patrol	http://www.surfcontrol.com/products/cyberpatrol_for_home/product_overview/index.html
Cyber Snoop	http://www.pearlsw.com/
CYBERsitter	http://www.solidoak.com/
Disney's Blast Online	http://www.disney.com/
EdView – Secure and Smart Channel to the Internet	http://www.edview.com/
ESRB	http://www.esrb.org/
evaluWEB	http://calvin.ptloma.edu/~spectre/evaluweb/
GuardiaNet	http://www.guardianet.net/
IBM Web Traffic Express	http://www.ics.raleigh.ibm.com/
The Internet Filter	http://www.turnercom.com/
The Internet Kids & Family Yellow Pages	http://www.netmom.com/
KidDesk Internet Safe	http://www.edmark.com/prod/kids
Kids CyberHighway	http://www.att.net/
Mail Gear	http://www.urlabs.com/
Net Nanny	http://www.netnanny.com/
Net Rated	http://www.netrated.com/
Net Shepherd World Opinion Rating Service	http://www.netshepherd.com/
NetFilter	http://www.netfilter.com/
PlanetView	http://www.planetview.com/
Platform for Privacy Preferences Project	http://www.w3.org/P3/
RSACi	http://www.rsac.org/
SafeSurf	http://www.safesurf.com/
Scholastic Network	http://www.scholasticnetwork.com/
SmartFilter	http://www.smartfilter.com/
WatchGuard SchoolMate	http://www.watchguard.com/schoolmate.html
WebChaperone with iCRT	http://www.webchaperone.com/
WebDoubler	http://www.maxum.com/WebDoubler/
WebSENSE	http://www.websense.com/
WinGuardian	http://www.webroot.com/
X-STOP	http://www.xstop.com/

Encryption and Privacy Software

This appendix lists several software products that can assist you in protecting your system and privacy. This is not a complete list of all such products, nor are these necessarily recommended products, but they are good resources for you to look into.

Product	Web Site	Category
Ad-aware	http://www.ad-aware.com	Ad blocker
AdSubtract	http://www.adsubtract.com	Ad blocker
WebWasher	http://www.webwasher.com	Ad blocker
Anonymizer	http://www.anonymizer.com/	Anonymous browsing
Cloak	http://www.the-cloak.com/ homepage/index.php3	Anonymous browsing
Freedom	http://www.freedom.net/products/ index.html	Anonymous browsing
IDzap	http://www.idzap.com/	Anonymous browsing
Rewebber	http://www.rewebber.de/	Anonymous browsing
SafeWeb	https://www.safeweb.com/	Anonymous browsing
COTSE	http://webmail.cotse.com/ servicedetails.html	Anonymous e-mail
Jack B. Nymble	http://www.skuz.net/potatoware/ jbn2/index.html	Anonymous e-mail
Amnesia	http://www.consultcom.com	Browser cleanup
Don't Panic	http://www.popupstopper.net/	Browser cleanup

Product	Web Site	Category
History Kill	`http://www.historykill.com`	Browser cleanup
Quick Clear Pro	`http://www.macrospeed.net/qc/`	Browser cleanup
Surf Secret	`http://www.surfsecret.com/`	Browser cleanup
Cookie Cruncher	`http://www.rbaworld.com/Programs/` `CookieCruncher/`	Cookie manager
Cookie Crusher	`http://www.thelimitsoft.com/` `cookie.html`	Cookie manager
Cookie Jar	`http://www.lne.com/ericm/` `cookie_jar/`	Cookie manager
Cookie Pal	`http://www.kburra.com/`	Cookie manager
MagicCookie Monster (for the Mac)	`http://download.at/drjsoftware`	Cookie manager
International PGP	`http://www.pgpi.org/`	Encryption
Pretty Good Privacy (PGP)	`http://web.mit.edu/network/` `pgp.html`	Encryption
SafeBoot (for Windows)	`http://www.controlbreak.co.uk/` `products/safebootv40.html`	Encryption
Scramdisk	`http://www.scramdisk.clara.net/`	Encryption
12 Ghosts	`http://12ghosts.com/`	Privacy protection
Bugnosis	`http://www.bugnosis.com`	Privacy protection
Complete Cleanup	`http://www.softdd.com/`	Privacy protection
Ghost Surf	`http://www.tenebril.com/`	Privacy protection
IEClean	`http://www.nsclean.com/` `ieclean.html`	Privacy protection
Junkbuster	`http://internet.junkbuster.com/`	Privacy protection
Norton Internet Security 2001	`http://www.symantec.com`	Privacy protection
Ponoi	`http://www.ponoi.com/`	Privacy protection
Privacy Companion	`http://www.idcide.com/`	Privacy protection
TraceEraser	`http://www.traceeraser.com/`	Privacy protection
Window Washer	`http://www.webroot.com/`	Privacy protection
Certified-Mail.com	`http://www.certifiedmail.com`	Secure e-mail
Disappearing Email	`http://www.disappearing.com/`	Secure e-mail
Ensuredmail	`http://www.ensuredmail.com`	Secure e-mail
HushMail	`http://www.hushmail.com`	Secure e-mail

Product	Web Site	Category
Lok	http://www.lok.com	Secure e-mail
Mail2Web	http://www.mail2web.com	Secure e-mail
Ziplip.com	http://www.ziplip.com	Secure e-mail
ZixMail	http://www.zixmail.com	Secure e-mail
PrivacyX	http://www.privacyx.com/	Secure messaging
SafeMessage	http://www.safemessage.com/	Secure messaging

Selected References

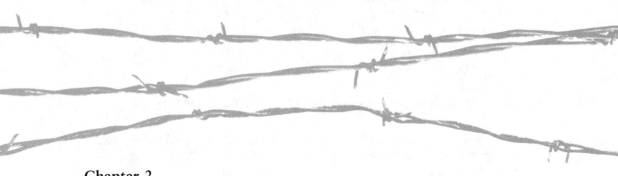

Chapter 2

- "FTC Chief's New Privacy Agenda Attacked," Brian Krebs, *CNN Newsbytes*, October 4, 2001.
- "Hacker Steals Huge Credit Card Database," staff writer, CNN, December 13, 2000.
- "Health Care: Making HIPAA Happen," Kim S. Nash, *Computer World*, August 13, 2001.
- "New York Life Names Chief Privacy Officer," Maria Trombly, *Computer World*, April 23, 2001.
- "When Privacy Is Job 1," Lee Schlesinger, *ZDNet*, May 7, 2001.

Chapter 3

- "GLB Privacy: Where We Are, Where We're Going," staff writer, *Privacy Headquarters*, July 1, 2001.
- "Legal Deadline Looms for Web Sites Collecting Data from Children," Steven Zansberg, *Computer World*, April 21, 2000.
- "Patriot Act Draws Privacy Concerns," Stefanie Olsen, staff writer, CNET News.com, October 26, 2001.

- "Say Ahh, Then Remain Silent," Jeffrey Benner, *Wired News*, June 5, 2001.
- "Web Enters Privacy 'Safe Harbor'," Chris Oakes, *Wired News*, November 2, 2000.

Chapter 4

- "Online Merchant Emails Out Customer Credit Card Details," John Leyden, *The Register*, September 13, 2001.
- "The Politics of Privacy," Mark Hall, *Computer World*, August 13, 2001.
- "Privacy and Human Rights—An International Survey of Privacy Laws and Practice," Privacy International, 2000.
- "U.S.: Fear Countries, Not Hackers," Declan McCullagh, June 22, 2001.

Chapter 5

- "15 Steps to Protecting Your Privacy," Matthew P. Graven, *PC Magazine*, January 3, 2001.
- "The Extent of Systematic Monitoring of Employee E-mail and Internet Use," Andrew Schulman, Workplace Surveillance Project, July 9, 2001.
- "Hackers to the Honey," BBC staff writer, July 31, 2001.
- "Know Your Enemy: Statistics Analyzing the Past...Predicting the Future," Honeynet Project, July 22, 2001.
- "Playing by Europe's Rules," Deborah Radcliff, *Computer World*, July 9, 2001.
- "Whom Do You Trust?" Matthew P. Graven, *PC Magazine*, January 3, 2001.

Chapter 11

- "Got Broadband? You're Under Attack," Brett Glass, *Extreme Tech*, June 12, 2001.
- "Make Your PC Hacker-Proof," staff writer, *PC World*, September 2000.
- "Making Your Hardware Firewall Connection," Les Freed, *PC Magazine*, May 24, 2001.
- "Personal Firewall Comparison," Robert Richmond, Sysopt.Com, November 4, 2000.
- "Tough Times for High-Speed ISPs Despite Demand," Corey Grice, CNET News.com, December 5, 2000.
- "The Truth About Cable," staff writer, *CNET News*, July 2001.

Chapter 14

- "Carnivore Could Eat into Wireless E-mails," Erich Luening and Ben Charny, staff writers, CNET News.com, August 24, 2001.
- "Disposable Cell Phones Spur Debates," Ben Charny, CNET News.com, September 17, 2001.
- "New Wireless LAN Vulnerabilities Uncovered," Dan Verton and Bob Brewin, *ZDNet*, August 9, 2001.

Chapter 16

- "Collecting Electronic Evidence After a System Compromise," Matthew Braid, SANS Institute, April 17, 2001.
- "Know Your Enemy: Statistics Analyzing the Past...Predicting the Future," Honeynet Project, July 22, 2001.

Index

Numbers

A

FBI (Federal Bureau of Investigations), 106, 127, 182, 277

FCRA (Fair Credit Reporting Act), 62, 67

Federal Intrusion Detection Network (FIDNet), 128

Federal Trade Commission (FTC), 51, 87

Felten vs. RIAA, 90

FIDNet (Federal Intrusion Detection Network), 128

Fight The Fingerprint, Web site, 146

fighting (online), 596

FileCrypto (F-Secure), Web site, 564

files, 469
    encryption, 503
    Linux
        monitoring, 397
        security, 394
        system log, host security, 398
    security, 368, 403-404
    NTFS (Windows NT), 379
    PGP (Pretty Good Privacy), 505
    PWL (Windows 95), 364-366
    security, 368
    settings (Windows 2000), 385
    sharing, 141, 363, 535-536
    storing (LokVault), 311
    Unix
        monitoring, 397
        ownership, 396
        permissions, 395
        security, 394
    viruses, 469

filter rule settings, 539

FilterGate, Web site, 256-257

filtering software. *See* blocking software (Internet)

filters, 281, 534

Financial Services Antifraud Network Act of 2001 (H.R. 1408), 105

Financial Services Modernization Act. *See* GLB (Gramm-Leach-Bliley) Act

fingerprints. *See* biometric technology

firewalls, 620
    appliances, 422-423
    BlackICE, 533-534
    BlackICE Defender, 424-429
    definition, 39
    NPF (Norton Personal Firewall), 437-440
    OpenBSD, 541
    personal, 416
        architecture, 417
        blocking traffic, 423-424
        NAT (Network Address Translation), 418
        problems, 420
        proxies, 418
    SPF (Sygate Personal Firewall), 443-447
    TPF (Tiny Software Personal Firewall), 448-451
    Web sites, 421-422, 653-654
    WinRoute, 528-533
    WinRoute Pro, 452
    WinRoute Pro 4.1, 452-460
    ZoneAlarm, 260
    ZoneAlarm Pro, 430-437

first-party cookies, 232

FOIA (Freedom of Information Act), 59, 66

folder sharing, 379, 536

footprinting, 547-548
    host identification, 350-352
    open ports, 353-354
    OS (operating systems) identification, 356

forms, disabling
    Netscape 6.1, 598
    Opera 5.12, 603

Foundstone, Web site, 67, 335

fraud, 150, 183-187

FRCA (Fair Credit Reporting Act), 179

Freedom 2.0 (Zero Knowledge), Web site, 210-211

Fscan, Web site, 353

FTC (Federal Trade Commission), 51, 87-88, 182, 187, 614

FTP (File Transfer Protocol), 319

I

X – Y – Z